101 STORIES OF THE GREAT BALLETS

Also by George Balanchine and Francis Mason:

BALANCHINE'S NEW COMPLETE STORIES OF THE GREAT BALLETS

101 STORIES OF THE GREAT BALLETS

George Balanchine
and
Francis Mason

ANCHOR BOOKS
DOUBLEDAY
NEW YORK LONDON TORONTO SYDNEY AUCKLAND

An Anchor Book
PUBLISHED BY DOUBLEDAY
a division of Bantam Doubleday Dell Publishing Group, Inc.
1540 Broadway, New York, New York 10036

Library of Congress Cataloging in Publication Data
Balanchine, George.
101 stories of the great ballets.
1. Ballets—Stories, plots, etc. I. Mason, Francis, joint author. II. Title.
MT95.B3 1975 792.8'4 74-9140

ISBN 0-385-03398-2

PRINTED IN THE UNITED STATES OF AMERICA
FIRST ANCHOR BOOKS EDITION: 1989

6 8 10 11 9 7

CONTENTS

PREFACE ix
ACKNOWLEDGMENTS xi
After Eden 1
Agon 2
Anastasia 6
Apollo 11
Astarte 17
As Time Goes By 21
At Midnight 26
La Bayadère 29
Bhakti 33
Billy the Kid 34
Brahms Quintet 41
The Cage 42
Celebration 46
Cinderella 49
The Clowns 66
The Concert 68
Concerto Barocco 70
The Consort 73
Coppélia 75
Dances at a Gathering 93
Dark Elegies 112
Deuce Coupe 114
Don Quixote 116
Duo Concertant 126
The Dream 129
Dybbuk Variations 132
The Dying Swan 137
Early Songs 140
Enigma Variations 143
The Eternal Idol 146
Eugene Onegin 147

An Evening's Waltzes 151
Façade 152
Fancy Free 154
Fête Noire 159
La Fille Mal Gardée 160
Firebird 170
The Four Temperaments 181
Gaîté Parisienne 183
Gala Performance 187
Gartenfest 192
Giselle 193
Goldberg Variations 210
Harbinger 220
Harlequinade 222
In the Night 225
Initials R.B.M.E 228
Intermezzo 229
Jewels 231
Journal 233
Kettentanz 234
Konservatoriet 236
Liebeslieder Walzer 239
Lilac Garden 241
Manon 247
A Midsummer Night's Dream 253
Monument for a Dead Boy 256
The Moor's Pavane 258
Mutations 261
Napoli 263
Nijinsky–Clown of God 266
Les Noces 272
The Nutcracker 277
Orpheus 284
Parade 291
Pas de Quatre 296
Petrouchka 305

Pillar of Fire 317
Prodigal Son 322
Pulcinella 330
Remembrances 336
Requiem Canticles 339
Reveries 341
The River 345
Rodeo 347
Romeo and Juliet 354
Sacred Grove on Mount Tamalpais 379
Le Sacre du Printemps 381
The Seasons 387
Serenade 388
The Sleeping Beauty 393
Spartacus 421
Spectre de la Rose 427
The Still Point 430
Swan Lake 432
La Sylphide 459
Les Sylphides 473
Symphonic Variations 480
Symphony in C 484
Symphony in Three Movements 487
Tales of Hoffman 489
Taming of the Shrew 491
Tchaikovsky Suite No. 2 494
Three-Cornered Hat 495
Three Virgins and a Devil 498
Triad 500
Trinity 502
Undertow 505
Unfinished Symphony 509
Violin Concerto 510
Watermill 513
Who Cares? 519
INDEX 528

PREFACE

This book contains stories of 101 ballets. Fifty are old favorites, ballets in the standard repertory that are performed regularly, plus a few ballets of major historical importance. The fifty-one others are among the many new ballets that have appeared in the past six years, since *Balanchine's New Complete Stories of the Great Ballets* appeared in 1968. The idea behind this paperback edition is to keep up with main trends in the repertory while also providing the background of the standard repertory. It is plainly impossible to include the majority of the new works that has appeared recently; that will be the job of the next hardcover edition.

When we first began to put together stories of ballets, there were all too few ballet ensembles performing in the United States. Few of us, unless we lived in the largest cities, had an opportunity to see ballet with any regularity. In those days it was even imagined that only foreign ballet companies could present the really old pieces with any authority! Today, we know better and through performances by numerous ensembles, domestic as well as foreign, we are able to make certain comparisons and distinctions. We are fortunate, too, to have new regional ballet groups and young ensembles like Arthur Mitchell's Dance Theatre of Harlem and the Eliot Feld Ballet that represent the special preoccupations of their directors.

More persons, too, are writing about dance. Describing ballets, which few of us were doing twenty years ago, is now an obligation many critics perform very well. It is a pleasure to acknowledge and to quote from the work of acute dance observers in this book.

I must not say more here. Ballet is not for words (the poet and critic Edwin Denby once said that at a ballet performance no one said a foolish word all evening!) and no amount of words is going to substitute for what you might see in the theater. On the other hand, if the words are not so bad and if they are not so many, you might say to yourself, Well, maybe I should go see for myself. That is certainly all I want, that you should try, if you have not been to ballet performances regularly. Open your eyes, your ears, your hearts, your minds. We are all happier when we admit the possibilities of a new awareness through the arts. For the arts help us not only in our everyday living, and make some of that exhilarating, they are in fact an inspiration. The arts point to the glories we might attain as human beings, perfecting as they do God-given gifts some are lucky to have.

My partners in this book are the ones I have had in the past, the writer Francis Mason and the editor Harold Kuebler. The three of us have thought often of the interest Lawrence Sherman and Marion Patton showed us when a book of ballet stories was first suggested years ago.

GEORGE BALANCHINE

ACKNOWLEDGMENTS

The Dance Collection of the New York Public Library, the world's most comprehensive archive of materials, past and present, relating to dance, has been consulted regularly throughout the writing of this book. Genevieve Oswald, Curator of the Collection, and her knowledgeable and helpful staff have been consistently obliging, and it is a pleasure to acknowledge indebtedness to all of them, especially to Marta Lucyshyn, Lacy McDearmon, Henry Wisneski, Natalie Bassein, Andrew Wentink, Paul LePaglia, Madeleine Nichols, and Winifred Messe. The Dance Collection has recently completed, at its premises in the New York Public Library's Library and Museum of the Performing Arts at Lincoln Center, the *Dictionary Catalogue of the Dance Collection.* This major bibliography represents the first time that all materials related to dance have been assembled in dictionary-catalogue form. One can find in it not only who danced what ballet when, but all the complementary details of music, libretto, choreography, and design. Its availability to the layman as well as the specialist is another historic step in the Collection's achievement.

We are extremely grateful to the critics and writers on dance whose work is quoted in this book: Jack Anderson of *Ballet Review, Dance Magazine,* and the *Dancing Times;* Robb Baker of *FM Guide;* Clive Barnes, dance and drama critic of the New York *Times;* Patricia Barnes of *Dance and Dancers;* Ann Barzell of *Dance News;* Alexander Bland of *The Observer* (London); Jane Boutwell of *The New Yorker;* Erik Bruhn for his treatise *Beyond Technique* (*Dance Perspectives 36*); Mary Clarke, editor of the *Dancing Times* (London); Selma Jeanne Cohen, editor of *Dance Perspectives;* the filmmaker Gardner Compton in *Dance Magazine;* the art critic and collector Douglas Cooper in *Dance and*

Dancers; Clement Crisp of the *Financial Times* (London); Arlene Croce, editor of *Ballet Review,* U.S. correspondent of the *Dancing Times,* and dance critic of *The New Yorker;* Edwin Denby, critic for many publications, especially *Dance Magazine* (for his historic interview with Jerome Robbins on the occasion of *Dances at a Gathering*) and for his two books, *Looking at the Dance* and *Dancers, Buildings, and People in the Streets;* Joseph Gale in the New York *Daily News;* Nancy Goldner of *Dance News, The Nation,* and for her book, *The Stravinsky Festival of the New York City Ballet;* Robert Greskovic of *Ballet Review;* John Gruen in the New York *Times;* Henry Haslam in *Ballet Review;* Doris Hering in *Dance Magazine;* Marian Horosko in *Dance Magazine;* Allen Hughes of the New York *Times;* Lydia Jaffe in *Dance Magazine;* Deborah Jowitt of the *Village Voice;* Oleg Kerensky of the *New Statesman* (London) and for his books *World of Ballet* and *Pavlova;* Lincoln Kirstein for innumerable sources, most importantly his recent book, *Movement and Metaphor: four centuries of ballet,* and the masterly volume, *New York City Ballet;* Anna Kisselgoff of the New York *Times;* Jean Battey Lewis of the Washington *Post;* John Martin of the New York *Times;* P. W. Manchester, U.S. correspondent of the *Dancing Times* (London); Don McDonagh of the New York *Times* and *Ballet Review;* Jacqueline Maskey of *High Fidelity;* John Percival of the *Times* (London), *Dance and Dancers,* and the New York *Times;* Andrew Porter of the *Financial Times* (London) and *The New Yorker* and for his book, *A Musical Season;* Robert J. Pierce of the *Village Voice;* Kay Rinfrette in *Ballet Today;* Peter J. Rosenwald of the *Wall Street Journal;* Hubert Saal of *Newsweek;* Marcia B. Siegel, dance critic of the *Hudson Review* and the *Soho Weekly News,* and for her collection of criticisms, *At the Vanishing Point* (1972); Anna Greta Stahle of *Dance News;* Walter Terry of *The Saturday Review;* David Vaughan of *Ballet Review;* and Peter Williams of *Dance and Dancers* and *The Observer.*

We are grateful, too, to the editor of *Dance Magazine,* William Como, for permission to reprint the interview between Jerome Robbins and Edwin Denby on the subject of the Robbins ballet *Dances at a Gathering* and the filmmaker Gardner Compton's article on *Astarte*. Also helpful have been interviews published in *The New Yorker* with Maurice Béjart; Leonard Bernstein and Jerome Robbins; and Kenneth MacMillan; in *Show* magazine with Rudolf Nureyev; in *Dance and Dancers* with Eliot Feld. Eric Walter White's crucial text, *Stravinsky: the Composer and his Works* (1966), has been consulted throughout. Macmillan St. Martin's Press has kindly given permission to quote excerpts from Dame Marie Rambert's autobiography, *Quicksilver* (1972). We are grateful also to George G. Harrap Co., Ltd., London, for an excerpt from *Frederick Ashton, a Choreographer and His Ballets* (1971).

The press and public relations representatives of ballet companies have been extremely generous in responding to frequent requests: Virginia Hymes and Irene Shaw of American Ballet Theatre; Isadora Bennett, Rima Corben, and Robert Larkin of the City Center Joffrey Ballet; Judith Jedlicka of the Harkness Ballet; Virginia Donaldson, Marie Gutscher, and Clarence Hart of the New York City Ballet; Vivien Wallace of the Royal Ballet; Tom Kerrigan for the many dance ensembles appearing at the Brooklyn Academy of Music; Sheila Porter, press representative for S. Hurok, and her associate John Gingrich.

For helpfulness and interest we wish also to thank: Jane Allison; Betty Cage, Edward Bigelow, Carole Deschamps, and Mary Porter of the New York City Ballet; Eugenie Ouroussow, Nathalie Molostwoff, and Elise Reiman of the School of American Ballet; Mrs. Norman Lassalle; Barbara Horgan; Robert Irving; Darryl Dodson of American Ballet Theatre; Harvey Lichtenstein of the Brooklyn Academy of Music; Arthur Mitchell of the Dance Theatre of Harlem; and Marion Patton and Lawrence and Joan Sherman. In 1950 it was Lawrence Sherman's initiative and uncommonly lively interest in Balanchine, music, and ballet that made possible George Balanchine's first book. Marion Patton nurtured that interest to produce with us *Balanchine's Com-*

plete Stories of the Great Ballets (1954). Harold Kuebler keenly sponsored the second volume, *Balanchine's New Complete Stories of the Great Ballets* (1968), and proposed this new paperback form for keeping up with rapid changes in the repertory and for giving the newcomer to that repertory some knowledge of the dances. He is thus responsible for whatever merit this venture might have. His assistant, James Menick, has been consistently helpful throughout. George Balanchine and I are grateful to them, as we are also for the editorial assistance of Shields ReMine and Lisa Ray.

F.M.

101 STORIES OF THE GREAT BALLETS

AFTER EDEN

Music by Lee Hoiby. Choreography by John Butler. Scenery by Rouben Ter-Arutunian. First presented by the Harkness Ballet at the Broadway Theatre, New York, November 9, 1967, with Lone Isaksen and Lawrence Rhodes.

After Eden is a dramatic ballet about Adam and Eve after the Fall and the expulsion from the Garden of Eden. It shows in dance terms, with no narration, something of the agony, regret, defiance, and resignation of the two lovers as they face the fate they had not imagined. In the process, their dependence on each other varies and it is this that makes the drama of the piece: Will they, after what they have come through, be able to stay together? At the start of the dance they are united in their misery and therefore mutually dependent. Later, realizing their new, appalling freedom, it seems briefly possible for them to separate or to entertain that notion. But not for long, for they have survived much and cannot go their separate ways. They are like magnets, alternately attracting and repulsing as they turn in different directions. In the end, they are newly united and apparently resolved to encounter the future together.

After Eden was revived by the City Center Joffrey Ballet, March 21, 1972, with Starr Danias and Dennis Wayne.

AGON

Music by Igor Stravinsky. Choreography by George Balanchine. Lighting by Nananne Porcher. First presented by the New York City Ballet at the City Center, New York, November 27, 1957, with Diana Adams, Melissa Hayden, Barbara Walczak, Barbara Millberg, Todd Bolender, Roy Tobias, Jonathan Watts, Arthur Mitchell, Roberta Lubell, Francia Russell, Dido Sayers, and Ruth Sobotka.

While the New York City Ballet has in its repertory many works by Igor Stravinsky, *Agon* is the third Stravinsky ballet composed especially for our company. Lincoln Kirstein and I had always wanted a new Stravinsky work to follow *Orpheus,* and at first it seemed possible that this might be based on another Greek myth. We looked into a number of possibilities, but none of them seemed to work out. We began nevertheless to discuss possibilities of a new ballet with the composer. It was Stravinsky who hit upon the idea of a suite of dances based on a seventeenth-century manual of French court dances—*sarabandes, gaillards, branles*—he had recently come across. We all liked the idea, especially as Kirstein and I recalled Stravinsky's other masterful treatment of polkas and other dance forms, including ragtime rhythms. The title of the ballet, *Agon,* the Greek word for *contest, protagonist,* as well as *agony* or struggle, was a happy inspiration of Stravinsky's. It was to be the only Greek thing about the ballet, just as the dancing manual, the point of departure, was to be the only French.

Stravinsky and I met to discuss details of the ballet. In addition to the court dances, we decided to include the traditional classic ballet centerpiece, the *pas de deux,* and other more familiar forms. Neither of us of course imagined that we would be transcribing or duplicating old dances in either musical or dance terms. History was only the takeoff point.

We discussed timing and decided that the whole ballet should last about twenty minutes. Stravinsky always breaks things down to essentials. We talked about how many minutes the first part should last, what to allow for the *pas de deux* and the other dances. We narrowed the plan as specifically as possible. To have all the time in the world means nothing to Stravinsky. "When I know how long a piece must take, then it excites me." His house in California is filled with beautiful clocks and watches, friends to his wish for precision, delicacy, refinement. We also discussed in general terms the character each dance might have and possible tempos.

When we received the score I was excited and pleased and set to work at once. Sounds like this had not been heard before. In his seventy-fifth year Stravinsky had given us another masterpiece. For me, it was another enviable chance to respond to the impulse his music gives so precisely and openly to dance.

Music like Stravinsky's cannot be illustrated; one must try to find a visual equivalent that is a complement rather than an illustration. And while the score of *Agon* was invented for dancing, it was not simple to devise dances of a comparable density, quality, metrical insistence, variety, formal mastery, or symmetrical asymmetry. Just as a cabinetmaker must select his woods for the particular job in hand—palisander, angelique, rosewood, briar, or pine—so a ballet carpenter must find dominant quality of gesture, a strain or palette of consistent movement, an active scale of flowing patterns which reveals to the eye what Stravinsky tells the sensitized ear.

I was fascinated by the music, just as I had been fascinated and taught by Stravinksy's *Apollo* in the 1920s. As always in his ballet scores, the dance element of most force was the pulse. Here again his pulse built up a powerful motor drive so that when the end is reached we know, as with Mozart, that subject has been completely stated. Stravinsky's strict beat is authority over time, and I have always felt that a choreographer should place unlimited confidence in this control. For me at any rate, Stravinsky's rhythmic invention gives the greatest stimulus. A choreographer cannot invent rhythms, he can only reflect them in movement. The body is his medium and, unaided, the body will improvise for a little while. But the organizing of rhythm on a large scale is a sustained process, a function of the musical mind. To speak of carpentry again, planning a rhythm is like planning a house; it needs a structural operation.

As an organizer of rhythms, Stravinsky, I have always thought, has been more subtle and various than any single creator in history. What holds me always is the vitality in the substance of each measure. Each measure has its complete, almost personal life; it is a living unit. There are no blind spots. A pause, an empty space, is never empty space between indicated sounds. It is not just nothing. It acts as a carrying agent from the last sound to the next one. Life goes on within each silence.

Agon was written during the time of Stravinsky's growing interest in the music of Anton Webern and in twelve-tone music. He has said: "Portions of *Agon* contain three times as much music for the same clock length as some other pieces of mine." The score begins in an earlier style and then develops. The piece contains twelve pieces of music. It is a ballet for twelve dancers. It is all precise, like a machine, but a machine that thinks.

Like the score, the ballet is in three parts, performed without interruption. The first part consists of a *pas de quatre* for four boys, a double *pas de quatre* for eight girls and a triple *pas de quatre* for all twelve dancers. The curtain goes up before the music begins. There is no setting, only a plain backdrop. Four boys in practice clothes stand facing the back. They turn toward us quickly; as they step forward, the music begins, with a bright trumpet fanfare. The boys soon give way to eight girls. To a faster rhythm they, too, seem to be warming up. Then the boys come back and as the music, now a variation and development of the previous section, becomes more familiar and Stravinsky gives short solo passages to some of the principal instruments, the dancers stand in a state of readiness. Supported by the full confidence of the orchestra, all twelve dance.

There is another fanfare and three of the dancers, two girls and a boy, face us. They dance a *pas de trois*. The boy then dances a *sarabande*. Stravinsky's scoring is for solo violin, xylophone, tenor and bass trombone. This seems an odd combination on paper, but it is lovely in fact, and the contrast between the instruments is very interesting to the ear. The music changes then and we have the two girls dancing a *gaillard* featuring three flutes, chimes, mandolin, harp, and the lower strings in marvelous combinations. This gay dance with leaping steps merges into a coda for all three, as the boy comes back. The coda is the first piece in twelve-tone style and, now that our ears have been tuned in, we are ready for its complexities.

After a fanfare and a brief orchestral interlude again, the first *pas de trois* is replaced by another and the second part of the ballet begins with three *branles*. Descriptions of many old *branles* are available in dance histories, but my dances of course are improvisations. The two boys show off the girl, lifting her, balancing her, then she leaves.

Robert Craft says in his notes to the recording of *Agon* that Stravinsky saw an engraving in the old French manual depicting two trumpeters blowing accompaniment to a *branle simple* and that suggested the brilliant combination of those instruments for the next part, which is canon form. The two boys each take the part of one of the trumpets.

The *branle gai* is a solo for the girl, dominated by the rhythmic sound of castanets and the sort of dance style they suggest. The full orchestra then intervenes and the boys rejoin the girl for a final *branle double*.

Next comes the *pas de deux*, again after the fanfare and a short interlude. The music of the adagio is scored for strings, with a concertante part for the solo violin. There are variations for the boy, the music of which recalls the second *branle*, and the girl, and a coda. A brief quartet for mandolin, harp, violin, and cello is especially memorable in the score.

Four horns then recall the opening fanfare. The music for the first movement of the ballet is repeated and the piece ends as it began, with four boys dancing alone. They face the backdrop as the curtain falls.

ANASTASIA

Scenario and choreography by Kenneth MacMillan. First performed in a one-act version by the Ballet of the Deutsche Oper, Berlin, June 25, 1967, with Lynn Seymour in the title role. Music by Bronislav Martinu (Symphonic Fantasy). *Introductory score by the Studio for Electronic Music of the Berlin Technical University. Designed by Barry Kay. Film scenes from the Aero Film production* From Tsar to Stalin. *Conducted by Ashley Lawrence. First given in three-act version by the Royal Ballet at the Royal Opera House, Covent Garden, London, July 22, 1971, with Lynn Seymour as* Anastasia, *Derek Rencher and Svetlana Beriosova as the* Tsar *and* Tsarina, *and Antoinette Sibley and Anthony Dowell as* Kschessinska *and her partner. Music for Acts One and Two by Peter Ilyich Tchaikovsky (Symphonies Nos. 1 and 3). Scenery and costumes by Barry Kay. First presented in the United States by the same ensemble with the same principals at the Metropolitan Opera House, New York, May 5, 1972.*

The nursery was the center of all Russia's troubles.

SIR BERNARD PARES

Anastasia tells the story of the royal Russian princess who survived, some believe, the Bolshevik Revolution to live on and recall her past. Robert Massie in his book about the last Russian tsar and his wife, *Nicholas and Alexandra,* quotes an older relative of the real Anastasia, who knew the child well, the tsar's sister, Grand Duchess Olga: "My telling the truth simply does not help in the least, because the public simply wants to believe the mystery." This three-act ballet relates the young Anastasia's early life in the Russian imperial family and concludes with a scene in a Berlin hospital in 1920 where A Woman Who Believes She Is Anastasia looks back on her story. The same dancer depicts both. Through Anastasia's personal history the Russian past and cataclysmic public events are telescoped and recaptured.

Tsar Nicholas II came to the Russian throne in 1894 at the age of twenty-six. His wife, Alexandra, bore him four daughters—Olga, Tatiana, Marie, Anastasia—and one son, his first heir, the Tsarevitch Alexei, a hemophiliac. The tsarina believed implicitly in the power of the Russian priest and mystic, Rasputin, to treat her son's bleeding.

The boy's tutor, the Swiss Pierre Gilliard, later wrote: "The illness of the Tsarevitch cast its shadow over the whole of the concluding period of Tsar Nicholas II's reign and alone can explain it. Without appearing to be, it was one of the main causes for his fall, for it made possible the phenomenon of Rasputin and resulted in the fatal isolation of the sovereigns who lived in a world apart, wholly absorbed in a tragic anxiety which had to be concealed from the world." And Alexander Kerensky, the Russian revolutionary leader removed by the Bolsheviks, declared: "Without Rasputin, there could have been no Lenin."

In March 1917 the tsar abdicated as a result of the outbreak of revolutionary activity and, following the Bolshevik October Revolution that same year, the imperial family was imprisoned. On the night of July 16/17, 1918, the tsar and his family were killed by Bolshevik forces at Ekaterinburg.

It was in 1920 that a woman patient in a Berlin hospital was recognized by some as one of the daughters of the tsar. Since then this woman has endeavored to prove her identity as the Grand Duchess Anastasia.

ACT ONE IN THE COUNTRYSIDE, AUGUST 1914 The imperial family is at a picnic in a birch grove by a lake with guests, who include the tsarina's great friend Madame Vyrubova, Rasputin, and a group of naval officers. The party ends as the tsar receives news of the outbreak of World War I.

The royal family is seen here to be a loving, close-knit group who have a congenial but necessarily distant relationship with the officers and courtiers who surround them. On this informal occasion, a picnic in the country, where the young can romp and play, where the tsar can relax and take snapshots of his children, there is an illusion of tranquility broken only by the presence of young officers. Dominating the scene is the tsarina's concern for her son and her faith in Rasputin's power to keep him from any dangerous accident. One of her relatives later recalled: "The Empress refused to surrender to fate. She talked incessantly of the ignorance of the physicians. She turned toward religion, and her prayers were tainted with a certain hysteria."

Anastasia, in a sailor blouse, enters on roller skates. She soon establishes a forthright, playful character, yet is considerate of others. She dances with three of the young officers who attend the family and, later, dances with her mother, who shows her the steps of an old Russian dance. When a telegram is brought to the tsar and news of war breaks the calm, the soldiers and sailors in attendance begin to practice drills and maneuvers. The tsar dances reassuringly with his wife, Rasputin leads them all in prayer, and there is a hope of victory. But one senses that it is a thin hope. The critic Peter Williams, remarking on the silver-birch setting of the scene, noted that some of the trees "have been cut down, with just their stumps showing, to suggest that the ballet opens where Chekhov's *Cherry Orchard* left off—a warning wind symbolic of the passing order."

ACT TWO PETROGRAD, MARCH 1917 Despite rapidly growing unrest, the tsar is giving a ball to celebrate the coming out of his youngest daughter, Anastasia. He has invited his favorite ballerina—with whom he had a liaison before his marriage—to dance for his guests. Anastasia is puzzled by the outburst of revolutionary activity.

The setting of the ballroom, like the first act, is circular in form, with a circular staircase descending like a vortex just off-center. Before the ballroom, however, an outside scene, with slogans and discontent in the streets, reminds us of unrest among the Russian people.

In the ballroom itself, which contrasts vividly with the poverty we have just seen, there are ceremonial dances for the tsar, the royal family, and their guests. Anastasia, who has come of age, looks lovely and has a new maturity. The ballerina Mathilde Kchessinska, one of the great Russian ballerinas, first dancer of the Maryinsky Theatre for more than twenty-five years, enters and with her partner performs a *pas de deux* to the second movement of Tchaikovsky's symphony. Favorite of the tsar before his accession to the throne and later the wife of the Grand Duke Andrei, the real Kschessinska in fact left Russia to live in Europe, where she danced triumphantly and taught for many years. Margot Fonteyn, and numerous other dancers were among her students. She died in Paris, in 1971, at the age of 99.

Later, when the ballerina has changed from her costume to a ball gown and joined the party, there is a *pas de quatre* in which she appears with the tsar, the tsarina, and Rasputin. Kchessinska's partner later joins in that dance, where old and new relationships excite the participants. The young Anastasia watches her parents and their friends and is bewildered; coming of age is more complicated than she has imagined if life, and love, are like that. An officer who tries to involve Anastasia herself is repulsed.

Now the action shifts back to the unrest in the streets of St. Petersburg. Soon the populace and troops outside the palace interrupt the processions and formal dances of the ballroom. They invade the premises and the ball ends in disaster.

ACT THREE SOME YEARS LATER For the woman who believes she is Anastasia, past and present intermingle. She relives incidents from the years since the massacre of the tsar and his family; her rescue by two brothers; the birth of her child; her marriage; the death of her husband; the disappearance of the child; her attempted suicide; the confrontation over the years with relatives of the imperial family who deny her identity as the Grand Duchess Anastasia.

The scene here is a Berlin hospital, where Anastasia sits on a white iron bed. She has recovered from a long period of unconsciousness and, reliving the past, is trying to find out who she is. Is she a plain person named Anna Anderson who has suffered simply a series of personal tragedies, or is she the Grand Duchess Anastasia who, in addition to personal misfortune, symbolizes another world? Filmed flashbacks of the past aid her memory of historic events, shown in newsreels and still photos, while her personal history and relationships are danced and depicted on stage. We see her rescue, the man who becomes her lover, their child, their happiness. This, too, is destroyed by another firing squad, for her husband is shot. She escapes yet again with his brother. Intermingled with the recapitulation of history and personal tragedy are confrontations the girl endures with members of the imperial family who refuse to recognize her as Anastasia. She herself, however, has no doubt; transcending all of her prolonged personal misfortune is her vivid recollection of the lovely past, when families might picnic under the silver birches and a young girl in a sailor suit might be so beloved by her parents that she would surely have a happy life. The ballet ends as we see Anastasia poised high at the foot of her hospital bed. The bed begins to move, coming toward us like an open royal limousine, it progresses; Anastasia, still and triumphant, receives silently the homage of the world.

Reflecting on Kenneth MacMillan's achievement in the three-act ballet form, Arlene Croce wrote in *The New Yorker* in 1974: "Of the three full-evening ballets MacMillan has produced so far, *Anastasia* seems to me the best, not so much because of what it achieves as because of what it attempts. In *Romeo,* MacMillan had before him both Leonid Lavrovsky's version for the Bolshoi and Cranko's for the Stuttgart; in *Manon* he is working à la Cranko. But in *Anastasia* he produced a personal fantasy about a global cataclysm entirely from nothing. I don't think he was being pretentious, and the insults that were showered upon him for missing the mark themselves missed the mark. MacMillan's taste, musical instinct, and technical skill place him first among those British and European choreographers whose careers began in the fifties."

APOLLO

APOLLON MUSAGÈTE

Ballet in two scenes. Music and book by Igor Stravinsky. Choreography by George Balanchine. Scenery and costumes by André Bauchant. First presented by Diaghilev's Ballets Russes at the Théâtre Sarah Bernhardt, Paris, June 12, 1928, with Serge Lifar as Apollo, *Alice Nikitina as* Terpsichore *(Alexandra Danilova alternated with Nikitina in this role in the original production), Lubov Tchernicheva as* Polyhymnia, *and Felia Dubrovska as* Calliope. *First presented in the United States by the American Ballet at the Metropolitan Opera House, New York, April 27 1937, with scenery and costumes by Stewart Chaney. Lew Christensen was* Apollo; *the three* Muses *were danced by Elise Reiman, Holly Howard, and Daphne Vane.*

To the Greeks, the god Apollo was many things: he was the god of prophecy, the god who punished wrongdoers, the god who helped those in trouble, the god of vegetation and agriculture, and the god of song and music. Apollo received different epithets, different names, for each of his various powers. Because of his powers of song and music, he was also closely associated with the Muses, goddesses who represented the different arts and derived inspiration from Apollo's teaching. This ballet concerns itself with Apollo, leader of the Muses, the youthful god who has not yet attained the manifold powers for which he will afterward be renowned among men.

The three Muses of the ballet were selected for their appropriateness to the choreographic art. In the words of the composer, "Calliope personified poetry and its rhythm; Polyhymnia represents mime; Terpsichore, combining in herself both the rhythm and the eloquence of gesture, reveals dancing to the world and thus among the Muses takes the place of honor beside Apollo."*

* From Igor Stravinsky, *An Autobiography,* Simon and Schuster, Inc., New York, 1936.

The ballet begins with a brief prologue that depicts the birth of Apollo. Before the opening curtain, the string orchestra intimates the theme that will become identified with the god as the ballet progresses. This theme receives a rhythmic accompaniment from the lower strings, and the curtain rises.

The scene is Delos, an island in the Aegean Sea. It is night; stars twinkle in a dark blue sky. Back in the distance, in a shaft of light, Leto gives birth to the child whom the all-powerful Zeus has sired. She sits high on a barren rock and holds up her arms to the light. The music quickens, the woman buries her face in her hands, a hurried crescendo is cut off sharply, the strings are plucked, and Apollo is born. Leto disappears, and in the shaft of light at the base of the high rock stands the infant god, wrapped tightly in swaddling clothes. He hops forward stiffly to a swift, flowing melody.

Two handmaidens leap softly across the stage and come to Apollo. The newborn god falls back in their arms; his mouth moves in an inarticulate cry for help, and the two women begin to unwrap his swaddling clothes. They circle the god, unwinding the rich cloth, but before they can finish, Apollo spins suddenly and frees himself of the garment and looks about the dark world, not seeing clearly, not knowing how to move. After this burst of energy, he is frightened. His head is crowned with golden vine leaves and his body is endowed by nature with sinuous strength, but the young god is bewildered.

The two handmaidens bring to him a lute, sign of his future greatness in music. Apollo does not know how to hold the instrument. They place it in his hands and stand behind him, reaching out their hands to pluck the strings. Apollo follows their example and finds the first clue to his immortality. There is a blackout.

The musical statement that marked Apollo's birth is repeated sonorously. When the lights come on again, the scene is brilliant, as if a flash of lightning had been sustained and permanently illuminated the world. Apollo, dressed now in a short gold tunic, stands in the center of the stage. To the music of a solo violin, he plays upon the lute. He whirls his arms around and around in a large circle over the strings, seeming to draw music from the instrument with his youthful strength. Other strings now accompany the solo violin softly. Apollo places the lute on the ground and dances alone. He reaches out to the lute for inspiration and moves tentatively, carefully, but with a new-found ease. Now that he has proved his potential grace in movement, Apollo picks up the lute again. He turns slowly in attitude, holding the lute before him. The solo violin concludes the theme.

Three Muses appear to Apollo, walking slowly and respectfully toward him from three corners of the stage. With a godlike gesture, the god welcomes them. The young goddesses bow to him, then in unison bend in low arabesques about the lute he holds high in his hands. They break this pose and stand together. The melody is strong yet moving, vigorous yet simple, like the youthful, inexperienced quality of the dance that now begins.

Apollo reaches out and, touching their hands gently, draws the Muses close to him. The three girls stand close together, one behind the other. Apollo takes their hands one by one. They pose in arabesque for an instant and move to the center of the stage. He motions two of the girls aside; Terpsichore, Muse of song and dance, falls back in his arms. He leaves her kneeling alone and, enclosing the other two girls in his arms, he lowers them slowly to the ground so that they also kneel.

Terpsichore rises and, dancing on point, slowly takes the hands of her sister Muses and encircles their kneeling figures. Now the three Muses stand again in a close line. The lower strings play the poignant theme with deep strength, and Apollo circles the stage in broad, free leaps as the girls move their arms in rhythm to the music.

The god returns to the Muses and supports each as she turns close to the ground. The girls form a line behind Apollo and move across the back of the stage, their bold, youthful figures imitating the dance of their leader. The girls pause and kneel, then rise at once. Apollo, arms outstretched, supports them as they hold hands and form a circular tableau.

When this tableau is broken, the Muses form a close line in front of Apollo. This line moves backward as one, the young god and goddesses shuffling awkwardly on their heels. The line comes to a rest. The three girls stand motionless; Apollo bends down and tenderly pushes them into motion with his shoulder. Led by Terpsichore, the Muses dance alone. The melody ends.

Apollo presents each of the Muses with the symbol appropriate to her art. To Calliope, Muse of poetry, he presents a tablet; to Polyhymnia, Muse of mime, a mask that symbolizes unearthly silence and the power of gesture; and to Terpsichore, Muse of dancing and song, he gives a lyre, the instrument that accompanies those arts. The Muses accept these gifts with delight and respect, form a line, and hop like pleased children to the side of the stage. Apollo commands the Muses to create and sits to watch what they will do.

Calliope comes forward with her tablet. She holds it out before her, then clutches it to her heart. Placing the tablet on the ground, she dances. The melody she moves to is based in form on the Alexandrine, the classical heroic measure of French poetry. Her dance is emotional, yet not weakly so; as she circles the stage before Apollo, her leg boldly sweeps the air before her. She is scribbling hastily on the palm of her hand when her dance nears its end, wondering if she has done well. She becomes a little sad, the music seems to cry out softly with her, and she goes to show Apollo what she has written. He does not approve.

Brilliant chords herald the dance of Polyhymnia, who soon puts her mask aside and dances rapidly to a sprightly, rhythmic melody. The girl holds her finger to her lips throughout the dance, as she tries to maintain the dignity of her mask, but her youthful enthusiasm gets the best of her: she forgets—as she responds to the happy, worldly music—and before she knows what has happened, her lips have moved and she has spoken. Terrified, she claps her hands over her mouth, punishing her own naughtiness, but Apollo sees what she has done and censures her.

Terpsichore comes forward and dances in profile with her

lyre. She holds the instrument high above her head, her curved arms suggesting the shape of the lyre, and her feet pluck at the ground as if they played upon it. She moves adroitly and sharply, with assured grace; the gestures she makes with her arms as she poses in a series of balanced arabesques show us that her whole body is coordinated to beauty. The music she dances to is similar in melody to Calliope's, but the rhythm is different; like her dance, it is more pointed, less romantic. Of all the Muses, she alone dances perfectly, and Apollo commends her.

Now the young god dances alone. Majestic chords announce the theme of his variation. He reaches his arms up toward Olympus, leaps grandly into the air, then kneels. To the quiet rhythms of the music, Apollo performs with ideal perfection, setting an example to the Muses and reminding us that he himself has acquired the skill he demands of them.

As his dance ends, Apollo sits on the ground in a graceful, godlike pose. Terpsichore appears before him and touches his outstretched hand. The young goddess steps over his arm and bends low in extended arabesque beside him. Now the girl rises and sits on Apollo's knees. He holds his arm up to her, she takes it, and both rise to dance a muted *pas de deux.* The melody is softly lyrical, but at the same time strong; it depicts in sound an awakening of Olympian power and strength, beauty and grace.

Apollo supports Terpsichore in extended arabesque, lifts her daringly high so that her body curves back over his shoulder, holds her as she extends her legs and sinks on the ground to rise on point in graceful extensions. She pirouettes swiftly and sharply in his arms then entwines herself around Apollo. The music brightens, they separate, dancing playfully, then meet again. Both kneel. Apollo puts his head in Terpsichore's open hands. Now, at the end, she falls across Apollo's back as the god bends down to give the Muse a short swimming lesson as a reward for her beautiful dancing. Her arms push the air aside as if they were moving in the water. When Apollo rises, Terpischore's body is curved against him.

Calliope and Polyhymnia rush in and join Apollo and

Terpsichore in a joyous coda in which the Muses surround Apollo with their new-found pleasure in movement. The young god, in their midst, holds out his arms; two of the girls grab hold, and he swings them through the air. The quick grace of the Muses is accompanied by lively, shifting rhythms in the music that rushes to a finish. Apollo takes them by the hand and drives all three across the stage in a swift chariot race. As the music ends, Apollo stands alone. The three girls walk toward him together and in unison clap their palms. Apollo leans down and places his head against their hands.

From on high, Zeus calls his son Apollo home with mighty crescendos of sound. Apollo stands motionless, as if under a spell, listening. The three Muses sit upon the ground. Apollo walks slowly around them. As he stands in back of them and reaches out over them, the three girls lift their feet to meet his hand. Apollo blesses them with a noble gesture. The Muses reach their arms up, and Apollo lifts them up beside him. For a moment the arms of the four figures are entwined, then the three Muses pose in arabesque behind Apollo's profiled figure to form a tableau in which the goddesses are as one with him.

Now Apollo takes their hands and draws them like a chariot across the stage. He takes them to the foot of the high rock, then walks forward and begins to climb to the summit, pointing the way to Olympus. The Muses follow. The four figures are silhouetted against the sky, holding out their arms to the sun. Leto, Apollo's mother, falls back in the arms of his handmaidens as she reaches up to her son in farewell.

ASTARTE

Created and choreographed by Robert Joffrey. Music performed by Chamberlain, conducted by Hub Miller. Commissioned score composed by Crome Syrcus. Lighting design and set by Thomas Skelton. Costumes by Hugh Sherrer. Film created and photographed by Gardner Compton. Produced by Midge Mackenzie. First presented by the City Center Joffrey Ballet at the City Center, New York, September 20, 1967, with Trinette Singleton and Maximiliano Zomosa.

Astarte, moon goddess of love and fertility, borrowed from the Babylonian-Assyrian Ishtar by the Greeks, is the heroine of this multimedia work. Astarte gave herself to all men, but was owned by none. She has been called the patron goddess of Women's Liberation, lover and destroyer, bestower of both life and death. The ballet that celebrates her powers uses music (an acid-rock score specially commissioned) amplified dramatically, lights (incandescent and strobe), film, and dance in the first combination of these elements in the theater of ballet. Techniques and impressions familiar in the discothèque are here, melded with dance to produce a dramatic *pas de deux* unlike any seen before.

What happens in general is simple. As the music starts full volume, the darkened theater is suddenly filled with varied kinds of light. A steadily blinking strobe stares out from the front of the stage so that no one in the audience can see for a moment of necessary adjustment; the stage itself begins to have some light on it, and searching spotlights are aimed at the audience, trying to find we know not what.

We soon find out. The backcloth of the setting on stage is a tightly stretched white cloth pulled in at the center like a belly button, and, against a drop farther back, a frantic film is being projected, of frantic birds and a hypnotic girl—the goddess Astarte. The seeking spotlights find a boy seated on the aisle in the audience as the eye of the goddess winks. He rises, transfixed by her glance, and slowly makes his way down the center aisle of the theater as we all watch. He crosses then to the right, toward steps to the stage, meanwhile looking at the stage at the goddess who has materialized before us. He goes up on stage and, standing there, still staring alone at the eyes of the goddess, begins to take off his clothes—all of them, down to his briefs, as her image looms huge above him on the screen. Soon his image, too, is seen to merge with hers. The rock singer has begun to sing, and the boy puts his clothes tenderly on the ground under the watching eye of the mysterious girl. He now goes to her, holding out his hands and, reaching her, molding them to her body. She steps forward then, and he begins to hold her in a dance that is anticipated, gesture by gesture, by the film that wraps around them and shows through them. The dance is slow, cool, collected, as the music blasts, and the boy and the goddess who controls him are in a different world, out of all contact with those who watch. There is no appeal here for attention to the spectator; there is only attention to each other, and the spectators are beyond reality. The boy in his dance worships the girl as he maneuvers her, lifts her, touches her. He attempts in mounting frenzy for a moment to control and subdue her as an erection rises in the stretched jersey of backcloth, and to kiss her. Then the music quietens. In the film we see his body branded with the impress of the goddess's as his passion is spent. She lets down her hair, and the dance of engulfment continues relentlessly, he, as always, powerless to resist her beauty and powerless, too, completely to claim her. He falls back, and, in the film, we see him somersault in pain and fall forward so that she in triumph can cause him to writhe at her feet.

She hovers over him as the rapid pulse of the strobe illumines them. She raises her leg over him, and the boy crouches there below her. Then, holding her above him, he rises and, before we realize it, he is carrying her and displaying her curved body aloft, as the filmed image has already anticipated, her legs locked about his head, his hands clasping her ankles. It is a posture of glory for the remote goddess and proud submission for the boy. He kneels at last so that she can step down. Before he realizes it, she is gone. The backdrop dissolves, and the boy walks back, back, through the back wall of the stage, where huge, high doors open for him, through the storage of scenery and props, to the exit to the street. These doors, too, open for him and, still transfixed by the goddess and his joy in her, he moves out into the light and traffic, perhaps to rejoin the world.

NOTES Gardner Compton, who created the films for *Astarte,* has had some interesting things to say about its composition. Writing in *Dance Magazine,* he said: "The discothèque is the temple of electricity with its light shows, audio-visual devices such as film (which, in essence, is merely the reproduction of light), and other visual effects. In these new temples, some dance to electronic music while others sit in small groups on the floor watching the God Electricity (Light) perform on the walls and ceilings. The milieu of *Astarte* was precisely this new house of worship.

"One of the elements of this new creed is the use of multimedia devices to obtain involvement. *Astarte* sought to bridge the gap between the loose, unrefined area of the happening and a legitimate art form—in this case, ballet. What Robert Joffrey and I tried to avoid was the looseness of form characteristic of the happening. Our concept was more classical in nature. The choreographer was using movement in a magnificent sustained counterpoint to the amplified acid-rock music. It was the dancers who were receiving the audio massage, a massage that tuned them *out* on the world of the audience. In so doing we hoped that the fantasy of the film media combined with the reality of the dancers would tune *in* the audience on the ritualistic milieu of the discothèque.

"But *Astarte* was merely a beginning, a primer for what is to come. It is only one of the first steps in the direction of a totally involved multi-media theatre experience. And I believe this will be a vital concept of the whole.

"In order for choreo-cinema to be successful, there must be a perfect blending of these concepts to form one unified artistic viewpoint. . . . I remember Martha Graham giving an image in class that made first position a reality to me. The essence of that image was as follows: Your arms are carried from the back as though you are standing in a shower and the water is like energy draining down the arm and off the middle fingers of the hands. A cameraman should film a dancer so that the last object to leave the frame is that portion of the body that moves the energy from space to space. The camera itself should also move the energy from one space to another, or it is not contributing. Timing and framing are the essential tools of a dance cameraman. One must frame on space and let the dancer move into it. Space is the dancer's canvas, whether on stage or on film. Both space and movement, too, may have to be modified or distorted to make the choreo-cinema effective to an audience.

"The camera is the eye of the audience, the establisher of the involvement, the point of view, the movement. Why should the joy of movement be limited to the dancers? The members of the audience, too, can enjoy it, but only if the camera works for them. Thus if someone were to ask me the difference between a *pas de deux* on stage and a *pas de deux* on film I would answer as follows: A *pas de deux* on stage is a dance for two people (usually a boy and a girl), whereas a *pas de deux* on film is a dance for a boy, a girl, *and* camera. If cinematographic movement techniques are used successfully with dance, a successful marriage can result. One must wed the movement of one art to the movement of the other in order to achieve a true choreographic end.

"In *Astarte,* Robert Joffrey choreographed for the stage. What I filmed was Joffrey's choreography (even the abstract images are derived from images of the dancers themselves). However, I selected and chose for my camera, making the film very different from what the dancers were doing on stage. Often to reach a total choreographic concept, I borrowed the fugue form from music. I repeated themes in such a way that the movement would start with the live dancers and then be repeated and built through film, although the dancers on stage were then doing something altogether different. At other times the film would initiate the theme and then the dancers would echo it and build it to climax which the film would again pick up. . . ."*

* Reprinted by courtesy of *Dance Magazine.*

AS TIME GOES BY

Music by Franz Josef Haydn. Choreography by Twyla Tharp. Lighting by Jennifer Tipton. Costumes by Chester Weinberg. Assistant to Miss Tharp: Harry Berg. First presented by the City Center Joffrey Ballet at the City Center, New York, October 24, 1973. Conducted by Seymour Lipkin.

As Time Goes By is a dance ballet to wonderful music by Haydn—the third and fourth movements of the *Symphony No. 45 in F-Sharp Minor.* Mozart once said, I think, that Haydn's music had given him immense amusement and also the deepest reflections. Mozart, as usual, was right. The music here is the famous *"Farewell" Symphony,* where the players get up and leave the stage one by one. What the choreographer does with that situation, and with other plots and developments of the music, is her own special business. The critic Marcia B. Siegel described it for *Dance Magazine:* "Beatriz Rodriguez' opening solo in silence is allegro ballet laced with those odd dislocations of body parts, those big transformations with smooth, almost lazy recoveries that we've come to think of as Tharpian. As Haydn's minuet begins, five other dancers join her and they slip through a long chain of decorous attitudes and preparations that melt or click into surprise partnerships. Haydn leaves the music dangling on an unfinished cadence, and the dancers redeploy themselves to begin The Four Finales, a glorious rout in which you can just pick out elements of various overworked dance endings, exits, and climaxes, all overlapped and out of joint and meticulously mistimed. Finally, to Haydn's famous adagio, where the musicians leave one by one, Larry Grenier spins out an extraordinary solo in one long, sinuous, self-involved phrase of movement, while the stage fills with dancers and empties again. You can't remember where he came from and you can't imagine where he'll stop. The curtain goes down while he's still dancing.

"I'm not inclined to take the title of *As Time Goes By*

too seriously—it might have come about by accident. A harried person from the Joffrey publicity department runs into the studio a week before the première and pleads: 'Twyla time is going by. The papers are screaming. We've got to have a title for your ballet!' Without taking her eyes off the rehearsal, Tharp mutters: 'Okay, call it *As Time Goes By*. Now don't bother me.'

"However that was, the ballet seems more concerned with continuity than with time itself. It shows us the bridges between things, the awkward foldings that precede the beautiful unfoldings, the movements that connect rather than the poses that separate. The beginning is the end is the beginning. Amen."

Arlene Croce, dance critic of *The New Yorker*, has written of Twyla Tharp's work in the November 19, 1973, issue of that magazine:

"Twyla Tharp is the Nijinska of our time. *Deuce Coupe*, an unidealized portrait of American youth in the nineteen sixties, is her *Les Biches*, and *As Time Goes By*, an abstract fantasy about individuals against the blank canvas of a tribal society, is her *Les Noces*. Of course I'm generalizing, but not, I hope, idly. *As Time Goes By*, created this season for the Joffrey Ballet and employing an all-Joffrey cast and Haydn music, is a study of classical dancing. Its 'tribal' ethos is that of young, hard-working New York-American dancers, subspecies Joffrey, and its light-speckled fancies and serene inversions of classical principles are as far from the iron wit of *Les Noces* as the heterogeneous home-style social dances of *Deuce Coupe* are from the monolithic encounters of that Parisian salon in *Les Biches*. Nevertheless, the parallel persists between Twyla Tharp and ballet's greatest woman choreographer. I think that, like Nijinska's, Twyla Tharp's work exacts a primitive force of expression from its subject, which is classical ballet. It seems to seek out first principles and turn them over with curiosity, finding new excitement in what lies on the other side of orthodoxy. And it gains a secondary kind of raw power from what seem deliberate lapses from ballet decorum and refinement. Sometimes, a classical step is resolved with a new twist; it forms itself and then re-forms itself backward. But sometimes the step isn't all there; it seems truncated or only half-quoted; the effect is of a surgical cut, a slash at the fat body of unusable style. The negations and distortions of Nijinska's choreography cut away rhetorical flab. The turned-in toes and obsessive stiff pointwork of *Les Noces* were a radical distortion, necessary if women's feet and not simply their points were to become significant once more on the stage. In much the same way, Twyla Tharp is moving toward a new quality of plain speech in classical choreography. At times, she seems to be on the verge of creating a new style, a new humanity, for classical-ballet dancers. If she doesn't go all the way to a full enunciation of that style, that is probably because the ballet is not long enough. Time, in this ballet, goes by much too fast.

"*As Time Goes By* is in four sections, quasi-dramatic in their progression. Beginning with the Individual, it moves on to the Group, then to the Mass, and finally back to the Individual. (These designations are my own; I prefer them to the unevocative titles in the program.) The opening solo is danced by Beatriz Rodriguez in silence. It is a concise statement of the material that will be developed, a ball of string that will be unwound. We see semaphore arms, snake hips, pirouettes stopped in mid-whirl, a paroxysm of flexions in *relevé*. Rodriguez, who looked childlike in *Deuce Coupe*, is transformed again. She is monumental, like a Nijinska iron woman. Three boys and two girls join her (Adix Carman, Henry Berg, William Whitener, Eileen Brady, and Pamela Nearhoof) and the music begins—the Minuet and Trio of Haydn's '*Farewell*' *Symphony*. The dance that accompanies it is not one dance but six—one for each member of the sextet. All six dances go on at the same time, now linking up, now separating, and all the whole moving from one tight cellular cluster to another. This sextet, which builds up the fascination and the deadpan humor of a clockwork toy, is a classical arrangement of the Tharpian group dance and typically democratic. The multifocal viewpoint makes a special event of the partnering (which keeps changing hands). It also eliminates the conventional hierarchy of the ballet ensemble. No one here is a ballerina; anyone may partner or be partnered. The sextet builds up pressure, too. The little hexagonal unit seems to become more and more confining, but the sweet musicianship of the choreography keeps the scene clear, its density unharrowing.

"The music breaks off, and one of the girls does a little walk-around in silence as new dancers enter. The Presto movement of the symphony starts. Suddenly, the stage seems to expand to unbelievable size. Dancers pour on and spread out. The broadened pattern has released us, but the tempo has stepped up the pressure, and we redouble our concentration. Now, against a complex background of moving dancers, solo variations occur; one, for Nearhoof, is galvanically funny, though at this breathless speed the laughs can't keep up with the jokes. Nor can we keep up with the ballet. There is no time to ponder the new logic of the steps—new in the way they combine close musical fit with a 'natural' loose look suited to each individual dancer; there's just time enough to enjoy it. One would like the key to that new logic; what makes it work at this tempo? Whatever it is, the result is a hyperkinesthesia that takes hold of the audience and doesn't let up until, once more, Haydn waves his wand and the dancers stroll nonchalantly away.

"The end of the piece is as Haydn would have wished it. To the Adagio finale of the '*Farewell*'—so called because the instrumentation thins out until only two violins are left—a dancer (Larry Grenier, whose attenuated lyrical style is itself a statement of slackening force) moves alone while others set about disappearing in a fashion that is unpredictable and sometimes chancy. A girl leaves, only to return a moment later. A boy lifts a girl off, turning her twice in the air, so another girl has to duck three times to avoid being hit. Ultimately, Grenier is *all* alone, having spun out the last thin skein of movement.

"*As Time Goes By* is not a pretentious enough ballet to make people feel that they have witnessed a heroic new undertaking in choreography. Its fifteen minutes are loaded with interest, but, like all of Twyla Tharp's work, the piece is peculiarly horizonless. Although each work she has made is self-contained and perfectly lucid in its own terms, each seems almost accidentally bound by the rise and fall of a curtain, and to be part of a larger continuity that exists out of time—out of the time, that is, of this ballet we have just seen. Somewhere, perhaps, there are unseen dancers unrolling the patterns and following up every implication, but we in the audience are spared their tortuous zeal. Twyla Tharp makes us feel that a ballet is nothing more than divisions of a choreographer's time. Although she understands cheap sensation and uses it well, there is no gloss, no appeal for attention, no careerism in her work. It's amusing to think of what a promoter like Diaghilev would have done with her. First, I think, he would retitle the sections of this ballet *Ariadne, Athens, The Labyrinth,* and *Theseus.* Cocteau would write the program notes and design the costumes. (The ones we have, by the Seventh Avenue designer Chester Weinberg, are examples of modest chic in shades of taupe.) Diaghilev would call the whole piece *The Minotaur,* because there's no Minotaur in it, and he would proclaim 'La Tharp' the herald of a new age. Which she is."*

* "A Moment in Time," by Arlene Croce. Reprinted by permission; © 1973 The New Yorker Magazine, Inc.

AT MIDNIGHT

Music by Gustav Mahler. Choreography by Eliot Feld. Décor by Leonard Baskin. Costumes by Stanley Simmons. Lighting and scenic supervision by Jean Rosenthal. First presented by American Ballet Theatre at the New York State Theater, Lincoln Center, December 1, 1967, with Bruce Marks, Christine Sarry, Terry Orr, Cynthia Gregory, and Eliot Feld in the principal roles. Sung by William Metcalf. Conducted by Kenneth Schermerhorn.

Danced to four of the "Five Rückert Songs" of Mahler, lyrics arranged by the composer to poems by Friedrich Rückert, *At Midnight* is named for the first of those songs. But the ballet is not based on what the songs say. They are rather an accompaniment to a danced narrative that reflects the motto of the ballet, a quotation from Thomas Hardy: "In the ill-judged execution of the well-judged plan of things, the call seldom produced the comer, the man to love rarely coincides with the hour for loving. Nature does not often say *'See!'* to her poor creature when seeing can lead to a happy doing or answer *'Here!'* to a body's cry of *'Where?'* till the hide-and-seek has become an irksome, outworn game."

The curtain rises on a dark stage. Illumined in the back is a painting of a face in torment surrounded by two ravens. We make out on stage toward the left a crouching group of men. A half-naked boy climbs onto their bent backs, lying there for support in an hour of need in the middle of the night. He stretches out and rolls off onto the floor as the baritone begins the song "At Midnight." The men cluster around the boy, covering his face with their hands. He is lifted high and then let down to dance alone. At the end, he leaps back into the arms of the men, where he first curls up, then stretches, his arms reaching out in an agony that has not gone away.

The backdrop changes to a painting of a figure crouching in despair. To the song "Ich atmet' einen Lindenduft" (I breathed a fragrance soft and sweet), a boy and girl, she in flowing yellow, he in gray, move in an intense yet lyric dance. Two extraordinary catches at the end of this buoyant *pas de deux* yield to a high lift, and the boy carries the girl away as she rides on his shoulder.

A boy, lost and never a part of a group of other boys and girls who dance happily and unaware about him, laments his loneliness and tries to imitate them. The music is the song "Ich bin der Welt abhanded gekommen."

The second song is now repeated. To its music, a girl joins the couple of the second song. There is no real communication between them, however, as she dances along and the couple, preoccupied, stands and sits together. They remain after the girl leaves and seem to waken from their reverie. Four other couples join them now, as do the lone girl of the last song and the boy of the third. Here, too, each of the single figures is so engrossed in trouble and separation that they have no eyes for each other. Amidst all these persons there is no new personal contact. They remain on stage as the song ends, alone as we first saw them.

NOTES Anna Kisselgoff of the New York *Times* has called *At Midnight* a "landmark ballet, poetic in its depth but accessible to everyone on its theatric level." Reviewing the ballet in the *Dancing Times*, the critic P. W. Manchester wrote that Eliot Feld's "first ballet, *Harbinger*, premièred in the 1967 spring season, indicated that a new talent had arrived. *At Midnight* more than confirmed the promise of *Harbinger*. Feld has set it to four of Gustav Mahler's songs. The first one provides the title for the ballet and is also the finest part of the work. It is a study in man's aloneness. The choreography, marvelously interpreted by Bruce Marks, aches with the doubts and loneliness of the fears that come only in sleeplessness. The second song . . . is a *pas de deux* for young lovers, done with exquisite, unsentimental sweetness by Christine Sarry and Terry Orr. . . . *At Midnight* is both moving and masterly. And . . . Feld is entering on his career as a choreographer while he is also just beginning his best years as a dancer. . . . His closeness to his company as colleague as well as choreographer may well be a major factor in what everyone is hoping will truly be a new era for American Ballet Theatre, one in which it will at long last have its own choreographer, creating for its particular talents, moulding its special and unique style."

Writing of the première in the *Jersey Journal*, the critic Patrick O'Connor said: "It is a unique privilege to be present at the first presentation of a great American work of art. But that's what happened to me last night at the American Ballet Theatre. In truth, there's no such thing as an American work of art. There are only works of art sometimes, too rarely, I'm afraid, composed, put together, by an American. Last night it was *At Midnight* by Eliot Feld. I won't say choreographed. It seemed much more than a dance composition. Feld is involved in what Doris Humphrey once called the art of making dances.

"Movement is, of course, the essential element but so is the painter's brush, the dynamics of stillness, the sacrifice of the mass, the crucifixion, the resurrection, the healing power of love. The whole piece was bathed in love and so was the audience; they knew it, felt it and were grateful.

"It seems almost profane to talk about the dancing. It wasn't dancing; it was another kind of activity—exalted movement. Cynthia Gregory in pentecostal lavender made one weep, and Christine Sarry in pentecostal yellow sustains stillness miraculously. She also danced brilliantly. Bruce Marks —as the Christ figure?—gave a shattering performance. Feld the dancer served Feld the choreographer like a ministering angel. A rare privilege, an historic occasion, something to tell my grandchildren."

LA BAYADÈRE

Ballet in four acts. Music by Ludwig Minkus. Book by S. N. Khudekov. Choreography by Marius Petipa. First presented at the Maryinsky Theatre, St. Petersburg, February 4, 1877. First presented (Act IV) in the United States by the Kirov Ballet at the Metropolitan Opera House, New York, September 14, 1961, with Kaleria Fedicheva as Nikiya, *and Sergei Vikulov as* Solor.

The libretto for this ballet, which is still active in the Soviet repertory, tells the story of a hapless Indian bayadère—a temple dancer—named Nikiya. The bayadère is loved but badly treated by Solor, a young warrior who breaks his pledge to her and marries another. Nikiya is poisoned by a confidante of her rival and dies. In the final act, the repentant Solor dreams that he seeks his beloved in the "Kingdom of the Shades." Though, like Orpheus and Albrecht, he finds her, she eludes him, despite his pledge that he will never forsake her again.

But the important thing about Act IV of *Bayadère* is not the story but the dancing. What happens is that the wraith-like inhabitants of the "Kingdom of the Shades" descend upon the stage down a long ramp at the back, parallel to the audience, all in profile in *arabesque penché* at each step. There are thirty-six Shades. These and their ensuing steps, while basically simple for dancers to perform, so direct the attention by their repetition that an otherworldliness results. Next there is a *pas de trois* for three of the Shades, followed by variations for each. Solor now dances a variation that reasserts his humanity in this atmosphere of immortals. The *pas de deux* between the two lovers ties them together as it were by a long diaphanous scarf. As Nikiya holds one end of the scarf with one hand, Solor at the other end supports her in a series of turns that is rivaled only by the lifts in the final act of *Giselle* for an expression of close spirituality.

NOTES Rudolf Nureyev's fine production of *La Bayadère* for the Royal Ballet has become well-known in the United

States. Another production, by Natalia Makarova, was presented in July 1974 by American Ballet Theatre. Arlene Croce wrote in *The New Yorker:* "It is an astounding success—more evidence that self-exiled Russian stars have as much to give as to gain in the West. *La Bayadère* (short for *La Bayadère,* Act IV: The Kingdom of the Shades) is an old Petipa classic of which most Westerners were unaware until the Kirov Ballet toured it in 1961. When Rudolf Nureyev, who defected on that same tour, produced it two years later for the Royal Ballet, it seemed that a miracle of transposition had taken place. Makarova has wrought an even greater miracle. She's not only reproduced a masterpiece of choreography, she's taken Ballet Theatre's corps and recharged it from top to bottom.

"The process of transformation is as yet incomplete, but never in my experience had the company danced a classical piece in so strict a style, on so broad a scale, and with such clarity of rhythm. Without these qualities, *La Bayadère* wouldn't be fun—it wouldn't even be *La Bayadère*—and what's *most* fun about this production is that every girl on the stage seems to be aware of the sensational progress she's making. . . . What matters . . . is that the motor impulse is there, solidly pumping energy into the right channels.

"Makarova's direction has been faithful and revealing. That motor impulse is basic to Petipa's exposition of movement flowing clean from its source. It flows from the simple to the complex, but we are always aware of its source, deep in the dancer's back, and of its vibration as it carries in widening arcs around the auditorium. This is dancing to be felt as well as seen, and Petipa gives it a long time to creep under our skins. Like a patient drillmaster, he opens the piece with a single, two-phrase theme in adagio tempo (arabesque, cambré port de bras), repeated over and over until all the dancers have filed onto the stage. Then, at the same tempo, with the dancers facing us in columns, he produces a set of mild variations, expanding the profile of the opening image from two dimensions to three. Positions are developed naturally through the body's leverage—weight, counterweight. Diagonals are firmly expressed. Returning to profile, the columns divide and flutter one by one to the rear. The final pose is of two long columns facing the wings with annunciatory arms. Now, to a collection of beer-garden tunes (the composer is Ludwig Minkus), Petipa sets dances for five soloists —a ballerina, a danseur, and three principal Shades—while behind them the vast, tireless corps responds in echoes, diverges, vanishes, regathers into garlands, into gateways, tosses, and freezes. The choreography is considered to be the first expression of grand-scale symphonism in dance, predating by seventeen years Ivanov's masterly designs for the definitive *Swan Lake*. But our first reaction is not to how old it looks but to how modern. Actually, the only word for this old-new choreography is immemorial. *La Bayadère* (1877) looks like the first ballet ever made: like man's—or, rather, woman's—first imprint in space and time.

"The subject of 'The Kingdom of the Shades' is not really death, although everybody in it except the hero is dead. It's Elysian bliss, and its setting is eternity. The long, slow repeated-arabesque sequence creates the impression of a grand crescendo that seems to annihilate all time. No reason it could not go on forever. And in the adagio drill that follows, the steps are so few and their content is so exposed that we think we'll remember them always—just like dancers, who *have* remembered them for a hundred years and for who knows how long before Petipa commemorated them in this ballet. Ballets, passed down the generations like legends, acquire a patina of ritualism, but *La Bayadère is* a ritual, a poem about dancing and memory and time. Each dance seems to add something new to the previous one, like a language being learned. The ballet grows heavy with this knowledge, which at the beginning had been only a primordial utterance, and in the coda it fairly bursts with articulate splendor. My favorite moment comes in the final waltz, when the three principal Shades are doing relevé-passé, relevé-attitude cambré to a rocking rhythm, and the corps, seeing this, rush to join them in the repeat. They—the corps—remember those cambré positions from their big dance.

"It's the corps' ballet—a fact the management should recognize by allowing a company call after, as well as before, the soloists have taken their bows. But the soloists in the performance I saw—Cynthia Gregory, Ivan Nagy, Karena Brock, Deborah Dobson, and Martine van Hamel—deserved their applause. Gregory was at her greatest. She took her grand port de bras the way it was meant to be taken—straight up out of the floor and through the body. Van Hamel, who may be the most talented of the company's younger ballerinas, did her variation the hard way by not coming off point until she was well up and into arabesque, and the excessively slow tempo made it even harder. Nagy has a way of filling a role superlatively without actually doing the steps. In his variation, he gathered himself powerfully and unfurled something that started like double assemblés and ended halfway to double sauts de basque. In the *pas de deux* with the veil, he didn't parallel the ballerina's steps and poses—but this is one of the differences between Makarova's staging and Nureyev's. Another difference is that she doesn't stroke the upbeat, or break the path of a gesture in order to point it. The way these two have staged the piece corresponds to their styles as performers—hers, musically more fluid; his, more emphatic. Also, her arabesques are not penchées, the solos are arranged in a different order, and she ends the ballet with the corps stretched along the floor in a semicircle rather than backbent in a sunburst. I prefer the Royal Ballet's orchestration, with its drumrolls and its protracted climax that accompanies the sunburst, and I think I prefer the sunburst, but apart from those things there's little to choose between these productions. They're both marvellous. Marcos Paredes' costumes for Ballet Theatre are in the Victorian style traditional to this ballet, and I liked his headdresses for the women—beaded circlets à la Anna Pavlova."*

* From "Makarova's Miracle" by Arlene Croce. Reprinted by permission; © 1974 The New Yorker Magazine, Inc.

BHAKTI

Based on a Hindu theme and musical setting. Choreography by Maurice Béjart. Costumes by Germinal Casado. First presented by the Ballet of the Twentieth Century in 1968. First presented in the United States by the same ensemble at the Brooklyn Academy of Music, New York, January 25 1971.

A Hindu love poem in dance, *Bhakti* is a ballet in three parts. The themes of those parts have been described by their creator, Maurice Béjart: "It is through love that the worshiper identifies with the divinity; and each time he relives the legend of his god, who is himself only one of the faces of the supreme and nameless reality." The three parts of the work are *pas de deux* between certain girls and their heroes:

RAMA an incarnation of Vishnu. His love affair with Sita, symbol of purity, is related in the celebrated Hindu epic *Ramayana.* This poem forms the basis of every classical dance or theatrical production in India.

KRISHNA another incarnation of Vishnu. He is the God of Youth and Beauty, the divine Player of the Flute whose affairs with the shepherdesses and the lovely Radha are sung in the *Gita Govinda.* He is also the teacher par excellence, and it is he who speaks in the *Bhagavad-Gita,* one of the most important books of all.

SHIVA the third person in the Hindu Trinity (*Trimurti*): Brahma, Vishnu, Shiva. As the "Destroyer," he kills illusion and personality. God of the Dance, his wife Shakti pursues the vital energy that flows from and returns to him, immobile, yet forever in motion.

Introduced by three young men, the ballet proceeds to representations of these gods and their ladies, each supported by appropriate ensembles.

BILLY THE KID

Ballet in one act. Music by Aaron Copland. Choreography by Eugene Loring. Book by Lincoln Kirstein. Scenery and costumes by Jared French. First presented by Ballet Caravan at the Chicago Opera House, Chicago, October 16, 1938, with Eugene Loring as Billy, *Marie-Jeanne as the* Mother *and* Sweetheart, *Lew Christensen as* Pat Garrett, *and Todd Bolender as* Alias.

The story of Billy the Kid is already a legend in America, a part of the larger legend we know as the Opening of the West. The facts known about him—that his real name was William H. Bonney; that he was born in New York City in 1859; was taken to Kansas when he was three; killed his first man in Silver City, New Mexico, when he was twelve; and by the time he was hunted down and shot, at the age of twenty-one, had killed a man for every year of his life—these facts remind us of a gangster movie. But actually these facts do not tell us the whole story of the Kid. They do not tell us that, although Billy the Kid was regarded as the most dangerous desperado of his time, he was loved and admired as much as he was feared, and that the Far West after the Civil War was a place where these emotions could interchange and resolve—to make of his life the heroic myth it has since become. This ballet is not, therefore, a simple biography of a wild West killer: it is the story of the life of Billy the Kid as it became a part of the life of his time.

PROLOGUE The first, slow notes of the music are subdued and eerie, like sounds in the wilderness at night. The curtain rises. Across the front of the stage a spotlight shines, making a path of brilliant orange light. The rest of the stage is suffused in a semidark glow, as if bathed in the light of the golden sun. An arid khaki-colored desert and tall, branching cacti are seen in the distance. From the right, a man dressed in a cowboy outfit steps boldly into the path of light. Later we shall learn that this is Pat Garrett, the sometime friend of Billy the Kid who becomes sheriff and kills him. But at the moment he is simply any American pioneer, moving westward toward the blaze of the setting sun. He moves stiffly, with determination; for each step forward he will take none back. Then his progress becomes a dance, the movements of which remind us of the frontiersman's work: he circles his arm high over his head to lasso invisible cattle; he pulls back roughly on invisible reins to halt a covered wagon, then drives the horses on with a lash of a whip; he kneels motionless, gun pointed, to catch the imaginary Indian. The music gains in strength with his vigorous movements. It becomes stronger still, as Garrett is followed by another man and a woman. The man copies every one of his leader's gestures, while the woman sets a dance pattern for the pioneer mother who rocks her children to sleep even when danger surrounds her. Other couples enter, and the orchestra builds gradually to sound a mighty processional as the pioneer figures follow their leader in this formalized march to the West. Now Garrett thrusts his arms forward, pushing back the frontier. He faces directly into the light. He pirouettes rapidly, spine in the air, and repeats these movements as all the men in the caravan follow his lead. All the dancers catch the full vitality of the music, which itself pushes forward to a resistless, persistent climax. Then, at its fullest volume, the music is cut off sharply. There is a blackout.

STREET SCENE When the lights come up again, the backdrop still depicts, as it will continue to do, the same arid desert, but before the curtain move a group of particular characters—not pioneers simply—who place this episode in the hot and sunny main street of an early Western town, just north of the border. Woodwinds play an old Western tune that the rest of the orchestra takes up gaily and playfully. A smiling, sinuous Mexican in a wide-brimmed hat struts about, pawing the street with his boots like a tame but unbridled stallion. Pioneer women, dressed for the town in close-fitting bonnets, pass him by, their arms crooked to carry invisible burdens. The Mexican ignores them. Cowboys ride across the scene, spurring on the imaginary horses they straddle. Three dancing girls enter, their hands on their tightly corseted hips in an impudent attitude. Two women look them up and down and, noting their high-buttoned gold shoes and garish red tights, turn up their noses in disapproval, sniff at the air, and walk away. Eight cowboys ride on, and there is a short rodeo. At the end three of them stop and take up with the dance-hall girls. A group of lovely Mexican girls come onto the scene, and now the street seethes with activity. The people stand about, some talking, some flirting, others going about their private business.

Then suddenly the music is quiet. An oboe sounds a theme, and on the left a small, attractive woman comes in. She is dressed in city clothes and is clearly a stranger to the community. A big, gangling boy, dressed only in overalls and a straw hat, hangs onto her skirts, and they move through the crowd. This is Billy the Kid. The boy looks about and appears to want to stop, but his mother walks on ahead and they exit. The Mexican and the four Mexican girls dance together briefly, and then the Kid and his mother return. This time the Kid shows off his strength by softly lifting his mother around for several measures. She pushes his cheek to tell him how silly he is, and he turns his face away, blushing, but he persists at the game and the two waltz off.

Meanwhile something has happened to the crowd. They stand closely packed together, watching an argument between the Mexican and a man in red. The argument becomes a fight. They hit each other in slow motion, neither falling. The music accompanies their blows with retarded rhythm that increases in volume and speed as the fight becomes serious. The people in the crowd begin to sense that they should stand back. Now, as a trumpet sounds the theme militantly, the Kid enters with his mother. Both of them are fascinated by the brawl and stand on the fringe of the crowd. Just as they join the group, the Mexican pulls a gun. The man in red turns quickly to defend himself and steps against the crowd, right next to Billy and his mother. The Mexican fires. He misses. Billy's mother doubles up in agony. She falls against her son, who stands transfixed, staring straight ahead, not comprehending. She grasps his arm, slides down slowly to the ground, and dies. The people are horrified, but they, too, are motionless. They remain still and shocked as the Kid shakes off his dream, grabs a knife, and dashes over to the Mexican. Billy kills him with one quick stab in the back. He topples over. Everyone steps back, unbelieving. Billy looks about wildly, wondering where to go. Pat Garrett steps in to help him, but the Kid ignores him and runs off. Already he has chosen his way.

One of the men stoops to pick up the body of the Kid's mother, and the whole crowd leans over in unison, expressing the common grief. Another man kneels down beside the dead Mexican, throws him over his shoulder, and carries him off. But the Mexican will reappear. He becomes Alias, a character of many disguises who haunts the Kid constantly throughout his life and finally helps to kill him.

The crowd begins to disperse. Couples walk away, shaking their heads, still stunned by the two murders. But instead of leaving the stage, they mill about, circling slowly, and we see after a few minutes that perhaps they are not the same men and women who saw Billy the Kid's first crime. The men lift their women affectionately, just as Billy lifted his mother, but everyone is wary and suspicious. The people have changed. They have grown older and, as we have been watching them, years have passed in the street. Finally, one by one, the couples leave and the stage is empty.

THE DESERT The Kid enters in the back. He is no longer a child. He is dressed in black and white striped riding breeches, boots, a wide-brimmed hat; there is a skull on his shirt pocket. He dances alone. In this dance we understand a little of how the Kid has grown up. The proud pose that begins and ends the dance is confidently self-assertive, and in between the Kid performs a series of difficult movements with ferocity rather than grace. He stomps loudly with his heavy boots, circles an imaginary foe with his gun ready to fire, spins swiftly in the air, lands, and kicks out at his victim. He is going through the only vocabulary he possesses, and we realize that all of his life, every waking moment, is a practiced preparation for the next time he will have to kill. His dance gesture for shooting is a quick aim at the target, then a spin in the air that matches the speed of a bullet, and finally a vicious kick. It is the gesture of a man who hates his dead foe and the whole world. And there follows inevitably the same pose of self-assertion. Never does this man doubt that he has done the right thing, never has he supposed himself guilty of a crime. Shooting happens to be his way of living: a murder is just like lighting a cigarette.

As the Kid nears the end of his soliloquy, he is interrupted by the arrival of a small posse. Three men canter across the stage in formation, circle, and try to close in on the Kid. He hides. Then he aims, spins, and kicks. The leader of the three men falls dead. The Kid prances slowly and softly, then draws himself up to his full height and stands triumphant. The scene blacks out.

A spotlight at the front of the stage comes on. Sitting close to the footlights, around a campfire, the Kid and Pat Garrett are playing cards. Garrett is now sheriff, but still a friend to the Kid. The light from the fire makes enormous silhouettes of their figures against the backdrop. The orchestra plays a quiet, wistful melody. The Kid shuffles the cards and deals. The two men draw their cards. A man and two cowgirls, all friends of Billy, approach the fire. The man stoops down to watch the card game. Garrett is distracted for an instant, but turns back to find the Kid cheating. He protests. The Kid is patient with him at first, denies cheating, and attempts to humor him. Pat continues to protest, but when he sees that the Kid will not accept his friendship, will not even admit to overt cheating, he rides off into the night. Billy's three friends gather about the fire and take up the cards while the Kid stands aside. His rage mounts. Pat has got the better of him. He stomps angrily, regretting that he did not kill his friend. The group at the fire turn and stare at him; they are frightened at what he may do. But the Kid does not have time to act. Shooting is heard in the distance, and before he can flee, the stage fills with people. The drums boom with gunfire as Pat Garrett leads a posse on in pursuit of the Kid. Billy moves to defend himself, shoots wildly as his friends gather about him and his attackers fall on their faces to protect themselves. A fierce gun battle ensues, during which the Kid continues to shoot out indiscriminately at all comers. He and his friends are hemmed in by two lines of gunfire. They are all killed except Billy. As he is about to fire another round, he trips over the body of one of his own men. Two men move in to hold him. One of them is Alias. The Kid kills Alias. The other is Pat Garrett. Pat is quick: he sticks a gun in the Kid's back and rides him off to jail. The Kid does not seem to care in the least.

The posse that has helped capture Billy—cowgirls and cowboys—now join together to celebrate and dance joyfully. In the midst of their frolic, the Kid's sweetheart, a beautiful Mexican girl, walks in and tries to find her lover. No one pays any attention to her. She leaves the scene disconsolate. The celebration is blacked out.

THE JAIL Billy stands on one foot, shuffling cards. Naked above the waist, he wears a kerchief about his neck, arm bands, and black riding togs over white tights. His jailer, Alias, stands at his side, ready to receive his cards. Billy bides his time, shuffles the cards slowly, and shifts to the other leg. The jailer grows impatient and turns away for an instant. Billy moves openly to grab his gun, as if the jailer expected him to. The jailer, of course, sees the move but ignores it. He suggests that it is all part of the game and that Billy won't do anything wrong. He walks away. The Kid sneaks up on him softly and this time does grab his gun. The jailer turns back, expecting the Kid to hand it over. The Kid laughs. He kills the jailer and stands again triumphant. Blackout.

THE DESERT The Kid gallops across the stage to his hide-out. He disappears. A posse follows, but they are unable to pick up the trail. Billy enters again, screened by two Mexican girls, who stand between him and the posse. Alias, now disguised as an Indian guide, leads him away. The Kid arrives at a quiet spot, and Alias leaves him. Pat Garrett and his riders pass by, but see nothing. Billy takes his hat off and undresses to go to sleep. He is so tired he seems to be asleep already. He crouches on the ground to the right and stacks his clothes automatically, as if in a dream. His sweetheart enters on the left, behind his back. She dances on point, formally. He does not turn and see her, but looks up, seeing her in his mind's eye. He looks back down at his clothes. The girl touches his shoulder and poses briefly. He stirs, first swings his right leg out and back from his crouching position—a movement in stylized keeping with the girl's remote intimacy. She stands close beside him, but he is never aware of her real presence. He rises, stretches; the girl holds onto him and poses again beautifully, and they begin a short *pas de deux* to a sensuous waltz. He lifts her gently and swings her body slowly, not looking at her at all; he might be dancing with any girl and she with any man. Almost immediately he abandons her and goes back to stretch out to sleep. The girl dances off as quietly as she came, with no protest. The dream is over.

Pat Garrett, led by Alias, comes in and watches Billy asleep. Billy has not heard them, but wakes up as if warned by something. He reaches for his gun, holds it ready. The night is black: he sees nothing. For an instant he is afraid. Garrett and Alias stand stock-still, holding their breath. Billy calls out "*¿Quien es?*" ("Who is it?"), his voice hoarse with fear. There is no answer. He waits. Still no sound. He laughs to himself, silently. To reassure himself, he laughs harder; his body shakes with laughter. He stops, takes out a cigarette, strikes a match, and illuminates his face for a flickering moment. Garrett fires. Billy falls. He is dead.

Long-robed Mexican women enter and stand over his body. They pass by slowly, mourning, to music of lamentation, and the light fades.

EPILOGUE The setting sun shines across the stage, and Pat Garrett walks in boldly, as he did at the beginning of the ballet, leading a host of pioneers. All march facing west, then turn back east, then west again, as the music impels them forward.

BRAHMS QUINTET

Music by Johannes Brahms. Choreography by Dennis Nahat. Costumes by Willa Kim. Lighting by Nananne Porcher. First presented by American Ballet Theatre at the Brooklyn Academy of Music, New York, December 1969, with Cynthia Gregory, Ivan Nagy, Mimi Paul, Gayle Young, Naomi Sorkin, Ian Horvath, Eleanor D'Antuono, and Terry Orr as principals.

This dance ballet to a masterpiece by Brahms uses the score for its narrative. The music critic Donald F. Tovey referred to the Brahms *Quintet in G Major, Op. 111*, as "an immensely powerful outburst of high spirits. . . . The first movement seems unlimited in its capacity for expansion. The adagio . . . is one of Brahms's tragic utterances. Its tempo is slower than that of any other piece of classical music since Beethoven's C Minor Concerto." Tovey found the third movement to be an "exquisite plaintive little scherzo and trio" and the finale "vigorous. . . . At the end its coda breaks away into a completely new dance tune, the phrases of which reel down in bacchanalian irregularity to explain themselves with impudent assurance as connected with the main theme by ties as intimate as a borrowed visiting card." (From *Cobbet's Cyclopedic Survey of Chamber Music*, 1963.)

Reviewing the ballet for the Washington *Post*, the critic Jean Battey Lewis said that "Nahat's *Brahms Quintet* is one of those flowing, floating dance works so appealing to us these days. It has a lovely, curving wind-swept quality and an abstraction that still celebrates the affection between the dancers."

THE CAGE

Ballet in one act. Music by Igor Stravinsky (Concerto Grosso in D for Strings). *Choreography by Jerome Robbins. Costumes by Ruth Sobotka. Lighting by Jean Rosenthal. First presented by the New York City Ballet at the City Center, New York, June 10, 1951, with Nora Kaye as the* Novice, *Yvonne Mounsey as the* Queen, *and Nicholas Magallanes and Michael Maule as the* Intruders.

This ballet is a dramatic demonstration of a phenomenon common to insect and animal life and to Western mythology too: the phenomenon of the female considering the male as prey. The mantis devours her partner after mating; the spider kills the male unless he attacks first; and the Amazons, in Greek mythology, were a cult of warlike females who did not associate with men, except for procreation. The Amazons despised their male children and maimed or destroyed them. Woman was sufficient; Man was accidental. *The Cage* shows us such a tribe of women.

Before the ballet begins, the auditorium is completely dark. The footlights come up before the curtain, then go out; the lights in the orchestra are extinguished. There is no music. The curtain rises. The light is obscure and misty, but we see hanging over the stage a tangle of multicolored strands, like the web of some huge spider. Mysteriously, as if it were a living thing, the web rises, stretches, and hangs over the floor. On the left stand a group of female figures arranged in a tight tableau; they are clustered together like bees in a hive.

The music begins with three notes sounded sharply on the strings. The women stir. In the center of the group sits the queen of the tribe. The lights come up gradually. A still, shrouded creature is drawn out from between the queen's legs; the novice has been born. The queen strips the confining membrane from the novice's body. The new member of the tribe crouches slightly. Her body is marked with endless, tangled viscera. Her face is still covered. She is motionless. The queen stands behind her, extending her arms grotesquely, seeming to enclose the novice with her long talons.

The orchestra begins a vibrant march. The twelve members of the tribe turn their backs, rise on point, and commence a grotesque ceremonial dance. As their bodies turn, we see that their backs are insectlike: strands reach out from their black spines to cover their backs, and they seem to resemble scuttling beetles. The queen leaves the novice and dances among the tribe. The women circle her and bow low obediently as she dances. The novice remains inert.

Now two of the women go to the novice and drag her to the center, before the queen. The queen tears off the membrane covering her face. The novice's hands reach up to protect her eyes from the sudden light. Her face is a mask; her hair, dark and wet, clings to her head. The queen is well pleased at her ugliness. The birth rite is over; the queen and her creatures leave to watch the novice from the surrounding darkness. Just as she departs, the queen touches the novice's dark head in blessing.

The melody changes; the music slows in tempo. The novice's untrained limbs do not yet know how to move and she squats alone. She tests her arms and legs, pushes her body up on them, rises on point. Her gestures are sudden and sharp, her body angularly contorted. Her fingers are clawing and knifelike blades cutting at the air tentatively; her arms are sinuous, serpentine. She walks with knees open and bent, arms ready to enlace her prey.

The music breaks into a loud, rapidly rhythmic burst of sound. A man rushes in and seizes the novice by the waist. She twists away in revulsion. The intruder attempts to pull her close to him and falls to the ground. The novice falls upon him, and they roll over together. The exhausted intruder lies quiet as the novice rises and steps upon his chest with the sharp point of her foot. Now she straddles his body, grabs his head between her legs, clenches her fists, tightens and twists her body, and cracks his neck with her knees. He is dead.

The music quietens. The novice kicks the body over on its face. As the orchestra resumes the opening march, she dances alone, her knees rising high, driving her feet hard against the ground. Her head is thrown back and her mouth hangs open in a shriek of triumph.

The queen leads the tribe back to the novice. The hideous women stalk into the light, surround the novice, and congratulate her. She has met the test, her instinct has obeyed the law of the tribe: she has killed her first male. The novice kicks at his body contemptuously, and he is dragged off.

The queen embraces the novice. Other women in the tribe pair off and rest together. The women are content with their own society and relax without fear of intrusion. Then the music sounds a warning. The couples separate. The light dims. The queen signals the others to hasten away. The novice, suddenly afraid, is running off after them as her swift body is caught up in the arms of a dark, handsome intruder. Her legs try to kick her body free as he holds her, but she cannot loosen his grasp. The warning in the music ceases; the melody flows yieldingly. The novice is now unsure. Gradually she succumbs to the superior strength of the intruder and dances with him a romantic love duet. He holds her on his knee, and she sharpens her claws together, not for battle now, but for love. Their bodies separate and their fingers approach and entwine like bristling antennae. She tries to make herself graceful as she dances and falls back into the intruder's arms. He catches her body between his legs; her face turns up toward his, and their arms embrace in a cocoon. The novice's feet beat at the floor as the intruder becomes her lover.

The lights go down for a moment. The music whirrs ominously. The frightened intruder moves and the woman falls to the ground. The two lovers cower together, trying to conceal each other in the darkness, as the queen and the tribe enter. Then, as the intruder sees the women who would claim the novice, he revolts and pushes the woman, now hideous to him, into the arms of her Amazon queen.

This is what the tribe have waited for. The queen directs her creatures to attack the intruder as the novice is held secure. The women climb upon the intruder like ants on a stick of candy. He is released briefly and rolls helpless on the ground. The novice's native instinct begins to return. She falls upon him, straddles him, and slides her body over the passive male. She squats guiltily as the women seize him and carry him aloft. The queen orders her fellow creatures to carry the novice on their shoulders and hold her poised above him. The novice's claws are straight and sharp for the kill. She aims carefully and deliberately and slashes.

The body of the intruder lies again on the ground. The hungry women crawl over him, devouring his limbs. The novice strangles him between her knees. His body curls for a moment, then straightens. He is dead. His body is rolled across the stage. The victorious women leap over it as they dance triumphantly.

The novice cleans her talons. The queen joins her to accept her as a true member of the tribe. The two grotesque figures whirl together, then stand motionless, their deformed bodies dominating the dark cage. The music stops. The great spidery web loosens and falls about them to the ground.

CELEBRATION

Ballet by Jerome Robbins. Music and choreography as specified below. Scenery by Rouben Ter-Arutunian. First presented by the Festival of Two Worlds at the Teatro Nuovo, Spoleto, Italy, July, 1973, with Antoinette Sibley and Anthony Dowell (England), Violette Verdy and Jean-Pierre Bonnefous (France), Carla Fracci and Paolo Bortoluzzi (Italy), Patricia McBride and Helgi Tomasson (United States), and Malika Sabirova and Muzafar Bourkhanov (Soviet Union).

Subtitled "The Art of the *Pas de Deux,*" *Celebration* combined in a few historic performances classical *pas de deux* of the past with contemporary dance. The basic idea was to show the classic *pas de deux* in all its glamor but to show, too, the depth of feeling of contemporary ballet duets. The original intention was for *Celebration* to begin with a brief talk and demonstration of the art of the *pas de deux* by Anton Dolin, the famed partner of many ballerinas. Jerome Robbins decided instead to introduce his ballet himself, saying simply that it would be a "celebration of dancing by dancers."

The dancers are five couples from England, France, Italy, the United States, and the Soviet Union. Heralds carrying flags introduce the action. All five dancers enter to a fanfare and dance to the music of a Tchaikovsky waltz. Then one by one, the couples performed some of the great *pas de deux.* First, Sabirova and Bourkhanov in *The Corsair Pas de Deux* then Fracci and Bortoluzzi in the love duet from *La Sylphide,* the oldest work of the evening. A *grand pas classique* for Verdy and Bonnefous came next, followed by Robbins's own *Afternoon of a Faun* by McBride and Tomasson. The *grand pas de deux* from the final act of *The Sleeping Beauty* by Sibley and Dowell concluded the first act of the presentation.

The second part consisted of the Balanchine *Tchaikovsky Pas de Deux* (McBride and Tomasson), the Ashton *Pas de Deux* from *Thaïs* (Sibley and Dowell), the Petipa/Minkus display piece from *Don Quixote* (Sabirova and Bourkhanov), Robbins's new *Bagatelles* to music from Beethoven (Verdy and Bonnefous), and the celebrated final *pas de deux* from the Mérante/Delibes *Coppélia.*

The finale was an arrangement by Jerome Robbins for all five couples of the Ivanov adagio from *Swan Lake,* Act Two.

NOTES The Robbins *Bagatelles,* called then simply *A Beethoven Pas de Deux,* had been performed initially at a preview in New York, May 16, 1973, at the New York City Ballet's Annual Spring Gala. It was danced by Violette Verdy and Jean-Pierre Bonnefous to *Four Bagatelles* of Beethoven, played by the pianist Jerry Zimmerman: Nos. 4, 5, and 2 from *Opus 33* and No. 4 from *Opus 126.* The costumes were by Florence Klotz and the lighting by Ronald Bates.

Reporting to the New York *Times,* the critic John Gruen wrote of the première of *Celebration* at the Spoleto Festival: "Bringing together five celebrated ballet couples (by no means an easy feat), and devising a work that would focus on international ballet styles, Robbins made clear both his magnetism as one of the world's great choreographers and his deep love of classical traditions."

The Ashton *pas de deux,* to the Meditation from the opera *Thaïs* by Jules Massenet, was first performed by Antoinette Sibley and Anthony Dowell at a gala ballet performance at the Adelphi Theatre, London, March 21, 1971. The critic Peter Williams wrote about the performance in *Dance and Dancers* magazine: Ashton "has created one of those oriental dream sequences that so reflect the whole mood of occidental awakening to the orient of the mid-nineteenth century. At least I imagine that Sibley must have been a dream figure, since she first appears with a light veil over her face as she approaches the kneeling Dowell. Everything about this dance evoked Pavlova, whom Ashton adored without reservation and whom he delighted in imitating until once, while staying at a country house, he seriously damaged his foot in an impromptu performance of *The Dying Swan.* But although the accident put a stop to any further imitations, Pavlova continued to cast a loving shadow over his life. This new *pas de deux* is all drifting and swooning and some fiendishly difficult lifts which have to look as though she is a wraith, and in which Dowell managed to make Sibley look as though she was. . . . It was lovely, and they were lovely, and to those that remembered, it must have brought on waves of nostalgia for Pavlova with Mordkin. . . ."

Writing after the first repertory performance of *Four Bagatelles* by the New York City Ballet, January 10, 1974, with Gelsey Kirkland and Jean-Pierre Bonnefous, Anna Kisselgoff said in the New York *Times:* "The very structure of *Four Bagatelles* follows the conventional sequence of the nineteenth-century classic *pas de deux:* adagio, variation for the man, then the woman, coda. In the first part, Mr. Robbins throws out almost subliminal quotes from three styles. A fleeting reminder of Denmark's Bournonville school, as in *Flower Festival at Genzano,* occurs in the beginning with the girl's *penchées arabesques,* head tilting and the man's leaps. Later, as Miss Kirkland slowly extends her leg to the side from on-toe position, while Mr. Bonnefous supports her in an image directly culled from the *grand pas de deux* of *The Sleeping Beauty,* there is a flashing allusion to the Russian style of Petipa.

"The adagio ends with Miss Kirkland down on one knee and Mr. Bonnefous behind her, in a reversal of the traditional pose that closes the adagio of Act Two of *Giselle*—a nod toward French Romantic ballet.

"These are, of course, whiffs of history wafting through a contemporary work, and the allusions are absent from the solos. Mr. Bonnefous's variation has folk touches that are echoed in the coda and some interesting experiments in phrasing. It is a tricky solo, somewhat short on transitional steps, and Mr. Bonnefous could not quite conceal the effort involved. Miss Kirkland, obviously most suited to the Robbins choreography, danced with brilliant technique and demure appeal. Mr. Zimmerman played with his customary excellence."

CINDERELLA

Ballet in three acts and seven scenes. Music by Sergei Prokofiev. Choreography by Rotislav Zakharov. Libretto by Nikolai Volkov. First presented by the Bolshoi Ballet at the Bolshoi Theatre, Moscow, November 15, 1945, with Olga Lepeshinskaya in the title role. Designed by Pyotr Williams. Presented in a new version with choreography by Konstantin Sergeyev at the Kirov State Theatre of Opera and Ballet, Leningrad, April 8, 1946, with Natalia Dudinskaya in the title role. A new production, revised by Sergeyev, was presented at the Kirov Theatre, July 13, 1964, with Irina Kolpakova. Designer: Tatiana Bruni. This production was first presented in the United States by the Kirov Ballet at the Metropolitan Opera House, New York, September 11, 1964, with Irina Kolpakova and Yuri Soloviev.

Prokofiev wrote that he conceived of *Cinderella* "as a classical ballet with variations, adagios, *pas de deux*, etc. I see Cinderella not only as a fairy-tale character but also as a real person, feeling, experiencing, and moving among us." The Russian composer began work on the score in 1940, but because of other commitments during World War II did not finish the orchestration until 1944.

ACT ONE—A ROOM IN CINDERELLA'S HOUSE It is evening and Cinderella's stepsisters—Krivlyaka (Affected) and Zlyuka (Furious)—are embroidering a silk scarf while their mother dotingly looks on. Cinderella sits alone at the fireplace, polishing a pot. The two sisters begin to quarrel over the scarf; their tempers are so bad that the mother can resolve the fight only by cutting the scarf in two. They now tease Cinderella, whom no one, not even her loving father, will defend. When they leave her alone finally, she sets about her routine of cleaning up the room. She finds a piece of the scarf and, forgetting herself, dances. But a mirror brings her back to reality; she sees her miserable dress and realizes that such a scarf is not for her. Her sadness induces memories of her beloved mother; she shuns the portrait of her cruel stepmother and tries to cover it with a curtain.

Her father returns and wants to comfort Cinderella. She sits on his knee and cries. But he fears his wife more than he loves his daughter, and, observing the covered portrait of his spouse, is apprehensive. Meanwhile, Zlyuka and Krivlyaka, who have been watching, alert their mother, who rushes in in a rage. She attacks her husband and taunts Cinderella mercilessly, finally collapsing in a fit of anger.

A beggarwoman appears, asking for alms. While the stepmother and the two sisters want to chase the woman away, and the father is too frightened to do anything, Cinderella turns and gives her a piece of bread.

Now preparations begin for the gala ball to which the family—all except Cinderella—have been invited. Dressmaker, hairdresser, dancing master, and musicians come to prepare the ladies. When everything is ready, they all depart for the castle, and Cinderella is alone.

Wishing also to be at the ball, Cinderella lets herself be carried away by unattainable dreams. She curtsies, as if before the prince himself. Suddenly the old beggarwoman appears again, but this time as Cinderella's fairy godmother. She promises to make the girl's dreams come true in gratitude for Cinderella's kindness. The fairy presents the girl with a pair of crystal slippers and orders four fairies representing the seasons of the year to prepare and dress Cinderella for the ball. The fairy of Spring brings her a gossamer dress, light as a cloud; Summer brings lovely roses; Autumn a splendid cloak glowing like the sun; and Winter diamonds and jewels, glistening like icicles. Dressed and ready now for the ball, Cinderella is truly a princess out of a fairy tale.

Before she leaves for the castle, however, the fairy godmother warns her that she must return home exactly at twelve o'clock, or she will turn back into her original state forever. She will be reminded of the approach of midnight by twelve dwarfs whom the fairy godmother will cause to emerge from the ancient clock at the castle. The fairy godmother wishes her godspeed and leaves, as a golden coach magically appears before Cinderella to take her to the ball.

ACT TWO—THE BALL AT THE PRINCE'S CASTLE While waiting for their host to appear, the splendidly dressed ladies and gentlemen dance a stately measure. The stepmother and her two daughters arrive and, grotesquely imitating the manners of their betters, attract considerable attention. Two men are finally persuaded to ask the two sisters to dance.

The prince appears, greets his guests, and ascends the throne. As the ball continues, a new strain of enchanting music is heard, and, accompanied by attendants, a lovely young girl enters. The prince cannot take his eyes off her, and asks her to dance. The court is curious about her identity. No one, not even her own family and least of all the ugly stepsisters, realizes that the beautiful guest is Cinderella.

When Arab boys present Cinderella with three oranges, she is so moved by the envious glances of Krivlyaka and Zlyuka that she gives the fruit to them. The prince and Cinderella are then briefly alone. They have both fallen in love at first sight and dance together to declare their love.

When the guests return, the court festivities continue. But at the height of the celebration, before she has even contemplated that such an evening should ever end, the clock strikes twelve. True to the fairy godmother's word, twelve dwarfs emerge from the clock. Cinderella, terrified, flees the castle. The prince runs after her. The prediction of the fairy godmother is fulfilled: Cinderella is again as she first was, and only the crystal slippers remain from her ball dress. She loses one slipper as she dashes home, and the prince, as he pursues her, finds it. He comforts himself that to find the girl all he has to do is find the owner of the slipper!

ACT THREE, SCENE ONE—COURTYARD OF THE CASTLE In an effort to find the maker of the shoe, the prince summons cobblers throughout the kingdom. No one can name the shoemaker and the prince decides to set out himself on his search for his beloved.

ACT THREE, SCENE TWO The prince searches far and wide, and every lovely girl in the land weeps that the slipper will not fit. The prince remains determined to find his true love.

ACT THREE, SCENE THREE—A ROOM IN CINDERELLA'S HOUSE Cinderella sleeps, pressing the remaining slipper to her breast. The slipper falls to the floor. Waking up the next morning, she recalls the splendid ball and her meeting with the prince. She decides that it must all have been a dream. But in the course of going about her daily chores, she finds the glass slipper. So it was not a dream after all! She cannot believe it.

The stepsisters come and relate the fine time they had at the ball, how popular they were, and how a princess gave them oranges.

Noise from the street heralds the arrival of the prince, who is going from house to house in search of the unknown beauty. When he enters, both stepsisters try in vain to force their feet into the shoe, and even their mother tries her luck. Then the prince notices Cinderella standing in the corner. She is so stunned by her lover's presence that she does not know what to do. She becomes so confused that she drops the other slipper. There is now no doubt as to who she is! Her fairy godmother appears and blesses Cinderella and her prince.

ACT THREE, SCENE FOUR—A FLOWERING GARDEN Cinderella and the prince have found each other. They celebrate their reunion and live happily ever after.

Ballet in three acts. Music by Sergei Prokofiev. Choreography by Frederick Ashton. Scenery and costumes by Jean-Denis Malclès. First presented by the Sadler's Wells Ballet at the Royal Opera House, Covent Garden, London, December 23, 1948, with Moira Shearer as Cinderella, *Michael Somes as the* Prince, *Robert Helpmann and Frederick Ashton as* Cinderella's Stepsisters, *Pamela May as the* Ragged Fairy Godmother, *Nadia Nerina, Violetta Elvin, Pauline Clayden, and Beryl Grey as the* Fairies, *and Alexander Grant as the* Jester. *First presented in the United States by the Sadler's Wells Ballet at the Metropolitan Opera House, New York, October 18, 1949, with Margot Fonteyn as* Cinderella *and the same principals.*

Cinderella is a story everybody knows and in the past it has attracted a great number of choreographers—French, Russian, and English. This particular ballet on the story, however, is important for a special reason: it is the first classic English ballet in three acts, the first full-length English work in the style and manner of the great nineteenth-century classics. But *Cinderella* is entertaining as well as important. Here the familiar tale is embellished with dramatic and comic differences, with *divertissements,* and with the grace and warmth of the grand academic style.

ACT ONE—A ROOM IN THE HOUSE OF CINDERELLA'S FATHER

The curtain rises on a somber scene. Cinderella crouches on the hearth of a high stone fireplace on the right. On the left, at a plain table, her father sits reading. Near him sit Cinderella's two stepsisters, busily sewing a scarf. They are elderly and hideous, and there is an obvious tension in the room. Cinderella is sitting by the fireplace because she is not allowed to sit anywhere else. Dressed in worn, unbecoming brown, she makes a pathetic figure. The light shines on her face and, despite her sadness, we note that she is beautiful. The music is quiet but expectant; strings are plucked rapidly to sound curiously like the clicking of knitting needles.

The stepsisters, old maids that they are, have been invited to a ball this very night and they work at their sewing with some haste. They finish the scarf and begin to fight about who shall wear it. Cinderella glances at them as if their bickering were all too familiar: in this house there is either quarreling or silence. But she is afraid to interfere. She is no longer the daughter of the house but its servant. The daughters of her father's second wife now rule the house, and she, like her father, can exist only by conforming to their wishes.

The father tries to calm his stepdaughters, but abandons hope when they ignore him. Each tugs at her end of the scarf, and it is torn in two. The stepsisters leave the room, still quarreling, and he follows after them despondently. Cinderella is alone. She takes up a broom and moves wistfully about the room, posing gracefully. She is thinking of happier days, when her mother was alive and there was love for her to respond to. She picks up a piece of the scarf her stepsisters have left behind and puts it around her shoulders: now she is a lady, the lady her mother would have wanted her to be. She takes a candlestick from the table, crosses the darkened room, lights the candle at the fireplace, and holds it high to look upon her mother's portrait, which hangs above the mantel. The father returns, sees his daughter's despair, and attempts to cheer her. But he, too, is sad. The ugly stepsisters come in and reprimand him for keeping Cinderella from her housework. They warn the girl to return to her cleaning.

The orchestra sounds a new, magical melody. The stepsisters hear it, too. Cinderella looks up expectantly, and into the room hobbles a hunchbacked woman in rags. Her face is grotesque, her rags are filthy, but Cinderella seems to welcome her. The old hag begs for money, and the two stepsisters go into a tizzy of silly fear, running away to the other side of the room. Cinderella would like to comfort the old hag, but she knows that she has nothing to give. When the woman begs from her, Cinderella can only give her a bit of bread. The elder stepsister is annoyed at this generosity and threatens the woman. But, like an omen fulfilled, she is suddenly seized with a toothache and flees back to her sister. As Cinderella watches, wishing she could help more, the old hag glances at her gratefully and gently and disappears.

No sooner has the father reminded his two stepdaughters that they must begin to dress for the ball, than purveyors arrive—a tailor, dressmakers, a shoemaker, a jeweler, a hairdresser, a dancing master, each taking advantage of the sisters' new-found popularity to sell all their wares and talents. The old women are delighted at this attention, costly as it may be, and titter constantly like debutantes. Soon they are decked out in extravagant dresses. At this point the dancing master reminds them of the courtly steps in which they must be perfect. The women practice their bows and try to dance, as two violinists play a gavotte. The elder stepsister, old as she is, manages to execute the gavotte more or less to the dancing master's satisfaction, while the meek, shy sister despairs of learning. The dancing master sees that neither will ever learn and finally pretends that both are perfect.

The time of the ball is drawing near, and the stepsisters hurry with their makeup, primping extravagantly, as if all the powder and rouge in the world would reduce their ugliness. Their coach is announced, there is a final flurry of activity, and the sisters, absurdly proud in their bearing, depart.

Again Cinderella is alone. She looks into the fire. The

women did not even bother to say good night to her. She wonders what the ball will be like, what any ball is like. She dances again with the broom, holding it before her as if she were not waltzing alone, and moves happily about the room, imagining herself at the ball. Soon she sees how silly she is being, puts the broom down, and goes back to sit at the hearth.

The harp is plucked gently, and again the eerie, high, piercing cry that heralded the arrival of the old beggar-woman causes Cinderella to look up and smile. The music is magical, like the loveliness of a dream; it grows in volume as the lower strings sound a full, promising melody. The room in which Cinderella sits seems to disappear, its walls vanishing. The old woman stands in the center of the room. She looks at Cinderella, and then something more extraordinary happens. In a flash, the old hag is transformed into a lovely, kind fairy: the ragged cretin becomes a beautiful creature dressed in a shimmering gown.

Cinderella cannot believe her eyes and when her fairy godmother tells her that she must prepare for the ball, that now, really, she *is* going to the ball, the lonely girl almost cries with happiness. The fairy godmother waves her wand, calling forth four fairies to dress Cinderella for the ball.

First comes the fairy Spring, then the fairies Summer, Autumn, and Winter. One by one, the fairies each dance a variation. After each one appears, the accompanying backdrop vanishes and Cinderella's room stretches back into the distance farther and farther. The scenery is transformed completely for each fairy, changing in color from green to icy blue, in surroundings from abundant garlands to a pinnacle of ice, and the fairies and their attendants are dressed charmingly in the habits of their seasons.

Cinderella sits on the floor at the feet of her fairy godmother, taking in the full magic of her great powers. Now she understands. The fairy godmother tells her to bring a pumpkin. Before the girl's astonished eyes, she changes the pumpkin into a magnificent coach. Cinderella is surrounded by the fairies, who present gifts to her and dress her for the ball. Almost at their touch, the lonely girl becomes as beautiful as a fairy tale princess, dressed splendidly in white and gold, wearing a crown and a long, flowing cape with a high pearl collar that encloses her shining face.

Her godmother tells Cinderella not to delay, that a new-found happiness awaits her at the ball. But she warns the girl that she must leave the ball before the clock strikes twelve. If she remains after midnight, the magic will vanish as mysteriously as it came and she will be just a lonely girl again, dressed in shabby clothes. Cinderella promises that she will not tarry and bows to her in gratitude. The fairies and a multitude of stars surround Cinderella as she goes to her coach and proceeds to the ball.

ACT TWO—A BALL AT THE PALACE The ball has already begun when the curtain rises. Members of the court are dancing a formal measure in a ballroom that has been set up in the palace garden. Two great trees and their overhanging branches enclose the festive scene. To the left and right, spectators watch the ball in low stage boxes. In the back, on either side of a flight of low steps, are two high elegant structures, pavilions set up especially for the ball. On the ground floor of these pavilions we can see other guests amusing themselves. Farther back, by the light of a distant chandelier, we can make out a splendid formal garden. At the top of the steps is the prince's throne. The prince has not yet arrived, and the court jester sits on the royal stool.

Cinderella's stepsisters make an absurdly grand entry in keeping with the elegance they have assumed for the occasion. Cinderella's father accompanies them and is made visibly ill at ease by their pretensions. The older sister is determined to enjoy herself and acts unimpressed by the beauty of the palace garden: it is all her due, designed for her enjoyment, and she imagines herself attractive. The younger sister is more honest and cannot so easily disguise the fact that all this elegance is strange to her. She tugs plaintively at her sister's dress and wants to go home. She is, of course, refused and resolves to see the evening out only when a courtier begins to pay her some attention, thus reviving her spirits. She is disenchanted when her jealous sister takes her suitor away.

Now, as another courtly dance commences, the two sisters have a chance to perform the measures the dancing master taught them. The older sister watches with disgust as the younger dances. She starts out well, and for a moment we think she is really going to make it, but her steps become tentative and it is apparent that she's forgotten every step she knows. The older sister laughs, executes the dance with grotesque accuracy, and then, to show off, tries to balance on one foot. The younger sister is terrified, and, of course, the show-off begins to topple over. The jester catches her as she stumbles about trying to keep from falling flat on her face.

Four friends of the prince enter and prepare the guests for the arrival of their host. The handsome prince enters with a regal but lively flourish, and all the guests bow to him. The two sisters attempt to make their reverence so that the prince will take particular notice of them, but he does not even glance at them. The prince's companions dance a *pas de quatre,* which is followed by another general dance by the court.

One guest has not yet arrived. The light, mysterious music that heralded the first appearance of Cinderella's ragged fairy godmother interrupts the court music, and everyone pauses. The jester, at the prince's order, goes to welcome the newcomer in the garden. The twelve girls representing stars and the four fairies with their pages enter at the rear, and the court wonders what to expect with such an elaborate preparation. All look toward the entrance to the ballroom as the prince awaits the guest. Finally the royal coach of Cinderella draws up to the garden gate. The girl steps out, and all are dazzled by her natural beauty and the loveliness of her costume. The prince, who is immediately charmed, takes Cinderella's hand and leads her forward. Two pages hold Cinderella's train while the stars and fairies kneel about their mistress. Wishing to discover more about this ravishing girl, the prince escorts her for a walk through the palace grounds.

The other guests, who have watched the entrance of Cinderella from the boxes at the sides of the ballroom, now mingle on the dance floor and begin a masked dance. The ugly stepsisters, of course, have not recognized Cinderella and accept her simply as visiting royalty. Soon the prince returns alone and dances a variation, after which he leaves the scene. Now Cinderella dances and in her movements she conveys the youthful and tender joy she feels at the ball. It is as if she belonged there, for she is unembarrassed and confident in her natural graciousness.

The two sisters, alone for a moment, spend their time gossiping about the unattractive girl who has gained the prince's favor. The two lovers return. The harp is plucked against a deep, flowing melody, and they begin a *pas de deux*. The dance is soft and considerate, yet strong in its regal elegance and the personal elegance of the handsome young pair. The prince kneels before Cinderella as their dance finishes. She responds to his love by dancing a variation that reflects her new-found pleasure in loving and being loved. She is so happy that she has no memory of her misery at home; she pirouettes rapidly, and her two stepsisters are a million miles away.

A Negro page brings to the prince an orange on a silver tray. This is the most highly prized fruit in all the kingdom and the finest gift he can give Cinderella. She accepts it graciously. Then the prince turns to the ugly stepsisters and bestows an orange on each of them. Instantly they begin to quarrel about whose orange is larger, and the dominating sister snatches the choice one away from the timid creature.

Cinderella and the prince lead the court in an ensemble dance. The music is a bright, sparkling waltz that gradually gains in sonorous force, and all the guests are caught up in the spirit of romance. Suddenly—as the waltz gains relentless force, cymbals shimmer, and we hear the loud ticking of a clock—a flourish of trumpets announces the approach of midnight. The cymbals crash, to warn Cinderella that she must hasten. The girl rushes from the prince's arms. He watches, astonished, as she tries to make her way through the crowded guests to the gate. The girl is desperate lest her secret be discovered. When she arrives at the gate, midnight has come. Her beautiful dress becomes her ragged work clothes, and she flees into the night, leaving behind one of her slippers. The prince cannot understand; he looks after her as the orchestra restates the theme of their *pas de deux* and the curtain falls.

ACT THREE, SCENE ONE—AFTER THE BALL When the curtain rises on the first scene, again Cinderella is seen sitting by the fire in her father's house, just as she was at the entrance of the fairy godmother. She is asleep. She wakens, looks about, and thinks she has dreamed of the ball. Only the slipper she finds hidden in her apron convinces her that she really was there, that there was a handsome prince, and that he did love her. She dances again with the broom, reflecting in her steps her unhappiness before the ball, her recollection of her first love, and her resignation to her everyday life.

Her sisters return. They are so tired that they don't even wish to gossip until they have undressed and cast off the weight of their excessive finery. They sigh as they remove their shoes from their swollen feet. But soon they are taunting Cinderella with tall tales about the ball, the prince, and his attentions to them. They toy with the oranges he gave them, and Cinderella is thinking too much of what the ball was really like to care much about their prattling.

The women hear a disturbance in the street. Townswomen rush in and excitedly announce that a royal procession is waking everyone up, that the prince, enamored of a girl he cannot find, is determined to discover the owner of a shoe left behind at the ball. He vows that he will marry the girl whom the shoe fits.

The sisters are apprehensive lest the prince visit their house when they are not fully dressed and scurry about putting on their formal gowns and their tight shoes again. The prince enters with the jester and an entourage. He holds Cinderella's lost slipper in his hand and declares that the woman it fits shall become his wife. He does not notice the girl in rags who crouches at the fire. The stepsisters do obeisance before the prince, who responds to them so graciously that they imagine one of them might be the chosen one. First, the shy stepsister tries on the shoe. She knows it is silly to pretend that it will fit and gives up wistfully. The other sister is delighted at her failure, but has no more luck herself, despite much straining and pinching in an effort to force her foot into the shoe.

When it is apparent that she, too, is a misfit, Cinderella helps her pull the shoe off. As the girl kneels before her sister, the other slipper falls from her apron pocket. The prince sees it and asks the girl if she will try on the shoe. Her stepsisters rail at her, but the prince insists. The shoe fits perfectly. At first the sisters cannot believe it, but when the prince announces that Cinderella will be his bride, they attempt in several reverential gestures to make up for the years of misery they have caused the girl. Cinderella understands them, pities them, and touches them lovingly as they bow before her. The prince and Cinderella embrace. The fairy godmother appears and raises her wand.

ACT THREE, SCENE TWO—AN ENCHANTED GARDEN The scene is transformed. We find ourselves in a magical place, a colorful garden where the light seems to sparkle. There a great boat awaits the arrival of the lovers. The prince's friends and the fairies dance together, and Cinderella and the prince enter. Six of the stars surround them as they dance, the fairies pose gracefully with their cavaliers, and the music sounds soaringly the theme of ideal romance that marked the couple's first recognition of love. The fairy godmother and all the magical creatures wish the lovers godspeed, and they step into the waiting ship. The surging music falls off into soft measures that predict eternal joy. The prince holds Cinderella in his arms as they sail off on a happy voyage that will never end.

Yet another important version of this ballet came into the American repertory in 1970:

Music by Sergei Prokofiev. Staged and choreographed by Ben Stevenson. Scenery by Edward Haynes. Costumes by Norman McDowell. First presented by the National Ballet at the Lisner Auditorium, Washington, D.C., April 24, 1970.

The synopsis of this version of the ballet is close to others, but has some important differences:

ACT ONE Cinderella's father watches his two stepdaughters embroidering scarves to be worn to a ball given that evening by the prince. The cruel stepdaughters tease their stepfather with the scarves. Cinderella enters and stops them. The stepsisters are furious and order Cinderella to clean the kitchen as they drag their father from the room. Her only friend now seems to be the broom.

Cinderella, remembering a picture of her mother, takes it from its hiding place and sits gazing at it. Her father enters and is overcome with remorse when he sees how much Cinderella resembles his first loving wife. She tries to comfort him when the stepsisters enter and are enraged to see Cinderella in her father's arms. They pull them apart and snatch the picture away. Suddenly the door opens and an old beggarwoman enters. The stepsisters decide to give her the picture, but the old woman sees the resemblance between the picture and Cinderella and returns it to Cinderella. Cinderella gives the old woman her last crust of bread.

The dressmaker and the wigmaker arrive to ready the stepsisters for the ball. A dancing master also arrives with the impossible task of teaching the stepsisters how to dance. Cinderella is alone again, pretending she is at the ball, and dances with the broom, then bursts into tears realizing it is only a daydream. The old beggar returns and much to Cinderella's amazement is transformed into a beautiful fairy godmother. The kitchen changes into a magic glade with dragonflies swooping among the trees. The fairy godmother asks Cinderella to find a pumpkin and four lizards and gives them to one of the dragonflies, who darts off into the trees. The fairy godmother gives a pair of glass slippers to Cinderella. The fairies of Spring, Summer, Autumn, and Winter arrive and dance for Cinderella, changing the seasons as they do. Cinderella's rags become a beautiful dress. The fairy godmother shows Cinderella a magic clock and warns her that at midnight her magic clothes will turn again into rags. The fairy godmother changes the pumpkin and lizards into a coach and horses and Cinderella drives to the ball like a princess.

ACT TWO A jester greets the guests as they arrive in the ballroom. The guests are amazed when the ugly stepsisters arrive. The prince enters, and he too is amused by the sight of the sisters; however, he asks them each in turn to dance with him to the amazement of the crowd. Cinderella arrives in her coach, and the prince falls in love with her at first sight. He offers his guests oranges, as they are the very rarest fruit in the land. One of the sisters is left without an orange; Cinderella sees this and gives up her own. The stepsister accepts without recognizing Cinderella.

While the Prince and Cinderella are dancing together, the clock strikes midnight and Cinderella's beautiful clothes turn to rags. The prince rushes after her to find only one of her glass slippers on the stairs.

ACT THREE Cinderella waits among the cinders in the kitchen thinking the ball only a dream until she finds the other glass slipper in her pocket. She quickly hides it as the ugly sisters arrive. They show Cinderella the oranges they received from the prince. Suddenly the jester enters the room, heralding the arrival of the prince and two of his friends who have with them the glass slipper. The stepsisters vainly try to squeeze their big feet into the tiny slipper. The prince sees Cinderella sitting by the fire and asks her father if she may try it. As Cinderella gets up from the stool, she drops the other glass slipper. The prince is overjoyed! The stepsisters beg Cinderella's forgiveness and the fairy godmother arrives, accompanied by the fairies of the seasons.

The prince returns the glass slippers to them and the kitchen once again changes into a magic glade. Cinderella and her prince dance a romantic *pas de deux,* and at its conclusion, the guests arrive for the coronation of Cinderella, the cruelly mistreated girl who rose from the cinders to a royal throne.

NOTES Reviewing this production of *Cinderella* in the British magazine, *Ballet Today,* Kay Rinfrette wrote: "Ashton's *Cinderella* for the Royal Ballet influenced Stevenson's ballet in several aspects: Like Ashton, Stevenson employs the English pantomime tradition by having the stepsisters played *en travesti,* and he excludes the stepmother who usually appears in Russian productions. Also, Stevenson omits the prince's search around the world. Unlike Ashton, Stevenson changes the sequence of musical numbers in the ballroom scene to give the *grand pas de deux* a traditional, formal structure. (The adagio is followed by the man's, then the ballerina's variation.) The choreography, especially effective in solos and group work, and character development are Stevenson's exciting, original conceptions (with only a few distant reverberations of some Ashton choreography).

"The choreographic structure of the ballet—Stevenson's use of thematic materials—is magnificent. Two primary movement themes (motifs), used separately and in combination, are introduced in the four-seasons sequence in Act One: (1) sudden or unexpected changes in direction of movement, and (2) traveling lifts which give an impression of weightlessness. The feeling of lightness created in this sequence emphasizes a fairy-tale quality and contrasts to the heaviness of the previous fireside scene (the cumbersome, heavy awkwardness of the stepsisters, the figurative 'burden' falling on Cinderella's shoulders).

"Specifically, the thematic movements include the 'dragonflies' transporting the fairy godmother in multiple traveling lifts with quick changes of direction—at one point she is carried back and forth across the stage three times without pause—and the sudden direction changes in the solos for Spring and Autumn. The same movement themes appear in the ballroom scene, especially in the *corps de ballet* work: many lovely lifts in unexpected directions, often backwards; at the waltz's climax, the girls, arching their backs, fall forward sequentially into their partners' arms, only to be weightlessly lifted and wafted away. The ballroom grand adagio, with its many extend traveling lifts (in fact, some lifts looked awkward and unnecessarily difficult), is also a part of weightless fantasy—the ballerina is swept away by the fairy-tale grandeur both literally and figuratively.

"The adagio in the last act is less involved with fantasy, closer to a real-life love relationship. This meaning is underscored by the choreography which includes thematic elements but in different combinations: there are fewer lifts, more *terre à terre* work, including swift runs with sudden direction changes, as if the lovers were blown by the wind. Structurally, this adagio is the climax of the ballet, combining and reconciling the literary themes of fantasy versus reality and the choreographic motifs of floating lightness versus heaviness or a sense of weight. In the final coronation scene, heavy-looking imperial crowns are placed on the heads of Cinderella and the prince—the fantasy (lightness) becomes a reality (weight).

"Character and dancing aspects are well balanced in this production, meaning that the stepsisters do not monopolize the show. Their hilarious antics are most clever in sequences with the dancing master and at the ball when they 'send-up' ballet steps—such as one sister holding an *attitude* for several seconds and then collapsing in a heap. The polarization of characters is clearly established in the beginning, when the stepsisters angrily snatch away from Cinderella a painting of her mother, and when Cinderella is kind to the old hag visitor (fairy godmother in disguise). The father, depicted as a multiple-henpecked man unable to cope, is a kind of transition figure between the 'good' Cinderella and the 'evil' stepsisters. Even minor characters are sharply drawn—the snobbish, prim dancing master and the eccentric, dissatisfied wigmaker."

Reviewing this new production of *Cinderella* in the New York *Times*, the critic Clive Barnes wrote: "The result is most pleasing. This is a good *Cinderella*. The settings by Edward Haynes and the costumes by Norman McDowell are simple but elegant, and Mr. Stevenson's unaffectedly classical choreography is a model of good taste.

"This is a formidable undertaking for a small company—it does not have so many dancers as the City Center Joffrey Ballet—and it survived grandly. Mr. Stevenson's choreography is strongly influenced by Frederick Ashton—Mr. Stevenson being a former member of the Royal Ballet—yet not slavishly so. Often he has gone to some lengths to be different from the Ashton version of the score, and his concept is always attractive.

"It is the kind of choreography that suits dancers—graceful and understated. He is not afraid of virtuosity, and certainly Mr. Stevenson has made more demands upon these Washington dancers than any previous choreographer. He cannot prevent the first scene of Cinderella and her sisters from appearing prosey—it always does in any production —but he does give his two lovers the most intricately stylish *pas de deux*.

"The dancing was splendid. Mr. Stevenson has mounted his ballet on two couples, Gaye Fulton and Desmond Kelly, and Marilyn Burr and Ivan Nagy. At the performance I saw it was given by Miss Fulton and Mr. Kelly.

"Miss Fulton, a delicate figurine of a princess in hiding, made an enchanting Cinderella, and Mr. Kelly, elegant and assertive, was the most perfect of Princes.

"Another young man of more than usual promise is Kirk Peterson, from the Harkness Youth Company, who was dancing the Jester. He had a brilliant technique and was very cleverly used by Mr. Stevenson. I also admired the roistering humor of Frederic Franklin (the company's director) and Larry Long as the Ugly Sisters, and the style of Judith Rhodes and Christine Knoblauch among the fairies. But the entire company extended and excelled itself."

THE CLOWNS

Music by Hershy Kay. Choreography by Gerald Arpino. Costumes by Edith Lutyens Bel Geddes. Lighting by Tom Skelton. Assistant to Mr. Arpino: James Howell. First presented by the City Center Joffrey Ballet at the City Center, New York, February 28, 1968, with Robert Blankshine, Frank Bays, Erika Goodman and Maximiliano Zomosa in principal roles. Special effects by Vernon Lobb and Kip Coburn. Conducted by Hershy Kay.

The Clowns is a dramatic metaphor about life as it is lived by those perennial reflectors of the human spirit—the floppy white clowns of the *commedia dell' arte*. The piece begins with a bang, as if all the world had exploded, and a lone clown, battered and bruised, appears to be the only remnant of civilization. But he is not quite alone, for bodies begin to fall out of the sky like hail, bodies of fellow clowns. Mournfully but doggedly determined and not stopping to grieve, the survivor piles them all up into a kind of pyre. But mysteriously, at least one of them is alive, for a girl emerges to join the clown. The two clowns dance together joyously. Their dance is a dance of renewal and liveliness and the life is contagious: before we know it, the whole pile of bodies is revived and the clown tribe lives again.

Not content, however, with renewal and resumption of their old funny and antic roles, the clowns now reveal their human side, too. They begin to plot against each other and to employ weapons—big balloons that seem to envelop the opposition. The original survivor, however much he tries not to get involved in this dark side of human nature, is soon caught up in it, too. The fellows he has helped revive turn hostile and he is the victim. In retaliation, he brings in the biggest balloon imaginable, a huge, long cylinder that becomes a transparent tunnel. What this instrument soon becomes is a clown catcher and all the opposition are entrapped in it, beating against its walls, helpless to get out. They can *see* out and the walls of the prison are soft but they cannot penetrate them. They are all sucked down into it. Except for one. The first survivor, who again survives.

THE CONCERT

A charade in one act. Music by Frédéric Chopin. Choreography by Jerome Robbins. Costumes by Irene Sharaff. First presented by the New York City Ballet March 6, 1956, at the City Center, New York, with Tanaquil LeClercq and Robert Barnett in principal roles.

Jerome Robbins subtitles this ballet "The Perils of Everybody" and writes in a program note: "One of the pleasures of attending a concert is the freedom to lose oneself in listening to the music. Quite often, unconsciously, mental pictures and images form; and the patterns and paths of these reveries are influenced by the music itself, or its program notes, or by the personal dreams, problems, and fantasies of the listener. Chopin's music in particular has been subject to fanciful 'program' names such as the Butterfly Étude, the Minute Waltz, the Raindrop Prelude, etc."

During the overture to the ballet, we look at an amusing drop curtain, by Saul Steinberg, depicting the interior of an old-fashioned concert hall. When the curtain rises, a pianist crosses the stage, dusts the piano, and slumps down in meditation. Finally, he begins to play, and the audience begins to arrive, each carrying a folding chair: a man in a scarf who sits and meditates seriously, then two girls who clearly disturb him, then a girl in a huge wide-brimmed hat. She is so enthralled by the music that she snuggles right up to the piano and embraces it. A very serious student indeed follows, and then a husband and wife and a man on tiptoe. An usher tries to straighten out a mix-up over seats. When everyone is quieted down a bit, their fantasies begin to take over.

The husband envisages the murder of his wife and dreams of her substitute nearby. As the pianist pounds out a Mazurka, he sees himself as a brave hussar carrying off his beloved. His beloved, meanwhile, only wants to be a poor butterfly and acts that way. The wife intervenes, the poor girl is put down, and her husband is compelled to back down.

These are but some of the jokes that are played and acted out by these people to Chopin's music. To reveal all of them is to miss the fun of seeing the ballet, called by Patricia Barnes, in *Dance and Dancers*, "dance's funniest creation."

NOTES *The Concert* was extensively revised for Jerome Robbins's Ballets U.S.A. presentation at the Spoleto Festival June 8, 1958, with settings by Saul Steinberg that are used in the New York City Ballet revival (first presented December 2, 1971, at the New York State Theater with Sara Leland, Francisco Moncion, Bettijane Sills, Shaun O'Brien, Robert Weiss, Bart Cook, Stephen Caras, Gloriann Hicks, Delia Peters, and Christine Redpath in principal roles. Jerry Zimmerman was the pianist).

CONCERTO BAROCCO

Classic ballet in three movements. Music by Johann Sebastian Bach. Choreography by George Balanchine. Scenery and costumes by Eugene Berman. First presented by the American Ballet at the Theatre of Hunter College, New York, May 29, 1940, with Marie-Jeanne, Mary Jane Shea, and William Dollar in the principal roles.

The only preparation possible for this ballet is a knowledge of its music, for *Concerto Barocco* has no "subject matter" beyond the score to which it is danced and the particular dancers who execute it. Set to Bach's *Concerto in D minor for Two Violins,* the ballet tries to interest the audience only by its dancing, its treatment of the music, just as Baroque art and architecture interested people not because of their subjects but because of the decorative treatment that embellished those subjects.

Bach's great concerto can stand alone. Some people then wonder, why arrange a ballet to such music? Why not arrange ballets to music that is more dependent, music that dancing can "fill out"? The answer is that bad music often inspires bad dancing, bad choreography. It is not an accident that the dance masterpieces of Saint-Léon, Petipa, and Fokine all have scores that are also masterworks. *Coppélia, The Sleeping Beauty,* and *Petrouchka,* with their scores by Delibes, Tchaikovsky, and Stravinsky, suggested to each one of these choreographers an advance in the development of ballet.

Choosing pieces of music for dancing is a matter for the individual choreographer. A choreographer disinterested in classical dancing will not care to use scores by Bach and Mozart except for theatrical sensational reasons; he will select music more to his immediate purpose. But if the dance designer sees in the development of classical dancing a counterpart in the development of music and has studied them both, he will derive continual inspiration from great scores. He will also be careful, as he acts on this inspiration, not to interpret the music beyond its proper limits, not to stretch the music to accommodate a literary idea, for instance. If the score is a truly great one, suitable for dancing, he will not have need of such devices and can present his impression in terms of pure dance.

FIRST MOVEMENT—VIVACE The curtain rises. The music begins. There are eight girls on stage. Dancing variously as one group, as two groups, and in duets, the girls correspond to the music the orchestra plays, but not in any strict or literal sense; they do not mirror the music, rather they move in accordance with its length, the space between its beginning and end being filled by a dance picture of the music. Just as the portrait is different from the news photograph, so the dance picture tries to tell something independent of an exact, bar-by-bar, rhythm-by-rhythm, mirror image of the music.

As the two violins take up their parts in the music, two soloists enter. Singly, together, and with the *corps de ballet,* they become a part of the dance orchestration. They support each other as the music of one violin entwines the other; they depict and develop dance themes that recur with the repetition and development of themes in the orchestra.

SECOND MOVEMENT—LARGO MA NON TANTO Now the soloists leave the stage. The orchestra sounds the touching, lyrical melody. One of the soloists returns, accompanied by a male partner, who lifts her softly and slowly, turns her as the *corps de ballet* bend low before her, and leads her in and out of a maze formed by the *corps.* The music is tender, but it possesses a warm nobility and strength that the ballerina's partner allows her to imitate as its development proceeds. When the music gathers toward a full statement and the theme repeats again and again, climbing with each repetition to a climactic rest, the ballerina's partner lifts her without pause high over his head, over and over again, to the accumulating sound. Then, toward the end of the movement, the boy slides the girl low across the floor in three daring movements. The ballerina rises each time in an open pose that reflects the strength underlying the lyricism of the theme.

THIRD MOVEMENT—ALLEGRO The music is now quickly rhythmic. All ten dancers seem to respond to it spontaneously, marking the beat of the music with soft, light jumps, crisp arm gestures, and syncopated groupings. As the joyous music ends, all the dancers kneel.

THE CONSORT

Music by Dowland, Neusidler, Morley, and anonymous composers. Orchestrated by Christopher Keene. Choreography by Eliot Feld. Costumes by Stanley Simmons. Lighting by Jules Fisher. First presented by the American Ballet Company at the Brooklyn Academy of Music, New York, October 24, 1970, with Marilyn D'Honau, Christine Kono, Elizabeth Lee, Olga Janke, Cristina Stirling, Larry Grenier, Kenneth Hughes, Daniel Levins, Richard Munro, and John Sowinski.

Seventeenth-century music, mostly English, with some bawdy German songs for salt, provides the musical base for this dance ballet, orchestrated by the then musical director of the American Ballet Company, Christopher Keene. There is no plot here, and at first it appears that we shall be watching simply a stately but vigorous period piece, expressive of the Elizabethan age. But a curious thing happens. The long, formal dresses of the girls yield to short shifts, and before we know what has happened, the boys are whirling them about, courtiers have become peasants and, perhaps, themselves. While the stylization of the dances suggests a time long ago, the best of the orchestration and its demanding rhythms suggest the music of our own time, too, which is reflected in a rustic dance difference. Set for ten dancers, there are combinations of ensembles, boys and girls alone as well as *pas de deux* and solos, that merge the two styles of dancing.

NOTES Writing about *The Consort* in the *Village Voice*, the critic Deborah Jowitt said: "The first part of *The Consort* is courtly, restrained, with that faint undercurrent of unpleasantness that you feel in a real pavane. Within the elaborate ritual, everyone is sizing up his partner and engaging in an almost invisible thrusting and parrying. Feld keeps the feeling of social dance; many instances of couples doing unison movement based—very remotely—on period dances. There are a few interludes that are more irregular. For example, there's an interesting bit in which Olga Janke dances very slowly and minimally, involved with her own skirt and a path that she is not quite progressing along, while John Sowinski keeps circling her lightly, but not lightheartedly—doing some of the subtly complex Feld steps that Sowinski performs with such luminous intelligence. They are aware and yet not aware of each other, and you are not quite sure which is the moth and which the star.

"As the court section ends, some of the women begin to help each other undress on stage. Quietly and naturally, they remove headdresses, take off boleros, loop their skirts up to above their knees. Daniel Levins examines and strokes his feathered cap for quite a time before tossing it into the wings. Again there is something faintly sinister in the air. When all the dancers are ready, the peasant section begins and begins mildly, with some of the same steps from the court part. You almost feel that these could be the same aristocrats playing at being peasants. Yet the stage gets more crowded (five couples as opposed to the three who began the piece), the dancers' bodies begin to look more weighty and sprawling, the harp (Keene's lute surrogate) is less noticeable, and the brasses begin to bray. These are still social dances, but with a coarseness and an increasingly ribald air. Two men do a fast rowdy dance, each with two girls, to Hans Neusidler's marvelously strange "Der Juden Tanz." *The Consort* ends with a debauch—the men wobbling like scarecrows, clutching the women to them; just drunk enough to be singlemindedly lecherous and with enough control left to do something about it. As the curtain comes down, the women have their legs about the men's waists and are being tossed and worried at. It reminded me of one of those Breughel scenes: you feel that because most of the time the peasants must have worked so hard, their appetites for play and drunken oblivion must have been immense, simple, and quickly sated."

COPPÉLIA
or
THE GIRL WITH ENAMEL EYES

Classic ballet in three acts. Music by Léo Delibes, Choreography by Arthur Saint-Léon. Book by Charles Nuitter and Arthur Saint-Léon, after a story by E. T. A. Hoffmann. First presented at the Théâtre Impérial de l'Opéra, Paris, May 25, 1870, with Giuseppina Bozacchi as Swanilda *and Eugenie Fiocre as* Franz. *First presented in the United States by the American Opera at the Metropolitan Opera House, New York, March 11, 1887, with Marie Giuri and Felicita Carozzi in the leading roles. First presented in England at the Empire Theatre, London, May 14, 1906, with Adeline Genée as* Swanilda.

Just as *Giselle* is ballet's great tragedy, so *Coppélia* is its great comedy. Both ballets are love stories and both have their roots in real life as well as in fantasy. In *Giselle* there are ghosts to test the quality of the hero's love for the heroine, and in *Coppélia* there is another romantic device by which the heroine makes sure of her lover's devotion. This device is the beautiful, lifeless doll, whose quiet, mechanical beauty contrasts with the charming liveliness of the real-life heroine. Because the hero in *Giselle* can only meet his lost love briefly in fantasy, and thereafter she is lost to reality, the ending of the ballet is tragic. But in *Coppélia* the inadequacy of the fantastic wax doll leads the hero back to his real love, and the ending is happy. And where Albrecht in *Giselle* learns an unhappy lesson from which he will never completely recover, Franz in *Coppélia* learns a lesson that makes his life happy forever after.

ACT ONE—THE SQUARE A spacious overture sets the tone for the whole ballet. The music begins with a melody of quiet dignity, first stated by the horns, then swept up by the strings. A muffled drum sounds, and the mood changes spontaneously to open gaiety as the orchestra plays a spirited robust mazurka. At its conclusion, the curtain rises.

The scene is a square in any small town in Central

Europe; the time is a sunny afternoon several hundred years ago. A small house in the back faces the audience; on the side, a higher dwelling with a balcony projecting from the second floor dominates the street. Other buildings cluster about the square in a pleasantly haphazard fashion. All the façades are clean and painted in bright colors, and the walls and roofs seen in the background confirm our impression of an old village whose charm has not been worn away by changing times. The square is empty. An old man, bent with age, hobbles out of the door of the house on the right. This is Dr. Coppélius, the town's most mysterious citizen. He is said to dabble in alchemy and magic, but no one knows precisely what he does. Coppélius looks up at the balcony of his house, and we see that a lovely young girl is sitting there, reading a book. She is hidden a little from the full light of the sun, is wholly preoccupied with her reading, and takes no notice of the old doctor. Coppélius points up at the studious girl, rubs his hands with satisfaction as if he were a delighted chaperone, and re-enters his house.

The door of the little house in the back opens in a moment, and Swanilda emerges. She is dressed in bright colors particularly becoming to her dark beauty. From her movements we know almost immediately that she is very young and very much in love. The music to which she dances is piquant in the unembarrassed fullness of its melody, and Swanilda dances to it with obvious pleasure at some inner happiness. She walks rapidly on point, looking about the square anxiously to see that she is alone. She is expecting someone, but has some business of her own to attend to first. She glances up at the balcony of the large house and sees there the charming young girl, just as attractive as she is. The girl is intensely occupied and, holding the book rigidly before her, she does not look down to see Swanilda waving to her. Swanilda is annoyed. First of all she is annoyed because the girl is clearly snubbing her, but she is chagrined mostly because she has noticed that Franz, her fiancé, has also waved at this strange girl and has never mentioned it to her. Everyone calls the girl Coppélia. She is said to be the old man's daughter, but Coppélius has never appeared with her in the streets of the town and their relationship is just as unfathomable as Coppélius himself. Swanilda imitates her, holding an imaginary book before her. Then she bows low to Coppélia, in mock ceremony. Still the girl will not notice her. Swanilda stamps her foot in annoyance and dances briefly. She does not understand why Coppélia sits there reading on such a beautiful day and suspects she might be in a trance. On the other hand, she might be waiting for Franz! Swanilda approaches the house to see the girl more closely, shakes her fists at her, but quickly turns away as she hears Franz coming down the street. She is carefully hidden by the time he enters and she observes him secretly.

Franz is a high-spirited young peasant dressed in country costume. Like Swanilda, Franz is open and carefree by nature, but his heartiness masks a certain conceit: he seems not to have a care in the world and would not think it odd if every girl in the village adored him as much as Swanilda does. He does not go directly to Swanilda's door, but strides over to the house of Coppélius. After making sure that he isn't being watched, he glances up at the balcony. He waves to Coppélia flirtatiously, but also casually, as if he were in the habit of greeting her every time he passed. He points to Swanilda's door and remembers his love for her in the midst of this new infatuation. He clearly enjoys not knowing which lovely girl to choose. He clutches his heart as he looks up at Coppélia, then blows a kiss to her. Swanilda's worst suspicions of Franz's fickleness seem to be justified. Her suspicions becomes fears when Coppélia looks up from her book and waves back to Franz. Neither she nor Franz can see that behind the girl Coppélius stands concealed. He watches the flirtation with obvious disapproval, steps forward quickly, and closes the window curtains in Coppélia's face. Franz is abashed by this sudden disappearance of his new love. He is so distressed that he doesn't notice Swanilda, who has come into the square and stands right behind him. Swanilda refuses to attract his attention when he won't even turn away from the balcony; she walks off.

Now Franz consoles himself by remembering his rendezvous with Swanilda. But he does not have time to reach her door before Swanilda returns, bringing a beautiful butterfly she has just caught.

Franz takes the butterfly from her and pins it to his shirt. To Swanilda, this harmless gesture is a stab at her own broken heart. She bursts into tears and angrily accuses Franz of being unfaithful to her. He demurs, but she has no patience with his offhand answers and suggests that they come to him just as readily as his flirtations. Now that he sees how serious she is, Franz sincerely denies that he loves anyone else. But Swanilda is firm in her disbelief; she will not listen. Now Franz begins to lose his temper: how can she fail, he wonders, to see that he loves only her? Swanilda leaves the square, and Franz hails a party of peasants, their friends, who are unaware of the tension between the two lovers. They dance the rollicking mazurka that the orchestra first played in the overture, and when Swanilda joins them, her anxieties are momentarily dispelled. But she is determined to keep clear of Franz and, even at the sacrifice of her happiness, will accept no explanations.

The dancing of the peasants halts as the burgomaster enters the square. Everyone stands aside to make room for him and listens attentively as he tells them that on the next day the village will receive a great new bell for the town clock as a gift from the lord of the manor and that they must prepare themselves for the celebration attendant upon the ceremonies. The peasants are delighted at the idea of an unexpected festival. Their pleasure is so great that they do not pay much attention to strange noises emanating from the house of Coppélius.

The burgomaster goes on to say that the gracious lord will present handsome dowries to the girls who marry on the festival day. Several couples look at each other expectantly, but Swanilda is unmoved. Franz watches her closely. The burgomaster turns and asks her if she will be wed tomorrow. Unwilling to expose her broken heart to her friends and perhaps still hoping that she may be wrong about Franz's love, Swanilda resorts to fate and takes up an ear of wheat which the burgomaster offers her and shakes it near her ear, looking at her fiancé. The custom is—if she hears anything, her lover "loves her true"; if the wheat is silent, her lover "loves her not." Franz supports Swanilda in lovely deep poses as she bends low to listen to the wheat. Swanilda hears nothing. Franz, who thinks this pretense is silly, also hears nothing. She beckons to a friend and shakes the wheat again. The friend claims there is a sound, but Swanilda will not believe it. She throws the straw to the ground and announces that she and Franz are no longer engaged. Franz stalks away in disgust at the ways of women, while Swanilda joins her friends to dance a bright, gay tune as if nothing had happened to disturb their good time. A drum roll sounds, and Swanilda's friends dance a czardas, a Hungarian folk dance that starts out with slow, formal dignity and then increases in both speed and humor to become delirious with joy. The light grows darker and the group soon disbands. The stage is empty as night falls.

The door to Coppélius's house opens, and the wizened old man totters out. He pulls out a large key, locks the door, tries it several times, puts his key away, pats his pocket, and proceeds slowly across the square, leaning heavily on his cane. Obviously reluctant at leaving his house, Coppélius is easily frightened by a band of pranksters who rail at him good-humoredly, dance about him, and boisterously try to overcome his reluctance to join in. He loses his temper, which only encourages the fun. As they push him about, Coppélius drops his key. The villagers do not notice this and soon leave him. He shuffles across the street on his errand, shaking his head at their impertinence.

Swanilda and a group of her friends pass him as they enter on their way to supper. Swanilda is delighted to find that he has lost his key. She looks back toward Coppélius, who has now disappeared, and then at his house. Her friends easily persuade Swanilda to try the key in Coppélius's door. At last she will discover the illusive Coppélia alone! She goes to the door, fits the key to the lock, and signals pleadingly to her friends to follow. She steps in. She backs out hurriedly, frightened at her own audacity and the dark interior. Her friends line up behind her in single file, trembling with fear, and one by one they enter the house.

The square is deserted for a moment, then Franz comes in, armed with a ladder. The petulant youth is determined to have his love acknowledged by Coppélia, now that Swanilda has renounced him, and he places the ladder against the house. He is climbing up to a window when Coppélius, who has finally missed his key, rushes in to look for it. He apprehends Franz, attacks him with his walking stick, and chases him off. He then continues to search for the key. When he fails to find it and discovers that his door is wide open, he throws up his hands in despair and with great agitation runs into the house. The persistent Franz re-enters, places his ladder again, and climbs toward the mysterious Coppélia. The curtain falls.

ACT TWO—COPPÉLIUS'S HOUSE The scene is a large room with dark walls. There is a large window at the back, and on the left is a curtained enclosure. Curious immobile figures, staring straight ahead, sit and stand about the stage in fixed attitudes, each as if cut off in the middle of a gesture. But there is not time to observe them before Swanilda and her friends walk in on tiptoe. The girls take in the weird room and are clearly sorry that they have let Swanilda talk them into coming. A small light throws their shadows against the walls, and they retreat into the center of the room. More curious than afraid, but still treading softly, Swanilda roams about looking at the woodenlike characters.

They seem to be dolls, but they are all life-sized and the suspended gestures in which they are fixed are alarmingly human. On the right, seated on a cushion, sits a tall Chinaman dressed in a richly embroidered native costume. A one-man band in resplendent parade dress stands with arm out, ready to strike the huge drum he carries. An astronomer in long black robes and a high, peaked hat, a poised juggler in the middle of one of his tricks, a Harlequin in typical diamond-patched costume, and a king holding scepter in hand—all these characters occupy Coppélius's room as if it were their home. [In the Sadler's Wells Theatre Ballet production, the figures are a Chinaman, a Crusader, Pierrot, an astrologer, and an Oriental dancer.] They are all individuals, each seems to exist apart from the others, yet to

Swanilda and her friends the silent, still figures have no animate existence at all and resemble nothing so much as oversized dolls. Still, the girls are terrified by the darkness and the strange silence. Swanilda is instinctively moved to investigate the curtained alcove, for nowhere does she see Coppélia. She goes over, starts to peep through the curtain, and then runs back to her friends. Her knees are trembling so much that one of the girls holds her shaking legs. The girls force Swanilda to return to the curtain, and this time she is a little bolder. She looks behind the curtain, runs back to her friends, and gestures with automatic movements to music that might accompany the dance of a mechanical toy! Coppélia is a doll! One of the girls accidentally collides with the sitting Chinaman, and the interlopers are aghast as the Chinaman throws out his arms like an automaton, wags his head knowingly, and does a little rhythm act. The terrified girls approach him carefully, but the Chinaman does not change his position. He is a doll, too, but a wonderful mechanical doll, so close to reality that the girls have never imagined his like before. They stare rapturously at his jerky, automatic gestures, laugh delightedly, and search for the hidden clockwork that makes him move. They find nothing. The music peters out. The doll stops as he began.

Swanilda and her friends examine the doll Coppélia. Swanilda reaches out tentatively and touches her. Coppélia is cold as ice, utterly lifeless, a wax doll like all the rest! Swanilda takes her book away, and the frozen girl sits as before, her stilted hands grasping nothing. Swanilda can make neither head nor tail of the book and turns back to be absolutely certain that the lovely girl will not look up and wave to her, as she did to Franz. She leans over to feel her heart. She feels nothing. Sure now that the charming creature of whom she was so jealous is merely an absurd doll, Swanilda gathers her friends about her and laughs with glee at the prospect of Franz paying court to her.

All the girls are tremendously relieved that they have no one to fear in the empty house and prankishly run to each one of the dolls. They wind the dolls up, and soon all the mechanical creatures are in motion. The one-man band plays his music, the juggler commences his act, the astronomer lifts a telescope to his eye—and the fascinated girls can't decide which they like best. They are so enchanted by the dolls that they do not hear Coppélius enter. The music imitates his fierce anger.

He runs in, cape flying behind him, speechless with rage. He shakes his stick at the intruders and rushes about to catch them. All the girls retreat toward the door—all of them except Swanilda, who sneaks into Coppélia's booth while the toymaker shakes his stick at her fleeing friends and pulls the curtains closed. Coppélius comes back into the room and makes straight for the curtains to see if the girls have harmed his most cherished creation. A window opens at the back, and Coppélius stops. Another intruder! He stands close against the back wall, ready to pounce on the stranger. Franz climbs into the room. Coppélius waits patiently until the youth cannot return to the window and then sets upon him. Franz pleads that he means no harm, that he has entered merely to see the girl he loves, and that he will die unless he talks with her.

Gradually Coppélius realizes that Franz is quite serious and he ceases to threaten him. He wants to hear more and astonishes Franz by becoming quite friendly. Coppélius insists that he stay, telling him that his daughter will be in very shortly, and invites the unbelieving youth to sit down and have a drink. When the drink is poured, Franz has no more apprehension and accepts it with relish. The toymaker chatters constantly, pretends to drink too, and Franz—gloriously happy now that he has neared his goal—fails to see that Coppélius is providing him with one drink after another. He tries to describe the beauties of Coppélia to the old man with drunken gestures, and his host nods repeatedly in agreement as Franz's intoxication is increased by a potion he has poured into the drink. Franz's head falls back against the chair, his arms hang limp in sleep, and in this room filled with dolls he is almost like a doll himself.

Coppélius checks to be sure that he is unconscious and wrings his hands in glee in anticipation of his next move. He takes out a huge leather volume, puts it down on the floor, and hurriedly leafs through the pages looking for a secret formula he has never used before. He finds it, leaps up, looks back at Franz, and approaches the drawn curtains of Coppélia's closet. He yanks back the curtains, peers in, and examines carefully every feature of Coppélia's face and dress. The clever Swanilda no longer resembles herself as she sits rigidly in Coppélia's costume, holding up her little book. Coppélius goes behind her chair and wheels Swanilda into the middle of the room as the orchestra sounds a beautiful melody on piercing, muted strings. He glances down at the book and makes magical gestures in Swanilda's face. Swanilda does not blink. Now the toymaker runs over to Franz and, moving his hands down the youth's body from head to foot, seems to pull the power of life from him like a magnet. Coppélius holds the life force tight in his hands and goes back to the doll, whom he tries to endow with this potency. He consults the book again and repeats the ritual. To his astonishment and happiness, Swanilda tosses away the book, and Coppélius believes his wooden doll has actually come to life.

Swanilda's arms move stiffly as the music mimics the mechanics of her strength. She raises her head and stands up, her body still bent over in a sitting position. The delighted Coppélius straightens her up, and she stands still for a moment. Her face is expressionless. Then she begins to try out her arms and legs, pushing her feet out before her in a simulated walk. Coppélia's master encourages Swanilda's every step with more incantations; the girl is excited at her success in deceiving him. She looks over at Franz and can hardly wait until he wakens. Meanwhile she lets Coppélius imagine that he alone is responsible for her new-found vitality. Her stance is rigid and her face assumes an equally artificial smile. At Coppélius's command, her legs move less mechanically, and soon she is dancing to a light, sparkling waltz, perfecting her steps as she circles about. Now that he has taught her to dance, the toymaker wishes her to continue showing off his magical powers. The doll smiles ingratiatingly, but instead of dancing she walks about the room, as if she were exploring it for the first time. She goes over to Franz, shakes him, sees the discarded wine mug, and raises it to her lips. Coppélius snatches it from her in the nick of time. He is beginning to find out that this live doll can be as exasperating as any young girl.

Swanilda keeps up her fun with him, but still maintains her mechanical characteristics. Like a child, she pretends in each one of her tricks merely to be doing what her teacher has told her to do in the first place. The tormented Coppélius beseeches her to dance again; she stares at him dumbly. Finally, to keep her out of any more mischief, he distracts her by placing a black mantilla about her shoulders. Swanilda responds instantly by dancing a bolero. The music is subdued, but the girl intensifies the impassioned Spanish dance as the tempo mounts. Coppélius now supposes that there is nothing he cannot make her do; he experiments further by investing the doll with a Scottish plaid. Sure enough, as the orchestra pipes a sprightly jig, she follows its rhythms like a good Scottish lass. At the end of this dance, however, Swanilda has had enough. She kicks the pages of his magic book and runs berserk about the room.

She tries to awaken Franz from his stupor. Coppélius, fraught with anxiety lest she harm herself as well as the other dolls, finally succeeds in grabbing her. He sets her down hard on her chair, shakes his finger in her face, and rolls the chair back into the curtained alcove. Franz stirs, stretches, and looks about. Coppélius allows him no time for questions and tells him to get out. Franz leaves eagerly, climbing back out of the window. Swanilda, no longer a doll, pushes the curtains aside and dashes about the room knocking over every one of Coppélius's precious toys except the king, who stands in ridiculous majesty over the chaotic scene. Then, all too lifelike, Swanilda escapes through the door to catch up with Franz.

The shocked Coppélius cannot believe his eyes. He pulls back the curtains, and there, thrown across her chair, he sees the naked, limp body of his beloved Coppélia.

ACT THREE—THE WEDDING The festival day has arrived, and all the villagers have gathered in the sun on the manor house lawn to take part in the celebration. The town's new bell has been blessed, and the lord of the manor awaits the presentation of dowries to those who will marry on the holiday. Swanilda, radiant in her wedding costume, and Franz, also in formal array, approach the lord with the other couples. Franz cannot take his eyes off Swanilda, who has taught him the lesson he unconsciously yearned to know. He knows now that, as his wife, she will be to him all women—all the other girls the beautiful Coppélia represented. The assembled villagers share the exuberant joy of Franz and Swanilda. The lord of the manor congratulates them and presents the dowries.

The irate and pathetic Coppélius marches in and upsets the happy throng by reminding them of the damage he has sustained. Coppélius is so intent on securing compensation, rather than explanations and apologies, that the crowd does not sympathize with him readily. The only one who sympathizes is Swanilda, who steps forward understandingly and offers him her dowry. The sullen Coppélius is about to take it, but the lord of the manor motions Swanilda away and rewards the toymaker with a bag of gold. The old man leaves the scene, wondering whether it will ever be possible for him to create a doll as lovable as his ill-fated Coppélia.

The pageant of the day now commences. The peasants dance the familiar "Dance of the Hours," in which the arrangement of the performers imitates the progress of the hours around an enormous clock as the hurdy-gurdy music tinkles the time away. The twelve girls form a circle like the face of an enormous clock, kneel toward the center, and one by one rise, pirouette, and kneel again, telling the time away.

Soft woodwinds herald the arrival of Dawn, danced by a lovely young girl. Her dance, with the music, is at first slow and tentative, like the gradual approach of light; then her body responds to bright wakening music and she celebrates the rising sun.

Now Prayer—a demure girl who clasps her hands before her and turns slowly in deep arabesques—delights the villagers. She kneels as the harp ends the music for her dance.

A peasant couple perform a vigorous betrothal dance to

rhythmic, piping music. They bow to the lord of the manor, and all await the arrival of the bride and groom.

Franz bows and holds out his hand to Swanilda. Together they dance a moving adagio to a deep melody from the strings. Franz carries Swanilda high on his shoulder, sets her down gently, and the girl kneels before him. She rises on point, pirouettes swiftly in his arms, is lifted again, released, and caught as her lover holds her across his knee. He turns her in arabesque, and the dance that symbolizes their reconciliation and pledged happiness comes to an end. Their dance together and the variation each now performs alone reveal the youthful strength and tenderness each possesses for the other. When they have finished, all the villagers join the smiling couple in a fast, constantly accelerating dance in which the whole company becomes a part of the breathless happiness reflected in the shining faces of Swanilda and Franz.

American Ballet Theatre revived *Coppélia,* in a new production by Enrique Martinez, during their 1968 season at the Brooklyn Academy of Music in New York. Carla Fracci and Erik Bruhn danced the first performance. Others dancing the principal roles were Cynthia Gregory and Gayle Young, Alexandra Radius and Ted Kivitt, and Eleanor D'Antuono and Ivan Nagy. When she joined the company, Natalia Makarova danced the role of Swanilda.

In 1974 I decided that we should stage *Coppélia* at the New York City Ballet (we needed another evening-long ballet) and asked the ballerina and teacher Alexandra Danilova, celebrated for many years for her Swanilda, to collaborate with me on the choreography. Rouben Ter-Arutunian designed the scenery and costumes, which were executed by Karinska. The ballet was first presented by the company July 17, 1974 at the Saratoga Performing Arts Center, the New York City Ballet's summer home at Saratoga Springs, New York.

Coppélia was first danced, of course, in France. It was introduced in Russia in 1884, with Marius Petipa's own version of Saint-Léon's original choreography. I remember very well performances by the Russian Imperial Ballet of *Coppélia* and as a member of the company danced in the mazurka. (It is said that the czardas and the mazurka were first introduced into ballet in *Coppélia* and, from then on, divertissements based on national and folk dances became very popular in ballet.)

I have often said that Delibes is one of my favorite composers for dance. In our new *Coppélia,* we used the entire score of the three-act version. The first dance drama of really uniform excellence deserves no less! No part of the ballet is subordinate to any other; most important of all, ballet music in *Coppélia* participates in the dance drama as never before, Delibes' charming, melodic music assisting the plot and unifying the music and dance. As we know, Tchaikovsky was directly inspired by Delibes' scores to write his own ballet music. Delibes is the first great ballet composer; Tchaikovsky and Stravinsky are his successors.

The first American performance of *Coppélia,* though greeted with applause by press and public in 1887, was not as memorable as a later one, when Anna Pavlova, making her début in the United States, appeared as Swanilda at the Metropolitan Opera House, New York, February 28, 1910.

Most major ballet companies round the world dance *Coppélia* and many distinguished dancers have performed its leading roles. The Ballet Russe de Monte Carlo staged the ballet for Alexandra Danilova who was identified with it for many years. The noted dance critic and poet Edwin Denby called her "the most wonderful *Coppélia* heroine in the world." Madame Danilova now teaches at the School of American Ballet in New York, where we began our work on our production.

Writing of the first performances at Saratoga, the critic Arlene Croce said in *The New Yorker:*

"In the New York City Ballet's new *Coppélia,* which had its première at the company's summer home in Saratoga, Patricia McBride gives a great and a great *big* performance—big in scale as well as spirit. The role comes as a climax to the present and most exciting phase of her career. The scale on which she has been dancing this year is a new development in her style, and to reach it she hasn't sacrificed any of her speed or sharp-edged rhythm or subtlety of intonation. And although the role of Swanilda gives her plenty of unaccustomed material (such as extended pantomime), she sweeps through it without ever once looking like anyone but herself. She persuades you that Swanilda is Patricia McBride and always has been. This is a remarkable triumph for an artist whom the world knows as the flag-bearer of the New York City Ballet, the embodiment of its egoless-star ethic. McBride is fundamentally inscrutable. She doesn't exist outside her roles, and when you try to place her among her peers in world ballet—Gregory and Sibley and Makarova and the other great Russians whose names mean more to the public than McBride's does—her image dissolves in a succession of ballets: *Donizetti Variations, Rubies, La Valse, Brahms-Schoenberg Quartet, Who Cares?, Dances at a Gathering, Harlequinade.* McBride doesn't throw us cues to let us know how we ought to take her; she doesn't comment, doesn't cast herself as an observer of life. All she knows about life she seems to have learned through dancing, and all she has to tell she tells through dancing. How durable a bond of communication this is she proves once again in *Coppélia,* and in the very first moments.

"Swanilda's *valse lente* is the opening dance. By custom, it's a straight classical solo, and it gives us the ballerina in full flight almost as soon as the curtain has gone up. But in the New York City Ballet version McBride runs down to the footlights and, on the first notes of the waltz, addresses the audience in a passage of mime. 'This one up there,' she says, pointing to Coppélia on her balcony, 'she sits and reads all day long. That one, who lives over there, is in love with her, but she never notices him. Me, I just play.' And she plays (dances), first for her own pleasure, then for Coppélia's, with enticing steps that seem to say, 'Come down and play with me. See how nicely I play.' The structure of the waltz is mime, dance, dance-mime; in one stroke the means by which the story of *Coppélia* will be told are laid before us, and the fact that it's all done to an unvarying waltz rhythm lets us see easily how these different effects—of a mime gesture or a dance movement or a dance movement that functions as a mime gesture—depend for their force and clarity on having a different relation to an over-all rhythm. 'Mime' time is not 'dance' time, and each has to be established to musical time in a different way. This isn't as elementary as it sounds. The big catch in keeping the time values disparate is that the rhythm which connects them may disintegrate, and the worst danger of *that* is that the dancer will seem to be switching personalities on us, much as if she were a singer whose speaking voice didn't resemble the voice she sang with. (A lot of the modern distrust of mime comes from the schizoid effect of miscalculated rhythm.) In McBride's variation, and through her whole radiant performance, she plays excitingly close to the danger point. But the values of dance and mime, distinct in their time sense, are equalized in their scale—the largest scale that one could hope to see. So the meanings that are conveyed by all these sharply differentiated rhythms are always absolutely clear; they fly at you and away, or loom and settle, but there's no break in her consistency. She 'reads' at every moment. She is a character. McBride has never struck me as a particularly strong actress, and her method baffled me for years. How else, if not by acting, could she have made her character in 'La Valse' so vivid—a character unlike anyone else's who does the part? But for McBride acting is not the key; dancing is. And now that she's become so grand I don't see how anyone could miss that. She is a great dancer and a great star.

"The new production of *Coppélia*, staged by George Balanchine and Alexandra Danilova, is a combination of old and new choreography, the old being a first and second act built largely around the excellent 'after-Petipa' version in which Danilova used to star for the Ballet Russe de Monte Carlo, and the new being a glittering Act III, all of it Balanchine's except for the grand adagio and the ballerina's variation, which belong to Danilova-Petipa. Balanchine's dances are not uniformly masterpieces, but, taken all together, they ought to extend the life of this ballet another hundred years. In their unique blend of light irony and ingenuousness, they are a mirror of the music—serious music that was not meant to be taken too seriously.

"For his third act, Delibes envisioned a village wedding, with the villagers putting on an allegorical pageant of man's works and days. Most productions get through Dawn and Prayer and then give up in confusion, either reassigning the rest of the music (Work, Hymen, Discord and War) or dropping it altogether. Balanchine uses all the music Delibes wrote, and he does not mistake its spirit. His choreography really does present a plausible (though not a realistic) village pageant stuck together with metallic threads and parchment and candle wax, but noble nonetheless, with an anti-grand-manner grandeur. The Waltz of the Hours, that sublime gushing fountain of melody, is danced by twenty-four grinning little girls in gold tunics, who line the path of the soloist, Marnee Morris, and form choral borders for the solos that follow: Dawn (Merrill Ashley), Prayer (Christine Redpath), and Work, or La Fileuse, here called Spinner (Susan Hendl). The entrance of these three graces—posed motionless as beauty queens in a carriage that circles the stage twice—is one of the most piercing visions in the ballet. And the solos for Ashley and Hendl are outstanding—complete summations of their gifts. There's a dance for Four Jesterettes in padded motley sewn with bells. (In the Monte Carlo production, this entrée—originally Hymen—was called Follies, which seems more to the allegorical point than Jesterettes.) Discord and War is a romp for boys and girls in horned helmets, a flourish of capes and spears waved as idly as picket signs—a witty number, shakily danced. Then, after the bridal *pas de deux*, comes an exhilarating finale, with climax piled on smashing climax. Best of all is the ballerina's fish dive into her partner's arms, instantly followed by the only thing that could top it—the return of the twenty-four golden tinies cakewalking on in a wide curve, with Morris in the lead tearing off *piqué-fouetté* turns.

"Balanchine's hand is evident elsewhere in the production, too—in that first-act entrance of Swanilda, and in the Mazurka and Czardas, which surely have never before been so thick and bushy with (musical) repeats, so fertile with invention. Their one weakness is that they are isolated from the action and don't serve any purpose. But the weakness is very likely not a permanent one. This is not a finished production, and by the time it reaches New York, in November, Balanchine is sure to have taken over more of it—filling up gaps in the staging, refurbishing or replacing some of the less effective old dances, and straightening out a few discrepancies, such as the sudden, unmotivated shift to a sunnier mood that follows Swanilda's solemn ear-of-wheat dance. Possibly he'll find more for the hero to do, too. At present, Franz has only one dance—an interpolation in the third act which old-timers will recognize as Eglevsky's variation from the *Sylvia Pas de Deux*. It's nice to have this great solo back again, especially as danced by Helgi Tomasson, but Tomasson, who is a charming Franz, doesn't get a chance to display his true dance power until the finale. I hope, too, that a way can be found to make the meaning of the ear-of-wheat episode (a direct descendant of the petal-plucking scene in *Giselle*) at least as clear to a modern audience as it is in the Ballet Theatre version.

"The part of the ballet that is, right now, just about perfect is the second act. Here, again, Balanchine has obviously been at work; you can almost feel him assuming command of the action the moment Coppélius enters his workshop to find it overrun by Swanilda and her friends. Coppélius is Shaun O'Brien, giving the performance of his career. He is not a buffoon, and Swanilda is not a zany. He's a misanthrope, a tyrant, believably a genius who can create dolls everyone thinks are alive. She is a shrewd, fearless girl who grows into womanhood by accepting as her responsibility the destruction of Coppélius. She must break his power over gullible, romantic Franz, who has chosen the perfect woman, the doll Coppélia, over the natural woman, herself. The conflict between idealism and realism, or art and life, is embedded in the libretto of *Coppélia*, and Coppélius's passion is in the music. I enjoy burlesque versions of the second act (and in this tradition there's no Swanilda more enjoyable than that gifted zany Makarova), but the heart of the music isn't in them. Balanchine's Coppélius is kin to other Balanchine artist-heroes—not only Drosselmeier of *The Nutcracker* but Don Quixote and Orpheus and the Poet of *La Sonnàmbula*. And when he raises Swanilda-Coppélia onto her points and she remains locked there, upright or jackknifed over them, he's the strangest of all alchemists, seeking to transform his beloved twice over: doll into woman, woman into ballerina. Swanilda must become as totally manipulatable, totally perfectible, as a Balanchine ballerina. She must be a work of art, and then burst out of her mold. I once saw a brilliantly horrifying performance given by the Royal Danish Ballet, in which Solveig Østergaard and Frank Schaufuss confronted each other as monsters equal in might if not in cunning. But there was nothing in it like Shaun O'Brien's 'speech' to McBride, conveyed in a paroxysm of joy: 'I have made you and you are beautiful.'

"Rouben Ter-Arutunian's costumes are attractive, and his scenery is modest and quite pretty in several styles. Act I is like a child's pop-up picture book, with exaggerated perspectives. Act II, a cutaway of Coppélius's lab, ranges from Ensor to Burchfield, but the backcloth for Act III looked sketchily realized. A number of bells hanging above the stage (the pageant celebrates, along with everything else, a *fête de carillons*) bear the monograms of those associated with the original production—the choreographer, Arthur Saint-Léon; the librettist, Charles Nuitter; and E. T. A. Hoffmann, whose tale of Coppélius inspired the ballet—and those responsible for the present one. The largest bell, for which I forgive this somewhat presumptuous idea, is inscribed 'J'étais créé par Léo Delibes, 25 Mai 1870.' It is Coppélia herself who speaks. G.B., for George Balanchine, happen to be the initials also of Giuseppina Bozzacchi, who has no bell of her own. She was sixteen when she made her début at the Paris Opéra, appearing as the first Swanilda. Giuseppina took Paris by storm. Then Discord and War came in earnest. Six months later, in the siege during the Franco-Prussian War, she died of smallpox on the morning of her seventeenth birthday."*

* "I Have Made You and You Are Beautiful" by Arlene Croce. Reprinted by permission; © 1974 The New Yorker Magazine, Inc.

DANCES AT A GATHERING

Music by Frédéric Chopin. Choreography by Jerome Robbins. Costumes by Joe Eula. Lighting by Thomas Skelton. First presented by the New York City Ballet at the New York State Theater, Lincoln Center, May 8, 1969. Pianist: Gordon Boelzner. Dancers: Allegra Kent, Sara Leland, Kay Mazzo, Patricia McBride, Violette Verdy, Anthony Blum, John Clifford, Robert Maiorano, John Prinz, and Edward Villella. Dedicated to the memory of Jean Rosenthal.

Dances at a Gathering is a ballet for ten dancers to piano pieces by Chopin. Five girls and five boys dance in an open space as a pianist plays to the left of the stage. He plays mazurkas, waltzes, études, a scherzo, and a nocturne—eighteen pieces in all—as the dancers, distinguished in the program by the color of their costumes, respond to the music.

The curtain goes up on a bare stage with a background of blue sky and amorphous clouds; we are outdoors in a clearing, a field, a meadow, a grove. A boy enters on the right, informally dressed in open white shirt, brown tights, and boots. He walks slowly, quietly looking the place over, glancing up at the sky, thinking. Then he is lifting his arm and his walk becomes a stride, a dance, as the piano begins, *Mazurka, Opus 63, No. 3*. His dance reflects a pleasure in being where he is on a day like this. As the music ends, he leaves, meditating.

A girl and a boy enter and dance to the *Waltz, Opus 69, No. 2*, moving arm in arm, at first a bit tentatively as if nothing will come of it, but the music changes all that as they follow its flow in lifts, leaps, and a rushing exit with the girl poised high on the boy's shoulder. Another girl and boy come in and dance a little more formally, responding to the character of the *Mazurka, Opus 33, No. 3*, with arm gestures, too. But they, too, get carried away with the music and she, too, is lifted off in a rushing conclusion.

A girl enters alone and dances fast to the staccato beat of a new, more demanding *Mazurka, Opus 6, No. 4.* She is still on stage as the next part begins.

Six dancers in different groupings respond to the music of four fresh *Mazurkas, Opus 7, Nos. 5* and *4, Opus 24, No. 2* and *Opus 6, No. 2.* There are two boys, dancing back to back in a kind of jig, one of the boys interested in one girl, who watches, the other in another. And not the same ones they were dancing with earlier. Rhapsodic as particular partnerships become, in the group commitments dissolve with no regrets and everyone begins again. In the dancing and watching of dances, in the joining in, partnerships shift. The dances become full of character and there is a feeling that we are in real Mazurka country as gesture identifies with music and place. There are friendships between the girls, too, and both boys and girls play at posing each other in groups for photographs.

Now to the *Waltz, Opus 42,* a girl and boy try to outdo each other in speed and virtuosity, each showing off to the other, he cartwheeling to victory, all of it a serious but affectionate competition. She touches his hand and he lifts her up to his shoulder, wrapping her about his head closely as they leave.

Three girls dance the *Waltz, Opus 34, No. 2,* entering in a dim light, strolling, doing solos, then all three dancing together. A boy comes to lift one girl away. They dance together as the other two watch. These two look into the distance. Then as quietly as he came the boy is gone, leaving his girl kneeling. She rises to join her two friends, they pose in a group, then separate with separate dreams, only to join arms and leave together.

The lights come up and two boys compete now to the music of *Mazurka, Opus 56, No. 2,* each trying to outdo the other, throwing each other about, making dramatic exits backward.

As the lights fade, a girl enters to dance thoughtfully alone to the *Étude, Opus 25, No. 4.*

To the big *Fourth Waltz, Opus 34, No. 1,* six couples dance, responding dramatically to the pulse of the music. There is an exhilarating series of slides and lifts, at the end of which the boys line up to pass the girls down a diagonal line, lifting them so that the next boy lifts them higher still to the demanding rush of the piano.

Now in dimmer light come a boy and girl. She clearly likes him and tries to make it clearer. He leaves her but another boy enters. She dances all around him, surrounding him with attention but he ignores her and goes off. With a third boy she has the same result, but more amused than despairing, she flicks her wrist and goes off.

Next a *pas de deux* to the *Étude, Opus 25, No. 5,* then a fast solo for a boy to the *Étude, Opus 10, No. 2.* The *Scherzo, Opus 20, No. 1* involves six dancers in dramatic declarations, fulfillments, and disappointments. As the three girls fall back in the boys' arms, they are a bit embarrassed and leave in a rush.

For the final piece, the *Nocturne, Opus 15, No. 1* and its slow melody, the lights come down. Gradually all ten dancers appear, singly and in couples, together now for the first time. One of them, the boy who began the dances at this gathering, touches the ground of the place. They all look at him and then up at the sky, which they watch intently. They pair off then and walk away. All move forward as the music dramatizes their situation. Then they look to the ground and raising their arms start a dance that does not develop. They go to the back of the stage, the boys to one side, the girls on another, and bow. The curtain falls.

NOTES *Dances at a Gathering* came about in an interesting way. "I started out to do a *pas de deux* for Eddie Villella and Pat McBride," Jerome Robbins told Hubert Saal of *Newsweek.* "Then I got turned on by the music. It all started to pour out as if some valve inside me had opened up and the purity of working with dancers took over. I had to find the form. Usually I work with a structured music, as in Stravinsky's *Les Noces,* where the literary material is built in. In this case I took whatever appealed to me and let it happen, trusting it. It's nice to work loosely and intuitively."

Shortly before the première, Robbins said to Clive Barnes of the New York *Times,* "I'm doing a fairly classical ballet to very old-fashioned and romantic music, but there is a point to it. In a way it is a revolt from the faddism of today. In the period since my last ballet (*Les Noces,* 1965), I have been around looking at dance—seeing a lot of the stuff at Judson Church and the rest of the avant-garde. And I find myself feeling just what is the matter with connecting, what's the matter with love, what's the matter with celebrating positive things? Why, I asked myself, does everything have to be separated and alienated so that there is this almost constant push to disconnect? The strange thing is that the young people are for love. Is that bad?"

Shortly after the première of *Dances at a Gathering,* Robbins was interviewed for *Dance Magazine* by the critic Edwin Denby. The complete text of the article, reprinted by courtesy of *Dance Magazine,* follows: "Robbins's *Dances at a Gathering* is a great success both with dance fans and the general public. And it is a beautiful piece. But it wasn't planned as a sure-fire piece—it wasn't planned at all beforehand and began by chance, as Robbins explains in the interview (taped shortly after the official première) which appears on the pages that follow.

"The ballet is set to Chopin piano pieces and the program lists ten dancers but tells you little more. The curtain goes up in silence on an empty stage. It looks enormous. The back is all sky—some kind of changeable late afternoon in summer. Both sides of the stage are black. Forestage right, a man enters slowly, deep in thought. He is wearing a loose white shirt, brown tights and boots. He turns to the sky and walks slowly away from you toward center stage. You think of a man alone in a meadow. As he walks you notice the odd tilt of his head—like a man listening, inside himself. In the silence the piano begins as if he were remembering the music. He marks a dance step, he sketches a mazurka gesture, with a kind of pensive vigor he begins to improvise and now he is dancing marvelously and, in a burst of freedom, he is running all over the meadow at its edge. Suddenly he subsides and, more mysterious than ever, glides into the woods and is gone. Upstage a girl and boy enter. At once they are off full speed in a double improvisation, a complexly fragmented waltz, the number Robbins speaks of as the 'wind dance.'

"As one dance succeeds another—the ballet lasts about an hour—you are fascinated by the variety and freshness of invention, the range of feeling, and by the irresistibly beautiful music which the dance lets you hear distinctly—its mystery too. You see each dancer dance marvelously and you also see each one as a fascinating individual—complex, alone, and with any of the others, individually most sensitive and generous in their relationships. The music and the dance seem to be inventing each other. For a dance fan, the fluid shifts of momentum are a special delight. For the general theater public, Robbins's genius in focusing on a decisive momentary movement—almost like a zoom lens—makes vivid the special quality of each dance, and all the charming jokes.

"But it is a strange ballet.

"Our talk began before the tape machine arrived. Robbins had been telling me how the ballet developed. He had been asked whether he would care to do a piece for the 25th Anniversary City Center Gala, May 8. Delighted by the way Patricia McBride and Edward Villella had been dancing *The Afternoon of a Faun,* he thought he would like to do a *pas de deux* for them—perhaps to Chopin music—and he accepted. As he listened to records and became more and more interested in the possibilities—it occurred to him to add two more couples—and he began rehearsal. In the course of rehearsals, however, all the six dancers he had chosen were not always free, so he went on choreographing with four others, using those who happened to be free. Gradually he made more and more dances, but without a definite plan for the whole piece. When about two-thirds of the ballet was done, he invited Balanchine (who had just returned from Europe) to rehearsal. At the end of it he turned to Mr. B and said, 'Don't you think it's a bit long?' Mr. B answered, 'More. Make more!' He did.

"Robbins said to me, 'As you see, there are still never more than six dancers dancing at once.' He told me that as the dances and relationships kept coming out of the different pieces of music and the particular dancers available, he began to feel that they were all connected by some underlying sense of community (he said, laughing, 'Maybe just because they were dancers') and by a sense of open air and sunlight and sudden nostalgia perhaps.

"We spoke of one of the many lovely lifts—this one at the end of Eddie's *pas de deux* with Pat where it looks as though he were lifting a sack onto his shoulder and, up on his shoulder, the sack suddenly changes into a beautiful mermaid. Robbins explained how it came out of a sudden metamorphosis in the music. And he illustrated how the lift is done.

"We were talking of Villella's gesture of touching the floor in the final minutes of the ballet, and Robbins mentioned that he was perhaps thinking of the dancers' world—the floor below, the space around and above. I was saying that I liked that gesture better the second time I saw it because it was slower and I wondered if he (Robbins) had changed it. At that point the tape begins:

"ROBBINS No, that's just a very subtle thing of acting and where the human being is at the time. I think two weeks ago at the preview, Eddie was under more difficulties and pressures—down more—and perhaps that made the difference.

"I think the ballet will seem different in almost every performance, not vastly, but shades like those you saw, they will happen, depending on the dancers. You said it, I remember, way back—the dancers read (in a review) what the ballet is about, then they change because now they *know* it (they know it in words)—before they just *did* it. And that can happen—there was a modesty and a sort of not knowing in the first showing. They may start to think now that maybe they should do it more like what everyone says it is. I don't know what to do about that except to ask them not to.

"I always tell them to do it for themselves, and to think of 'marking' it—Don't think of doing it full out.

"DENBY Well, that's another quality the ballet has. I was very happy to see that with Eddie, who is used to 'doing it full out'—he does that very beautifully, it's not vulgar selling at all—he's not forcing it. But the inner business he also does very well—in *Giselle*. He's remarkable, you know, wonderful.

"ROBBINS I like watching ballets, anyway, best of all at

rehearsals when a dancer is just working for himself, really just working. They are beautiful to watch then. I love to watch George's (Balanchine) work that way. Just love to.

"DENBY How beautiful everything is before it gets its name. Did I hear you say that Melissa (Hayden) will be covering Violette (Verdy)?

"ROBBINS Yes, I think she'll be marvelous.

"DENBY And so is Verdy. Someone told me that you're working to add a much longer number for her. So I said, 'Oh, wonderful.'

"ROBBINS I haven't been around ballet for so long, I forget how scuttlebutty it gets around here. If you say to someone, 'I want to work with you tomorrow,' the next day someone asks you, 'Are you doing a new ballet?' It already has gotten that big.

"But it was nice working with them. I did enjoy it very much. Patty McBride, I just *love* working with her.

"DENBY Yes, she's remarkable. . . . And I am very happy about what you did with Bob Maiorano. Because this year he's suddenly become a very good dancer wherever I look at him. He was beginning last year and, all of a sudden, there he is—now you can really see it.

"ROBBINS Yes.

"DENBY He has a marvelous Italian beauty of gesture. Maybe he was afraid of it all this time. The arm is so heavy the way he moves it. But the weight is right for all of them—the boys especially.

"ROBBINS Bobby Weiss, have you seen him? In one of the performances he is going to do Johnnie Clifford's part.

"DENBY He was wonderful in a school performance last year, too. Especially in the end of *Sylphides,* when he lost his nervousness in the finale. He looks as though he were not letting go as much as is his nature.

"ROBBINS He is beautiful when he lets go. In rehearsal, I just made him go.

"DENBY Clifford was remarkable too; he is so positively there. But it's not so simple. There is also something private about it. And Tony's (Blum) great—so much livelier than he's been . . . often.

"ROBBINS That's the fun of having another choreographer work with the dancers. Like in Ballet Theatre, Eliot Feld was doing a ballet, and I looked at his dancers and thought, Now, those are people I bypassed, but he saw something in them and brought out another whole aspect of them. It's always charming. But every choreographer—Agnes (de Mille) has people she works with I can't see—people I work with that she can't see. That's nice for the dancers, isn't it?

"DENBY And for the choreographers if you are going to travel around. You should try out your dances on the Russians. I'm sure they would like to have a dance of yours, they like to gather things—archives in their minds. It would be so much fun.

"ROBBINS I'm going to Russia. I *would* like to see if I can get it either to the Bolshoi or Kirov. I would like to see them dance this. I really would. It might finally turn out to be a peasant parody, you never know (*laughter*)—that folk part of it—I was surprised.

"DENBY I was surprised that people made so much of it, because the dancers are always so elegant. They might be landowners, if they were anybody in Europe.

"ROBBINS At first I also thought they were very elegant people, maybe at a picnic, maybe doing something—their own thing.

"And also to me—and this I'm very careful about—I don't want it to be a big thing—but the boys and the whole period are very hippie-ish.

"DENBY At first you had the beards, I was quite pleased with that.

"ROBBINS The boys still had them at rehearsal because of the long lay-off. Tony had long hair and a moustache and John Prinz had long hair and a beard and it was marvelous looking. It really affected what I was doing. I liked the boots —and the sketches are much more hippie than they appear on stage, in the sense of belts and open blouses for the boys and long hair and ballooning sleeves. There is something in the nature of knowing who they are and having love and confidence in them.

"DENBY Competence? . . .

"ROBBINS Confidence—which I feel is in the work, finally. Loving confidence in themselves and in the other people.

"DENBY That is in there very strongly.

"ROBBINS It has some strangenesses in it too, I'm sure, but I can't yet quite see it. Every now and then I look at a step and think that is a very odd step. There is a strange step that Eddie does in his solo—he should play with it the way one does this (*hand gesture*).

"DENBY There was an eight-year-old Negro boy in the street and he was running; he suddenly started throwing his feet around—with such pleasure.

"ROBBINS I saw something nice in the park. Near Sheep Meadow there was a black boy and a white boy, both happened to be wearing blue. The black boy had a blue sweat shirt and the white boy had a blue sweater and open collar. They were running toward each other and it was more than a game. They ran and reached out hands. Not just shook hands, because that's what it was about, but they took hands and swung around each other with their heads thrown back with laughter. And then let go and embraced each other. Oh, it was so beautiful, I was thrilled by it. There was so much rapture and ecstacy and friendliness and openness about it. Then they quieted down and began talking, (*laughs*).

"DENBY There are things in the ballet that are a bit gruesome. And, you know, very interesting.

"ROBBINS Gruesome?

"DENBY It's partly in the lifts, partly sometimes in the way the boys treat a girl.

"ROBBINS Well, opening night there was an accident. I want to be sure you know that it was an accident. There was a place where Sally (Sara Leland) was being swung around and they fell off the lift and it turned into a—it looked like she was in outer space—like she'd been released from a capsule. She was just swirling around. Horrifying for a moment. But there are?—I don't know, I can't tell.

"DENBY It's definitely in the music. It's much stranger than one. . . .

"ROBBINS Yes, than one thinks.

"DENBY Than one is supposed to think.

"ROBBINS There's a nocturne. I began late listening to one nocture—it was like opening a door into a room and the people are in the *midst* of a conversation. I mean, there's no introduction, no preface; it's like a cut in a film; it's almost like Chopin had finished the previous nocturne, finished it properly, and there was a fade-out. And suddenly (*clap*) you're on somebody's face who's talking. But in the middle of a sentence! You don't even get 'and then,' it's right in the middle of a word and he's very strange, really quite strange. He knew a lot, I think. Much more than I thought before I began. It was fascinating that way—just like some connection happened between all those sounds that he thought of, and where I was at.

"DENBY The movement through a piece is always so interesting, and that you catch so well and do so many things with.

"ROBBINS I listened to a lot of recordings, different people playing the same piece. I used mostly Rubinstein and Novaes and some Brailowsky. I listened to some of the Dinu Lipatti. Then it was enough for me and after that I knew I would start to get confused. There are hardly any liberties taken at all—I would say none. Only one where at the end of Eddie's first dance it's marked *fortissimo*—da da da *whoosh* —I don't even know if it's Chopin's indication—I choreographed it that way—and Eddie was gone, *whoosh*. I didn't like it, it was a little obvious, like I was trying for a hand and the piece was trying for a hand, I thought there was something else there, so I took it on retard and soft, and let him take that poetic thing he does there. The dancers are beautiful.

"DENBY Gordon (Boelzner) plays it very well because he also plays it for movement, without those extra questions of pianism.

"ROBBINS There are no sentimentalities.

"DENBY If you were listening to the music at a concert you might want more nuances, but this way you don't because the dancers are doing it, the nuances.

"ROBBINS And he's tireless, that boy. It's fantastic. He

plays it all day long, and does the other rehearsals, too. Some of those pieces are killers. I suddenly thought, Look at a Chopin concerto—they play a piece and go off and rest. They do maybe half an hour or twenty minutes and go and have a fifteen-minute intermission. But he's tearing off those *Études* written for these two fingers. You know about the one Eddie dances to—the little fast one—sort of chromatically going up and down the scale? Well, Chopin devised it to give these two fingers which are the weakest, a workout.

"DENBY I am so glad you didn't orchestrate it. Not that it would be possible, but there's that temptation.

"ROBBINS I got worried for a while before we got it down on the big piano because it began to sound very hollow to me. And I thought, Well when people come to this big theatre and they have just seen a big ballet with a lot of marvelous sounds, the piano is going to sound like a little rehearsal piano. But it doesn't, where it is. It seems it fills the house and sustains—a good combination, I think, between what you are seeing and what you hear.

"DENBY It isn't miked?

"ROBBINS No, not at all!

"DENBY And you're so glad to see him, too. I wondered whether he can see the dancers.

"ROBBINS Most of them, but not the ones on the side of the stage he is on. But there is a place where we have a mirror—rigged way up high on the wings so that if he looks up he can see someone come in for just a cue. And I thought Tom Skelton did a very good job in a very little time. He did the lighting.

"DENBY Some of it looks ominous, sometimes. I mean weather. It changes. I suppose you wanted that too. I liked it.

"ROBBINS I didn't mean it to look ominous, but I suppose that vast sky, it is almost like nature changing on you. You're a little worried about what is going to happen next, it doesn't matter if it goes up or down. It's just that it changes. Everything changes.

"I didn't know it was going to be that long a ballet or

what it was going to be. I originally thought, we'll do it using the wings and the cyclorama because it's just going to be a *pas de deux*. But by the time it was all done, I thought, Wow, who should do a set? Is it Jane Freilicher, or is it one of those watery sort of places, or is it—? Now I'm used to the way it is. I don't know if I want a set, or anything softer around the edges. That's a very hard line, those black wings. But once it starts, I don't suppose you are particularly aware of it any more.

"DENBY When you watch you realize that there are woods there, and you're in a meadow and there are trees.

"ROBBINS Isn't that funny, odd how that all got evoked. My names for the dances themselves, for instance, the second dance for John Prinz and Allegra (Kent), I call it 'wind waltz' because to me they are like two things that are on the wind that catch up with each other. There is something about air—breezes which are clawing them and pushing them almost like two kites. And 'walk waltz' or 'the three girls' to me is somehow in the woods. On a Chekhov evening. It just is. I can't see it any other way. It has that quality.

"DENBY The whole piece is a Chekhov piece. There are so many things suggested and not explained. The business of looking around at the end is the trickiest. I didn't like it at all the first time. Yesterday I didn't mind it so much. It is like looking at an airplane, I think of missiles and war.

"ROBBINS They must do it very softly. That is almost one of the hardest parts to be able to do. It is very hard for them just to walk on and be confident and just raise their heads or eyes and look at something without starting to make it dramatic. I keep telling them, 'Relax, don't be sad, don't get upset, just see it, just whatever you want to pick, just see. It's a cloud passing, if you want. Take it easy on it, don't get gloomy.'

"DENBY It's because they all do it together.

"ROBBINS Together—right—they all follow one thing. And that upset you? You thought it was airplanes and missiles?

"DENBY The atom bomb comes in and everything else. The sort of thing about Hitler attacking Poland. Your mind gets full of ideas that you don't want, that don't have anything to do with the piece.

"ROBBINS If I had to talk about it all, I would say that they are looking at—all right—clouds on the horizon which possibly could be threatening, but then that's life, so afterwards you just pick up and go right on again. It doesn't destroy them. They don't lament. They accept.

"DENBY That's what I told myself. It must be that they are looking at clouds—clouds rarely go that fast, but it might be a storm coming up and they're wondering if it's going to happen.

"ROBBINS That section, it was the last piece I did, though. I spent about two weeks after I finished the bulk of the choreography—it was almost all done about two weeks before the eighth of May. But that last two weeks I spent in arranging, trying to get the right order. Not only who danced what, but also that sense of something happening—making the dances have some continuity, some structure, whether I knew specifically what it was or not. At one point I had the scherzo finishing the ballet and the grand waltz opening it. All different sorts of ways. It was just—it was a marvelous sort of puzzle. Here I have all these people and these situations and I know they belong to each other—now let me see how. It was almost like rearranging *things.* And suddenly a picture was there. I am surprised by a lot of it. I am very surprised by the reaction to it. I didn't expect it at all. Something is there that I didn't know I was doing.

"DENBY The reaction?

"ROBBINS To the ballet.

"DENBY That everybody liked it so much.

"ROBBINS So much. The questions you are asking me about it seem to—I was originally going to call it *Some Dances.* That's all they are, just a series of dances. But something else takes over.

"DENBY I don't know that the title is exactly the best.

"ROBBINS It's a hard one to find. I was going to say *Dances: Chopin, In Open Air,* but that isn't the right title. In French *Quelques Danses* is nice, but in English *Some Dances* is sort of flat. If you say *Eighteen Dances* or *Nineteen Dances,* it divides them into compartments.

"DENBY And it's of no consequence. Once you see the piece, you figure it is a piece. That end is quite prepared for all along when it happens. You really didn't want a big dance at the end. Since they are walking so much anyway, it is natural to make the end out of that.

"ROBBINS Also the end of it had to come out of the scherzo, that very restless piece which ends with them all sort of *whoosh* running out—disappearing like cinders falling out into the night, and it couldn't end there, either. That's not the end of it, that's not how I feel about these people—that they went *whoosh* and disappeared. They are still here and they still move like dancers. They are a community. They take—what's the Italian word?—'a *passegiata*'—they take a stroll, like in an Italian town, around the town's square at sundown. They may have felt a threat, but they don't panic, they stay.

"I was very touched by Maria (Tallchief) last night. She was moved by the ballet, and I suddenly realized how much it meant to me that she *was* and that it pleased her, because she is such an image in my mind of what a dancer should be, and I can't think of her as a cinder which went *whoosh* and was gone.

"So coming back after the scherzo to the stage and the floor that we dance on, and putting your hand on it—if it's the earth or a ballet dancer's relationship to a wood floor—*that* somehow is the ending I knew I had to get to somewhere. Very little of this was conscious, Edwin. I don't like to make theory afterwards. I'm just trying to get at it—there may be seven other reasons I'm not mentioning, well, you understand.

"DENBY I don't want to pull it out of you—

"ROBBINS Well, besides, you have your thoughts about it anyway.

"DENBY Of course. Everyone is very happy that you've done a ballet again.

"ROBBINS So am I.

"DENBY And the dancers are happy. And it's nice you want to do some more.

"ROBBINS I'm surprised. I didn't know which I would do or how I would do. It's almost like an artist who has not been drawing for a long time. I didn't know how my hand would be. And I was so surprised that the dances began to come out and began to come out so gushing, in a way. And I worked in a way I hadn't worked before. Whether I knew the details or not, I pushed through to the end of the dance. I sort of knew where it was going, and then I'd go back and clean it up and fill it up. Quite often the dancers weren't even sure how they got through the steps to the next step. But they went with me. Well, what I started to say was that I was pleased to be choreographing again and to have it coming out, and it's given me a sort–it's unplugged something. And I want to do a lot of ballets. I want to go on and see if I can work a little bit more the way I've worked this time–that sort of trusting the intuition more than self-controlling the intuition. I'd like to see what happens with some other kind of music now. That music I feel I am very identified with and always have been. It may go all the way back to my sister's dancing days as a Duncan dancer. I think a lot of that's in there.

"DENBY I imagined you and your sister at the piano—you were seven or eight. The first thing that came from it was *The Concert* which, the first time, I was quite offended by.

"ROBBINS (*laughs*) I made up for that.

"DENBY I miss it now. I'd love to see it. But your jokes this time are adorable.

"ROBBINS I love them in the section where they're posing, just love them. . . . I had a researcher call me from a magazine to ask me some questions. The first one was something very close to this: 'Where do you place your newest ballet in the mainstream of the trend of abstract dancing today?' (laughter) I've also been asked, 'What is the relationship between *Les Sylphides* and your ballet?' Well, I guess we used the same composer.

"DENBY Did you use any of the same pieces?

"ROBBINS No, I didn't, except one, the adage that Tony

and Pat do, the third dance. Evidently, that music was used as the man's variation at one point, which I didn't know. It's a lovely piece.

"DENBY You told me that you are going to do another Chopin ballet.

"ROBBINS I've finished one nocturne and I've about three-quarters of another one, and I have an idea for a third. I've started them and want to see how they come out. One for Millie, one for Allegra, and I think one for Kay Mazzo.

"DENBY She's beautiful.

"ROBBINS Isn't she lovely?

"DENBY Sally is wonderful. She gets more and more of that giving-without-thinking.

"ROBBINS She has a kind of toughness, not tough as much as a practical quality. But then I'll say something and can see in her eyes that she's suddenly grasped it, and you can see it explode inside her—such joy.

"DENBY The dance of the girls comes off so wonderfully. Allegra is wonderful all through.

"ROBBINS That's the way about all of them. At so many rehearsals, they didn't dance all out. They sort of walked. That's how I got Eddie to do that first variation the first night. He came into rehearsal and had to save himself for the performance and just marked through it. I ran back and said, 'Now, that's what I want.' The same with Allegra—when she marks something, she shows you what it is. I don't think they realize how trained they are—so clear. Like someone with a great voice who can whisper and you hear it. And that's what you see. And that's what they do.

"DENBY They are so completely clear, it's extraordinary how clear they are because whatever is passing through is never a blur or an uncertainty or a conventionalism.

"[Postscript from Robbins to Denby (sent the following day from Stockholm where Robbins was supervising final rehearsals of *Les Noces* for its June 6 première with the Royal Swedish Ballet. He went from there to Moscow to attend, by invitation of the U.S.S.R., its International Ballet Competition.)]"

May 27, 1969

"Dear Edwin:

"Something bothered me terribly after we met—one of your remarks about the people looking up and watching something cross the sky at the end of the ballet. You said something about planes—A bomb—war today, etc., and it jarred me very much. I couldn't figure out 'the why' right away—but then I did on the trip over. First of all I feel you are imposing a terribly out-of-context meaning to what they are seeing. The ballet stays and exists in the time of the music and its work. Nothing is out of it, I believe; all gestures and moods, steps, etc. are part of the fabric of the music's time and its meanings to me. I couldn't think of planes—A bomb, etc. Only clouds—and the flights of birds—sunsets and leaves falling—and they, the people's reactions are all very underplayed, very willing to meet whatever threat is *in the music.*

"Well, those people knew their disasters—felt them, maybe felt that at a certain time their being would come to an end—but they faced it as a part of living.

"I hadn't thought of *all* of this when I did it. All I knew is that they weren't afraid, had no self-pity, and stayed—didn't leave.

"And I do feel that last piece is the logical end of the whole ballet. To me it is very much the only possible result of all that's come before.

". . . Stockholm is lovely, limpid skies at midnight—looking clear and blue as a New York fall—It was so good to see you—J"

Dances at a Gathering has been acclaimed in the United States and in London, where it was first performed by the Royal Ballet, October 19, 1970. Marcia Marks in *Dance Magazine* found it "the most significant work for many a season. For Robbins, it is the most spontaneous outpouring of sheer creative force in his balletic career, and for the dancers, it is an unexpected revelation." Patricia Barnes in

Dance and Dancers magazine said, "*Dances at a Gathering* is, by general consent, a masterpiece. . . . It has been interpreted by different people in different ways, but all seem agreed on one aspect. This is a ballet about people, recognizable human beings rather than mere ciphers. There is no story, but a strong mood and atmosphere are present. There are ten dancers, five boys and five girls—they could be Americans, Poles, Danes or Russians. Their nationality is unimportant. What is significant in the fluent, utterly captivating series of dances is a love of humanity, an observation and understanding that is remarkably conveyed by the dancers involved. It seems impossible to leave the theatre having seen *Dances at a Gathering* and not feel one's soul uplifted."

In London, where the first performance was danced by Rudolf Nureyev, Monica Mason, Antoinette Sibley, Anthony Dowell, Laura Conner, Ann Jenner, David Wall, Lynn Seymour, Michael Coleman, and Jonathan Kelly, the editor of the *Dancing Times*, Mary Clarke, wrote: "Genuis is a word to be used sparingly in the small artistic world of ballet but genius is the only word for Jerome Robbins, as choreographer and man of the theatre. . . . It may sound exaggerated to say that this ballet, just about people dancing, is profoundly moving but it is true. There is more dancing than in some three-act ballets and certainly more emotion because it is happening here and now. It is an hour of delight and if you catch it on a program with Ashton's *Enigma Variations* or *The Dream*, your faith in ballet will be restored. The Press has been unanimous in praise. I echo Clement Crisp of *The Financial Times:* it is a ballet 'that will enrich our lives for years to come.'"

In 1972, Jerome Robbins wrote to *Ballet Review* the following letter, which is of general interest:

To the Editor:

For the record, would you please print in large, emphatic and capital letters the following:

"THERE ARE NO STORIES TO ANY OF THE DANCES IN DANCES AT A GATHERING. THERE ARE NO PLOTS AND

NO ROLES. THE DANCERS ARE THEMSELVES DANCING WITH EACH OTHER TO THAT MUSIC IN THAT SPACE.

Thank you very much.

New York, N.Y.

Jerome Robbins.

DARK ELEGIES

Music by Gustav Mahler. Choreography by Antony Tudor. Scenery and costumes by Nadia Benois. First produced by the Ballet Rambert at the Duchess Theatre, London, February 19, 1937, with Maude Lloyd, Antony Tudor, Walter Gore, John Byron, Agnes de Mille, Hugh Laing, Daphne Gow, Ann Gee, Patricia Clogstoun, Beryl Kay, and Celia Franca. First presented in the United States by Ballet Theatre at the Center Theatre, New York, January 24 1940, with scenery and costumes by Raymond Sovey after the Benois originals. The principal dancers were Nina Stroganova, Miriam Golden, Antony Tudor, Hugh Laing, Lucia Chase, and Dimitri Romanoff.

Dark Elegies is a dance ballet to the *Kindertotenlieder* (Songs of Childhood Death) of Mahler. The singer on stage tells of the grief of a father over the death of his children. The setting is somber, rough, jagged, with lowering clouds over water and mountains and trees that seem to have been lashed relentlessly by the wind. As the music laments, a small group of villagers begin to dance. Their grief over a disaster that has befallen them all is communal and also private. We do not know what the tragedy is, there are no specifics, but with the expression and gesture of the dancers, we have no need. Their movement universalizes the particulars of Mahler's songs and we watch, as at a religious rite, the unfolding of desperate grief to mourning, to resignation and perhaps hope.

NOTE *Dark Elegies* has been in the active repertory of the Ballet Rambert since it was first performed. It is now danced by the National Ballet of Canada and other companies. Jerome Robbins has said: "Fokine inspired me as a performer; he made me feel I could really dance. Tudor didn't; he made it complicated. He brought psychological motivation into ballet; he conveyed through movement emotions that could not be put into words. And he had the courage to persevere along this line in the face of adverse criticism. But he did wonderful things in pure dance, as well. *Gala Performance* and *Dark Elegies* stand alone, and I think they will last longest because they are more formal in structure . . . Tudor had a great influence on my early work and a great influence on all contemporary ballet."*

* From "Antony Tudor" by Selma Jeanne Cohen, in *Dance Perspectives 18,* 1963.

Deuce Coupe

Music by the Beach Boys. Choreography by Twyla Tharp. Setting by United Graffiti Artists. Costumes by Scott Barrie. Lighting by Jennifer Tipton. First presented by the City Center Joffrey Ballet at the City Center, New York, March 1, 1973, with Erika Goodman, Twyla Tharp, and dancers from the Joffrey Ballet and the Twyla Tharp Company.

Described as a juxtaposition of classical ballet and choreography based on social dances of the 1960s, *Deuce Coupe* was the first major work to be staged with an important ballet company by the modern dancer and choreographer Twyla Tharp, who appeared in the piece with members of her company. The title refers both to an automobile and to the piece *Little Deuce Coupe* by the Beach Boys, the rock group whose music, on tape, is featured in the ballet. Another major feature of the ballet is the setting—a background of three high strips of translucent paper (at first they look like windows we can't see out of) that a group of young people gradually fill with graffiti. As they inscribe the long sheets of paper, the paper is rolled up until the full height of the stage reflects their handiwork.

What happens on stage can be simply suggested but inadequately described. While a ballet dancer, Erika Goodman, performs an alphabetical but not-so-straightforward rendition of steps from the classical ballet dictionary, beginning with *Ailes de pigeon,* the rest of the dancers, in various combinations and permutations, perform dances both ancient and modern.

There are nineteen dances: *Matrix I, Ailes de pigeon* through *Attitude,* for the ballerina type and a couple; *Little Deuce Coupe, Balancé* through *Ballon,* with eighteen dancers and the persistent ballet performer; *Honda I, Balloné battu* through *déboulés,* for a *pas de trois* and the ballet girl; *Honda II, Changement de pieds* through *Dégagé à la quatrième devant en l'air,* for a couple and the girl; *Devoted to You, Dégagé en tournant* through *Failli,* for two couples and the girl; *How She Boogalooed It, Faux* through *Manège,* for the girl and a large ensemble; *Matrix II, Pas de basque sur les pointes* through *Pas de chat,* for the girl and six; *Alley Oop, Pas de cheval* through *Répétition,* for the girl plus eight; *Take a Load Off Your Feet, Retire* through *Sissone Tombée,* for three girls and two boys; *Long Tall Texan, Six* through *Suite,* for three girls; *Papa ooh Mau Mau,* for six; *Catch a Wave,* for five; *Got to Know the Woman, Temps de cuisse* through *temps lié,* for two girls; *Matrix III, Temps lié grand* through *Voyage,* for the ballet girl; *Don't Go Near the Water,* for six girls; *Matrix IV,* for a girl and boy; *Mama Says—"Eat a Lot, Never Be Lazy,"* for five boys and a girl; *Wouldn't It Be Nice,* for ten; and *Cuddle Up,* a finale for the whole company.

NOTE: Writing on the première in the *Daily News,* the critic Joseph Gale said that *Deuce Coupe* "is all the sadness, joy, cynicism and flavor of the beat generation . . . and the ballet is a smash.

"It is never less than exciting in crazy whorls of frenzied choreography that races, expires, picks up, jets ahead, pauses, and finally lays itself bare in unshed tears of last hopes.

"Through it all, there is the shining thread that holds it together and is the ballet's signature. That is Erika Goodman, unruffled and serene, who goes through a fair lexicon of classical dance, from *ailes de pigeon* through *pas de cheval,* while the world breaks up around her. She is the symbolic glory and salvation, the one who, after all else has failed, proffers hope in the palm of her outstretched hand. . . .

"There is also the schizoid passion of Miss Tharp's own dancing and, too, the United Graffiti Artists, who scrawl up a wall with the best decor of the season."

See comments on *As Time Goes By,* another Twyla Tharp ballet, for other views of this choreographer.

DON QUIXOTE

Ballet in four acts, eight scenes, and a prologue. Music by L. Minkus. Choreography by Marius Petipa. First presented by the Bolshoi Theatre, Moscow, December 26, 1869. First presented in the United States by the Bolshoi Ballet at the Metropolitan Opera House, New York, April 21, 1966, with Petipa's choreography revised by Aleksandr Gorsky and Rostislav Zakharov. Scenery and costumes by Vadim Rindin. Maya Plisetskaya appeared as Kitri, *Vladimir Tikhonov as* Basil the barber, *Pyotr Khomutuv as* Don Quixote, *and Nikolai Samokhvalov as* Sancho Panza.

Miguel Cervantes's masterpiece *Don Quixote* has a long ballet history. Beginning with a danced version by Noverre in the mid-eighteenth century, the story has attracted dancers and choreographers many times. The two principal versions of Cervantes's novel are described below.

PROLOGUE—DON QUIXOTE'S STUDY Don Quixote's servants, anxious about his growing obsession with ancient chivalry, are seen trying to throw his books away. He enters, reading, and sits at his table. He rejoices in heroic tales of brave knights and beautiful ladies. In a vision, he beholds the lady of his dreams, Dulcinea. Sancho Panza enters, pursued by angry shopkeepers from whom he has stolen a goose. The Don rescues him, appoints him his squire, and sets out on his adventures.

ACT ONE—THE SQUARE IN BARCELONA Basil, a barber, is in love with the innkeeper's daughter, Kitri, but her mother wishes her to marry Gamache, a foppish nobleman. Don Quixote arrives with Sancho. The Don assumes that the inn is a famous castle. Sancho is teased by the townsfolk and tossed in a blanket. Don Quixote rescues him. Don Quixote now sees the beautiful Kitri. He is bewitched and acclaims her as his Dulcinea.

ACT TWO, SCENE ONE—INSIDE THE INN Kitri's mother, still determined to marry her daughter to the nobleman, so distresses Basil that he pretends to stab himself. As he lies dying, he begs Kitri's parents to unite them.

ACT TWO, SCENE TWO—A GYPSY ENCAMPMENT Gypsies and strolling players, alerted to the imminent arrival of Don Quixote and Sancho, prepare to trick the knight. Don Quixote enters and pays homage to their leader as king. The leader then calls for dances to begin. This is followed by a command performance of the puppet theater. Watching the play, Don Quixote mistakes the heroine for Dulcinea, sees her under attack, and rises to assault the puppet stage. Pursuing her further to windmills nearby, he imagines Dulcinea is being concealed. Mistaking the windmills for menacing giants, he tilts at them, only to be caught up in one of the wings and tossed in the air. Sancho revives and comforts him.

ACT THREE, SCENE ONE—A FOREST The Don and Sancho lie down to rest in a wood. But still stunned from his fight with the windmill, the Don is troubled by fantastic dreams where he sees himself a knight in shining armor surrounded by lovely ladies.

ACT FOUR—PROLOGUE Hunting horns proclaim the arrival of the Duke of Barcelona, who has heard about Don Quixote and wishes to see the curious knight himself. He awakens the Don and invites him to accompany a *fiesta*. The Duke then persuades Basil to dress up and pretend to be a Knight Errant to play a trick on Don Quixote.

ACT FIVE—THE MAIN SQUARE OF BARCELONA It is *fiesta* time. The Duke and the Duchess and the Don watch the dancing. Suddenly the Don thinks that he recognizes his Dulcinea in a girl carried on by mysterious figures guarded by a strange knight. The Knight challenges the Don to a duel and the old man is soon vanquished. His opponent, removing his disguise, reveals himself as Basil the barber. The Don is so crestfallen by this trickery that the Duke and Duchess have pity and comfort him. Kitri and Basil then celebrate their betrothal in a *grand pas de deux*. Don Quixote realizes that he has not yet found his Dulcinea and with Sancho sets off for more adventures.

NOTES This *Don Quixote* includes the *grand pas de deux* that is often presented independently in various versions on ballet programs. The part of Kitri has been performed over the years by many famous ballerinas, Pavlova and Karsavina among them. Pavlova produced a shortened version of the ballet for her tours. Rudolf Nureyev produced his version of the Petipa ballet for the Vienna State Opera on December 1, 1966, himself appearing as *Basil* with Ully Wuehrer as *Kitri*, Michael Birkmeyer as *Don Quixote*, and Konstantin Zajetz as *Sancho Panza*.

In 1970, Nureyev staged his version of the ballet with the Australian Ballet in a production designed by Barry Kay. This production was first presented in the United States by the Australian Ballet in San Francisco, January 4, 1971. In 1972, Nureyev and Robert Helpmann made a film of this production.

Interviewed by Laura Bell for *Show* magazine in 1971 about certain aspects of his production of *Don Quixote*, Nureyev commented about the duel between the Don and his foppish rival Don Gamache: "The duel is mine but the stabbing is all in the original Petipa, and in the book. There, you may remember, it is even broader. Basilio has a bladder of sheep's blood hidden under his arm and when he stabs it, blood spurts everywhere. I decided this was going a bit far in literalness, and it would be messy. The duel, though, was originally between the knight and the heroine's father, an innkeeper. But I think it proper Don Quixote should fight his own kind, not a commoner, so I have him fight Don Gamache, who, in the bargain, is wearing the proper white gauntlets to throw down. I try all through to keep the six main characters together, playing off each other, as in *commedia dell'arte*—you can even match up characters. Quixote is Pantalon, Kitri is Columbine; Basilio, Pierrot, and so on. I wanted the story not to be about Don Quixote but about how people react to him, how they take advantage of him and devise ways to mock and laugh at him. Yet they go crazy doing this, they are as fanatic as the knight is.

"And Don Quixote himself . . . At first, I hated him quite a lot. I didn't understand for a long time. I was on the side of the people. To me he was just a clown. And then I read the book! There is so much there, but in a ballet you can only skim the surface. I tried to put in a lot of things I felt about the book, like impressions of the Callot lithographs, but you daren't put too much comment in. It really is largely a lot of dances and great zest and comic spirit . . . and yet, everybody seems to think of this ballet as kind of foolish.

"I can't take any credit for these productions which I do only to provide another vehicle for myself and to preserve what is left of Petipa. With *Don Quixote* I wanted a comic part and since no choreographer has ever offered me one, I did this. With original choreography you have to sit down and think and spend a lot of time. I do *not* like improvisations. If you want to create a ballet, you have to have a certain point of view, something you want to say, not just steps or variations that just 'come' to you. And even with *Raymonda* and *Don Quixote*, they took a lot of working out and research. Perhaps in time . . ."

A film of Nureyev's production of *Don Quixote* was made in Australia in 1972 with the Australian Ballet. Codirected by Nureyev and Sir Robert Helpmann, the film starred Lucette Aldous as Kitri-Dulcinea and Nureyev as Basilio. It was first presented in the United States, November 1, 1973, at a Gala Benefit for the Dance Collection of the New York Public Library.

Ballet in three acts. Music by Nicolas Nabokov. Choreography by George Balanchine. Scenery, costumes, and lighting by Esteban Francés. Assistant to Mr. Francés: Peter Harvey. Costumes executed by Karinska. First presented by the New York City Ballet at the New York State Theater, May 27, 1965, with George Balanchine as Don Quixote, *Suzanne Farrell as* Dulcinea, *Deni Lamont as* Sancho Panza, *and the entire company.*

I first read Cervantes in Russian, but I have read parts of *Don Quixote* many times since, in English and French as well. The idea of doing a ballet about the Don has always seemed to me natural and inevitable, something I would want to do whenever time and opportunity came. Other ballets to *Don Quixote* I had perhaps seen but scarcely remembered.

The Petipa ballet, with music by Minkus, was in the repertory of the Maryinsky when I was a boy (I danced in this production in 1916, when I was twelve), but it was not a serious work and not one of my favorites. Twenty years ago I discovered that my friend the composer Nicolas Nabokov had a similar enthusiasm for *Don Quixote.* He had written an orchestral suite on the Don and Dulcinea which I liked. We then spoke of doing a full-scale ballet on the subject one day, but it was some years before this came about. We began to work out a scenario in detail. We did several scenarios, in fact, arriving at a final one in June 1964. Throughout the composition of the score we were in frequent communication and saw each other as often as possible to discuss the music and the action. As a musician with a deep knowledge of ballet, Nabokov knew what he was getting into. Three-act ballets are difficult compositions. Nabokov's score has everything, it *has* to have everything to do its job properly, for music written to accompany a danced narrative with *divertissements* cannot preserve the unities designed for the concert hall. Nabokov worked within three traditions, the musical one, the ballet tradition, and the dramatic. His score in essence amounts to symphonic dance variations.

The action of the ballet follows closely the scenario Nabokov and I worked out together.

The form the novel took for us naturally does not follow the sequence of the book, but I must say we never had any difficulty in our ideas. The problem was always what we had to cut and put aside. Don Quixote's anguished search for human perfectibility, the intricate shifts from fantasy to reality that take place in his mind, are vividly expressed through his adventures and the dream of the Lady Dulcinea, who appears in many guises to him. Guises these always are —the Magdalen, the Virgin Mary, the Shepherdess Marcela, the Lady of the Silver Moon—and although he gives his whole life for her, he never really sees her. He is, if you like, a kind of secular saint whom no one believes in. Finally, his death brings him face to face with himself, seemingly defeated, but having lived as he believed.

PROLOGUE—DON QUIXOTE'S STUDY Don Quixote sits alone

and reads his books about chivalry. He searches through them for the answers to his dreams of knight errantry. He falls off to sleep. A mist covers the stage and strange figures from his dream take over the scene: a girl seems to materialize right out of the pages of a book; a dragon appears. The Don rescues the girl. He rests. A young girl, a maidservant, enters and washes his feet, drying them with her hair. He kisses her forehead and she leaves and Don Quixote rises.

Sancho Panza enters carrying the Don's clothes, does a pratfall but quickly rises to dress his master. The Don, with sword held high, follows the girl toward the brilliant sun she has let into the room. This is the only sun he will see. As Cervantes said, "Misfortunes always pursue men of talent." Don Quixote's study is now transformed, becoming:

ACT ONE, SCENE ONE—LA MANCHA Don Quixote stands alone surrounded by earth and sky. Windmills in the distance. In the piercing light of midday there appears to him a vision of the Madonna, a girl with a resplendent headdress standing on a cart much as if a statue of the Virgin being carried in a village procession has suddenly come to life. It is the servant girl of the Prologue. He kneels before the vision, takes the oath of a knight, and receives the Madonna's blessing.

Don Quixote encounters a child being beaten by a man. He challenges the man and chases him off. The rescued child runs away, mocking the Don. Next he comes upon a group of prisoners being led in chains. He attacks the jailers and frees the men, who thereupon set upon the Don and Sancho and give them a good trouncing.

ACT ONE, SCENE TWO—A VILLAGE SQUARE There are folk dances in front of an inn. Sancho runs out, pursued by guards and fishwives from whom he has stolen a huge fish. He is caught, beaten up, and tossed in a blanket. Don Quixote appears on his horse, dismounts and liberates Sancho. Sancho kneels at his feet, weeping. The Innkeeper brings food and the Don comforts Sancho. A cortege enters. A poet is being mourned. A beautiful country girl, Marcela, is seized and accused of causing his death. We see that she is the same girl as in the first scenes, dressed now as a shepherdess with a long crook. She is grateful to the Don and dances. In

Cervantes, she explains that she is not to be blamed for the poet's death: "If every beauty inspired love and won hearts, men's fancy would become vague and bewildered and not know where to stop, for as beauty is infinite, desire must likewise be infinite. If this is so, as I believe it to be, why do you ask me to surrender my will under pressure for no other reason than that you say you love me? For beauty in a modest woman is like distant fire or a sharp sword; the one does not burn, the other does not cut the man who does not go near it. Now if modesty is one of the virtues and the fairest ornament of the body and the soul, why must the woman who is loved for her beauty lose it to gratify the desires of a man who, for his pleasure alone, tries with all his strength and ingenuity to rob her of it? I was born free, and to live free I chose the solitude of the fields. The trees of those mountains are my companions; with the trees and the brooks I share my thoughts and my beauty. I am the hidden fire and the distant sword . . ."

Now a puppeteer comes into the courtyard with his cart and arranges his puppet show. In the midst of the show Don Quixote becomes indignant about what he sees. Here again is the tiny blond heroine who emerged from his books. To him, she is Dulcinea and when he sees her being persecuted by Saracens, he charges the puppet show with his sword. The puppet theater falls down on his head. Just then, to solemn music, heralds announce the arrival of the Duke and Duchess of the region. The Duchess observes the wreckage of the theater and orders it cleared out. She congratulates the Don on his victorious adventure with the puppet. Supported by Sancho, Don Quixote kneels before her. Recognizing him from Cervantes's book, the Duchess gives him wine and invites him to come to the castle. He is lifted onto his horse, Sancho mounts the donkey, and the villagers wave them farewell.

ACT TWO—THE PALACE The curtain rises on the sumptuous ballroom of the Duke's palace. Don Quixote enters with the Duchess, who places him to her right as she sits on the throne. He stands by her side like a true gentleman. Courtiers enter and as they bow to the royal couple, they also pay mocking deference to Don Quixote, sensing the joke the Duchess is playing on the knight. The courtiers and their ladies now dance a stylized courtly ballet: first, a sarabande by the entire assembly, then a series of danced *divertissements: a danza della Cacia*, a *pas de deux Mauresque*, a *Courante Sicilienne*, a *Rigaudon Flamenco*, and a *ritournel*. Now eight masked men enter. The Duchess whispers to the Duke. All salute as Don Quixote escorts the Duchess down to the dance floor to dance a *pavane*. The court has decided to end the charade they have been playing with the Don. Sancho senses this and tries to take the Don away, but the courtiers close in on them. They are blindfolded, tickled by ladies' fans, pricked by swords. A wooden horse is brought in, they are placed on it, fireworks are set off in its tail and at the explosion Don Quixote and Sancho fall to the ground, where they are beaten. There then appears to Don Quixote a vision of Dulcinea. The whole court freezes like waxworks. She gestures to him, seems to be calling to him to renew his adventures. He lays his sword at her feet and kneels before her. Dulcinea helps him up and just as Don Quixote is about to follow her, a masked lady approaches and beards him with whipped cream, a final mockery. He ignores her scorn and in a trance stumbles after Dulcinea to start again on his quest.

ACT THREE, SCENE ONE—A GARDEN OF THE PALACE The Don and Sancho enter. They lie down to rest under an old oak tree. He sleeps and begins to dream. Masked courtiers arrive and cover him with a fishing net. Dulcinea appears. In his dream he sees a ballet in the Elysian fields. In the midst of the dancing is the Lady of the Silver Moon in whom is embodied "all the impossible and chimerical attributes of beauty which poets give to their ladies." There follows a classical *pas d'action*, consisting of a set of four variations, a *pas de deux* and a coda. Dulcinea is challenged by a girl in black, the Night Spirit, reminiscent of the Duchess, and tormented by the magician Merlin. She goes to Don Quixote, and he rouses himself to help her. As he does so, dragging the net behind him, the magic landscape of his dream vanishes. He is alone on an empty field with mills turning their big wheels in the wind and seeming to move ominously toward him and Dulcinea.

ACT THREE, SCENE TWO A huge giant bears down on Don Quixote as high as a windmill. The Don attacks him but his long lance is caught in a sail of the windmill and he is tossed high into the air and falls back to earth. Sancho runs to him and binds his head. Strange creatures cross the stage; like pigs they swarm all over the place. Now four courtiers of the Duchess disguised in masks bring in a wooden cage. Don Quixote crawls into it like a wounded dog. Weeping, Sancho follows, holding his master's sword.

ACT THREE, SCENE THREE—DON QUIXOTE'S STUDY To a *pavane funèbre* the Don is carried to his home. He is taken from the cage and undressed for bed. He asks for the last rites of the Church. In his delirium he sees a procession of Bishops, Cardinals, monks, earls, and dukes, all hooded figures, march in to a Gloria. His books are burned by these Inquisitors. Then, in another vision, he sees again the vision with which his adventures began, the Madonna of the cart, the lovely blond girl with a halo. He reaches out to her yearningly, rises high in his bed as if by a miracle, she looks at him, then vanishes. The hooded figures are grouped around his bed as in the painting of the burial of the Count d'Orgaz by El Greco. But in a changing light, they are changed into the simple people of his village, the serving girl, the priest, Sancho. He recognizes them, blesses them, and dies quietly as the first lights of dawn come through the open window. The servant girl makes a cross of two sticks, places it on his body, and kneels to weep at his side. ". . . If he like a madman lived, at least he like a wise man died," said Cervantes.

NOTES My interest in *Don Quixote* has always been in the hero's finding an ideal, something to live for and sacrifice for and serve. Every man has a Don Quixote in him. Every man wants an inspiration. For the Don it was Dulcinea, a woman he sought in many guises. I myself think that the same is true in life, that everything a man does he does for his ideal woman. You live only one life and you believe in something and I believe in that.

For criticism of this ballet, readers may wish to consult "The Story of 'Don Quixote'" by Elena Bivona in *Ballet Review,* Vol. 2, No. 2; and Andrew Porter's review of the 1973 performances of the ballet in *The New Yorker,* reprinted in his book.

The composer Nicholas Nabokov contributed to the January 1973 edition of the New York City Ballet program *Playbill* an entertaining and informative essay about his career and our collaboration on this ballet. Many of us look forward to Nabokov's autobiography.

DUO CONCERTANT

Music by Igor Stravinsky. Choreography by George Balanchine. First presented by the New York City Ballet at the Stravinsky Festival, 1972, at the New York State Theater, Lincoln Center, June 22, 1972, with Kay Mazzo and Peter Martins as the dancers, Lamar Alsop and Gordon Boelzner as the musicians. Lighting by Ronald Bates.

This work for violin and piano was composed by Stravinsky in the early thirties. It is a short piece in five movements and a marvelously lyrical one in several of its parts. It is not surprising that the composition of the *Duo Concertant* was associated in Stravinsky's mind with a book on the classical poet Petrarch by his friend Cingria, which appeared about the time he was writing this music. Stravinsky in one of his recollections quotes this passage from Cingria: "Lyricism cannot exist without rules, and it is essential that they should be strict. Otherwise there is only a faculty for lyricism, and that exists everywhere. What does not exist everywhere is lyrical expression and composition. To achieve that, a craftsman's skill is necessary and that must be learned."

This is exactly a thought I have tried so unsuccessfully to say myself on a number of occasions and it is wonderful to find it so finely expressed in connection with a composition I so much admire.

I am trying to recall the first time I heard the *Duo Concertant.* It was, I think, in France in a performance by Samuel Dushkin, the violinist, and the composer himself, both of whom in the early thirties toured Europe performing Stravinsky's music. It has always been a favorite of mine and when we were planning the Stravinsky Festival at the New York City Ballet, I decided to make a ballet to the music.

The less I say about the ballet, the more I think you may enjoy watching it. It is nothing very unusual, only two dancers, a girl and a boy, standing on stage next to a piano, where the two musicians begin to play. The dancers listen intently; we listen to them. The music for piano and violin is questioning at first, then declarative, open; it then tightens in rhythm and assertiveness of melody. Before we know it, the dancers are moving to the music. Sometimes they stop to listen. The second movement, Ecloque I, begins with a jocular tune and develops into a brisk dialogue between the two instruments. In Ecloque II, the violin takes the lead and in a slowly paced cadenza sings an idyll. For the fourth movement, there is a vigorous and lively Gigue. The stage darkens for the finale, the Dithyramb. Eric Walter White calls this a "noble rhapsody . . . a movement of grave beauty. The high-pitched violin part leads the piano into an increasingly elaborate passage. . . . The effect is that of an exalted threnody." The stage darkens for this music, one spotlight shining on the two musicians, another on the two dancers. The lights close down about the artists as the music ends.

A girl and a boy, a piano and violin. Perhaps, as Lincoln Kirstein says, that is what ballet is all about.

NOTES Reviewing this ballet in *The Nation*, Nancy Goldner wrote: "*Duo Concertant*, for piano and violin, is one of the most beautiful duets Balanchine has ever done. As a metaphor on the idea that the festival celebrates music, Mazzo and Martins listen to the musicians, who are on the stage, almost as much as they dance. Watching them listen is a theatrical experience in itself. Their faces speak a multitude of unknown thoughts, but the intensity and sweet concentration with which they listen suggest that the notes are running through their bodies. Finally, they are moved to dance. At first they stick closely to the music's beat, almost 'conducting' it with arms and legs; torsos are still.

"Becoming more free, the dance turns into a melting duet, each phrase winding down on slightly bent knees, as in a whisper. They dance with seeming spontaneity. Even when Balanchine arranges an unusual means of partnering—as when Martins scoops her from the floor holding only the underside of her thigh—the movement spins off them with utter simplicity and naturalness. In other sections, they occasionally stop dancing to listen. At those times, Martins firmly takes hold of her hand or slips his arm around her waist. She is shy, but the music pleases her and so does he. She does not move away. They listen in repose, arm in arm. In the last part, the stage darkens except for a white spotlight. She places her arm in the light and raises it above her head. No longer is it her arm; it exists independently, like a segment of a statue. He kisses the back of her hand, a supplicant at the throne of beauty. She is now a goddess-ballerina; he, her servant. She steps out of the light. He steps into it. Not finding her, he leaves. She returns. He kisses her hand again. The jump from intimate hand-holding to ceremonial hand-kissing is theatrically daring. It is also inevitable, and those who cannot accept the leap or the brazen display of sentiment cannot ultimately accept one of the underlying themes of Balanchine's work. In his most noble ballets, he elevates the dancer into an image of love, a Muse-ballerina who inspires but is unreachable. And so this ending is an apotheosis of Balanchine's art."

THE DREAM

Ballet in one act. Music by Felix Mendelssohn, arranged by John Lanchbery. Choreography by Frederick Ashton. Scenery by Henry Bardon. Costumes by David Walker. Lighting by William Bundy. First presented by the Royal Ballet at the Royal Opera House, Covent Garden, April 2, 1964, with Antoinette Sibley as Titania, *Anthony Dowell as* Oberon, *Keith Martin as* Puck, *Alexander Grant as* Bottom, *Carole Needham as* Helena, *Vergie Derman as* Hermia, *David Drew as* Demetrius, *Derek Rencher as* Lysander, *and Alan Bauch as the* Changeling Indian Boy. *First presented in the United States by the Royal Ballet at the Metropolitan Opera House, New York, April 30, 1965, with the same cast, with Rennie Dilena as the* Changeling Indian Boy.*

Frederick Ashton arranged his ballet to *A Midsummer Night's Dream* for the Royal Ballet's observance of the four-hundredth anniversary of Shakespeare's birth. Based on Shakespeare's play. Using Mendelssohn's music, the ballet tells the magical story of the quarrel between the King and Queen of Fairyland and its outcome.

The King and Queen, Oberon and Titania, quarrel over the Changeling Indian Boy. Whom shall he belong to? Oberon sends his sprite Puck through the forest to pluck a strange flower, the juice of which when dropped in the eyes during sleep brings love for the first living thing seen on waking. Oberon plans to use this drug to spite Titania. Into the forest meanwhile have strayed a happy pair of lovers, Lysander and Hermia, and their unhappy friends Helena and Demetrius. Helena's desire for Demetrius is unrequited, for he mistakenly desires Hermia. Oberon has watched these mortals, and when Puck returns with the magic flower he sends him with the potion to charm Demetrius into love with Helena.

Now Oberon drops some of the charm into his Queen's eyes and causes her to be awakened by a rustic called Bottom on whom the returning Puck, to heighten his master's

* See also A MIDSUMMER NIGHT'S DREAM.

revenge, has fixed an ass's head. On waking, Titania at once falls in love with Bottom the Ass, but Puck, for all his cleverness, has complicated the affairs of the other, mortal lovers by charming the wrong man, Lysander, into love with Helena. Oberon commands Puck to create a fog, under cover of which all that is awry is magically put right. Titania, released from her spell, is reconciled to her master and the mortal lovers are happily paired off. Bottom, restored to human form but with dreamlike memories of what lately happened to him, goes on his puzzled way.

NOTES *The Dream* was staged by John Hart for the City Center Joffrey Ballet in 1973. The first performance, at the Wolf Trap Performing Arts Center in Virginia, near Washington, D.C., August 9, featured Rebecca Wright, Burton Taylor, Russell Sultzbach, Larry Grenier, Alaine Haubert, Charthel Arthur, Robert Talmage, Robert Thomas, Richard Coleman, Robert Estner, Phillip Hoffman, Jeffrey Hughes, Ted Nelson, Donna Cowen, Denise Jackson, Eileen Brady, Diane Orio, and Vinod Sahl. Writing of this production after its first New York performance (October 9, 1973), Clive Barnes said in the New York *Times:* "Ever since Ashton created *The Dream* for Britain's Royal Ballet nearly ten years ago, it has been one of that company's special treasures. This new production, authoritatively staged by John Hart, is a charmer, full of the original's mixture of Shakespeare, poetry, Mendelssohn, moonshine and fun. It is an extraordinarily English ballet, but the New York dancers have adopted it for their own.

"The costumes, fanciful and glamorous, are the same as David Walker designed for the original production, but Mr. Walker has devised a completely new setting to replace the earlier scenery by Henry Bardon. The setting, a sylvan glade, looks appropriately Victorian, but does not have the full romantic exuberance of the Royal Ballet's first staging. Yet what is more important is the style of the dancing, and here the Joffrey company does splendidly.

"Rebecca Wright made a Titania of glistening eyes and the most entrancing delicate footwork. It was a performance of gossamer and thistledown. As Oberon, Burton Taylor—making his welcome return to the stage after nearly two years off through injury—danced cleanly and forcefully. His presence was admirable, his partnering secure and his elegance always completely natural."

DYBBUK VARIATIONS

Music by Leonard Bernstein. Choreography by Jerome Robbins. Scenery by Rouben Ter-Arutunian. Costumes by Patricia Zipprodt. Lighting by Jennifer Tipton. First presented by the New York City Ballet at the New York State Theater, Lincoln Center, May 15, 1974, with Patricia McBride and Helgi Tomasson as the principals and a cast headed by Bart Cook, Victor Castelli, Tracy Bennett, Hermes Conde, Daniel Duell, Stephen Caras, Nolan T'Sani, Peter Naumann, Muriel Aasen, and Stephanie Saland. Conducted by Leonard Bernstein. Baritone: David Johnson. Bass: John Ostendorf.

The composer Leonard Bernstein and the choreographer Jerome Robbins first conceived of the idea of a ballet to the dybbuk theme in 1944, at the time of their first brilliant collaboration, *Fancy-Free*. A dybbuk, in Central-European Jewish folklore, is a spirit, first and restless, that enters and persists in the body of a living person. The possessed body acts and speaks with the voice and behavior of the dead one. The most famous treatment of the theme is the play by S. Ansky, *The Dybbuk*, renowned in its original Yiddish version and through many subsequent international productions, among them the Habimah presentation in New York in the 1940s. The restless spirit dominates the action.

Jerome Robbins has said that the ballet is not a retelling of Ansky's play, "but uses it only as a point of departure for a series of related dances concerning rituals and hallucinations which are present in the dark magico-religious ambience of the play and in the obsessions of its characters."

An understanding of the play is useful background to the ballet. It tells the story: In friendship, two young men pledge that their children will wed each other, should one have a son and the other a daughter. The friends part and go out into the world, where each marries and has a child, boy and girl, as hoped for. Chanon and Leah meet when grown and, unaware of their parents' commitment, fall in love. But because Leah is from a wealthy family and Chanon is a poor but devoutly orthodox theological student, their love is undeclared. Chanon is also regarded as a wanderer and seeker of truths that are perhaps best always hidden.

Leah's father arranges a suitable match for her; Chanon desperately turns to the Kabbala, book of mystic wisdom and dark magic. (This text, developed by rabbis from about the seventh to the eighteenth centuries, was based on a mystical technique of interpreting Scripture; by this method the initiated were empowered to foretell the future and penetrate sacred mysteries.) He seeks in the Kabbala for a way in which to win Leah for himself. As a last resort, he invokes the powerful but dangerous other-worldly formulae of ancient usage. At the supreme moment of discovering the secret words that unleash the dark forces, he is overwhelmed by the enormity of it, faints and dies.

At Leah's wedding, Chanon returns to her as a dybbuk and, claiming her as his rightful bride, clings to his beloved. Finally, through prescriptive counterrituals instituted by elders of the religious community, Chanon is placed under formal ecclesiastical curse and the dybbuk is expelled. Leah, unable to survive without her predestined bridegroom, dies to join him.

Throughout the Ansky play, a supernatural being called "The Messenger" is an omniscient and prophetic witness to each evolving phase of the drama.

The action of the ballet is divided into eleven parts: 1) IN THE HOLY PLACE: Variations for Seven Men; 2) THE PLEDGE: Male duet; two couples; three couples; 3) ANGELIC MESSENGERS: Variations for three men; 4) THE DREAM: *Pas de deux;* 5) INVOCATION OF THE KABBALA: the quest for secret powers; VARIATIONS: a. Solo with six men; b.c.d.e. Soli; f. Solo with six men; 6) PASSAGE; 7) MAIDEN'S DANCE; 8) TRANSITION; 9) POSSESSION: *Pas de deux:* allegro, adagio; 10) EXORCISM: Entire cast; 11) REPRISE AND CODA.

NOTES. Talking with *The New Yorker* about the ballet shortly before its première, the composer, Leonard Bernstein, described how he and Jerome Robbins had approached the dybbuk legend. "Ansky's story is a kind of ghetto version of

The Ring of the Nibelung. Greed versus love. A compact that is broken. Two young men pledge that their children will marry, but one of them eventually disregards the oath because he wants a wealthy husband for his daughter, Leah. Chanon, the son of the other man, becomes a wandering scholar, a very *farbrente* Talmudist, and a Cabalist. He comes to this little town, sees Leah, and, even though he doesn't know about the pledge, falls in love and desperately tries to find Cabalistic ways of winning her. In (one) dance . . . Chanon calls on the dark powers to help him, and at the moment of revelation he dies, because no human vessel can contain that much fire and knowledge and survive. His soul becomes a dybbuk and finds its resting place in the body of his beloved. And when the rabbi exorcises the dybbuk from her body, Leah joins him in oblivion.

". . . You have to remember that this is a story about ghetto people who have nowhere to go, no professions they can be in, no place in the world except the isolated provincial town in which they live. They are forced in on themselves, and they turn to their Torah and live their whole lives in terms of that. And they get to such a point of intensity, of concern, of concentration on their relationship with God that they come to believe the whole universe depends on it. That is the reason behind all the diagrams, the mysticisms, and the calculations. Where else could these people look except to heaven? Jerry suggested a marvellous line for the program note. He said that this ballet deals with the visions, hallucinations, and magical religious manifestations of an oppressed people. And that's exactly it. All they had for centuries was a book with the words of God."*

Writing after the première of *Dybbuk Variations* in *Newsweek,* the critic Hubert Saal said: "Robbins's ballet does not tell the detailed story . . . of S. Ansky's 1914 play, a classic of the Yiddish theatre . . . but extracts highlights of the drama, making a superdrama of such abstractions as the conflict between light and dark, the individual and so-

* From "Possession" by Jane Boutwell in "The Talk of the Town." Reprinted by permission; © 1974 The New Yorker Magazine, Inc.

ciety, love and law. Sometimes what occupies a long scene in the play takes a moment in dance—and vice versa. In reorganizing what Ansky called a 'realistic play about mystic people,' Robbins and Bernstein have created a work that is theatrical without being showy, stylized without being stilted and Hebraic without being parochial.

"The eleven scenes, starkly and effectively designed by Rouben Ter-Arutunian, begin with the important mood setter, the dance of the seven elders, who with pious grace assume the shape of a Menorah, the Jewish candelabrum. Throughout the ballet they act as an irresistible force in their faith and fanaticism, embodying the inexorable power of Jehovah's Law and of social custom. Among the most dramatic scenes are the brilliant, complex variations for Chanon and his fellow scholars, who vainly try to dissuade him from the cabalistic investigation that ends in his death. Of all the dance sequences, perhaps the most satisfying is the long *pas de deux* in which the dybbuk takes possession of Leah. Their agitated bodies, trying to adjust to the violent collision of two souls, gradually fuse into one, through their love for each other.

"The climax is spine-tingling, with some magical stagecraft, as the exorcising elders force Chanon to leave the body of Leah and she abandons her own flesh to join him as pure spirit in the hereafter. As this Jewish Romeo and Juliet, the brilliant Helgi Tomasson and the radiant Patricia McBride dance with fire and tenderness.

"No one could have provided Robbins with a more resilient musical floor than Bernstein, who has remained in close touch musically with his Jewish origins. His first symphony, the 'Jeremiah,' was dedicated to his father, a noted Talmudic scholar, and his third symphony is called 'Kaddish.' With obvious eagerness, Bernstein has seized this opportunity to invent music with old-fashioned Hebrew lilt and cadence, an intonation that is part laughter, part tears, and a range from simple folk tunes to complex inversions of tone rows. . . .

"Robbins and Bernstein, two 55-year-old partners and friends, are complementary opposites. . . . Robbins emphasized that the new work 'is a ballet, not a play. It says things that the play doesn't. There are whole areas in the play that are non-verbal.' Bernstein was amazed by the performance of the New York City Ballet Orchestra. 'They're fantastic,' he exclaimed, 'the most wonderful theatre orchestra in the world.'

"Both men remembered the time 30 years ago when the idea for *Dybbuk Variations* came to them—standing on the stage of the old Metropolitan Opera House after the triumph of *Fancy Free*. 'I love the dark, lyric quality of Ansky's play,' says Robbins. 'The astonishing faith. Of all kinds.' Two years ago they isolated themselves in Jamaica and devoted a concentrated three weeks to finding an approach that lay between Robbins's feeling for the abstract and Bernstein's for the concrete drama. 'After that,' Bernstein says, 'I just wrote music and played it for Jerry and he would say that excites me or it doesn't.'

"Earlier Robbins had said, 'Choosing the *Dybbuk* had nothing to do with my being Jewish.' Now Bernstein said, 'In a larger sense what success we've had is based on our experience of Jewishness. Isn't that right, Jerry?' Robbins paused and said, 'I don't know,' and then smiled and added: 'But we are what we are and that feeds into it.'"

THE DYING SWAN

LE CYGNE

Music by Camille Saint-Saëns. Choreography by Michel Fokine. First produced at a concert in the Nobleman's Hall, St. Petersburg, Russia, in 1905, with Anna Pavlova. First presented in the United States at the Metropolitan Opera House, New York, March 18, 1910, by Anna Pavlova.

Perhaps the most famous of all dramatic solos for the ballerina, *The Dying Swan* shows the last minutes in the life of a stricken swan. Slowly, trembling, trying to hold on to life for a brief last flight but then giving up, she dies. It only takes about two minutes to perform. When Pavlova first danced it at the Metropolitan, Carl Van Vechten wrote that it was "the most exquisite specimen of her art which she has yet given to the public."

The choreographer, Michel Fokine, recalled that the dance was composed in a few minutes. One day Pavlova came and asked him to do a solo for her for a concert being given by artists from the chorus of the Imperial Opera. She had just become a ballerina at the Maryinsky Theatre. Fokine was at that time a mandolin enthusiast and had been playing at home—to the piano accompaniment of one of his friends—Saint-Saëns' *Swan*. He said right then, "What about Saint-Saëns' *Swan*?" She immediately realized, Fokine wrote, that a swan would be a most suitable role for her. "As I looked upon the thin, brittle-like Pavlova, I thought—she is just made for the *Swan*." A rehearsal was arranged and the dance completed very quickly. "It was almost an improvisation. I danced in front of her, she directly behind me. Then she danced and I walked alongside her, curving her arms and correcting details of poses.

"Prior to this composition, I was accused of barefooted tendencies and of rejecting toe dancing in general. *The Dying Swan* was my answer to such criticism. This dance became the symbol of the New Russian Ballet. It was a combination of masterful technique with expressiveness. It was like a proof that the dance could and should satisfy not only the eye, but through the medium of the eye should penetrate into the soul" (*Dance Magazine*, August 1931).

In 1934 in Paris, Fokine told Arnold Haskell (see his *Balletomania*): "Small work as it is, and known and applauded all over the world, it was 'revolutionary' then, and illustrated admirably the transition between the old and the new, for here I make use of the technique of the old dance and the traditional costume, and a highly developed technique is necessary, but the purpose of the dance is not to display that technique but to create the symbol of the everlasting struggle in this life and all that is mortal. It is a dance of the whole body and not of the limbs only; it appeals not merely to the eye but to the emotions and the imagination."

The French critic André Levinson has written of *Le Cygne:* "Arms folded, on tiptoe, she dreamily and slowly circles the stage. By even, gliding motions of the hands, returning to the background from whence she emerged, she seems to strive toward the horizon, as though a moment more and she will fly—exploring the confines of space with her soul. The tension gradually relaxes and she sinks to earth, arms waving faintly as in pain. Then faltering with irregular steps toward the edge of the stage—leg bones aquiver like the strings of a harp—by one swift forward-gliding motion of the right foot to earth, she sinks on the left knee—the aerial creature struggling against earthly bonds; and there, transfixed by pain, she dies."

The dancer and teacher Hilda Butsova, who became Pavlova's leading dancer (1912–25) in the company that toured the world, has recalled with Marian Horosko in *Dance Magazine* the joy and hardships of those days: "It was not that she wanted to make money or had a big ego. She wanted people to see dance. . . . It was Anna Pavlova, and no one else, who opened the world to ballet. It was she who did the back-breaking work of pioneering. It was Pavlova who found and cultivated audiences for contemporary ballet companies. Her service to ballet is priceless. No other single human being did more for ballet than she. To all the millions of people for whom she danced, she brought a little of herself; she brought a little happiness to them all. Her genius was as intangible as the legacy she left behind. What remains of Pavlova today is not a movement in the art, not a tendency, not even a series of dances. It is something far more concrete, but possibly far more valuable: inspiration."

EARLY SONGS

Music by Richard Strauss. Choreography by Eliot Feld. Costumes by Stanley Simmons. Lighting by Jules Fisher. First presented by the American Ballet Company at the Brooklyn Academy of Music, New York, April 5, 1970. Soprano: Eileen Shelle. Baritone: Steven Kimbrough. Pianist: Gladys Celeste Mercades.

Early Songs is a dance ballet arranged to fourteen songs by Richard Strauss, songs of the composer's youth, when he wrote with fervor and passion to accompany poems he admired about love, dreams, separation, longing, despair, night. *Early Songs* can be said to be about love and the way different young couples are involved in it, how they show it, hide it, seek it, find it, languish in it, rejoice in it. There is no story, only the dance and gestural images we seek on stage. Sometimes they are reflective of the music; sometimes they suggest things beyond the music.

The music is sung by a soprano and a baritone, accompanied by the piano. The words are not directly relevant to the danced picture which is best seen beyond words, in the theater. Successful dance ballets are the hardest things in the world to describe outside their own language!

The ballet is in fourteen parts that flow together, accompanying the Strauss songs. While an understanding of the words of the songs, which are sung in German, is certainly not essential to enjoyment of the dances, you may wish to listen to recordings before coming to the theater. The English of the German words will be found at the end of this account.

The curtain rises in silence on two boys and a girl. The music is quiet as the baritone starts to sing of meadows at twilight and the pursuit of a beautiful woman "Dream at Twilight." As the song continues in that vein, rising slowly in intensity, one of the boys, in green, responds to the girl and the others among the couples who materialize about him. He would be with them, but is not, as they come and go. He is left, seeking but not finding, but not absolutely forlorn; after all, they have not rejected him: perhaps it is the other way round.

To the tempo of the rapid "Serenade," sung by the baritone, the boy dances with a girl quick in movement and flirtatiousness. He kneels at her feet and they dance together. Her legs tremble at the beauty of it. Two other couples, the girls responding similarly to the romantic ambience, appear to attend them; the boy then lifts the girl to his shoulder and takes her off into the wings. It is not surprising that the song should invoke the nightingale dreaming of kisses and a rose that, in the morning, should remember and shine with the recollection of the night.

Four couples dance pensively to a poem about "The Star." Next, in the fourth dance, again a *pas de deux* ("Tomorrow"), a young couple move quietly together as the soprano sings of a tomorrow that will unite happy persons, who will look into each other's eyes with muted recognition of their joy. Gently, the boy carries the girl off into the wings.

The baritone sings now a bright tune ("To What End, Maiden?") in which he wonders amusingly at the deceitfulness of a young maiden. There is a dance for three couples, then just one, where the boy seems to question the girl and to find her wonderful at the same time.

"Strolling at Night" follows, under a silvery moon, where an enraptured couple dance of their intense happiness. He falls at her feet. Now, two boys and a girl, hand in hand, dance to a song ("Beautiful, Yet Cold"); the soprano sings about the beautiful but cold stars of heaven that cannot compare to the eyes of the beloved.

Next, a girl moves toward dancing couples, seeming to see a vision of her own ideal and truly finding him in her thoughts, if not in reality ("Rest, My Soul"). The girl in lonely torment is joined by a boy who makes an effort to make her forget. Gentle at first, he fails to comfort her and then almost forces her to forget. She is then in torment, held by him agonizingly and turning her face from him. They leave, her arms folded and her hands curled over her face.

Bright light comes up and five couples rush on to celebrate with the baritone the coming of spring ("Sir Spring"). Next, a boy alone dances, introspectively and thoughtful ("All My Thoughts"). Then he faces three girls. He tries to lead them in a dance ("Ah, Woe Is Me, Unhappy Man!"), partnering them one after another, but does not succeed. He is alone again at the end.

A radiant couple swirl to a song by the baritone about the uselessness of descriptions of his beloved ("Nothing"). What do we know about the sun, the giver of life and light?

Two other lovers dance their joy as the soprano recalls the magic of the time they first looked into each other's eyes and love showered down on them ("Ever Since Your Eyes"). The girl leans against the boy as the lights dim. He touches her hand. Other lovers join them as the song speaks of night, which may steal one's love away ("Night").

NOTES Writing about *Early Songs* in the New York *Times*, the critic Clive Barnes said that the ballet "is a picture of a world lost, a world full of gentle nuance, of literary feeling, of a rapture impassioned by the poetry of poetry rather than the poetry of life. Love is pure here, and its heartbeat is a kind of exquisite stylization of lust. It is the end of a civilization, and empty-handed cavaliers bearing silver roses are about to be everywhere. . . . It is a fantastically beautiful work; it lilts, it rises, it flies like a kite above our all-too-average dance works. . . . Feld offers a choreographic viewpoint that extends our view of the dance."

Walter Terry wrote in *The Saturday Review: "Early Songs,* tastefully costumed by Stanley Simmons and sensitively lit by Jules Fisher, is a work of superior craftsmanship choreographically, but more, it is an art experience that lifts the spirit. At its première, it was faultlessly danced by its cast of thirteen, including Feld himself, (Christine) Sarry, Elizabeth Lee, John Sowinski, and Richard Munro among the most impressive."

ENIGMA VARIATIONS

Music by Edward Elgar. Choreography by Frederick Ashton. Scenery and costumes by Julia Trevelyan Oman. First presented by the Royal Ballet at the Royal Opera House, Covent Garden, London, October 25, 1968, with Derek Rencher, Svetlana Beriosova, Stanley Holden, Brian Shaw, Alexander Grant, Robert Mead, Vyvyan Lorrayne, Anthony Dowell, Georgina Parkinson, Desmond Doyle, Antoinette Sibley, Wayne Sleep, Leslie Edwards, and Deanne Bergsma in the principal roles. First presented in the United States by the same ensemble, with the same cast, at the Metropolitan Opera House, Lincoln Center, April 22, 1969. Conducted by John Lanchbery.

Subtitled, in the composer's words, "My Friends Pictured Within," *Enigma Variations* is a dance portrait of the artist among friends and family in Victorian England. The ballet is based on its score, which characterized thirteen friends and relations "who were there," and a fourteenth, "absent on a sea voyage" at the time, who remains the "enigma."

Describing one aspect of his composition, Elgar said it was "written at a time when friends were dubious and generally discouraging as to the composer's musical future." The action of the ballet, which is set in an English country house in the Cotswolds in 1898, occurs at a point when the composer needed friends most. It follows very closely the true story that Elgar had sent the completed score of his *Variations* to the celebrated Viennese conductor Richter, in the hope of interesting him in the work. Elgar's various friends, who visit him during the trying period of his awaiting a reply, pass an afternoon in the customary, relaxed pursuits of a Victorian autumn day. Only his wife, a constant source of inspiration and encouragement throughout his life, understands and watches over him to offer comfort. One by one the friends enter the action, identifying their separate personalities with each danced variation to the music Elgar wrote to characterize them. A chamber-music comrade, an amateur cellist, a tricycle-riding crony, a contemplative scholar, a romantic young girl, a gracious and sedate lady, and an eccentric dog lover all pass in review. Those closest to him, his wife and his friend "Nimrod" (who also knew the conductor Richter), continually reflect their understanding and the significance of the anxious waiting period. From time to time, Lady Mary Lygnon appears and reappears as a mysterious background figure, symbolic of the enigma of the long anticipated reply. At the end of the ballet, a telegram arrives for "Nimrod" from Richter, announcing that he will indeed conduct the first performance of *Enigma Variations.*

NOTES Unanimously regarded as a masterpiece when it was first presented in England, the ballet was called by John Percival, in the *Times,* "a rare and moving expression of the quality of friendship." It received wide acclaim after its U.S. première. Writing in the *Village Voice,* the critic Deborah Jowitt said: ". . . I am astonished at its power to move me. The key—or one of them—to the enigma of the ballet's beauty is the nostalgia inherent in certain things. Lorca once wrote that a flock of sheep bears nostalgia about with it; it need not matter whether one has longings at all relevant to a flock of sheep. I don't think that one needs to have known era, place, or people involved in Ashton's ballet to be beguiled.

"The setting is Elgar's house in Worcestershire in the late years of Victoria's reign and of the nineteenth century. Everything about the ballet has an air of lateness: the composer's lateness in achieving recognition, the ripe late-Romantic music, the autumn garden, the amber of the sunlight. Julia Trevelyan Oman's set and costumes are carefully and poetically authentic. It's the kind of set I loved as a child—so super-real that it's hard to believe that there actually is a backstage area and not just more lawns and paths. There is a brick entrance, a cutaway view of an interior stairway, hammocks, bicycles, trees from which occasional yellow leaves float. Those friends of Elgar's cryptically enshrined in the musical variations are conveniently brought together. . . . They wander about . . . each emerging to do his (or her) variation and then strolling off. At the end a telegram is brought. . . . Elgar's friends rejoice in his good fortune.

"I see most clearly in this ballet what Ashtonophiles rave about. He is best at being quiet; his effects are modest, unflamboyant, but extremely sensitive to the nuances of character. . . . Sometimes he creates character through rhythm and through subtle gestural grafts onto the ballet vocabulary. Other times . . . he suggests eccentricities by requiring an eccentric manner of performing straightforward classical steps. He has a fine way with small understated lifts that seem to come with no preparation; the girl's feet make shy conversational steps barely off the ground. There are several of these in the bittersweet duet for Elgar and a very young girl (beautifully done by Derek Rencher and Antoinette Sibley), and in one of more promise of fulfillment between Matthew Arnold's son and Isobel Futton (Robert Mead and Vyvyan Lorrayne). I especially liked two delightfully brusque, erratic solos performed by Alexander Grant and Anthony Dowell; some affectionate conjugal passages between Elgar and his wife (Svetlana Beriosova); and a signified . . . touching duet between Elgar and a friend (Desmond Doyle) to the famous *Nimrod* variation."

THE ETERNAL IDOL

Music by Frédéric Chopin. Choreography by Michael Smuin. First presented by American Ballet Theatre at the Brooklyn Academy of Music, December 4, 1969, with Cynthia Gregory and Ivan Nagy.

A romantic narrative ballet, *The Eternal Idol* is appropriately set to the *Larghetto* of Chopin's *Concerto No. 2 in F Minor*. The theme and inspiration for the ballet is Rodin's famous sculpture "The Eternal Idol," where a boy kneels at a girl's feet and rests his head on her breast. The ballet begins that way, reminding us of the pose of the sculpture. It then explores in a *pas de deux* for the lovers the beginnings and growth of their love for each other. As the critic Walter Terry has noted, the ballet evokes such images as Bernard Champigneulle speaks of in his book *Rodin:* ". . . Songs and sighs of love, cries of pleasure and pain, cries of pain and pleasure mingled, the eternal call of woman, the call of man . . . all found expression in Rodin."

EUGENE ONEGIN

Ballet in three acts and six scenes after Alexander Pushkin. Music by Peter Ilyich Tchaikovsky, arranged and orchestrated by Kurt-Heinz Stolze. Choreography by John Cranko. Scenery and costumes by Jürgen Rose. First presented by the Stuttgart Ballet at the Wuerttemberg State Theatre, Stuttgart, Germany, April 13, 1965, with Marcia Haydée and Heinz Clauss in the principal roles. First presented in the United States by the same ensemble at the Metropolitan Opera House, Lincoln Center, New York, June 10, 1969.

The ballet tells the story of Pushkin's great poem. The music, by Tchaikovsky, is not from that composer's opera *Eugene Onegin,* but has been arranged from his lesser-known compositions.

How is it possible for me to speak of Pushkin's poem *Eugene Onegin* without emotion? It is like asking an Englishman to speak of Shakespeare without emotion. Alexander Pushkin produced the first great Russian poem, or "free novel" in verse, in *Eugene Onegin* (1823–30). His work is the beginning of greatness of the Russian language. There are problems about the translation of *Eugene Onegin* into English. Many have tried to render the poem into English. Vladimir Nabokov's complete version is the best we have, but for the reader with no Russian, it is difficult to explain the poem's greatness. For it is not what we think of as an epic or a huge, classic poem. It is a story, first of all, a work in poetry in a language that was unknown before, a language that became with Pushkin the Russian language of literacy and spoken liveliness. At any rate, John Cranko chose to make a ballet of this narrative, having known it as a poem, and also as an opera in Tchaikovsky's profound version. He arranged his ballet not to the music of Tchaikovsky's opera, but to other work by Tchaikovsky researched, arranged, and orchestrated by Kurt-Heinz Stolze.

Interviewed by *The New Yorker,* Cranko spoke of his ballet: "'I see *Onegin* as a myth in the same way that Charlie

Chaplin is a myth. . . . Myths always have double meanings, and in this sense Chaplin is both funny and terrifying. Onegin is a young man who has everything—good looks, money, charm—and yet he adds up to nothing. Which makes *him* terrifying. His problem is a very contemporary one—lack of recognition. Then, of course, the plot of the Pushkin poem is balletic—explainable in three different dance styles. The first act is a youthful peasant dance, the second is a bourgeois party, the third is an elegant St. Petersburg ball. And like a thread going through the labyrinth you have your soloists, with their problems, their stories.'

"Mr. Cranko . . . added that when he choreographed a ballet he tried to create visual images that speak for themselves. 'A diamond has no color, but it takes light, and when you look at it you see red, blue, green, and yellow,' he said. 'A ballet image should be like a diamond. No meaning. No color. But hard, not sloppy. I have a specific feeling which maybe I can only shape for myself. So the ultimate definition of the images comes from the eyes of the public, not from my eyes.'"

A synopsis of the ballet follows:

ACT ONE, SCENE ONE—MADAME LARINA'S GARDEN Madame Larina, Olga, and the nurse are finishing the party dresses and gossiping about Tatiana's coming birthday festivities. Madame Larina speculates on the future and reminisces about her own lost beauty and youth. Girls from the neighborhood arrive, their greetings and chatter are interrupted by gunshots.

Lensky, a young poet, engaged to Olga, arrives and tells them there is no cause for alarm; he was hunting with a friend from St. Petersburg. He introduces Onegin, who, bored with the city, has come to see if the country can offer him any distraction. Tatiana, full of youthful and romantic fantasies, falls in love with the elegant stranger, so different from the country people she knows. Onegin, on the other hand, sees only a coltish country girl who reads too many romantic novels.

ACT ONE, SCENE TWO—TATIANA'S BEDROOM Tatiana, her imagination aflame with impetuous first love, dreams of

Onegin and writes him a passionate love letter which she gives the nurse to deliver.

ACT TWO, SCENE 1—TATIANA'S BIRTHDAY The provincial gentry have come to celebrate Tatiana's birthday. They gossip about Lensky's infatuation with Olga and whisper prophecies of a dawning romance between Tatiana and the newcomer. Onegin finds the company boring. Stifling his yawns, he finds it difficult to be civil to them: Furthermore, he is irritated by Tatiana's letter which he regards merely as an outburst of adolescent love. In a quiet moment, he seeks out Tatiana and, telling her that he cannot love her, tears up her letter. Tatiana's distress, instead of awaking pity, merely increases his irritation.

Prince Gremin, a distant relative, appears. He is in love with Tatiana, and Madame Larina hopes for a brilliant match; but Tatiana, troubled with her own heart, hardly notices her kindly and elderly relative.

Onegin, in his boredom, decides to provoke Lensky by flirting with Olga who lightheartedly joins in the teasing. But Lensky takes the matter with passionate seriousness. He challenges Onegin to a duel.

ACT TWO, SCENE 2—THE DUEL Tatiana and Olga try to reason with Lensky, but his high romantic ideals are shattered by the betrayal of his friend and the fickleness of his beloved; he insists that the duel take place. Onegin kills his friend and for the first time his cold heart is moved by the horror of his deed. Tatiana realizes that her love was an illusion, and that Onegin is self-centered and empty.

ACT THREE, SCENE 1—ST. PETERSBURG Years later, Onegin, having traveled the world in an attempt to escape from his own futility, returns to St. Petersburg where he is received at a ball in the palace of Prince Gremin. Gremin has recently married, and Onegin is astonished to recognize in the stately and elegant young princess, Tatiana, the uninteresting little country girl whom he once turned away. The enormity of his mistake and loss engulfs him. His life now seems even more aimless and empty.

ACT THREE, SCENE 2—TATIANA'S BOUDOIR Tatiana reads a letter from Onegin which reveals his love. Suddenly he stands before her, impatient to know her answer. Tatiana sorrowfully tells him that although she still feels her passionate love of girlhood for him, she is now a woman, and that she could never find happiness or respect with him. She orders him to leave her forever.

NOTES The critic Walter Terry, reviewing a performance of *Eugene Onegin* in New York in 1971, wrote in *The Saturday Review:* "How Cranko tells a story in dance! He is a theater man through and through, as was his illustrious predecessor of two centuries ago in Stuttgart, Jean-Georges Noverre, whose revolutionary esthetics carried the ballet away from mere steps to *ballet d'action*—that is to say, to dramatic ballet, to movement with dramatic meanings.

"Cranko's *Onegin* has its virtuosic steppings—the cross-stage leaps by the company at the close of Act One, Scene 1, or the great pinwheel pattern in the ballroom scene—but of equal importance are the acted, not danced, duel and death scene that takes place way at the back of the stage (the late Doris Humphrey, among the great choreographers of our age, once stated that tragedy worked best in upstage remoteness and that comedy was for downstage familiarity), the finale in which the heroine stands alone center stage, and the remarkable mirror dance that combines acting and dancing as Tatiana literally draws her dream lover from the image in her mind and has him step from behind her own reflection in the mirror and into her arms.

". . . Marcia Haydée was Tatiana, a role identified with her very special artistry as both an actress and a dancer, and Heinz Clauss was Onegin, stern, strong, remote yet romantic. . . ."

AN EVENING'S WALTZES

Music by Serge Prokofiev. Choreography by Jerome Robbins. Costumes by Rouben Ter-Arutunian. First presented by the New York City Ballet at the New York State Theater, Lincoln Center, May 24, 1973, with Patricia McBride and Jean-Pierre Bonnefous, Christine Redpath and John Clifford, Sara Leland and Bart Cook in leading roles.

The music for this dance ballet is five waltzes by Prokofiev from his *Symphonic Suite of Waltzes.* There is no story, only these persons dancing to these waltzes. Each of the waltzes is different, and a different atmosphere and mood are established for the dances. The three leading couples as well as the soloists and *corps de ballet* are formally dressed, as if they were attending a formal party.

Writing in the *Wall Street Journal* about the ballet, Peter J. Rosenwald said that "it has so much beautiful movement that it could almost bring back ballroom dancing as a national pastime. . . . From beginning to end it has that Robbins romantic style, warm and eloquent, full of effortless and thrilling lifts which are never showy for their own sake."

Deborah Jowitt in the *Village Voice* wrote: "Over the decorous unison waltzing of the *corps,* pairs of soloists enter one at a time to make violent small talk in dance. Small outbursts of movement, sudden changes of heart and direction interrupt the smooth surface of the waltzing. These couples are, perhaps, dancing out the thoughts and the verbal exchanges that occur at grand parties such as these, where a current of fashionable melodrama flows through the ballroom. The duet for Redpath and Clifford (replacing the injured Gelsey Kirkland and Helgi Tomasson at the last minute) is particularly effusive, with a hint of drastic coquetry."

FAÇADE

Ballet in one act. Music by William Walton. Choreography by Frederick Ashton. Scenery and costumes by John Armstrong. First presented by the Camargo Society at the Cambridge Theatre, London, April 26, 1931, with a cast that included Lydia Lopokova, Alicia Markova, and Frederick Ashton. First presented in the United States by the Sadler's Wells Ballet at the Metropolitan Opera House, New York, October 13, 1949, with Moira Shearer and Frederick Ashton in featured roles.

The music to *Façade* was originally written as a setting to certain poems by Edith Sitwell. The poet recited her verses accompanied by the music. The ballet has nothing to do with the poems and uses only the music, to which the choreographer has arranged a series of nine comic *divertissements* that poke fun at their subjects. The scene shows the façade of a large, light-colored house of the Victorian era.

First, two girls and a boy amble out on stage and dance a "Scottish Rhapsody" in appropriate native costume. This is followed by a number called "Yodeling." A milkmaid enters with a stool. Soon she is disturbed by three mountaineers, who turn her around as she stands posed on the stool and pay tribute to her fresh beauty. There is a yodeling contest, in which the girl enters with gusto. The music ripples and laughs with the happy young people. Next comes a "Polka," danced by a smart young lady.

Now two couples dance a "Fox Trot," which is followed by a "Waltz" executed by four girls. Two vaudeville dandies take up the "Popular Song" and perform it with quick, funny precision. The "Country Dance" features a silly country girl, a yokel, and an irate squire. A gigolo, overslickly dressed in evening clothes, and a debutante, who wears a long red dress and an absurd feather in her hair, now come forward and dance the "Tango." The gigolo bends the debutante backward, dips her low, runs a scale down her back with his fingers, and with a devilish air tries to overexploit her good nature. The debutante is amenable to any treatment, however, and finishes the dance considerably disheveled. All the dancers come forward now and join in a "Tarantella Finale."

FANCY FREE

Ballet in one act. Music by Leonard Bernstein. Choreography by Jerome Robbins. Scenery by Oliver Smith. Costumes by Kermit Love. First presented by Ballet Theatre at the Metropolitan Opera House, New York, April 18, 1944, with John Kriza, Harold Lang, and Jerome Robbins as the three Sailors; *Muriel Bentley, Janet Reed, and Shirley Eckl as the three* Passers-by.

This modern American ballet tells what happens to three sailors who go out on liberty in New York City. The time is "the present": any hot summer night. The scene is a side street in Manhattan.

The music is quiet when the curtain rises. Outlined against the dark city night is the interior of a bar. The entrance to the bar, on the right, leads out onto a street corner. There a bright street lamp shines down on the sidewalk. Inside the bar there are no customers; the lone bartender lazily dries and polishes beer glasses. He begins to read a newspaper. In the background the myriad lights of distant skyscrapers penetrate the sultry night like stars.

Through the side windows of the bar we can make out three sailors walking toward the corner. The music blares out. They rush toward the corner, pivot on the lamppost, and begin to dance in the street in front of the bar. Dressed in clean summer whites, the sailors are out to make the most of the night. They preen a little, adjust their hats to jazzy angles, and strut along the pavement in anticipation of the good time that must naturally come their way. Their dance is like an improvised vaudeville act; it's clear that the three are friends and that they can kid each other and laugh about it. If they have their way, this is going to be an evening to beat all the rest. They try to outdo each other with brief trick dance steps and laugh. Two of them push the third high up in the air between them. Inside the bar the bartender smokes and reads his paper.

The rowdy music that accompanies the sailors' dance slows

down and softens. The three men know from experience that simple determination isn't going to get them a good time. They straighten their jackets, readjust their hats, and wonder what to do next: which do they want first—women, drink, or music? One of the sailors leans against the lamppost to consider the problem seriously. One of his pals joins him. Before these two have made up their minds completely, the third sailor enters the bar. His friends race in after him.

The three sailors strut up to the bar with a special salty air for the bartender's benefit. They order three beers, clink their glasses together, down the drinks in unison, and slam the glasses back down on the bar. The bartender eyes them suspiciously: who's going to pay? The sailors look at each other as if such a thought had never entered their heads. Finally one of them is tricked into paying by the other two. As he puts down the money, he tries to shrug off the fact that he always ends up with the short end of the stick.

Now that they've had one drink, the sailors remember that they don't want to drink alone. They look around the empty bar with amused disgust, hitch up their pants, and head for the door. The music is moody, waiting for something to happen. The sailors are getting slightly tired of each other; they wonder if the evening is going to turn out to be a bust, after all. One of them pulls out a stick of gum. He starts to unwrap it, then remembers his friends and splits it with them. The three chew thoughtfully and, one by one, flick the pieces of gum wrapper out into the street to see which one can flick it farthest. The winner wonders what difference it makes.

At this point, just as the three are about to relax into boredom, they straighten up as if lightning had struck. The music breaks out into loud, rhythmic boogie-woogie, and a terrific-looking girl walks by. She wears a tight-fitting blouse and skirt, high patent leather shoes, and carries a red handbag. The girl knows she is being watched; she smiles and by her walk suggests all the things the sailors are imagining. The sailors are struck numb; standing close together, they move as one body—bending so far forward to watch the girl that they almost fall on their faces.

The girl pretends that she hasn't seen them, which sends the boys into action. Suddenly they are three very different individuals, each trying to interest the girl in his own special way. They imitate her walk, laugh at her, grab her purse and toss it around, and all but lie at her feet to get the girl to recognize their existence. The girl wants to be angry and tries to act as if she is, but the boys sense that she's just kidding. When she laughs in warm, friendly recognition, the three sailors smile back and wonder—who saw her first? A small fight breaks out. Two of the boys lift the girl high. She kicks free and stomps off impatiently. The battle has left one sailor lying in the street. He watches as his two friends follow the girl, then lazily picks himself up.

He smoothes out his uniform and starts to go back into the bar. Then, as in a dream, he bumps into a small, cute girl, younger than the first. He apologizes for his clumsiness, smiles winningly, looks her up and down adroitly, and introduces himself. The girl smiles back. The sailor looks over her shoulder to be sure his friends have disappeared and asks her into the bar for a drink. The girl consents.

Inside, the bartender is still reading. The sailor and his girl climb up on two stools and order drinks. He is feeling his way with the redhead, but decides on the old routine. The music stops as he gives her a dazzling, rapid display of What-I've-Been-Through. His hands circle the air and zoom down to attack imaginary ships, and his body vibrates to machine-gun fire as he describes the terrors of life at sea. When the girl takes this in and doesn't laugh at him, just watches, the boy decides that she's not only cute, she's adorable. He asks her to dance.

The orchestra plays a low blues number as they move together slowly. The *pas de deux* they dance is instinctively intimate, and the intimacy—their mutual liking and attraction—is so natural and unforced that formality and doubt would be out of place. This is a made-for-each-other dance that makes sense in its alternate casualness and conviction. He dances with her as he would with any girl, then holds her closely, and she responds warmly to this way of showing how special she is. When the dance is over, he bends down and kisses her softly. The girl smiles and wipes her lipstick off his face. They move together back to the bar.

The sailor picks the girl up and sits her on a stool. He has started to pay for the drinks when a roaring rattle of sound breaks the romantic spell and ushers in his two friends. The two gobs barge into the bar with the first girl and stop dead in their tracks when they see him with a date. He grabs his girl and pulls her toward the door to avoid the intruders. But the girl stops him. The girls are old friends, apparently, and begin to carry on together as girls will.

The boy sees that the situation is hopeless and goes to join his pals at a table. More drinks are ordered. The girls sit down. There are only four chairs, and one of the sailors is left standing. He tries to sit on the first girl's lap—she seemed more experienced and tolerant—but she pushes him off. Two of the sailors dance with the girls, and the boy who found the redhead sits alone for a moment. Now he cuts in. The snare drum signals the quarrel that ensues: who's going to dance with whom? The situation is hopeless. One of the boys has got to clear out or the night will be ruined.

The three sailors finally get together and agree that they'll have a contest to see which one of them can dance best. The girls will be the judges of the two winners, and the third man will scram. Two of the sailors join the girls at the table, and one of the boys begins a solo.

His dance is rowdy and energetic as he tries to outdo all the steps he thinks his friends might try. The girls are delighted at his fresh and arrogant skill and begin to applaud as he finishes his number by jumping up on the bar with one leap. There he poses for an instant, then jumps down, grabs up a beer, and flourishes his glass. The other two sailors razz him as the girls clap their hands.

The next variation is danced by the cute girl's first partner. His dance is subtler, relying more on sinuous, flowing rhythm than boisterousness, more on false modesty than overt bragging. The girls respond to his quiet dance with a sigh, and his friends hold their noses. He lies on the floor with his legs in the air as his number ends. The last sailor tries to combine the two styles of his friends and succeeds brilliantly in a snaky, Latin dance at the end of which he jumps down from a bar stool to kneel on the floor before the girls.

The girls don't know which ones to choose! They argue about it; then the boys argue with them and start to fight among themselves. The competition that began when the first girl passed by on the street turns into anger and rage, and they begin to tear each other apart. The girls cringe against the bar, thinking at first that this can't be serious, but as the battle goes on in earnest, they decide to get out of there fast. The sailors dive behind the bar in a tussle and don't notice that the girls have walked out on them. When they pause and wake up to this fact, they look at each other frantically and dive for the door. Out on the street they can't find the girls. They look at each other with amused disgust, straighten out their uniforms, nurse their aches and pains, and relax again.

What are they to do now? Maybe another drink will help. They re-enter the bar, down a drink apiece, and again the same sailor pays. The friends head back for the street. They stand there under the lamppost, as they did before they first entered the bar at the beginning of the evening. They split another piece of gum three ways; they tear off the paper and flip it into the street.

The music sounds noisily, and a beautiful babe promenades across the street—terrific, you understand? As before, the three bodies slant in unison as they follow her every step and wiggle. The girl struts off down the street on the left. The sailors seem to recover from her fascination and remember the bruises of the battle royal the last girls got them involved in. Each watches the others carefully, to be sure that this feeling is unanimous. This is just a stall. They begin to idle away from each other, laughing the blonde off, when one sailor strikes off like a streak of lightning after the girl. His friends follow. The cycle is endless.

FÊTE NOIRE

Music by Dimitri Shostakovich. Choreography by Arthur Mitchell. Scenery and costumes by Bernard Johnson. Lighting by Fred Barry. Pianist: Craig Sheppard. Conducted by Isaiah Jackson. First presented by the Dance Theatre of Harlem.

When the Dance Theatre of Harlem presented *Fête Noire* at the Spoleto Festival in July, 1971, the critic William Weaver called the ballet "a kind of black version of *Graduation Ball*, danced with precision and brio," and so indeed it is. The music is the *Concerto No. 2 for Piano and Orchestra* by Shostakovich. The setting is a huge ballroom where, responsive to the developing themes and moods of the music, the dancers celebrate an important occasion that demands of them their very best.

LA FILLE MAL GARDÉE

THE UNCHAPERONED DAUGHTER

Ballet in three scenes. Music by Ferdinand Hérold. Choreography by Jean Dauberval. First presented at Bordeaux, France, 1789, and at the Grand Theatre, Paris, July 1, 1789. First presented in the United States in various versions beginning in 1794. Revived by Ballet Theatre, with music by Wilhelm Hertel and choreography restaged by Bronislava Nijinska and Dimitri Romanoff, at the Center Theatre, New York, January 19, 1940, scenery and costumes by Serge Soudeikine.

Many people who go to the ballet and chance to come across a work that was originally presented more than a hundred and fifty years ago imagine that such a ballet must be sad—perhaps an antique tragedy. But *La Fille Mal Gardée* is a comedy. The earliest of all the ballets in the current repertory, its universally comical situations are no doubt responsible for its survival.

Soon after the music begins, a painted drop curtain depicts the principal characters of the ballet. On the left are Lisette and Colin, the two lovers. A rotund Cupid painted at the top of the scene directs a pointed arrow at the heroine. Lisette's mother, Madame Simone, dominates the scene, trying to watch her daughter and be pleasant to the suitor she has chosen for her. The story contained in this picture gradually unfolds as the drop curtain rises. The ballet is set in a small provincial French town. The time is about two hundred years ago.

SCENE ONE—THE FARM OF MADAME SIMONE Alongside the steep-roofed house of Madame Simone, a "rich farmerette," is the family barnyard. In back, a rushing stream cascades down a hill. Madame Simone sits on a bench at the left, whiling away the time of day. Two neighbors join her to gossip. She bustles off with them.

The music suggests the arrival of the heroine, and Lisette enters on the left. Dressed in a light-blue skirt with a red bodice, with blue ribbons in her hair, she is the picture of innocent, country prettiness. The day has just begun, and because she is supposed to be busy at one task or another, Lisette pretends to arrange several flowerpots on the bench. She bows to several of the village boys, bound for the fields with their scythes, as she waters the flowers. Colin, a good-looking farmer, enters on the left, carrying a rake. He sits down on the bench, and Lisette, anxious to be surprised by his arrival, absent-mindedly waters his head. Colin jumps up, and he and Lisette immediately begin to dance together. Their dance reveals that the two have been attracted to each other for some time, that this is not their first rendezvous. Colin lifts Lisette boldly, yet gently.

The love duet is interrupted by Lisette's mother. Directly she approaches, the two lovers rush to hide behind the bench. Madame Simone discovers them, however, and chases Colin around the stage. Hastily he embraces Lisette and rushes off. Madame Simone, in a high temper, proceeds to lecture her daughter on her duty to make a proper marriage. Lisette protests that she is absolutely innocent of any flirtation, but her mother persists in her rage. The two neighbors come in to watch the scene. Lisette finally secures her mother's forgiveness by offering her, with a sweet smile, one of her own flowers.

Trumpets announce the arrival of four of Lisette's friends. They are followed by a group of villagers. The young people want Lisette to join them. Dutifully she asks her mother's permission and she begins to dance. Colin sneaks in at the back and conceals himself in the crowd. He runs out and takes Lisette's hand when her mother stalks off. The two dance a lively duet, surrounded by their friends. The music is gay and sparkling. The conviviality is short-lived, however, for Madame Simone returns, sees Colin, and sends him packing. She makes a point of her daughter's idleness by presenting scythes to her four friends.

Lisette attempts to console herself by dancing with her friends as they celebrate the harvesttime. She tries to leave with them when they go, but her mother pulls her back. Lisette herself is now in a temper. She stomps, shakes her fists pathetically, cries, and hides her face in her hands. Her mother takes her hands away and tries to make amends. Colin has entered quietly and stands in back of Madame Simone. That is consolation enough for Lisette. She waves to him. Her mother notes the gesture, but cannot find a reason for it. Colin does not conceal himself for long, however. The impetuous girl rushes to him. They embrace briefly before Madame Simone leaps at them to drag Lisette back toward the house.

She sits her daughter down on the bench. Lisette rises and brings out a butter churn. Her mother fills the churn with cream and orders her daughter to work. Lisette churns away, and her mother leaves the scene. Colin leaps in behind Lisette. He places his hands on hers and easily persuades her to stop her work. He sits down on the bench beside her; Lisette, suddenly embarrassed at being alone with her lover, rises and dances. She turns softly and slowly, beguiling Colin with her sweet motion. When she finishes her dance with a series of rapid turns, Colin throws out to her a long blue ribbon. Lisette catches it and, holding the flowing ribbon above their heads, the two dance together romantically. Lisette tosses the ribbon back to Colin, who fixes it halter-fashion around her shoulders, after which the girl performs her steps as if by his command. Lisette pirouettes into his arms, Colin ties the ribbon about her, and the girl poses against her lover. The two then leave the stage.

Thomas, a vinegrower, enters with his son, Alain. Come to see Madame Simone by appointment, the obese Thomas is decked out in a bright-green suit; he is determined to be formal and correct. His son, determined to be playful and completely oblivious to his surroundings, leaps about the stage trying to catch butterflies in a net. Thomas reprimands him and pulls him to a bench.

Madame Simone, dressed in her best purple, arrives to greet the guests. With ceremonious gestures, she and Thomas discuss the suitability of a marriage between their children. Madame Simone is readily persuaded of Alain's eligibility when Thomas dangles a bag of gold in her face. The woman approaches to examine the young man, ascertains that he is sound of limb if not of mind, and gives her approval. She drags Lisette out to meet her fiancé. Dutifully the girl has changed her clothes for the occasion, but she has no idea of its real meaning. Both parents push their children toward each other. Both children step back in horror as they realize the meaning of their parents' interview. Each tries to escape, but the parents hold them secure. The curtain falls as they both kneel, their faces turned away from each other. Lisette's white dress and pink ribbons are for the wrong man. Madame Simone stands over them in an attitude of supreme happiness. During the scene change, Thomas and Madame Simone, accompanied by the neighbors, drag the engaged couple off to the village notary to make the marriage settlement final.

SCENE TWO—THE VILLAGE GREEN On the painted backdrop, wheat fields are seen in the distance. Sheaves of freshly cut wheat are propped up where the workers have left them. A windmill stands over the fields on a hill at the back. On the right is a great tree; two cows meditate near by. The workers of the village, colorfully dressed girls and their companions, pause for a general dance. Lisette and Alain are pushed into the scene by their parents. Despite all their complaining, the two are made to stand close together. They are able to separate only when Thomas asks Madame Simone to dance. The aged couple cavort grotesquely about the green; it has suddenly occurred to Madame Simone that she, too, might be quite a match, and she flirts with the vinegrower.

Meanwhile Colin has entered quietly on the right. He sees that his sweetheart has been promised to another and turns away. Madame Simone and Thomas race off to pursue their flirtation elsewhere, and some of Lisette's friends, noticing Colin's plight, encourage the girl to comfort the poor lad. Lisette touches his arm. By her soft, endearing gestures the girl convinces him that she herself has had nothing to do with the proposed match. Colin puts his arms about her, and their foreheads touch. He kneels, and the two begin an adagio to the melody of solo strings and an accompanying harp. The villagers sit on the ground to watch the lovers. Lisette leaves the scene after the dance is over, and Colin performs a bright, dazzling variation. Lisette returns for a winsome, engaging dance in which she lifts her skirt softly, with innocent coquetry. Her variation increases in momentum; at the end she turns brilliantly and cuts her movement off suddenly with a swift, pert pose.

Alain, who has been off chasing after butterflies, runs onto the scene, brandishing his net before him. He circles the stage in long, high leaps. Two of the girls try to engage his attention. The youth ignores their flattery, but the girls persist and dance on either side of him. Alain abandons them, jumping off into the wings in pursuit of his hobby.

Thunder is heard and the scene darkens; lightning flashes illumine the hurried dashing back and forth of the villagers. Lisette and Colin follow as their friends run for cover. Alain rushes in, trembling with fright at the lightning. He hides his head under a girl's skirts and pushes her off toward safety. The drop curtain falls.

SCENE THREE—MADAME SIMONE'S HOUSE Lisette enters quickly to escape the storm. Her mother follows and bustles about the room. Lisette pours coffee for her, then sits at her feet as Madame Simone begins to work at her spinning wheel. Lisette tries to sneak away, but her mother orders her to read a book she gives her. Lisette looks at a page or two, then asks her mother the meaning of one of the words. Madame Simone is horrified: she has given her daughter the wrong book! A romantic novel, no less! The girl succeeds in crawling away a few feet until Madame Simone seizes her from behind and draws her back to her chair. She takes up her sewing again.

Colin opens the transom above the door and throws in a flower to Lisette. Lisette turns around and sees him. Immediately her mother senses her agitation and commands her to be still. Colin, by passionate signs, beseeches her to dance for him. The girl persuades her mother to play the tambourine so that she can practice her dancing. Lisette dances flirtatiously for Colin's benefit. The old woman tires of the tambourine and falls off to sleep. Lisette approaches her on tiptoe. As the girl takes her key, her mother wakens and beats the tambourine. Lisette continues her dance, and at its conclusion Madame Simone kisses her in reward.

Boys and girls of the village enter, bringing with them sheaves of wheat, which they stack against a table. Lisette would like to follow them off, but her mother commands her to take her turn at the spinning wheel. Lisette stamps her foot and throws herself down in the chair to sulk. Her mother leaves the room.

The orchestra repeats the melody to which she and Colin danced so happily, and Lisette imagines what it would be like to be married to the man of her own choice. She puts her hands on her heart and blows a kiss toward the door. She sees herself surrounded by Colin's children, whom she scolds; she rocks her arms as if they held a child.

To Lisette's embarrassment, Colin is there in the room watching her. The sheaves of wheat are thrown aside, and her lover sits smiling at her. She sits beside him for a moment, then jumps up as he proposes to her seriously. Colin pleads with her—after all, she has just imagined herself as his wife—but the girl in her embarrassment and confusion denies her love and shoves the boy toward the door. Colin begins to lose his temper at her stubbornness and is delighted to find her even more flustered when she finds that the door is locked!

Lisette runs to the chair and sees that she can keep up the pretense no longer. Colin kneels at her feet and places his head in her lap. The two trade their scarves as a pledge of their love. Madame Simone can be heard approaching. Lisette tries to hide Colin—under the little table, in a small chest. In desperation, she pushes him into the hayloft and slams the door shut just as her mother enters.

Lisette thinks she is safe but she has forgotten Colin's scarf. Madame Simone spots it instantly and fetches a large switch to beat the girl. Lisette runs, but the old woman catches up with her, spanks her soundly, and, as an additional penalty, locks her in the hayloft!

Visitors are heard outside. Madame Simone admits Thomas and Alain, the village notary and his secretary following in their wake. Villagers accompany them to witness the marriage contract. The notary buries his face in his registry, the parents rejoice, and the preoccupied Alain toys with the spinning wheel. Madame Simone presents him with the key to the hayloft and tells the youth where to find his bride. Alain unlocks the door. Lisette and Colin step out sheepishly, their clothes and hair covered with hay.

Madame Simone is scandalized. Before all the village, her daughter has ruined the family's reputation. Lisette begs her to understand. Colin joins Lisette, and both lovers kneel before her. At first Madame Simone refuses to listen. Then she realizes that the notary can quite easily make another marriage contract and consents. Lisette kisses her joyfully. Colin kisses her. The two lovers kiss, and Madame Simone embraces them both.

Ballet in two acts. Music by Ferdinand Hérold, freely adapted and arranged by John Lanchbery. Choreography by Frederick Ashton. Scenery and costumes by Osbert Lancaster. First presented by the Royal Ballet at the Royal Opera House, Covent Garden, January 28, 1960, with Nadia Nerina, David Blair, Stanley Holden, and Alexander Grant in the principal roles. First presented in the United States by the Royal Ballet at the Metropolitan Opera House, New York, September 14, 1960, with the same principals.

Although other versions of the ballet are often danced, Frederick Ashton's re-creation of *La Fille Mal Gardée* is now permanent in the modern repertory. In 1960 Tamara Karsavina, the ballerina who danced in the ballet in Russia, recalled an earlier production in the Covent Garden program: "This production we now regard as the turning point in the history of ballet; a break-away from the formal, pseudoclassical tradition; a ballet of action instead of a succession of conventional dances which use the plot as a peg on which to hang a succession of *entrées, pas seuls, pas d'ensemble* . . . The story lends itself admirably to ballet treatment; there is not a dance in it that does not flow directly out of a natural situation. It is a charming period piece singularly compatible with the artistic trends of today . . ."

The music for the ballet, entirely restudied and arranged by John Lanchbery after consulting varied scores for the ballet by Hertel, Feldt, and others, is based on the 1828 score of Ferdinand Hérold, then chorus master of the Paris Opéra. After a pleasant overture, the curtain rises. An inner drop curtain depicts a charming rural landscape with a village in the distance. Arnold Haskell in the Covent Garden program describes the action when this inner curtain rises:

ACT ONE, SCENE ONE—THE FARMYARD "Lise, the only daughter of Simone, a widow and owner of a prosperous farm, is in love with Colas, a young farmer, but her mother has more ambitious plans.

"The dawn of a busy day on the farm is heralded by the cock and his attendant hens. Lise, disappointed at not seeing Colas, leaves a ribbon tied in a lover's knot, as a token of her devotion. He finds it and ties it to his staff. The lovers meet, but are interrupted by Simone, who sets her daughter a task of churning butter. Colas, in hiding in the loft, joins her. The work is shared and then forgotten as they declare their love.

"The farm girls summon Lise to play, but her mind is elsewhere. Her suspicious and ever-watchful mother catches hold of her and chastises her. Just then Thomas, the prosperous and wealthy proprietor of a vineyard, arrives with his son Alain. Simone, aware of their mission, dismisses Lise. Thomas asks her hand for his son, and when Lise returns, Alain, coy and clumsy, shows off his paces. She is amused and a little shocked by his antics, but definitely not interested. They set off for the harvest.

ACT ONE, SCENE TWO—THE CORNFIELD "It is harvest time, and after working in the fields the harvesters, led by Colas, relax in a joyful dance. Lise and Alain dance, but Colas intervenes, and the young girl makes it clear where her preference lies. One of the harvesters plays the flute to the general merriment, and Alain thinks he will have a turn, but the harvesters mock him and he is rescued from their horseplay by his indignant father.

"The field is now left for the triumphant Colas, who dances with Lise. Simone joins in the merriment. But suddenly they are interrupted by a storm that drenches them, scattering them far and wide.

ACT TWO—INTERIOR OF THE FARM "Mother and daughter, soaked by the storm, return to the farmhouse. They sit down to spin: work, thinks the mother, should keep Lise out of mischief. But she is overcome by sleep and Lise, who has seen Colas through the gate, tries to take the key from her. Simone awakes and, in order to remain watchful, plays the tambourine for Lise to dance. But the tap grows feebler, she begins to nod, and now she is fast asleep. Lise runs to the door and makes love to Colas through the unfriendly bars. The knocking of the harvesters, coming for their pay, awakens Simone. Colas enters with them and conceals himself in a pile of straw. Simone tells her daughter to get on with her chores as she leaves to give the harvesters a drink. Lise, thinking she is alone, dreams of the delights of married life. Colas cannot resist, and comes out from hiding. She is bashful at first having been taken by surprise, but once again they declare their love, exchanging scarves as a token.

"As Simone reappears, Lise hustles Colas into her bedroom. The ever-suspicious mother realizes that the lovers have been meeting, and in her turn hustles Lise into the bedroom, locking the door.

"Alain and his father now arrive with a notary to complete the marriage contract. When it is signed, Simone hands Alain the key to the bedroom. After a moment of idiotic indecision, he opens the door, and to everyone's dismay, Colas and Lise emerge. The lovers fall on their knees to ask Simone for forgiveness and a blessing. In spite of the fury of Thomas and Alain, urged on by the notary and the villagers, she finally gives in amidst general rejoicing."

NOTES Andrew Porter, music and dance critic of *The Financial Times*, London, has said of this ballet: "The first act, in two parts, lasts just over an hour; the second, thirty-six minutes. There is not an ounce of padding. Invention tumbles on invention, and the whole thing is fully realized in dance. The second act, in fact, is continuous, *durchkomponiert;* there is no possible break for applause except between the sections of the *grand pas de deux;* just before the final gigue. The choreography is wonderfully fresh, and the shape of the scenes is beautifully balanced.

"There is comedy, sentiment, jollity, romance, flowing one into another. There is a clog dance for Widow Simone, brilliantly sustained; a 'parade' before the drop curtain which must be the most delightful of its kind ever done; a *valse des moissoneurs* in the first act which one would like to be twice as long; a stave dance; breathtaking 'Russian' lifts; passages which seem to be inspired by the virtuosity of the Georgians.

"Ribbons run like a motif through the first two scenes. They are used in a score of ingenious and beautiful ways, reaching their climax in a great maypole where the fleeting kaleidoscope of stage patterns is recorded by the plaited thread.

"To a far greater extent than any of the classics as we now know them, *La Fille Mal Gardée* seems to be all 'highlights,' without any of the stretches that we sit through for the sake of the best bits. And this cunningly varied and ceaseless flow of dance is constantly enlivened by the most brilliant inventions by the way, comic or touching, that give fullness to the ballet—far more of them than can be taken in at once."

FIREBIRD

Dramatic ballet in three scenes. Music by Igor Stravinsky. Choreography by Michel Fokine. Scenery and costumes by Golovine and Bakst. First presented by Diaghilev's Ballets Russes at the Théâtre National de l'Opéra, Paris, June 25, 1910, with Tamara Karsavina as the Firebird, *Michel Fokine as* Prince Ivan, *and Enrico Cecchetti as* Kastchei.

Firebird marks Igor Stravinsky's entry into the field of ballet music. Perhaps his most famous score, the original ballet to the music remained dormant for many years. In 1954, to commemorate the twenty-fifth anniversary of the death of Diaghilev, under whose auspices the original had been created, the Royal Ballet produced in London a reconstruction of the original, with scenery and costumes by Natalie Gontcharova. This was made possible by Serge Grigoriev, Diaghilev's régisseur for many years, Lubov Tchernicheva, and Tamara Karsavina. The revival was first presented at the Empire Theatre, Edinburgh, August 23, 1954, with Margot Fonteyn as the *Firebird,* Michael Somes as *Prince Ivan,* Svetlana Beriosova as the *Tsarevna,* and Frederick Ashton as *Kastchei.* This production was first given in the United States at the Metropolitan Opera House, September 20, 1955, with the same principals.

Fokine has described in his book *Memoirs of a Ballet Master* how he envisaged the action of the ballet, and the background to the collaboration that produced the final work. In the Royal Ballet revival, the curtain rises on the enchanted garden of the sinister Kastchei. A high golden fence protects his golden fruit and the lovely princesses he has captured. The Firebird now appears, followed by Prince Ivan. The Firebird attempts to steal the golden apples from Kastchei's magic tree but Ivan captures her. He vows that he will not let her go unless she gives him one of her feathers. With her feather as talisman, he is assured of her magic intercession if he should ever need it. The Firebird yields to his entreaties and leaves.

Now in the growing darkness Ivan learns from the most beautiful of the captive maidens held prisoner by Kastchei how the evil magician entraps innocent travelers and turns them into stone. Ivan is attracted to the lovely creature who tells him this strange story and they dance. At dawn they kiss and part, the girl warning him not to follow her.

Ivan does not heed the warning. Following after his beloved, he opens the gate to Kastchei's magic garden and alarms sound, bells peal, and swarms of monsters rush out. Kastchei emerges, his enslaved creatures do him homage, and he approaches Ivan menacingly. The wicked magician tries to turn him to stone but just then Ivan remembers the Firebird's feather. He waves the feather in Kastchei's face and the Firebird instantly reappears. She compels Kastchei's monsters to dance until they collapse. Then, remembering the great egg that holds the soul of the magician, she orders Ivan to steal it. Finding it, Ivan throws the egg into the air. As it falls and breaks, Kastchei dies. Ivan then is free to marry his princess. All at the ceremony rejoice. The Firebird flies away forever.

Music by Igor Stravinsky. Choreography by George Balanchine. Setting by Marc Chagall. Lighting by Jean Rosenthal. First presented by the New York City Ballet at the City Center, New York, November 27, 1949, with Maria Tallchief as the Firebird *and Francisco Moncion as* Prince Ivan.

The composer of *Firebird*, Igor Stravinsky, once said that Russian legends have as their heroes men who are "simple, naïve, sometimes even stupid, devoid of all malice, and it is they who are always victorious over characters that are clever, artful, complex, cruel and powerful." Prince Ivan in this ballet is such a hero: he is a simple hunter who stumbles into the eerie garden of an evil monster, there falls in love with a beautiful princess held captive by the ogre, and rescues her with a supernatural power granted him by a magical bird of fire.

SCENE ONE—A FOREST As the music to the ballet begins, we have that first suggestion of the mystery and magic that will control Ivan's destiny. No sooner has the orchestra—with its low, throbbing strings and baleful trombones—given us a hint of darkness and foreboding, than the curtain rises to present us with an enormous painting of the ballet's heroine, the Firebird who will help the prince to free the world of one of its monstrous evils. The Firebird is depicted as bright, glorious, and triumphant—a fantastic creature, half bird, half woman. She has the face and arms of a charming young girl and a body of shimmering feathers that tapers off in orange-speckled flame. This colorful figure is painted against a background of amorphous, purple shapes. The music now suggests unimagined giants plodding across the earth and a fairyland peopled with primeval beings sadly singing an accompaniment.

Now the painted curtain rises. It is dark, and as the stage brightens slightly, we can see in the background trees so thickly crowded that the sun can scarcely penetrate. Here in the forest we are transported visually to the world of fantasy at which the music has hinted, and when the prince enters, his bow stretched tightly, ready to destroy any creature concealed in the thicket, we understand why he hunts with care. Ivan wears a costume more becoming to an untutored Russian peasant than to a royal prince, but this serves only to remind us that we are watching a story of a time before the primitive court of the tsar was altered by European opulence.

Subdued, half-uttered cries come from behind the dark trees. Ivan looks about him, searching for the beasts that may lie waiting in the shadows, when a low, steady drum, followed by an answering horn, indicates that he is about to meet his prey. Suddenly the music whirs rapidly and brightly and from above a bright amber light races around and around the prince. Ivan, almost blinded, throws up his arms in astonishment and tries to avoid the shadow the light makes of his startled figure. He runs off, seeking the safe darkness. The music increases its speed, and on stage to its swift accompaniment dances the dazzling Firebird.

Her entrance is as strong and brilliant as the bright red she wears. As she crosses the stage in a series of swiftly executed leaps and poses, followed by that same amber light which announced her arrival, glints of light catch her figure in various attitudes to reveal the long red feather that rises high on her head. Her arms and shoulders are speckled with gold dust, and the shimmering red bodice reflects spangles of brilliance about her moving form. She dances frantically, in continuous movement, to music that mirrors her great joy in displaying vivid images of flight. Even here, in the secluded forest, the Firebird refuses to be earth-bound and seems to resist nature by performing dashing movements that whip the very air about her.

The prince emerges from the shadows to watch unseen. Wishing to capture this creature who moves so magnificently, he reacts with wonder as he discovers that this marvelous bird is also a ravishing woman. He follows her surreptitiously while the Firebird, unaware of the hunter who pursues her, darts about the stage climaxing her solo with rapid turns on point across the stage. This movement increases in momentum with the music, and just as her accelerating spin reaches its fullest force and the music its highest pitch, Ivan dashes forward and reaches out to catch the Firebird about the waist. Brought down to earth, she freezes at his touch, all movement ceasing. Slowly she backs away, in terror of the hunter, in modesty at sight of the man. She turns to escape, but Ivan, fascinated at her daring now that she is in his power, holds her secure. The Firebird, rigid with fear, her arms stiff across her body, falls back against him reluctantly, apparently resigned, but now her arms fly out and beat the air in a frantic effort to free herself.

Ivan will not release his prey, and the frightened Firebird, certain of death by his hand, pleads for mercy. The prince is moved to pity by this appeal for freedom and gently loosens his grasp. He holds out his arm, and the Firebird, in extended arabesque, falls across it, bending her head so that her headdress almost touches the floor at the prince's feet as she bows in tribute to his pity and courtesy.

Encouraged now by the prince's tenderness, the Firebird moves back to dance again. When she turns full circle, Ivan comes forward to support her. Moved by his compassionate strength, as Ivan is moved by her unclaimed love, the Firebird walks toward this man so strange to her. He holds her hand high, then she runs toward him, her body falling back full-length in mid-air. Ivan catches her swooping body and supports her again, as she repeats this movement of ultimate sacrifice and trust. Assured of his sympathy, the Firebird now dances with the prince.

Standing behind her, Ivan supports her arms with his own as the Firebird, standing on point, bends her knees to the floor, then rises to his embrace. Legs spread wide, she slides across the stage as Ivan holds her. The haunting melody of their *pas de deux* soars to its height as the Firebird is held motionless on point, her right leg extended in stillness. Then she falls back, and Ivan swings her around and around in great circles as her free arm flutters in flight. Reminded by this of her greater freedom in the air, the Firebird moves as if to leave the prince. He bows to her formally in homage, and in gratitude for his generosity in releasing her, the Firebird takes from her breast a brilliant red feather. She indicates to the prince that this feather is a magic charm: he need only wave it in the air and she will come to his aid, should he ever require it. Ivan, in respectful deference to the truly supernatural being he now understands the Firebird to be, thanks her and watches regretfully as she turns and leaps gloriously into the wings. The prince follows, transfixed as the music ends in enchanted serenity.

SCENE TWO—KASTCHEI'S GARDEN While Ivan remains in the shadows, marveling at his encounter with the Firebird, we hear a gay melody from the orchestra. Ten young princesses run in, happily dancing to its tune. They wear long peasant dresses with little caps, and their innocent, carefree gambols make it impossible for us to believe that they are, in reality, captives of the monster Kastchei who rules over the forest. Two of the young girls carry scarves and, as the group dances with simple but elegant grace, these two playfully direct the dancing of the others. They are all dancing together when Prince Ivan startles them. Shocked at the intrusion of a stranger in their dangerous world, the princesses gather together and whisper excitedly. Ivan is amused at their fear and approaches them. From a respectful distance, in mock seriousness and formality, he beckons one of the maidens to come to him. The princesses are agitated by this request and wonder at Ivan's audacity. Ivan insists, and one of the girls at last leaves the group. Ivan bows to her, then whispers softly in her ear. The girl is shocked by what he says to her and runs back to tell her friends. The maidens confer, and then the most beautiful one of them all, in sweet and nervous modesty, steps forward to greet the prince.

The two bow formally and, linking hands, lead the group in a *khorovod* or Russian round dance, to the accompaniment of folklike themes. The chorus of girls become so entwined about their two leaders that it is impossible for the prince and the princess to remain long together. They close their arms about one another, but their partners come amusingly to break their embrace. The two lovers dance with their friends until the light begins to fade. A trumpet is heard in the distance, and the girls gather together quickly in fear. The princess then hastily bids Ivan farewell and runs off with her companions. Ivan stands alone, bewildered at their behavior, as the music takes on mysterious darkness and hints of things unseen.

Ivan stares into the dark thicket about him and is suddenly afraid, but before he can leave the threatening darkness that seems to close in on him, a sharp crash of sound comes from the orchestra and dozens of weird monsters leap with a single bound into the stage and surround him. Green, brown, and multicolored creatures with hideous features and maimed limbs cavort about Ivan to fierce, militant beats from the orchestra. The monsters—some masked with the head of animals—divide into four groups and race backward and forward and sideways, each group trying to outdo the others in grotesque gestures of threat. One of the creatures is held upright, then thrown straight up into the air and caught by the others, only to be tossed up again. The music subsides, and all the creatures of this fantastic underworld fall on their faces as their master, Kastchei, enters menacingly. He is surrounded by the princess and her friends. Kastchei flourishes his dark cap at his creatures, and we glimpse his skeletonlike body. On his head he wears a spiked crown of burning gold. His fingernails, long as his hands, clutch at the air for victims to satisfy an insatiable appetite.

As Kastchei's slaves surround him in frantic attitudes of homage, Ivan moves to flee. But then he remembers the pledge of the Firebird, remembers that he need fear no danger, and brings out the magic feather. He runs, weaving in and out among the monsters, waving the charm in the air. The monsters try to close in on him. Kastchei stamps the earth in indignation and vows to kill the prince. To the theme to which they danced so playfully just a few moments before, the princesses encircle their evil lord and plead for mercy for Ivan. Kastchei dismisses them with curt disgust, but the prince, encouraged by the confusion he is causing among the monsters, races about with the brilliant red feather. The ogres step back, astounded at his fearlessness in the presence of the all-powerful Kastchei. Enormous snarls from the orchestra follow the prince as he provokes the demons to madness. Kastchei moves in to attack. Then a quick whir in the music proclaims the imminent arrival of the Firebird, come to Ivan's rescue.

The Firebird runs onto the scene with a magnificent leap, carrying over her head a naked golden sword. She hurriedly presents the sword to Ivan, then circles the stage in so rapid and fierce a spin that all the monsters are set to twirling with her. She exits quickly as Ivan falls upon Kastchei with the golden sword. The monster falls dead and Ivan, bathed now in the Firebird's brilliant light, holds the gleaming sword high in triumph as the music sounds his victory in a final crescendo.

The stage is dark. The prince stands alone among the fallen bodies of the monsters. The Firebird approaches. Harp strings are plucked gently. The prince finds the princess; he helps her rise. Both bow low before the beautiful Firebird, thanking her for saving their lives. The princess' friends rise and do obeisance before the magical bird, and the Firebird bows to them in return.

Free now of mortals, the Firebird dances alone. The stage is completely dark save for the light that follows her. She rises on point, extends one leg straight out, and whips the air in daring turns. The Firebird now revives the fallen monsters. She gestures over them as the harp sounds swooping arpeggios and consigns them to an endless sleep. The orchestra plays softly a flowing lullaby. The mysterious eerie forest of Ivan's adventure becomes serene as she sets all at peace with graceful, birdlike movement. Her mission over, the Firebird moves across the stage in a flowing dance, now turning, now stepping softly. Her feet tremble to release her body back into the air. Compelled to leave the earth, she moves away, her body thrown back. The last we see of her is her golden hand fluttering against the dark curtain at the side of the stage. The scene blacks out.

SCENE THREE—THE COURT OF PRINCE IVAN The music begins a quiet, subdued statement of an ancient Russian folk song. The melody that seems simple at first is changed gradually into a majestic song of thanksgiving. The music mounts in dignity and volume as light slowly comes up to show us a blue-green drop curtain. On this curtain are represented all those figures in fairyland who never will have any trouble in living happily ever after. Now that the music has asserted itself fully in praise and gratitude, we see two guards enter. They stand at attention in front of the curtain. The stage is fully lighted. Courtiers enter and bow to each other with each mighty chord from the orchestra, then join hands with the princesses who trip in to meet them. Now the drop curtain rises. Before another curtain of magical deep red, Ivan and his princess stand together. Pages enter with royal standards. A crimson carpet is pulled down the center of the stage, and onto it step Prince Ivan and his bride, in regal costume. All pay homage to the royal couple, and a page comes running out to present to the prince and princess a great wedding cake, aglow with hundreds of candles. The curtain falls as he kneels before them with his gift.

NOTES The New York City Ballet production of *Firebird* has been revised over the years, like all ballets of any interest, and most importantly perhaps by Jerome Robbins and me at the New York State Theater, May 28, 1970. Marc

Chagall had wanted for some time to do new designs for the costumes and to make other changes. The new *Firebird* was an attempt, in fact, to present Chagall's paintings in action, with Stravinsky's accompaniment. This provided an opportunity to make changes, too, in the choreography. Jerome Robbins and I shared the work, he taking responsibility for the scenes involving large ensembles. Gelsey Kirkland, Jacques d'Amboise, and Gloria Govrin were the principal dancers in this revival. Barbara Karimska's costumes to Chagall's designs were acknowledged masterpieces of art and craft, like all her marvelous work. Karinska's supremacy was appropriately acknowledged at this period by an exhibition of her designs at the Library and Museum of the Performing Arts, New York Public Library, Lincoln Center.

Music by Igor Stravinsky. Choreography by Maurice Béjart. First presented by the Paris Opéra Ballet at the Palais des Sports, Paris, October 31, 1970, with Paolo Bortoluzzi in the principal role. First presented in the United States by the Ballet of the Twentieth Century at the Brooklyn Academy of Music, New York, January 25, 1971.

To the choreographer Maurice Béjart, *Firebird* is a revolutionary act, a Maoist gesture. Béjart writes: "The Firebird is the Phoenix reborn from ashes. The Bird of Life and Joy, immortal, whose splendor and strength remain indestructible, untarnishable. . . ."

Referring to the original version of the *Firebird*, Béjart says: "Since then, the . . . ballet seems lame. What remains now is pure music that is true to a certain choreographic vision, but inappropriate to the complicated wanderings of the complete scenario" of the original. "There is no question about replacing one story with another of even transforming the original. Instead, let us try to free the emotion that fills the succession of scenes in a reduced version, and therein find the two major elements that startled at the creation: Stravinsky, Russian musician; Stravinsky, revolutionary musician. Let the dance become the abstract expression of these two elements that are always present in the music: a profound feeling of Russia and a certain rupture with traditional music, translated above all by an inhabitual rhythmic violence. The Firebird is the Phoenix reborn from ashes. The Poet, like the revolutionary, is a Firebird."

Interviewed in *The New Yorker* magazine (February 6, 1971), Béjart was even more specific about his viewpoint on *Firebird:* "The music is so strong, so modern, so full of life, but the Russian legend on which the ballet was based—the magical Firebird who enables a Prince to rescue a Princess from a wicked sorcerer—is impossible to translate on the modern stage. So I thought there must be a way to reach the spirit of the music. The ballet was composed shortly before the Russian Revolution, and as I started to read revolutionary poets such as Esenin and Mayakovsky, I discovered that there was a small group of avant-garde writers, artists, composers, and dancers working in this period who called themselves the Firebird. So I did an abstract ballet but tried to give the feeling of young intellectuals grouped around one boy searching for something new in life. The Firebird leader is a phoenix. He is destroyed, but he rises from the ashes and lives again. That is why we have two men dancing the Firebird instead of one ballerina. . . . Ballet has been a woman-dominated art since the middle of the nineteenth century, but in every folklore the male dancer is more important. In seventeenth-century France and Italy, where ballet was born, women were at first not even allowed to participate. For example, Louis XIV was a very good dancer, but never his queen. They called him the Sun King because he always took the part of the sun in his ballets. In the classic repertoire, we have the *entrechat,* the jump in which the dancer changes the position of his feet several times. The *entrechat-trois* is always called *le royal,* because the Sun King performed it exceptionally well. I think the day of the prima donna in dance, theater, and opera has passed into the history of our civilization. Now we begin to go in the other direction."*

* From "Béjart" by Jane Boutwell in "The Talk of the Town." Reprinted by permission; © 1971 The New Yorker Magazine, Inc.

Following this conviction, the action of the ballet depicts the history of a vigorous revolutionary band: their rise, fall and, miraculously, their rise again at the will of a dynamic boy. A group of young partisans in dungarees declare their faith in a revolt, making a pledge of faith in blood in a red spotlight. One of the group, a vigorous boy, discards his denims for a red costume and asserts leadership. He is hailed by the group and leads them in battle. While he loses the fight and his army is defeated, he rises from the dead, hailed by his band of Firebirds.

THE FOUR TEMPERAMENTS

Classic ballet in five parts. Music by Paul Hindemith. Choreography by George Balanchine. Scenery and costumes by Kurt Seligmann. Lighting by Jean Rosenthal. First presented by Ballet Society at the Central High School of Needle Trades, New York, November 20, 1946, with Gisella Caccialanza, Tanaquil LeClercq, Mary Ellen Moylan, Elise Reiman, Beatrice Tompkins, Todd Bolender, Lew Christensen, Fred Danieli, William Dollar, José Martínez, and Francisco Moncion as the principal dancers.

Subtitled "A Dance Ballet Without Plot," *The Four Temperaments* is an expression in dance and music of the ancient notion that the human organism is made up of four different humors, or temperaments. Each one of us possesses these four humors, but in different degrees, and it is from the dominance of one of them that the four physical and psychological types—melancholic, sanguinic, phlegmatic, and choleric—were derived. Greek medicine associated the four humors and temperaments with the four elements—earth, water, fire, and air—which to them composed the human body as well as the world.

Although the score is based on this idea of the four temperaments, neither the music nor the ballet itself make specific or literal interpretation of the idea. An understanding of the Greek and medieval notion of the temperaments was merely the point of departure for both composer and choreographer.

The ballet is in five parts that correspond to the divisions of the score. The first section, Theme, features three couples, who dance three *pas de deux* to different statements of the basic musical theme. The music is languidly paced at first; the strings carry the melody carefully, but effortlessly. The bright assertiveness of the piano interrupts this passage, and the music becomes syncopated, with a quick, tinkling brilliance. In the third statement the string orchestra and the piano combine to state the theme fully.

Melancholic, the first variation on the theme, begins sadly and slowly; a solo violin sings despondently against the piano's accompaniment. A dancer performs a helpless, despondent, and lonely variation. The tempo changes, and he is joined by two girls as the full orchestra plays with muted strings. Four mysterious girls stalk in fiercely, majestically, to the tune of a strong and vibrant march in which the piano joins percussively.

The second variation, Sanguinic, is bright and effusive in its waltz tempo. A ballerina and her partner dance with open gestures that are alternately sharp and flowing. A secondary group of four dancers accompanies them.

To the third variation, Phlegmatic, a dancer dances at first alone. His mood changes suddenly with the music. He is joined by four girls and with them dances a sequence of adroitly measured lightness to a gay, humorous melody.

After a brief variation by a ballerina who represents the choleric temperament, the entire ensemble returns to the stage for a recapitulation of their dances; this merges with the music for a finale characterized by high, extended lifts.

GAÎTÉ PARISIENNE

Ballet in one act. Music by Jacques Offenbach. Choreography by Leonide Massine. Book by Comte Étienne de Beaumont. Scenery and costumes by Comte Étienne de Beaumont. First presented by the Ballet Russe de Monte Carlo at the Théâtre de Monte Carlo, April 5, 1938, with Nina Tarakanova as the Glove Seller, *Eugenia Delarova as the* Flower Girl, *Jeannette Lauret as* La Lionne, *Leonide Massine as the* Peruvian, *Frederic Franklin as the* Baron, *and Igor Youskevitch as the* Officer. *First presented in the United States by the Ballet Russe de Monte Carlo at the Metropolitan Opera House, New York, October 12, 1938, with Alexandra Danilova as the* Glove Seller; *the other principals were the same as those who danced the première in Monte Carlo.*

The trumpets and snare drum, which begin the overture to this ballet with loud and persistent good humor, proclaim a tale of the night life of old Paris, a story of romance, convivial dancing, and perpetual high spirits. The jubilant rhythm and sparkling melody of the music remind us of a time when love was brief and casual, but intense, of a time when the day began at nine o'clock in the evening.

The curtain rises on the most popular room of a fashionable restaurant in nineteenth-century Paris. High green draperies are looped back against brass pillars; brass chandeliers flood the room with light. Marble-topped tables and gold chairs stand at the back. Four waiters and four cleaning girls are preparing the *salon* for the evening's entertainment. The boys flick the tables and chairs with their towels and dance comically to amuse the girls. They run forward and sit at the front of the stage at the end of their act.

A girl with flowers in her hair enters gaily. She shakes hands with the waiters, who gather around her adoringly. This is the flower girl. She presents each boy with a bouquet. They reward her with a drink, and the flower girl joins them in a dance in which she toasts her admirers. One of the boys lifts her up to his shoulders and another kneels below her.

Three ladies of easy virtue—the *cocodettes*—enter with their escorts. The girls are dressed cheerfully in loud, candy-striped dresses; their companions wear black jackets and berets. The flower girl sets up her tray of flowers and leaves with the waiters. The *cocodettes* dance a lively mazurka with their partners. The waiters return to watch, but soon the company is distracted by the entry of the ballet's heroine, the beautiful glove seller. The men desert their partners and cluster around her. She carries a basket of gloves on her arm and tries to attend to her business, but the men insist that she dance with them. She is lifted high, then circles the stage as all stop to admire her. The glove seller is not as pert and flirtatious as the flower girl, yet her beauty is more striking.

Everyone is watching her when the gay Peruvian, just arrived in Paris, hustles in to a whistling tune. He has been so eager to get to the café and enjoy the proverbial night life that he has brought his bags with him. He scuttles about the stage in uncontrollable excitement at the possibilities of the evening, amusing the girls, who know that—though his pockets may be filled with gold—he is incapable of stopping long enough to spend it on any one of them: he will always pursue pleasure, but never enjoy it. Finally he drops his bags and goes over to the flower girl, who places a *boutonnière* in his white lapel. He wiggles with delight as the girls watch him. Only the glove seller does not notice him. The Peruvian is fascinated. He sneaks up on her and asks for a pair of gloves. The girl obliges and tries to fit him. The Peruvian dances even as he stands still.

The baron enters. A waiter takes his cape, and the flower girl, attracted by his handsome uniform, immediately goes over to him. The baron, however, has seen the glove seller; gently ignoring the other girl, he turns to her, introduces himself modestly, and asks her to dance. The glove seller responds graciously, and the guests retire as the two come forward and dance to a romantically rhythmic waltz. The couple move together not as if they had just met, but as if they were predestined to know one another; their dance is touching, in its quiet, flowing warmth.

In the background the jovial Peruvian entertains the *cocodettes.* With a flourish, he ceremoniously orders a bottle of champagne. He sips a glass, spits, and stamps his feet. The girls encourage him as he orders another bottle. He approves the new wine and offers it to the ladies. His flirtations are interrupted by the arrival of five soldiers and an officer, who strut into the café as if they expected all the girls to notice only them. The girls oblige them. The couples perform a martial dance at the conclusion of which the girls hang about the soldiers' necks in mock farewell as the soldiers salute them.

All are startled by the sudden entrance of La Lionne, the fashionable beauty of the day. She sweeps into the café in her red velvet dress and greets the group condescendingly; the girls are furious, the men anxious to please her. La Lionne's escort, the duke, is unable to make up his mind whether to be pleased or annoyed. Her companion, the lady in green, seeks an alliance among the men.

La Lionne makes eyes at the officer, who abandons his attempt to take up with the beautiful glove seller. The Peruvian returns. He douses himself liberally with perfume and approaches the glove seller. As he whispers in her ear, she plagues the baron by pretending to agree to the Peruvian's suggestion. The baron is furious with her. The duke is furious with La Lionne. Both fight with their rivals, and the guests, who seem to have been waiting for such an outbreak, take sides and join in the contest. The scene becomes riotous. It is too much for the Peruvian, who crawls under a table, his limbs quaking. The restaurant is cleared. The waiters return and see the Peruvian, who doesn't dare look up. They pound on the table, and the terrified playboy rushes off, carrying the table on his head.

The baron and the glove seller re-enter and, to a sumptuous waltz, dance together. Their mutual love now assured, the two dance in reunited harmony. No sooner have they finished than the café comes to life again. The dazzling cancan dancers enter with their dancing master, and all the guests regather to watch them display their high, bold kicks. The girls form in a line as the dancing master commands, one by one they fall to the floor in a split. The crowd is delighted and everyone joins in the boisterous dance, some taking the cancan girls for their partners. The Peruvian enters with his top hat. The girls circle him and rotate his hat about their slippers.

The whole cast is assembled on the stage for the finishing bars of the heated dance. All the girls are lifted high; their legs fall back in the air. The girls fan themselves briskly. The lights dim; wraps are brought. The girls take their partners' arms; the music becomes soft and mellifluous; and the couples glide away as if they were carried by quietly moving gondolas into the night—the baron with the glove seller, the flower girl with the duke, La Lionne with the officer. The glove seller, her hair covered with a black mantilla, waves farewell and falls back in the baron's arms. The Peruvian is left alone. The couples wave at him. He sulks.

GALA PERFORMANCE

Ballet in two parts. Choreography by Antony Tudor. Music by Sergei Prokofiev. Scenery and costumes by Hugh Stevenson. First presented by the London Ballet at Toynbee Hall, London, December 5, 1938, with Maude Lloyd, Gerd Larsen, Peggy van Praagh, Hugh Laing, and Antony Tudor in principal roles. First presented in the United States by Ballet Theatre at the Majestic Theatre, New York, February 11, 1941. Scenery and costumes by Nicolas de Molas. The cast was headed by Nora Kaye, Nana Gollner, Karen Conrad, Hugh Laing, and Antony Tudor.

Gala Performance is a comedy, telling a joke about ballet and three different ballerinas. Today many of us are inclined to stay away from ballet because we think it's made up of silly mannerisms. *Gala Performance* shows us these mannerisms (exaggerates them in the style of its period) and makes us laugh. Three famous ballerinas—the Queen of the Dance (from Moscow), the Goddess of the Dance (from Milan), and the Daughter of Terpsichore (from Paris)—are performing on the same stage for the first time in their lives. In their attempts to outdo each other, the dancers invoke every trick of their trade: they not only compete in respect to their dancing, but resort to any ruse that will secure the most applause.

The time of this *Gala Performance* is about sixty years ago; the place is the Theatre Royal in London. The music is by Prokofiev: the first movement of the *Concerto No. 3 in C for Piano* (for Part One) and the *Classical Symphony* (for Part Two).

PART ONE The curtain rises on a backstage scene. The closed curtain of the Theatre Royal is the backdrop of the setting, and in the harsh light before the performance begins we watch the nervous, hurried preparations for an unprecedented program of ballet. Two *coryphées* come out through the wings and begin to warm up. Others join them. These girls are members of the Theatre Royal's *corps de ballet,* the chosen few who will have the honor of appearing with the three guest ballerinas. They are quite naturally frightened and wait apprehensively for the arrival of the great dancers. They practice dance steps, turn their backs to us, and pose in the direction of the audience behind the curtain. Other girls and a number of boys—attendant cavaliers to the ballerinas—come on stage.

A woman in black, the theater dresser, enters and adjusts the costumes of the *coryphées*. Next comes the ballet master, who watches the *corps de ballet* as they quickly run through the steps they will dance when the curtain rises. All the company turn expectantly as the Russian ballerina approaches the stage. She walks commandingly. Everyone on stage is beneath her notice, and she accepts the homage of the company with marked indifference. Then, as she scrutinizes the *corps de ballet*, she notices that one of the *coryphées* is wearing a necklace. She motions to the girl, reprimands her, and orders her to remove it. She herself is loaded down with jewelry, to which she now directs her attention while the distraught girl dashes off, weeping.

The ballet master and the conductor hover about the ballerina. The conductor promises to heed her warning about the proper tempo, while the ballet master can only assure her that his *corps de ballet* will be impeccably unobtrusive. The Queen of the Dance makes final adjustments in her richly embroidered red dress, fixes the high feather in her hair, and turns toward the curtain to rehearse her bows. Her way of acknowledging applause seems to be more important than the dance that will apparently receive it, and the girls and boys are secretly amused at the number of kisses she expects to throw to her audience. She is watching out of the corner of her eye, however; she snaps her fingers at the *corps* and orders them to practice their routine.

This severe scene is interrupted by the arrival of the Daughter of Terpsichore, the sparkling French ballerina, who bounds onto the stage in a fluffy, delicate costume appropriate to her exuberance. She can hardly keep still long enough to be introduced to her Russian peer, who naturally scorns her, and has no time to be regal and domineering. But she has time to be demanding and takes the conductor aside to instruct him about the tempo *she* will require. Where the Russian ballerina will make her every wish a command, the scatterbrained French dancer imagines that everything will be all right because everyone loves her and wants to please her. We are suddenly thankful that this is a ballet and not a play, for the silly French ballerina must surely never stop talking.

But if we think that the Russian and French ballerinas are vain and absurd, we have not yet seen their peer in mannerism. The Italian ballerina, the famed Goddess of the Dance, now enters. She is dressed in dignified black and walks across the stage with slow, studied elegance; her steps are carefully measured: every time she puts a foot forward, it seems to hesitate, as if it were considering the worthiness of the floor she deigns to walk upon. Automatically she holds out her hand to be kissed. The cavaliers, prompted by the ballet master, pay tribute to her. Now she orders the dresser to hold up a mirror so that she can make final adjustments to her coiffure and elaborate headdress. The dresser's attention wanders for a moment, and the Goddess of the Dance rewards her with a smack.

The ballet master huddles with the *corps de ballet*, giving them their final instructions. The stage lights come up; some of the dancers make a final rush to the rosin box so that their shoes will not slip on stage; others wish themselves luck by repeating private superstitious gestures; and one wonders how the performance will ever begin. But suddenly everyone is miraculously in place. The drop curtain rises, and the scene blacks out.

PART TWO—GALA PERFORMANCE When the lights come up again, we are the audience at the Theatre Royal. Instead of the backstage picture, we now see an ornate setting, draped in orange and red, that might represent any regal hall. Eight *coryphées* are on stage. They wait tremulously for their cue and begin to dance. They are nervous, but not too nervous to try to ingratiate themselves with the audience: each tries to outleer the others with absurd chorine smiles.

Four cavaliers lead the Russian ballerina on stage. They bow and leave the stage. The ballerina comes forward slowly, almost to the footlights, and begins to dance when she has played upon the anticipation of the audience to establish what she doubtless imagines is a personal, lovable relation. In her dance she attempts to hit the audience between the eyes with the most elementary pirouettes, staring them down, *daring* them not to like her. And she wins our applause. When she leaps off into the wings, one of her cavaliers, invisible to the audience, catches her, and she poses in endless midflight. She accepts applause with no modesty whatsoever and finds it difficult to leave the stage for an instant while it continues.

Now the Italian ballerina comes on. She comes forward to the footlights, tantalizing us with possibilities, rises on point as if it were the supreme sacrifice, and nods curtly at the conductor. The dance she executes is an adagio, in which she eschews the assistance of her partner. No one can serve her great art but herself; the audience should be grateful to be watching her. She balances as long as possible in every pose and is coldly indifferent to gasps of amazement from the audience: to her, nothing is impossible. When her dance ends, she allows a cavalier to lift her off into the wings. As she returns for her curtain calls, she walks with the measured steps of her backstage entrance. After obligingly taking applause with the company and her cavaliers, she finally shoos them off so she can acknowledge her due alone.

The French ballerina now takes the stage and covers it with rapid leaps. She responds to applause by inflicting upon the audience an ingratiating and somewhat irritating charm.

The solos are over, and the three ballerinas appear together in the coda. They come out on stage and stand together and for a moment they are equals, but directly they begin to dance, competition is rampant. The French and Russian ballerinas try every means to attract the attention of the audience and thereby lose the contest, for the Italian "goddess" makes the audience love her by treating them as if they were idiots. She is surely in command of the whole situation and only at the final curtain does she give any sign of respecting any gift the audience might bestow on her. When the three ballerinas receive flowers, she manages to grab more bouquets than the other two. Not to be outdone, the French ballerina steps in front of the curtain to pick up more bouquets which the audience has thrown to her. But when the curtain rises again, the Italian still has the most flowers. The other two ballerinas look at her and then at us and smile and smile and smile.

GARTENFEST

Music by Wolfgang Amadeus Mozart. Choreography by Michael Smuin. Scenery by Jack Brown. Costumes by Marcos Paredes. Lighting by Jean Rosenthal. First presented by American Ballet Theatre at the Brooklyn Academy of Music, December 18, 1968, with Sallie Wilson and Paul Nickel, Ted Kivitt and Ivan Nagy, and Cynthia Gregory in principal roles. Conducted by Jaime Leon. Soli violinist: Guy Lumia.

Gartenfest is a dance ballet to Mozart's early *Cassation No. 1 in G* (he was but thirteen at the time), music suitable for use in the open air, where much great eighteenth-century music was performed. The scene is appropriately, therefore, a garden, where dancers perform a series of diversions, varying in character with the music. There is no plot, only the inherent dance quality of the score and its design. The ballet is in six movements: *Menuetto,* for a lead boy and girl and four couples; *Allegro,* a bright and vigorous dance for two boys who compete in varied complex combinations of steps, beats, and jumps; *Andante,* a solo for a ballerina, supported by an ensemble of six girls; *Menuetto,* a dance for three couples; *Adagio,* a *pas de trois* for a ballerina and two boys; and *Finale: Allegro assai,* a dance for the ballerina who introduced the ballet, with the entire cast.

NOTES Reviewing *Gartenfest* in *Dance and Dancers* magazine, Patricia Barnes said that "Ballet Theater has been lucky enough to find within its ranks another young man, Michael Smuin, who with his latest work shows himself to have genuine choreographic potential. . . . *Gartenfest* was a genuine success, most notable for the way in which it exploited the talents of its dancers, mostly drawn from the younger principals and the most promising soloists. . . . The choreography had the same fluent charm as the score."

GISELLE

Fantastic ballet in two acts. Music by Adolphe Adam. Choreography by Jules Perrot and Jean Coralli. Book by Vernoy de Saint-Georges, Théophile Gautier, and Jean Coralli. Scenery by Pierre Ciceri. Costumes by Paul Lormier. First presented at the Théâtre de l'Académie Royale de Musique, Paris, June 28, 1841, with Carlotta Grisi as Giselle, *Lucien Petipa as* Albrecht, *Adèle Dumilâtre as* Myrtha, Queen of the Wilis, *and Jean Coralli as* Hilarion. *First presented in England at Her Majesty's Theatre, London, March 12, 1842, with Carlotta Grisi and Jules Perrot in the principal roles. First presented in Russia at the Bolshoi Theatre, St. Petersburg, December 30, 1842, with Elena Andreyanova as* Giselle. *First presented in Italy at the Teatro alla Scala, Milan, January 17, 1843, with choreography by A. Cortesi and music by N. Bajetti. First presented in the United States at the Howard Atheneum, Boston, January 1, 1846, with Mary Ann Lee and George Washington Smith in the leading roles.*

Giselle is such an important and popular ballet that people who know something about dancing are always talking about it. They speak of Pavlova's Giselle, Karsavina's Giselle, Spessivtzeva's Giselle, Markova's Giselle, and those who are unfamiliar with ballet think it strange: it's as if the habitual theatre-goer spent all of his time talking about *Hamlet,* without paying much attention to modern plays.

But there is good reason for the balletgoer to be preoccupied with *Giselle.* Like *Hamlet, Giselle* is a classic: it is not only important historically, it also happens to be good. It is just as popular today as when it was first performed, more than 130 years ago. People go to see *Giselle* and to see new ballerinas dance it for the same reason we go to see new interpretations of *Hamlet:* the work is such a good one that we always discover something in it we hadn't seen before, some variation in performance that brings out an aspect that seemed previously concealed; we learn something new.

There are many ballets important to history: the ballet in

which the ballerina first discarded her heeled slipper, the ballet in which she first stood on the tips of her toes, and the ballet in which she jumped dangerously but effortlessly from a height of twenty feet to be caught in her lover's arms. But these ballets, with all their innovations, haven't come down to us; they are important only in a narrow academic sense. *Giselle* has come down to us, has been performed by one ballet company or another ever since its first performance, because it combines innovation with drama and dancing that make us forget all about history.

Giselle's innovation is its summing up of what we know as the Romantic ballet. To be romantic about something is to see what you are and to wish for something entirely different. This requires magic. The mysterious and supernatural powers that romantic poetry invoked to secure its ideal soon became natural to the theatre, where dancers attired in billowy white seemed part of the world and yet also above it. Marie Taglioni in the ballet *La Sylphide* (see page 459), popularized this fashion so completely that the sylph became ballet's symbol for romantic love—the girl who is so beautiful, so light, so pure that she is unattainable: touch her, and she vanishes.

Poets and novelists of the time were all interested in stories of the romantically supernatural, stories that told of lovely young girls whose love was never fulfilled because of intervening powers. One of these stories told of girls known as Wilis, who were engaged to be married yet died before their wedding days. In the evening they rose from their graves and danced alone in the moonlight. Their dancing was impassioned with their anger at death; but, dressed in their flowing bridal gowns and endowed with unearthly gifts of movement, their ghostly forms seemed never to touch the ground.

The Wilis were so beautiful that it was simple for them to attract young men into their midst. But they were as dangerous as they were irresistible. They danced with the young men who came only to trap them: their suitors were compelled to dance until they died.

This story of the Wilis seemed to be ideal for ballet: it made the story of *La Sylphide* look like merely the first step in the attainment of the romantic ideal. For the heroine of that ballet was purely a creature of the imagination, a figure in the hero's dream. We had admired her beauty and pitied her, but she was too illusory a character to make us feel deeply. What would accomplish this, what would make us care about such a character, would be to give her a basis in real life, to make her real and unreal at the same time—like the Wilis.

The poet, novelist, and critic Théophile Gautier read the story of the Wilis as it was related by Heinrich Heine, and thought it would make a good ballet and would be particularly fine for Carlotta Grisi. Gautier had seen Grisi's début in Paris and had fallen in love with her. Under the tutelage of her husband, Jules Perrot, the great dancer and choreographer, she had become the potential rival of Marie Taglioni and Fanny Elssler.

However, the story of the ballet required considerable work before it was resolved. There was the problem of how the heroine would become a Wili, under what circumstances would she die? Gautier presented this difficulty to the popular librettist Vernoy de Saint-Georges. Within three days they had contrived a suitable story and the libretto had been accepted at the Paris Opéra. Within a week the score had been written and the ballet was in rehearsal. At its first performance, a few days later, *Giselle ou les Wilis* was proclaimed the triumphant successor to *La Sylphide* and the greatest ballet of its time. For the Giselle he created for her, Grisi owed Gautier her greatest triumph and Gautier's attachment later obliged the ballerina to leave Perrot.

ACT ONE—A VILLAGE ON THE RHINE The first curtain is preceded by a brief overture. The contrast between the strong, virulent opening measures and the light romantic melody that follows gives us an indication of the pitiless fate that will govern this love story. When the curtain rises, we see a part of a wooden village on the Rhine. It is vintage time, and the people of the village are preparing to celebrate. Peasant couples cross the stage, talking to each other affectionately; a few girls enter alone, wave in greeting to their friends, link arms, and follow them off to the left, near the entrance to a cottage. This is the cottage of Giselle, the lovely village maiden who lives with her mother, Berthe. On the right we discern the entrance to another cottage.

The stage is empty for an instant. Trumpets sound a warning. Hilarion, a gamekeeper, enters. He is dressed somewhat rudely and his gestures are not refined, but he is a man of genuine feeling. Almost directly he walks over to the door of Giselle's cottage. He is in love. Hilarion is about to knock on the door when he hears someone approaching. He looks around hurriedly and hides behind Giselle's cottage to watch.

Two men enter. They are Albrecht, Duke of Silesia, a handsome young man who wears a royal cape over his peasant clothes, and his squire, Wilfrid. Albrecht, too, goes to Giselle's door. Hilarion, who watches the scene jealously, is interested in the cape and sword that Albrecht wears, for Hilarion, like Giselle, knows this young man only as Loys, a peasant. Albrecht stands before Giselle's cottage and holds his hands over his heart. He, too, is in love and has put on peasant disguise in order that his love may be returned. Wilfrid, his attendant, is not in favor of his master's love for Giselle and begs him to come away. Albrecht refuses. He gives his cape and sword to Wilfrid and dismisses him. Wilfrid conceals the cape and sword in the cottage on the right and reluctantly withdraws.

Albrecht, at the door of Giselle's cottage, listens, then knocks. The music anticipates. He runs and hides. Giselle emerges from the house. She is expecting Albrecht and runs out happily. She dances joyfully and beautifully, as if she wanted to be watched. But no one is there! She looks about, acts as if she were indifferent, and begins to dance again. Now she hears something. She stops and poses as she listens carefully. Albrecht is blowing kisses to her! But still he will not show himself. Giselle is annoyed at this teasing, stamps her foot impatiently, and prepares to go back into the house. At this point Albrecht steps out before her. Giselle frowns and pretends that she is not glad to see him. He nudges her shoulder, and she bows low before him, still unsmiling. She runs to the cottage door, lest her pretense break down. Albrecht stands before the door to prevent her escape, then reaches out and gently takes her wrist. Now she smiles, looking up at him with amused reproach.

The two lovers dance across the stage together and sit on a crude wooden bench at the right. Albrecht tries to sit close to Giselle, but she edges away every time he moves closer. Again she tries to go back into the house, and again Albrecht prevents her.

Suddenly Albrecht is completely serious. He expresses to Giselle his eternal love and vows that he will always be faithful to her. Giselle acts as if she did not take him at his word and, to prove this, she picks a flower and begins to pluck its petals in a game of he-loves-me-loves-me-not. Albrecht vigorously nods his head when the petals say he-loves-me, but the last petal she chooses to pick turns out to be loves-me-not. Giselle throws the flower to the ground and begins to cry. To comfort her, Albrecht picks up the flower again and declares that the last petal is really he-loves-me. Giselle is fully consoled and, linking her arm through Albrecht's, dances again with him.

The lovers are so absorbed in each other that they do not notice Hilarion, who has emerged from his hiding place. The gamekeeper boldly interrupts their rendezvous and separates them. Before they know what has happened, Hilarion is attacking Albrecht and warning him not to make love to Giselle. Giselle thinks that Hilarion is simply jealous and upbraids him for eavesdropping. Hilarion kneels before her and assures her that he alone truly loves her. Her anger mounting, Giselle dismisses Hilarion with rude laughter. The gamekeeper regards Albrecht with suspicion and hatred and, as he leaves the scene, shakes his fists at him.

Giselle is still shaken by this scene. Albrecht holds her in his arms and reassures her softly. They walk together. Village girls now enter, carrying huge baskets of grapes. They are all friends of Giselle's, and when they begin to dance, she joins them, dancing in their midst to a bright, melodious waltz. Albrecht watches Giselle from the bench near by. She soon runs over and asks him to join in. Boys join the girls as Albrecht and Giselle dance around the stage. The two lovers blow kisses to each other as the music accompanies their dance with a soft, hesitant theme that tinkles gently. The waltz ensemble ends as Albrecht holds Giselle on his knee.

Berthe, Giselle's mother, opens the cottage door and steps out. She does not wish to interfere with the festivities, but she is genuinely worried. Giselle playfully hides behind her friends, but her mother discovers her. She upbraids her daughter for dancing so much and reminds her that her heart will fail. Berthe attempts to impress Giselle with the truth of what she says by warning her that if she dies, she will become one of the Wilis, one of those creatures doomed to dance forever, even in death.

Giselle's friends take Berthe's tale more seriously than her daughter does. She wishes to dance again and goes to Albrecht. Berthe, however, takes her by the hand, and together they go into the cottage. The door closes. The disappointed Albrecht wanders off, and the villagers disperse.

Now that the stage is empty, Hilarion, bent on vengeance, approaches Giselle's cottage. He does not know how he can convince the girl that she is being deceived. A hunting horn sounds in the distance. Hilarion hears a hunting party come his way and seeks concealment in Albrecht's cottage.

Wilfrid, Albrecht's squire, is the first of the hunting party to enter. He looks about apprehensively, lest his master still be present. The prince of Courland and his daughter, Bathilde, follow with huntsmen and members of the court. The prince gestures to Wilfrid that they are in need of refreshment and rest and orders him to knock at Giselle's door.

Berthe responds to Wilfrid's knock. Seeing the prince and his daughter, she bows low before them and invites them to partake of whatever humble refreshment she can offer. She signals inside the house, and two girls bring out a table and stools, metal goblets, and a pitcher of wine.

Giselle steps out of the house and is astonished to see the royal party. She bows to Wilfrid, thinking him a prince. Wilfrid indicates the true prince; Giselle curtsies to him and his daughter and tries to assist in their entertainment.

Bathilde is kind to the girl and indicates to her father, "How beautiful she is!" Wilfrid pours the wine, and the prince and Bathilde drink. While they sit at the table, Giselle kneels surreptitiously at Bathilde's feet and touches the hem of her long dress. Giselle has not seen such expensive fabric before and remarks its beauty when Bathilde looks down and sees her. Bathilde takes Giselle aside and asks her how she spends her day. "Weaving and spinning," Giselle replies. "But are these the things you like to do best?" Bathilde wonders. "No," Giselle indicates, "I like best to dance," and so saying dances several steps before Bathilde.

Giselle's mother disapproves and is about to reprimand her daughter, but the dance is quickly over. Bathilde wishes to express her admiration for the peasant girl by giving her a present. With the prince's consent, she takes off her necklace and, calling Giselle to her, places it about the girl's neck. Giselle, in rapture, kisses her hand and proudly shows the necklace to her mother.

The hunting party now accepts Giselle's invitation to rest within the cottage. Wilfrid remains without, ready to rouse the prince with the hunting horn should there be good cause for the hunt to continue. Wilfrid dismisses the huntsmen and follows after them.

Hilarion comes forth from Albrecht's cottage. He carries Albrecht's sword in his hand. He looks about quickly, sees no one, and gestures in triumph: now perhaps Giselle will believe him! He exits as the peasant girls and boys return to resume their dancing. They knock at Giselle's door and finally persuade her mother to allow her to join them. The girls and boys recline in a semicircle about Giselle, who dances a brilliant solo. Albrecht appears as the girls dance. He and Giselle join her friends, and as the dance ensemble ends, the lovers embrace.

The music crashes ominously. Hilarion runs out, tears the lovers apart, and tells Giselle what he has learned: "You might love this man, but he is an impostor." He rushes out, retrieves Albrecht's sword, and places it in Giselle's hand. Albrecht is motionless with horror. He knows that the gamekeeper is right, but he knows that this is not the way for

Giselle to learn the truth. She will never believe him again, never believe his love. Giselle seems to think Hilarion is lying; it does not occur to her that her lover has wronged her.

Wilfrid enters and attempts to protect his master. Hilarion persists in reminding Giselle that the sword is Albrecht's. She goes to Albrecht. With great faith she asks him if the gamekeeper is speaking the truth. Albrecht bows his head; he cannot speak. Then, looking up at Hilarion, who imagines that a duke cannot love as truly as a gamekeeper, seizes the sword and attacks him. Only Wilfrid prevents him from murdering the gamekeeper. The sword falls to the ground. Hilarion is glorying in his revenge so much that he does not notice what he has done to Giselle. He takes down the hunting horn and blows on it to summon the prince. Sobbing in her mother's arms, Giselle cannot yet believe what she has learned.

The prince and his daughter come out of the house with their party. The prince is surprised to see Albrecht in peasant's clothes; Bathilde goes to Albrecht and asks him what is wrong, why he is dressed like this? Giselle watches him closely. When he kneels before Bathilde and kisses her hand, Giselle tears herself from her mother's arms and accosts Bathilde. Albrecht tries to caution Bathilde, but before he can prevent it, she has pointed to the ring on her finger: she is engaged to Albrecht, Duke of Silesia.

Giselle, her heart broken, is so defenseless that her reason begins to disintegrate. Fiercely she tears the necklace Bathilde gave her from her neck and dashes it to the ground. She falls before her mother. Berthe comforts her as best she can and tries to quiet her and loosens her hair. Albrecht attempts to speak to her, to assure her of his love, but she will not listen. The girl is so stricken with grief, so helpless without the love she lived by, that all present, courtiers and peasants alike, pity her.

Giselle staggers to her feet. She moves about the stage slowly and pathetically, reliving her moments of happiness with Albrecht. With her reason gone, this is all she can think of. She picks up an imaginary flower and to herself plays another game of he-loves-me-loves-me-not. She circles the stage, and all the people stand back. Suddenly Giselle sees Albrecht's sword lying forgotten on the ground. She runs to it and, taking it up at the pointed end, holds it in front of her. Hypnotized by her madness, her friends do not move. Giselle bends low and drags the sword about with her, its handle rattling as she trails it around the stage at the feet of her friends. Then, before anyone can move, she raises the sword high and forces its point into her heart. Albrecht leaps across to her and seizes the sword.

The prince and Bathilde withdraw. Here they can only cause agony. Giselle, dying in her mother's arms, rises and goes to Albrecht. Her mind is now completely gone and she imagines that there has never been anything wrong, that he is her lover as before. She begins to dance with him, and again the soft, hesitant theme of romance that accompanied one of their happy dances together is repeated. Giselle awkwardly, falteringly, repeats the steps that she formerly danced with such grace. Then, in the midst of the dance, she is frightened. She runs to her mother, but falls to the ground before she can reach her embrace. Albrecht despairs as Berthe bends over her daughter. But Giselle asks for him. He comes to her and looks down into her eyes, which even now seek only his. He declares again his imperishable love. Giselle reaches up to touch his face in a gesture of forgiveness; then her hand falls. She is dead.

Albrecht rises and drags Hilarion to see what his jealousy has accomplished. As the gamekeeper weeps and kneels beside Giselle, Albrecht seizes the sword and again tries to kill him. Wilfrid again prevents him. Albrecht weeps beside Giselle. The dead girl lies before him, her arms crossed on her breast. The villagers turn their faces away to hide the grief they share.

ACT TWO—WITHIN A FOREST GLADE AT MIDNIGHT In the second act we pass to a scene and a mood entirely different from that of Act One. Our first hint of this comes in the music. The strings sing softly against a rippling harp; all is quiet and ethereal. The curtain rises on a scene misty with the dewy night. The moon penetrates the thick trees occasionally; its light is reflected in a nearby lake, and in this dimness we discover Giselle's grave at the left. Her name is inscribed on a large cross that stands above the grassy mound. In the dark-blue sky, small shimmering lights appear.

Three huntsmen with a lantern enter to rest. They sit down near the lake. Hilarion joins them. Soon the men are disturbed by the eerie atmosphere of the place. They have heard tales that Wilis danced here and they fear the place is haunted. The lights in the sky are not constant, they appear to shimmer at will. Hilarion, aware that Giselle's grave is close by, becomes apprehensive. He approaches the grave. The men warn him to leave. Hilarion is reluctant, but joins his friends as they depart.

Across the back of the stage a veiled figure in a long white dress moves flowingly. She is Myrtha, Queen of the Wilis. She enters, crosses the stage rapidly, and again appears at the back. At her second entry, she has removed her veil. She bows, poses in deep, still arabesque, and begins to dance. Her movements are confident, controlled, beautiful, but they possess no warmth. The supernatural powers Myrtha possesses allow for nothing but perfection. She moves more rapidly now; the quickness of her dancing is brilliant and hard, like a diamond. She gathers two fern branches from the lakeside, throws them into the forest to dedicate the place to her awful purpose, and circles the stage in a brilliant display of virtuosity.

Now, with her wand, she calls forth the Wilis. Instantly obedient to her command, they appear on either side of the stage, their hands crossed over their breasts. Myrtha orders them to remove their white veils. They obey her and arrange themselves for a dance. Led by two attendants to the queen, the Wilis move with a perplexing, almost automatic, grace, as if they danced only at Myrtha's will. Myrtha dances among them, dances with relentless, abandoned force, as if she could not restrain herself, then orders the dancing to end. All the Wilis turn toward Giselle's grave, kneel, and bend low. A new creature is to be initiated.

Myrtha bends over the grave with a magical branch. The

earth parts, and Giselle rises from the mound. She is dressed in white, veiled, her arms crossed over her breast. Instinctively, as if hypnotized, she responds to Myrtha's commands. She walks toward the queen and stands motionless as Myrtha removes her veil. Now Giselle opens her eyes. Following Myrtha's example, she begins to dance, imitating her movements exactly. Myrtha declares that she is now a member of the ghostly tribe and orders Giselle to dance alone. The girl suddenly seems to come to life and, turning around and around, rejoices in her liberation from the grave.

Surrounded by her sisters, Giselle dances as they, too, have danced at their first appearance from their graves—before the dreadful power of the queen dominated them completely. Giselle leaves the scene at the end of her dance, and Myrtha orders the Wilis to conceal themselves.

The stage is empty when Albrecht enters. He moves slowly, dejectedly. He has come to visit the grave of his beloved and is filled with memories of her tragic death. Wilfrid follows his master and attempts to dissuade him from reminding himself of Giselle. Albrecht dismisses him and kneels before Giselle's grave. As he thinks of her, Giselle appears. Albrecht cannot believe it; he looks again; she was not there, after all. He rises and looks about the scene. Now Giselle runs fleetingly in a swift diagonal before him. Albrecht catches her in his arms briefly, lifts her in midflight, and again she disappears. Albrecht's brief touch is like a glance; he thinks that he must be dreaming, yet prays that the dream is true.

As he kneels in prayer, Giselle re-enters and dances about him. He does not see her. Then Giselle walks up in back of him and lovingly touches his shoulder. Albrecht rises and watches her. Joyful that his prayer has been answered, he wishes to touch her. They begin to dance together, Giselle leading the way. Then suddenly she vanishes.

She returns, picks two white lilies, and, dancing in swift diagonals, throws the flowers back over her head. Albrecht, pursuing her closely, picks up the flowers and follows her into the forest as she exits.

Hilarion returns to the scene. No sooner has he done so than Wilis appear before him. He turns to escape them, but in every direction other winged creatures enter and surround him. Myrtha enters with her attendants to examine the captive. At her command, all the Wilis encircle Hilarion, then stand in a long diagonal line, reaching from the right front of the stage to the lakeside. Myrtha stands at the right, at the head of the line. Hilarion, now sure of her intent, begs her for mercy. The queen gestures grandly, "No." Hilarion rushes down the line, beseeching the Wilis to intervene for him. They all refuse. Myrtha declares that he must die. She points to the lake. Hilarion is turned around and around as he is thrust down the long line of Wilis. At the end, two Wilis seize him and cast him into the lake.

Myrtha, unrelenting and triumphant, crosses the stage in light, unremembering leaps and exits at the rear. Two by two, all the Wilis follow her, imitating her step precisely. When Myrtha leads them back on stage, Albrecht confronts the queen. He, too, asks that his life might be spared, and again the queen denies the request. Giselle pleads in his behalf, but her intervention serves only to increase Myrtha's anger. Giselle, determined to save Albrecht at all costs, gestures to him to take refuge beneath the cross at her grave. Myrtha quickly orders the Wilis to intercept Albrecht, but he succeeds in reaching the cross in spite of their efforts to ensnare him. Giselle stands before him in an attitude of protection, and the queen is helpless.

Determined that Albrecht shall die, and offended at this sudden curtailment of her power, the queen orders Giselle to descend from the cross and dance. The girl obeys her, dancing alone between the Wilis, who are arranged in lines down the sides of the stage.

At the conclusion of the dance, Albrecht leaves the protective cross, steps down, and the two lovers go down the lines of Wilis, pleading for their intercession. All obstinately refuse. Now Giselle and Albrecht begin a *pas de deux*. As Albrecht supports Giselle in the adagio, Wilis contrive to come between them and separate them. But the two are now so reunited, so reassured of their lasting love, that they escape these Wilis without even noticing them.

Myrtha commands Giselle to dance alone again. This is followed by a variation for Albrecht. Giselle rejoins him. He lifts her again and again, higher and higher, straight into the air, her phantomlike body seeming a part of the air. Giselle dances another solo. The queen of the Wilis knows that Giselle will never tire, that, like all Wilis, she has a passion for dancing. She knows also that Albrecht will wish to please Giselle and will dance with her. Albrecht will dance to his death.

Albrecht commences another variation. When he has finished, he pleads with the Wilis to make him dance no longer. They ignore his request and, in the midst of continuation of the dance, he falls exhausted to the ground. Giselle tries to help him up, but he cannot move. Giselle turns to the queen and dances to divert her. Finally Albrecht stirs as Giselle beckons to him. They resume their dance; Albrecht makes a new plea to Myrtha, and the dance is resumed as she again denies him. When Albrecht collapses and kneels on the ground, Giselle stands over him protectively. She humbly approaches Myrtha and when the queen obstinately rebuffs her, Giselle asks each of the Wilis to help her. They can do nothing; they are all in the queen's power.

Albrecht attempts to leave the scene, but the watchful Wilis prevent his escape and force him to dance again. He leaps again and again high into the air, then falls to the ground.

Dawn approaches. Four o'clock sounds in the distance. The Wilis must vanish, for with the coming of day, they are powerless. Giselle rejoices that Albrecht has been saved! The Wilis again bow at Giselle's grave, consigning her back to the earth. Giselle embraces Albrecht as she kneels beside him. She knows that this is farewell. The Wilis rush away into the coming dawn, followed by their queen. Albrecht succeeds in rising. Giselle, with mysterious longing, yearns to return to the earth. She goes to her grave. Albrecht follows her, but before he reaches the tomb, she has fallen back and been covered with earth. Albrecht despairs and falls to the ground where he first knelt beside the grave of his beloved.

NOTES Two recent performers of the title role in *Giselle* have attracted special attention, both in the Royal Ballet's production. Writing in the New York *Times* of Merle Park's performance of May 10, 1970, at the Metropolitan Opera House, New York, Clive Barnes said: "She is gorgeous—one of the greatest Giselles I have ever seen and to be ranked with Ulanova, Markova, Alonso, or Chauviré. Miss Park conveys all of Giselle—her innocence, her simple love of play-acting, her vanity, her nervousness, her compassion. Her portrayal is not only beautiful in its dramatic detail—never in my life have I seen a more consummately convincing mad scene—but is also marvelously danced. Once again, as with Antoinette Sibley, with these classic English ballerinas, one looks to Leningrad for their peers, and here you find Natalia Makarova. Makarova has more elevation, more ethereality. Park has more force, more honesty, and more technical finesse. Miss Park is a Giselle for people who never want to see that ballet again."

In June 1972, Natalia Makarova danced *Giselle* with the Royal Ballet in London. Peter Williams reviewed her performance in *The Observer:* "The first time that Natalia Makarova ever danced *Giselle* with her parent company, the Kirov, was in London. In this city, some years later, she broke the umbilical cord and decided to remain in the West. It was right that in *Giselle* she should return to dance as guest with the Royal Ballet at Covent Garden, since the company has its roots deep in the Leningrad School.

"Giselle is probably the most deceptive role in all classical ballet since sheer dancing ability is simply not enough to make it work. The ballerina has to be totally convincing as a human and, later, as a supernatural being. It is the conviction Makarova brings to both aspects of the part, combined with her great schooling, that makes her possibly the finest interpreter of our time.

"She *is* the simple village girl, overpowered by the attentions of Albrecht, whom she believes to be a swain of peasant stock; her trust in him is complete and touching. Her madness, following the moment of truth, is achieved by none of those contrived ballerina gestures but with the inconsequential movements of a deranged mind—she scrabbles at the ground for imagined flowers; in her aimless wandering she already imagines the Wilis; she is a lost soul with just the right glimmer of confused recognition as she confronts one of the figures in her tragedy.

"In the opening moments of the first act, Makarova had a bit of trouble with the tempi; gradually, as the ballet progressed, she and conductor Lanchbery moved together until, in the second act, any disparity was smoothed out. Her control, never overstepping the bounds of the role, is wonderful: slow turns which even leave time for extra beaten steps in their progress; a softness that is never coy; a quiet exultation in all her phrasing. Her arms are so expressive that, in the second act, their fluidity seemed to become a part of the mists encircling her unhallowed grave.

"There is no doubt that Makarova's performance was enriched by the accord which existed between her and Anthony Dowell's anti-hero Albrecht. What for him started as a flirtatious game gradually developed into true tenderness; his partnering all through became a moving expression of a love that believably went beyond death and the grave. Dowell's dancing and subtle playing matched so perfectly with Makarova's that this might well be the beginning of an historic partnership."

Writing of his famous roles, the *premier danseur* Erik Bruhn recalled his impressions of Albrecht in the essay "Beyond Technique" for *Dance Perspectives:* "I think I consider Albrecht as something of a playboy, with a definite background that James (in *La Sylphide*) does not have. He is just James. He could be a peasant boy from the country with not much sophistication. Albrecht belongs to the aristocracy. A marriage has been arranged for him, as was customary at that time, and he accepts this without protesting or rebelling. At the same time he feels that he is free to do what he wants to do as well. So here is this playboy playing with something as lovely, as innocent, as serious as Giselle. Yet there is a certain innocence in Albrecht too, or he would have been smart to conceal the fact of his disguise as a peasant and nobody could have discovered that he had a fiancée already. His fancy for Giselle is earnest enough as long as he can keep it secret. For he is quite prepared to do what he is supposed to do and marry his proper fiancée and continue the family tradition. He does not dream that Giselle will take his attentions so seriously.

"She is attracted to him because he is different. After all, she has plenty of peasants to choose from. Whether the audience sees him first dressed as a count or as a peasant does not matter. There is something different about him. It is like we see someone on the subway and he may stand out because of his mod clothes and long hair (though even that we pass by now), or he may dress like anyone else and we don't know why but suddenly we turn and look. Giselle recognizes his difference though she doesn't know where he comes from.

"After she dies from the shock of Albrecht's deception, he realizes some sincerity in life that he might not otherwise have known. His awareness of guilt makes him mature. His going to her grave at night is like a nightmare. The wilis, of course, are not real because today we cannot believe in terms of wilis flying around. They are in Albrecht's mind. They are all the things we are afraid of, that we have tried to escape. In his nightmares a man's wrong deeds come back to him, carrying a message that he must look at right in the face. Then he can accept his guilt without pushing it away; he can face reality. Albrecht survives because he can admit his guilt and realize his responsibility. After that night he will go into the future with an awareness that makes him mature. And this proves a strength in him too.

"My first *Giselle* was with Alicia Markova in 1955 and, unlike my first *La Sylphide*, it was a success. We did it in three days. I had never done *Giselle* before but I had seen it and maybe I wanted to do it for years. Markova was so clear in what she told me about the ballet that I felt ready to go on stage that night after only one rehearsal. She never had to repeat herself and she said once, 'We seem to speak the same language.' Thanks to her, it worked out just right. Some things were sketchy because we had worked alone and there was just one runthrough before the performance with everyone on stage, and suddenly I realized that people were there in those places and they were all moving. I chose to do nothing rather than try to act something I didn't know anything about. Yet I later relied on the work I had done with Markova and based my future performances on it.

"It seemed there was nothing wrong with my first *Giselle;* in fact it set me up like I was supposed to be *the* Albrecht. But if I had not on occasions revived my idea about Albrecht, I couldn't do the character today and the memory of my Albrecht would belong to the books. It had only a momentary truth that worked for a time as life. Now I can bring more to a role. I can go back to roles I have done for ten years to get a picture of how I see James or Albrecht today. When I first did them I had less of a past to return to and therefore was not able to give that much to a role. I think the more experience you have got the more need there will be for you to use it. And there will be a youth and vitality in the characterization that it didn't have originally. In a more mature state, one has more imagination as to what a youth would do. When I was his age I could only be me which was the beginning of a James. Now I can give a more complete portrayal of James and Albrecht because I have used my imagination. And the portrayal of the character is always true as long as we bring to it what we have within us."

GOLDBERG VARIATIONS

Music by Johann Sebastian Bach. Choreography by Jerome Robbins. Costumes by Joe Eula. Lighting by Thomas Skelton. First presented by the New York City Ballet at the New York State Theater, Lincoln Center, May 27, 1971. Pianist: Gordon Boelzner. Part I: Theme, Renée Estopinal and Michael Steele. Variations, Gelsey Kirkland, Sara Leland, John Clifford, Robert Weiss, Robert Maiorano and Bruce Wells; Bryan Pitts, David Richardson, Delia Peters, Christine Redpath, Bettijane Sills, Stephen Caras, Hermes Conde, Richard Dryden, Francis Sackett, Suzanne Erlon, Gloriann Hicks, and Virginia Stuart. Part II: Variations, Karin von Aroldingen, Susan Hendl, Patricia McBride, Peter Martins, Anthony Blum, and Helgi Tomasson; Merrill Ashley, Rosemary Dunleavy, Renée Estopinal, Johnna Kirkland, Deborah Koolish, Gail Kachadurian, Colleen Neary, Susan Pilarre, Giselle Roberge, Polly Shelton, Marjorie Spohn, and Lynne Stetson; Stephen Caras, Victor Castelli, Hermes Conde, Richard Dryden, Bryan Pitts, David Richardson, Francis Sackett, Nolan T'Sani.

Because this dance ballet is based on its music, Bach's *Goldberg Variations*, it might be well to consider the score first. The popular name of "*Goldberg*" *Variations* attached itself to the work because of the circumstances of its composition. It was hoped that they would be a sure cure for the insomnia of one Count von Kayserling. As the story goes, Bach was commissioned by the count, the Russian ambassador to the Dresden Court, who suffered badly from insomnia, to write some pieces "of a smooth and lively" character in order to relieve the tedium of his sleepless nights. Johann Theophilus Goldberg, a pupil of Bach, was harpsichordist to the count. He was the one who played the finished variations for the count and his name has attached itself to the work ever since.

Published in 1742, the *Goldberg Variations* consist of an aria or theme and thirty variations. It is the only work of Bach's in the form of a theme and variations. But it differs from most compositions of this work in an important respect. We usually think of a series of musical variations as an exploitation or development of a theme or melody that is stated at the beginning of the piece; we expect the same music to appear again and again in different dress. Bach's variations, however, are harmonic variations, rather than melodic; they develop the bass of the original aria rather than its melody. The result is that in the thirty variations that follow, the melody of each is always fresh while the original bass accompaniment is developed anew underneath. The fundamental pattern in the bass can be heard in the first few bars of the aria, a *sarabande* that Bach wrote for his wife.

But first of all, the *Goldberg Variations* are a pleasure. The pianist Charles Rosen writes in the notes to his recording: "It is the most open and public of Bach's keyboard works, the one that most absorbs and transforms the popular styles of his time. The *Goldberg Variations* are, in fact, an encyclopedia: a survey of the world of secular music . . . a social work: it was meant mainly to delight, and it instructs only as it charms. . . . There are canons, a fugue, a French overture, a *siciliana,* a *quodlibet,* accompanied solos and a series of inventions and dance-like movements."

A hearing of a recording of the work is certainly not essential before seeing the ballet (Bach's music is immediately likable in any case), but it is enjoyable to listen to so entertaining and danceable a masterpiece. Come to think of it, I would suggest, if the piece is not familiar to you already, that you hear it first as you see the ballet. In this case, both what you see and what you hear will be marvelous.

What you see begins, and ends, with a *sarabande* or stately dance. Two dancers in eighteenth-century costume perform an elegantly simple *pas de deux* at the beginning. They are still as the curtain rises, posing formally, then they step toward us as the music begins. Their somewhat courtly manner of movement and gesture sets the style for much that follows. Their dance is slow, a bit grave, "yet happy, tranquil and at the same time vibrant with internal life," as Wanda Landowska described the music.

The theme stated, dancers in modern attire come to accompany the inventiveness of the score: there is a trio for a girl and two boys, then a series of variations for different groupings—solos, quartets, *pas de deux*, a sextet, in a continuing flow of dance discovery of the music.

After the fifteenth variation, a middle point is reached. The second part of the ballet has a different character from the first, as do the costumes, which become more formal. Dominated by the dancing of three couples, with solos by the principals, and a *corps de ballet* of twenty, the new part is an exploration of the classic *pas de deux* and concentrates more on the few rather than the many. Just before the end, all the dancers return, and in costumes recalling eighteenth-century court dress, celebrate the final variation. The restatement of the opening aria at the end is danced by the couple we saw first at the start of the piece, but dressed now in contemporary costume. The circle is closed.

The general outline I have tried to give here is all you need, assuming, in fact, that anything is needed but open eyes and ears. Those who want to recollect some details after they have seen *Goldberg Variations* may find the following map useful:

The piece begins, and ends, with an aria, a *sarabande*. The harpsichordist Ralph Kirkpatrick calls the whole work "an enormous *passacaglia* . . . framed as if by two monumental pylons, one formed by the aria and the first two variations, the other by the two penultimate variations and the *quodlibet*, the variations are grouped like the members of an elaborate colonnade."

After the aria is stated by the piano, the curtain rises on a girl and boy, she in a white ballet dress, he in eighteenth-century attire with black knee britches, white stockings, and a white ruffled shirt. They are quite still for a moment, posing formally, then they move toward us. Their dance is slow, a bit grave, yet, in Wanda Landowska's words about the music, "happy, tranquil and at the same time vibrant with eternal life." The boy kneels before the girl briefly.

1. A girl in a light olive-green tunic and two boys in tank suits replace the first couple as the introductory aria finishes and we are in another century altogether. The music is brisker, too, within the flowing melodic line and after the

girl begins, the boys dance too, at her signal. She joins them at the close.

2. In what Landowska calls a "serene and pastoral mood," a girl in violet and two other boys dance; it is a friendly, thoughtful occasion, both boys lifting the girl to the trills of the score.

3. A boy, like a watchful teacher, leads four couples in an ensemble. One of the girls joins him. As he takes her off, the music changes, becoming openly declarative, with a kind of flourish.

4. These "jocose imitations" (Landowska) are danced by three couples and a boy who gesture in formal greeting and thanks.

5. The music, very fast, a contest for the performer, is for crossed hands (crossed keyboards on the harpsichord), an "outburst of irrepressible joy," in George Malcolm's words; two boys compete in the dance.

6. To new, slower music, the boys rest, lie down, stretch, look up briefly at the sky, then at each other. Then they sit up, rise, approach each other in a friendly way and begin to dance.

7. Their dance is a *saltarella*, a kind of jig, the rhythms of which were very popular in old French ballets. They greet a group of newcomers.

8. Six boys who watch a girl dance to tripping rhythms. She bows to them and goes. A boy in green leads the boys in a dance, girls join them and there is an ensemble.

9. As the music slows down four beats to the bar, the lead boy moves toward the lead girl, as do other couples in the group. They face each other across a circle of dancers. They simply walk, aimlessly, without any intention. The circle is broken; they are individuals again, then the walk becomes a promenade and they are all moving together and it is a dance. For twelve dancers.

10. A *fughetta*. Here, as George Malcolm puts it, the solemn *aria* melody is "slyly turned into a lithe and witty subject" for a little fugue. A dance for four boys, somersaults, cartwheels, and rolls.

11. To very rapid runs on the keyboard, three girls and three boys dance like the wind.

12. Three other couples dance to a stately measure in a dim light, then the six dancers from (11) return for varied combinations and separations. The boys watch the girls a bit and there is a final ensemble.

13. To a *cantilena* with a delicately ornamented upper melodic line, two girls and two boys dance. The light is subdued, the atmosphere friendly and thoughtful. There, hinting, in the words of the critic Emory Lewis, "at the differing ways of love," the two boys dance together, as the girls watch, then the girls dance together, as the boys relax. Then again the boys dance with the girls.

14. Again the boys dance with the girls. The lights come up. To brilliant music of crossed keyboards, there is an ensemble led first by the boy in green.

15. The mood quietens again and the first of the variations in a minor key is danced by six girls, who back in from the right, and six boys, who back in from the left. They become a group of varied partnerships. The girls are lifted off gently into the wings at the close.

16. One boy remains, his arm raised before his face when suddenly to the right, to flourishing music, a phalanx of twelve girls ushers in three couples. In George Malcolm's words, this is "a specially grand variation and acts as a prelude to the second half, taking the form of an overture in the French style with the typical pompous opening and lively fugato. The aria is transformed by great technical skill into a splendid piece of Baroque grandeur."

17. A group of girls in blue begins this sparkling variation in which the music seems to cascade across the stage. The three couples who are to dominate this last half of the ballet take over but the girls return to finish the dance.

18. To a marchlike rhythm, a girl in pink and her partner dance an exhilarating, witty *pas de deux* in which the two dancers openly enjoy the mocking laughter in the music. Four boys and four girls watch.

19. Another *pas de deux* to music of gentle syncopations that floats, in Landowska's phrase, "like a barcarolle."

20. Excitement returns and the same two dancers seem to counteract the impulsive rhythm of the music by deliberately slow movement. The lights dim and before we know it they seem to have caught up with the music in rapid combinations of motion and gesture. The dancers perhaps embody George Malcolm's description of the music here, where "differing voices take up a living pursuit of each other."

21. The light darkens. A supported adagio for the third couple, this variation in G minor is reflective of the tragedy and pathos implied in the score.

22. A "massive" variation to Landowska, "its voices interlacing after the fashion of Palestrina," is danced by the boy who, left alone, dejected, seeks comfort in expression, then returns to his memories.

23. The lights come up. Brilliant again and almost "vertiginous in its joy" (Landowska), this variation accompanies a swift dance for four couples; the boys, then the girls racing diagonally across the stage, then all leaving together.

24. Calm again and in a stately dance rhythm, the music accompanies the girl who left the boy. She dances a variation. Three of her friends are with her and appear to want to be soloists, too.

25. The last variation in a minor key, somber, restless, romantic, a "richly ornamented adagio that overwhelms us" (Landowska), is danced by the girl in pink and her partner.

26. This sparkling variation is a combination of 18/16 time in one hand and 3/4 in the other, the two hands temporarily changing places once in a while. Girls and boys in new costumes, like the eighteenth-century couple at the start, enter and watch as the other two lead couples dance.

The 27th variation (Landowska saw "humor and malice" here), the 28th (memorable for its tinkling trills), and the joyful 29th bring all six of the principals before us as each dances before the *corps de ballet*. All now are dressed in eighteenth-century costume.

For the 30th variation, a *quodlibet,* or fantasia, involving two folk tunes as well as the fundamental base melody, the dancers cluster at the center of the stage. They stand there briefly in a quiet pose. The lights come down; they all seem to promenade off. But as the aria is played again, the first two dancers, now in modern dress, come back to show again the beginning.

NOTES Few ballets have been so praised, and at such articulate length, as *Goldberg Variations*. After a performance of what the choreographer called a "work in progress" at the Saratoga Performing Arts Center on July 23, 1970, Don McDonagh wrote in the New York *Times* that "the New York City Ballet has presented many premières in its history but none has had the informal and charming intimacy of *Goldberg Variations*."

After the New York première, *Variety* said the ballet was not only "a pinnacle of 20th century art but gave rise to the notion that it may be the most perfect dance work ever made. No better dancing can be seen than in this work. . . . Few other companies could have provided such superior execution by 42 dancers. . . . It is difficult to overestimate the contribution of pianist Gordon Boelzner, who played the immense work with brilliance, insight and rhythmic subtlety."

Winthrop Sargeant in *The New Yorker* called *Goldberg Variations* "a magnificent spectacle. . . . The ballet is abstract in the sense that music is abstract, but, like music, it contains moods ranging from sombre to playful. Mr. Robbins's feeling for the music is extraordinarily sensitive, and his treatment of rhythmic movement is—like his treatment of stage space—fluid, sometimes eccentric, but always deeply conscious of musical values. The première of the *Goldberg Variations* was to me the high point of a busy ballet season, and it places Mr. Robbins among the great, original masters of the art."

In *The Saturday Review*, the critic Walter Terry, admiring the ballet, recalled that Jerome Robbins had used the harpsichord at the working rehearsal of *Goldberg Variations* at Saratoga. "At a subsequent matinee, the harpsichord was tried again. In both forms of accompaniment, Gordon Boelzner was the admirable, laudable musician. Robbins himself says that he prefers the support of the piano since 'I worked with the piano in rehearsal when the ballet was being created, and it is closely related to those sounds. As for the length of the ballet . . . I could not violate the music. It is there, all there, and if the mind wanders, let it rest and then come back.'"

Writing in *Dance and Dancers* magazine, the critic Patricia Barnes described many of the performers:

"The first variations are dominated by the performances of the six soloists—among the company's most brilliant. The two girls are rewardingly contrasted. Sara Leland, lithe, daring and intensely musical, has an abandon and fearlessness that is exciting to watch; while Gelsey Kirkland, more restrained in her personality, offers us dancing that is as delicately precise as the finest embroidery. Her manner is touching too. Just 18, she is poised on the threshold of womanhood, but retains the charming innocence of a young girl. She has one solo, outstandingly danced, sympathetically watched by six young men casually seated on the floor, that perfectly catches in its unselfconscious coquetry her individuality and special grace.

"John Clifford, Bruce Wells, Robert Weiss and Robert Maiorano have equally enhanced their reputations. Each has had his artistry extended in this work. Clifford has never looked so elegant, while losing nothing of his appealing ebullience. Wells, a sure *premier danseur* in the making, is superb, smooth and effortless in everything he does, demonstrating a perfect line, buoyant elevation and a radiant personality.

"Another dancer who has caught the eye ever since he joined two years ago has been Robert Weiss. His brio, neat footwork and fine *ports de bras* are always in evidence, and Robbins has here exploited his mercurial gifts to splendid advantage. A slight stiffness in his upper torso at present prevents this slim and promising young dancer from total elegance, but this should come.

"One of Maiorano's first major opportunities came with *Dances at a Gathering*, and he has once more found himself in a Robbins ballet that gives him a chance to shine. His developing stage presence and ever-improving technique need this sort of exposure, for when given the opportunity he has shown himself most capable. . . .

"It would be impossible, in this dense and lengthy ballet, to describe fully the variations in detail, so isolated examples must suffice. One particularly striking section for four dancers, two boys and two girls, stands out. The two boys (Bryan Pitts and David Richardson) dance together, watched by the two girls (Leland and Kirkland), and while they relax the two girls dance.

"My own favorite variation is performed by two couples. Maiorano with Leland and Weiss with Kirkland, while Wells and Clifford slowly, in musical counterpoint, walk around them. The dance turns into two pas de trois, as the two boys weave their way in and out of the dancers to form two trios. The subtle transition is so beautiful, natural and elegant that one almost holds one's breath at Robbins's dazzling craftsmanship. . . .

"The final half of the ballet revolves around the six dancers, supported by the ensemble, and is far more formal in its construction while the choreography is more intricate. There is room only for the mention of highlights.

"The opening couple, McBride and Tomasson, backed by the ensemble, reflect in their pas de deux something of the bucolic humours of the 18th century, as hands on hips, backs to the audience, their bodies seem to shake with merriment, but this humour is touched with a 20th-century jazziness that perfectly fits the music's rhythms. The pas de deux from Blum and Hendl, at the start cool and classical, deploys Hendl's clean lines and Blum's strong presence. There is a gradual and subtle change of mood as the choreography becomes more sensual. The convolutions of the two dancers as they entwine around each other, while within the framework of the classic technique, succeeds in looking very new and very arresting.

"The loose-limbed and pliant qualities of von Aroldingen are shown off well in her quirkily individual solo, backed by three girls, but even better is the appearance of Peter Martins. He has never seemed more spirited, more dexterous. He was a joy to watch as he revelled in the musical rhythms and choreographic complexities. This elegant and beautiful dancer has sometimes in the past appeared a little too reserved. In *Goldberg* he was a powerhouse of excitement and physical strength. . . .

"Musically the work is yet another gift to City Ballet by its remarkable pianist, Gordon Boelzner. As in the previous Robbins masterworks, Mr. Boelzner, calm and implacable, is at his keyboard on a platform to the left of the proscenium arch and, as always, playing with modest majesty. He has become one of City Ballet's gilt-edged assets. Typically, when for one performance he was asked as an experiment to play on the harpsichord rather than the piano, he was willing, able and of course brilliant."

Admirers of *Goldberg Variations* must also be referred to Elena Bivona's indispensable essay on the ballet in *Ballet Review*, Vol. 3, No. 6, 1971.

HARBINGER

Music by Sergei Prokofiev. Choreography by Eliot Feld. Setting by Oliver Smith. Lighting by Jean Rosenthal. First presented by American Ballet Theatre at the New York State Theater, New York, May 11, 1967, with Christine Sarry, Edward Verso, Paula Tracy, Cynthia Gregory, Marcos Paredes, and Eliot Feld in leading roles.

Harbinger tells no story; its plot is outlined by the music of Prokofiev's *Concerto No. 5 in G for Piano.* Usefully for the listener and spectator, both the composer and the choreographer have given notes on their own impressions of this work.

Prokofiev writes: "The first movement is an *Allegro con brio* with a *Meno mosso* as middle section. Though not in sonata form, it is the main movement of the concerto and fulfills the function and maintains the spirit of the traditional sonata form. The second movement has a march-like rhythm. I would not think of calling it a march because it has none of the vulgarity of commonness which is so often associated with the idea of march, and which actually exists in most marches. The third movement is a toccata. This is a precipitate, displayful movement of much technical brilliance and requiring great virtuosity; it is a toccata for orchestra as well as for piano. The fourth movement . . . is the lyrical movement of the concerto. It starts off with a soft, soothing theme; grows more and more intense in the middle portion, develops breadth and tension, then returns to the music of the beginning. The finale has a decided classic flavor. The coda is based on a new theme, which is joined by the other theme of the finale. There is a reference to some of the material of the preceding movements in the finale."

The choreographer and dancer Eliot Feld described his view of the work in an interview with Jack Anderson in *Dance Magazine.* He said that in choreographing *Harbinger,* he wishes to "explore certain patterns of human relationships. . . . The first movement, in which a solo boy ambles lazily among a group of girls, is about 'being by yourself and having fantasies.' The impetuous second movement is conceived as a chase. The third movement is a slightly melancholy duet with *corps de ballet* serving as background. . . . The fourth movement, a competitive trio for two boys and a girl, is 'just what it appears to be.' The finale is composed of movement motifs taken from the preceding sections. 'I guess that in all of *Harbinger* I'm talking about myself and the people I know. It's like showing some of the kinds of personal games we play.'"

Harbinger attracted considerable attention when it was first presented in New York. Clive Barnes of the New York *Times* wrote that Mr. Feld was "the most important indigenous talent in classic ballet since Jerome Robbins."

Interviewed by the British magazine *Dance and Dancers,* Eliot Feld was asked when, as a dancer in American Ballet Theatre, he got the idea of doing choreography. He replied: "I don't really know. When I started to try out choreography I really had no idea of doing a ballet. I had listened to the Prokofiev fifth piano concerto for some time and I had the idea of doing this duet—very allegro, very short. I worked with a dancer just as a favour and we choreographed this dance, which turned out to be the eventual duet in *Harbinger,* my first ballet. It took us about 300 hours of rehearsal time to choreograph two minutes of choreography. I don't indulge in that way of working any longer. Then I got another idea for another of the movements and I began to choreograph that, but it became difficult because I needed three people, and Royes Fernandez helped me out at that time. Gradually I realised that I had a ballet, but I don't really think that I had thought of myself as wanting to be a choreographer before that. Before *Harbinger* I had never put any steps together. I have a lot to thank Robbins for, because after I had completed about four minutes of choreography he came in and saw what I had done and seemed very excited about it. He asked me what I intended to do, and I told him it depended a lot on what he could do for me; would he be willing to speak to Lucia Chase about producing the ballet? He did, and on the basis of his approval it was put on by Ballet Theatre."

HARLEQUINADE

Ballet in two acts. Music by Riccardo Drigo. Choreography by George Balanchine. Scenery, costumes, and lighting by Rouben Ter-Arutunian. First presented by the New York City Ballet at the New York State Theater, February 4, 1965, with Edward Villella and Patricia McBride in the leading roles.

Most of us know the old *commedia dell'arte* story of how Harlequin wins Columbine from her rich father.

The original ballet to this story, *Harlequin's Millions* was first presented at the Hermitage Theatre in St. Petersburg in 1900. It was the last success of the brilliant creator of dance, Marius Petipa. I remember very well dancing in this production when I was a student at the Imperial Ballet School. What I liked about it was its wit and pace and its genius in telling a story with clarity and grace. It was a very different kind of ballet from *The Sleeping Beauty,* and showed the range of his genius.

Les Millions d'Arlequin had a great deal of influence, I think, on ballet history, becoming the model for comedy narrative. It is the other side of the coin from *Swan Lake,* if you like. I don't of course remember details of the old production. In 1950 I arranged a *Harlequin pas de deux* for Maria Tallchief and André Eglevsky that used some of Drigo's music in a *demi-caractère* display piece. I remember thinking at the time that one day we should try to do the whole ballet. That came about in the usual accidental way when it was suggested that the settings Rouben Ter-Arutunian had designed for the New York City Opera production of Rossini's *Cenerentola* might be usable for a full-length *Harlequinade.* We were able to borrow the scenery, which the designer adapted for the ballet, and I began to work.

During the overture we see a drop curtain painted in the style of Pollock toy theaters with boxes right and left and a paper proscenium. When this rises the scene shows the exterior of the house of the rich merchant Cassandre, father of the beautiful Columbine. The action shows how Harlequin, helped by La Bonne Fée, succeeds in rescuing Columbine from the wealthy suitor her father has picked out for her. The enraged Cassandre tries to have Harlequin killed but is foiled. The Good Fairy brings a cornucopia of gold pieces, Harlequin outbids his rich rival, and the lovers are united. There is a dance celebration of their love in an enchanted park.

NOTES When I was studying ballet in Russia, I much admired Petipa's original version of this ballet (*Les Millions d'Arlequin,* first performed at the Hermitage Theatre, St. Petersburg, February 10, 1900). The fun and slapstick as well as the occasional deeper meaning of the popular Italian comedy, the *commedia dell 'arte,* have always appealed to me with their strength and warmth, and in *Harlequinade* I have attempted to remain faithful to the spirit of Petipa's dances and drama without reproducing any of the actual steps of his time. Who, in fact, remembers them?

As I often do with my ballets, I changed *Harlequinade* somewhat in 1973, adding sequences at certain points and filling out the piece so that, hopefully, with one intermission, it makes for an evening-long diversion. Among the additions are a tarantella in Act One and a polonaise in Act Two. Children are used among the dancers, and the music is now the complete score by Riccardo Drigo.

The critic Nancy Goldner described the revision in *Dance News*: "*Harlequinade* is now filled out so that it fills an evening. The main addition is a 'ballabile des enfants' for polichinelles, little harlequins, scaramouches, and pierrots and pierettes—in other words, small editions of all the adult roles. They do a series of *divertissements* in the beginning of Act II, and, as is his way, Balanchine gives them simple but utterly charming steps. Their dances most closely resemble the polichinelle dance in *Nutcracker;* in fact, the *Harlequinade* polichinelles are now wearing the *Nutcracker* costumes. At the end of the variations, all the children do a grand polonaise, and they do it with more style and belief than the adults. Watching all 32 children dancing with proper deportment and happy faces is enchanting. Inevitably, it reminds one of Balanchine's childhood and his statements about how exciting it was to appear on stage. So here is Papa giving his kids what he had. That knowledge gives an extra charm to the ballet.

"There is also a new blaze-of-color ensemble dance for adult revelers in the first act. The idea is to cram hordes into a small area, so that all you see are many bright colors in squished motion. But the costumes are garish, the paper lanterns carried by the dancers kept falling off, and it went on too long.

"Gelsey Kirkland was beautifully shy and sweet in her solemn way as Columbine. Her delicate articulation suits the choreography well, yet this is still Villella's ballet. His brute strength is here quieted by humor and something that is almost lyricism, especially in the beautiful serenade dance. His strength is still felt, but from the underside. It is very compelling."

IN THE NIGHT

Music by Frédéric Chopin. Choreography by Jerome Robbins. Costumes by Joe Eula. Lighting by Thomas Skelton. Pianist: Gordon Boelzner. First presented by the New York City Ballet at the New York State Theater, Lincoln Center, January 29, 1970 with Kay Mazzo and Anthony Blum, Violette Verdy and Peter Martins, Patricia McBride and Francisco Moncion.

At the time of his ballet *Dances at a Gathering*, Jerome Robbins said, "There is more Chopin that I like—the nocturnes, for example—that I may use for another ballet." *In the Night* continues the exploration of Chopin's music, using for its score the Chopin *Nocturnes, Opus 27, No. 1; Opus 55, Nos. 1 and 2; and Opus 9, No. 2.*

When we speak of a nocturne, the critic Harold Schonberg has pointed out in his fine book on Chopin and Schumann, we think automatically of Chopin's "night pieces." They were, in the composer's lifetime, his most popular compositions, captivating all of Europe from the amateurs who found them comparatively easy to play, to the connoisseurs who liked their dreamlike form. "We live in a non-sentimental age, or pretend to," Schonberg remarks, and the nocturnes are not now so much played. Perhaps after this ballet we will listen to them more. Many consider the first nocturne used in the ballet to be Chopin's greatest; the last, *Opus 9, No. 2*, is surely the most popular of the twenty works in this genre.

In the Night consists of dances for three couples. They dance in sequence and then appear together briefly. The curtain rises on a starry night. A boy and a girl enter to the slow introductory music. Their dance develops with the pulse of the score, which quickens dramatically, then returns to simplicity and melody. The boy lifts the girl into the wings.

There is a more formal atmosphere for the second *pas de deux*, a suggestion of chandeliers above the stage. The music is tender, but in the midst of the dance the girl breaks away from the boy. When she returns, their dance has a real abandon until holding the girl upside down as her limbs tremble, passions subside. At the end, he lifts her, facing him, and away.

In the third *pas de deux*, almost melodramatic in response to the piano, there are declarations, rejections, pleadings, rapid swings from one emotion to another. She hangs onto the boy. He leaves her and she seems helpless. But after a short reunion, both leave. She returns, to walk across stage, kneel before him, and touch him. He cradles her in his arms.

To the most familiar nocturne, the three couples enter, meeting as if accidentally at a dance. The girls acknowledge each other, then the boys, but all clearly have eyes only for each other and do not know quite what is happening. Each couple goes its own way.

Deborah Jowitt wrote in the *Village Voice:* "I shall not vex myself with wondering whether Jerome Robbins intended his new ballet, *In the Night,* as a companion piece to his *Dances at a Gathering* or as a sequel, prelude, epilogue, cadenza. I think that it is probable that Robbins simply had more Chopin in his ears and more movement ideas in his head so he made another ballet—not as long as *Dances at a Gathering* but equally astonishing.

"The two ballets are certainly related. The movement has the same beautiful ease in space. We do not notice 'choreography,' but see dancing. Even ballet steps that we know melt into the long phrases before our eyes can freeze them. The special kind of contemporary Romanticism that Robbins is interested in is expressed in dance that burgeons and branches and grows like leaves—startling, perhaps, by its eventual shape, but never seeming inorganic. . . .

"Kay Mazzo and Anthony Blum perform the first duet. The gracious rapture of their relationship is punctuated by little confrontations. They appear to leave each other for the pleasure of rushing together again.

"The chandelier projection creates a half-indoor feeling—a ballroom with all the doors and windows flung open. In this duet for Violette Verdy and Peter Martins, there is a delight in each other, but also a slight and charming decorousness. Occasionally they do little steps arm in arm as if they were at a dance, or remembering a dance. She looks very small, very trusting beside him.

"The third duet is full of passion and artifice. The lovers, Francisco Moncion and Patricia McBride, are being melodramatic for each other. One minute they are involved in flashy, tempestuous lifts; the next minute one of them disappears from sight. Their very anger seems to be exciting them. Even her final kneeling at his feet to touch him is extreme as well as truly humble.

"At the end the three couples, still alone, occupy the same fragrant patch of night. The women come together and are surprised to see each other: you can almost see them blinking awake. The men greet each other. Then the couples separate and again take their own paths.

"The choreography serves the dancers, and they in turn serve it beautifully. Each seems completely real in what he is doing. Ballet technique disappears as artifice and becomes —as it rarely does—a means to dancing, a transparency for spirit to be seen through."

In the Night has also been described, with an interesting commentary, by the critic Robert Sealy in *Ballet Review*, Vol. 3, No. 3.

INITIALS R.B.M.E.

Music by Johannes Brahms. Choreography by John Cranko. Décor by Jürgen Rose. First presented by the Stuttgart Ballet at the Wuerttemberg State Theatre, Stuttgart, Germany, January 19, 1973, with Richard Cragun, Birgit Keil, Marcia Haydée, Heinz Clauss, and Egon Madsen in principal roles. First presented in the United States by the same ensemble with the same principals at the Metropolitan Opera House, New York, May 30, 1973. Conducted by Stewart Kershaw. Piano solo by Katsurako Fujiwara.

This dance ballet is named for its principal dancers—*R*ichard Cragun, *B*irgit Keil, *M*arcia Haydée and *E*gon Madsen, the stars of John Cranko's Stuttgart Ballet. Cranko called it "a ballet for four friends to music of Johannes Brahms, whose passionate feeling for friendship and love is confirmed by his compositions, in his letters and by the testimony of others."

The first movement of the Brahms *Piano Concerto No. 2*, to which the ballet is arranged, was set for Richard Cragun; the second for Birgit Keil. Marcia Haydée and Heinz Clauss are featured in the third movement and Egon Madsen in the fourth. Each of the sections is supported by the *corps de ballet.*

NOTES Writing of this ballet's success on the Soviet tour of the Stuttgart Ballet (1973) in *Dance Magazine*, Lydia Jaffe notes that each of the four stars of *Initials R.B.M.E.* are "all dancers with whom Cranko has had a long and friendly association at the Stuttgart. They started with him as beginners, and his guidance brought them to artistic accomplishment.

"The ballet was enthusiastically acclaimed, and Vera Krasovskaya, the Soviet ballet critic, remarks: 'What a wealth of fantasy. The dancers execute these virtuosities with precision, discipline and feeling. It is an homage to the whole company.'"

INTERMEZZO

Music by Johannes Brahms. Choreography by Eliot Feld. Costumes by Stanley Simmons. Lighting by Jules Fisher. First presented by the American Ballet Company at the Festival of Two Worlds, Spoleto, Italy, June 29, 1969, with Christine Sarry, Elizabeth Lee, Cristina Stirling, David Coll, John Sowinski, and Alfonso Figueroa. Pianist: Gladys Celeste Mercades. First presented in the United States by the American Ballet Company at the Brooklyn Academy of Music, New York, October 23, 1969, with Olga Janke replacing Cristina Stirling in the original cast.

Intermezzo is a set of dances to piano music by Brahms—the *Op. 117* and *118 intermezzos* and some of the *Op. 39* waltzes. The piano is on stage to accompany the dances throughout the ballet. The story is what the dancers do.

They are seen entering gradually onto a darkened scene, three couples in formal dress. They listen to the first bars of the music as the light rises. Then a girl begins to move to the music. The others follow, responding to the flow of the music in speed and stillness. Two couples leave, and the remaining one dances a *pas de deux* to a romantic sequence. They yield the stage to another, faster duet, this one buoyant and full of brio; then the third couple returns and all six finish the piece.

This is the ballet's pattern, a series of duets and ensembles, all of them distinct in character with the music, all of them a contrast. There is a tempestuous waltz, and, in one duet, the boy is distracted by the girl so much that she seems to blind him. After another duet in which the dancers appear to be driven in the demanding pace of the music, a girl dances pensively alone. The *pas de deux* resume, their variety accumulating with shifts in the music. Toward the end, as the lights begin to fade, the three girls are cradled in their lovers' arms. They realize it is late and say good night.

NOTES *Intermezzo* was the new major work created by Eliot Feld for the first performances of his American Ballet

Company. Writing about these performances in *Dance and Dancers,* Patricia Barnes said:

"For a choreographer still only in his middle 20s to create within a couple of years six ballets is an achievement in itself; that they should all be interesting, and at least three of them major works by any standard, sets Feld up in the ranks of the leading contemporary choreographers. Choreographed during the spring of 1969 and seen for the first time in Spoleto, *Intermezzo* is a real beauty. Performed to a backdrop of curtains and with the piano placed to the left of the stage, the dances have a flow and musicality that is both subtle and natural. Using just six dancers and varying his work with ensemble, *pas de deux* and solos, the choreography has an ecstasy and technical dexterity that is gorgeous . . . it is Feld's genuine invention and originality that make *Intermezzo* so rewarding. He dares a great deal in his choreography and asks almost impossible things of his dancers. Lifts abound in his work, some like none I have ever seen before. When performed by dancers such as the nimble Christine Sarry and David Coll, who is, quite simply, one of the best partners I have ever seen, the effect is dazzling.

"Another striking *pas de deux* is that created for Elizabeth Lee and John Sowinski, which is strongly atmospheric, a tiny choreographic gem almost complete in itself. With Sowinski's arm protectively round her waist, Lee seems to perceive strange and fearful visions. Sowinski gently removes her hands from her eyes and tenderly, reassuringly, he helps her face life. This small sequence is danced with a beauty, gravity and compassion that is altogether memorable."

Writing of the ballet in the *Village Voice,* the critic Deborah Jowitt said, "*Intermezzo* . . . is all ardent swoops and dips, runs and waltzes, light and breathless lifts. Occasionally a mysterious melancholy comes in like gathering dark. John Sowinski reaches toward the invisible while his partner, Elizabeth Lee, tries gently to turn him back toward her. They and the other two couples (Christine Sarry and David Coll, Olga Janke and Alfonso Figueroa) do not so much formally replace each other on stage in *pas de deux* as sweep in and out as if flashing different facets of a relationship between two people."

JEWELS

Ballet in three parts. Music by Gabriel Fauré, Igor Stravinsky, and Peter Ilyich Tchaikovsky. Choreography by George Balanchine. Costumes by Karinska. Scenery by Peter Harvey. Lighting by Ronald Bates. First presented by the New York City Ballet at the New York State Theater, April 13, 1967, with Violette Verdy and Conrad Ludlow; Mimi Paul and Francisco Moncion; Patricia McBride, Edward Villella, and Patricia Neary; and Suzanne Farrell and Jacques d'Amboise in the leading roles.

This is a dance ballet in three parts to music by three different composers. The music for the three parts is very different and so are the dances. The dancers for each part of the ballet are dressed like jewels, emeralds for Fauré, rubies for the Stravinsky, and diamonds for the Tchaikovsky. (I thought of using sapphires, too, and had Schoenberg in mind, but the color of sapphires is hard to get across on stage.) The idea for a new ballet using jeweled costumes came about some years ago when my friend Nathan Milstein introduced me to Claude Arpels, the jeweler. I saw later the splendid stones in his collection in New York. Of course I have always liked jewels; after all, I am an Oriental, from Georgia in the Caucasus. I like the color of gems, the beauty of stones, and it was wonderful to see how our costume workshop, under Karinska's direction, came so close to the quality of the real stones (which were of course too heavy for the dancers to wear!).

The first part, "Emeralds," is arranged to music by Fauré, from *Pelléas et Mélisande* and *Shylock*. It is danced by two leading couples, three soloists, and a *corps de ballet* of ten girls. There is first of all a *pas de deux* to soft, melodious strings with eight girls accompanying, then a variation for a girl to light, lilting music. This is followed by a dance by the other leading girl. There is a *pas de trois* and then to music of muted strings another *pas de deux,* quiet and alone. All the dancers join in the finale.

To try to describe for you the dances themselves would be boring, for they have no literary content at all. I suppose if this part of the ballet can be said to rèpresent anything at all, it is perhaps an evocation of France, the France of elegance, comfort, dress, perfume.

Others seem to have found the second part, "Rubies," representative of America. I did not have that in mind at all. It is simply Stravinsky's music, which I have always liked and which he and I agreed to use, arranged for a leading couple, a soloist, and a *corps de ballet* of girls and boys. The couple and the soloist alternate in leading the ensemble.

Stravinsky's *Capriccio for Piano and Orchestra* was first performed in 1929, with the composer as soloist. The work is in three movements, *Presto, Andante rapsodico,* and *Allegro capriccioso ma tempo giusto.* In naming this piano concerto *Capriccio,* Stravinsky relates in his *Chronicle* that he was thinking of definitions of a *capriccio* given by Praetorius: "he regarded it as a synonym of the *fantasia* which was a free form made up of *fugato* instrumental passages."

"Diamonds," the final part of the ballet, is danced to Tchaikovsky's *Symphony No. 3 in D major,* which has five movements. I did not use the first movement, which is not really suitable for dancing, and concentrated on the remaining four, which include two scherzos, a slow movement, and a superb polonaise. This ballet is arranged for a girl and her partner, a group of soloists, and a large *corps de ballet.* The movements are marked: 2. *Alla tedesca, Allegro moderato a semplice;* 3. *Andante elagiaco;* 4. *Scherzo, Allegro vivo;* and 5. Finale: *Allegro con fuoco (tempo de Polacca).* The first is danced by twelve girls and two soloists, the second is a *pas de deux* for the two principals, the third an ensemble with variations for the two principals, and the finale a polonaise for the entire group of thirty-four dancers.

JOURNAL

Music by Burt Alcantara. Choreography by Louis Falco. Décor and costumes by William Katz. First presented by the Netherlands Dance Theatre at the Royal Theatre, The Hague, October 27, 1971. First presented in the United States by the same ensemble at the Brooklyn Academy of Music, New York, March 30, 1972.

Journal is a dance narrative with music and words, a collage with a new dimension. The words, like news headlines or quick entries in a diary, punctuate the action, rising over and above the music and the action, sometimes reflecting the action, sometimes calling attention to a complementary feeling or situation; they do not literally describe it or cogitate it; like *Strange Interlude,* they accompany the action. The action is about men and women and what they seem to mean to each other and what they might really mean. The dance endeavors to expose, often comically, actual situations that are concealed from the participants, sometimes by themselves.

NOTES Deborah Jowitt in the *Village Voice* wrote of *Journal:* "The dancers engage in monologues, dialogues, bouts of screaming. Some of the material is autobiographical, and it's all angry. Much of the movement is casual, scrambling. Some of it more formal—non-specific but colored by the arguments and flung by dancers at other dancers as if it were cursing. Many of the dialogues have to do with male-female bickering, and in one extremely effective final scene between one couple, other dancers stand for the possessions that she is taking with her when she leaves. The dancers stumble off with her like good little animals. The dance is scraps of human hostility jumbled together, spilling out of the bright, bitter little games Falco has set them. Grownups on a playground, using the swings to bash each other. . . ."

KETTENTANZ

Music by Johann Strauss and Johann Simon Mayer. Choreography by Gerald Arpino. Costumes by Joe Eula. Lighting by Thomas R. Skelton. First presented by the City Center Joffrey Ballet at the City Center, New York, October 20, 1971.

Kettentanz (Chain Dance) is a ballet of six couples who begin the piece, hands joined, to a vigorous *galop* by Strauss. It is Strauss's music (and a finale by his contemporary Johann Mayer) that gives the ballet its character, although it is used here through no sentimental screen of Old Vienna. It is, rather, the zest and energy of the polkas, galops, and other dances that have been used, with gestures of the past, to show new dances of contemporary interest. There are nine dances in all, performed in an unbroken chain: Strauss's *Gitana Galop, Opus 108; Annen Polka, Opus 137; Erste Kettenbrucke Walzer, Opus 4; Eisele und Beisele Sprunge, Opus 202; Chineser Galop, Opus 21; Seuzer Galop, Opus 9; Hofball Tanze, Opus 51; Cachucha Galop, Opus 97;* and Mayer's *Schnofler Tanz.*

NOTES Writing in *Dance Magazine,* the critic Doris Hering said that "superlatives are the province of second-rate movie critics, but I can't resist one in connection with Gerald Arpino's *Kettentanz.* It is his loveliest ballet. . . . Arpino has soared blithely above the music to create a suite of tender miniatures, all growing out of an opening chain formation and eventually returning to it with the gleaming casualness of a meadow stream filtering through cluster after cluster of brightly nodding flowers."

In the *Christian Science Monitor,* Nancy Goldner wrote of the dances in *Kettentanz:* "They are . . . purely virtuoso essays. As such they are immensely enjoyable . . . as in a pensive duet for Rebecca Wright and Dermot Burke; a bobbing, sprightly exercise in small and quick footwork for Scott Bernard and Glenn White; and a brilliant *Cachucha Galop* for Susan Magno and Miss Wright, a dance that Fanny Elssler made famous about a century ago. . . ."

Reviewing *Kettentanz* in the *Daily News,* Joseph Gale said that the ballet "is one of Arpino's half-dozen or so neoclassical masterpieces. It is folk—perhaps even countryside—Viennese. . . . It is all ravishing—gay, insouciant, tender, frothy, and as is characteristic of Arpino's works of this genre, bravura."

KONSERVATORIET
CONSERVATORY

Music by H. S. Paulli. Choreography by Auguste Bournonville. First presented by the Royal Danish Ballet at the Royal Theatre, Copenhagen, May 6, 1849. First presented in the United States by the Royal Danish Ballet at the New York State Theater, 1965. Revived by the City Center Joffrey Ballet at the City Center, New York, February 20, 1969, in a staging by Hans Brenaa, with Barbara Remington, Pamela Johnson, and Paul Sutherland in principal roles. Scenery by William Pitkin.

Most students of ballet are familiar with the name of the great Danish ballet master, August Bournonville, whose work has been familiar to audiences for 150 years. We know it in the dancing of great stars like Erik Bruhn, who was schooled at the academy set up by Bournonville and who has written a book about it. We know it in the repertory of Bournonville's own Royal Danish Ballet and we know it, too, in fortunate revivals like this one of *Konservatoriet*—which is simply the Danish word for what we mean by conservatory, or a place of study.

The place of study here is a school of ballet, where a ballet master is in charge of a group of brilliant pupils. The dance style of the ballet is what Bournonville learned in France from Auguste Vestris, the *premier danseur* of his time. In the setting of an old Paris ballet studio, with crystal chandelier, covered with cloth to protect it from dust, and to the accompaniment of a violinist (the violin, we realize, was the instrument for ballet classes in those days), we watch a ballet master put his students through their paces.

NOTES The fact that *Konservatoriet* is, in fact, the first act of a much longer ballet (called *A Proposal of Marriage Through a Newspaper*) need not divert us, for that ballet tells the story of two girls, Elisa and Victorine, who come to Paris for adventures, beginning with the study of ballet. The ballet master prompts them to show their best form and he, too, shows them what he means by form, by dancing a solo of his own.

Writing of *Konservatoriet* in *Ballet Review* in 1969, Henrey Haslam described the work's importance for both history and the present: In this particular work, he said, "could be seen the quintessence of the French school. It was choreographed by Bournonville in 1849 from memories of his stay in Paris more than twenty years earlier as a student of the great Vestris, a brilliant dancer in the age of male supremacy in the ballet world. Bournonville taught the French school of Vestris in his classes in Denmark. One of his students, Christian Johannson, went to St. Petersburg, where his teaching combined with the influence of the Italian school, which was then reintroduced to Paris and western Europe in 1909 by the Diaghilev Ballet. This Russian school is the background of many of the great teachers in America today. But the branch of the French school remained in Denmark, cut off from the mainstream of the dance world until the early 1950s.

"Hans Beck, a pupil of Bournonville who succeeded him as director of the company, was responsible for the revival of *Konservatoriet*. Hans Brenaa, who was dancing under Beck, is one of the foremost authorities on Bournonville and staged *Konservatoriet* this year for the City Center Joffrey Ballet. The ballet was originally in two acts, titled *Konservatoriet or A Proposal by Advertisement*. It had a very complicated plot about dancers and their adventures and flirtations in Paris. It is regrettable that the second act did not survive, for in it was a *can-can*, which was probably one of the first times such a dance appeared on a ballet stage. Only the first act remains, in which the ballet master, Victorine, and Elisa are introduced—the leading roles which still use the names but have lost their distinct characterizations. The scene is a ballet studio, with the ballet master conducting a class that contains a series of *enchaînements* which are exacting both technically and stylistically.

"I was delighted that an American company had obtained *Konservatoriet* for its repertoire, and I applauded Robert Joffrey, artistic director of the City Center Joffrey Ballet, for his decision to have the ballet staged for his company by Brenaa, who is a fine teacher and coach. The dancers were privileged to be able to work with him in a style and technique not part of their background."

LIEBESLIEDER WALZER

Music by Johannes Brahms. Choreography by George Balanchine. Scenery by David Hays. Costumes by Karinska. First presented by the New York City Ballet at the City Center, New York, November 22, 1960, with Diana Adams, Melissa Hayden, Jillana, Violette Verdy, Bill Carter, Conrad Ludlow, Nicholas Magallanes, and Jonathan Watts.

"Brahms and waltzes! The two words stare at each other in positive amazement on the elegant title page of the score. The earnest, silent Brahms, a true younger brother of Schumann, and just as north German, Protestant, and unworldly as he—writing waltzes!" So wrote the music critic Eduard Hanslick when Brahms published his first group of *Liebeslieder Walzer* in 1869. Brahms had written them during his first year in Vienna and they were so successful that five years later he wrote a new series. They have been popular ever since, in the concert hall and in the home but most of all at home, for this music for piano, four-hands, and a quartet of voices was perhaps designed for the pleasure of performers. All the *Liebeslieder Walzer* performed together last about an hour, which is a very long time to hold an audience's attention in the theater, especially if the music is all in three-quarter time. But I felt I had to do dances, set to this music. And the music would seem to me the best preparation one can have for watching the dances, unless one wants simply to be naturally surprised at what might happen. What happens on stage is dancing and gesture and music. The setting is a ballroom of an earlier time. There are small tables with candles at the side. A piano stands on the left, a man and a girl in evening dress sit down to play and four singers join them. Four couples in formal dress stand in this ballroom. As the music starts, they begin to dance. The music is a waltz in slow time, the words are about love. The waltz does not last long. Neither does the second, which is more vigorous. It is sung first by the baritone and is then taken up by the other singers. Two couples dance this one, as the others watch. And so it goes, one waltz after another, all different, for changing combinations of voices, for changing couples, for changing aspects of love.

Sometimes friends ask me why we do not print the words to all of these long songs in the program so that everyone will understand the original German. I always answer that the words really have nothing to do with the dances; to print them would suggest that the dances were illustrations and I never had that in mind.

After the eighteenth waltz and the end of Brahms's first group of *Liebeslieder*, the curtain comes down for a few minutes. When it rises again, there is a new setting, still a ballroom, but one without walls and illumined by the stars. The dancers are dressed differently, too, in costumes for ballet dancing. The atmosphere here is more theatrical, if you like, than the intimacy of the first part. So, I think, is the music.

At the end, after fourteen waltzes, the dancers leave the stage. The last song is to words by Goethe:

Nun, ihr Musen, genug!
Vergebens strebt ihr zu schildren
Wie sich Jammer und Gluck
Wechseln in liebender Brust

(*Now, Muses, enough! You try in vain to portray how misery and happiness alternate in a loving heart.*)

As these words are sung, the dancers come back and listen. That is all.

The words ought to be listened to in silence.

LILAC GARDEN

Dramatic ballet in one act. Music by Ernest Chausson. Choreography by Antony Tudor. Setting and costumes by Hugh Stevenson. First presented by the Rambert Ballet Club at the Mercury Theatre, London, January 26, 1936. Maude Lloyd, Hugh Laing, Peggy van Praagh, and Antony Tudor were the principals. First presented in the United States by Ballet Theatre at the Center Theatre, New York, January 15, 1940, with Viola Essen, Hugh Laing, Karen Conrad, and Antony Tudor in the principal roles.

This ballet is a tragedy of manners. It portrays the problem of a young woman who is about to marry a man she does not love. The time is the latter part of the Victorian era. It does not occur to the girl that her marriage can be put off: that she can escape from its "convenience." *Lilac Garden* depicts her mute acceptance in the kind of world where confession of any difficulty would be impossible. The drama of the ballet arises from a social situation that seems to demand confession and release.

The name of the girl is Caroline. She is giving a party for all of her friends and relations before the wedding. The scene is a lilac garden; the time is evening. The music is Chausson's *Poème*, for violin and orchestra.

When the curtain rises, Caroline and the man she must marry are standing together in the center of the garden. Giant shrubs of lilac surround the small open space. The light is misty. The girl wears a long white dress and white flowers in her hair. Her fiancé wears a formal suit with a long, formal coat reaching to his knees. There is a boutonnière in his buttonhole. They are a handsome couple, but each is preoccupied; they seem to have nothing to say to each other, no gestures to make. The man looks off to the left as if he were searching for someone. On the right, Caroline's lover enters. As she sees the man she really loves, the girl motions him away. The dark young man in uniform turns away. Caroline takes her fiancé's arm and they walk off, side by side. She glances back over her shoulder as they disappear. Another guest arrives at the party, a woman in a slate-blue dress. This is the former mistress of Caroline's husband-to-be. Other women come onto the scene. Caroline re-enters. She greets the newcomer. She does not know that this woman loves her fiancé. Now Caroline is alone. She moves backward toward the right. Her lover emerges; she falls back against him. He slips his arms under hers, and the two begin to dance. Their steps are so in harmony that it is apparent they have danced together many times before. Now the occasion is different. Caroline nervously looks to left and right whenever they pause in motion.

The woman in blue, her back turned, moves ominously across the back of the garden. The boy kisses Caroline's hand. The girl draws her hand back quickly; the woman in blue turns around. Caroline nervously introduces her two guests. Her hand moves to her lips; perhaps she should have kept them apart. The three dance forward together. As soon as she dares, Caroline draws her lover aside, and they dance away. Two men leap onto the stage and exit with the woman in blue.

Caroline re-enters, alone. She dances plaintively to the threnody of the violin's romantic theme. She holds her hand to her forehead in a gesture of hopelessness. As a group of her guests disturb her solitude, the girl moves her hand slightly, pretending that she is smoothing her hair. The melody mounts in intensity. The guests leave as two of the girls are lifted high by their escorts. Caroline pirouettes desperately toward the other side of the garden. Her lover appears while she turns frantically, and he catches her in his arms. He lifts her high above him, then the two kneel together. Then Caroline is afraid, suddenly, and hurries off.

Three couples and a girl come into the garden. Caroline's lover takes the girl for a partner, and the couples separate and bow, preparatory to a formal dance. Caroline disturbs the pattern by entering swiftly and dancing down the line between the couples. She moves off to the right.

The woman in blue joins the couples. She is searching for Caroline's fiancé, her former lover. By common instinct, the other women turn away and leave the garden. The woman bows to Caroline's lover. He turns away and follows the other men off. One man is attracted to the woman and remains until it is apparent that she will not notice him.

Caroline's fiancé steps out into the garden. The woman in blue runs to him, though the man turns aside, afraid to acknowledge her. He catches her as she leaps toward him, and the woman is poised for an instant high over his shoulder, looking down on his head. She has been his mistress, he has loved her, perhaps still does. He wishes to see her, but not here. He releases the woman he has renounced for Caroline, and they move together, mutually fearful of the consequences. The guests rush across the garden, and their rendezvous is interrupted swiftly. In what is apparently a single movement, the woman is lifted high and carried by Caroline's lover as Caroline is caught up in mid-movement by her fiancé.

All the guests dance together in a wide circle, as if nothing had happened. All leave the stage but Caroline and her lover. Her arms are rigid as she falls back into his arms. They dance forward; the music builds to a climax. He lifts the girl up straight and catches her body at full length as he lets her fall. He dips her body gently toward the ground and releases the girl to kneel at her feet.

Two of the older married women at the party see the lovers together. The boy rushes off. One of the women whispers to her companion, revealing Caroline's secret. Now she bows to Caroline. She approaches her softly and takes her hand, and the two move back to the rear of the garden. The woman reassures Caroline by her sympathy for her situation: all women, she suggests, love the man they do not marry. Caroline buries her face in her hands for a frantic instant. This is the first sympathetic advice she has ever received about her lover; she understands, to her horror, the sympathy that she in turn may someday give to someone else. The girl pulls her hands away from her face before she can weep. Caroline walks off.

Her lover re-enters. He gestures after Caroline, his hands clasped before him, hoping. The woman who has befriended Caroline and two other women repeat his gesture, then stand aside with bowed heads as the man sees that he can do nothing. They try to comfort him, but Caroline returns. The women leave the lovers alone. Now the music of the violin piercingly responds to the unhappiness of their passion; their fear that it will be perceived increases. Their ecstasy in being close is destroyed as they turn away from each other curtly and cruelly, lest they be seen. They stand apart, holding hands, as Caroline's fiancé enters. Her lover releases her, and the engaged couple walk away together. Now that all seems to be known, the boy rushes off alone.

The fiancé's former love, the woman in blue, dances into the garden, her movements quick, unyielding, and desperate. She leaves as Caroline and her own lover approach with two other couples. The three couples dance with stilted, subdued steps. The woman in blue tries to approach her lover. Fiercely he motions his former mistress away with his hand. The other couples walk away. He is afraid that Caroline may see, but directly the woman approaches her fiancé, Caroline disappears. The man is desperate: he has lost them both. He follows after the woman in blue, his hand shaking in anxiety.

Caroline and her lover enter and dance frantically, oblivious to their surroundings, and go off together. The entire orchestra takes up the theme of the violin fully. As the music gathers volume, the fiancé enters. The woman in blue leaps to his arms. Caroline and her lover run across the back. When they enter the garden, Caroline's fiancé turns away from the woman in blue and catches Caroline about the waist to lift her high above him. Caroline's arm points straight up over her head; she will not touch him. He lets her down. The other guests have come in; the orchestra sounds the climax of the melody. Caroline's fiancé bends down to kiss her hand. The girl stands beside him in stiff resignation; all movement is frozen: the guests are caught, with the engaged couple, in a tense, frigid tableau.

Caroline is the first to break the spell. Her fiancé stands holding the hand of an imaginary girl as she moves out to her lover; the music subsides. The guests move, the woman in blue approaches the fiancé, and all four lovers move forward in a slow line—Caroline and her lover at either end, reaching out into space. The two couples dance, the rejected lovers moving in unison with Caroline and her husband-to-be. The dresses of the girls flow with their retarded movement.

Suddenly the fiancé walks away. The woman in blue opens her arms. Caroline's lover runs off and returns to present to her a bouquet of lilacs. He kneels and kisses her hand. Caroline holds the flowers listlessly in her hand. Her fiancé returns with her cloak. He places it about her shoulders. The girl in white steps toward her and places her head on Caroline's shoulder in farewell. Caroline gestures to all of her guests, bidding them good-by. The violin mirrors her movement. As she reaches out her hand to her lover, her fiancé draws her hand back to her side. Caroline takes his arm and walks away with the man she must marry. The other guests depart. Her lover remains in the garden, his back turned.

NOTES *Lilac Garden* was one of the first ballets by the English choreographer and dancer Antony Tudor to be staged in the United States. It immediately became popular and has been so ever since. The New York City Ballet staged a new production of it on November 30, 1951, at the City Center, New York. This production provoked the following remarks from John Martin of the New York *Times*: "*Lilac Garden*, a modern classic, begins a new phase of its existence with the notable restudying it has received. Antony Tudor has given it back its choreographic substance . . . All its esthetic values have been deepened; so, too, have its emotional values. Nora Kaye, who has danced her role many times, has found new warmth, new womanliness, new quiet eloquence of movement and of spirit, and Tanaquil LeClercq, who has never danced the role of the other woman before, illumines it with electric tensions that are taut and tragic. As a crowning glory, Horace Armistead has provided a setting that actually participates in the drama by its subtly authoritative establishment of the mood and the mores of the action."

Alicia Markova, Nora Kaye, Diana Adams, and Alicia Alonso have all danced the part of Caroline. Maria Tallchief danced the part of the other woman in guest appearances with Ballet Theatre in 1949. Tanaquil LeClercq and Yvonne Mounsey have danced it in the New York City Ballet revival. Hugh Laing and Antony Tudor resumed their customary roles in first performances of this revival; Tudor's role has been taken since by Brooks Jackson.

Dame Marie Rambert, in whose ballet company *Jardin aux Lilas* (*Lilac Garden*) was created, has recalled its beginnings in her book *Quicksilver:* "Tudor wrote *Jardin aux Lilas* in 1936. The subject was suggested to him by Hugh Stevenson, who did a perfect, though obvious, setting of clumps of lilac bushes and beautiful costumes, very expressive of the various characters. Here is the synopsis as printed in the program: Caroline, on the eve of her marriage to the man she does not love, tries to say farewell to her lover at a garden reception, but is constantly interrupted by guests and in the end goes off on the arm of her betrothed with hopelessness in her eyes. The situation is complicated by the presence of her betrothed's former love.

"The interplay of feelings between these characters was revealed in beautiful dance movements and groupings, with subtle changes of expression, which made each situation clear without any recourse to mime or gesture. It could be called a '*ballet psychologique*' on the same ground as Stendhal's '*roman psychologique.*' It had one quite startling moment: at the height of the drama the movement froze and the music continued alone for several bars. It made you hold your breath. The whole ballet was perfect and has become a classic. Although it had been composed on the small stage of the Mercury, it bore transference to the Metropolitan Opera House in New York. In fact, as I have indicated, those of our Mercury ballets that were good became even better on big stages, because the dancers could take wing after the restricted space of our own stage—and the integrity of the work itself shone the brighter."

MANON

Ballet in three acts. Music by Jules Massenet, orchestrated and arranged by Leighton Lucas with the collaboration of Hilda Gaunt. Produced by Kenneth MacMillan. Choreography by Kenneth MacMillan. Designs by Nicholas Georgiadis. First presented by the Royal Ballet at the Royal Opera House, Covent Garden, London, March 7, 1974, with Antoinette Sibley, Anthony Dowell, David Wall, and Derek Rencher in principal roles. First presented in the United States by the same ensemble, May 7, 1974, at the Metropolitan Opera House, New York.

Based on Abbé Prévost's great eighteenth-century romantic novel *Manon Lescaut* and not on the famous operas derived from that work, this ballet tells the story of a girl who has much charm but little character. She suffers accordingly, but not before she has brought down with her a lover who persists in finding in her charm a character no one else can see. The choreographer, Kenneth MacMillan, has said that what interested him from the start was Manon's amoral nature, which shifts from scene to scene, and within scenes.

ACT ONE, SCENE ONE takes place in the courtyard of an inn near Paris. The music that introduces it is not the familiar music by Massenet we might expect from that composer's opera to this story; indeed, all of Massenet's music used in the ballet comes from any work of his except his opera *Manon*. This particular inn is frequented by actresses, gentlemen, and the demimonde from Paris; it is artificially gay, a set-up and a snare for the unwary; it is not surprising to find a ratcatcher one of the principal personages in the courtyard. Coaches come and go, depositing pretentious ladies with large muffs who are escorted by gouty gentlemen. In the crowd we begin to distinguish a young man, Lescaut by name, who seems to know what everything is all about and has it all under control; he dances a vigorous solo. After an interlude featuring a bunch of ragpickers, we notice, too, a young divinity student who walks about in a broad-brimmed hat reading, preoccupied with his holy studies. This is Des Grieux, a handsome boy who seems to shun the world. The worldly persons who dominate the courtyard are Lescaut, who is there to meet his sister, Manon, on her way to join a convent, and Monsieur G.M., a wealthy Parisian. A coach arrives bringing Manon and an old gentleman who has been very much attracted to her. Manon is young, about sixteen she seems (as in Prévost), and much dazzled by the bustle of the courtyard. But it is clear that she has the old gentleman under control and shuns his advances. Des Grieux does not notice her, nor she him, at first; he sits reading. Monsieur G.M. does notice her and wants her as much as the old man does; he asks Lescaut to intercede on his behalf and secure Manon's favors for him. Lescaut is happy to oblige and all but auctions his sister off between Monsieur G.M. and the old man. In the midst of this undertaking, Manon is horrified to see a ratcatcher in the crowd. Des Grieux, watching a bit now, moves over to a table on the right, fanning his face with his hat and removing his jacket. He and Manon, both all innocence, watch as a courtesan dances for Lescaut and G.M. Then suddenly Des Grieux has forgotten his book and is staring at Manon. The old man kisses her hand. Des Grieux rises. The old man gives money to Lescaut. Manon is suddenly face to face with Des Grieux. The lights dim; they seem to be all alone; he dances for her, then kneels at her feet and kisses her hand. She is embarrassed, touched, and clearly attracted. To soft strings, he openly adores her. When she rises, he takes her in his arms and they begin to dance together of their growing passion. The dance is cool, detached from its environment.

Manon and Des Grieux, now much in love, decide to escape to Paris with the help of the money she has meanwhile taken from the old gentleman. Lescaut and the old gentleman, having made a bargain about Manon, emerge from the inn. To their dismay, Manon has gone: Des Grieux has mounted the driver's seat in the coach and taken her away. Monsieur G.M., always eager to join the crowd, at this point informs Lescaut that he, too, is interested in Manon. G.M.'s wealth is known to Lescaut, who promises to find his sister and persuade her to abandon Des Grieux and accept the rich G.M.

In SCENE TWO, Lescaut remarkably succeeds. The setting is Des Grieux's rooms in Paris, where he writes a letter, by candlelight, to his father asking him for money. Manon, languishing near the large bed at the left, does not like to be unattended and tries to interrupt her lover. They dance, reassuring each other of the depth of their love. Manon then helps Des Grieux into his overcoat and he goes off to mail the letter. In his absence, her brother, the perpetual fixer, arrives with Monsieur G.M. When the latter presents her with a fine gown and jewelry, it is as if she had never been a sweet sixteen-year-old on the way to any convent. She forgets Des Grieux, although she does hang on to the bed draperies a bit in fleeting recollection. There is a *pas de trois* in which her brother guides the girl and with G.M. swings Manon between them as if she were a toy. Lescaut swings her up to G.M.'s shoulder and, seeing the self-satisfaction that has matured between the two "lovers," asks for payment from G.M.

Manon says "adieu" to the bed and leaves with G.M. while Lescaut jiggles the purse he has received. Des Grieux returns and, sharing the purse with him, Lescaut tries to persuade him that they will all be rich if he, Des Grieux, will sanction the liaison between Manon and G.M. Lescaut is thoroughly in control of this situation and the impoverished Des Grieux consents.

In ACT TWO, the first scene is a gambling house and bordello, a "*hôtel particulier* of Madame." This Madame bustles about in her hall of mirrors and shiftily clad young girls making matches with the men who turn up. It is all *ancien régime* and polite; the men put their swords away upon arrival and even with the raucous music there is an agreed on code of behavior that prevents the expression of true feeling.

Lescaut, drunk, brings in Des Grieux, who is horrified at it all. Lescaut dances brilliantly of his spirited exhilaration and the girls try to close in on Des Grieux. When Manon arrives on the scene with G.M. and finds Des Grieux there, she gradually is seen to be torn between the wealth of her present lover and her recollection of the impetuous youth who saved her from the convent. Wearing a black and gold dress of rich embroidery and brilliant jewelry, Manon dances with her assembled admirers at the party while Des Grieux watches. She is manipulated in the *sarabande* and passed from one man to another as G.M. watches. Finally, she is lifted to G.M. and placed at his feet.

Although Manon is increasingly shattered by Des Grieux's presence and tries to avoid him, he at length tries to persuade her to leave with him. She tells him that the time is not right and engineers an arrangement for Des Grieux to cheat at cards with G.M. Her older lover is highly suspicious, however, and in the midst of the card game catches Des Grieux cheating. Des Grieux and Manon rush away.

In SCENE TWO, back at Des Grieux's lodgings, he and Manon once again declare their love for one another. She touches the curtains of their bed. G.M. interrupts them, however, just as Des Grieux has succeeded in reminding Manon that if she is to stay with him, she must give up the jewelry G.M. has lavished on her. It is precisely the jewelry's return that G.M. in his vengeance seeks. Lescaut is brought in, in handcuffs, and G.M. is triumphant. In the ensuing struggle and her arrest as a prostitute, Manon's brother is killed. Manon and Des Grieux look on in horror. Monsieur, holding Manon's arm, is gleeful.

In ACT THREE, the scene shifts to New Orleans, then a penal colony for the French. In his office, the jailer of the penal colony has a rendezvous with his girl. Two soldiers enter to remind him of certain duties and he leaves for the port.

The port dominates the second scene, busy with the unloading of ships. Cargo and passengers descend onto the dock while the soldiers and natives watch. Many of the exiled prisoners are girls, prostitutes like Manon, who lament their lot in a dance. Yet the jailer flirts with them and, above all, with Manon, who enters with Des Grieux. The jailer's girl despairs of her lover and tries to deflect his attention from the new riffraff from France, but the man persists and she is dragged away by his soldiers. Manon is also taken away to his room. Here the jailer, strangely drawn to this pathetic emaciated creature who has seemingly lost all her charm, is completely captivated. He is a displaced G.M. all over again and can offer her much. The dance he compels her to perform is done passively on her part and she appears to despise the man. He does not notice, however, and places a bracelet on her wrist in gratification. Des Grieux enters and stabs him. Manon throws the bracelet on the jailer's body and flees with Des Grieux.

Trying to escape capture, the lovers hide in a swamp, where mists and menacing foliage envelop their passage. Exhausted from their flight, Manon and Des Grieux rest. In a kind of delirium, the girl recalls her past and sees it travel in the mist before her—the jailer, the Madame of the bordello, the ratcatcher, G.M. Roused by her delirium, Des Grieux tries to comfort her. The two perform an impassioned dance in which Manon seeks a comfort as yet unknown; in a turmoil of abandonment, she is flung high into the air and spins there hysterically, only to be caught again in her lover's arms. All her former notions of wealth and splendor have been renounced for her love for Des Grieux. As she gradually expires, the demented man tries to revive her and to prop her up, but he cannot succeed. She has given up the ghost and Des Grieux laments.

NOTES The music for *Manon* by Massenet, arranged by Leighton Lucas and Hilda Gaunt, is taken from the operas *Le Cid, Griselda, Thérèse, Cinderella, Cléopâtre, Don Quixote, Eve, Thaïs, Bacchus, Ariane,* and *Le Roi de Lahore,* the orchestral works *Scènes alsaciennes, Scènes pittoresques, Scènes dramatiques, La navarraise, Valse très Lente, Chanson de Capri,* and *Aubade de Chérubin.*

The music for the Prelude to the ballet is from *Le dernier sommeil de la Vierge* and the *Cantata de la Vierge.* The score for Act One, Scene One is derived from *Aubade de Chérubin, Scènes dramatique, Scènes pittoresques, Le Cid, Créspuscule, Pastorale* from *L'esclaramonde, First Orchestral Suite, Scènes dramatiques, Si tu le veux, mignonne*—a song, *Griselda, Thaïs, Ariane, Élégie, Menuet d'Amour* from *Thé-*

rèse. Act One, Scene Two: *Cendrillon, Ouvre tes yeux bleus*—a song, *Cendrillon,* and a salon piece.

Act Two, Scene One: *Scènes dramatiques, Au Cabaret—Scènes alsaciennes, Ariane, Bacchus,* a salon piece, *Don Quixote, Cléopâtre, Le Roi de Lahore, Crépuscule, Air de ballet, La navarraise, Élégie, Il pluvait*—a song, *Griselda, Cléopâtre.* Scene Two: *Adam and Eve, Bacchus.*

Act Three, Scene One: *Cendrillon, Griselda, Don Quixote, Cendrillon, Don Quixote, Don Quixote, Crépuscule, Sappho,* and *Adam and Eve.* Scene Two: Symposium of hallucinations. Scene Three: *La vierge, La vierge.*

Interviewed in *The New Yorker* in 1974 about *Manon,* Kenneth MacMillan said: "The characters fascinate me. You have a sixteen-year-old heroine who is beautiful and absolutely amoral, and a hero who is corrupted by her and becomes a cheat, a liar, and a murderer. Not exactly our conventional ballet plot, is it? One of the intriguing things about Prévost's Manon is that there doesn't seem to be any logic in the way she thinks. One minute, she tells Des Grieux that she loves him, the next minute she's deceiving him with an elderly count. My clue to her behavior is her background of poverty. Manon is not so much afraid of being poor as *ashamed* of being poor. Which brings me to the other theme of the ballet—the contrast between great wealth and great poverty in eighteenth-century France. . . ."*

* From "MacMillan's Manon" by Jane Boutwell in "The Talk of the Town." Reprinted by permission; © 1974 The New Yorker Magazine, Inc.

A MIDSUMMER NIGHT'S DREAM

Ballet in two acts and six scenes. Music by Felix Mendelssohn. Choreography by George Balanchine. Scenery and lighting by David Hays. Costumes by Karinska. First presented by the New York City Ballet at the City Center, New York, January 17, 1962, with Arthur Mitchell as Puck, *Jillana as* Helena, *Edward Villella as* Oberon, *Melissa Hayden as* Titania, *Roland Vasquez as* Bottom, *Francisco Moncion as* Theseus, *Patricia McBride as* Hermia, *Nicholas Magallanes as* Lysander, *Bill Carter as* Demetrius, *Gloria Govrin as* Hippolyta; *Violette Verdy, Conrad Ludlow, and the entire company.**

Shakespeare's *A Midsummer Night's Dream* has always been a favorite of mine ever since I first saw it and appeared in the play as a child in Russia. I was an elf in a production at the Mikhailovsky Theatre in St. Petersburg when I was about eight years old. I suppose it was then that I came to know so many lines from the play; even now I can recite in Russian speeches like the famous one of Oberon's beginning:

> *I know a bank where the wild thyme blows,*
> *Where oxlips and the nodding violet grows . . .*

I worked on a production of the play at the Shakespeare Memorial Theatre in Stratford, Connecticut, in 1950, arranging some dances. But what has really interested me more than Shakespeare's words in recent years has been the music that Mendelssohn wrote to the play, and I think it can be said that the ballet was inspired by the score.

Mendelssohn did not, however, write music for the whole play. To fill out the danced action that developed as the ballet was being made, I selected other scores of Mendelssohn's that neatly fitted into the pattern we were making. (The pieces incorporated along with the incidental music in the first act are the overtures to *Athalie, The Fair Melusine, The First Walpurgis Night;* in the second act the *Symphony No.* 9 and the overture *Son and Stranger.*)

* See also THE DREAM.

The story of the ballet, of course, concerns the adventures and misadventures of a group of mortals and immortals in their resolutions of the confusions and problems of loving and being loved. It is called a "dream" because of the unrealistic happenings that occur to the characters . . . real yet unreal events such as crossed loves, meaningless quarrels, forest chases, and magic spells woven by the infamous Puck. I think it is possible to see and enjoy the ballet without knowing the play. At least that was my hope in creating the piece.

The first act takes place in a forest near the duke's palace. Oberon, King of the Fairies, and Titania, his queen, quarrel. Oberon orders Puck to bring the flower pierced by Cupid's arrow (which causes anyone coming under its influence to fall in love with the first person the eyes behold), and while Titania is asleep and unknowing, he casts the flower's spell over her.

Meanwhile, Helena, wandering in the wood, meets Demetrius, whom she loves but who does not love her. Demetrius rejects her and goes his way. Oberon watches and tells Puck to use the flower on Demetrius that he may return Helena's affection.

Another couple, Hermia and Lysander, very much in love, are also wandering in the forest. They become separated. Puck, eager to carry out Oberon's orders, mistakenly anoints Lysander. Helena appears and Lysander, under the flower's spell, at once and to her amazement tells her how much he loves her.

Hermia now returns. She is astonished and then dismayed to see Lysander paying attention only to Helena. Puck manages to bring Demetrius, too, under the flower's spell, much to the delight of Helena, who doesn't care for Lysander at all.

Demetrius and Lysander, now both in love with Helena, begin to quarrel over her. Puck, at Oberon's order, has separated Bottom, a weaver, from his companions, transformed his head into that of an ass, and placed him at the sleeping Titania's feet. Awakening, Titania sees Bottom, thinks him fair, and pays him close and loving attention. At last Oberon, his anger over, has Bottom sent away and releases Titania from her spell.

Hermia now gets no attention, Helena too much. The men, completely at odds, quarrel seriously and begin to fight. Puck by his magic causes them to separate, lose one another and wander apart in the forest, until exhausted they fall asleep, with Puck arranging for Helena to fall asleep beside Demetrius and Lysander (his spell removed) by Hermia.

The duke and Hippolyta discover the lovers asleep in the forest, awaken them, find their differences are resolved and proclaim a triple wedding for themselves and the two couples.

The second act opens in the duke's palace with parades, dancing, and *divertissements* in honor of the newly married couples. When the celebrations are over and the mortals retire, we return to the demesne of Oberon and Titania, who are now reunited and at peace. And at last Puck having put order into disorder sweeps away the remnants of the night's doings. The fireflies twinkle in the night and reclaim the forest.

MONUMENT FOR A DEAD BOY

Music by Jan Boerman. Choreography by Rudi van Dantzig. Scenery and costumes by Toer van Schayk. First presented by the Het National Ballet, 1966. First presented in the United States by the Harkness Ballet, November 3, 1967, with Lawrence Rhodes in the principal role.

This ballet traces the history of a young boy who, at his death, looks back. It is preceded by a quotation from Truman Capote: "Unafraid, not hesitating, he paused only at the garden's edge where, as though he'd forgotten something, he stopped and looked back at the bloomless, descending blue, at the boy he had left behind." Verbal themes for the eight parts of the narrative are derived from *The Inner Wallpaper* by Hans Lodeizen. The music is an electronic score by Jan Boerman.

Six huddled dark figures, perhaps the furies who haunt the boy's life, are seen in shadow as the ballet begins. The mature boy and his younger self, protrayed by a smaller dancer, enter and move together, identifying and differing in gesture and emphasis. ("I am playing with the sad rope of time.") Then suddenly the older boy is lifted away to watch the youth. ("Springtime makes doors, the wind is an open hand, we must yet begin to love.") His parents enter and soon, in an excess of affection, they all but tear the child in two in a tug-of-war. ("Soon we will all have died; What is memory? What is love?") The boy seeks refuge in the arms of his older self. Where can I go, he seems to ask, but to myself?

Two visions now haunt him, one a girl in blue ("As I am standing in the yellow night on the blue floorcloth of my heart"), the other a girl in white. ("In a block of buildings I live as a child, suspecting fingers everywhere, darkness and kisses.") Both attracted and repelled, the boy finds alternating comfort, understanding, and tenderness with another boy at school. (". . . happiness with you means the past.") Next, a painting of a playground, the back wall embellished with graffiti and five boys spaced in front of it, comes suddenly alive. The hero is attacked, hurt, humiliated. (". . . like jellyfish on a beach, they soil the horizon.") The Girl in Blue finds him. They dance together in sympathy and passion but it is too late. Back at home, the boy watches in horror the aggressive lust of his parents. At this point the older boy and his youth portray his despair, a hopelessness that finds release only in death. (". . . like a curtain I jerked open darkness, to see the night.") As the hero dies, his younger self grieves, hailing him, celebrating him forever, in a silent lament, and remembering.

NOTES Revived by American Ballet Theatre at the City Center, New York, January 11, 1973, *Monument for a Dead Boy* starred Ivan Nagy as the Boy. Scenery and costumes were by Toer van Schayk. Lighting by George Bardyguine.

The critic Robb Baker of *FM Guide* wrote of this revival: *Monument for a Dead Boy* "is a powerful psychological dance drama depicting a teenaged boy looking back at his own homoerotic fantasies." Rudolf Nureyev and Helgi Tomasson have danced the principal role in this ballet. The English critic Oleg Kerensky has said in his book *The World of Ballet* that "it is a powerful theatrical work. . . . It grips its audience at least as much by its subject matter, its psychological interest, and its skillful staging as by its dance content."

THE MOOR'S PAVANE

Music by Henry Purcell (arranged by Simon Sadoff). Choreography by Jose Limon. Costumes by Pauline Lawrence. First presented by Jose Limon and Company at the Connecticut College American Dance Festival, Palmer Auditorium, New London, Connecticut, August 17, 1949, with Jose Limon, Betty Jones, Lucas Hoving, and Pauline Kohner. First presented by American Ballet Theatre at the New York State Theater, Lincoln Center, June 27, 1970, with Bruce Marks, Sallie Wilson, Royes Fernandez, and Toni Lander. Assistants to Mr. Limon: Daniel Lewis, Clive Morgan, and Jennifer Muller. Conducted by Akira Endo.

Long acknowledged as a masterwork of modern dance and performed in the United States and abroad by Jose Limon and his company, *The Moor's Pavane* is fortunately available to the public also in the repertories of American Ballet Theatre, the City Center Joffrey Ballet and other ensembles. Subtitled "Variations on a Theme of Othello," it is assumed that the spectator is familiar with Shakespeare's play. Here all subplots, or non-essentials of that story, are eliminated, and in a stately quadrille, the four principals—Othello, Desdemona, Iago, and Emilia, called here the Moor, his wife, the Friend, and his wife, dance a minuet of love, comradeship, jealousy inflamed, betrayal, death, and discovery.

NOTES Reviewing this revival of *The Moor's Pavane* in the New York *Times,* Clive Barnes wrote: "*The Moor's Pavane* is a totally engrossing work and likely to remain among Mr. Limon's most enduring ballets. . . . What Mr. Limon has set out to do is to picture the corrosive force of jealousy and the destruction of good by evil, and to encapsulate this into the patterns of a ballroom dance.

"The dance starts simply enough, with bows and graces, and all manner of Elizabethan furbelows. But as it proceeds, the undercurrents of feeling beneath the courtly observances make themselves felt, the dance takes on a new urgency, moves into a new dimension. . . . Mr. Limon has been fortunate here in an ideal cast. I will never forget Mr. Limon himself and Lucas Hoving as the original Othello and Iago. They were fantastic—a bull and a matador come to judgment. Yet now Bruce Marks and Royes Fernandez are no less impressive. Mr. Marks, bearded, noble, anguished, and with all the passion and agony of the world on his broad shoulders, is brought low by a sinuously insinuating Mr. Fernandez, a very proper villain with the graceful movements of a snake.

"This admirable cast is completed by Sallie Wilson as the wicked Emilia (Mr. Limon is less charitable with her than is Shakespeare) and Toni Lander as the yielding and wronged Desdemona. It is a shrewd and subtle work that will be a credit to Ballet Theatre."

Writing in the Washington *Post* of Jose Limon's work after his death in 1972, Jean Battey Lewis said: "Perhaps his best-known work is *The Moor's Pavane*, his conception of the Shakespearean tragedy of Othello. He and his company danced the work at the White House before President and Mrs. Johnson in 1967 and the dance is in the repertoire of several ballet companies here and abroad. (It was danced at the Kennedy Center last season by American Ballet Theatre.)

"Eric Bentley once said that of all the works created on the American stage the one he would choose above all others to send abroad as a showcase of our art would be *The Moor's Pavane*.

"Describing himself as 'either the most atheistic of Catholics or the most Catholic of atheists,' Limon was often inspired by Biblical themes—*The Traitor*, based on the betrayal of Jesus; *There Is a Time*, and *The Exiles*, a dance about Adam and Eve, are among them. *A Choreographic Offering* to the music of Bach was his tribute to his mentor, Doris Humphey.

"A few years ago the dancer declared, 'I try to compose works that are involved with man's basic tragedy and the grandeur of his spirit. I want to dig beneath empty formalisms, displays of technical virtuosity, and the slick surface; to probe the human entity for the powerful, often crude beauty of the gesture that speaks of man's humanity.

"'I reach for demons, saints, martyrs, apostates, fools, and other impassioned visions. I go for inspiration and instruction to the artists who reveal the passion of man to me, who exemplify supreme artistic discipline and impeccable form: to Bach, Michelangelo, Shakespeare, Goya, Schonberg, Picasso, Orozco,' he continued.

"This wrestling with elemental themes is obviously not a currently fashionable approach in an art that in recent years has leaned toward abstraction, impersonality and a structure based on chance. Talking to Limon last year after a rehearsal at Julliard School in New York it was clear that he had no use for fashion in the arts.

"He was working at the time on a new dance, *Dances for Isadora,* which he said he was composing in memory of his wife.

"*Dances for Isadora* is a study of Isadora Duncan, the first great revolutionary American dancer. Somewhat as a companion piece (*Isadora* was a dance for five women), Limon was completing *The Unsung,* a suite of male solos on eight American Indian chieftains—our unsung heroes.

"Of his choice themes, Limon said at the time, 'What are we here on earth for if not to illuminate our experience, for ourselves and others?'"

MUTATIONS

Music by Karlheinz Stockhausen. Choreography by Glen Tetley. Cine-choreography by Hans van Manen. Film visualization by Jean-Paul Vroom. Production designs by Nadine Baylis. Costumes by Emmy van Leersum and Gijs Bakker. Lighting by John B. Read. First presented by the Netherlands Dance Theatre at the Circustheater, Scheveningen, Holland, July 3, 1970. First presented in the United States by the same ensemble at the Brooklyn Academy of Music, New York, March 29, 1972.

With the presentation of *Mutations,* New York saw a nude ballet performed for the first time by a major company on a major stage. In addition to nudity, unusual aspects of the work include film episodes, shown on three screens at the back of the stage while live dancers perform in front of them, and action which extends from the stage along a ramp into the center aisle.

The first of the ballet's films is of naked Gérard Lemaitre and is in such slow motion that his body appears to float freely and effortlessly through space. The final scene is a nude *pas de deux* danced by Anja Licher and Lemaitre while all three films are shown behind them. The *pas de deux* repeats in part some of the filmed choreography as well as sections of the live choreography.

The ballet is not entirely nude, for it also concerns the emotional influences of costume. The clothed dancers have movements that are correspondingly rigid. Those half-undressed use their freedom for aggression and competition. And finally, the totally nude dancers explore the possibilities of fluid, unencumbered motion.

NOTES: Glen Tetley says, "You construct a game, you set your own restrictions, and then you challenge yourself to find your way through these restrictions."

Writing after the first performance of *Mutations* in London, in 1970, the critic Alexander Bland said in *The Observer*: ". . . It is sincere, shapely, rich in those plastic movements which Tetley excels in. . . . Nudity is used in this ballet as a stimulating but serious ingredient which completely justifies itself artistically. The scene is a kind of arena (by Nadine Baylis) into which white-clad figures gradually fight their way. Once arrived, the mood changes. A nude figure appears dancing on film, and this is followed by a nice trio for girls . . . and some all-in applications of red paint suggesting violence. A couple dance, clad and unclad on screen and stage, to gently variegated electronic sounds by Stockhausen; more join in and the film triplicates until some mysterious figures in transparent suits sweep the action off stage—naked and strangely vulnerable—alone as the lights fade."

NAPOLI

Romantic ballet in three acts. Music by E. Helsted, Gade, and Paulli. Choreography and book by Auguste Bournonville. Scenery by Christensen. First presented by the Royal Danish Ballet at the Theatre Royal, Copenhagen, March 29, 1842.

Napoli is the great ballet by Auguste Bournonville, the dancer, choreographer, and ballet master of the Royal Danish Ballet for many years and the founder of its famous continuous tradition of training and performance. Since 1829, when Bournonville mounted his first ballet in Copenhagen, ballets by him have been danced by the Royal Danish Ballet more than four thousand times. *Napoli,* the finest of them, is but a year younger than *Giselle;* but unlike *Giselle, Napoli* has not been changed by succeeding generations of choreographers, dancers, and musicians: it is still danced in Copenhagen today as it was more than one hundred and twenty-five years ago.

ACT ONE—NAPLES, BY THE BAY OF SANTA LUCIA—EVENING Three boys are in love with the beautiful Teresina, the daughter of a watchful widow. Teresina loves only one, a fisherman, Gennaro. Her two suitors—Giacomo, who sells macaroni in the town, and Peppo, who sells lemonade—try to persuade her mother that Teresina will be better off married to one of them. Teresina, the mother indicates, will make up her own mind. Teresina ignores her suitors as she waits for Gennaro, who is returning to port with all the other fishermen of the town.

Soon the fishermen return. Gennaro embraces Teresina, and her mother reluctantly consents to their marriage. A monk, Fra Ambrosio, enters and asks the fishermen and the assembled townsfolk for alms. Gennaro and Teresina both contribute. Teresina's suitors, Giacomo and Peppo, still persist in bothering her and her mother; they try to make the girl jealous as Gennaro jokes with a girl who has come to buy fish from him. But when Gennaro places an engagement ring on her finger, Teresina is convinced that her happiness lies only with him.

The two lovers go out into the bay in order to be alone. After they have been gone for some time, thunder and lightning fill the air. A violent storm breaks over the Bay of Santa Lucia. Gennaro, out in the bay, rows frantically, trying to reach shore. His fellow fishermen go to help him, and he is rescued. But Teresina has been swept overboard by the giant waves, and no one can find her. Gennaro curses his destiny. The girl's mother accuses him of drowning Teresina, and all the people of the town abandon him.

Gennaro is alone. He is about to despair, but then he prays beneath a likeness of the Madonna. Fra Ambrosio comes to him and, giving him an image of the Madonna to carry with him for protection from harm, tells Gennaro not to give up hope: he must take a boat and go out to sea and there find his love. Gennaro goes to find a boat. Fra Ambrosio kneels in prayer.

ACT TWO—CAPRI—A BLUE GROTTO In Act Two, the scene changes to an entirely different world. Here, in a blue grotto, we are in the abode of Golfo, a powerful sea sprite who rules over the sea around and about him. Two of Golfo's naiads approach the grotto in the great sea shell they use for a boat. They bring to their master Teresina, whom they have rescued. Teresina still holds the guitar she was playing to Gennaro in the fishing boat before the storm broke over Naples.

Teresina asks Golfo to return her to her home, but the sea sprite is fascinated by the girl's beauty and wishes to keep her by him. Over her head he pours the magical water of the grotto, and the girl becomes a naiad; she forgets entirely that she was ever a mortal.

All of Golfo's naiads and Tritons forgather and celebrate the initiation of the newcomer. Golfo himself makes love to her, but Teresina repulses his advances.

Gennaro's boat enters the grotto. Golfo signals his slaves to disappear: he, alone, will deal with the intruder. Gennaro beaches the boat and looks about him. He sees Teresina's guitar. He knows now that she is alive! Golfo tries to induce him to leave the grotto by causing fire to engulf the grotto, but Gennaro refuses to go. He asks for Teresina, and finally the other naiads bring the girl to him.

Of course, since she is no longer a human being, the girl does not recognize her lover. Gennaro tries to bring back her memory by speaking of their life together in Naples and by playing upon her guitar, but still the girl is unmoved. Gennaro is about to give up, when he remembers the image of the Virgin which Fra Ambrosio gave him. He beseeches the Madonna that Teresina's memory may be restored. Slowly Teresina recognizes him. She remembers their love, and the two lovers embrace.

Golfo, enraged at the reconciliation of the lovers, contrives to kidnap Teresina. But the girl will not leave Gennaro. The Tritons and naiads cannot separate them. Teresina realizes though, that they will never be able to return home unless Golfo's rage is calmed. She holds up the image of the Madonna and commands Golfo and his sea creatures to bow to the Queen of Heaven. Golfo and his Tritons and naiads submit, and the two lovers set sail for Naples in a boat weighed down with gifts.

ACT THREE—MONTE VIRGINES, NEAR NAPLES The people of the city are gathered together on a religious pilgrimage outside Naples, when Teresina appears with her mother. The people are astonished. Gennaro arrives, and Teresina informs her friends that her lover rescued her. But her friends, who believed her dead, find that such a claim is too mysterious: perhaps witches are at work. Teresina's mother separates her from Gennaro.

Gennaro rails at Teresina's mother for believing such nonsense. The people flee in fear of witchcraft. Only Fra Ambrosio can set them right. He is sent for, blesses Gennaro, and tells the crowd how Teresina was rescued through the power of the Virgin.

Everyone believes the monk instantly, and all gather about Teresina and Gennaro. They dance to celebrate the reunion of the lovers, and Teresina and Gennaro are lifted into a cart, in which their friends draw them toward their home, marriage and a happy life together.

NIJINSKY–CLOWN OF GOD

Ballet by Maurice Béjart. Music by Pierre Henri. Costumes by Joelle Roustan and Roger Bernard. Lighting by Roger Bernard. Sound direction by Pierre Henri. First presented by the Ballet of the Twentieth Century at the Forest National Auditorium, Brussels, October 8, 1971, with Jorge Donn as The Clown of God, *Paolo Bartoluzzi as the* Rose, *Daniel Lommel as the* Golden Slave, *Jorg Lanner as the* Faun, *Micha Van Hoecke as* Petrouchka, *Suzanne Farrell as the* Girl in Pink, *Angele Albrecht as the* Nymph, *Jaleh Kerendi as the* Woman of the World, *Cathérine Verneuil as the* Ballerina, *Hitomi Asakawa as the* Doll, *and Pierre Dobrievich as* Diaghilev *in the principal roles. First presented in the United States by the Ballet of the Twentieth Century at the Felt Forum, Madison Square Garden, New York, October 24, 1972.*

The ballet is given in two parts, the whole consisting of eleven scenes. During the work, extracts from *The Diary of Vaslav Nijinsky* are read over the loudspeaker. It is largely upon this book, which Maurice Béjart reread in 1971, that his ballet on the life of the most renowned of all dancers is based. Béjart has said: "Of all the famous names connected with that rich and strange era of Diaghilev and the Russian Ballet, the person of Nijinsky is perhaps the most perplexing and fascinating. Even to those not particularly interested in ballet, the name and the phenomenon of this great dancer must be familiar. It is generally known that he was one of the most spectacular dancers the world has ever seen, that he was especially renowned for his sensational leap, and that his career was tragically curtailed by madness. Yet Nijinsky's personality and the forces that led to his madness are widely unknown.

"In one of his works Henry Miller, alone on an island, talks about the books he could not live without; among the two or three great titles which he cites appears *The Diary of Nijinsky*. He adds: 'I never grow tired of reading it.' The key to Nijinsky is in that *Diary*–a disturbing document about an exceptional human being.

"The *Diary* was written as his total madness was approaching and records his most inward feelings, emotions, and fantasies. In life, Nijinsky was described by his contemporaries as quiet, slow, and rather awkward, yet when he emerged upon the stage his personality was transformed and his body expressed grace, poetry, and dynamic energy. In the *Diary* yet another side of his personality is revealed—a quick, restless, and highly cultured mind reacting with intensity to the events and people around him. The *Diary* is a frightening yet uplifting book, for we watch Nijinsky's mind gradually giving way under the pressure of its own sensitivity to the horrors of the First World War, to Diaghilev's cruel treatment of him after his marriage, and to the artistic pressures of creativity. Yet beyond all this we feel his burning conviction in his role as 'Clown of God' and in his need to preach the gospel of universal love.

"This ballet does not attempt to be a biographical reconstruction of Nijinsky's life, but, taking its inspiration from the *Diary*, it tries to create a marginal note, a secret path where the heart, ideas, emotions, memories, and fantasies can live and dance an imaginary ballet on lines similar, perhaps, to those of his own thoughts during the last conscious moments of his life. Imaginative and allegorical figures come alive and enact the conflicts in Nijinsky's mind—representations of characters from his ballets and from his life. Most important among these are the three principal characters in the action: NIJINSKY HIMSELF—the artist and poet in search of Truth, who sees himself as the apostle of universal love, a mystic messenger of God; WOMAN—not just Nijinsky's own wife, but a symbol of love and poetry, a vision and a creature of the spirit; DIAGHILEV—Nijinsky's master, father, creator. In short, his God, at once feared and adored."

The setting of the ballet is a large open stage dominated by a large black cross. From left and right, high ramps descend to the open area. Everything is dark. A voice sounds: "The world was made by God, Man was made by God. It is impossible for man to understand God, but God understands God."

Béjart's "Clown of God" theme for this work is also taken

from Nijinsky's *Diary:* "I will pretend to be a clown, because then they will understand me better. I love Shakespeare's clowns—they have a lot of humor, but nevertheless they express hate, they are not from God. I am a clown of God, and therefore like joking. I mean that a clown is all right when he expresses love. A clown without love is not from God."

A synopsis of the ballet follows.

PART ONE THE NIJINSKY OF THE RUSSIAN BALLET 1. *The Creation of the World:* Inert, naked, and faceless bodies cover the stage. Under God's eyes they become animated, organized, breathing. The circle is formed. Life!

A being detaches itself from the anonymous mass and places itself in the center of the Circle. God gives him a face. It is man: The Clown of God. Slowly the Creator forms him, teaches him to live, to walk, to jump, to *Dance.*

2. *Earthly Paradise:* God creates Earthly Paradise for his most favored creature. . . . It is the age of the Russian Ballet, that torrent of images of Paradise, that revelation of color, sound, and light which, in five years, was to conquer the world. As a companion, God gives him *Dance,* personified by the Ballerina and, for friends, four guardian angels, four fantastic creatures: a Rose, a Faun, Petrouchka, and a Golden Slave, symbols of the four elements: Air, Earth, Water, and Fire.

3. *The Woman:* But his craving for a great and constant love, and his tenderness force him to create a new image of love. A woman, unreal at first, grows in his soul. Little by little she takes a tangible shape and he seeks in her the support of a creature of flesh and blood. The face of his dreams suddenly becomes the face of one woman—his WIFE.

4. *The Fall:* Nijinsky is tempted during the absence of God. He marries suddenly in South America and incurs the wrath of Diaghilev, who when informed of the event, banishes him from the Russian Ballet. Earthly paradise crumbles. It is 1914—the end of an era.

PART TWO THE NIJINSKY OF GOD The search for love, for true love, is long. Diaghilev is no longer God. A god who rejects his won creation, a god who will not pardon is not a god of love, not a true god.

His companion is by his side, but she cannot follow him in his search for the Divine, in his love of Humanity. He is alone, and alone he has to suffer a long Calvary at this time, troubled as it is by the horror of war; it is this that will lead to the famous day which he called his "Marriage with God," the day of his last dance recital on January 19, 1919, when in a series of sublime improvisations, he portrayed in mime the horrors of war, the absurd, senseless, and grotesque features of his times, and his love of God and Humanity. Vaslav Nijinsky no longer exists, but may this ballet help the world to love and know this unique, angelic being, in whom physical grace reflected spiritual grace, and whose technique and genius were immense because they serve God and brotherly love.

NOTES Writing of the ballet *Nijinsky* in the *Wall Street Journal*, Peter J. Rosenwald said: "'People want to have sports and mystery,' says Maurice Béjart, an innovative Belgian whose Ballet of the Twentieth Century comes to New York tomorrow. Mr. Béjart's company will be performing a controversial work called *Nijinsky, Clown of God*, but not at Lincoln Center or some other chaste establishment of the dance.

"Rather, *Nijinsky, Clown of God*, will get its first New York viewing at that midtown palace of cheers, boos, sweat, and liniment, Madison Square Garden's Felt Forum. As in Europe, where this ambitious work also has played in large sports arenas—such as the 5,000-seat Palais des Sports in Paris—Mr. Béjart hopes to attract some new converts to the dance from among people who might know more about Nijinsky, the race horse, than Nijinsky, the dancer. The ballet has drawn enthusiastic, animated crowds in Europe, even though it has been alternately praised and damned by European critics.

"In a masterpiece of dance theater, Mr. Béjart has fashioned a work which perfectly uses the many talents of his versatile company to tell factually and metaphorically the story of the great Ukranian dancer, Vaslav Nijinsky, from his discovery by choreographer Serge Diaghilev of the Ballet Russe to his agonizing death in 1950, insane and lonely, believing himself to be incarnate God. Using extracts from Nijinsky's diary, the work concentrates on Nijinsky the man, Nijinsky the dancer, and Nijinsky's deeply religious yearnings. Said Nijinsky in his diary, 'I appear as a clown to make myself better understood. . . . I think that a clown is only perfect when he expresses love, otherwise he is no longer a clown of God.'

"What gives the work its vitality (and what seems to offend most academic critics) is the fusion of Nijinsky the man and the four most famous roles he portrayed: The Rose in *Spectre de la Rose*, the Golden Slave in *Scheherazade*, the Faun in *L'Après-Midi d'un Faun* and Petrouchka, the puppet with a soul, in the ballet of the same name. Not only has Mr. Béjart created five Nijinskys who often appear on the stage at the same time but he has given each of them a clown whose purpose is to symbolize their inner souls.

"From the moment when a giant papier-maché figure of Impresario Diaghilev points its finger at a mass of dancers and chooses Nijinsky, the stage is a whirl of action. Giant crosses rise from it, whole ballets within the ballet seem to take the focus of activity. The music varies from the familiar strains of Tchaikovsky's *Pathétique* Symphony to contemporary Pierre Henri's electronic score.

"There is a brilliant madness in Mr. Béjart's superimpositions of sight and sound, past and present, real and imagined, to produce a surprisingly integrated and intimate picture of Nijinsky's strange genius, his search for the relationship between art, love, and religion and an ultimate sense that the world which rejects his gifts of love is to blame for his madness and his death. Perhaps it is.

"If Mr. Béjart is sometimes excessive in his symbolism and uneven in his choreography, his dancers more than make up for these failings with stunning performances which give life to the characters and credibility to their actions. Jorge Donn's Nijinsky, Clown of God, and Suzanne Farrell as the Girl in Pink, who becomes Nijinsky's wife, are memorable and unique expressions of dance theater at its best.

"If *Nijinsky, Clown of God* has a major flaw, it is in proving that nothing exceeds like excess. It is so rich that it sometimes overwhelms itself and the spectacle overcomes its meaning. But it is never dull, never intellectual for its own sake, and never uninteresting."

LES NOCES

THE WEDDING

Cantata with dances. Music and words by Igor Stravinsky. Choreography by Bronislava Nijinska. Scenery and costumes by Nathalie Gontcharova. First presented by Diaghilev's Ballets Russes at the Théâtre Gaîté-Lyrique, Paris, June 14, 1923, with Felia Dubrovska as the Bride *and Leon Woizikowski as the* Bridegroom. *First presented in the United States by the League of American Composers at the Metropolitan Opera House, New York, April 25, 1929, with scenery and costumes by Serge Soudeikine and choreography by Elizaveta Anderson-Ivantzova.*

Stravinsky's dramatic cantata *Les Noces* depicts the ancient Russian peasant marriage ritual. Singers on the stage sing words which the dancers accompany with meaningful movement.

SCENE ONE—BENEDICTION OF THE BRIDE—THE TRESSES The voice of the bride is heard chanting before the rise of the curtain. The scene is the interior of a peasant home in old Russia. The bride stands in the center of the stage, surrounded by her mother and her friends. Her friends help to calm the grief she feels at leaving her home, her fear of life with a man who seems to her now a stranger, and her hatred of the person who has arranged the match. The women tell her that her husband's father will accept her in their home and that her life will be much as it has been, that she must go through with everything for her own parents. At the bride's request, the women comb and bind her hair. They tell her that the birds outside the house are singing happily. Can't she be happy too? They ask God to bless her marriage.

SCENE TWO—BENEDICTION OF THE BRIDEGROOM—THE BRIDEGROOM'S HOUSE The bridegroom's father and friends help him to prepare for his wedding. His hair, too, is combed and anointed. All wish him good luck. The parents of both the bride and the bridegroom lament the loss of their children, who are no longer children. The friends of the families congratulate the parents.

SCENE THREE—THE BRIDE'S DEPARTURE—THE WEDDING The bride is prepared to go forth from her house to meet the bridegroom at the church. Her friends tell her she is a princess this day. At the church, the bridegroom kisses the cross. The best man declares his friend is present to greet his bride. The guests pay tribute to the bridegroom's love for his parents. The bride enters, and the wedding ceremony takes place. As the couple leaves, all congratulate them. Their parents lament.

SCENE FOUR—THE WEDDING FEAST At the wedding feast, the father of the bride presents her to the assembled guests. Men in the company inform her of the household duties she must perform. The bridegroom is informed of his responsibilities to his wife. Everyone drinks and is joyous.

An older married couple is selected, from among the guests, to warm the marriage bed. There is a toast to the young couple, after which they are conducted to the door of their room. The older couple returns to the feast.

The guests gather about the parents of the bride and the bridegroom as they sit beside the door to their children's room. The bridegroom sings of his love for his wife.

NOTES *Les Noces* was first performed in the United States in concert form, at Aeolian Hall, New York, in February 1926, under the auspices of the International Composers Guild.

Leopold Stokowski conducted the first United States performance of the complete cantata with dances. Marc Blitzstein, Aaron Copland, Louis Gruenberg, and Frederick Jacobi were the four pianists on this occasion.

Bronislava Nijinska's staging of *Les Noces* was first presented in the United States by the Ballet Russe de Monte Carlo in 1936, with Irina Baronova and Yurek Shabelevsky in the principal roles.

Nijinska's ballet was revived by the Royal Ballet in London March 23, 1966, with Svetlana Beriosova and Robert Mead in the principal roles. This production was first presented in the United States at the new Metropolitan Opera House, New York, May 2, 1967. After the London première, Mary Clarke reported in *Dance News* that the London press "has never acclaimed a ballet so unanimously." Alexander Bland wrote in *The Observer:* "The curtain rises on the Bride flanked by her companions holding her long ritual pigtails. 'Oh fair tress of my hair' sings the soprano—and this could be the motif of the whole ballet. The score weaves a crisp embroidery of words and music, poetry and slang. On the stage, in place of delicate classical curlecues and filigrees, Nijinska plaits her dancers together, kneads them into knotted mounds, tugs them backwards and forwards like lengths of thick hemp.

"The patterns are stiff and new as linen. The steps are complicated but rough, repeating like a sampler pattern. The groups are blunt and tight and rounded. Without a hint of rural charm, she evokes a peasant world where a wedding means . . . a vow, a bed, having children, dying and leaving them money and a cow. *Les Noces* is a superb example of the Diaghilev ideal—contributions of individual, almost independent merit, bound together into a single perfect skein."

A dance cantata. Music by Igor Stravinsky. Choreography by Jerome Robbins. Set by Oliver Smith. Costumes by Patricia Zipprodt. Lighting by Jean Rosenthal. First presented by the American Ballet Theatre at the State Theater, New York, March 30, 1965, with Erin Martin as the Bride *and William Glassman as the* Bridegroom.

Preparing program notes for *Les Noces*, Jerome Robbins wrote: "Stravinsky used as material for *Les Noces* the ritualistic elements found in the ancient customs and traditions of Russian peasant weddings, but reserved the right to use them with absolute freedom, paying little heed to ethnolographical considerations. His purpose was not to reproduce the wedding or show a stage dramatization with descriptive music, but rather to present a ritualized abstraction of its essences, customs, and tempers.

"The text is adapted from folk songs and popular verse,

typical wedding remarks, clichés of conversations, but again they are not used realistically but rather as a collage of the words spoken or sung during these traditional rites. The first half of the 'scenic ceremony' deals with the preparations, and revolves around religious elements. Alternating with these intense invocations and blessings are continual lamentations by the parents for the loss of their children, and by the bride against the matchmaker, on leaving home, and on losing her virginity.

"In the second half (the wedding feast) the grief and religious elements are forgotten in robust celebrations with food, drink, songs, toasts, boasts, bawdiness, rough jokes, etc. A married couple is selected to warm the bed and finally the marriage is allowed to be consummated while all sit outside the nuptial chamber."

The composition is divided into four tableaux which run without interruption:

TABLEAU I—PREPARATION OF THE BRIDE Before a backdrop with two huge ironlike figures of saints, the musicians, four pianists, and a chorus file on stage. Then from both sides of the stage come the dancers in rough brown and white peasant dress. They bow to each other, to the musicians, and begin to dance. The bride flings out her two long braids on both sides and the women take up the strands and begin to plait her hair. The bride weeps and laments, her father and mother are entangled in the strands. Her tresses sing: "In the evening my mother braided you with care, she combed you with a silver comb, she combed you, she braided you. Ah, poor me, poor me. Alas, poor me." Then she is picked up like a child and taken out.

TABLEAU II—PREPARATION OF THE GROOM The bridegroom is pushed out before the guests by his friends. As his mother berates him, we see that he is indeed her child as he crouches while his friends dance. Then one of them insists that he join them. There is a dance with his parents. Two bass voices sing: "Bless me, my father, my mother, bless your child who proudly goes against the wall of stone to break it."

TABLEAU III—DEPARTURE OF BRIDE. CODA—LAMENTATION OF MOTHERS The bride enters in a white dress trimmed with orange and with an orange bow. She crouches in *plié*, then as her friends dance about her, she is lifted up and carried off in triumph. The lights dim and the two mothers lament: "My own dear one, child of mine, do not leave me, little one."

TABLEAU IV—WEDDING FEAST When the lights come up, the bride and bridegroom are seen in the center. During a ritual dance both are raised high and then set down. The chorus sings realistic advice: "Love your wife, cherish her like your soul, shake her like a plum tree." The girl then dances to her friends and the boy to his. Then, after their bed has been warmed, they are placed together on a platform like two lost children and the marriage is consummated in quick trembling. The pianos and a bell strike a bell chord fortissimo and a solo bass sings, as a bridegroom would sing to his bride: "Dear heart, my own little wife, let us live in happiness so that all men may envy us." The bell chord tolls throughout his song, he finishes, the pianos alone take the chord, we hear it on every eighth beat, then there is no more singing, the pianos stop and we have only the persistent bell chord. The time between its sounding measures an infinity of happiness.

NOTES Jerome Robbins's ballet was acclaimed by all the critics after its first performance. Allen Hughes in the New York *Times* called it "an overwhelming fusion of animal energy, ritualistic ardor, and rhythmic attack." Doris Hering in *Dance Magazine* said that the dancers in performance were in "what might be called a state of rhythmic grace . . . The dancers bowed . . . and then the surge began! They were drawn into a relentless sea of stamping, jumping, and somersaults. Sometimes there were brief allusions to national style in the use of squared arms or the digging of one heel into the ground and curving the feet outward. Always they seemed to be caught in something jubilant and ominous at the same time."

THE NUTCRACKER

Classic Ballet in two acts. Music by Tchaikovsky. Choreography by Lev Ivanov. Book by Lev Ivanov. Scenery by M. I. Botcharov. First presented at the Maryinsky Theatre, St. Petersburg, December 17, 1892, with Antoinetta Dell-Era and Paul Gerdt as the Sugarplum Fairy *and the* Prince. *First presented in Western Europe by the Sadler's Wells Ballet at the Sadler's Wells Theatre, London, January 30, 1934, with Alicia Markova and Harold Turner. This version was staged by Nicholas Sergeyev, after Ivanov. First presented in the United States in an abbreviated form by the Ballet Russe de Monte Carlo at the Fifty-first Street Theatre, New York, October 17, 1940, with Alicia Markova and André Eglevsky. Scenery and costumes by Alexandre Benois. Presented in the United States in complete form by the San Francisco Ballet, 1944, with choreography by William Christensen. Presented by the New York City Ballet, with choreography by George Balanchine, February 2, 1954, with Alberta Grant as* Clara, *Susan Kaufman as* Fritz, *Michael Arshansky as* Herr Drosselmeyer, *Paul Nickel as the* Nutcracker *and Maria Tallchief and Nicholas Magallanes as the* Sugarplum Fairy *and her* Cavalier. *Scenery by Horace Armistead. Costumes by Karinska. Masks by Vlady. Revived in a new production by the New York City Ballet with scenery by Rouben Ter-Arutunian and costumes by Karinska at the New York State Theater, December 11, 1964.*

It is another sign of how popular ballet has become that today many companies perform *The Nutcracker*. It has almost become a kind of annual Christmas ritual in many American and Canadian cities. Of course this was not always so. We used to rely on a touring company to give us a truncated version of this full-length work, a ballet people used to call *Nutcracker Suite* because they knew the music better than the ballet. Now that is all different. I have heard that more than fifty groups do this ballet. The one we do in New York every Christmas was first presented in 1954 and we have been doing it every year since. There have been changes in the production (I am always making them) but in its main outlines the story and the action are about the same.

I have liked this ballet from the first time I danced in it as a boy, when I did small roles in the Maryinsky Theatre production. When I was fifteen, I danced the Nutcracker Prince. Years later in New York, when our company decided to do an evening-long ballet, I preferred to turn to *The Nutcracker,* with which American audiences were not sufficiently familiar. I accordingly went back to the original score, restored cuts that had been made, and in the development of the story chose to use the original story by E. T. A. Hoffmann, although keeping to the outlines of the dances as given at the Maryinsky. A prologue was added and the dances restaged.

The three scenes of the ballet are arranged in two acts. In the first act, we are in the real world but begin a journey to the magical kingdom of the second.

The overture to the ballet is bright and delicate. Pizzicato strings and tinkling triangles create a light, intimate atmosphere that sets the stage for the action.

ACT ONE When the curtain goes up, we are in a hallway of a large house looking at the door to the living room. This is the home of Dr. Stahlbaum, a city official, and his wife. It is Christmas Eve. Their children, Marie and Fritz, have fallen asleep by the door as their parents decorate the Christmas tree. Behind the keyhole, the parents and the maid are putting the finishing touches to the tree and arranging presents underneath. The children awaken and eagerly await the arrival of the guests. For there is to be a Christmas party, a family affair for relatives and close friends, but most of all a party for children.

Soon the other children arrive with their parents, and the doors are opened. All rejoice in the large, lighted tree. The grown-ups greet each other and there is much speculation among the children about what is in the packages. Now the parents organize things. Dr. Stahlbaum divides the children for games and dances. The boys do a brisk march and then there is a polite formal quadrille for the girls and the boys. Some of the grown-ups join in. Soon grandparents come to join the party, refreshments are served, and, most important of all, presents are given out.

The children are sitting quietly looking at their presents when suddenly everyone looks up. Something seems to have gone wrong. The lights flicker and over the huge grandfather clock a terrifying old owl flaps his wings as the hour is sounded. Then at the door an old gentleman looking very much like the owl comes in. This is Herr Drosselmeyer, an old family friend who is also Marie's godfather. He wears a black patch over one eye. He is a mysterious man, a marvelous inventor of moving toys, and he has brought with him three large boxes and also his handsome young nephew. Drosselmeyer kisses Marie and introduces her to his nephew, whom she likes at once. The gifts in the huge boxes delight everyone—a Harlequin and Columbine and a Toy Soldier who dance to jolly tunes. Then Drosselmeyer brings out a large Nutcracker, a soldier, for Marie. He shows everybody how it works and Marie is clearly delighted with it. She is so pleased with it that Fritz is furious. He grabs the Nutcracker and stamps on it. The nephew chases him away as Marie weeps. Drosselmeyer plays doctor and ties a handkerchief around the Nutcracker's head.

Marie and her friends sit and rock their dolls to sleep, only to be interrupted by the rowdy boys, who disturb them with drums and bugles. The nephew brings Marie a toy bed for the Nutcracker and he is tucked in and put under the tree. All the children are tired and upset and clearly in need of sleep. Dr. Stahlbaum and his wife now lead all the guests in a final dance, Marie dancing with the nephew. At the end, they shake hands solemnly, reluctant to say good night to each other, hoping that they will meet again soon. Everyone goes off to bed, the room darkens, and only by the lights of the Christmas tree can we make out the empty space.

It is midnight. Marie enters in a white nightgown. She comes slowly into the room, being careful not to make any noise. She goes directly to the Nutcracker, takes him up and cradles him in her arms. Then she goes to her bed and sleeps. Drosselmeyer enters, takes the Nutcracker from her, and fixes his jaw with a screwdriver. He restores the Nutcracker to her. There is a rustle, the Christmas tree lights flash on and off. Marie wakes. She puts the Nutcracker back in his bed and just then old Drosselmeyer from on top of the clock flaps his arms like the owl and Marie is thoroughly terrified. What is he doing in the house, anyhow, at this time of night? Marie just manages to hide behind a curtain when a big fat rat comes in. She dashes to the couch and huddles there. Suddenly the Christmas tree and everything under it seem to be growing—even the toy soldiers. The walls of the room grow. The tree grows taller and taller, to a huge height. The mice are big too, and it is good that the soldiers are there to protect her. They battle the mice, but the mice, led by their fierce king, seem to be winning. Then the Nutcracker, grown to life size, rises from his bed and leads the soldiers.

The Nutcracker orders cannon brought and candy is fired at the mice. Marie throws her slipper, which hits the king of the mice by surprise. The Nutcracker runs him through with his sword, and the battle is won.

Marie falls onto the bed, which begins mysteriously to glide out of the room into the snowy evening. She arrives at the Kingdom of Snow and is met by the Nutcracker, who before her very eyes suddenly turns into a handsome young prince. He bows to Marie, gives her the crown taken from the king of the mice and leads her away on a magic journey. In a snowy forest, snowflakes dance.

ACT TWO—KONFITUERENBURG (THE LAND OF SWEETS) When the curtain rises, we are in the inside of a huge box of candy. Twelve angels enclose the stage, each dressed in white and gold. The Sugarplum Fairy, who rules over this Kingdom of Sweets, makes a regal entry. She dances a charming variation to the tinkling celesta. The angels enclose her in a semicircle of love. Then leading the angels off, the Sugarplum Fairy welcomes the full candy box: Chocolates and Coffee and Tea sweets, Candy Canes, Marzipan, Polichinelles, and lovely Dew Drops. At this point, to majestic heralding music, a walnut boat arrives bringing the Nutcracker Prince and Marie. The prince escorts Marie to the shore and introduces her to the Sugarplum Fairy. The fairy then asks the prince what happened. The prince then relates in pantomime how they came from far away, how the Mouse King and his men attacked Marie and the toy soldiers, how the mice were defeated finally when Marie at just the right moment threw her slipper and the King of Mice had his crown cut off, which was given as a present to Marie. The Sugarplum Fairy congratulates the prince warmly on his victory and escorts him and Marie to a candy throne high on a dais. Before the pair are placed numerous sweets and creams to eat as they watch the entertainment that has been arranged for their pleasure.

We now watch a series of dances by the creatures of the candy kingdom. When they are finished, the Sugarplum Fairy and her cavalier perform the grandest dance of all, a *pas de deux* to climax the occasion. This is exactly the kind of dance that Marie would like to do, too, one day, and she and the prince rejoice in the splendid tenderness of the royal couple. All of the candies then come back in as the Sugarplum Fairy and her cavalier bid the young couple farewell. Marie and her prince step into a royal sleigh drawn by reindeer and before our very eyes the sleigh rises right into the sky and away.

Ballet in two acts after the story "The Nutcracker and the Rat King" by E. T. A. Hoffmann. Music by Tchaikovsky. Choreography and production by Rudolf Nureyev (the Prince's variation in Act Two by Vassily Vainonen). Scenery and costumes by Nicholas Georgiadis. First presented by the Royal Swedish Ballet at the Royal Swedish Opera House, Stockholm, November 17, 1967. Presented by the Royal Ballet at the Royal Opera House, Covent Garden, London, February 29, 1968, and introduced by that ensemble to the United States at the Metropolitan Opera House, New York, May 10, 1968.

ACT ONE It is Christmas Eve early in the nineteenth century. The wealthy mayor, Dr. Stahlbaum, is giving a party for his friends and their children. The children are dancing and playing in excited anticipation of the approaching Christmas festivities and of their presents. Herr Drosselmeyer, an old friend of the family, arrives bringing the children gifts and amuses them by his conjuring tricks. He gives Clara, his favorite, a Nutcracker, which delights her. Her brother Fritz spitefully breaks it but Herr Drosselmeyer mends it for her. After the grandparents arrive and join in the dancing Clara becomes very tired and falling asleep in her chair, has a vivid dream. The room and the Christmas tree seem to grow . . . from the wainscot a swarm of rats appears trying to capture the Nutcracker, but Clara rushes to his rescue, throwing them her favorite dolls in an effort to distract them from him. From their toy fort an army of soldiers led by the Nutcracker (who suddenly springs to life) comes to help the fight against the rats and their leader, the Rat King. A company of Hussars and another of marines fight the rat army but are overwhelmed. The Nutcracker and the Rat King are left on the battlefield. Desperately Clara flings her shoe at the Rat King. As it strikes him he falls dead and a sudden transformation takes place revealing the Nutcracker as a young, handsome prince.

ACT TWO Together the Nutcracker Prince and Clara are carried away to an enchanted grotto. There Clara becomes frightened by bats but when the prince comes to protect her she realizes that they are actually her family and friends transformed by her nightmare.

The grotto mysteriously changes into Clara's own toy theater where she finds many of her favorite dolls brought to life. The mood changes to one of happiness and everyone dances. As Clara's dream closes she is found still sleeping in her chair. Her mother and father waken her and, as the guests take their leave, the party comes to an end. Clara is left alone, enthralled by memories of her adventures.

NOTES Rudolf Nureyev's version of *The Nutcracker* for the Royal Swedish Ballet was Reviewed for *Dance News* by Anna Greta Stahle: "The Christmas party takes place in a palace—suggesting old St. Petersburg. The parents and children are dressed in directoire style, and the old people, like Drosselmeyer, keep to the fashion of their youth and are in rococo. The acting and miming is staged with imagination and humor; it is indeed an elegant and lively party.

"Clara is a girl of an age between child and woman, and consequently her dreams are both childish and tinged with an erotic element. Nureyev has omitted the visit to the Kingdom of Sweets and has built the *divertissement* entirely on dreams in which Clara's family and Drosselmeyer appear in different shapes. The same dancer is seen as Drosselmeyer, the Rat King, and the Prince. Clara is herself all through the ballet, dancing the usual Sugarplum Fairy *pas de deux* with the Prince as though it were a dream of herself as a princess."

ORPHEUS

Ballet in three scenes. Music by Igor Stravinsky. Choreography by George Balanchine. Scenery and costumes by Isamu Noguchi. Lighting by Jean Rosenthal. First presented by Ballet Society at the New York City Center, New York, April 28, 1948, with Nicholas Magallanes as Orpheus, *Maria Tallchief as* Eurydice, *Francisco Moncion as the* Dark Angel, *Beatrice Tompkins as the* Leader of the Furies, *Tanaquil LeClercq as the* Leader of the Bacchantes, *and Herbert Bliss as* Apollo.

This ballet is a contemporary treatment of the ancient myth of Orpheus, the Greek musician who descended into Hades in search of his dead wife, Eurydice. With his music, Orpheus charms the God of the Dead into returning Eurydice to him. He promises not to look at her until they have reached the earth again. Eurydice, unknowing, persuades Orpheus to break this promise, thereby bringing about her irrevocable death. The ballet tells this story and its aftermath as simply as possible with its music, its dramatic action, and its dancing.

SCENE ONE—THE GRAVE OF EURYDICE The first notes of the orchestra remind us that Orpheus's instrument was the lyre. A harp sounds descending scales in a slow, mournful rhythm accompanied by quiet strings. Eurydice is dead, and Orpheus cannot console himself with his own song. The curtain rises. Orpheus stands alone beside Eurydice's grave with his back turned. His arms hang limp, his lyre is discarded at his feet, and his head is bowed to the intensely blue sky that would pierce his sorrow with brightness. Three friends enter on the left, cross over to the grave, and place upon it relics of Eurydice. Orpheus does not notice them; he remains motionless when they place their hands on his shoulder to console him. He ignores their departure. The music ceases its slow lamentation, and Orpheus wakens from his grief. He takes up his lyre and begins a dance that expresses physical grief as well as mental anguish. He raises the lyre high above him in supplication, then holds the instrument in one hand as he dances. The song of the lyre is inadequate to his bereavement; yet the lyre is the only possession Orpheus has left, and in his dance he tries to make the instrument a partner to his woe. This effort fails, and Orpheus places the harp on Eurydice's grave, where he beseeches it to speak for her. Then he falls in despair at the grave and reaches out to pluck the lyre's strings. At this sound, a satyr and four wood sprites leap out from behind rocks in the background and attempt to distract Orpheus. Orpheus rises to meet these creatures who have been moved by his song and he darts in and out among them for a moment, but soon leaves them, to dance alone with his lyre. His misery is unabated and his pathetic figure seems to demand the sympathy of the gods he invokes to aid him. Again he stands beside Eurydice's grave with downcast eyes.

Now the prayers of Orpheus are answered. In the back, against the vivid blue sky, appears a strange, dark figure whose body is enveloped in black coils. The Angel of Death poses briefly, then moves forward toward the grieving poet. He approaches softly, so as not to disturb Orpheus in his reverie, and touches him. Orpheus stands immobile. The Angel of Death frees himself of the black coil that represents his power in Hades, raises Orpheus's arms high, and entwines the coil between his outstretched hands. As he wraps the coil about the silent musician, the Angel of Death by his intimate presence endows Orpheus with the power to accompany him on the long journey across the River Styx to Eurydice. The angel stands away from Orpheus and dances triumphantly for a moment, then prepares for the trip into Hades. He frees Orpheus of the bonds of death, then places over the minstrel's eyes a golden mask which must not be removed until the journey is over. Then he picks up the lyre, slips his arm through it, and beckons to Orpheus. Orpheus moves toward him hesitatingly; pliantly he stretches out his hand to grasp the angel's upturned palm. The open, widespread fingers of the angel close about his hand with the strength of steel. A trumpet sounds. The angel moves the lyre down his arm to rest on their clasped hands and begins to lead Orpheus on the downward journey. The music is slow and spacious as the two figures move toward the front of the stage. From above, a flowing white gauze falls in slow motion, and in front of this curtain the Angel of Death leads the blinded Orpheus on the tortuous journey. The progress in their descent into Hades is marked by bright objects that can be seen moving upward in back of the transparent curtain. The passage becomes difficult as the two figures cross the stage toward the left, and as they disappear, the angel, exhausted, pulls Orpheus over the ground. When they have gone, mysterious figures in back of the gauze push the curtain forward with a movement similar to the helpless beating of wings against a cage.

SCENE TWO—HADES The gauze curtain rises swiftly, and crouched about the stage in fearful attitudes are the Furies, creatures of Hell who would destroy those who enter the Land of the Dead unlawfully. Bright cones of light from above illuminate their hideous and fantastic attire. The leader of the Furies proceeds to direct them harshly in a rapid, rhythmic dance. Orpheus and the angel enter on the left. The leader of the Furies turns and points at them menacingly, followed by her weird creatures. But the angel and Orpheus stand motionless. The Furies finish their dance, and their leader directs them to gather in a group. Tortured souls who have remained in the background now stir with great effort. They carry heavy burdens of rock on their shoulders and bend painfully under the strain. They set boulders down behind the group of Furies, as if to protect themselves, and all turn toward the two interlopers.

The Angel of Death moves away from Orpheus, slips the lyre from his arm, and, standing in back of the minstrel, places the lyre for Orpheus to play. But Orpheus does not understand—he cannot see—and the angel moves his hands so that they touch the strings of the harp. The angel plucks the strings, and now Orpheus comprehends and begins to play. His music is accompanied closely by two oboes and the orchestra. The lovely, soft melody of his lyre enchants the Furies, who are lulled to silence and rest. Yet Orpheus is still reluctant to play the harp as he once did, before Eurydice died, and the angel continues to exact the music from him. He knows that only by his great music will Orpheus persuade the ruler of Hades to release Eurydice. The two figures dance to the beautiful song, the angel constantly encouraging Orpheus to prolong the melody. The burdened, tortured souls move closer to hear more perfectly, and the music reflects their agony, which Orpheus's song has temporarily relieved.

But now the song is over. Orpheus bows stiffly in obeisance toward the back. In the dark recesses of the stage a strange shape begins to turn toward him. This is Pluto, God of the Underworld. Standing before him, her hands resting on his shoulders, is Eurydice. Orpheus does not move. Although he cannot see, he senses her presence and waits for Pluto's answer to his prayer. Eurydice moves forward, haltingly at first, with a slight limping motion, then more freely as her dance becomes syncopated. She turns to Pluto and beseeches him to come forward. Eurydice's arms move constantly to express her desire for freedom, and Pluto moves toward her. The Furies take Orpheus by the hand and bring him to Eurydice. Pluto joins their hands, and for a moment the two stand motionless before the god as Orpheus pledges not to look at his wife until they have ascended to earth. A blue stalactite descends from on high to symbolize the reunion, and the Dark Angel comes forward to lead Orpheus and Eurydice back to earth. He takes Orpheus by the hand, and all the inhabitants of the underworld circle the three figures, who move with hands joined to the front of the stage. The gauze curtain falls behind them, and the Dark Angel proceeds ahead, holding out Orpheus's lyre as a guide to the couple.

Orpheus and Eurydice dance together to a sumptuous melody as their journey begins. At first Eurydice merely follows Orpheus, imitating his steps as he leads the way. But the ascent is difficult, and their dance becomes for a short time a kind of portrayal of the hardships they undergo in passing unseen obstacles. Orpheus is blind, and when Eurydice is not holding him by the hand, she is lost to him. Eurydice puts herself in his way constantly: she longs increasingly for Orpheus to see her. Her longing is infinitely tender and appealing because of the warmth of the love in her own eyes; she therefore seems to tempt Orpheus to tear the mask from his face not so that he can see her, but so that she can see him as she remembers him. She wishes to help him as they proceed along the way, but the one way in which she cannot help him is by showing her love for him. Eurydice is tormented momentarily by the fact that, although they are really together once again, they are actually remote to each other: Orpheus, because he cannot see; Eurydice, because she cannot be seen by the man she loves.

The tempo and the theme of the dance change briefly as Eurydice moves away and dances before the blind Orpheus a gay and pleasant measure. She holds in her hands an invisible pipe, and plays upon it in celebration of their reunion. Orpheus catches the mood of her dance and joins her in it. Both are attempting to suppress the impassioned longings they feel so deeply. But Orpheus becomes even more intently aware of his lack of sight as Eurydice beguilingly dances out of his reach, and the principal theme of their *pas de deux* returns, this time prefaced with a short musical warning from the harp. On the extreme left, the arm of the Dark Angel still holds out the guiding lyre, and the two lovers turn to follow it. They start out as before, Orpheus leading and Eurydice duplicating his movements, but now Eurydice moves close to him in intimate contact. Orpheus tries to hold her, but she slides down to the floor, where his arms reach out desperately to find her. The melody mounts to a brief crescendo. Now that he cannot touch Eurydice, Orpheus abandons all patience and takes his head in his hands. Eurydice stands beside him, her face close to his, and he tears the mask from his eyes. There is absolute silence. Instantly she falls against him and dies. At first too stunned to move, Orpheus stretches out his arms, eager to touch her and to feel her touch. Invisible creatures of Hades push forward the gauze curtain to make good their promise and slip Eurydice away. Orpheus kneels alone, his open arms clasping the empty air.

Now that he has lost Eurydice until he himself shall die, Orpheus is afraid. Horns sound in terrifying judgment upon his fatal error. He remembers that the Angel of Death is still with him, just ahead, and he turns, half crawling, half running, to grasp his lyre. But just before his fingers reach the lyre, it disappears. Powerless now in the Land of the Dead, Orpheus knows that he is powerless, too, on earth; he crawls off in search of his lyre.

The gauze curtain rises rapidly when Orpheus has left the stage. Here again on earth the sky is still blue, but now it is bathed also in blood-colored lights. There is a small hillock in the background. At the crash of a drum, there comes in from the left a tall Thracian woman with long red hair. This is the leader of the bacchantes, pleasure-seeking women who have not known love. She stalks the scene as if seeking desirable prey, moving with quick thrusts of legs and arms, looking to the right and left. She is soon followed by eight bacchantes, all with brilliant yellow hair. Orpheus enters carrying his mask. Immediately the bacchantes surround him. Their leader seems to demand his favor. Orpheus repulses her, indignant that she should try to sully his grief. The woman smiles her contempt and tries to take the mask from him. He runs, but the bacchantes are all around him. The leader embraces Orpheus savagely with her long arms, and the two fall to the ground. They roll over and over, and Orpheus frees himself, but the bacchante rises in triumph, holding his mask. Her face contorted with demoniac delight, she throws the mask out of sight. Orpheus cannot escape. The entire orchestra imitates his terror and the ferocity of the bacchantes with frenzied, rhythmic fortissimos. The bacchantes move in for the final attack. They push Orpheus back toward the hillock. He does not resist. They push him again. His head is bowed, his body listless. The bacchantes raise his arms, and for a brief moment they seem open in supplication. The leader stalks in on Orpheus and cuts off his right arm, then his left. He raises his head; she decapitates him. The body of Orpheus lies behind the hillock, torn to pieces. The bacchantes exit, strutting proudly, unregretfully.

SCENE THREE—APOTHEOSIS The stage is empty. Gradually the red disappears from the blue sky and the earth is bright once more. Again we hear the harp play the theme that opened the ballet, but now the accompaniment is different: this seems but a mere imitation of Orpheus's music. Apollo comes in slowly and approaches the grave of Orpheus. He kneels beside it and takes from behind the hillock a golden mask of the minstrel's face. Apollo holds the mask high, invoking the spirit of Orpheus as the God of Song, then holds it gently with his arm, as Orpheus held his lyre. The harp sounds as Apollo plucks the air before the mask, but the music—accompanied as it is by two horns—makes us all the more aware of the death of Orpheus and of Apollo's inability to call forth his music alone. Finally Apollo sets down the mask and stands poised over the grave of Orpheus. Slowly he moves his arm upward, and from the grave rises the lyre of Orpheus entwined in a long garland of flowers. The lyre rises higher and higher, carrying with it for the ages the tenderness and power of his song.

PARADE

Music by Erik Satie. Book by Jean Cocteau. Choreography by Leonide Massine. Scenery and costumes by Pablo Picasso. First presented by Diaghilev's Ballets Russes at the Théâtre du Châtelet, Paris, May 18, 1917, with Leonide Massine, Lydia Lopokova, Nicholas Zverev, Maria Chabelska, and Leon Woizikowski in leading roles. First presented in the United States by the City Center Joffrey Ballet at the City Center, New York, March 22, 1973, with Gary Chryst, Eileen Brady, Gregory Huffman, Donna Cowen, and Robert Talmage in leading roles.

Renowned collaboration of the Diaghilev era, unique combination of the gifts of Satie, Cocteau, Massine, and Picasso, *Parade* proves yet again in the 1970s the genius of the Diaghilev Ballets Russes in generating artistic collaboration of the highest order. When relatively few of the ballets created under Diaghilev's direction can be seen in our theaters (only *Petrouchka, Firebird*—in another version, *Spectre de la Rose, Apollo,* and *Prodigal Son*), in a recent season, it is refreshing to have the impresario's incomparable gifts demonstrated again for a new generation. Until its American revival, *Parade* had not been seen for forty-seven years.

Parade has long been considered a landmark for its introduction of cubism into the theater. The idea of the ballet was Jean Cocteau's. It was he who persuaded Satie and Picasso, who had never worked with the Ballets Russes, to collaborate on this undertaking in the midst of World War I. Subtitled a "Realistic Ballet," the work was intended to heighten realism; Guillaume Apollinaire, writing in the program, put the word *surrealism* onto the printed page for the first time to describe *Parade*. This would seem to point to a contrast the ballet makes visible on the stage—a contrast between performers in a traveling circus, the real people, and their managers or impresarios—public relations men who attempt to persuade the public to enjoy their arts.

Street circuses used to be common in Paris, and it is one of these that is the subject of the ballet, where the huckstering managers parade their talent to passers-by before the start of the show, with the hope that they will pay to come inside.

Massine, *Parade*'s choreographer, has said, in describing his method of making ballets, that it is sometimes the music, sometimes the theme, or the period and atmosphere of the action. With *Parade*, "the music was supreme, although the theme, too, interested me." Satie's score, like Picasso's settings and costumes visually, radically reflected new directions in sound and sense, mixing everyday noises, the real, with the imaginative expectation.

The action of the ballet is direct and straightforward, with none of the mystery associated so often with the avant-garde. After a series of almost solemn, quasi-religious chords in a brief musical prelude, there is a brief quiet that reveals a drop curtain of "early Picasso" portraying a rustic backstage scene of players relaxing before a performance. This inner curtain rises to show a scene by the same artist that is clearly different: a curtained booth, askew but making sense at once as a stage for the public to view a performance. Here parades an odd creature, the like of which has never been seen walking—a huge, pipe-smoking man made up of angles and planes and no softness. This is the French Manager, who introduces the Chinese Conjuror, who emerges from the curtained booth to amuse us with tricks—sword swallowing, etc.—to simulated oriental music. In a splendid multicolored costume he fairly dazzles us with his entertainment and then disappears behind the curtain.

There is a flourish and another huckster comes out, this the Manager from New York, his costume an amalgam of skyscrapers and curious angles. He carries a megaphone and a sign reading PARADE. He consults and commiserates with his French colleague, then introduces his specialty, a Little American Girl, a perpetual child in white middy blouse with a bow in her hair. To the menacing sound of multiple typewriters and gun shots, she dances a machine-age number, all winsomeness and cute charm. But her dance is more than that—it epitomizes, in small compass, the European image of America as heard by an acute ear and reflected by an acute eye in 1917. The imagery is almost totally derived from popular songs and movies. As the music imitates American dance rhythms, the little girl runs the gamut of stock U.S. melodrama—cops and robbers, rescue from a storm at sea, etc., at the end of which she bounces off as cheerily as she entered. At the end, her Manager is just as disappointed as his predecessor: no audience responds enough to come into their theater. He and the French Manager cannot understand this indifference.

Now in silence comes a brown-and-white Horse, grinning from ear to ear. Somewhat bashfully he entertains us, too, and prances out. The curtains close behind him. When they part again, we see two Acrobats, a girl and a boy, who dance a circuslike *pas de deux,* simulating tricks of the ring and high wire.

After the Acrobats finish, to the sound of a screaming siren the two Managers and the American Girl return. Next, the Horse and the Conjuror, finally the Acrobats, all in a reprise of their acts. In unison, they urge us, the audience, to come into their theater to see more. When we do not, they form a kind of cortege and the Horse lies down. The curtain falls as the music of the beginning is heard again.

NOTES There are many accounts of the origins of *Parade* but none more complete than those in *Cocteau,* Francis Steegmuller's biography of the librettist, in Leonide Massine's autobiography, and in Douglas Cooper's book, *Picasso Theatre.* Cooper, Picasso's collaborator, assisted the revival by the City Center Joffrey Ballet, and also wrote about it at length in *Dance and Dancers* magazine. He said of the presentation, which had been re-created by Leonide Massine himself:

"The famous drop curtain, revealed during the opening section of the music, showed one of the most romantically evocative and tender of all Picasso's circus compositions. But behind it lay a surprising and colorful contemporary reality. A proscenium opening, decorated with scrolls and a lyre, was painted red and yellow, and set among whitish buildings, with dark windows, and some dark-green foliage. The Chinese Conjuror had a scarlet tunic, strikingly patterned in yellow and grey, over black trousers with a yellow pattern. The two Acrobats had sky-blue tights with bold ornamental motifs in white, while the Little American Girl had a dark-blue middy jacket over a white skirt.

"Each of these turns was presented successively by one of the two so-called Managers, dancers raised to eleven-foot-high figures by an elaborately carpentered, descriptively symbolic superstructure rising from their shoulders. Both wore a sort of formal evening dress and a top hat, but were equipped with buildings and other attributes to establish their national character: thus the American had the Woolworth building, a megaphone and some flags, while the French Manager had houses, trees, a staff and a long-stemmed pipe.

"Massine cleverly characterized each role in his choreography, which made much use of mime. The subtly emphasized rhythms beaten out by the four legs of the Horse, in an enchantingly comic, acrobatic dance without music, was a triumph of his invention. While the Managers were made to convey the force of their huckstering and despair by ungainly movements, by demonstrative and angry steps and by towering over all around them.

"Massine had the good fortune to find in the Joffrey Ballet a marvelous group of young dancers who worked with him brilliantly in this recreation of *Parade*. For it is a ballet which requires the performers to show style, precision of movement, perfect timing, athletic prowess, great powers of mime and especially a sense of enjoying what they are doing. Gary Chryst, assuming Massine's original role (the Chinese Conjuror), displayed that nervous intensity, speed, suavity, and air of mystery which is required for the character. His flickering hands, his shuffle, his leaps and especially his elevation were superbly timed and amazing to watch, as were the mimed passages of his dance where he finds an egg in his pigtail, digests it and recovers it from the toe of his shoe, or swallows a sword or eats fire.

"Donna Cowen, the first native-born American ever to dance the role of the Little American Girl, showed a marvelous sense of ragtime and was by turns pert, droll and captivating as she danced and mimed her way through the episodes of the ungainly typewriter, of the encounter with Indians, of the wreck of the *Titanic* or of the rosy dawning. The graceful and wistful *pas de deux* for the two Acrobats, who tumble, climb ropes, perform trapeze and walk a tightrope, was danced with great feeling and dexterity by Brady and Huffman. The Managers and the Horse gave their numbers with great distinction and all the fun and noise of the fair. The music was rendered in strict accordance with Satie's published score so that the incidental sound effects were confined to a typewriter, a ship's siren and some revolver shots at the appropriate times."

Cooper recalls that in staging the ballet, Massine was able to consult with dancers living in New York who had once appeared in various roles, notably Maria Chabelska, Vera Nemtchinova, Lydia Sokolova, and Michel Pavloff, while Boris Kochno also made a contribution from Paris. Lydia Sokolova in her memoirs had written prophetically: "*Parade* was so delightful that I am sure it would be a favorite if it could be done today."

PAS DE QUATRE

Divertissement. *Music by Cesare Pugni. Choreography by Jules Perrot. First presented at His Majesty's Theatre, London, July 12, 1845, with Marie Taglioni, Carlotta Grisi, Fanny Cerrito, and Lucile Grahn.*

This short ballet is probably the most famous *divertissement* in the history of dance. It displayed in one work four of the greatest ballerinas of its time, bringing these talents together for several memorable performances that have excited the curiosity of dance lovers for more than a hundred years. At this distance, it is impossible for us to tell exactly what *Pas de Quatre* looked like as a ballet, but information about what it resembled, and the unprecedented occasion it undoubtedly was, has come down to us in lithographs and reviews. If the greatest ballerinas of the United States, France, England, and the U.S.S.R. were to appear together in a ballet today, we should have some approximation of the excitement caused by the original *Pas de Quatre*. If such a *Pas de Quatre* seems impossible today, we must remember that it also seemed impossible in 1845.

Among all artists there is bound to be competition, and in the 1840s it seemed unlikely that any four of the great ballerinas would consent to dance on the same stage. Marie Taglioni had been acknowledged the finest dancer in the world when she created the title role in *La Sylphide* in 1832, and even thirteen years after her first famous role, she was still considered supreme in the realm of the romantic ballet that she had helped to create. But with the coming of the romantic era, there were also other ballerinas who danced in similar ballets: exceptional among these dancers were Fanny Cerrito, who was acclaimed in the early 1840s, Carlotta Grisi, who danced in 1841 the first performance of *Giselle*, and the Danish ballerina Lucile Grahn, who had successfully danced Taglioni's role in *La Sylphide*. The fact that each ballerina had danced *Giselle* (Taglioni, Cerrito, and Grahn undertook Grisi's original role in 1843) gives us an indication of their rivalry. There was, in short, so much natural jealousy between these four—and each faction of the public showed so great an amount of enthusiasm for its chosen goddess among them—that it appeared unlikely that the ballerinas would expose themselves to any common venture.

The man who thought otherwise and acted with persistence until he achieved his goal was the enterprising manager of His Majesty's Theatre in London, Benjamin Lumley. "The government of a great state was but a trifle compared to the government of such subjects as those whom I was *supposed* to be able to command," he recollected almost twenty years after the event. "These were subjects who considered themselves far above mortal control, or, more properly speaking, each was a queen in her own right—alone, absolute, supreme."

Lumley was encouraged to assemble the four ballerinas by a success he had brought off in 1843, when Fanny Cerrito danced at his theatre in a *pas de deux* with Fanny Elssler, the fifth great ballerina of this period. Why Elssler was not invited to participate in Lumley's assembly of ballerinas in 1845 is perhaps partially explained by this earlier triumph, but not altogether so. For Elssler's fame equaled, if it did not actually exceed, Taglioni's. No doubt that is exactly the point. Taglioni's superiority was unquestioned throughout Europe until Elssler made her début at the Paris Opéra in 1834. From this point on, the rivalry between the two was bitter. Elssler taunted Taglioni and her admirers by threatening to dance *La Sylphide,* which no other dancer yet dared to do. When Elssler essayed Taglioni's famous role in this ballet in 1838, open war broke out, and seven years later it must have been clear even to Benjamin Lumley that between these rivals there could never be peace. Théophile Gautier, who was to become the originator of *Giselle,* the friend and critical sponsor of Carlotta Grisi, wrote in 1837 that Fanny Elssler's dancing had a special quality that distinguished her from all other dancers and proceeded to make his point clear in a fashion that must have made the rivalry between the newcomer and the "Sylphide" intense:

". . . it is not the aerial and virginal grace of Taglioni, it is something more human, more appealing to the senses. Mademoiselle Taglioni is a Christian dancer, if one may make use of such an expression in regard to an art proscribed by the Catholic faith; she flies like a spirit in the midst of transparent clouds of white muslin with which she loves to surround herself, she resembles a happy angel who scarcely bends the petals of celestial flowers with the tips of her pink toes. Fanny is a quite pagan dancer; she reminds one of the muse Terpsichore, tambourine in hand, her tunic, exposing her thigh, caught up with a golden clasp; when she bends freely from the hips, throwing back her swooning, voluptuous arms, we seem to see one of those beautiful figures from Herculaneum or Pompeii which stand out in white relief against a black background . . ."

And Elssler was not praised only in Europe. She came to the United States in 1840 for a three-month tour and did not return to Europe for two years—two years during which she became the toast of the nation. She was welcomed by President Martin Van Buren, escorted by his son, entertained by Congress, carried on the shoulders of adoring crowds, and so universally acclaimed that she could declare, with accuracy, that "never was an artiste more completely seated in public sympathy." In nineteenth-century America she anticipated the exclusive success enjoyed by Anna Pavlova seventy years later.

But Benjamin Lumley also had grounds for being discouraged. His predecessor at His Majesty's Theatre had announced, but had been unable to present, Taglioni, Cerrito, and Elssler in a special performance. Circumstances, too, contrived against him. He had chosen Jules Perrot, the former partner of Taglioni and the choreographer who had collaborated on *Giselle,* to arrange the dances for the *Pas de Quatre,* and everyone was ready to begin—except one of the ballerinas. Carlotta Grisi, Perrot's wife, seemed unable to fulfill her engagement on time. She was dancing in Paris; how was she to get to London for rehearsals? Lumley tells us how: "A vessel was chartered . . . to waft the sylph at a moment's notice across the Channel; a special train was engaged and ready at Dover; relays of horses were in waiting to aid the flight of the *danseuse*, all the way from Paris to Calais."

When Grisi arrived, Perrot began to work on the most difficult assignment a ballet master ever had. He had not only to invent an ensemble that the four ballerinas would perform together, he had also to devise individual dances that would display ideally the particular artistry of each performer without distracting from the excellence of her sisters. In Lumley's words, "no one was to outshine the others—unless in their own individual belief." Perrot had worked closely on other projects with each of the four dancers previously and knew their temperaments; as the finest *danseur* of his time and a choreographer of equal fame, he also knew his job.

He seemed to succeed. The ballerinas were content with what they were to dance together and pleased with their variations; the costumes were ready, the theater sold out. And then came the problem of who was to dance first—or, rather, last, for the final variation in every ballet, as in regal processions, according to Lumley, is performed by the superior artist. Cerrito, Grisi, and Grahn agreed that Taglioni, because of her unprecedented fame, should occupy this place of honor. But as to the penultimate variation, the ladies disagreed: who was to be closest to Taglioni? Cerrito and Grisi vied for the position and quarreled on stage. Finally Grisi lost her temper, called Cerrito "a little chit," and the two ballerinas vowed they would never appear together.

Perrot, in despair, told the bad news to the manager. Lumley recalled what the choreographer said: "*Mon Dieu!* Cerrito won't begin before Carlotta, nor Carlotta before Cerrito, and there isn't anything that will make them change their minds: we're finished! And Lumley also recalled what he replied: "The solution is easy . . . In this dilemma there is one point on which I am sure the ladies will be frank. Let the oldest take her unquestionable right to the envied position."

Perrot returned to the stage to try this ruse. When he told the two ballerinas the manager's decision, everything suddenly changed: they "tittered, laughed, drew back, and were now as much disinclined to accept the right of position as they had been eager to claim it." The trick worked! Taglioni was at this time forty-one, Cerrito was twenty-eight, and Grisi twenty-six: the reverse order was thus established, with Grahn, who was twenty-four, leading with the first variation. Lumley says that "the *grand pas de quatre* was finally performed on the same night before a delighted audience, who little knew how nearly they had been deprived of their expected treat."

What this audience saw was recorded by several critics, and approximations of the performance have been given us in modern representations of this *divertissement*. When the curtain went up, the four ballerinas appeared before a romantic background. They entered in a line, holding hands; each was dressed in billowing muslin and each wore in her hair a crown of white flowers, except Cerrito, who wore flowers in the knot at the back of her head. The ballerinas smiled, walked to the footlights, and bowed. The audience could not believe it. One member of the audience did not want to believe it and threw down from the gallery a shower of placards that declared Cerrito the peer of all dancers in the world. The audience was embarrassed and frightened of the possible consequences, but then someone laughed, the dancers smiled, and the music began.

The *Pas de Quatre* commenced in soft stillness as the four ballerinas moved toward the backdrop and arranged themselves in charming tableau about Taglioni, who looked down upon her sisters with an expression of sincere sweetness. Even the slightest display of jealousy was impossible now, for each artist was thoroughly aware that the ballet would surely fail if any of them failed to be as perfect as Perrot imagined they were and that they would be responsible. And so they knelt about Taglioni, opened their arms to her in a gesture of affection and respect, and smiled as innocently as she did. They changed their position, and the graceful Taglioni seemed to fall back in their welcoming arms.

The actual dancing began with a short variation by Grahn

to quick, lively music. This was followed by a *pas de deux* by Cerrito and Grisi, which came to an end as Taglioni crossed the stage in high, light leaps that seemed to make her a part of the air. This introduction was merely a hint as to what was to follow in the four virtuoso variations. Grahn came first, dancing quickly, lightly, turning and hopping on point, moving about the stage with the controlled vigor of shining youth. Next, as the music changed, Carlotta Grisi stepped forward and danced with a sharp but airy vibrancy, a solo that summed up in a few short minutes her great fame.

Taglioni and Grahn, the oldest and the youngest, now danced together to a brief romantic measure. Cerrito was posed gracefully on stage with them, apparently waiting for them to finish their duet. Suddenly she cut this dainty and quiet sequence short, darting forward like an arrow released from the taut bow and describing a long, swift diagonal of accelerated turns. She finished her variation in a display of still, balanced poses contrasted with unparalleled verve and speed.

Taglioni, as the last of these great dancers, had the most difficult variation of all: she had to show the audience that what they had rejoiced in so far could be climaxed. And this she did, not by dancing in any fashion novel to her, but in a manner that epitomized her reputation: she moved with supreme lightness and she moved effortlessly, dazzling the audience with controlled poses even in midflight. And she moved with unquestioned authority, with the highest knowledge of her great gift and of her own faithful obedience to it, pausing in perfect balance with the grace and refinement of the mature artist.

Now, at the end, the three other ballerinas joined her. They all danced together, each trying to outdo the others in a final display of virtuosity. Then, as if they all understood that competition was in vain, they arranged themselves again in the tender tableaux with which they had begun. Taglioni raised her arms over her head and looked down upon the other three, who gathered about her quietly and looked toward the audience with pensive, beguiling smiles, as if they had never moved.

NOTES And what was the critical opinion of this *Pas de Quatre?* The *Times* of London called it "the greatest Terpsichorean exhibition that ever was known in Europe . . . Never was such a *pas* before. The excitement which a competition so extraordinary produced in the artists roused to them to a pitch of energy which would have been impossible under other circumstances, and hence everyone did her utmost, the whole performance being a complete inspiration . . . The whole long *pas* was danced to a running sound of applause, which, after each variation, swelled to a perfect hurricane . . . Bouquets flew from every point, an immense profusion, as each *danseuse* came forward, so that they had to curtsy literally in the midst of a shower of floral gifts. Cerrito's wreaths and nosegays were more than she could hold in both her arms . . . The front of the stage was almost covered with flower leaves."

The critic of the *Illustrated London News* reported: "No description can render the exquisite, the almost ethereal, grace of movement and attitude of these great dancers, and those who have witnessed the scene may boast of having once, at least, seen the perfection of the art of dancing. . . ."

The best accounts of three of the four ballerinas are given by their contemporary Théophile Gautier. Gautier did not review the *Pas de Quatre,* but he speaks here of Taglioni the year before the London *divertissement:* "Mademoiselle Taglioni is not a dancer, she is the embodiment of dancing . . . Fortunate woman. Always the same elegant and slender form, the same calm, intelligent and modest features; not a single feather has fallen from her wing; not a hair has silvered beneath her chaplet of flowers! As the curtain rose, she was greeted with thunders of applause. What airiness! What rhythmic movements! What noble gestures! What poetic attitudes and, above all, what a sweet melancholy! What lack of restraint, yet how chaste!"

Gautier speaks of Cerrito two years after the *Pas de Quatre:* "Fanny Cerrito's principal qualities are grace of pose, unusual attitudes, quickness of movement, and the rapidity with which she covers ground; she bounds and rebounds with an admirable ease and elasticity; there is a charming grace about her whole body. . . . She radiates a sense of happiness, brilliance, and smiling ease which know neither labor nor weariness. . . ."

Of Carlotta Grisi, Gautier had this to say at the time of her début at the Paris Opéra (1841): "She is possessed of a strength, lightness, suppleness and originality which at once place her between Elssler and Taglioni." Two years later he was to write that "Grisi's dancing has a quite special style; it does not resemble the dancing of either Taglioni or Elssler; each one of her poses, each one of her movements, is stamped with the seal of originality."

Pas de Quatre with its original cast was performed only four times (July 12, 15, 17, and 19, 1845). Queen Victoria and the Prince Consort attended the third performance. Three of the original cast—Taglioni, Cerrito, and Grisi—danced in a revival of the *divertissement* that was performed twice in Lumley's theater: on July 17 and 19, 1847. Carolina Rosati replaced Lucile Grahn in these performances. Rosati at this time was only twenty years old; fifteen years later, in Russia, she was to dance the leading role in *The Daughter of Pharaoh* (Pugni), the first great success of the ballet master Marius Petipa.

A year after the first performance of the original *Pas de Quatre,* Taglioni, Grahn, and Cerrito danced together at Lumley's theater in a ballet called *The Judgment of Paris* (Pugni-Perrot). The ballerinas danced the parts of three goddesses in this *divertissement,* which was hailed almost as loudly as *Pas de Quatre. The Judgment of Paris* was Marie Taglioni's last new ballet.

Marie Taglioni retired soon after she danced the revival of *Pas de Quatre* and died impoverished in Marseille, France, in 1884, at the age of eighty. Fanny Cerrito, at the time of her appearance in London, had yet to achieve her fullest fame and in the 1840s and 1850s secured for herself additional triumphs. She died in 1909 at the age of ninety-two. Carlotta Grisi had new successes after the famous *divertisse-*

ment, creating the title role in *Paquita* (Mazilier-Deldevez) in 1846 and dancing at the Imperial Theatre in St. Petersburg. She was seventy-eight when she died in 1899. Lucile Grahn, the youngest of the *Pas de Quatre* ballerinas, had danced in Russia before she came to London for Lumley's *divertissement*. Trained in her native Denmark by the great Danish ballet master Auguste Bournonville, Grahn made her début at the Royal Theatre, Copenhagen, in 1835. In this theater Grahn danced a version of *La Sylphide* created for her by Bournonville (1836). This production of the famous ballet has been in the repertory of the Royal Danish Ballet ever since it was first performed. Grahn died in 1907 at the age of eighty-six.

Another historic presentation of *Pas de Quatre* took place January 24, 1972, at the City Center, New York, at the Gala Performance for the Dance Collection of the New York Public Library. Anton Dolin, who had reconstructed the ballet for American Ballet Theatre in 1941, did so again, this time bringing together Carla Fracci as Taglioni, Violette Verdy as Grisi, Patricia McBride as Cerrito, and Eleanor D'Antuono as Grahn.

PETROUCHKA

Ballet burlesque in one act, four scenes. Music by Igor Stravinsky. Choreography by Michel Fokine. Book by Stravinsky and Alexandre Benois. Scenery and costumes by Benois. First presented by Diaghilev's Ballets Russes at the Théâtre du Châtelet, Paris, June 13, 1911, with Vaslav Nijinsky as Petrouchka, *Tamara Karsavina as the* Ballerina, *Alexandre Orlov as the* Moor, *and Enrico Cecchetti as the* Charlatan. *First presented in the United States by Diaghilev's Ballets Russes at the Century Theatre, New York, January 25, 1916, with Leonide Massine, Lydia Lopokova, and Adolph Bolm in the principal roles.*

Petrouchka tells the story of a puppet with a human heart, a creature of straw who comes to life only to be disbelieved. Characters similar to Petrouchka, half comic, half tragic, have been common to popular theatrical tradition in Europe for hundreds of years—characters such as Pierrot and Puck, clowns no one will ever take seriously, funny men who are always unlucky but who somehow manage to have in the end more wisdom than anybody else; funny men such as Charlie Chaplin's tramp. *Petrouchka* is ballet's representation of this universal character, of what the creators of the ballet knew in their youth as the "Russian Punch and Judy Show." At first the puppet is happy to be a mere automaton. Then he falls in love with a beautiful dancer and tries to win her, though all the world seems against him. He loses her, dies, and everyone laughs. He wins by returning for the last laugh himself.

SCENE ONE—THE SHROVETIDE FAIR The first scene of the ballet is set in a great public square in old St. Petersburg. The year is 1830; the season, winter—the last week before Lent, when all the populace gather together for final feasting and celebration. Even before the curtain rises, the orchestra tells us it is carnival time, as the cheerful blatancy of the music swells and varies to bring up images of a surging festival, where everyone is determined to have a good time in his own way. Peasants, gypsies, soldiers, and well-dressed folk, all in holiday attire, mingle in the snow-covered square. Fair booths decorated with bright bunting and flags surround an open area, and in the back stands the largest booth of all. It has blue curtains drawn across it like a stage. Above the booth, in Russian, are the words "Living Theater." Behind it are the spires of government buildings topped with flags. The crowd tries to keep warm by moving constantly; its members stamp and throw their arms around their chests as they talk to each other; some buy hot tea at a booth with a large, steaming samovar. But the cold weather serves only to intensify their good spirits. Everyone seems to be happy and carefree in the pursuit of a traditional pleasure all can share. The open, undisguised merriment of the music whirls with the circling crowd and its quick-changing rhythms accentuate the variety of noises that refuse to blend into one tune—the loud, comradely greetings, the laughter, the shrieking of persistent barkers, the vigorous dancing of three enthusiastic peasants.

The crowd hears a barrel organ grinding away in the distance, but its small sound is almost immediately drowned out by the hubbub in the square. The organ-grinder enters, playing a street song, and the people stand aside to watch his approach. With him comes a girl who carries a little rug under her arm and a triangle. She spreads the rug over the snow, strikes the triangle in a steady beat to secure everyone's attention, and begins to dance to a gay tune. Her dance is clearly designed to show the crowd how rapidly she can turn on one point without stopping; and as people begin to be impressed by her virtuosity, the organist shows off too, by grinding out the song with one hand and duplicating it on a cornet he holds with the other. When he finishes, he begins to play again his rather mournful street song, while on the other side of the stage a rival team of entertainers has appeared to attract the crowd away. There another dancer begins to turn to the tune of a hurdy-gurdy, and a new group forms about the girl and her accompanist. The organist and his partner glance over at the newcomers and speed up the tempo of their act. The two dancers and the two instruments compete openly: each of the girls imitates the other's movements, and the crowd watches first one and then the other as if they were looking at a tennis match. Finally the girls have spent all their energy and the contest is over. Both end their dances in identical positions; the spectators applaud, reward both couples, and everyone is delighted.

The square is now packed with people, who mill about greeting one another and conversing as the orchestra renews the raucous overture. Rowdy peasants come in and dance an animated Russian folk dance to the amusement of some of the crowd. The scene is now feverish with liveliness and hearty good spirits, and the music reaches a high volume to duplicate this enthusiasm. Two drummers step out from behind the blue-curtained stage at the rear and walk forward. The crowd stands back. The drums roll commandingly; everyone looks toward the stage; a loud chord from the orchestra is cut off sharply. A man with a high-peaked hat pokes his head through the curtains. This is the Charlatan, the showman in charge of the "Living Theater." Everyone is silent as they watch him. He is a showman who entertains by magic, and when he steps out from behind the curtains, no one is quite certain what he will do. His long black robe decorated with mysterious signs, his white face, and his menacing gestures attract the crowd strangely. He takes out a flute. The orchestra sounds a few weird bars suggestive of incipient evil. Then the Charlatan surprises us by playing on his instrument not an Oriental incantation, but a pleasant melody, beseeching in its repetitions. This is his magic song, the music that will bring to life the unseen show behind the closed curtains. The crowd waits, fascinated. The Charlatan gives a sudden imperious signal. The curtains fly back. We see a stage separated into three small compartments. In each compartment rests a motionless puppet, staring out at the audience with blank expression. The three figures are supported by high armrests. In the center is the prima Ballerina, with perfect, Dresden-china features and pink cheeks. She poses rigidly, waiting to be wound up. On the left is the Moor, with white eyes and a white mouth set in a coal-black face. He wears a turban, a bright blouse with a sash about his waist, and trousers of gold brocade. On the right, completely relaxed, is Petrouchka. His face is a white mask, his body is limp, like that of a rag doll. His costume has no conventional design: the loose-fitting trousers that hang down over black boots, the blouse ruffled at the neck, the haphazard cap—all make his figure absurd. While the ballerina and the Moor hold themselves erect, Petrouchka's head lolls to the side. Of the three, he is the least eager to move or to be moved. Lifeless as he is, Petrouchka therefore seems to be more natural. The ballerina and the Moor are posed tensely, ready to spring into activity, but Petrouchka's attitude suggests that perhaps he is tired of being a puppet.

The three puppets remain still as the Charlatan finishes his invocation to his magical gods. The ensuing music is low and mysterious. The Charlatan cuts it short by sounding his flute three times, whereupon Petrouchka, the ballerina, and the Moor instantly wake up and move their feet to the sharp and lively rhythms of a Russian dance. The puppets still stand, and their feet move so fast on and off the floor that their bodies seem suspended. They have come to life so spontaneously, and their feet mark each accent of the dance with such energetic unison, that it is difficult to believe they were inert but a moment before. The music becomes more demanding in its tempo, but the puppets follow the dance perfectly, as if they were toy soldiers obeying the beat of a snare drum. Now they abandon their armrests and step down. The crowd gives them room, and, to the great pleasure of the spectators, the puppets act out a dumb show almost as mechanically as they danced. Both the Moor and Petrouchka are enamored of the ballerina. The Moor flirts with her, and the ballerina seems to favor him, upon which Petrouchka, in a jealous rage, attacks his rival. The Charlatan signals for the drama to stop, and the three puppets involuntarily return to their dance routine. The stage grows darker, and the crowd begins to wander off. The Charlatan makes another signal, and the puppets immediately cease all movement and become rigid and still. The curtain falls.

SCENE TWO—PETROUCHKA'S ROOM Now we are taken behind the scenes, into the private lives of the puppets. Petrouchka's room is a barren cell. The peaks of icy high mountains are painted all along the walls, near to the floor, while up above, near the ceiling, is a border of puffy white clouds. The room has been decorated, the set implies, for a character not altogether of this world. On the right wall hangs a large portrait of the Charlatan. A door on the left is embellished with satanic figures carrying pitchforks. Petrouchka is suddenly tossed into the room through this door by the Charlatan. The door slams shut. Petrouchka makes a feeble effort to pick himself up, but wonders whether it is worth it. His wooden gestures indicate that everything is hopeless. Here he is in prison again, with nothing to look at but a picture of his master. A piano takes up a despondent theme that embodies Petrouchka's despair, while the rest of the orchestra tries to drown it out. He moves about the room helplessly, he tries to open the door, he pounds on the walls, hoping that someone will release him. Then, all alone, he rages against the world that ignores him. As trumpets blare a loud fanfare, Petrouchka turns to the portrait of the Charlatan and shakes his fists in challenge to the evil magician who limits his life to public performances.

As if to prove that he is worthy of a better fate, Petrouchka then does a little dance in which he imitates human expression of feeling. The piano accompanies him. His arms are stiff, but when he holds them close to his heart and then opens them in a gesture of hope, we see that the puppet understands more than the dumb-show version of love. He is a marionette who might become human, but cannot because of the Charlatan who made him. His hatred of the Charlatan is his hatred of his inarticulate self, that part of his dual nature that can but pathetically copy the human gestures for the human emotion his other nature feels so intensely. He arouses our pity because we see that his rage against the world is also his rage at himself. His clumsy wooden limbs try in vain to express their freedom, and his white face is a mask of sorrow.

But Petrouchka's whole attitude changes when he turns to see that the ballerina has entered his prison. Now the music is gay and lighthearted and Petrouchka jumps about joyfully. The ballerina, who stands motionless on point, registers shock at this inelegant expression of pleasure. She makes the appropriate formal gestures of delicate disapproval and turns to go. Petrouchka is beside himself with anxiety and proceeds to increase the ballerina's distaste by leaping higher to attract her attention. Clearly, the ballerina has had enough of the uncontrollable puppet. She turns and leaves.

Once again Petrouchka is in despair and again, to the accompaniment of the piano and the overpowering orchestra that represents the world he fights against, he gives himself up to his grief. The Charlatan will always think him a mere puppet; the ballerina will never regard him as anything but an idiotic buffoon. He flings his exhausted body about the room, bangs against the walls, finally succeeds in tearing open a large hole in the right wall, and collapses when he sees that it leads nowhere.

SCENE THREE—THE MOOR'S ROOM The Moor, too, has been imprisoned by the showman, but his abode is ornately decorated and sumptuously furnished. Everything is splashed with color. A large couch, covered with the skin of a tiger and backed with cushions, is on the left. Tall, bushy palm trees are painted on the walls. Serpents and ferocious beasts depicted in bright colors peer out into the room through thick jungle foliage. On the right is a door ornamented with a snake rampant. On the couch lies the Moor. He is playing idly with a coconut. The music is slow, almost lazy, as the Moor amuses his indolence by tossing the coconut and catching it. Unlike Petrouchka, the Moor is satisfied with his abode and appears happy whiling away the time of day like the caged beast contentedly resigned to an imitation jungle. He is also unlike the clown in his inhumanity: he is all puppet. He is soon bored with his simple pastime and tries to vary it with complications: by grasping his toy with his feet and letting it fall, by catching it in many ways. But this is not sufficient for the Moor's entertainment. He grows angry with the coconut. He shakes it, as an animal would shake the head of a helpless victim. He hears something inside, but he cannot break the coconut. He pulls out his scimitar, places the coconut on the floor at his feet. The music crashes with his effort to break the coconut in two, but it is hard as a rock.

The Moor is astonished. He stares at the mysterious object that can withstand his mighty blow and decides that it must be magical. He kneels then, bows and worships his plaything as he would worship a god.

The door moves aside, and a roll on a drum signals the entrance of the ballerina. She dances in, horn held to her lips, and steps gaily about the room, the beat of the drum accompanying the tune she plays. The Moor forgets his fetish and watches her with great pleasure, a pleasure which the music expresses with brief cries. The ballerina is charmed by this simple response, so different from the open approval of Petrouchka, and obliges the Moor by dancing a waltz. He is delighted beyond mere approval by this performance and insists upon dancing too. His motions are primitive alongside her elegant steps, but he nevertheless tries to make his crude dance fit the rhythm of the ballerina's waltz. He fails miserably and persists in his own private rhythm as the orchestra imitates the chaos of their duet by opposing different melodies. The Moor is now infatuated with the dainty ballerina and demonstrates his affection by pulling her toward the couch. The ballerina pretends to be aghast at this behavior, but secretly she is charmed also and scarcely resists when the Moor holds her on his lap. Their amorous dalliance is interrupted, however, by strange noises from outside. One of Petrouchka's melodies is proclaimed on the trumpet, and the clown thrusts his arm in at the door in an effort to wedge himself into the room. He has imagined the plight of the ballerina and has come to her aid! The couple jump guiltily as he forces his way in; they spring apart. The jealous Petrouchka berates the Moor for his behavior and approaches him menacingly as the music resounds his rage. The Moor recovers from the surprise of Petrouchka's sudden appearance and replies with animal grunts. Then he draws his scimitar and begins to chase the clown around the room. The ballerina faints on the couch, the Moor closes in on Petrouchka, whose end seems certain until he makes a quick dash for the door and escapes. The Moor is about to pursue the interloper, when he remembers the ballerina. He drops his sword, goes back over to the couch, and pulls the ballerina back onto his lap. The curtain falls as his head bobs up and down in savage satisfaction. The private lives of the three puppets have turned out to be almost identical to the dumb show they acted before the public: Petrouchka always loses.

SCENE FOUR—GRAND CARNIVAL The Shrovetide Fair, the outside world, has gone on while we watched the inner drama backstage, and the music now takes us back to the festivities. Very little time has elapsed, for the stage is not yet dark and the celebrating crowd is by no means ready to go home. The puppet theater in the back is dark and silent. Stimulated by their continuous refreshment, the peasants are all laughing and whipping themselves up to a final high pitch of excitement. A group of nursemaids emerge from the multitude, line up, and start a traditional dance to a Russian folk song that is exhilarating in its open melody; the crowd sways to the rhythm of the dance. The nursemaids' round is interrupted by deep, plodding notes from the orchestra, which herald the arrival of a trained bear. The bear swaggers clumsily onto the scene, led by his trainer, who laughs at the fears of the spectators and directs the bear in a few simple tricks. Then follows the dance of the coachmen, whose performance outrivals all the others in color and vigor. The theme to which the nursemaids danced is heard again, and the nurses join the coachmen. The couples seem to exhaust themselves in joyous abandon, but gain fresh strength with each step. Garishly dressed masqueraders—a demon, various animals—scurry about in the square trying to frighten people, but almost everyone is involved in the dance, in watching it at first, then imitating it while standing still, then participating fully, so that the stage gradually becomes a mass of whirling color. The frenzied beat of the music, and its increasingly raucous volume, intoxicates the dancers, and—as night descends on the scene and snow begins to fall—their movements in this picture frame of old Russia surge with a final expression of carnival fervor.

The enthusiasm of the revelers has not allowed them to notice that in the back, within the puppet theater, there are signs of activity behind the drawn curtains. They all turn, as they hear strange noises inside the theater, and wait expectantly. Petrouchka comes running out, the music sounds his fanfare, and we see that he is trying to escape from the Moor, who dashes out after him. The crowd is struck dumb by this apparently spontaneous life in the puppets and looks on, fascinated, as the clown tries to avoid the blows of the Moor's scimitar. The Moor's animal strength overpowers Petrouchka. The clown is cornered. He covers his head with his arms, shaking with fright. The Moor, with one blow of his sword, strikes him down. Petrouchka doubles up in pain. The music reflects his agony and his great effort to remain alive, but his legs stretch out, his whole body quivers spasmodically, and he is dead.

His death has been so realistic that the people who surround his body cannot believe that he is a mere puppet; a crime seems to have been committed. Someone calls a policeman, who observes the dead clown and hauls out the Charlatan to give an account of the strange goings on. The Charlatan is much amused at his suspicions and picks up the body to show everyone they are mistaken. Petrouchka is now a limp rag doll, a creature who could never have been anything but lifeless. The policeman is satisfied, people shake their heads, the crowd begins to leave slowly. The Charlatan remains alone, holding the puppet, and the stage is almost completely dark. He turns to re-enter the theater—perhaps to put the errant clown back in his cell—when Petrouchka's fanfare blares out loudly to stop him in his tracks. He looks up: on the top of the theater the ghost of Petrouchka shakes his fist at the Charlatan—and at everyone else who will not believe he is real.

NOTES The idea of *Petrouchka* was first of all a musical idea. Stravinsky had finished *Firebird* and was about to begin work on his next project for Diaghilev—*The Rite of Spring*—when he interrupted his plans to compose a purely nonballetic piece. He wanted to write a piece for piano and orchestra in which the piano would seem to be attacked by the mass of instruments. It would fight back, flourish a bit, but then the large orchestra would win out.

Stravinsky began to think of this composition as a contest between a puppet, represented by the piano, and the orchestra. After he had finished it, he tried to find an idea that would express the image that had been in his mind as he composed. He found it in a word, *Petrouchka,* "the immortal and unhappy hero of every fair."

He conveyed his idea to Diaghilev, who, upon hearing the music, decided to produce a ballet on this theme as soon as possible. The painter and designer Alexandre Benois collaborated with the musician and the impresario on the story, which Michel Fokine choreographed for Nijinsky, Karsavina, Orlov, and Cecchetti.

Although it is perhaps the most famous ballet in the modern repertory, *Petrouchka* has but recently been revived with sufficient competence to remind us that its first production was a very great one indeed. Stravinsky has written in his *Autobiography* (1936): "I should like . . . to pay heartfelt homage to Vaslav Nijinsky's unsurpassed rendering of the role of Petrouchka. The perfection with which he became the very incarnation of this character was all the more remarkable because the purely saltatory work in which he excelled was in this case dominated by dramatic action, music and gesture. The beauty of the ballet was greatly enhanced by the richness of the artistic setting which Benois had created for it. My faithful interpreter Karsavina swore to me that she would never relinquish her part as the dancer, which she adored. But it was a pity that the movements of the crowd had been neglected. I mean that they were left to the arbitrary improvisation of the performers instead of being choreographically regulated in accordance with the clearly defined exigencies of the music. I regret it all the more because the *danses d'ensemble* of the coachmen, nurses and mummers, and the solo dances, must be regarded as Fokine's finest creations.

Carl Van Vechten describes Nijinsky's Petrouchka in this way: "He is a puppet and—remarkable touch—a puppet with a soul. His performance in this ballet is, perhaps, his most wonderful achievement. He suggests only the puppet in action; his facial expression never changes; yet the pathos is greater, more keenly carried over the footlights, than one would imagine possible under any conditions. I have seen

Fokine in the same role, and although he gives you all the gestures the result is not the same. It is genius that Nijinsky puts into his interpretation of the part. Who can ever forget Nijinsky as Petrouchka when thrown by his master into his queer black box, mad with love for the dancer, who, in turn, prefers the Moor puppet, rushing about waving his pathetically stiff arms in the air, and finally beating his way with his clenched fists through the paper window to curse the stars? It is a more poignant expression of grief than most Romeos can give us."

Many famous dancers have since appeared in the role—Massine, Woizikowski, Jerome Robbins, Michael Kidd, Børge Ralov. Fokine revived the ballet for the Royal Danish Ballet in 1925, and for Ballet Theatre, October 8, 1942.

Petrouchka was revived by the Royal Ballet on March 26, 1957, with Alexander Grant, Margot Fonteyn, and Peter Clegg in the principal roles. Rudolf Nureyev danced the role for the first time with this company on October 24, 1963. Nadia Nerina was the doll and Keith Rosson the blackamoor. Mary Clarke wrote in the *Dancing Times:* "Let it be said at once that Nureyev captures to perfection the sawdust quality of the part. His first fall in the opening scene is just a crumble of a puppet body and all the way through one feels that the gloves contain no hands, just useless stuffing. This, of course, heightens the pathos of the character, the little pigmy soul that aspires to human loves and fears without a human body to support them. The scene in Petrouchka's cell is, as yet, only sketched; it will develop with more performances . . . but the final moment on the top of the booth, when the immortal soul asserts itself for the last time, is marvelously done. Everybody's heart must have trembled just a little bit when watching this."

Petrouchka is a ballet for which I have some sentimental recollection. In the Diaghilev production, whenever anyone was sick or unable to dance I took his part in the ballet. At one time I thought I had danced almost every male part in the ballet!

Petrouchka was revived in New York, March 13, 1970, by the City Center Joffrey Ballet under the supervision of Leonide Massine, assisted by Yurek Lazowski and Tania Massine. The principal roles were taken by Edward Verso, Erika Goodman, Christian Holder, Yurek Lazowski, and Zelma Bustilio. Noting that the ballet had not been seen in New York for twelve years, the critic Anna Kisselgoff wrote in the New York *Times* that "the spell of the decor, based on the original designs of Alexandre Benois, the magic of Igor Stravinsky's miraculous score and the radically expressive choreography of Michel Fokine are as strong as ever."

American Ballet Theatre revived *Petrouchka* June 19, 1970, at the New York State Theater, with Ted Kivitt, Eleanor D'Antuono, and Bruce Marks in the principal roles. Clive Barnes in the New York *Times* called this production, staged by Dimitri Romanoff and Yurek Lazowski "A sumptuous and authentic new staging that is part homage to the past and part reaffirmation of Ballet Theatre's historically classic role in American dance's future."

PILLAR OF FIRE

Ballet in one act. Music by Arnold Schoenberg. Choreography and book by Antony Tudor. Scenery and costumes by Jo Mielziner. First presented by Ballet Theatre at the Metropolitan Opera House, New York, April 8, 1942, with Nora Kaye as Hagar, *Hugh Laing as the* Young Man from the House Opposite, *Lucia Chase as the* Eldest Sister, *Annabelle Lyon as the* Youngest Sister, *and Antony Tudor as the* Friend.

This ballet tells a story to a piece of music that was inspired by a story. Schoenberg's *Verklärte Nacht* (*Transfigured Night*) is based on a nineteenth-century German poem called *Weib und die Welt* (*Woman and the World*), which had a theme daring for its time. In the poem there are two characters, a man and a woman who walk together in a cold, moonlit wood. They are lovers. First the woman addresses the man. She tells him that she has sinned, that she is going to have a child that is not his. All this happened, she tells her lover, before she was sure of his affection, at a time when she was desperate for any kind of security. She has learned since that sensuality is no security at all and that her new love for him is the blessing she really sought. The man replies that she must not feel guilty, that their mutual love is so great that even her child will be unblemished, that it will be in reality his child. He says that, as the light of the moon embraces the dark night, her love for him will transfigure the child, just as his love for her has transformed him. There is no need for forgiveness: they have love.

Such is the story of *Pillar of Fire;* but because it is a ballet, it takes this story and presents it dramatically, introducing additional characters, giving us a picture of the community in which such an event can take place, motivating the principal characters and their actions as completely as possible. The time is about 1900. The place is any town. The curtain rises to a low throbbing of strings. We see a wide street, lined with houses, under a darkening sky. The street narrows and vanishes in the distance. In the foreground, on the right, stands a high, narrow house, its woodwork embellished with Victorian scrolls. On the front steps a girl sits, brooding. She is plainly, almost severely, dressed; her long dark hair is braided about her head. She sits absolutely erect, her whole body seeming to delight in an intense placidity that is belied only by the clenched fists in her lap. This is Hagar, who lives in this house with two sisters.

The music is dark, heavy, oppressive; yet within this gloom, the principal melody cries out yearningly. Hagar watches the townspeople pass by in the twilight. Young people walk in the street, young people in love, and we sense immediately that Hagar has never been like them. Spinsters walk down the street with exaggerated daintiness, and Hagar turns away in disgust. She herself is not a young girl, but already she is frightened: she cannot be like the beautiful young girls in love, and the spinsters suggest the only alternative. She smooths back her hair, and we see that she is not unattractive.

Her two sisters emerge from the house. One is older, prim, and straitlaced; the other is young, a blond girl with long curls, soon to become a woman. The contrast between these two is apparently the same as the difference Hagar has noted in the passers-by. The younger sister is obviously spoiled, and when the older sister seems to reprimand Hagar for sitting apart from them, the young girl pokes fun at her. A young man comes across the street to their door. Hagar is delighted to see him. He is her only friend, and she is in love with him. Now she is no longer moody, but she hesitates to display her true feelings before her family. She knows them too well. The friend observes this and, being a very polite, conventional young man, is pleasant to her sisters.

The sisters, in turn, are more than civil to him. They are thoroughly aware that he has come to the house mainly to see Hagar, but the one—older, strong, possessive—and the other—young, demanding, accustomed to having anything she wants—soon draw his attention to themselves while Hagar watches. The young sister sidles up to him, flirting with cunning innocence. The friend observes her manner, is charmed by her blind youth, and ignores Hagar. The spinster is delighted at this sudden success of her favorite and asks the friend into the house. He goes in, and Hagar again is alone. It occurs to no one that she would enjoy going with them.

Hagar's despair turns to anger and hatred. It is not enough that her sister has dominated her family; she must also dominate all those who come in contact with it. The girl sees her last hope of freedom gone: her friend is hopelessly ensnared. And so she tries to forget her hope that he will respond to her love. The house across the street aids her forgetfulness. Lights come up inside the house, and Hagar sees through the walls all she has imagined must take place within it. For this is a place where love is celebrated all night long, where bold, unpolite men come to meet their women.

Shadows of lovers embracing are thrown against the walls of the house, and Hagar reaches out in open longing. She is taken aback when a man comes out of the house and glares at her. He walks jauntily, confidently, putting himself on display a little. She pretends to be embarrassed when he looks at her boldly and openly. Under any other circumstances this man would seem absurd to her, but now he embodies all the longings that Hagar cannot satisfy in a normal way, and she is attracted to him and the mysterious life in the house across the street. The man gives her a final look and goes back inside.

Now Hagar's young sister returns with the friend. The friend observes Hagar and has no understanding of her dilemma. Instead of questioning her, instead of helping her, it is much easier for him to succumb to the designs of the younger girl. Now more a woman than a child, the girl curls herself around his affections with the sinuousness of a cat. Hagar sees that her older sister has succeeded in making of the younger a frightening, pretty projection of her own willful selfishness and turns away in horror at the contrast between the girl's innocent beauty and inner evil. Should she warn the friend? How can she? He would laugh and not believe her. And so she watches as the girl takes her friend's arm and goes off with him for a stroll in the moonlight.

As they disappear, Hagar is frantic. She despises not only her sisters, but the man who will be duped by them. She contorts her body obscenely to express the depth of her disgust. Feeling now completely severed from all she might hold dear, she turns instinctively toward the mysterious house. The man who watched her in the street sees that she is still alone and leaves the house to join her.

Hagar welcomes him, and the two dance together. The girl loses all sense of modesty and decorum and for the first time in her life gives open expression of her feelings. The man encourages her passion. When Hagar leaps across the stage, he seizes her in mid-air, cutting short her flight of freedom, directing her warmth only to himself. He takes her by the hand and leads her to the house. Now eager to learn its secrets, Hagar enters ecstatically.

When she leaves the house a little later, she is alone. The conventions she renounced to discover love renew their hold on her to expose her act as sin, and she is filled with remorse. Now she has nothing, for she has rapidly learned the inadequacy of the kind of life led by the bold young man.

Her older sister enters and sees the guilt on Hagar's face. Neighbors passing by seem to know of her guilt, and Hagar, bitterly ashamed, seeks some friendly response from the crowd. She is shunned by everyone, even by the sordid people who frequent the house she has just left. These lovers-in-experience look at her in contempt while the youthful lovers-in-innocence scarcely see her.

The younger sister and the friend return from their walk. While the older sister mingles with a group of spinsters, confirming the shame Hagar has brought on the family, the young girl cavorts with new playmates from the house across the street. She is delighted to discover how nice they are.

The tormented Hagar can turn to no one. Obediently, like a child, she goes with her sisters toward the house. The two women say good night to her friend, as if to apologize for her behavior. The scene blacks out.

The street and the houses have vanished when the scene is lit again. The three sisters find themselves outcasts from society because of Hagar's indiscretion. Secretly her two sisters are delighted at her defection; but they are angry at what it has cost them and they repudiate her. The friend comes to her with his sympathy and help, but Hagar cannot bear to confront him with her evil. She seeks recognition instead from the townspeople, from the loose women, from men like her seducer. All are aghast at her downfall and will not help. Finally, in desperation, she reaches out pathetically to the seducer himself. He looks at her as if he'd never seen her.

Seeing her final despair, the friend returns. Hagar twists away to flee, but now the young man will not let her go. He holds her strongly, yet tenderly, tells her that she has forgotten his love and that he is there to stand by her and welcome her as his own. The girl is overwhelmed with his loving kindness and dances with him a *pas de deux* that is not only passionate, but tender. Hagar now possesses the permanent love that she despaired of finding. The lovers disappear for a moment, then we see them again, walking away in the distance, their hands clasped, their shoulders touching. They move slowly away out of sight in a deep green forest to the singing romantic music.

PRODIGAL SON

Ballet in three scenes. Music by Sergi Prokofiev. Choreography by George Balanchine. Scenery and costumes by Georges Rouault. First presented by Diaghilev's Ballets Russes at the Théâtre Sarah Bernhardt, Paris, May 21, 1929, with Serge Lifar in the title role, Felia Dubrovska as the Siren, *Michael Fedorov as the* Father, *and Leon Woizikowski and Anton Dolin as* Servants to the Prodigal Son. *Revived by the New York City Ballet at the City Center, New York, February 23, 1950, with Jerome Robbins as the* Prodigal Son, *Maria Tallchief as the* Siren, *Michael Arshansky as the* Father, *and Herbert Bliss and Frank Hobi as* Servants to the Prodigal Son. *Lighting by Jean Rosenthal.*

The story of the prodigal son is told first in the Bible: ". . . A certain man had two sons. And the younger of them said to his father, Father give me the portion of goods that falleth to me. And he divided unto them his living. And not many days after the younger son gathered all together, and took his journey into a far country, and there wasted his substance with riotous living. And when he had spent all, there arose a mighty famine in that land; and he began to be in want . . . And he would fain have filled his belly with the husks that the swine did eat: and no man gave unto him. And when he came to himself he said, How many hired servants of my father's have bread enough to spare, and I perish with hunger! I will arise and go to my father, and will say unto him, Father, I have sinned against heaven and before thee, and am no more worthy to be called thy son: make me as one of thy servants. And he arose and came unto his father. But when he was yet a great way off, his father saw him, and had compassion, and ran, and fell on his neck, and kissed him. And the son said unto him, Father I have sinned against heaven, and in thy sight, and am no more worthy to be called thy son. But the father said to his servants, Bring forth the best robe, and put it on him; and put a ring on his hand, and shoes on his feet: And bring hither the fatted calf, and kill it; and let us eat, and be merry: For this my son was dead, and is alive again; he was lost, and is found . . ." (St. Luke, 15:11–24)

This ballet tells the parable dramatically, with certain necessary omissions from and additions to the original story, but with the central theme preserved.

SCENE ONE—HOME The curtain rises almost immediately after the orchestra has played the first few bars of a strong, high-spirited theme. The scene is opulently colored. A painted backdrop depicts the distant view and imaginative sky line of the ancient Near East. A bright yellow sun hangs in a rich blue sky over a port with a lighthouse watching over the sea. At the right, in the back, is the opening to a tent; on the left, toward the front, stands a low picket fence with a small gate. Two boys, friends to the prodigal son, are busy about the scene, hurriedly arranging a store of large wine jugs as if they are preparing for a long journey. The prodigal son emerges from the tent, followed by two sisters. He is dressed in a short blue tunic and an open vest. His sisters, dressed in long, flowing garments, try to engage his attention, but the carefree youth ignores them to greet his friends. He picks up one of the wine jugs and throws it to one of them playfully. The music becomes terse in tempo, and the prodigal son dances vigorously in response to its pounding rhythm. With robust gaiety he seems to act out for his friends the adventures in store for them away from home and to reveal, at the same time, an innocent, headstrong spirit that urges him to seek those adventures. His sisters are frightened at his strong determination to leave home so selfishly and watch apprehensively. The prodigal son leaps about the stage with boundless energy, oblivious to their care. His dance stops in an open gesture when he looks up, to find himself face to face with his father, who has come out of the tent. He is embarrassed for an instant and steps back.

As a new, poignant melody begins, the father beckons to his children. They come and sit before him, the son unwillingly, but obediently. The son's attention wanders, and the father patiently turns his head back to the family circle. He holds up his arms over his children and looks upward in humble prayer. He touches their heads softly. The son turns away in protest at the ritual, but his father persists gently. When the son twists his body away, the father takes the boy's hand and places it on his sisters' hands.

The tension between the son and the father increases; the son turns away in disgust, leaps up, and flaunts his indifference in his father's face. The father rises and stands motionless and unprotesting in his grief, as his son dances in defiance before him. The son's temper is so high and his eagerness to leave home so intense that his sisters watch in terror and sadness. His dance is closely similar to his first dance, but here he is emboldened by anger. He ignores his family, beckons to his two friends, and points toward the open highway. They gather together their gear and run off through the gate, closing it hastily behind them. In a final gesture of rebellion, the son turns rapidly in the air before his father, dashes across the stage, and jumps high over the fence after his companions. The sisters stand close to their father in sympathy, but the old man walks forward slowly, raises his hand in unacknowledged farewell, and stands for a moment watching. Then he motions his daughters to the tent and follows them into their home. The scene blacks out.

SCENE TWO—IN A FAR COUNTRY The backdrop has been changed when the lights come up again. Still heavily colored, it now depicts an open tent furnished with a festive table. The small, symbolic fence that figured in the first scene stands as it was, on the left. A loud, crashing march heralds the arrival of a group of revelers, who enter on the left in a close line. They wear short tunics and white tights. All of them are bald. The manner in which they cross the stage to the raucous music is grotesque. As they separate, the beautiful, jubilant melody that will dominate the scene receives its first statement from the orchestra. They go over to the fence, turn it upside down, and we see that the prop is also a long black table. The table is moved back. The revelers form in short lines before it and hop across invisible lines toward each other, playing some fantastic game. Four of them lie down on the stage and spread their legs to form a star. One of the revelers lies across the middle of the star as the others move forward and rotate the pattern their companions have made. Their frolic is renewed until the prodigal son enters on the right with his two friends.

The revelers cease their play and gather in a close group on the other side of the stage; they are just as frightened as the intruders. The prodigal son doesn't see them at first. Then he approaches carefully, urging his friends to follow. They refuse, and he abandons his fears, to greet the strangers with open cordiality. He tries to shake hands with one of them, then with another, but all the revelers pull their hands back. He doesn't understand. They touch his rich clothes covetously and come closer. He hesitates and moves away apprehensively, but his friends force him back and he remembers the wine they have brought with them. He tells his companions to give the revelers drink, and immediately the situation changes. The revelers form a parade behind him, and the prodigal son is carried on the shoulders of his two friends. Everyone is now his friend. He is lifted up and, from above, shakes hands with all of his new companions. They throw him side to side in jovial welcome. Then he dances between his two fellows as everyone watches admiringly. He grasps their hands elatedly, and all the revelers rush to shake his hand. The whole group dances boldly and vigorously with the prodigal son. He jumps over the table as the dance ends, and all gather about him.

The siren comes in, dancing on point slowly and seductively to a tune of Oriental character. She wears a tight red tunic about her slim body, a high headdress, and from her shoulders there trails a crimson cape of velvet. The men watch her intently; the prodigal son is dazzled by her strange beauty and the confidence with which she fascinates. She turns slowly, wrapping the cape around the upper part of her body, then unwinds the garment. She handles the cape as if it were a part of her own body—an animate object obedient to her will. When the cape is fully extended behind her, the siren steps back over it, pulls it up between her legs, and winds it around them. Holding the cape with one arm, she dances proudly. She seems oblivious to the fact that she is being watched; this dance seems to please her more than it could please anyone else. She drops the cape and falls to her knees in an attitude of conventional despair. Then she rises, proud and assertive, to turn intricately on point. She throws the cape behind her, falls back on her arms, and, moving slowly on her hands and points, drags it across the floor slowly. Then she kneels low and pulls the cape up over her head, covering her body completely.

The prodigal son, now helplessly attracted, moves from behind the table and pulls the cape away. The siren rises on point, unsurprised. He tosses the garment aside as she turns to look at him. The prodigal son becomes now as obedient to her desire as the castoff raiment. He stands transfixed as the siren dances before him. She turns with strong, sinuous grace and holds out her arms in a gesture of approval and welcome. She approaches him closely; the prodigal son places his hands on her waist; they move backward in response to her lead. The siren pushes him back against the table. The revelers gather about them, and the siren is thrown back high above the table, into the waiting arms of her accomplices. She sits in triumph over the suppliant prodigal son, who lies on the table beneath her.

The siren is lifted down and sits facing the prodigal son. His eyes look down. His two friends begin a dance to amuse the group. Relieved by this distraction, the prodigal son watches with the others, but glances at the siren when her eyes leave his face. The siren touches his hand and moves her fingers up his arm to caress the golden medallion that hangs about his throat. He looks her full in the face.

His friends finish their dance, kneel before the table, and everyone applauds. The siren and the prodigal son come forward, watching each other intimately. They stand apart. It is as if he were imitating her movements. The siren falls back in his arms. She repulses his caress and entwines her arms back around his neck, and the two dance forward. They pause, and he puts his head between her legs, rises, and the siren sits proudly on his shoulders. Then she slides down his back. She stands on point before him and coils her leg about him, holding him fast, as he turns her. She releases him, and he pulls her over his back; the siren's hands reach out for her feet so that her body forms a hoop about him. Her body snakes about him completely, and slowly she slides to the floor. He steps out of the coil, rolls the siren upright, and holds her under her arms. Her knees rest on his feet as he moves across the stage. Now the prodigal son becomes bold and caresses the siren openly. He sits at her feet, his knees drawn up. She approaches him and sits on his head while resting her feet firmly on his knees. Now she rises straight up, arrogant in her voluptuousness and power. She steps away, and the prodigal son lies supine. She lies back across his body; their legs tangle. Now powerless, the prodigal son lies entwined in the siren's grasp. She gestures in insidious exultation.

The music pounds and shrieks fiercely. The prodigal's two friends pull the couple apart. Their companions are now reveling in drunkenness and force the prodigal son to join them. They drag his exhausted body about the stage while the siren watches from the table. He seeks her help, but the profligates carry her above the table and she pours wine down his throat as he slides down the table beneath her. They lift him high and carry the siren under him. Both are held by the waist as their bodies fall back hideously. They embrace frantically, are finally released, and two drunkards crawl under their legs. The prodigal staggers from group to group in his intoxication and falls against the table, where he cannot distinguish one of his companions from another. The siren watches him expectantly. He rushes up on the table, but the revelers tilt it up high under him and he slides down it, all his strength spent. The siren places her pointed toe on his chest in triumph.

The table now stands up on end. The revelers conceal themselves behind it. The prodigal is shoved back against the table, where he rests helpless. Hands reach out from either side and move down his body. The friends rush out from behind, turn him upside down, shake him, and collect his gold greedily. They stand aside as the siren is carried out. She stands upright on a man's shoulders, her arms akimbo. She gets down and gathers up all the remaining gold. Now the thieves rob the prodigal of all his outer garments, even his shoes. He is still unaware of what they have done to him, and the debauchers celebrate by crawling over and under each other, like eels. The siren yanks off the prodigal's gold medallion, kisses it, and exits. Her companions leave the scene, running across the stage, back to back, like many-legged insects.

The prodigal son wakens slowly from his stupor. He slides down the table to the ground and falls on his face. He pulls himself back up, gripping the table with agonized effort. He looks down at his hands, then at his body. He remembers and holds his head in disbelief. Stretching his hand up plaintively in despair, he acknowledges the betrayal of his friends and his own self-betrayal. He falls to the ground, sees water, crawls to it, drinks, and curls up like a child. He rises, looks behind him at the scene of his debauchery, and struggles off on his knees.

The profligates return, bringing their loot with them. The siren follows. The table is now turned upside down to form the gate and fence. The siren's companions run to the fence, arrange themselves within it, and the siren joins them. One of the men lifts high the end of her crimson cape, others begin a rowing motion, and the table becomes a ship, the siren's cape its sail, and her arched body its figurehead. Her companions blow their trumpets, and the scene blacks out.

SCENE THREE—HOME The stage is set as it was for the first scene. The prodigal son, covered now with a thin and tattered black cloak, crawls across the stage, supporting his exhausted body with a staff. The music is dark, almost funeral-like in its persistent beat. The traveler's progress is slow and, to him, endless, for he has no idea where he is. He looks about hopelessly. Suddenly he sees the gate to his home. He staggers toward it, reaches out his hand, touches it, and collapses with the effort.

His sisters emerge from the tent. One of them sees him and calls to the other. Together they go to him and open the gate to lead him in lovingly. The piercing melody of the music reflects their great joy. They stand on either side of their kneeling brother as their father comes out. They are so happy that they do not move. The father remains near the door of his home. The son slowly and hesitatingly raises his head and looks up at his father. He beseeches him with outstretched arms. The father does not move. The son twists away toward the fence, but he has no sooner moved than his father raises his hand to keep him. He turns back toward his home, bows his head to the ground, and stretches his arms out behind in self-denial. With head still bowed, he crawls toward his father slowly, wretchedly. He falls full length just as he nears him, reaches out to drag himself forward by grasping his father's feet. He pulls himself up, clinging to his father's arms. The father reaches out to gather him close in forgiveness, love, and protection and, holding him like a child, he covers his son with his cloak.

PULCINELLA

Dramatic ballet in one act. Music by Igor Stravinsky, based on scores by Giambattista Pergolesi. Choreography by Leonide Massine. Scenery and costumes by Pablo Picasso. First presented by Diaghilev's Ballets Russes at the Théâtre National de l'Opéra, Paris, May 15, 1920, with Leonide Massine as Pulcinella, *Tamara Karsavina as* Pimpinella, *Vera Nemtchinova as* Rosetta, *Lubov Tchernicheva as* Prudenza, *Stanislas Idzikowski as* Caviello, *Nicholas Zverev as* Florindo, *Enrico Cecchetti as* Il Dottore. *First presented in the United States by the New York Music Guild in Chicago, 1933, with choreography by Laurent Novikoff.*

Stravinsky's score for *Pulcinella* is based on music by the great Neapolitan, Giambattista Pergolesi. The story of the ballet is based on an early eighteenth-century Italian manuscript found in Naples, and its principal characters are taken from the *commedia dell' arte*, the popular Italian masked comedy, which, beginning in the sixteenth century, captured the imagination of all of Europe with its universal types: the pathetic Pierrot, the heartless and flirtatious Columbine, the deathless Pulcinella (Punch, to the English-speaking world), and others. The ballet tells a new variation of Pulcinella's immortality.

A narrow street in Naples is the scene. A volcano can be seen in the distance, over the bay at the end of the street. The end house to the left is that of Tartaglia, whose daughter, Rosetta, is beloved by the youth Caviello. The end house to the right is that of *Il Dottore* (the doctor), whose daughter, Prudenza, is beloved by Florindo.

At the beginning of the ballet Caviello and Florindo enter to watch the houses of their sweethearts. Soon Prudenza and Rosetta look out of their windows. They smile at their suitors, seemingly encouraging them, then pour water out over their heads. The doctor, meanwhile, has discovered the presence of the boys and drives them away.

Pulcinella enters—the familiar figure with a long, pendulous red nose. He dances in the street to the tune of a small violin he plays. His dance and his music attract the girls. Prudenza, who clearly adores him, tries to embrace him. Pulcinella chases her back into her house. Rosetta appears, properly chaperoned by her father, Tartaglia. She tells him that she is in love with Pulcinella and must marry him. Tartaglia upbraids her for loving the ugly little man, but Rosetta ignores him. She tries to interest Pulcinella, who is as indifferent to her as he was to Prudenza. She dances before him. Enchanted, Pulcinella kisses her and takes her for a partner in a dance.

Pimpinella, Pulcinella's wife, discovers the two dancing together. The husband protests that he is innocent, that he still loves only her; Pimpinella is at length convinced of it, and the couple dance.

Meanwhile the two suitors, Caviello and Florindo, have been watching the street. They have seen that Pulcinella is the favorite of both Rosetta and Prudenza, and they are furious with jealousy. Their rage is still more inflamed when it becomes obvious that Pulcinella dares to reject the advances of the girls.

They attack Pulcinella, both jumping on him at once. Pimpinella screams for help, and both Rosetta and Prudenza rush out to help. The boys flee, and poor Pulcinella, left in the hands of three women, all eager to assist him, is almost torn in two by their fierce sympathy.

Summoned by their fathers, the two girls return to their homes. Pulcinella dances with his wife.

Florindo and Caviello have been waiting for this moment. They re-enter the street, disguised in black cloaks, carrying swords. Just as they run for him, Pulcinella sees them. He crosses himself hurriedly and pushes his wife into their house. Before he can enter too, he is caught by the two boys. Florindo strikes him dead with his sword. The murderers leave. Pulcinella gets up as if nothing had happened to him. He turns down the street and disappears.

The stage is empty for a moment. Then an astonishing thing happens. Four little Pulcinellas enter, carrying on their shoulders a fifth Pulcinella, apparently dead. They lay the corpse down in the street and dance.

Tartaglia and the doctor come out with their daughters, to see what has happened. The two girls, horrified to see their Pulcinella lying thus in the street, helplessly hover over his body. The doctor examines Pulcinella and declares him dead.

A magician joins them and assures the girls that he can bring Pulcinella back to life. The four little Pulcinellas and the two girls anxiously await the result of his mysterious incantations. The two fathers stand aside, disbelieving. After pommeling Pulcinella's body thoroughly, the magician commands him to live again. Pulcinella gets up, and the onlookers rejoice. The two girls swear to him that he is their only love.

Their fathers, however, remain unconvinced, even by appearances. To prove these skeptics wrong, the magician takes off his long cloak and wig: *he* is the real Pulcinella! His friend, Fourbo, has been the body.

Fourbo and Pulcinella trick the two fathers into retreating into their homes. Pimpinella comes into the street and, seeing two Pulcinellas, runs away in horror. Fourbo, still alias Pulcinella, brings her back.

Now everyone tries to get into the act. Caviello and Florindo enter, wearing Pulcinella disguises, to renew their romances with Rosetta and Prudenza. The girls accept them. Pimpinella, Rosetta, and Prudenza are dancing with three fake Pulcinellas. The real Pulcinella intervenes and kicks each of his imitators. While his friend Fourbo seeks safety in the magician's costume, Pulcinella unmasks the other two impostors before their girls.

The doctor and Tartaglia, still astonished by the goings on, are persuaded by Fourbo, the magician, to permit their daughters to marry Florindo and Caviello. The fathers agree. Pulcinella dances joyfully with Pimpinella, and the magician declares that they and the other two couples are man and wife.

NOTES Massine's *Pulcinella* was first presented in the United States by the City Center Joffrey Ballet, in 1974.

The New York première was at the City Center, October 9, 1974.

Music by Igor Stravinsky. Choreography by Jerome Robbins and George Balanchine. Scenery and costumes by Eugene Berman. Lighting by Ronald Bates. First presented by the New York City Ballet at the Stravinsky Festival, 1972, at the New York State Theater, Lincoln Center, June 23, 1972, with a cast headed by Edward Villella and Violette Verdy. Conducted by Robert Irving.

I am proud that the painter Eugene Berman, who died December 14, 1972, soon after *Pulcinella* was completed, designed this ballet for us. His help, friendship, and collaboration were essential. I had long felt that the original idea of the ballet from the Diaghilev days was just not interesting enough for the stage any more. But Jerome Robbins and I loved the music. So did Stravinsky's friend Berman, who was of course almost an Italian, so immersed was he in Italy, living there, painting there, knowing that beautiful country, its art and its traditions and theater, too, in all its variations. Berman was a kind of specialist in the *commedia dell'arte*, the improvisational theater identified with the great natural mimicry of the clowns of Naples, what Lincoln Kirstein has called the "underground manual idiom of scurrilous tricks and gesture." It was just those tricks that inspired us to do this new ballet with Berman to Stravinsky's music and I am glad that we did it. Robbins and I enjoyed putting the piece on; we even enjoyed dancing in the first performances, and if the ballet doesn't last as we made it, both of us know that Berman's part in it ought to. Good painters go on forever.

You just have to read the story of the first *Pulcinella*, described above in the first version, to see how complicated it all was for the audience to understand. Our idea was to simplify so that everything would be clear, and we hit on a variation of not only the Pulcinella myths, but the Faust myth, too. We decided that Pulcinella, a Neapolitan scamp, would make a pact with the devil to save his skin. He would then, as would be expected, renege on his promise, but his girl would rescue him, in spite of his having given her a hard time all along. Jerome Robbins and I had worked together before on a compressed story ballet, *Tyl Ulenspiegel*, where he, as the hero, made the whole of a personal as well as political and religious plot idea wonderfully clear in a matter of minutes. (One of the reasons Robbins is such a great choreographer is his great gift as a dancer; we can't remember that too often.)

To see the ballet and enjoy it, I hope words are not really necessary. It might be good to hear the recording that Stravinsky conducted of his lovely music (Col. ML-4830) and to read Robert Craft's notes on that album. As for the action:

Berman's superb drop curtain of Pulcinella and Stravinsky's signature rises on a graveyard scene. Eight Pulcinellas as pallbearers bring to his tomb a white skeleton recumbent on a catafalque. The Pulcinellas are beside themselves with grief. They put the skeleton in the tomb, nevertheless, weeping and wailing all the time.

The Devil arrives. At the tomb, he obliges the skeleton to look over the list of sins the deceased Pulcinella has committed, etc. He then tempts the deceased to sign a pact by which he will rise from the dead if he obeys the Devil in the future. The skeleton signs and then, miraculously, comes out of the grave a full-fledged Pulcinella. His girl, who had despaired at his death, rejoices. She cannot believe that her love has been restored to her. Pulcinella, however, intent on a reunion with his fellow comics, repulses her cruelly. The Devil drags him away to meet several fascinating ladies. In a brief scene in a brothel, the ladies, at the Devil's command, respond to his desires.

Pulcinella leads on a group of his fellow clowns as the baby Pulcinellas watch. He dresses then in a woman's dress and in this disguise, suddenly becoming a beggar, is seen asking for alms at a street fair of acrobats. This is simply a disguise for thievery, of course. The police spot him. He eludes them, then just as the police think they have cornered him, all his identical Pulcinella friends turn up and they don't know *whom* they are chasing. Victorious over the law, Pulcinella passes out the loot among his friends. He gives too fast, however, and there is nothing left for himself! Alone, he laments. A skeleton appears, brought onto the scene by the Devil; Pulcinella shivers in terror at this reminder of the pickle the Devil got him out of. Now when his girl comes onto the scene, he does not dismiss her rudely. The chorus sings as the Devil gives him a scroll; this is the pact he has signed.

A funeral procession of another Pulcinella passes. The Devil reminds Pulcinella of the flames of hell that await him. Then a young boy appears, blond and attractive, especially to the Devil, who can't keep his eyes off the boy. Suddenly blind to all else, the Devil follows the boy. Pulcinella has again escaped.

He and his girl are reunited. Pulcinella indicates that for some reason he is terribly, terribly hungry; ravenous, in fact. So a long table and a huge pot are brought in. Quickly, a potful of pasta is produced out of the pot. Pulcinella and his friends eat so much they collapse. The Devil arrives with his scroll again. Before he knows what has happened to him, Pulcinella's pals put him in the pot and give the scroll to their friend.

The scene shifts now to a solo by the girl, followed by one for Pulcinella, dressed now all in a white costume festooned with black balls. The brass in the orchestra begins a richly melodic section and the *pas de deux* for the two lovers begins. A dance of celebration for all the villagers follows, after which Pulcinella and his girl come forward to the front of the stage, with all their friends, to blow kisses to the audience.

REMEMBRANCES

Music by Richard Wagner. Choreography by Robert Joffrey. Set by Rouben Ter-Arutunian. Costumes by Willa Kim. Lighting by Jennifer Tipton. First presented by the City Center Joffrey Ballet at the City Center, New York, October 12, 1973, with Francesca Corkle and Jonathan Watts as principals. Conducted by Seymour Lipkin. Pianist: Stanley Babin. She, Who Sings: *Donna Roll.* She, Who Remembers: *Jan Hanniford.*

Remembrances is a ballet about looking back. As a woman sings her recollections of past love, a woman who remembers remains at her side to watch and reach out toward a danced re-enactment of the past.

The program recalls that Richard Wagner, in 1849, having taken an active role in the revolutionary movement in Germany, was forced to flee with his wife, Minna, and to settle in Switzerland. There, in Zurich, he met a wealthy silk merchant, Otto Wesendonck, who, at his wife Mathilde's urging, became Wagner's patron. It was not long before "something dangerously like a love affair" developed between Mathilde and Wagner.

Some of Wagner's work is inextricably linked with his relationship to Mathilde. In 1853 he wrote for her personal album a sonata that is described by one of his biographers, Paul Bekker, as "a summary of the past and a promise for the future, a delicate act of homage to the woman who had inspired the music which was now to flow from him in an almost unbroken stream." Written on the manuscript of the sonata, as a motto, is the inscription: "Do you know what will follow?"

Mathilde Wesendonck and Wagner became artistic collaborators a few years later, when in 1857–58 he set to music five of her poems. The poems are entitled *Der Engel* (*The Angel*), *Stehe Still* (*Stand Still*), *Im Treibhaus* (*In the Greenhouse*), *Schermzen* (*Tears*), and *Traume* (*Dreams*). Wagner said that *Im Treibhaus* and *Traume* could be described as "studies" for *Tristan und Isolde.*

In 1935 Arturo Toscanini discovered a lost, unpublished piece of Wagner's known as the *Porazzi Theme,* which the composer had played on the afternoon of his death. Dating from 1859, this theme had been jotted down on the back of a sketch for *Tristan,* relating to the lovers' invocation to the night.

These musical works of Wagner's are the score for the ballet and set the scene for its backward look.

The ballet carries as its motto this quotation from Shelley:

> Music, when soft voices die
> Vibrates in the memory.

The pianist begins the music in the dimly lit auditorium. The house slowly darkens with the quiet music. Soon a girl in a long dress walks slowly across the stage. She reaches out in a gesture of longing and sits down. Following her now comes another girl, her double, who is to sing what the first girl feels and acts as she watches the scene that flows before her.

A girl dances with a boy, it is apparently long ago and almost lost to the memory but soon other images come back, the lovers are among friends, four other couples. The scene appears to be a clearing high above a cavernous bay, the sea shimmering in the distance; the setting resembles an oculus that is focused on a far-off place, the sea, mountains, enclosed in a curved landscape of the memory.

Two couples dance to the music of the first song. Then later, the lead girl, alone, dances and seems to suffer, but her lover rejoins her.

There is a recognition between the woman who watches her past and the girl who dances it. Others now dance to the low threnody of strings. Finally, the girl is left by herself, kneeling. She rises; her partner returns. Later among the happy couples, the lovers seem to expire. She, Who Remembers reaches out to them and gestures to She, Who Sings. But her young image only looks back at her.

NOTES Writing in *Dance and Dancers* about *Remembrances,* Patricia Barnes referred to the ballet as "perhaps the best thing Robert Joffrey has yet achieved. . . . It is a lushly romantic work, matching the music's soul and passion. . . . Corkle has always been a brilliant young technician. In *Remembrances* Joffrey has seen another side of her. One is tempted to say that this ballet has made her a great dancer. She performed it as if her heart was on fire, with a sincerity and depth that were remarkable. In her movement there was a dramatic tension and in her musicality a wealth of understanding of what can transform a simple movement into art.

"Jonathan Watts . . . was here making his first stage appearance in nine years. . . . He is now dancing better than ever, even after such a long lay-off period. Always an immaculate stylist, in *Remembrances* he was superb, partnering with tenderness, possessing elegant *ports de bras* and unforced dignity."

REQUIEM CANTICLES

Music by Igor Stravinsky. Choreography by Jerome Robbins. Lighting by Ronald Bates. First presented by the New York City Ballet at the Stravinsky Festival, June 25, 1972, at the New York State Theater, Lincoln Center, New York, with Merrill Ashley, Susan Hendl, Bruce Wells and Robert Maiorano as principals. Soprano: Elaine Bonazzi. Bass: William Metcalf. Conducted by Robert Craft.

Stravinsky's *Requiem Canticles,* for contralto, soloists, and orchestra, first performed in 1966 at Princeton, New Jersey, was selected by Jerome Robbins as one of his ballets for our Stravinsky Festival in 1972. That event, which marked the composer's ninetieth birthday, also mourned his death as we hope he would have wished us to do, with celebration. *Requiem Canticles* was the final ballet of the Festival.

Stravinsky had earlier informed the New York City Ballet that he planned the *Requiem Canticles* "as an instrumental work originally, and I composed the threnody for wind instruments and muffled drums, now at the center of the work, first. Later I decided to use sentences from six texts of the traditional Requiem service, and that time I conceived the triangulate instrumental frame of the string *Prelude,* wind-instrument *Interlude,* and percussion *Postlude.* The *Requiem Canticles* are concert music, but the celebration of death is to be played in memory of a man of God, a man of the poor, a man of peace."

Robbins's *Requiem Canticles* was an appropriate finale in dance to what was, for many of us on both sides of the footlights, a memorable week.

A *Village Voice* critic said of the ballet: "Mr. Robbins's piece, conducted by Robert Craft, accentuated the energy heard in the music. Here were granite blocks of black-clothed dancers staring out at the audience in the *Prelude* and shaking in tight spasms. The choral sections followed, with the *Exaudi* bringing in slow gestures and walkings, the *Dies irae* frenzied with lifts and aimless striding, the *Tuba mirum* showing Bruce Wells as a sort of Angel Gabriel ready to call everyone to judgment, the non-vocal *Interlude* leaving the stage to four dancers full of expectation, *Rex tremendae* bringing back the corps in their block phalanxes, Merrill Ashley bursting out of a semicircle of corps in *Lacrymosa*, the *Libera me* letting the corps members converge on one another on their knees and making room for short solos by Miss Ashley and Susan Hendl before the group goes into asymmetric attitudes; and finally the drums and bells of the *Postlude* setting off a mechanism of ticking bodies, limbs, and finally just heads in open-mouthed, silent cries of fear and marvel."

REVERIES

Music by Peter Ilyich Tchaikovsky. Choreography by John Clifford. Costumes by Joe Eula. Lighting by Ronald Bates. First presented by the New York City Ballet at the New York State Theater, December 4, 1969, with Conrad Ludlow. Anthony Blum, Johnna Kirkland, Gelsey Kirkland, and ensemble.

The fourth ballet by John Clifford, the New York City Ballet's youngest choreographer, to be mounted by that company, *Reveries* uses music from Tchaikovsky's *Suite No. 1* (the first, third, fourth, and sixth movements). The plot of the ballet is the plot of the music.

The curtain rises after a brief orchestral introduction. The first movement, marked *Introduction and Fugue,* is staged for a boy and twelve girls who, dressed in flowing pink, surround their romantic hero. He is seen in a spotlight, center. Detached at first, he kneels and watches the girls dance, then joins them under the dark, starry sky. His dance is like magic, and they all seem to respond like flowers in the wind. He leaves the girls then to commence to dance to the fugue. The boy returns to dance and fall at the feet of his Muses. They soon leave, the scene darkens and he, too, departs.

To the third movement of Tchaikovsky's Suite, *Intermezzo,* the dance begins in a diagonal of light on a dark stage. Four boys and four girls face each other. The stage brightens, a boy lifts on a girl in white, and the orchestra plays a romantic theme. The couple dances, he catching her under the arms as she leaps. As the music ends, he kneels before her, then holds her as she falls into his arms. A brilliant soloist in blue dances in dynamic contrast to the lyricism of the lovers.

The *Marche Militaire* is led by a girl who matches the brilliance of Tchaikovsky's melody with the help of a small group of four girls. The finale, *Gavotte,* brings the four principals together in a climactic ensemble of complication and exuberance.

NOTES Clive Barnes wrote in the New York *Times: "Reveries* is John Clifford's best piece to date, and is a lovely piece of choreography. . . . He really illuminates the music. There is a sumptuous and love-rapt *pas de deux* for Johnna Kirkland and Conrad Ludlow, and beautiful solos for Anthony Blum and Johnna's brilliant kid sister, Gelsey Kirkland. . . . The entire piece is elegant yet fun."

Arlene Croce, editor of *Ballet Review,* wrote of John Clifford in *Playbill* in 1969: "The youngest of the New York City Ballet's dancer-choreographers is twenty-one-year-old John Clifford. Clifford came to New York from Los Angeles and was awarded a scholarship to the School of American Ballet, where he entered the choreography workshop in 1966. He made his choreographic debut with *Stravinsky Symphony* in the spring of 1968 and has revised it steadily ever since. His second ballet, to Vaughan Williams' *Fantasia on a Theme of Thomas Tallis,* is a lyrical work about two real people and a dream couple whom the real people prefer to one another. Premièred early this year, *Fantasies* was a hit with both critics and audiences, and Clifford has been invited to stage his next ballet for the company's Sixth Annual Spring Benefit on May 8, on the same program with new works by George Balanchine and Jerome Robbins. Robbins, who returns this spring to choreograph for the company after more than a decade's absence, provided Clifford with his earliest inspiration. Shortly before spring rehearsals began, Clifford was to be found at the State Theater, where Robbins was taking class.

" 'I've been watching Jerry work on his new piece,' he told an interviewer. 'I'm rehearsing it but I don't know if I'm going to be in it yet. The way he squeezes everything he can get out of you! I can't do that yet. He's a rhythm choreographer of course—he uses every last bit of rhythm. And he's so thorough. I think he thought about *The Cage* for years before he did it, thought it all out and knew exactly what he wanted to do. When I first joined the company I would watch every performance of *The Cage* and people would say, "Well, John, what did you like this time?" The first large-scale choreography I ever saw was the film of *West Side Story.* I've seen it more than twenty times. When it came out again recently, I went back. I think it affected my spatial concepts when I began to choreograph. I used to try and set bits of movement in the background that only ended up confusing the stage picture. I was choreographing selectively as if for a camera. I didn't realize that in the theater the spectator has to have a central focus because he's stationary; he can't move around like a camera picking up this and that. You know those funny, insectlike things the girls do in *The Cage*? Well, they do a lot with their arms and hands you really can't see, but only because the stage is so dark. I wish it could be brighter. I'd like to do a horror ballet like that some day. Actually, whether you do story ballets or not depends on the music. I consciously try to do something different in each piece. The Stravinsky—a neo-classical abstract work. Mr. B. thought it would be good for me to work with that score. Next, a long romantic piece with a bit of a story. Now I'm using Bernstein's *Prelude, Fugue and Riffs.* It's a jazz score from the same period as Stravinsky's *Ebony Concerto,* but it's not going to be set as a "jazz ballet" in that sense because it would look dated. I don't read music or have a record-player. I go to the library and listen to records. When I hear something I like, I file it away in the back of my mind. I hadn't heard the *Tallis* until about a year ago, on the Coast, when somebody played it for me. I didn't care for it too much then. But it came back to me for *Fantasies.* When I'm making a piece, I don't try to get the dancers to consciously project a meaning. I don't tell them what they're supposed to do except over coffee. Ideally, you just want the dancer to be. You try and get the ones you know will look right for the part in the first place, then things happen. . . . I have projects going all the time. This company is so full of terrific dancers but we have such an enormous rep they don't often have the energy to show off. Right now, in addition to the Bernstein, I'm choreographing a Bartok ballet over at the school, and a rock ballet—rock music. It's only a 7½-minute piece but it's the hardest thing I've ever done. I tried doing classical *pas de deux* movements but it didn't work, it looked too contrasty. Then I did regulation discothèque and hated it. Now, last night, I had them all just walk. It was better. I want to do all kinds of things—multimedia . . . using singers and speech . . . opera. I have this terrific idea but I won't talk about it. I think Lincoln Kirstein thinks I'm mad.' "

THE RIVER

Original score by Duke Ellington. Choreography by Alvin Ailey. Costumes by Frank Thompson. Lighting by Gilbert V. Hemsley, Jr. Special lighting by Nicholas Cernovitch. First presented by American Ballet Theatre at the New York State Theater, Lincoln Center, New York, June 25, 1970, with a cast headed by John Prinz, Alexandra Radius, Hans Ebbelaar, Marcos Paredes, Eleanor D'Antuono, Cynthia Gregory, Ivan Nagy, Dennis Nahat, Sallie Wilson, and Keith Lee. Conducted by Jaime Leon.

A quotation from the musician Duke Ellington prefaces the ballet: ". . . of birth . . . of the well-spring of life . . . of reaffirmation . . . of the heavenly anticipation of rebirth. . . ." The work itself is the result of collaboration between Duke Ellington and Alvin Ailey. In its musical entirety, the work consists of a *Prologue*, an *Epilogue*, and eleven sections. These are entitled: *Spring, Spring Run, Meander, Giggling Rapids, Falls, Vortex, Lake, Mainstream* (*Riba*), *Two Cities, The Sea* (*Mother*), and *Spring*.

First presented by American Ballet Theatre in an unfinished state that was later completed, on June 29, 1971, *The River* was appraised by critic Jean Battey Lewis of the Washington *Post* as a work with "an alive and joyous quality, a life force that carries along its series of solos, duets and group dances in a headlong sweep. . . . *The River* is not only a well-spring of free, unforced, imaginative movement. It is also a tribute to Ailey's gifts as a director and developer of talent that he has created passages which capture so sensitively the strengths of some of Ballet Theatre's finest dancers."

Writing of *The River* soon after its première, in *The Saturday Review*, the critic Walter Terry said: "The Ailey ballet *The River*, with an original score by Duke Ellington, was not completed by première time, so for the season it was given in part as 'six dances from a work in progress.' A full appraisal, of course, must wait, but the Ailey dance brilliance—wonderful freshets of movement designs to delight the eye—are already there. There are patterns of mass motion that are utterly beautiful, but there are also such choreographic concentrates as Eleanor d'Antuono's incredibly fast solo *Vortex;* Cynthia Gregory (with either Ivan Nagy or Gayle Young) in a cool and graceful *pas de deux,* surrounded by ensemble movements, called *Lake;* Dennis Nahat's jaunty *Mainstream;* and the curiously haunting *Two Cities,* danced by Sallie Wilson and Keith Lee, each in separate pools of light, each lonely, each reaching out across the unseen barrier of river, of distance, of divisiveness of solitary spirit, however you care to interpret it, and, finally, bridging the abyss."

A year later, Deborah Jowitt wrote in the *Village Voice:* "Alvin Ailey has added three more sections to *The River*. One, called *Sea,* certainly rounds the whole piece out, since the sea people, Erik Bruhn and Natalia Makarova, can now open the ballet by pulling away from the 'spring' (Keith Lee) in a receding wave and return at the end in a slow, coiling floor duet that seems to spawn that wellspring again. *Meander*, for Mimi Paul, Ted Kivitt, and Ian Horvath, is a playful, jazzy, carelessly sensuous *divertissement*—very nicely danced, but not terribly compelling in its movement concept. *Giggling Rapids* features Bruhn and Makarova in a fast, almost kittenish exchange. She has a beautifully innocent body to go with her strength, and both are exuberant performers. As for the whole idea, well, the crowd loved seeing these two jazz it up (so good-sporty of them), but watching Bruhn reminded me of Cathy Berberian singing Beatles songs. Technique and persona not completely compatible with the material.

"There were other good things in *The River*. Dennis Nahat did marvelous things with the rhythmic shape and impetus of his little solo in *Falls*, and Eleanor D'Antuono has mastered *Vortex* completely, so that now her turns and swirls unleach little spurts of power without obvious effort or preparation."

RODEO

Ballet in two scenes. Music by Aaron Copland. Choreography and book by Agnes de Mille. Scenery by Oliver Smith. Costumes by Kermit Love. First presented by the Ballet Russe de Monte Carlo at the Metropolitan Opera House, New York, October 16, 1942, with a cast headed by Agnes de Mille as the Cowgirl, *Frederic Franklin as the* Champion Roper, *and Casimir Kokitch as the* Head Wrangler. *Revived by Ballet Theatre at Rhine-am-Main Air Force, Frankfort, Germany, August 14, 1950.*

Rodeo, subtitled "The Courting at Burnt Ranch," is a love story of the American Southwest. The problem it deals with is perennial: how an American girl, with the odds seemingly all against her, sets out to get herself a man. The girl in this case is a cowgirl, a tomboy whose desperate efforts to become one of the ranch's cowhands create a problem for the cowboys and make her the laughingstock of womankind.

SCENE ONE The corral of Burnt Ranch. The ballet's brief overture begins with a crash of cymbals and continues with a rowdy, rhythmic melody reminiscent of the wild west. The music becomes quiet, and the curtain rises on the corral of Burnt Ranch. The time is Saturday afternoon, the time of the weekly rodeo, about the turn of the century. Against an orange-red sky whose intense heat seems to bear down on the scene, a high wooden fence encloses the parched, dusty ground of the corral. Half a dozen lazy cowhands stand about, idling away the time. Among them stands the cowgirl, self-assertive in a bright red shirt, brown hat tilted back over her head, and brown pants and boots. Long pigtails hang down her back. One of the cowhands holds his hand up to shield his eyes from the glaring sun and looks out into the distance. Another cowboy rides in, twirling his arm over his head in a lassoing motion. The cowgirl hitches up her pants, as if to prepare for the rodeo that is about to begin. The cowboys tell her that she can't come along and ride off rapidly. Not to be outdone so easily, the cowgirl decides to follow them and rushes off to the right, roping the air with a fast-turning arm.

Three cowhands ride on vigorously. Six of their fellows join them, and all dance wildly, imitating in their movements the jolts and tricks of the rodeo. The music is fierce and a challenge to the dancers. The cowgirl re-enters and tries to join one of the groups. The cowgirl secretly hankers after the head wrangler, and watches him anxiously. He and the others motion to her to go away—she isn't wanted. The girl is used to this kind of treatment, however, and stays put, trying to compete in the rodeo. She disgraces herself, and the head wrangler is about to lose all patience with her.

But suddenly the corral is transfigured by the arrival of girls in city clothes—Eastern friends of the rancher's daughter, who have come out with her to get a taste of ranch life. The cowboys slap their thighs in enthusiastic welcome; the girls wave to them with their handkerchiefs and giggle among themselves in feigned bashfulness. The cowgirl is both contemptuous and envious of their finery; she is visibly disgusted by their silly flirting.

The champion roper steps out to show off his skill before the girls. When the head wrangler steps over to them politely and takes off his hat to the rancher's daughter, the cowgirl can bear it no longer and rides off in a jealous fit of petulance. Four women from the ranch come out to watch the rodeo. They are entertained until the cowgirl rides in on what appears to be a bucking bronco. All the women raise their hands in despair at this foolish show-off. The cowgirl falls. The Eastern girls rush over to her and can't control their laughter: never in *their* born days has a *girl* done anything like that. The cowgirl is furious. She gets up and thumbs her nose at the women. Soon, alone with the cowboys, the girl sees that she's made a fool of herself all around; the women may laugh at her, but the men are worse: their silence makes her despair. She tries to regain her old familiarity with them. They ignore her and stare into the distance. The head wrangler jerks his thumb toward the house, telling her to leave the corral. He is the one man in the world the girl respects; smothering her tears, she obeys him.

The rodeo is over. The girls wave at the champion roper as he leaps away. The scene darkens, the music softens, the womenfolk cross the stage, moving slowly, bravely, yet wistfully, and there is created an impression of what home is like after a tiring, busy day. The cowboys cross the stage behind the women, and when the girls step backward, hesitating in their homeward march, the men move forward to them, place their arms about their waists, and move forward again with them.

The couples disappear. The cowgirl re-enters and tries to attract the head wrangler's attention. But it's as if she weren't even there: he goes to the rancher's daughter, who stands demure in her long blue dress with ribbons in her hair, lifts her softly, and takes her off into the night.

The cowgirl dances for a moment alone, trying to shake off what she knows has happened to her. She isn't any good as a woman and she's a miserable failure as a cowhand. The head wrangler returns. He doesn't understand what's wrong with this strange girl. A cowboy calls to him, and he leaves before the girl can tell him. The womenfolk try to call the girl home; she ignores them. The champion roper crosses the back of the corral, snapping his fingers in private anticipation of the Saturday night dance at the ranch house. He disappears. The cowgirl falls to the ground, all alone now with her problem. The stage blacks out around her.

A bright blue drop curtain, decorated with galloping wild horses, falls in front of the scene. Four couples rush out and begin a square dance. A caller shouts out directions to the dancers, and the couples respond by moving quickly into more intricate patterns as he commands. Soon they are out of breath, but turning still more rapidly and now shouting as they run around and around in a circle, faster and faster. They run off into the wings.

SCENE TWO The ranch house. The curtain rises on the ranch house. The cowgirl is sitting alone on a bench at the left, watching three cowboys dance a jig to a jazzy piano accompaniment. One of the cowboys is the champion roper, dressed now in his Saturday-night best—violet shirt, a loud vest of cowhide, and striped yellow pants. He jumps high into the air and clicks his heels together repeatedly. The cowgirl, still dressed in the dusty clothes of the corral, feels out of place, though she is making an obvious effort to enjoy herself. The boys finish their jig. Three couples come in and dance about the room, oblivious to whether anyone is watching them. Two of the couples waltz into the parlor as the remaining pair quarrel: the boy kisses the girl, and she rushes out.

The boy despairs of women and sits down beside the cowgirl. She tries to comfort him, man to man. But another girl has come in looking for a partner. She sees the boy alone, lifts her dress flirtatiously, and runs out. He chases after her. The cowgirl can see no hope for such an idiot. The champion roper strides back in and notices the lonely girl. He doesn't know what the matter is; but since this is Saturday night and dancing time, he can see only one cure. He tells her to get up and dance. The cowgirl says she doesn't know how to dance. Well, first, he tells her, you'd better look a little cleaner. He tries to fix her face up and smacks the dust off her bottom.

Just as the girl is beginning to forget about the head wrangler, he comes in and goes over to the rancher's daughter. The cowgirl forgets all about the champion roper. He loses patience with her; after all, he's just as interested in other girls as she is in the head wrangler: He was only trying to make her have a good time. When the champion roper walks out on her, the girl begins to cry. She looks at the romantic dancing couple and falls to the floor in tears.

Gradually the room fills with people. The bench is moved back, and everybody gets ready for a community dance. The girls line up on one side, the boys on the other. Bravely, the girl decides to try again and hopefully stands in line with the girls. The boys approach and take their partners; the cowgirl is left standing alone! The music becomes sweet and lyrical; the couples form a circle; the boys lift the girls tenderly high above them; the girl turns away.

The champion roper dances in, jumping high in the air, clicking his heels together, breaking the romantic spell. When he finishes this bit of exhibitionism, he comes over and leans on the girl's shoulder. She stifles a sob. The other couples leave the scene. The roper puts his hand under her chin and tells her to cheer up, to try to dance with him again. He opens his arms wide, the girl smiles, hitches up her belt, comes close to him, and everything is all right for a few seconds while they dance.

Everything is spoiled, however, by the head wrangler and the rancher's daughter, who come back and remind the cowgirl of her real love. The roper catches her watching them; before he can do anything about it, she has run away. The roper sees a girl walking alone and pursues her into the wings.

All the cowboys and their girls dance now, filling the scene with violent color and vigorous movement. The couples clap their hands joyously in rhythm to the music. They stop dancing all at once and stare, as the cowgirl comes in, dressed from head to foot in bright red. The girls are shocked by this lack of taste; the boys are eager to find out what it means.

The champion roper goes to her, hitches up his pants, and asks her to dance. Even in her new dress the girl hitches up her clothes, too. They dance. The violins saw away at a square-dance theme, and the moving couples form a circle around them.

The cowgirl finds herself standing between the head wrangler and the roper. Both want to dance with her. The wrangler has forgotten the rancher's daughter long enough to notice the cowgirl. The roper and the wrangler throw the girl back and forth between them. She tries to escape, but the wrangler grabs her and tries to kiss her. The roper steps in and says, "No! She's my girl!" He takes her face in his hands and kisses her hard. He kisses her again, harder. Both of them wake up: they've both been wrong all along and didn't know what was happening. The head wrangler rejoins the rancher's daughter, and the whole group dances happily. As the curtain falls, the girls step into stirrups formed by the boys' hands and stand poised high over their heads. The cowgirl and the roper look into each other's eyes.

NOTES *Rodeo* has been a steady favorite in the United States and on American Ballet Theatre's many tours abroad.

That was proved especially true when the company revived the ballet in 1972, in New York, at their engagement at the City Center. Writing of that performance in *Dance Magazine*, the critic Nancy Mason said: "America was ripe for *Rodeo* when performed by Ballet Russe in 1942. We were at war; national feeling was running high. Although Women's Lib may now quibble about the theme—'How to get a man'—*Rodeo* isn't dated because it deals with basic emotions.

"The action's set on a ranch in the Southwest and concerns a tomboy (Christine Sarry) who prefers riding a horse to wearing a dress. She's the tag-along of the cowboys, desperately and unreciprocally in love with the Head Wrangler (Marcos Paredes). Aaron Copland's music offers rowdy and rhythmic accompaniment.

"There couldn't be better casting for the tomboy. Christine Sarry even looks the part with her cropped brown hair and stubborn expression. What's more, she's a superb actress and comedienne; a powerpacked little dynamo who can stir laughter or tears. One really feels for her plight and wishes her well. Projecting incredible energy, she'd meet any challenge by pushing back her hat, hitching up her trousers, then diving right in. Shyness underlies this gumption. Here's a girl more at home on the back of a horse than in any social situation.

"The turning point arrives at the Saturday night dance, where Chris is finally persuaded by the Champion Roper (Terry Orr, alternating with William Carter) to put on a dress and join the party. A few minutes later she dashes in and everything halts abruptly. Gone are the baggy trousers; in their place, a sensible red jumper and ankle-length boots; on her face, a triumphant, excited grin. The Head Wrangler does a double-take. Then there's a competition between him and the Champion Roper for her heart.

"In *Rodeo* virtuoso tap dancing was used for the first time in a ballet. It also focused international attention on utilizing American folk themes in ballets. It changed the course for the musical theater; the next year Agnes de Mille choreographed *Oklahoma*.

"What a happy thought that *Rodeo* is back in the active

repertoire. The company performs it with infectious zeal and good feelings. It's a perfect vehicle for Christine Sarry; Terry Orr delights with his easygoing and confident Roper interpretation. And it's good to see William Carter. . . . He created an honest and charming 'big brother' feeling."

ROMEO AND JULIET

Shakespeare's tragedy of *Romeo and Juliet* has been turned into dance by many choreographers. The five ballets described below are the most familiar:

Ballet in three acts, based on the play by Shakespeare. Music by Sergei Prokofiev. Libretto by Leonid Lavrovsky, Sergei Prokofiev, and Sergei Radlov. Choreography by Leonid Lavrovsky. Décor by Piotr Williams. First presented at the Kirov State Theatre of Opera and Ballet, Leningrad, January 11, 1940, with Constantin Sergeyev and Galina Ulanova in the title roles, A. V. Lopukhov as Mercutio, *and S. G. Karen as* Tybalt. *Revised and presented at the Bolshoi Theatre, Moscow, December 28, 1946. First presented in the United States by the Bolshoi Ballet at the Metropolitan Opera House, New York, April 16, 1959, with Galina Ulanova and Yuri Zhdanov in the title roles.*

The Soviet production relates Shakespeare's story in thirteen scenes, with a prologue and epilogue.

PROLOGUE Friar Laurence, sage and philosopher, blesses the marriage of Romeo and Juliet. The three figures stand motionless in tableau in front of three arches.

ACT ONE, SCENE ONE—THE MAIN SQUARE OF VERONA As dawn breaks, Romeo, son of Montague, is seen wandering alone about the deserted streets of Verona. Three servants leave the house of Capulet and walk across the square to join some girls in the inn. They are soon embroiled in a quarrel with two servants of Montague, the sworn enemy of their house. Swords are drawn and a fight starts. More and more people, including Benvolio, nephew of Montague, and Tybalt, nephew of Lady Capulet, join in the fray. Paris, who has come to Verona to seek the hand of Capulet's daughter, Juliet, reaches the square when the fighting is at its fiercest. Montague and his hated rival, Capulet, unsheathe their swords and attack each other. The tocsin rings; its sound, reverberating through the city, brings crowds to the square. The prince of Verona then appears. He stops the fighting and an edict, forbidding disturbances in the city streets, is proclaimed. Tybalt leaves, cursing the Montagues.

Before the curtain, in a transitional *Front Scene,* the Capulet household is preparing for a ball. Juliet's nurse, carrying a beautiful dress, stops to reprimand some servants who have stolen food from the kitchen.

ACT ONE, SCENE TWO—JULIET'S ROOM In her room, the walls covered with tapestries, Juliet plays hide-and-seek with her nurse instead of dressing for the ball. Lady Capulet comes into the room and tells Juliet that Paris has asked for her hand in marriage. Juliet protests that she is too young, but leading her to the mirror, her mother shows her that this is not so.

Front Scene: The preparations for the ball are almost finished. The servants carry in food and wine.

ACT ONE, SCENE THREE The guests, including Verona's most illustrious citizens, troubadours, and many friends of Juliet's, arrive for the ball; among the last to come are Paris and his page.

Front Scene: Hearing music, Romeo's friends Mercutio and Benvolio decide to disguise themselves and go to Capulet's ball. They persuade Romeo to join them. He puts on a domino mask.

ACT ONE, SCENE FOUR—THE BALLROOM OF THE CAPULETS' PALACE Juliet with all their guests awaits the arrival of her parents, who now enter. Paris presents Juliet with a bouquet. The ball now begins with a formal dance during which the men lay cushions at the feet of the ladies, kneel and kiss the hems of their skirts. The ladies and gentlemen then dance separately, followed by a slow and stately ensemble. Now Juliet, who has been arranging flowers and watching, dances herself. The dance of the guests is resumed briefly and then Juliet dances again. Romeo and his friends enter. He is enchanted by Juliet and approaches her. Paris, however, intercedes. Mercutio dances to distract the guests. As they dance together, Romeo tells Juliet how beautiful she is. His mask falls from his face and Juliet sees him for the first time. Juliet is captivated. This man she could really love. But then Tybalt appears and thinks he recognizes

Romeo, a sworn enemy of the family. He tells old Capulet. Romeo quickly puts his mask back on. Although Tybalt there and then wishes to attack Romeo, Mercutio comes between them.

Front Scene: After the guests have left, Juliet learns from her nurse that it is none other than Romeo, son of her father's enemy Montague, with whom she has fallen in love.

ACT ONE, SCENE FIVE—THE GARDEN Juliet cannot sleep and comes out on her moonlit balcony. She can only think of Romeo, whom she suddenly sees in the garden. They confess their love for each other and dance.

ACT TWO, SCENE ONE—THE MAIN SQUARE OF VERONA Revelers throng the square. There are dances for the crowd and waitresses at the inn. A procession enters carrying an image of the Madonna. Benvolio and Mercutio flirt with ladies at the cafe and dance with the waitresses and there is another ensemble for the revelers. The nurse pushes her way through the crowds, looking for Romeo to give him a message from Juliet. He enters the square and the nurse whispers to him.

Front Scene: Romeo reads that Juliet has consented to be his wife and rapturously presses the letter to his heart.

ACT TWO, SCENE TWO—FRIAR LAURENCE'S CELL On a simple table stand some flowers and a skull, which the friar is contemplating when Romeo enters. Romeo kneels before the friar and asks him to marry them secretly. Nervously waiting for Juliet to come, his hands play with the skull and the flowers. Juliet, wearing a black cape, rushes in. Friar Laurence marries them and hopes that their union will end the strife between the Montagues and Capulets.

Front Scene: The Montagues and Capulets are in the main square as the procession of the Madonna moves across. Mercutio buys fruit and gives it to his friends. Tybalt bursts into rage when a peddler's tray accidentally knocks into one of his companions. Both families are cruelly sensitive now to any possible offense.

ACT TWO, SCENE THREE—THE MAIN SQUARE OF VERONA Revels continue in the square with a tambourine dance. Mercutio dances with waitresses at the inn. Tybalt enters and challenges Mercutio to a duel. Romeo tries to call it off and make peace but Tybalt mocks him and goads Mercutio into fighting. Mercutio is hit, struggles bravely against death but dies. Tybalt leaves, laughing. Romeo tries to hear Mercutio's heart and mourns. The body is borne out. Just as Romeo follows after, Tybalt comes back, insolent, swaggering. Romeo draws his sword, dashes up the stairs, and kills him. Romeo flees. The Capulets rush from their palace with the nurse. Lady Capulet so laments her kinsman's death that she is carried out gesturing wildly on his bier. The prince of Verona declares Romeo an exile for life.

ACT THREE, SCENE ONE—JULIET'S ROOM At dawn the next morning, Romeo opens the curtain onto the balcony and watches the sun. Juliet pulls the curtain back and the two lovers dance an impassioned *pas de deux.* But the household is stirring and Romeo must go. He embraces Juliet for the last time. As he leaves by the balcony, Juliet's parents and Paris enter with the nurse. Paris tries to woo Juliet but is scorned. Hurt by Juliet's rebuff, Paris leaves. Juliet tells her parents that she will not marry him. They are angry and threaten to disown her. The mother and the nurse leave and the father tries to force Juliet to submit to his will. She dances in despair when he has finally left her alone. Then quickly she finds her cape and runs out.

Front Scene: Juliet rushes to Friar Laurence.

ACT THREE, SCENE TWO—FRIAR LAURENCE'S CELL Juliet prays and relates her plight. She sees a dagger on the table and seizes it. Gently taking the dagger from her, Friar Laurence gives her instead a phial of sleeping potion which she must drink. She will then fall asleep, he tells her, and her parents, thinking her dead, will bury her in the family tomb. Meanwhile, Romeo, warned by Friar Laurence, will return under cover of darkness and take her away from Verona.

ACT THREE, SCENE THREE—JULIET'S BEDCHAMBER It is evening and Juliet is with her family and Paris. She consents to marry Paris, they dance together, and her parents are jubilant. The nurse brings the wedding gown. Juliet is alone. She knows she must drink the potion but delays in a dance of indecision. She then quickly swallows the potion and falls back on the bed. Soon it is morning. Her friends come with troubadours to celebrate her engagement. Paris enters, eager to see his bride. But the wedding dress lies on a chair and Juliet still sleeps. Her mother comes and orders the nurse to waken her. She goes to the bed but starts back with a cry of terror. Juliet lies lifeless on the bed. All weep.

ACT THREE, SCENE FOUR—A STREET IN MANTUA Romeo, alone, expresses his sorrow at his separation from Juliet. Outpacing Friar Laurence's messenger, Romeo's servant Balthasar arrives from Verona with the news that Juliet is dead. Stunned by grief, Romeo does not know what to do, then decides that he must go to his beloved.

ACT THREE, SCENE FIVE—THE CAPULET TOMB Many attend Juliet's funeral and her body is placed in the family vault at the top of a flight of steps. Paris prays there and leaves. It grows dark. Romeo comes in, mounts the steps, removes her shroud and holds Juliet in his arms. He kisses her, then picks her up to carry her briefly down the steps. He ascends again, holding her high over his head, and places her on her tomb. He then drinks a phial of poison and dies, falling back down the steps. Juliet now awakes from her sleeping potion. She sees Romeo and at first thinks him perhaps asleep, as she has been, but he is dead. She takes his dagger at once and stabs herself. She falls back over his body.

EPILOGUE Over the bodies of their children, the Montagues and the Capulets, followed by the populace, take each other's hands and swear to end their feud. All kneel.

NOTES Prokofiev's score to *Romeo and Juliet* was completed September 8, 1935, soon after his return to Russia from Paris. It was first performed at a concert in Moscow in October of that year. Prokofiev's plan at that time was that the ballet should end happily, with Juliet resurrected in her tomb and a final joyous *pas de deux* for the two lovers. This idea received some criticism and the composer abandoned it. He said at the time: "I have taken special pains to achieve a simplicity that will, I hope, reach the hearts of all listeners. If people find no melody and no emotion in this work of mine, I shall be very sorry; but I feel that they will, sooner or later."

Some time elapsed before the score was first used for ballet, and this was in Brno, Czechoslovakia in 1938. Meanwhile, two suites arranged by Prokofiev were played in the U.S.S.R. and the United States.

The Soviet choreographer Leonid Lavrovsky published notes about his conception of the ballet, which was first produced in 1940: "The depths of passion and ideas, the intensity of feeling conveyed by the protagonists of Shakespeare's tragedy, demand the fusion of dance with mime. In ballet, words are absent and the effect of every phrase of mime must correspond with the spoken language of the stage characters. Mime should never descend to trivial, commonplace, imitative gestures, but become a genuine theatrical performance, in which characters, emotion, and passion are expressed by the movements of the body, instead of by the varied intonations of the voice. Ballet is a choreographic play in which the dancing must arise naturally from the mimed action, or the mimed action be the logical sequence of the dancing."

A film of Lavrovsky's *Romeo and Juliet* was produced in the U.S.S.R. in 1954, with Galina Ulanova.

Other ballets to Prokofiev's score include productions by Dmitri Parlić (Belgrade, June 25, 1948), Margarita Froman (Zagreb, June 1949), John Cranko (Venice, July 26, 1958), Frederick Ashton (Copenhagen, May 19, 1955), and Kenneth MacMillan (London, February 9, 1965).

Narrative ballet in one act, based on the play by Shakespeare. Music by Frederick Delius. Choreography by Antony Tudor. Scenery and costumes by Eugene Berman. First presented by Ballet Theatre at the Metropolitan Opera House, New York, April 6, 1943, with Alicia Markova as Juliet, *Hugh Laing as* Romeo, *Nicolas Orloff as* Mercutio, *Antony Tudor as* Tybalt, *and Jerome Robbins as* Benvolio.

This dramatic ballet compresses into one vivid act the tragic love story of Romeo and Juliet. Within a single-unit setting representing the ordered golden beauty of the Italy of the Renaissance, the narrative proceeds without scenic interruption; and what might be spoken of as "scenes," in an ordinary dramatic spectacle, move together and coalesce with a flow that suggests the inevitability of the tragedy itself.

The score for the ballet is an arrangement by Antal Dorati of selected works by Delius: *Over the Hills and Far Away, The Walk to the Paradise Garden, Eventyr,* and *Brigg Fair.*

PROLOGUE The curtain rises immediately on a drop curtain depicting the entrance to a palace in Verona. There are two great arches to the left and right, and in the center, cut out of the curtain, is a draped entry. A spotlight centers on this doorway, and Romeo steps out cautiously. He looks behind him, and Rosaline, a beautiful girl, follows him. Romeo takes her hand and attempts to embrace her. Rosaline warns him that he is too hasty, and Romeo follows her impatiently within.

Now members of the opposing families of Montague and Capulet dance onto the scene and challenge each other. The two leaders of the factions, Mercutio and Tybalt, are eager for a contest, and the two groups commence dueling. But the heads of the two houses at variance with each other enter with their wives and order their kinsmen to desist. The men reluctantly abandon their fighting and bow to the peers. It is apparent that their battle will be renewed at the first opportunity. Romeo and his friend Mercutio remain behind when the others have left. Only the entrance of the fair Rosaline persuades them that they have better business elsewhere.

BALL AT THE HOUSE OF THE CAPULETS The drop curtain rises on a wide, open area of red marble enclosed by a decorative colonnade. Couples in richly embroidered costumes are dancing in elegant, courtly fashion. The music softens, and Juliet enters on the right. She lingers slightly, hesitating to step into the ballroom, for she knows what awaits her. She greets her parents warmly, yet formally. Capulet turns to introduce her to a young nobleman, Paris, but Juliet seeks instead the company of her cousin Tybalt. The understanding Tybalt consoles her, but also reminds her of her duty and leads her to Paris. The assembled company begin to dance again, and Juliet accepts Paris as her partner.

Romeo enters on the right. He looks directly at Juliet. Juliet, her back to Paris for a moment, glances back at him. As Paris bends down to kiss her hand, Juliet looks across the room toward Romeo. The dance continues, and Romeo chooses a partner to join the ball. The two couples dance on opposite sides of the room. The set pattern of the dance separates them, and Juliet and Romeo despair of meeting. Soon the entire company circles the hall and the dance ends. The guests proceed to move toward the rear for refreshment, and Romeo and Juliet are alone.

Romeo falls at her feet and declares the overpowering love he has felt since he saw her. He rises, their faces touch, and they kiss. Then, formal again, the two bow to each other and begin to dance together a delicate, flowing measure. When the dance is over, they realize that they must separate and both say their farewells. But as they turn to go, they move together again and kneel.

Mercutio and Tybalt emerge from the banquet hall. Juliet's nurse urges her away, lest there be trouble. Tybalt warns Romeo and turns to Juliet questioningly, and all depart.

ROMEO WOOS JULIET IN THE CAPULET ORCHARD The lights dim. White drapes are drawn across the back colonnade. Four torchbearers enter on the right, followed by Romeo and Mercutio. Romeo is preoccupied and will not listen to his friend's appreciation of the beauty of the evening. Mercutio grows impatient and tells his friend that the romance he contemplates is out of the question. The music builds in intensity, and Romeo refuses to heed Mercutio's advice. Mercutio leaps to the back of one of the torchbearers and urges Romeo to follow them to a tavern. Romeo pretends to go, then conceals himself. The others return to look for him, but soon follow after Mercutio.

Two couples enter. Romeo holds his arm across his face, lest he be recognized. The couples disappear, and Romeo dances alone. Above the colonnade at the rear, Juliet looks down into the orchard and sees her lover. She is enchanted and rests her head sweetly on the balcony railing, wondering when he will look up and see her. Romeo glances up and blows kisses to her. She returns the kisses, but warns him away. Just as he hides behind a pillar on the right, Juliet's nurse comes into the garden. No sooner has she departed than Tybalt and Paris stroll by. When they are alone again, Romeo holds out his hands to Juliet and from above she gestures to him yearningly. Romeo gestures defiance of their families and proposes marriage. Juliet consents.

BETROTHAL OF ROMEO AND JULIET BY THE FRIAR Drapes are drawn across the colonnade, and Friar Laurence stands in his cell. Romeo enters. He is impatient and afraid and paces the floor. There is a sound at the door, and Romeo rushes to see who it is. Friar Laurence pulls him back warningly. Romeo's back is turned as Juliet runs into the room. He turns to her, and the two kneel before the friar, who blesses them. Juliet rises, turns rapidly, and falls low in Romeo's arms. Then she rushes off into the night, promising him that her nurse will bring him a message.

STREET SCENE The curtains are drawn back, the friar disappears, and the open area becomes the street. It is still night. A cripple and a blind man enter, followed by the gay Mercutio and a friend. Romeo enters, followed by Juliet and her nurse. The nurse beckons Juliet away. The concern of the lovers is contrasted with the friction between their families, for Tybalt has entered and threatened Mercutio in earnest. The two fight, their kinsmen join the battle, and the music is ominous, like the sound of an approaching storm. Mercutio is stabbed by Tybalt and dies in Romeo's arms.

Romeo recovers from his grief and attacks Tybalt. He leaps to his back, forces him down, and stabs him to death. Now there is no hope of reconciling the two families. Romeo does not know what to do. Friar Laurence enters and takes the dagger from him. Finally the youth is persuaded that he must flee for his life.

Juliet and her nurse enter the square and see what has happened. Juliet weeps for Tybalt, but then, suddenly desperate, instructs the nurse to run to Romeo and reassure him.

ROMEO'S FAREWELL TO JULIET The scene is Juliet's bedroom. Day is breaking. Juliet rises first and dances joyfully, with a sweet, youthful happiness, as Romeo watches her from the bed. She returns to him, he lifts her, and they embrace.

Romeo prepares to leave. He must escape from Verona. They will meet elsewhere. Juliet weeps because of her happiness and its quick ending. They kiss. Romeo departs, and Juliet falls back on the bed, still weeping.

PREPARATIONS FOR THE WEDDING OF JULIET TO PARIS Some time passes, and handmaidens to Juliet enter with her nurse to prepare her for the marriage her parents have insisted upon. They waken Juliet. Instantly she sits up and looks off into the direction that Romeo took when he left her. She cannot believe that this day she must marry another man. The nurse holds her in her arms and tries to comfort her. Juliet rises and protests to her father that she cannot marry Paris. Capulet refuses to listen to her or to his wife, who tries to intercede for Juliet.

Then, to the accompaniment of a melody almost unbearable in its sweetness and pathos, Juliet's four handmaidens form a tableau beside her. They hold before her a wedding dress of gold, and Juliet slips her arms into it as if the cloth were on fire.

When she is dressed, she weeps softly in her father's arms. Her father blesses her and places on her head a shining crown. She is presented with a bouquet of white flowers. Friar Laurence enters, and Juliet falls into his arms. When they are unobserved, the friar gives her a vial containing a secret drug and instructs her to drink it without delay: all may yet be well.

Juliet walks away, drinks the contents of the vial, whirls frantically, and swoons. Her family gathers about her. Six women bear slowly across the stage a great cloth trimmed in somber black.

PROCESSION TO THE TOMB Two of Juliet's attendants head her funeral procession. Juliet lies on a bier carried high by her black-cloaked kinsmen. Her father and mother follow behind. When the procession has passed, the women holding up the cloth of mourning disappear to reveal another scene.

SCENE IN THE VAULT OF THE CAPULETS We are in Juliet's tomb. She lies immobile on her bier, her hands pressed together at her breast. Romeo enters. He imagines that his beloved is dead and drinks a vial of poison. He falls at the foot of the bier.

Juliet gradually revives from the drug she has taken. She rises. Romeo sees her, pulls himself up with difficulty, reaches out for her, and—when Juliet comes to him—lifts her with his remaining strength. He falls. Juliet understands what has happened. She spins around and around frantically. Romeo rises again and lifts her in his arms. He holds her for a moment, then collapses across her bier. He dies. Juliet looks down upon him. She takes out his dagger, waits for a moment, and—rising suddenly on point, as if to meet the happiness only death can bring her—stabs herself in the heart. She falls across her lover's body and, with her last gesture, touches his face.

NOTES Tudor's *Romeo and Juliet* was revived by American Ballet Theatre, July 22, 1971, at the New York State Theater, Lincoln Center. The critic Deborah Jowitt wrote in the *Village Voice:* "What Antony Tudor did in his 1943 *Romeo and Juliet,* now revived by Ballet Theatre, makes it one of the most brilliant and interesting of recent ballets. In particular, he has worked with the structure of the play so as to situate it in the kind of Renaissance time and space with which Shakespeare's work has so many affinities.

"As Wylie Sypher pointed out in his *Four Stages of Renaissance Style,* the plot of *Romeo and Juliet* is an essay in symmetry and proportion. Capulet is weighed against Montague, Romeo's passion against Paris's suitability, love against hate, night against day, rashness against prudence, etc. Time is compressed into forty-two hours; space is defined and confined by the walls of Verona's chambers, gardens, piazzas. There is none of the depth, irregularity, or ripeness of the later *Hamlet* or *Macbeth.*

"Tudor has set his version of this sad and lyrical equation in what might be compared to a continuous Botticelli frieze. There is an emphasis on elegant, agitated, fastidiously sensual flow rather than on volume. It is as if Tudor had speeded up the heartbeat of the play, so tremulous is one's reaction to it. His space, like Botticelli's, is almost more medieval than Renaissance: depth is created by temporary hierarchies, events separated in time can coexist in space. When Romeo and Julie wind through the pillars of the piazza in an ecstatic return from their wedding, they are small upstage figures, seen through the minor bustle of the square. When Juliet, enveloped by the nurse, weeps over Tybalt down left, their figures are balanced by those of Romeo and Friar Laurence consulting hastily down right. And the two tableaux are separated by a temporary 'wall' formed by two watching women. Tudor's use of these women is another odd detail. They witness the action from different positions, like those little faces in the corners of certain medieval paintings.

"The effect of all this compression on the spectator is fascinating. There is no blood, thunder, bombast; the action is drawn lightly over you like a veil while you sit in a state of almost febrile tension. Events, briefly sketched, flow out of each other; even what Tudor has chosen to show or not show is revealing. Nothing seems to have any preliminaries. The Montague boys' decision to attend the Capulet ball is conveyed to Mercutio's brusquely beckoning finger, while the powerful effect of the lovers' first meeting on Romeo and his friends is shown more fully. Letters are not delivered, potions are drunk, marriages are arranged at high speed and with pictorial clarity.

"Eugene Berman's marvelous pillars, archways and porticos hold and shape the action, add to the morbid delicacy of atmosphere. When a curtain is drawn to reveal the ball in progress, the dancers first appear cramped, too large for the space they inhabit—another painterly touch. Tudor's choice of excerpts from Delius is extremely unusual. The music meanders along its own path—painting a lush, summer atmosphere that is neither dramatically nor rhythmically assertive, but full of feeling. Often it creates a curious tension between its dreamy flow and the action of the play. For instance, the insistent little tappings and steppings of the court dances begin to be almost ominous against the inconclusive music.

"Since nothing in this ballet ever really stops, pauses for large scale 'dance numbers' would have been unthinkable. Tudor has built the dancing out of gesture so subtly and naturally that you are not aware of anything but the continuous unfolding of this lyrical disquisition on action. There is a ball scene, of course, quietly and slowly built up. There is no *grand pas de deux* for the balcony scene: alone on the stage floor, Romeo bursts into an exulting stammer of leaps and postures and wide-flung gestures, while Juliet on the balcony above returns his passion with slow and happy stretchings and curvings of her body and arms. Even the morning-after-the-wedding scene turns into a dance imperceptibly through a series of muted rushings, claspings, near-swoons.

"Because nothing seems calculated, no particular moments of dance can be easily isolated. Pointe work has a special expressive function. Juliet steps up onto pointe as if some delicate emotional balance were at stake, or as if she were on unfamiliar ground. In some of her steps, she might be swooning upward."

The critic Marcia Siegel wrote in the Boston *Globe:* "Antony Tudor's *Romeo and Juliet* is a beautiful ballet. An extraordinary ballet. I think it's the best new ballet I've seen this year, even though it's really a revival, originally choreographed in 1943 for the infant Ballet Theatre. Restaged July 22 by that company, with Carla Fracci and Ivan Nagy in the opening-night title roles, it's a deeply moving and interesting work. I don't know when I've seen a ballet with such clarity and distinction of detail.

"Tudor saw the perennial story in quite intimate terms, encompassed in one act with several scenes. This makes for a tighter production—the story moves quickly, building to its powerful tragic end, without the long interpolations of swordplay and ceremony that pad out more grandiose Romeo and Juliet ballets. There's considerably less display dancing, smaller crowds, and less exposition, but I think this makes sense. Tudor's ballet is about the star-crossed lovers. The John Cranko and Kenneth MacMillan versions we've seen here in recent years are about the spectacular possibilities of a full-length ballet based on Shakespeare's play—quite a different thing.

"Fracci and Nagy are splendid as the doomed couple. Fracci is one of our best actress-dancers, and Nagy, released by Tudor's unstereotyped movement from the conventional suffering nobility of his other roles, was more convincing, more alive to the dramatic situation than I've ever seen him. All their scenes together breathed wonder and changeableness, joy touched with disbelief, a sort of shining despair.

"Tudor set the ballet in the Italian Renaissance, and much of the movement looks like the paintings and court dances of the period—the men with one leg turned out and pointing a fashionable toe, the women tilting back with their weight thrust mincingly forward. At times the company looked awkward with these stylizations, but Bruce Marks as Tybalt, Rosanna Seravalli as Lady Capulet, and Bonnie Mathis as Rosaline showed me immediately what the shape of the movement is, how it works. What intelligent character dancers these three are!

"There's more in this ballet, both in its dancing and production, than I can discuss in one day, but Tudor's choice of Delius' music is indicative of his unusual concept. The elegaic, rich-textured, but not especially dancy score seems at first too impressionistic to support the tragedy. But in fact it reinforces the ballet's delicate romanticism and isn't overpowering as the more familiar Prokofiev *Romeo and Juliet* usually is.

"Eugene Berman's multilevel set suggests both the scaffolded flexibility of a Shakespearean stage and the columns and perspective of an Italian painting. . . ."

"I went back to see Antony Tudor's *Romeo and Juliet,* given by American Ballet Theatre, and found it as fascinating as I had the first time. It's a ballet of ideas—not philosophical or moral preachings, but ideas about how to present a classic story.

"Ballets are produced in such quantity here, and with so little attention to durability, that they often seem to be a matter of choosing new spices to liven up the same old hamburger. Tudor's *Romeo* constitutes a rethinking of every aspect of the narrative ballet. He uses all theatrical elements to suggest the depth and universality of the theme, instead of just letting us recognize what we already know about it.

"Eugene Berman's opening drop shows a small Romanesque building, possibly a tomb, suspended against a blue sea or sky, just hanging there, a door to something insubstantial and timeless. Classical allusions keep recurring quietly. You notice during the principals' first duet that the other guests at the Capulets' ball have seated themselves beyond some pillars, at a dinner table in another room. Their backs are to the audience; they are too close to the stage for realism. They look flat, like the background of a Renaissance painting. Juliet's friends, dressed like Botticelli nymphs, lift a shroud across the stage where Juliet's drugged body lies, and stand there throughout the funeral procession, echoing the statues perched atop the colonnaded set.

"The changes of scene—there are about ten of them—are accomplished in a variety of ingenious ways, many involving characters in the ballet. In fact, two 'attendants' watch the whole ballet from a bench downstage, moving around to draw curtains and even, at one point, simulating a wall. They are spectators of the tragedy who also help present it to us, and at the same time they belong to the House of Capulet as servants. This is an Elizabethan device as well as a classical reference. Realistic theater didn't come along till the late nineteenth century, and Tudor isn't offering us a modern romance. Other critics have objected to the extremely stylized quality of this *Romeo,* as if that were a drawback, and as if *all* ballet weren't a stylization to begin with. I suggest that Tudor's concept of production has the same elevating effect on the story that Shakespeare's poetry has."*

Ballet in eleven scenes with prologue, based on Shakespeare's play. Music by Sergei Prokofiev. Choreography by Frederick Ashton. Scenery and costumes by Peter Rice. First presented by the Royal Danish Ballet at the Royal Theatre, Copenhagen, May 19, 1955, with Mona Vangsaae and Henning Kronstam in the title roles. First presented in the United States by the Royal Danish Ballet at the Metropolitan Opera House, New York, September 26, 1956.

Frederick Ashton's ballet follows this scenario:

At Verona there is constant feuding between the families of Montague and Capulet. A party of young men from Mon-

* From *At the Vanishing Point* by Marcia B. Siegel (Saturday Review Press); © 1972 Marcia Siegel.

tague's household are present at an entertainment at Capulet's house. Among them is Romeo, who falls in love at first sight with Juliet, Capulet's only child. Romeo and Juliet declare their love for each other. They are secretly married by Friar Laurence. The brawls are continued. Romeo's friend Mercutio is killed by Tybalt, of the House of Capulet. Romeo kills Tybalt and is forced to flee. He takes refuge with Friar Laurence.

Meanwhile, old Capulet decides that Juliet shall marry Count Paris. The friar, hoping to bring about a reconciliation, advises Romeo to say farewell to Juliet and to hide in Mantua. When he learns of old Capulet's decision, he gives Juliet a sleeping draught which will produce a deathlike sleep. Juliet is believed dead, and is buried in the vault of her ancestors. The friar's message to Romeo miscarries. Supposing that his wife is indeed dead, Romeo hurries to the tomb, and commits suicide over her body. Juliet wakes too late, finds Romeo dead, and kills herself with his dagger.

Ballet in three acts after William Shakespeare. Music by Sergei Prokofiev. Choreography and staging by John Cranko. Décor and costumes by Jürgen Rose. In the repertory of the National Ballet of Canada. First staged by John Cranko for the ballet of La Scala, Milan, at the Teatro Verde, in Venice, July 26, 1958; this production was extensively revised and first presented by the Stuttgart Ballet at the Wuerttemberg State Theatre, Stuttgart, December 2, 1962. The Stuttgart Ballet production was first presented in the United States at the Metropolitan Opera House, New York, June 18, 1969, with Marcia Haydée as Juliet, *Richard Cragun as* Romeo, *Jan Stripling as* Tybalt, *and Egon Madsen as* Mercutio.

The scene is Verona.

ACT ONE, SCENE ONE—THE MARKET PLACE As day breaks, Romeo, son of Montague, is found declaring his love to the fair Rosaline. With the sunrise, the market place fills with townspeople, among whom are members of the two rival families, the Capulets and the Montagues. Tempers flare and a quarrel develops. The Duke of Verona appears and warns the two factions that death will be the ultimate punishment if the feud does not stop. Romeo and his friends Benvolio and Mercutio make reluctant peace with Tybalt, a kinsman of the Capulets.

ACT ONE, SCENE TWO—JULIET'S GARDEN IN THE CAPULETS' HOUSE Juliet receives her first ball dress from her mother, Lady Capulet, and learns that she is to meet the noble Paris to whom she will be betrothed on the following day. Now she must bid farewell to her childhood.

ACT ONE, SCENE THREE—OUTSIDE THE CAPULETS' HOUSE Guests appear for the Capulets' ball, among them Rosaline. Romeo and his friends, masked, follow her to the ball.

ACT ONE, SCENE FOUR—THE BALLROOM Juliet dances with Paris but suddenly she and Romeo behold each other, and it is love at first sight. Tybalt, suspecting Romeo's identity, tries to start an argument but is prevented by Juliet's father who abides by the laws of hospitality.

ACT ONE, SCENE FIVE—JULIET'S BEDROOM On the balcony outside her bedroom Juliet dreams of Romeo. He appears below in the garden. They declare their eternal love.

ACT TWO, SCENE ONE—THE MARKET PLACE A carnival is in progress in the main square. Romeo, indifferent to the gaiety around him, is discovered by Juliet's nurse, who brings him a letter from her. She asks Romeo to meet her at the chapel of Friar Laurence.

ACT TWO, SCENE TWO—FRIAR LAURENCE'S CELL IN THE FOREST In his cell, Friar Laurence joins the young lovers in marriage.

ACT TWO, SCENE THREE—THE MARKET PLACE At the height of the carnival, Romeo returns to the square. Tybalt accosts him but Romeo declines to fight. Mercutio, angered, engages in a duel with Tybalt, and dies at his hands. Romeo, distraught, turns on Tybalt and kills him.

ACT THREE, SCENE ONE—THE BEDROOM In Juliet's bedroom the lovers are awakened by the sunrise, and Romeo, under sentence of exile, must leave Juliet and Verona. Lord and Lady Capulet enter with Paris, but Juliet rejects him.

ACT THREE, SCENE TWO—FRIAR LAURENCE'S CELL IN THE FOREST Juliet, appealing for help to Friar Laurence, receives a potion from him that will place her in a deathlike sleep. He explains that Romeo will find her in the family tomb and both can escape together.

ACT THREE, SCENE THREE—THE BEDROOM Juliet agrees to her marriage with Paris. After he leaves with her parents, she takes the sleeping draught and is thought to be dead when her family and friends discover her.

ACT THREE, SCENE FOUR—THE CAPULET FAMILY CRYPT Romeo, who has never received Friar Laurence's message revealing the plan, believes Juliet to be dead and rushes to her tomb. There he finds the mourning Paris and kills him. Embracing Juliet for the last time, he plunges his dagger into his heart. Juliet awakens to find Romeo dead. Grief-stricken, she kills herself.

Reviewing a performance of Cranko's ballet by the Stuttgart Ballet at the Metropolitan Opera House in the spring of 1973, the critic Andrew Porter wrote in *The New Yorker:* "There can be little dispute that Prokofiev's *Romeo and Juliet* is the most successful full-length ballet score written since Tchaikovsky's. I have seen it set to movement in six different versions, and only one of them—Serge Lifar's, for the Paris Opéra—was without marked merit. John Cranko's, created for the Stuttgart Ballet in 1962, and chosen for the opening night, last week, of the company's current Metropolitan season, is a very successful dance drama that has worn well. It continues to display the special virtues and strongly individual character of the troupe for whom it was made, and provides extended, uncommonly telling roles for the major stars—Marcia Haydée, Egon Madsen, and Richard Cragun—that shine in the splendid ensemble. The Royal Ballet, they say, dances best in New York; perhaps the Stuttgarters do so, too. I was bowled over on the first night by the power and eloquence of their presentation, and certainly Jürgen Rose's *Romeo* scenery and costumes never look as handsome and striking as they do on the Metropolitan stage. Dramatic force, potent projection, is a mark of German dancing; in Stuttgart, with his international team of dancers, Mr. Cranko has combined this force with Royal Ballet 'school,' developed his artists by composing new works for and 'on' them, and created one of the world's leading companies.

"Approaches to a Shakespeare ballet are almost as diverse as those to a Shakespeare opera. Prokofiev in his *Romeo* score devised appropriate melodies and motifs for the characters and their attributes (Juliet as a girl, Juliet as a woman, Romeo's ardor, Mercutio's wit, etc.), wrote movements that mount to passionate climaxes in the right places, supplied the necessary (and some unnecessary) ensemble dances, and achieved all this with his wonted flair for theatre music. Leonid Lavrovsky did the original choreography; his version was first performed, in Leningrad, in 1940. He worked on the piece with Prokofiev (and once told me how tiresome and silly the composer had been—wanting, for a while, a happy ending, not wanting to lose a Dance of Carpet Sellers that he had somehow managed to bring in). While Prokofiev's 'libretto' was, so to speak, the plot, the characters, and their emotions, the choreographer added a more detailed attention to Shakespeare; in his version specific lines from the play seem often to ring out from the motion of the dancers: Romeo's 'O! she doth teach the torches to burn bright' when first he sees Juliet, his 'I do protest I never injur'd thee' to Tybalt, and then, after Mercutio's death, 'Fire-ey'd fury be my conduct now,' Juliet's 'My only love sprung from my only hate,' her 'Is there no pity sitting in the clouds?,' and many others. By comparison, Ashton's version for the Royal Danish Ballet, in 1955, to the same score, was a Lamb's Tale that became lyric poetry in the duets for the lovers. Kenneth MacMillan's *Romeo* for Covent Garden, ten years later, borrowed Cranko's solutions to the structural problems set by Prokofiev's ensembles, and acquired its special character from the detailed concentration on Juliet's development. In the monologues and duologues of MacMillan's version there is the same sense found in Lavrovsky's of words just below the surface of the dance. The successive quatrains and couplets of the antiphonal sonnet spoken by Romeo and Juliet when first they meet ('If I profane with my unworthiest hand') are transmuted into plastic imagery. Cranko's *Romeo* is more generalized, less intense in its close-ups. We do not follow the balcony and bedroom scenes 'line by line'; his approach, like Prokofiev's, is less literary. But the dances do not lack emotion, and they flow effectively. Cranko's presentation of the world around the tragedy—the street scenes, the assembly of Capulet's guests, the ball—is the most successful of all; a theatre flair kin to Prokofiev's is apparent in his handling. I miss Juliet's pas de deux with Paris on the wedding morning, a poignant moment in both the Lavrovsky and the MacMillan versions; the Friar Laurence scenes are rather skimpy, and Act III passes too swiftly. (Lavrovsky did well to insert a solo for Romeo in Mantua, corresponding to 'Is it even so? then I defy you, stars!') Comparisons are helpful in description; in its own right, Cranko's *Romeo* is an excellently vigorous, youthful, unrhetorical yet affecting work, couched in a fluent, eclectic choreography that I suppose could be called free-Fokine with modern ingredients, and very skillful in its theatrical shaping.

"The first night presented the nonpareil cast of Miss Haydée and Mr. Cragun in the title roles and Mr. Madsen as Mercutio. The second brought a new Juliet, the young Joyce Cuoco, touching and vulnerable, a promising actress and fleet technician—prone, in fact, to phrase some of the lyrical choreography too crisply. The Romeo and Mercutio swapped roles: Mr. Madsen now made a courteous, romantic Romeo, rather less boldly ardent than Mr. Cragun had been, while as Mercutio Mr. Cragun lacked only the twinkling beats with which Mr. Madsen had tripped through the Queen Mab solo. Jan Stripling's cold, strong Tybalt, the contrasted interpretations of Paris from Reid Anderson (a formal wooer) and Vladimir Klos (more tender), and Andrew Oxenham's bright Benvolio deserve mention; so do the unforced buoyancy, verve, and warmth with which the whole company took the stage."†

Ballet in three acts. Music by Sergei Prokofiev. Choreography by Kenneth MacMillan. Scenery and costumes by Nicholas Georgiadis. Lighting by William Bundy. First presented by the Royal Ballet at the Royal Opera House, Covent Garden, February 9, 1965, with Rudolf Nureyev and Margot Fonteyn as Romeo and Juliet. *First presented in the United States by*

† From *A Muscal Season* by Andrew Porter (Viking Press); © 1973 Andrew Porter. Originally in *The New Yorker.*

the Royal Ballet at the Metropolitan Opera House, New York, April 21, 1965.

The English critic and editor Peter Williams has said, "The game of love and death is the theater's trump card, and Shakespeare was no fool about what made good theater, the rules of which have varied little in any language from the threshing floors of Greece until the present day." Kenneth MacMillan's version of *Romeo and Juliet,* while based on the Prokofiev score used by a number of choreographers, varies substantially in treatment and detail.

ACT ONE, SCENE ONE—THE MARKET PLACE The curtain rises on a dark stage. Then, to pizzicato strings, the stage is gradually lighted, revealing the market place. It is early morning, and the market is not yet busy. Romeo enters and tries to declare his love for the lovely Rosaline, who rejects him. Romeo joins his friends Mercutio and Benvolio, and, as day breaks and the market begins to fill up with butchers and farmers, Romeo takes off his cape and watches idly. A girl tries to entice him away. With two other harlots, she becomes involved with Romeo and his friends. A quarrel now develops between Tybalt, a nephew of Capulet, and Romeo. The Capulets and Montagues are of course sworn enemies and a fight begins. The heads of the two families join the dispute and do not assist a solution. The Prince of Verona appears and is obliged to order them to cease their feuding. All place their swords on the ground at his command, in front of the slain, but the two families stand opposite each other, obstinate in their rage.

ACT ONE, SCENE TWO—JULIET'S ANTEROOM IN THE CAPULETS' HOUSE After a brief musical interlude, the curtain rises on a bright and cheerful room. There are large bird cages to the right and left, and Juliet's nurse sits waiting. Juliet runs in and we are reminded at once that this girl who will become a tragic figure is at heart a child of fourteen. She plays with a doll. She reacts like a spoiled child, too, when her mother and father come in with Paris, whom she does not like. But Juliet is nevertheless interested somewhat in anyone who would express interest in marrying her; she yields to her father's insistence and is nice to him. When the Capulets and Paris leave, Juliet wants to resume her play with the doll, but the nurse points out that her childhood is over, that she is a young woman now, about to be beloved. Juliet clutches her heart. The curtain falls.

ACT ONE, SCENE THREE—OUTSIDE THE CAPULETS' HOUSE Two huge iron gates guard the entrance to the Capulet palace, where guests are arriving for a masked ball. Romeo, Mercutio, and Benvolio, disguised in masks, enter. Romeo flirts with a lady who drops a rose for him to pick up—the fair Rosaline. Then he and his friends dance a vigorous, high-spirited *pas de trois.* They decide then to follow the lady into the ball. They are aware that they do so in some danger.

ACT ONE, SCENE FOUR—THE BALLROOM Romeo and his friends arrive at the height of the festivities. Still infatuated with Rosaline, Romeo follows her. He comes face to face with Juliet for a moment. As Juliet dances with Paris, Romeo watches, bewitched. As Paris kneels to kiss her hand, Juliet turns, sees Romeo, and is visibly disturbed. She is given a mandolin and strums it as six of her friends dance. But their dance is interrupted by one for Romeo, as if Juliet could not get him out of her mind. He dances marvelously for her alone, and kneels at her feet, taking her mandolin. But Paris quickly intercedes and Juliet dances. Romeo, irresistibly drawn to her, comes to join Juliet, catching her about the waist. Mercutio, seeing that Romeo is entranced with Juliet, dances to distract attention from him. Later, Tybalt recognizes Romeo and orders him to leave, but Capulet intervenes and welcomes him as a guest in his house.

ACT ONE, SCENE FIVE—OUTSIDE THE CAPULETS' HOUSE As the ball breaks up and the guests depart, Tybalt follows Romeo out. Lord Capulet intervenes and Tybalt is restrained from pursuing Romeo.

ACT ONE, SCENE SIX—JULIET'S BALCONY Unable to sleep, Juliet comes out on her balcony, throws off her scarf and leans against a column. She thinks of Romeo. Suddenly he is there, below in the garden. She runs swiftly down the long flight of steps to him. He drops his cloak and goes to her. He puts his hand to her heart and then dances for her. Now they dance together, confess their love, and the die is cast.

ACT TWO, SCENE ONE—THE MARKET PLACE The market bustles with activity; buyers and sellers jostle together, hooded monks mingle with the crowd. Romeo, who can think only of Juliet, watches as a wedding procession passes and dreams of the day he will marry her. Her nurse enters on the right, seeking Romeo. She gives him a letter in which he rejoices: Juliet has consented to marry him, but with their families so opposed, they must do this secretly. Thinking only of his bride, Romeo dances joyfully, then embraces the nurse and rushes out.

ACT TWO, SCENE TWO—THE CHAPEL The music is somber as the curtain rises on Friar Laurence's cell. The monk enters and prays. First Romeo and then Juliet and the nurse come. All kneel before the monk. Friar Laurence joins the hands of the two lovers, hoping that their union will end the strife between the Montagues and the Capulets. The nurse weeps.

ACT TWO, SCENE THREE—THE MARKET PLACE Meanwhile, the crowd in the market place is still celebrating. Interrupting the revelry, Tybalt tries to pick a fight with Romeo. At such a time, Romeo will not duel his wife's kinsman. But Tybalt will be fought with and before anyone can intercede, Mercutio has accepted the challenge and the two enemies fight with swords. Romeo begs Mercutio to stop. Tybalt stabs Mercutio in the back. Mercutio staggers. He still tries to fight, but dies with gaiety, his sword becoming for a moment his guitar as he plays his own lament. As Mercutio dies, Romeo in revenge attacks Tybalt and kills him. Romeo is exiled. Lady Capulet holds the body of her nephew, swaying back and forth in her grief as her husband watches helplessly.

ACT THREE, SCENE ONE—JULIET'S BEDROOM Romeo and Juliet lie together on a canopied bed. He kisses her as the sun comes through the window. She sleeps on for a bit but soon they rise to dance ecstatically of their mutual joy. At the end they are sick with sadness that they must part. After a long kiss Romeo rushes to the balcony and away, while Juliet hurries back to bed just as the nurse enters. Her parents soon follow with Paris. Juliet, to her father's rage, repulses Paris. The nurse begs her to behave, but she cannot. She prays to her father to forget this marriage. When he will not she throws herself on the bed and cries like a child. But the family closes in on her, bearing down and insisting. Juliet seems to reconsider but instead of going to Paris and being nice to him she circles him on point. Capulet will tolerate this no longer; he and his wife take Paris away. They leave Juliet lying in despair. She sits up then at the foot of the bed, vulnerable yet sure, tormented but determined to find a way out for herself and her lover. She takes up her cloak, gestures toward the balcony as if that would bring Romeo back, prays frantically, and then rushes off to see Friar Laurence.

ACT THREE, SCENE TWO—THE CHAPEL Juliet falls at the friar's feet and begs for help. He gives her a phial of sleeping potion which will make her fall into a deathlike sleep. The monk further undertakes to warn Romeo that Juliet has taken the potion and is not really dead but that she must be rescued from the family tomb.

ACT THREE, SCENE THREE—JULIET'S BEDROOM Juliet, back in her room, hides the phial under the pillow. When her parents come, she begs her mother's pardon. Her father is pleased that she seems to have come to her senses. Juliet dances for Paris but resists any real contact with him. He kisses the hem of her dress. Her parents decide not to force matters and then Juliet is alone. She goes to the bed for the phial, but is frightened at the possible consequences of taking it. Suppose she will really die? What if the potion does not work at all and she is compelled to marry Paris anyway? She sits at the foot of the bed and again she is a child, younger than we saw even at the beginning, caught up in a fate beyond her. But she takes the phial, drinks the sleeping potion, and expires on the bed.

The next morning Juliet seems to be asleep when six friends of the bride enter with flowers. They remark how quiet she is and try to waken her. The nurse comes in with Juliet's wedding dress and then her parents arrive. The nurse falls full length beside the bed when Capulet declares that his daughter is dead. All lament.

ACT THREE, SCENE FOUR—THE CAPULET FAMILY CRYPT

The curtain rises on the grim interior of an underground cavern. Juliet lies on a bier in the center. Her family mourns and monks with candles lament her passing. Paris remains behind to bid farewell to Juliet, but Romeo, disguised as a monk, throws off his cloak and attacks him. Paris is killed. Believing Juliet to be dead (the message from Friar Laurence has miscarried), but not believing it possible, Romeo lifts her from the bier and holds her. He dances with the dead body of his beloved, trying to revive her, but she falls back always in his arms. He places her on the tomb, then drinks a phial of poison that he has brought with him. Juliet wakes, but as she moves off the tomb she sees Romeo's body. She takes his dagger, which he had dropped near Paris's body, plunges it into her breast, and embraces Romeo.

SACRED GROVE ON MOUNT TAMALPAIS

Music and lyrics by Alan Raph. Choreography by Gerald Arpino. Set designed by Robert Yodice from a concept by Ming Cho Lee. Costumes by David James. First presented by the City Center Joffrey Ballet at the City Center, New York, November 2, 1972, with Starr Danias, Russell Chambers, and Russell Sultzbach in leading roles. Conducted by Sung Kwak.

From antique times, men and women have gone to sacred groves to celebrate the earth's renewal every spring. Mount Tamalpais, in Marin County, California, overlooking San Francisco Bay and the Pacific beyond, is the scene of this extensive dance ballet that explores the drive, innocence, and sophistication of contemporary youth. There is a pastoral marriage and evidence of other commitments ". . . to build from a moment onward/to build a beginning./ Come to the wall around you/Come through the wall around you./ Come and see/look and see/follow me." The score, with lyrics, which includes the *Canon in D* by Johann Pacelbel, was commissioned by the Foundation for American Dance, Inc.

The action depicts a wedding ceremony and the attendant celebration, followed by the birth of a son who represents a kind of prophet to the young persons on Mount Tamalpais.

NOTES Writing about the ballet in the New York *Times*, Clive Barnes said that "Mr. Arpino has conceived his ballet as an exaltation of the human spirit. Californians (perhaps) in a Greek mood are dancing out fancies of renewal. Two lovers—Starr Danias and Russell Chambers—produce, quite suddenly, a full-grown son, Russell Sultzbach. . . . Miss Danias dances like a still thought in a quick world—there is a special quietness to her lyricism, a youthful melancholy, that Mr. Arpino so instinctively picks up. He creates beautifully for her, and Mr. Chambers, ardent and provocative, makes her a nicely matched partner. The assertive radiance of Mr. Sultzbach was also used to strong effect."

In a special portfolio by Olga Maynard on Gerald Arpino's

"Berkeley ballets" for *Dance Magazine* (September 1973), the choreographer is quoted as saying that *Sacred Grove on Mount Tamalpais* polarizes its audiences: "'For some (for whom the distance is too far from the real Mount Tamalpais, and the Berkeley life-style), the ballet is incomprehensible. It is not a work that should be approached intellectually, but as an experience. But people come to me, in every city that The Joffrey dances *Sacred Grove on Mount Tamalpais,* to say that it has made them feel beautiful again. I am very grateful for that. . . .

"'The choreographer cannot deliberately make a ballet to appeal to an audience; he has to start from personal inspirations. He has to trust the ballet, to let it stand on its own strengths—or fall on its weaknesses. If it reaches the audience, then he is lucky that round!

"'In *Trinity* and *Sacred Grove on Mount Tamalpais* I have been able to look at the world through the eyes of the young —to touch the heart of the matter of what it is to be young in this place and time. I could not have done this unless I had gone to Berkeley.

"'The choreographer (especially in the United States) needs Berkeley. Materialistic things, from which art cannot be separated, force us into certain perspectives, they sometimes narrow those perspectives, as tall buildings confine the sight of the sky. At Berkeley, The Joffrey had a true freedom, and our company was able to refresh and to replenish its spirit. Joffrey and I are very conscious of the free spirit that identifies this company; the dancers are very important to the company. They *are* The Joffrey.

"'As artists, they are very sensitive to an atmosphere and at Berkeley we all felt, very intensely, the free, open spirit that is the stamp of The Joffrey.'"

LE SACRE DU PRINTEMPS

THE RITE OF SPRING

Ballet in two parts. Music by Igor Stravinsky. Choreography by Vaslav Nijinsky. Book by Igor Stravinsky and Nicholas Roerich. Scenery and costumes by Nicholas Roerich. First presented by Diaghilev's Ballets Russes at the Théâtre des Champs-Élysées, Paris, May 29, 1913, with Marie Piltz as the Chosen One. *Rechoreographed by Leonide Massine and presented by Diaghilev's Ballets Russes at the Théâtre des Champs-Élysées, 1920, with Lydia Sokolova as the* Chosen One. *First presented in the United States, with new choreography by Massine, at the Academy of Music, Philadelphia, April 11, 1930, under the auspices of the League of Composers. Martha Graham danced the leading role in the first American presentation.*

Stravinsky has said that the "violent Russian spring" that seemed to begin in an hour was like the whole earth cracking. . . . It was "the most wonderful event of every year of my childhood." In 1910, when he was finishing *Firebird,* the composer had an unexpected vision: "I saw in imagination a solemn pagan rite: wise elders, seated in a circle, watching a young girl dance herself to death. They were sacrificing her to propitiate the god of spring." The ballet that resulted from this vision made musical and theatrical history. The score, long a masterpiece of the modern repertoire, has become more popular in the concert hall than in the theater, although there continue to be a number of ballet versions (one by Kenneth MacMillan for the Royal Ballet, with scenery and costumes by Sydney Noland, May 3, 1962, was introduced in North America the following year, May 8, 1963).

Subtitled "Scenes of Pagan Russia in Two Parts," the ballet returns us to a time when primitive rites dominated the lives of the Russian tribes. Every year spring was consecrated by a human sacrifice.

FIRST TABLEAU—ADORATION OF THE EARTH A musical prelude recalls man's first relations with the world about him.

The curtain rises. In a wasteland scene dominated by great masses of stone, young girls and boys sit in separate groups. They do not move, they wait and watch, as if expecting some sign from the stone shafts they revere. The girls rise, as if drawn by the abundance of nature to which the music calls their attention. A wise man stands among the dancers; the girls rush around and around him. Now he moves toward the sacred mound of the enclosure. The girls follow and bow before him. The opening phrase of the ballet—the quiet, plaintive cry of man against all-powerful nature—is repeated.

The strings sound strong, persistent chords that rouse the young men. To the virile beat of the music, they begin to dance, their movements accelerating at its demand, their feet stamping, stamping the earth. The girls join in the dance, the music becomes joyous, and the adolescents abandon themselves to the swift, exuberant rhythms of the orchestra.

This music changes sharply. A new, penetrating melody shrieks warningly and disturbs the young people. The happiness of the boys and girls shifts abruptly to fierce savagery. They split into different groups; the boys face the girls and move toward them. The boys seem bent on attack, but at the last minute they hesitate; they move back and forth in an almost helpless effort, ignorant of their own true intent. The rhythmic crescendos give place to the soft trilling of flutes. Now the boys break their formation, and each carries a girl away.

Four boys remain on the scene. They choose four girls, lift them up on their backs, and dance slowly, bending low under the weight of their burdens in imitation of the plodding chords of the music. This "Round Dance of Spring" gradually increases in volume, and all the adolescents participate. All the dancers step back as the trilling flutes repeat their love call.

Drums herald the beginning of a contest between two rival tribes. Groups of men from each tribe engage in vigorous games. In the midst of their activity, the wise man, represented in the orchestra by a portentous melody on the tuba, tries to interrupt the games. The stronger theme of the games at first drowns out the wise man's theme, then recedes. The men turn to the wise man. There is a brief, taut silence, then all the men fall to the ground and worship the earth.

The drum rolls loudly, and all rise to dance, as if they had felt the pulse of the earth and been renewed by its power. The dance grows frenzied in its intensity. The curtain falls.

SECOND TABLEAU—THE SACRIFICE Night is about to fall as this second scene begins; the setting sun has turned the sky scarlet. The girls sit near the wise man at a fire. One of these girls must be chosen by the others to make the sacrifice to the earth: this girl must dance herself to death. The music is calm; the figures on stage are quiet and they are unafraid. The girls regret what they have to do, but they are resigned to it with a kind of physical tiredness that the music reflects. They do not feel that they are victimized by Nature, but rather that they must obey what they believe to be its rules.

Soon the girls rise and move in the patterns of the "Dance of the Mysterious Circles." Their movements are trancelike, as if they themselves were not to make their dreadful decision. Their inspiration arrives, and they rush to the periphery of the scene; the chosen one stands alone in the center of the stage.

Now begins the dance that glorifies the victim. The chosen one remains motionless as the girls and men of the tribe whirl around her. All are transfixed at her power. They invoke the spirit of their ancestors, terrified anew by the force of Nature. Marking the relentless, sharp rhythms of the music with their feet, their dance reaches an ultimate expression of uncontrolled glory in sacrifice.

All the tribe members retire to watch the chosen one. The orchestra sounds strong, militant chords, trumpets blare harshly, cutting the air. The dance of the chosen one begins. The brutal savagery of the demanding music compels her to imitate it. Brief moments of comparative quiet, which seem at first to be periods of rest and release, are in reality more deadly because of the thrashing force that follows them. The girl is now wholly a part of the music, part of the earth. Hypnotized by her movements, the tribe joins in the violent dance. The chosen one begins to lose her strength, but—forced on by the convulsive violence of the music—is endowed with a new, superhuman compulsion. When it seems that Nature can demand no more, the girl is pushed into a fresh frenzy. Then she falls. She is dead.

The men of the tribe catch her up in their arms and hold her high over their heads before the sacred mound. The people of the tribe rush around her, holding up their arms. At the last slapping crescendo of the music, they fall to the earth.

NOTES The first assistant to Nijinsky in the creation of the first version of *Le Sacre du Printemps,* Dame Marie Rambert, who later founded ballet in Britain and developed the gifts of Tudor, Ashton, de Mille and many others, has written in a way no one else can match of the background of this ballet in her autobiography, *Quicksilver* (1972):

"It was the painter Roerich who first suggested the subject of *Sacre du Printemps.* He then worked on the theme with Diaghilev, Stravinsky and Nijinsky. It was to be prehistoric Russia and represent the rites of spring. Stravinsky had finished his magnificent score by 1912, and we started the rehearsals with the company that same year.

"Nijinsky again first of all established the basic position: feet very turned in, knees slightly bent, arms held in reverse of the classical position, a primitive, prehistoric posture. The steps were very simple: walking smoothly or stamping, jumps mostly off both feet, landing heavily. There was only one a little more complicated, the dance for the maidens in the first scene. It was mostly done in groups, and each group has its own precise rhythm to follow. In the dance (if one can call it that) of the Wisest Elder, he walked two steps against every three steps of the ensemble. In the second scene the dance of the sacrifice of the Chosen Virgin was powerful and deeply moving. I watched Nijinsky again and again teaching it to Maria Piltz. Her reproduction was very pale by comparison with his ecstatic performance, which was the greatest tragic dance I have ever seen.

"The first night of that ballet was the most astonishing event . . . at the first sounds of the music, shouts and hissing started in the audience, and it was very difficult for us on the stage to hear the music, the more so as part of the audience began to applaud in an attempt to drown the hissing. We all desperately tried to keep time without being able to hear the rhythm clearly. In the wings Nijinsky counted the bars to guide us. Pierre Monteux conducted undeterred, Diaghilev having told him to continue to play at all costs.

"But after the interlude things became even worse, and during the sacrificial dance real pandemonium broke out. That scene began with Maria Piltz, the Chosen Virgin, standing on the spot trembling for many bars, her folded hands under her right cheek, her feet turned in, a truly prehistoric and beautiful pose. But to the audience of the time it appeared ugly and comical.

"A shout went up in the gallery:

"'*Un docteur!*'

"Somebody else shouted louder:

"'*Un dentiste!*'

"Then someone else screamed:

"'*Deux dentistes!*'

"And so it went on. One elegant lady leaned out of her box and slapped a man who was clapping. But the performance went on to the end.

"And yet now there is no doubt that, musically and choreographically, a masterpiece had been created that night. The only ballet that could compare with it in power was Bronislava Nijinska's *Les Noces,* created in 1923. She, like her brother, produced a truly epic ballet—so far unexcelled anywhere."

Music by Igor Stravinsky. Choreography by Maurice Béjart. First presented by the Ballet of the Twentieth Century at the Théâtre Royale de La Monnaic, in December 1959. First presented in the United States by the same ensemble at the Brooklyn Academy of Music, New York, January 26, 1971, with Tania Bari and Jorge Dunn in principal roles.

The choreographer of this version of *Le Sacre,* Maurice Béjart, has written: "What is Spring but an immense primordial force, which after long sleeping under the mantle of winter, suddenly bursts forth, kindling new life in all things.

. . . Human love, in its physical aspects, symbolizes the act by which the divinity creates the Cosmos and the joy the divinity thereby derives. At a time when the borders that divide the human spirit are gradually crumbling, we must begin to speak in terms of the culture of all mankind. Let us avoid folklore that is not universal and only retain the essential forces of mankind which are the same the world over and throughout all periods of history.

"Let this ballet then be stripped of all the artifices of the picturesque in a Hymn to this union of Man and Woman in the innermost depths of the flesh, a union of heaven and earth, a dance of life and death, as eternal as Spring."

Rejecting, therefore, the original scenario of Stravinsky and Roerich, this *Sacre* celebrates instead the mating of a young man and woman. Writing in the New York *Times,* Anna Kisselgoff has said that Béjart's "use of group patterns and rhythmic pulse gives this *Sacre* an underivative look. . . . The chosen maiden is not sacrificed literally but thrown into a physical union with an equally virginal male. . . . The Puritans did not ban Maypole-dancing in England for nothing and Béjart has given his strikingly designed fertility ritual the primitive physical force it needs. It works."

The English critic Peter Williams has written in *Dance and Dancers* magazine: "The mass ritualistic movements leading up to the final orgasmic moment make pretty powerful theatre, in which the music plays a vital part."

Rudolf Nureyev danced Béjart's ballet on March 12, 1971, at the Palais des Sports, Brussels.

John Taras choreographed a new version of *Le Sacre* for La Scala, Milan, December 9, 1972. Natalia Makarova danced the principal role. Scenery and costumes were designed by Marino Marini.

THE SEASONS

Music by Alexander Glazounov. Choreography by Marius Petipa. First presented at the Hermitage Theatre, St. Petersburg, February 7, 1900. First presented by the Stuttgart Ballet, in a production by John Cranko, at the Wuerttemberg State Theatre, Stuttgart, June 15, 1962. Completely revised by Mr. Cranko in a new version which was first presented in the United States at the Metropolitan Opera House, New York, April 30, 1971.

While the first ballet to Glazounov's great score (one that is more familiar, from excerpts we know, than we suspect) included four danced tableaux of the seasons and an apotheosis, John Cranko's production also makes of the work a major opportunity for a reigning ballerina. He provides her with no less than three of the seasons—Winter, Summer, and Autumn. (Spring is led by two girls.) Each of these parts of the ballet is supported by soloists and *corps de ballet,* but the emphasis is on personal virtuosity and dance display. Summer and Autumn are both *pas de deux,* the latter rivaling the former in exuberance.

When *The Seasons* was first presented in America, Clive Barnes wrote in the New York *Times* that "Cranko has never choreographed with more authority. . . . The dancing has a range, scope and sheer bigness that have to be associated with the Bolshoi Ballet and nothing else. . . . Cranko's pure dance choreography has more vigor than it ever had. . . . The dancing is the best the Stuttgart has ever given us."

SERENADE

Classic ballet in four parts. Music by Peter Ilyich Tchaikovsky. Choreography by George Balanchine. Costumes by Jean Lurçat. First presented by students of the School of American Ballet at the estate of Felix M. Warburg, White Plains, New York, June 9, 1934. Presented by the producing company of the School of American Ballet at the Avery Memorial Theatre, Hartford, Connecticut, December 6, 1934, with Kathryn Mullowney, Heidi Vossler, and Charles Laskey in the principal roles.

Named after its music—Tchaikovsky's *Serenade in C major for String Orchestra*—*Serenade* tells its story musically and choreographically, without any extraneous narrative. Because Tchaikovsky's score, though it was not composed for the ballet, has in its danceable four movements different qualities suggestive of different emotions and human situations, parts of the ballet seem to have a story: the apparently "pure" dance takes on a kind of plot. But this plot, inherent in the score, contains many stories—it is many things to many listeners to the music, and many things to many people who see the ballet.

Most people would agree that a nonprogrammatic piece of music doesn't have to have a story to be a pleasure: we enjoy symphonies by Tchaikovsky and Mozart just as much as we enjoy a symphony with a story, such as Beethoven's *Pastorale*. *Serenade* is programmatic only insofar as its music is programmatic.

To tell a story about something is simply a very human way of saying that we understand it. Making a ballet is a choreographer's way of showing how he understands a piece of music, not in words, not in narrative form (unless he has in mind a particular story), but in dancing.

The four movements of Tchaikovsky's score are danced in the following order, without interruption: (1) Piece in the Form of a Sonatina: *Andante non troppo, Allegro;* (2) Waltz; (3) Tema Russo: *Andante, Allegro con spirito;* (4)

Elegy. Twenty-eight dancers in blue costumes dance the ballet before a blue background.

FIRST MOVEMENT The orchestra plays the strong and spacious opening chords of the brief Andante section and repeats them deeply before the curtain rises. When we see the stage, a group of girls stand in a tableau of crossing lines. It is night. The shadowed light that shines upon them is soft. They are motionless at first, then respond to the music as the light brightens and the new melodious Allegro is heard.

The girls dance in small groups, forming patterns on the stage. One girl dances alone, turning, posing, leaping among the others. Others seem to imitate her originality, but then all are whirling faster and faster in a wide circle together. Suddenly, quickly, each girl stands motionless in the same tableau that opened the ballet, and the familiar chords of the introductory Andante are repeated.

One girl comes in late. She finds her place in the group and stands with the other girls. A boy enters at the back of the stage. As he walks forward toward the girl, her friends leave the stage.

SECOND MOVEMENT A waltz begins as the boy reaches the girl. They begin to dance together, the girl moving away from him, then rejoining him. When her friends re-enter, the girl dances joyously among them; then she and her partner lead them in a dance, the boy lifting the ballerina high in front of the group. The waltz slowly and softly ends, and the group walks off to the tempo of its concluding rhythms.

THIRD MOVEMENT (the fourth movement in the original suite) Five girls remain on stage. They sit together on the stage as the music is quiet, turning toward each other in gentle movements. They rise and, at the first sound of the brilliant Russian melody, respond immediately and dance with open gaiety. A boy rushes on and meets a girl; they dance together; and when the ensemble runs off, as the music finishes, we see that the girl has fallen to the floor, her head buried in her arms. She is alone.

FOURTH MOVEMENT Another girl brings a boy to her. This girl walks behind the boy, guiding him forward: it is as if she moved him, as if he saw only what she wished. When they reach the fallen girl, the boy helps her to rise and now dances with the two of them. He remains with them, dancing with one of them alone, then both together, until there comes a time when he must choose. The girl who possessed him first, the girl who brought him to the other, claims him irrevocably and he leaves with her. The forsaken heroine collapses, revives briefly, and then is lost. Three boys lift her straight up above their shoulders. Her body arches back slowly as they carry her forward in a quiet procession; her arms open wide.

NOTES *Serenade* was my first ballet in the United States. Soon after my arrival in America, Lincoln Kirstein, Edward M. M. Warburg, and I opened the School of American Ballet in New York. As part of the school curriculum, I started an evening ballet class in stage technique, to give students some idea of how dancing on stage differs from classwork. *Serenade* evolved from the lessons I gave.

It seemed to me that the best way to make students aware of stage technique was to give them something new to dance, something they had never seen before. I chose Tchaikovsky's *Serenade* to work with. The class contained, the first night, seventeen girls and no boys. The problem was, how to arrange this odd number of girls so that they would look interesting. I placed them on diagonal lines and decided that the hands should move first to give the girls practice.

That was how *Serenade* began. The next class contained only nine girls; the third, six. I choreographed to the music with the pupils I happened to have at a particular time. Boys began to attend the class and they were worked into the pattern. One day, when all the girls rushed off the floor area we were using as a stage, one of the girls fell and began to cry. I told the pianist to keep on playing and kept this bit in the dance. Another day, one of the girls was late for class, so I left that in too.

Later, when we staged *Serenade*, everything was revised. The girls who couldn't dance well were left out of the more difficult parts; I elaborated on the small accidental bits I had included in class and made the whole more dramatic, more theatrical, synchronizing it to the music with additional movement, but always using the little things that ordinarily might be overlooked.

I've gone into a little detail here about *Serenade* because many people think there is a concealed story in the ballet. There is not. There are, simply, dancers in motion to a beautiful piece of music. The only story is the music's story, a serenade, a dance, if you like, in the light of the moon.

Serenade has seen a number of different productions. It was produced by the American Ballet, the company made up of our dancers at the School of American Ballet, in its first season, at the Adelphi Theatre, New York, March 1–15, 1935. It was staged for the Ballet Russe de Monte Carlo, October 17, 1940, at the Metropolitan Opera House, with costumes by Lurçat and a cast headed by Marie-Jeanne, Igor Youskevitch, and Frederic Franklin. In 1941 *Serenade* was mounted for the South American tour of the American Ballet Caravan in a new production with costumes by Alvin Colt. In 1947 it was staged for the ballet of the Paris Opéra. On October 18, 1948, *Serenade* became part of the permanent repertory of the New York City Ballet. This production has costumes by Karinska.

The leading role in *Serenade* was first danced by a group of soloists, rather than by one principal dancer. In a number of productions, however, I arranged it for one dancer. But when the New York City Ballet was to make its first appearance in London, at the Royal Opera House, Covent Garden, in the summer of 1950, it seemed appropriate to introduce the company by introducing its principal dancers and the leading role was again divided and danced by our leading soloists.

Serenade is now danced by many ballet companies in the United States and abroad. A few years ago I finally succeeded in expanding the ballet so that it now uses all of the score of the Tchaikovsky "Serenade for Strings," something I had wanted to do for a long time. The interesting thing is that while some knowing members of the audience noticed this change and spoke to me about it, the critics didn't seem to notice at all! Perhaps they had seen the ballet too often!

Serenade was danced by students of the School of American Ballet at their annual program in 1974, at the Juilliard Theater, Lincoln Center, New York.

THE SLEEPING BEAUTY

Classic ballet in three acts, with prologue. Music by Peter Ilyich Tchaikovsky. Choreography by Marius Petipa. Book by Marius Petipa and Ivan Vsevolojsky, after tales by Charles Perrault. Scenery and costumes by Ivan Vsevolojsky. First presented at the Maryinsky Theatre, St. Petersburg, Russia, January 15, 1890, with Carlotta Brianza as the Princess Aurora, *Paul Gerdt as the* Prince, *Marie Petipa as the* Lilac Fairy, *Enrico Cecchetti as* Carabosse, *Varvara Nikitina as the* Enchanted Princess, *and Enrico Cecchetti as the* Bluebird. *First presented in Western Europe by Diaghilev's Ballets Russes at the Alhambra Theatre, London, November 2, 1921. Staged by Nicholas Sergeyev after the choreography of Marius Petipa. Additional choreography by Bronislava Nijinska. Orchestration of Prelude to Act Three and the Princess Aurora's variation in Act Three by Igor Stravinsky. Scenery and costumes by Léon Bakst. The cast included Olga Spessivtzeva as the* Princess Aurora, *Pierre Vladimiroff as the* Prince, *Lydia Lopokova as the* Lilac Fairy, *Carlotta Brianza as* Carabosse, *Felia Dubrovska, Lydia Sokolova, Bronislava Nijinska, Lubov Egorova, and Vera Nemtchinova as the* Fairies, *Ludmilla Shollar as the* White Cat, *Lydia Lopokova as the* Enchanted Princess, *and Stanislas Idzikowski as the* Bluebird. *Revived by the Sadler's Wells Ballet at the Sadler's Wells Theatre, London, February 2, 1939, in a new production staged by Nicholas Sergeyev after choreography by Marius Petipa. Scenery and costumes by Nadia Benois. The cast included Margot Fonteyn as the* Princess Aurora, *Robert Helpmann as the* Prince, *June Brae as the* Lilac Fairy, *and Mary Honer and Harold Turner as the* Bluebirds. *Revived by the Sadler's Wells Ballet in a new production under the supervision of Nicholas Sergeyev at the Royal Opera House, Covent Garden, February 20, 1946. Additional choreography by Frederick Ashton and Ninette de Valois. Scenery and costumes by Oliver Messel. Margot Fonteyn as the* Princess Aurora, *Robert Helpmann as the* Prince, *Beryl Grey as the* Lilac Fairy, *and Pamela May and Alexis Rassine as the* Bluebirds *headed the cast. First presented in the United States by the Sadler's Wells Ballet at the Metropolitan Opera House, New York, October 9, 1949, with Margot Fonteyn and Robert Helpmann, Beryl Grey, Moira Shearer, and Alexis Rassine. Catherine Littlefield, Director of the Philadelphia Ballet, produced a complete version of* The Sleeping Beauty *with her own choreography at the Academy of Music, Philadelphia, February 12, 1937. This version was later produced at the Lewisohn Stadium, New York, July 29 and 30, 1937.*

The crashing, commanding chords of the brief overture to *The Sleeping Beauty* herald the special magic of the fairy tale the ballet relates, a fairy tale that is rich and formal in presentation, but warm and intimate in effect. Tchaikovsky and Petipa have so fashioned Perrault's story of the sleeping princess ("*La Belle au Bois Dormant,*" from *Mother Goose*) for the theater that notions of reality are suspended in favor of belief in characters who can live forever, in a curse of black magic that can put a forest to sleep for a hundred years, and in a beneficent fairy whose magic can rescue all goodness from evil. The time is unimportant, as is the place. The nameless mythical kingdom of the mythical King Florestan XXIV becomes the scene of our imagination.

The intensity of the music demands the attention, focusing it, as it were, on the splendor of the opening scene. The overture to *The Sleeping Beauty* also contains in miniature the story it introduces. Concealed within the opening regal chords is a theme that represents the fairy Carabosse, the evil fairy who will cast a spell upon the ballet's heroine and her family. This music is quickly interrupted by the melodious harp, which introduces a soft, slow, magical, compassionate theme—the melody of the Lilac Fairy, whose beauty and goodness will triumph over the evil fairy's challenge.

Now the music changes to a march tempo, quietly at first, then more assertively. The melody swells. The curtain rises.

PROLOGUE—THE CHRISTENING The hall of King Florestan's palace is high-ceilinged. Great arches of stone cross the back of the stage; through them can be discerned the foliage of the garden. Drapery of resplendent color and ornament warms the spaciousness of the scene. On the right, on a small platform, stands the canopied cradle of the Princess Aurora, guarded by two nurses on each side. Two heralds stand at the back. Almost immediately the king's master of ceremonies, Cattalabutte, enters in elaborate full dress. With great flourish, he busies himself seeing that all is ready for the ceremony. Satisfied, he comes forward, gives a page his stick of office, and scans the list of guests who have been invited to attend the christening of the princess.

Twelve ladies in waiting enter the chamber. They circle the stage and ceremoniously ask Cattalabutte if they may see the child. He consents and leads them over to the cradle, where they hover over the princess. Cattalabutte directs a page to notify the king that all the preparations have been made and nervously unrolls the guest list again to check his memory. The ladies retire from the cradle and stand to one side. A fanfare sounds in the distance; it grows louder; three pages enter. To the blaring of trumpets, the king and queen approach. They pause for a moment under the silk canopy that is held high above them by Negroes dressed in gold and survey the scene. Then their attendants drop their trains. The queen goes to the cradle. She kisses the princess and greets the ladies in waiting, who bow to her. She joins the king, who stands in conference with Cattalabutte. After a brief consultation with their servant, the two monarchs mount the steps to their thrones.

An arpeggio on the harp announces the arrival of the fairy godmothers of the princess. The royal fairies are preceded by their pages, who enter two by two and bow to their sovereigns. Five of the fairies enter in a group: the Fairy of the Crystal Fountain, the Fairy of the Enchanted Garden, the Fairy of the Woodland Glades, the Fairy of the Songbirds, and the Fairy of the Golden Vine. Eight maids of honor attend them. Last of all comes the Fairy of the Lilac, accompanied by six cavaliers, one for each of the fairies. The cavaliers carry, on plush cushions, the gifts the fairies have chosen for their godchild. The Lilac Fairy leads the group forward. The fairies bow low to the king and queen, who welcome them cordially, and arrange themselves about the royal cradle to bless the princess. They bow again to the king and queen and leave the scene.

The maids of honor come forward in two lines and, to the syncopated rhythm of a new melody, they dance in linear patterns. They are joined by the cavaliers, who leap boldly in the air. The fairies return, and all dance together briefly.

The queen thanks the Lilac Fairy for the dance and asks the group to continue. The Lilac Fairy bows.

A new tender theme is heard, accompanied by runs on the harp. The fairies and their partners arrange themselves in five moving circles, the Lilac Fairy in the center. Two of the girls in the back are lifted to their partners' shoulders and turned around and around so that they appear to be swimming high in the air. The fairies come forward to the footlights. One by one, the fairies pirouette rapidly and pose in attitude supported by their cavaliers. The maids of honor lie at their feet in respectful obeisance.

The tableau is broken; the music subsides, then regains in volume; in a hushed pause, the royal nurses bring the small princess to the center of the stage. There is a magical rushing run on the harp, and the Lilac Fairy is lifted high above the princess. She blesses the babe with her wand. The *pas de six* is over. The harp plays for a moment, the tempo changes, and the fairies leave the stage while the maids of honor dance a new sprightly measure in unison.

Now each of the fairies returns to perform a variation before the assembled court. These variations are very short; they have no literal significance, and the attributes of the different fairies cannot be read into them; but the different music and different dances that Tchaikovsky and Petipa devised for the six fairies gives each of the variations an individual, distinctive character. First is the Fairy of the Crystal Fountain. She enters and waits for her music to begin. Its movement is slow and leisurely; its melody, calm. The fairy dances forward and moves back and forth across the stage on her points, her body in graceful repose. As her feet mark the retarded rhythm of her music, her head and arms depict the quiet sweetness of the melody. She kneels to the king and queen as her variation ends and leaves the stage.

The Fairy of the Enchanted Garden emerges to dance with quick steps to a brighter tempo—music which carries her into swift pirouettes that accelerate as she moves across the stage. For the Fairy of the Woodland Glades, the music is characterized by a soft, tempered pizzicato. This fairy's skill in quiet, slow movement is revealed in the daring figure that highlights her dance: she dances forward on one foot, her other foot extended before her. With subdued brilliance her extended foot moves back, and the girl stands poised for a breathless moment in arabesque. This figure is repeated as she continues to move forward. Then her dance becomes luminous and light, with rapid dancing on point. She ends her variation standing on point, with open arms, one leg raised pertly before her.

In a flashing yellow costume, the Fairy of the Songbirds dances now to a hurried, tinkling melody, her arms moving ecstatically in simulated flight, her bright head turning to the shimmering elevation of the rhythm. She is followed by the Fairy of the Golden Vine, whose dance is characterized by the curt, staccato movement of her head and the quick pointing of the index fingers of both her hands—the so-called "Finger Variation." The tempo of the music increases sharply, and the brilliant fairy whirls to a quick, sudden stop.

The Lilac Fairy comes forward. She stands toward the back of the stage. The orchestra begins a sumptuously melodic waltz, and the Lilac Fairy accompanies its flowing line with extended, open movements in which her raised point traces small circles in the air. Then she turns in arabesque; she pauses briefly each time her body is seen in profile. In the rapid complexity of its movement and in the fullness of the magnificent waltz, the variation of the Lilac Fairy sums up in splendid grandeur the dances of all the other fairies.

Now the cavaliers dance. The maids of honor join them with light, precise movements. The fairies reassemble at the front of the stage. Their cavaliers hold them in attitude. The fairies' gifts are presented to the king and queen. The queen leaves the throne and delightedly examines the presents. There is a deep, rumbling sound, like an earthquake, off stage. Some of the courtiers imagine it to be only thunder, but the king is apprehensive. The queen trembles for the safety of her child, and the master of ceremonies cowers. A page rushes in and gestures helplessly to the king, pointing off to the left. The king understands suddenly and rushes over to Cattalabutte and demands to see the invitation list. He scans it rapidly, then dashes the scroll to the floor in a gigantic rage. Cattalabutte's fate is averted momentarily by the frightening appearance of two great rats, who emerge from the left and dance a few insidious steps. They run back out. Before the court has recovered, they return with other rats, pulling along behind them an enormous black coach. Standing majestically in the coach is the fairy Carabosse, the hunchbacked godmother of the Princess Aurora, whom the forgetful Cattalabutte has neglected to invite to the christening. She grasps at the air in her fury; her black chariot circles the stage, sweeping all the courtiers aside.

Assisted by her four rodent attendants, Carabosse steps down. The music gives a low warning. Her face is a hideous blue-white mask covered with moles and magical, shining spangles. Her long black dress is tattered and dusty, yet she wears it as if it were ermine. Carabosse hobbles forward on her stick and inquires fiercely of the king, by gesture, "Why was I forgotten? Do you realize what this will mean to the fate of your child?" Already, the king is afraid. He points to Cattalabutte as the real culprit. Carabosse approaches the cowardly master of ceremonies, who kneels at her feet. He throws up his hands, begging for mercy and to protect himself, but Carabosse reaches out her talonlike fingers and tears off his wig, which she throws at the hungry rats. Now, deprived of all his dignity, the courtier attempts to escape.

Carabosse raises her stick and, with a quick thrust in the small of his back, sends him flying. She caresses the rats, who form a small square about her as she dances blithely. She gestures to the royal couple, pointing to the cradle: "Your daughter will grow up . . . She will grow up to be a beautiful princess . . . the most beautiful princess of them all; and then"—Carabosse brings down her stick loudly; the music thunders—"and then . . . she will die! . . . She will prick her finger, no one will prevent it, and she will be a beautiful dead princess." The wicked fairy cackles with glee as the king tries to comfort the distraught queen. He motions Carabosse imperiously away, but the evil fairy persists in laughing at his discomfort. She whips her great black cape through the air to the sound of the harp.

The Lilac Fairy steps out. Carabosse tries to approach the

cradle to repeat her curse. The Lilac Fairy holds up her wand in quiet defiance; Carabosse stumbles back. All the other fairies gather around her to guard the cradle. She threatens them with her stick, but the good fairies stand placidly impervious. The hideous, servile rats surround the grotesque Carabosse, and she dances a final, frantic jig, at the end of which she holds up her hand in triumph. She climbs back into her carriage; as she stands under its high roof of black plumes, shaking her fists at the whole court, the obedient rats draw the black chariot off. The thunder subsides.

The queen weeps in the king's arms. He cannot comfort her. The Lilac Fairy comes to them. The lovely melody that identifies this good fairy fills the hall. She gestures toward the cradle and gives them this message in pantomime: "Your daughter, the princess, will grow up to be beautiful, and it is true that she will prick her finger and seem to die . . . but in reality she will only go to sleep . . . she will sleep for a hundred years, and all the court with her . . . but one day a prince, as handsome as she is beautiful, will come to the princess . . . she will wake at his kiss, and all will live happily ever after."

The king and queen bow to the Lilac Fairy and thank her. The release from the evil curse of Carabosse causes the court to be joyful. All the fairies bow to the king and queen, and then the entire assembly turns toward the cradle of the Princess Aurora. The queen stands over her daughter; the ladies in waiting and the maids of honor kneel in homage, and the fairies stand in attitudes of infinite protectiveness. The curtain falls.

ACT ONE—THE SPELL The scene is the garden of the palace. A colonnade of huge columns, topped by ancient statues, sweeps in a curve about a high fountain toward the right to support a great arch of stone over the back of the garden. Thrones for the king and queen are arranged at the right. On the left, a flight of wide stone steps leads up toward the palace. Peasants idle in the distance. Ladies in waiting and their cavaliers walk about the garden, marveling at its beauty and anticipating the day's festival. For today is the Princess

Aurora's sixteenth birthday, and the king has decreed a celebration in her honor. The king has also invited the court and kingdom to entertain four foreign visitors: princes from England, India, Italy, and Spain, who have come long distances to meet the young princess and pay court to her.

Three old hags in black, their dark hoods concealing their faces, stoop together over spindles. As they sew, they keep looking about cautiously. Cattalabutte enters. He has aged somewhat in the sixteen years that have passed, but still flourishes his cape and stick at every opportunity. The old women dance away from him. Cattalabutte regards them suspiciously. They try to escape, but the master of ceremonies catches them. He takes the spindles from them forcibly and stands over them threateningly. The women cower at his feet as Cattalabutte reminds them that for sixteen years, ever since the curse of the wicked fairy Carabosse, the king has ordered that no spindles be brought within a mile of the Princess Aurora. He is interrupted by the arrival of the king and queen, who are followed by the four princes. The old women scurry into a corner.

The king greets Cattalabutte and wonders what his courtier holds concealed in the hand behind his back. Reluctantly Cattalabutte holds out the dread spindles. The king is shocked and furious. Cattalabutte points to the weird women; the king commands them to come forward. He tells them that they must hang for this offense; how otherwise can he protect his daughter from the spell of Carabosse? The women kneel at his feet and plead for forgiveness. The king is adamant. To a sudden crescendo of surging, pulsating music, the queen steps forward and asks the king to relent. After all, this is Aurora's birthday and the women are truly sorry. The king smiles and consents.

The king and queen mount their thrones, carrying fresh garlands. A group of peasant girls enters. They bow deeply to their lord. The courtiers gather on the steps, and the four princes stand to one side as the girls commence to dance to a flowing waltz. The girls weave in and out under the garlands and arrange themselves in circles that travel around the stage in opposite directions. Cattalabutte thanks them when the waltz is over, and they bow to the monarchs.

Four musicians enter, carrying golden instruments, followed by eight girls—friends of the princess. The four foreign princes stand ready to greet the guest of honor. The music is expectant. The four princes look toward the back of the garden and peer down the colonnade, hoping for a glimpse of the princess. Softly the music hesitates. In the distance, under the arch, we see a beautiful girl in a pink dress embellished with silver. She poses for an instant and disappears like an apparition. Then, brilliantly, to a burst of music, she is on stage, dancing joyfully with the sweet, innocent exuberance of youth. The four princes approach her. The princess goes to her mother, who embraces her warmly, then to the king, who kisses her on the forehead. The king then introduces her to the foreign princes, who bow low to her. She responds gently. The harp plays a rushing cadenza; all the other instruments are silent, waiting; there is a brief hush, a momentary interval of preparation like the soprano's measured intake of breath before a great aria commences. The "Rose Adagio" begins.

The four princes move to the front of the stage in a line. One by one, the princes support the Princess Aurora as she dances softly and openly her preparatory steps. Then she steps back; standing on point in attitude, she greets the first prince. Holding her right hand, he turns her in attitude, as she maintains the graceful pose. When she has come full circle, the prince releases her hand; both hands are raised to form a crown above her head for a moment of balance; then the second cavalier steps forward to hold her right hand. This design is repeated. Finally, as the last prince releases her, the princess extends her body in arabesque and holds this position with breath-taking equilibrium.

One of her suitors now supports Aurora, who modestly displays her dancing skill without conveying the least impression that she is unlike any other young girl who is beautiful and happens to be dancing. Sweetly holding her hands to her cheek, the princess leans forward. She is lifted high in the air. When she is released, she dances alone in a small circle, her arms invoking the melody of the music, her strong points tracing its rhythms.

Each of the enamored princes now presents Aurora with a freshly picked rose. The theme is played softly by the oboe. One prince supports her as the others come forward, one by one, with their gifts. The princess pirouettes swiftly as she accepts each of the flowers. Then, charmingly, she leaves her suitors and presents their flowers to the queen. She moves to the back of the stage and dances forward. Armed with fresh roses, the princes kneel at her feet. As she pirouettes past them, the princes hold out their flowers; the princess pauses in her turning to receive each rose. She holds the flower to her breast for a moment, then tosses them in the air as her dance continues.

The music approaches its fullest, final expression. One of the princes holds her hand as the princess stands again on point in attitude. He releases her, and she sustains her pose as if it were effortless. Then, moving only her arm, she takes the hand of the second prince, to prepare briefly for a second, longer balance. Her modest confidence in balance increases as the adagio comes to a conclusion. When the fourth prince releases her, she stands in what seems perpetually perfect balance until the final chord breaks the enchantment. She runs off into the garden.

The eight friends of the Princess Aurora dance to a tinkling, blithe melody. Soon the princess returns. The four princes beseech her to dance again. She turns to her mother, who encourages her with a smile, and the princess begins a *pas seul.* After posing in attitude and arabesque, she goes to the corner of the garden. She dances forward on point in a diagonal line with slow precision. Step by step, she bends her right knee and brings her right leg up so that it touches gently the back of her supporting leg. The diagonal completed, she dances backward toward the corner in a series of pirouettes, each of which ends in secure, perfect position. The princess circles the garden, with brilliant, accelerating spins, and leaves the stage.

When friends commence to dance, the princess comes back. She dances toward the front with high, broad leaps in which she kicks her front foot forward—a movement that gives her dance a new urgency. She circles the stage again, this time with open, free turns rapidly executed. The tempo of the music builds with her speed, with her joy in dancing.

On the right, in the corner, half concealed by the crowd, an old woman in black emerges. She watches the happy princess, and when Aurora circles near her, holds out a present to the princess. Aurora, barely stopping, takes it and dances on, delighted with the strange, new object. The gift is a spindle! The king rises in terror and warns the court. Everyone attempts to stop Aurora's dance and take the spindle from her. But the innocent, impetuous girl is so charmed by the spindle that she cannot cease to play with it. Suddenly, she pricks her finger. Instantly, she falls to the ground.

The king and queen rush to her. The angry monarch orders the court to find the criminal who presented the princess with the fatal spindle. The princess herself has no idea of what has happened. She stirs, looks into her father's disturbed face, and shakes her head slowly, as if to say, "Don't worry, nothing is wrong." Similarly she comforts her distraught mother. To prove that everything is all right, the anxious girl rises and begins to dance again. She moves rapidly, the music accelerates ominously, and there is a clap of thunder. The princess falls into her father's arms. The cymbals clash in evil triumph, and the old woman in black steps out. She throws aside her cape: she is the fairy Carabosse, come back to court to fulfill her prophecy. She cackles with delight. The princess seems to die. Armed courtiers chase the evil fairy as she runs into the garden.

A trumpet sounds, then the harp, and the melody of the Lilac Fairy is heard. She enters with her wand and comforts the king and queen, telling them that the princess, as she foretold, is not really dead, she is merely asleep, and this is the beginning of the spell that will last a hundred years. The king and queen thank the Lilac Fairy and bow humbly. Courtiers take up the princess and carry her slowly up the steps to the palace. The Lilac Fairy ascends the stairs; the last members of the court disappear. She holds out her wand, casting a spell over the kingdom.

The stage grows dark; the garden fades in the distance. From the ground, enormous shrubs, great branches of foliage rise magically and seem to entwine the garden and the palace, smothering them in sleep. In a small point of light, the Lilac Fairy can be seen dancing softly, waving her magic wand, as the palace and its people, obedient to her command, go to sleep for a hundred years.

ACT TWO—THE VISION A brief orchestral introduction features the sound of hunting horns, and when the curtain rises on a wooded glen, we are prepared for the entry of the royal hunting party. The scene is the forest of King Florestan XXIV, a part of the forest remote from the sleeping palace; the time, one hundred years later. The setting sun glows in the distance over rocky hills that enclose a still stream. As the hunting party comes upon the scene, it is apparent that the style of dress has changed considerably. Duchesses and dukes, marchionesses and marquesse stride about the wood in their colorful riding habits. Gallison, tutor to Prince Florimund, the leader of the hunt, totters onto the stage exhausted. Prince Florimund follows. Dressed in red riding habit, with high red boots and a feathered hat, the prince bows to his guests. A countess approaches him and makes a suggestion. The prince responds lazily and motions her away gently. The persistent countess does not acknowledge the rebuff, however. She has in mind a game of blindman's buff and persuades the tutor to bind his eyes. The old man obliges her and chases after the royal couples, who egg him on by whipping their riding crops at his feet. He stumbles around, becomes dizzy, and takes the hand of what he imagines to be a beautiful lady. He is somewhat staggered as he takes the handkerchief from his eyes and finds himself embracing a peer.

The game has not amused the guests sufficiently and they turn to other entertainment. Reluctantly the prince yields to the countess' persuasion and takes her as his partner in a stately mazurka. Peasants enter the wood at the conclusion of the dance and perform a farandole, a round dance in which the boys and girls join hands and curve about the stage in a continuous serpentine line. Every member of the hunting party is diverted by the farandole except the prince, who is moody and preoccupied. The hunting horns sound again. Attendants bring in spears for the hunt, and the lords and ladies prepare to leave. But the prince has suddenly changed his mind and urges his guests to leave without him. He will remain in the forest for a little while and rejoin them later. The countess is visibly upset at her inability to attract the prince away; she attempts to change his mind; the prince dismisses her.

Now alone in the glen, the prince walks about. Night falls; the setting sun becomes the new moon. He stares out over the lake, hoping that the beautiful scene will settle his gloom. He turns away dejectedly and walks forward. Just as he turns his back, the theme of the Lilac Fairy is heard and a magical boat floats onto the lake from the right. Its gossamer sail hangs from a silver mast; motioning the boat forward is the Lilac Fairy, who stands with upraised wand in the great sea shell that forms the boat's hull. The boat stops at her command, and the fairy steps down to earth. Still preoccupied with his own thoughts, the prince does not see her. As he moves back toward the lake, he is astonished by her presence. He bows deeply.

The Lilac Fairy then begins to instruct the prince in the cause of his woe. In a palace not far from this forest, she tells him, sleeps a beautiful princess, a princess so lovely that his mind must have envisaged her all his life. This princess has been aleeep for a hundred years, yet she is only sixteen. She will sleep forever unless she is kissed by a prince who loves her.

The prince is enchanted, but somewhat skeptical, and impatiently asks the Lilac Fairy to let him see the princess. The fairy consents to show him a vision of the Princess Aurora. She points her wand to the left, and concealed within a dark tree trunk we see a misty vision of the princess. The specter disappears as quickly as it came. The prince demands to see more of her; already he is enamored of Aurora. The Lilac Fairy now allows the vision of the princess to enter in person.

The princess comes in on the right. Still the beautiful young girl of the first act, her movements are now soft and romantic. A haunting melody begins, dominated by the cellos, lending the scene a dark, mysterious atmosphere. The prince lifts Aurora high off the ground and, when he lets her down, attempts to embrace her. Fairies who have followed the princess pull him away from her, and he watches as she dances alone. The fairies form a circular tableau in the center of the scene. The princess moves about this circle, momentarily disappearing from the prince's sight. He pursues her softly, patiently, yet never catches up to her. Finally he holds her for a brief moment in his arms. The vision relaxes against him for an instant and then leaves him, like a phantom. He beseeches the Lilac Fairy to call her back again.

The sixteen nymphs dance for a short interval, and suddenly the princess returns to their midst. The flowing music becomes strongly rhythmical. Standing in the center of the stage, she dances quickly, with staccatolike urgency, a brilliant variation that excites the prince's love for her. He holds out his arms and she vanishes.

The nymphs fill the scene again with their dancing, and the princess makes a final, spinning, illusory appearance. The prince asks the Lilac Fairy, "Where has she gone? Where can I find her again?" The Lilac Fairy calms his curiosity and tells him that to find the princess, they must sail across the lake to her father's palace, where the princess lies asleep. She motions for him to follow, and the curtain falls as the Lilac Fairy's magical boat disappears in the midst of the lake.

ACT THREE, SCENE ONE—THE AWAKENING The orchestra plays a long overture, the composition that was designed originally to accompany the journey of the Lilac Fairy and the prince toward the palace, a slowly paced interlude during which the fairy's magic barge passed slowly across the lake, surrounded by a panorama of dense forest and splendid vistas of the enchanted palace.

When the curtain rises, the Lilac Fairy and the prince have already disembarked. The fairy leads the prince across the stage from the right. He follows several paces behind her, looking about him cautiously, both amazed and delighted at the sleeping forest. Only shadows can be distinguished in the background. The two walk off at the left and reappear almost immediately behind a gauze curtain. Light emerges from behind; the palace can be seen, rising high on the summit in the distance. On the ground, two guards, frozen in an attitude of perpetual slumber, sleep away their watch. The prince stares at them, unbelieving. The Lilac Fairy leads him off; the light is extinguished, only to come up again in a moment in a high-vaulted chamber—the boudoir of the Princess Aurora. The Lilac Fairy enters first, holding her wand before her. She enters through a maze of great columns entangled with cobwebs, beckoning to the prince to follow. In the half-darkness, on the left, a silken bed canopied with royal drapes dominates the apartment. Guards stand in a line, motionless, sleeping against their upright spears.

The prince enters, marveling at the oppression of the sleeping rooms and the splendor they still contain. He glances incredulously at the sleeping guards. The Lilac Fairy motions him forward to the bed. In the dim light, he sees the sleeping princess. He hesitates, not wishing to disturb her sleeping beauty. The Lilac Fairy waves her wand, and he steps forward toward the bed. Curled in an attitude of peaceful contentment, the princess lies in deep slumber, her head on an ancient, dusty pillow. The prince bends down toward her face; the Lilac Fairy gestures with her wand; he kisses her softly. The music mounts to a vivid crescendo. The princess stirs, wakens, and rises slowly as the prince gathers her in his arms.

The light flashes out, and miraculously the giant spiders who hover over the chamber rise and vanish; the cobwebs are disentangled from the great pillars and gradually fall away. The light comes up slowly, royal pages stand against the high columns, and we see before us the great hall of King Florestan's palace.

ACT THREE, SCENE TWO—THE WEDDING The lofty columns of stone support high-vaulting arches. In the distance, great, sweeping staircases climb up to the farther reaches of the castle. The thrones of the king and queen stand at the right.

With pomp and ceremony, as if he had not been disturbed by more than a night's sleep, the courtier Cattalabutte enters with all his old-time flourish. He struts about the hall as if he himself were responsible for the festivities that are about to follow.

The king and his queen enter regally. Cattalabutte bows to them and escorts them to the dais. Courtiers and ladies in waiting with their escorts dance in and promenade about the hall to the virile rhythms of a polonaise. Six other ladies enter. As the dance theme is repeated quietly, the special guests who have been invited to attend the wedding of Princess Aurora and Prince Florimund dance in to pay their respects to the parents of the bride.

These royal guests are perennial fairy tale characters. First comes the White Cat, held high on a pillow which her escorts carry on their shoulders. She paws the air plaintively and washes her face. Behind her comes Puss in Boots, who watches her possessively while waving his hat in greeting. Bluebeard and his wife, Goldilocks and her prince, Beauty and the Beast, and Florestan, the crown prince of the kingdom, and his two sisters follow behind. Last of all come the enchanted princess and the bluebird. Now, led by the Lilac Fairy, all six of the Princess Aurora's fairy godmothers enter in all their glory.

All the courtiers and guests arrange themselves in a great circle about the hall. Prince Florestan, Aurora's brother, and their two sisters step out and stand at the back of the stage toward the right. A lovely, lilting waltz begins; to its enchanting melody, the three dance a *pas de trois*. When the waltz ends, each of the two girls dances a short variation to music that is light and sparkling in its tinkling sound. Prince Florestan rejoins them, and all three leap off into the wings.

The next *divertissement* features the White Cat and Puss in Boots. This oboe mimes their mewing as Puss in Boots tries to ensnare the winsome cat in a love trap. The White Cat pretends to resist Puss's caresses, but actually she is delighted. Finally Puss can contain himself no longer and puts an end to the flirtation by carrying his ladylove off.

The Enchanted Princess enters with the Bluebird. Both flutter their arms in light, airy motions of flight and commence a *pas de deux*, perhaps the most dazzling dance duet of the entire ballet. The Bluebird, in his variation, seems to be suspended in soaring flight.

Another *divertissement* enacts the tale of Little Red Ridinghood. Four pages bring small trees onto the stage. Red Ridinghood walks lightly through the wood, treading as softly as possible, glancing behind her at every turn. The wolf enters with a bold leap and conceals himself behind one of the trees. The girl passes; he steps out in front of her. Red Ridinghood tries to pretend that he is just another passer-by, like herself, and, holding her basket close, proceeds on her way. The wolf is fooled only for a moment: quickly he throws her over his shoulder and runs off.

Now the moment for which all the court has been waiting finally arrives. Princess Aurora and Prince Florimund enter. A spotlight brightens the brilliant white the bride wears for her wedding day, and all the lords and ladies bow. The royal couple come forward and begin to dance. Their *pas de deux* is gracious and formal. The Princess Aurora reveals, in her mastery of movement and balance, a maturity and perfection for which the "Rose Adagio" was but a youthful rehearsal. Still charming, the youthful princess is now about to be married, and her radiant poise reflects the lesson her love has taught. Prince Florimund supports his bride gallantly, lifting her effortlessly, holding her confidently—by each of his gestures and motions drawing the court's attention to her loveliness. As the *pas de deux* concludes, its tender music ascends to a pitch of everlasting joy. The princess turns with incredible speed on point and dives toward the floor. The prince catches her falling figure and holds her in the daring pose.

A final *divertissement* is offered by the Three Ivans, who perform a virile, stomping Russian dance for the bride and groom. The court is now at the height of good humor, and when the Princess Aurora returns to dance briefly alone, everyone is suddenly saddened by the fact that soon she will go away with her prince. But everyone watches closely this last dance of their princess; the entire assembly is infected by her happiness. Now the whole court—all the fairies, all the nobles, all the fairy tale figures—joins the bride and groom in a spirited mazurka, at the end of which the guests form a circle about the prince and princess who, standing in close embrace, become, in reality, a part of that fairy tale world that brought them together. Everyone kneels to them.

NOTES The success of *The Sleeping Beauty* described here—as presented by the Royal Ballet (then the Sadler's Wells Ballet) in 1946, in London, and three years later in the United States—has led to many other productions. All of these, including new productions by the Royal Ballet itself, retain the main outlines of the story and the principal dances, while adding variations of character, new dances and ensembles to accompany changes in scenery and costume. Notable productions are those of the Leningrad Kirov Ballet (filmed in 1965, with Alla Sizova and Yuri Soloviev), the National Ballet of Washington (staged by Ben Stevenson), and the National Ballet of Canada (staged by Rudolf Nureyev). The latter, with Veronica Tennant as the Princess Aurora and, as guest artist, Rudolf Nureyev as Prince Florimund, was presented on film by Public Broadcasting Service television in the United States at Christmastime 1972 in color. Rudolf Nureyev first staged the ballet independently for La Scala, Milan, September 17, 1970, with scenery and costumes by Nicholas Georgiadis. Margot Fonteyn and Nureyev danced the première.

Nureyev has said of *The Sleeping Beauty* (in an interview in *Dance and Dancers,* January 1972): "It is really a kind of *Parsifal* of ballet and very important to the whole ballet world. It's very long and very lush, and there is nothing you can really cut. Since I had been brought up on the Kirov version, my production was naturally inspired by that."

In writing of Nureyev's *Sleeping Beauty* soon after its New York première in 1973, Andrew Porter in *The New Yorker* reviewed much of the ballet's history: "In ballet history, the usual order is reversed; the Romantic works come first, then the Classical. And the Petipa-Tchaikovsky *Sleeping Beauty,* first performed, in St. Petersburg, in 1890, is the grandest, fullest, and finest achievement of Classical ballet—its 'definitive statement' and an enduring inspiration to later choreographers. Balanchine, Ashton, and Kenneth MacMillan all proclaim their debt to the inventions of Petipa. Brought from Leningrad to London by Nicholas Sergeyev, *The Sleeping Beauty* became, in 1939, the foundation of the Royal Ballet's work, and the dancers, directors, ballet masters, and teachers who have gone out from Covent Garden to play leading roles in ballet across six continents have all been brought up on *Sleeping Beauty* as ballet's Bible. Meanwhile, in Leningrad itself, *The Sleeping Beauty* remains the work that shows Maryinsky-Kirov dancing at its purest and most poetic. The Kirov company brought its *Sleeping Beauty* to London twelve years ago, and left a new mark on all subsequent Western productions. The influence was continued, in a highly personalized variant, by the participation of the ex-Kirov dancer Rudolf Nureyev in the Royal Ballet performances and then by his own stagings of the work—at La Scala, in 1969, and now for the National Ballet of Canada. With a *Sleeping Beauty* 'produced, staged, and with additional choreography by Rudolf Nureyev after Marius Petipa,' the Canadian company made its Metropolitan début last week. It offered an exceedingly grand presentation of the piece—from a scenic point of view the grandest, in fact, that I have ever seen.

"When Auguste Bournonville, that great Romantic choreographer (whose *La Sylphide* is another work in the Canadian repertory), visited Petersburg in 1874, he was distressed by what he saw: 'Much as I wanted to, I could not discover action, dramatic interest, logical continuity, something that would even remotely remind one of common sense. And if, on occasion, I did succeed in finding a trace of something like it (as, for example, in Petipa's *Don Quixote*), the impression was immediately obscured by an endless number of monotonous bravura appearances.' Ivan Alexandrovich Vsevolozhsky, appointed Director of the Imperial Theatres in 1881, changed all that. He instituted production councils in which scenarist, choreographer, composer, and designer got together to plan a new work. Of *The Sleeping Beauty* he was both scenarist and costume designer; Tchaikovsky, 'in large letters,' dedicated the published score to him. Composer and choreographer worked closely together. Petipa told Tchaikovsky exactly how many measures he wanted for each episode, and specified the tempo, the style, even the scoring. Princess Aurora's first variation should be accompanied by violins and cellos pizzicato, and harps; at Carabosse's unmasking, at the end of Act I, 'a chromatic scale must sound in the whole orchestra'; the Sapphire of Act III, being of pentahedral cut, required an accompaniment in 5/4 time. When, during rehearsals, the Panorama music of Act II came to an end before the great panorama of painted canvas had rolled its full course, Tchaikovsky composed extra music, whose length was determined, literally, by the yard. The three collaborators played each his different role in giving unity to the elaborate *féerie.* Vsevolozhsky had his conception of a glittering dance pageant mounting to its climax in an apotheosispaean to imperial splendor (a paean in the precise sense, since the ending would show Apollo costumed as Louis XIV). Petipa had his sharp-cut scheme for a balanced and well-varied sequence of dances. And Tchaikovsky? He always delighted in the evocation of past centuries. Petipa's blueprint checked his tendency to sprawly form. And he poured out his heart. It is Tchaikovsky's music that gives character to the heroine and expresses the 'inner theme' which raises *The Sleeping Beauty* above the level of a pretty divertissement.

"Most of the fairy tales that adults go to the theater to see again and again—*Swan Lake, Cinderella, Hansel and Gretel,* the *Ring*—symbolically enshrine truths about human experience and human behavior to make their pleasures more than incidental. *Swan Lake,* for example, is a drama involving conflict and character; it gives scope for dramatic expression, for acting, and for diverse striking interpretations. By comparison with Prince Siegfried in *Swan Lake,* Prince Florimund of *The Sleeping Beauty* is a cipher. What does he do to deserve his princess? The briar thicket surrounding his bride is no dangerous Magic Fire through which only the dauntless can pass. And similarly, by comparison with the brave, pathetic Odette and the formidable temptress Odile, Princess Aurora is a passive heroine played upon by circumstance. Can we find a moral in *The Sleeping Beauty* beyond that guest lists should be kept up-to-date lest awkwardness result? Perrault, who wrote the fairy tale on which the ballet is based, suggested, 'What girl would not forgo her marriage vows, at least for a while, to gain a husband who is handsome, rich, courteous, and kind?' Not enough! In a preface to the Penguin edition of Perrault, Geoffrey Brereton remarks that it is 'tempting to adopt the nature-myth interpretation and see the tale as an allegory of the long winter sleep of the earth'—but adds that 'the allegory, if it is one, is obscure.' Tchaikovsky's interpretation was simpler. His *Sleeping Beauty* is a struggle betweeen good and evil, between forces of light and forces of darkness, represented by the benevolent Lilac Fairy and the wicked fairy Carabosse. The prelude, a straightforward exposition of the music associated with the two characters, suggests it; the consistent employment of melodies related to or derived from these themes—the Lilac Fairy's transformation of the Carabosse music at the close of Act I, the Carabosse figuration that propels Aurora's dance with the spindle, the opposition of the two themes in the symphonic entr'acte that precedes the Awakening—makes it clear. These two forces shape Aurora's destiny, and although she initiates nothing, with just a little stretching of the imagination we can accept the declaration of the Russian composer and critic Boris Assafiev that the heroine's three adagios (the Rose Adagio, in E flat; the Vision Scene appearance, in F; the Grand Pas de Deux, in C) tell 'the story of a whole life—the growth and development of a playful and carefree child into a young woman who learns, through tribulations, to know great love.' It is in this sense that Margot Fonteyn, since 1939 our leading Aurora, dances the role.

"That question 'Can we find a moral?' prompts others. Is it right to look for one? Does the 'meaning' of *The Sleeping Beauty* not lie simply in its patterns of movement, as does that of, say, *Ballet Imperial*, Balanchine's homage to Petipa and Tchaikovsky? While spectacle, pure dance, expressive dance, narrative, and symbolism must mix in any presentation of the work, what importance should be given to any single ingredient? Different productions have provided different answers. The Kirov's has modest décor; the dances shine as rich, perfectly cut jewels in a quiet, rather dowdy setting; this Leningrad *Beauty* is not a drama but a long, lyrical poem in varied metres, spun on a thread of radiant narrative. Kenneth MacMillan's presentation, at the German Opera, in Berlin, in 1967, was very grand indeed to look at (the epochs were moved forward, so that Aurora fell asleep in the reign of Catherine the Great and woke a century later, under Alexander II) and also rather dramatic—yet the main emphasis was again not on the story but on the dances, both Petipa's and those that MacMillan added, in brilliant emulation. The famous old Covent Garden version, which did more than twenty years' hard service (and in 1949 introduced the company to New York), balanced all the ingredients listed above, but toward the end it fell apart; though the central Petipa episodes were lovingly preserved, around them was a ragged patchwork. The 1968 replacement was softly romantic, lavishly sentimental in appearance, and did not last long; I have not seen its successor, which opened at Covent Garden in March.

"Nureyev's production for the National Ballet of Canada is different again. The décor, by Nicholas Georgiadis, is even more sumptuous than Barry Kay's in Berlin, though it does not sparkle so brightly. Mr. Kay produced a jewelled effect, of diamonds, rubies, sapphires, with the softer gleam of pearl and opal in the Vision Scene; Mr. Georgiadis prefers an impression of old gold, with touches of rich colors that are muted as if by a layer of fine dust; in the final scene the dominant tone becomes rust red. David Hersey's subtly elaborate lighting subdues the colors still further and blurs distinctions between them; a prevailing amber glow neutralizes all shades in the Vision Scene except when follow spots fall on the principals, or the attendant fairies enter pools of white light stage-front. Blackness at the back strikes an unsuitably sombre note at the christening party of the Prologue; Aurora's wedding, I think, also calls for a more splendid general blaze. All the same, the lighting is carefully and imaginatively wrought. There are some excellent stage effects: a streamer of red ribbon flies across the stage, to shape itself as Carabosse and her retinue; a boat for Florimund and the Lilac

Fairy glides magically through the obstacles on the way to the palace. The tableau of sleeping courtiers through which the prince, marvelling, picks his way is a triumph for designer, producer, and lighter at once. Mr. Georgiadis's architecture, substantial and imposing, leaves plenty of space for the dance. His multitudinous costumes are beautiful both in detail and in massed effect. Only the cut of the tutus, which are large, floppy, and thus line-obscuring, is unhappy.

"Nureyev's handling of the piece is extremely elaborate, from the first moment of the fairies' entrée; they come on four at a time, *bourréeing* hand-in-hand, each group with an attendant cavalier, who then lifts the leader while she draws her companions through the mazes of a most un-Petipalike procession. The second fairy variation is danced in duplicate, which is unusual, but in the score the variation does bear the names of two characters (Coulante, Farine). Nureyev's main innovation in the Prologue is to divide the role of the Lilac Fairy into two: a 'Principal Fairy,' who does the dancing, and a Lilac Fairy 'proper,' who turns up at the party, last guest to arrive, only after Carabosse has spoken her curse. Crinolined and heavily draped, an ambulant tea cozy, this fairy can do little more than glide about and wave her wand. Carabosse is played by a woman, as she was by Natalia Dudinskaya in Leningrad a decade or so ago, and she is played by Celia Franca in terms of offended dignity rather than evil malice. Her retinue roughs up the good fairies in a rather infelicitous sequence. Amid all this complication, and with the roles of good and evil genies reduced, the point of the Prologue is not clearly made. The fact that the fairies are endowing young Aurora with the gifts characterized in their variations is unstated, and a newcomer might watch the scene without even becoming aware that a royal infant is the focus of the festivities. The knitting bee, at the start of Act I, becomes another production number, involving slatterns, cat's-paws, halberdiers, hangmen, and a good deal of fussy activity. At the close of the act, the four minor princes, lunging at Carabosse, run one another through. But Petipa's lovely inventions for Aurora are respected, even if eight minstrel girls figure too prominently in parts of the Rose Adagio.

Veronica Tennant, Aurora at both performances I saw, places the choreography precisely, apart from a tendency to push forcefully into arabesque. She does not convey much sense of a developing character, and her dancing lacks, above all, legato—that feeling for a flowing line which links one image to the next. It is stop and start again—sequences chopped into short phrases. And this is a general company fault, observable in most of the solo dancing. The musical director, George Crum, has it, too; Tchaikovsky's long melodies do not flow smoothly enough. The anonymous orchestra is proficient but a bit short on strings. Some of Mr. Crum's rhythms are sludgy and undramatic.

"When, in Act II, Prince Florimund arrives, in the person of Rudolf Nureyev (who dances fourteen of the sixteen New York performances), he gives a splendid demonstration of that phrasing command which, so to speak, keeps the line going through the rests. In Petipa's original the Prince was not a large dancing role (the brilliant male technician of the Petersburg company, Enrico Cecchetti, created not the Prince but the Bluebird—and also Carabosse); Nureyev has enlarged it. He has given himself three variations in Act II, the second of them done to Panorama music shifted to an earlier point in the act. Aurora's second solo has been rewritten, without the alternating *relevés,* and not improved. The voyage to the palace and the Prince's entry are, as I said, strikingly achieved. After the Awakening, the climax of the story, there is a letdown. It is mainly Petipa's fault; here, surely, there should be a *pas de deux* for the Princess 'whose radiant beauty' (in Perrault's words) 'seemed to glow with a kind of heavenly light' and the Prince 'who hardly knew how to express his joy and gratitude'—but, instead, the curtain drops after a few bars. In the old Covent Garden version the difficulty was solved by moving straight into the wedding celebrations, and for the 1968 production Ashton composed a tender new *pas de deux* to the music of the entr'acte. In the Canadian version, on the opening night, Miss Tennant and Nureyev made things worse by expressing no great interest in one another. Reactions in this production were often inadequate. Earlier in Act II, the Prince showed little surprise when the Lilac Fairy joined him but behaved as if fairy apparitions were an everyday occurrence. Act III in the Canadian *Beauty* opens not brilliantly but quietly, with the Sarabande, originally the penultimate dance, brought forward. Then things follow much their usual course. The *pas de quatre* of Jewels becomes a *pas de cinq*, with the Diamonds a twin set. (The male Diamond is allotted Sapphire's 5/4 solo variation.) Bluebirds are placed before Cats; Red Ridinghood, Hop-o'-My-Thumb, and Cinderella are omitted; so, unfortunately, is the apotheosis. Again, the plot point—that all the characters of fairyland have assembled to pay homage to the royal couple—is not potently made, but again there is a display of dense dance patterns around the solos, with much rich 'doubling at the octave' in Nureyev's favored manner.

"The National Ballet of Canada was conceived when the Sadler's Wells/Royal Ballet, after its New York triumphs in 1949, went on to appear in Toronto. The official début was late in 1951; the company comes of age with a *Sleeping Beauty* that shows it need yield nothing in scale of presentation to the London company."*

March 15, 1973, the Royal Ballet produced a new version of *The Sleeping Beauty*. Designed by Peter Farmer, with lighting by William Bundy, the ballet used the choreography of Marius Petipa with new and additional dances by Kenneth MacMillan. Antoinette Sibley was the *Princess Aurora*, Anthony Dowell the *Prince*. The fairy variations were danced by Jennifer Penny, Laura Connor, Alfreda Thorogood, Anita Young, Lesley Collier, and Deanne Bergsma (the *Lilac Fairy*). Lesley Collier and Michael Coleman were the *Bluebirds*. Clement Crisp reviewed it in *The Financial Times*: "'A magical fantasy'—thus I. A. Vsevolozhsky, director of the Imperial Theatres and guiding spirit in the creation of *The Sleeping Beauty* as librettist and designer of the costumes, wrote to Tchaikovsky when he commissioned the score. *Beauty* is, of course, several things: the supreme achievement

* From *A Musical Season* (Viking Press); © 1973 Andrew Porter. Originally in *The New Yorker*.

of Petipa's genius; the pinnacle of nineteenth-century ballet; a *ballet féerie* designed to delight a court audience and pay discreetly flattering homage to the Czar, whose servants the artists of the Imperial Ballet were. For us it is the signature work of the Royal Ballet—symbol of the company's maturity in the 1946 staging, testimony to the international standing of the troupe at the triumphant New York opening in 1949.

"The 1946 staging was decorated by Oliver Messel, and after the austerities of the war it looked supremely opulent. Five years ago a new production, with designs by Henry Bardon and Lila de Nobili—*à la manière de Doré*—was a brave attempt at rethinking the piece; but it lacked airiness, space in which Petipa's inventions could breathe; and hence the new production by Kenneth MacMillan with designs by Peter Farmer, given at a gala in the presence of Her Majesty the Queen last night to pay tribute to the American Friends of Covent Garden whose generosity has paid for this much-needed revision.

"The result is entirely worthwhile. This new staging is Vsevolozhsky's 'magical fantasy,' with steps restored, some choreography renewed, other sections embellished. The *Beauty* has been reawakened, and the whole staging is a re-assertion of MacMillan's love and understanding of the classic tradition of which he is a product. To detail the various innovations must wait until later viewings of the production; suffice it to say that the spirit of this great ballet is honored throughout. MacMillan has done his homework—*Beauty* is a well-documented ballet—and both the spirit of the piece and its choreographic structure have been honorably displayed.

"It is the special merit of Peter Farmer's settings that they give ample room for the dances. Each act of the ballet is conceived in one color: the Prologue is almost entirely blue—the most difficult shade to bring off on stage—and in amid the soaring arches of King Florestan's palace, which suggest a properly magical setting for a fairy tale, the arrival of the fairy godmothers had been staged with extraordinary skill as they enter down mysterious flights of stairs hidden from our eyes.

"For Act One we are in a garden setting which, at first

viewing, seems too ingratiatingly pretty, but here—as throughout the evening—I was conscious of the care taken that nothing should obscure the impact of the dances. In the Prologue, the Fairy variations glittered diamond-sharp against the indigo darkness of the palace; with Aurora's appearance we could see the majesty of Petipa's inventions plain, and Antoinette Sibley was in superb form as the young princess, and later as the vision, and ultimately and most brilliantly as the bride.

"Carabosse—Alexander Grant, tremendous here as throughout the evening—is placed on stage under the guise of a courtier, and the spell is cast, and the Lilac Fairy intervenes, with a real feeling for the magical element that sustains the whole action of the piece. In this scene, as at every point during the action, there is a concern for dramatic credibility; MacMillan has reworked small incidents that have become dully traditional, and the action is carried forward with a nice appreciation for period style.

"The first two acts are set in a suitably fantastic and improbable realm of fairy enchantment; but with the hunting scene we enter a world which, as Vsevolozhsky intended, has some historical reality. The whole development of the staging moves from the imaginary, dream-like setting of Aurora's youth into the clarity and formal elegance of the age of Louis XIV in which she must awake from Carabosse's enchantment.

"The Prince Florimund is Anthony Dowell, princely in style and technique; his journey to Aurora's palace—with its use of panorama as demanded by Tchaikovsky's music—is true theatrical magic and the celebrations of the final act are grand and beautiful. Further comment must wait until the *Beauty* enters the repertory next week: until then a welcome for the production, and for the excellence of the company's performance."

For a contemporary Soviet Russian appraisal of Marius Petipa's achievement in *The Sleeping Beauty*, an essay by Vera Krasovskaya in *Dance Perspectives*, No. 49, is of interest. Yuri Slonimsky's monograph, *Marius Petipa*, translated by Anatole Chujoy in *Dance Index* VI, Nos. 5 and 6 (1947), remains the classic account of that master's work, by the renowned Soviet critic and historian. Also of interest is *Russian Ballet Master: the Memoirs of Marius Petipa,* edited by Lillian Moore and translated by Helen Whittaker (New York, Macmillan, 1958).

SPARTACUS

Ballet in four acts. Music by Aram Khachaturian. Choreography by Yuri Grigorovich. Scenery and costumes by Suliko Virsaladze. First presented in this version by the Bolshoi Ballet at the Bolshoi Theatre, Moscow, April 9, 1968, with Vladimir Vassiliev, Yekaterina Maximova, Maris Liepa, and Nina Timofeyeva in principal roles.

Not the first Soviet ballet to this story, this one by Grigorovich appears to have attracted the most acclaim. A synopsis of the action, based on classical sources such as Plutarch, relating the fate of the Roman slave Spartacus, follows:

ACT ONE, SCENE ONE—SUBJUGATION The Roman legions terrify their captive empire. The army leader is Crassus, cruel, ruthless, and coldly flamboyant. After campaigns in Thrace, where the land has been pillaged and burnt, he brings back Thracian captives to Rome to sell as slaves. Among them are Spartacus and his wife, Phrygia. Spartacus expresses his love of freedom and his refusal to be reconciled to his new state of slavery.

ACT ONE, SCENE TWO—THE SLAVE MARKET The captives are left at the wall of the capital. Men and women are separated so that each will get a better price for the slave dealer from the Roman patricians. Phrygia is parted from Spartacus. Phrygia is desperate in her grief. Her beloved Spartacus has been reduced to slavery, and she herself is subject not only to Rome but the Roman master who has purchased her, and taken her from her husband forever.

ACT ONE, SCENE THREE—ORGY Phrygia has been bought by Crassus, and taken to Crassus's villa in Rome. Aegina, Crassus's concubine, mocks Phrygia's unhappiness and fears. For her, wine, gold, lust, power, and murder are the only facts of pleasure. Crassus is holding an orgiastic party for his friends. As the climax to this, two masked gladiators are brought in. They are to fight blindfolded until one of them is killed. They fight with blind and deathly intensity until one is slain. The victor takes off his mask. It is Spartacus.

Spartacus looks down at his unwitting victim with a terrified compassion. He has been forced to murder a fellow man, a slave like himself. What has he done? What more will he be forced to do?

ACT ONE, SCENE FOUR—THE GLADIATORS' BARRACKS Spartacus, returned to the Gladiators' Barracks, is full of remorse. He calls upon the gladiators to break their chains and escape from their shameful captivity. With superhuman efforts they do this, and overcoming their guards flee to freedom.

ACT TWO, SCENE ONE—THE APPIAN WAY It is night. The gladiators, escaping in glory, meet shepherds resting by the wayside. Inflamed with the spirit of revolt they call the shepherds to join them, and Spartacus's band is joined by many brave men. It is now an army, dedicated to remove the yoke of Rome. Spartacus is proclaimed its leader.

Alone, Spartacus muses on his forced acceptance of power. He is determined to lead his slave army to victory and to free thousands of Rome's victims. But he realizes that he first must find Phrygia and release her from Crassus.

ACT TWO, SCENE TWO—CRASSUS'S VILLA Spartacus discovers Phrygia in Crassus's villa to the south of Rome, and they are joyfully reunited. Meanwhile Crassus is giving a feast for the Roman patricians at which Aegina is also present.

Aegina contemplates Crassus and herself. She not only wants power over Crassus, but wishes to dominate the entire world. He tries to achieve it with power and cruelty, and she with cunning and duplicity. But they share the same ambitions—power, glory, and riches. Both need to acquire all and relinquish nothing.

ACT TWO, SCENE THREE—CRASSUS'S DEFEAT The patricians pander to Crassus and praise his power and victories. But the praise is cut short by the terrifying news that the villa is all but encircled by the advancing army of Spartacus. Crassus, Aegina, and the patricians depart in defeat, leaving Spartacus in possesssion of the villa.

Spartacus ponders on his victory. The Roman legions' success rests solely on the weapons of the legionnaires and the submission of the conquered. The Roman leaders themselves are cowards.

ACT TWO, SCENE FOUR—THE CONTEMPTUOUS GENEROSITY OF SPARTACUS Crassus has been captured and is brought before Spartacus, whom he recognizes as his former gladiator. The rebel soldiers want to execute the Roman general out of hand, but Spartacus asserts his authority and permits Crassus to save his life with the same kind of trial the tyrant imposed upon gladiators. But this time the singlehanded combat will not be blindfolded. The rebels are warriors, not murderers. Crassus fights Spartacus but is no match for him. At point of death Crassus pleads for mercy. With a gesture of contempt the rebel leader lets him go.

ACT THREE, SCENE ONE—CONSPIRACY The dishonored Crassus swears revenge, and Aegina fans his hatred. He calls his soldiers once more into the field, and Aegina sees them off to battle. Left alone, Aegina is full of hatred for Spartacus, fearing she might lose Crassus. She vows vengeance.

ACT THREE, SCENE TWO—THE ENCAMPMENT OF SPARTACUS Aegina steals into Spartacus's camp by night. Phrygia's fears are not helped by Spartacus's attempts to console her. Spartacus is told by a messenger that the Roman legions are advancing on him. He now puts forward his plan of battle, and the weaker among his captains are frightened by the daring of his tactics. Spartacus now calls upon all of them to take an oath of loyalty.

Spartacus, left to his thoughts, notes that the rebel forces will be defeated if there is dissension among their leaders. For all this death in battle is preferable to life as a life.

ACT THREE, SCENE THREE—TREASON The faithful captains of Spartacus await his signal to start the combat and follow him at once. Those of weaker mettle might have followed their example, but Aegina appears out of the darkness bringing wine and whores. They succumb to temptation and fall easily to the advancing vanguard of Crassus's army. Crassus himself rewards Aegina for her help.

Crassus now knows that his revenge will not be complete until Spartacus has been killed, for he cannot forgive the humiliating stain to his honor he suffered as the captive of a slave. He will overtake the remainder of Spartacus's army and annihilate it.

ACT THREE, SCENE FOUR—THE FINAL BATTLE Spartacus's troops are encircled and his army is fast dwindling in the face of vastly superior forces. Spartacus is still fearless and begins to counterattack the legionnaires. Cunningly the Romans ambush him, triumphantly raising him on their spears as he dies a hero's death. Phrygia comes on to the battlefield to find his dead body. She is heartbroken.

NOTES The first Soviet ballet *Spartacus* had choreography by Leonid Yacobson, music by Khachaturian, book by Nikolai Volkov, décor by Valentina Khodasevich, and was first presented at the Kirov State Theatre in Leningrad, December 27, 1956, with Makarov and Zubkovskaya in the principal roles of Spartacus and Phrygia. Another treatment of the same story was made by Igor Moiseyev, with designs by Alexander Konstinovsky, and given at the Bolshoi Theatre, Moscow, March 11, 1958. This version, presented in the United States at the Metropolitan Opera House, New York, September 12, 1962, by the Bolshoi Ballet, featured Dmitri Begak and Maya Plisetskaya in the main roles.

Writing in the British magazine *Dance and Dancers* about her impressions of the Grigorovich *Spartacus*, Patricia Barnes said: "Grigorovich's choreography and conception are brilliant. This is an immensely moving work, filled with imaginative theatrical strokes and performed with blazing intensity by Mikhail Lavrovsky, who at this performance dominated the ballet. The dances are fairly clearly divided between the coldly neo-classic steps given to Crassus and his armies and the more plastique work, expressive and eloquent, for Spartacus and his followers.

"Particularly successful has been the way Grigorovich has used his male dancers. Never have I seen an ensemble used with such sweep and grandeur, and rarely has a dance work on such an ambitious scale succeeded so well in putting across its ideas and dramatic theme with such a minimum of mimetic fuss.

"The opening is startlingly effective. Crassus is seen standing in the center of the stage, arm raised, the lower half of his body surrounded by a wall of shields. Seconds later it is seen as the soldiers of his army spill forward filling the vast stage in a profusion of silver uniforms, shields and swords.

"The tragic ending is in its way as admirable as the ballet's opening. The black-clad grieving figure of Phrygia is lifted high by the followers of Spartacus and the body of her husband is handed up to her, together with his battle shield. She lays the shield on his chest and, eyes cast down, sorrowfully contemplates the dead Spartacus. It is a beautifully conceived scene and brings the curtain down on a work of truly heroic dimensions.

"Mikhail Lavrovsky's Spartacus is a wonder to behold. It is a superbly thought-out role and Lavrovsky has explored every dramatic nuance of it. From our first view of him as a slave in bondage, through his moments of resolution as he vows to free the slaves in captivity, until his final battle, he never departs from a characterization that is deeply felt and powerfully projected.

"A particularly superb episode is a gladiator fight. Two men, blindfolded, are brought in for the entertainment of Crassus's court, and fight for their lives. One kills the other—he takes off his helmet, and it is Spartacus, grieving over the fellow slave he has been forced to kill. As he stands there his face reflects the bitter anguish of his heart and with it we see the beginnings of his revolt, the first stirrings of his determination to free himself and his fellow-slaves from his ruthless captors.

"Almost as impressive was the sweetly passionate portrayal of Phrygia by Natalia Bessmertnova. Her dancing, so extraordinarily individual, had the elegiac beauty of a poem and her dark eyes and pale face caught at the heart.

"In a role that was created by Maris Liepa (and one could see how brilliant he must have been), young Mikhail Gabovich was extraordinarily good. If he looked on the young side, he could hardly be blamed, being under twenty, and he nevertheless gave a portrayal of genuine power. He presented Crassus as a warrior both arrogant and heartless, and his dancing was lithely elegant.

"The last of the four principal roles, Aegina, is the least interesting, being rather more of a stereotype. It was performed on this occasion by Svetlana Adyrkhaeva, who danced with a sveltely voluptuous allure.

"Finally, the dancing of the company, for which no praise could be too high. The men in particular outdid themselves in convincing one that the stage was filled with hundreds. Their attack and technical mastery was constantly outstanding."

Clive Barnes in the magazine of the Friends of Covent Garden, *About the House*, said that the Grigorovich *Spartacus* was "undoubtedly the most successful Soviet ballet since *Romeo and Juliet*." The Grigorovich *Spartacus* was performed by the Bolshoi Ballet in London for the first time July 17, 1969.

LE SPECTRE DE LA ROSE

Ballet in one act. Music by Carl Maria von Weber. Choreography by Michel Fokine. Book by J. L. Vaudoyer. Scenery and costumes by Léon Bakst. First presented by Diaghilev's Ballets Russes at the Théâtre de Monte Carlo, Monte Carlo, April 19, 1911, with Vaslav Nijinsky and Tamara Karsavina. First presented in the United States by Diaghilev's Ballets Russes at the Metropolitan Opera House, New York, April 3, 1916, with Alexander Gavrilov and Lydia Lopokova.

This is a ballet danced by two people, a romantic *pas de deux.* The ballet has a simple story, but the story is so slight that we must refer to the actual dancing for an impression of the ballet. Its first performances convinced audiences that it was possible for two dancers, alone on a stage, to create a story and at the same time to create a mood in which that story could become real, like a lyric poem.

Le Spectre de la Rose is based on a poem, a poem by the nineteenth-century French poet and novelist and great critic of the ballet Théophile Gautier. Just as Gautier adapted the work of another poet, Heinrich Heine, to produce the romantic classic *Giselle,* so his own creative work gave to another age the inspiration for another romantic ballet. In Gautier's poem a rose addresses the girl who wore it to a ball. The rose is grateful for having danced with her all evening, grateful even for death on her breast, and tells the maiden that his ghost will continue to dance, at her bedside, all night long, to express his love.

The ballet *Le Spectre de la Rose* has a real setting but, as in *Giselle,* it is a dream that comes to life within this setting that creates its romanticism. The music is Carl Maria von Weber's *Invitation to the Dance,* as orchestrated by Hector Berlioz.

The curtain rises on a young girl's boudoir. The room is formal, high, and cool, with immense windows that look on to a garden. There is a bed on the right and on the left a small dressing table. The colors are blue and white, and as we look at the walls and the furniture and see the moon through the French windows, we imagine that the girl who lives here is demure and innocent. The room is uncluttered, plain in spite of its elegance; it makes you interested in the life it contains. The young girl enters. She is dressed formally, in a long white gown. She takes off the cape she wears about her shoulders, unties her bonnet, and we notice that she holds in her hand a red rose. She refuses to relinquish it as she moves about the room, turning slowly, dancing with an invisible partner, remembering the excitement of her first ball. She has come back from the dance to her familiar surroundings and finds the room a little old-fashioned; it has not changed as she imagines she has changed. She is in love. She presses her lover's rose against her cheek and sits down in a white chair near one of the windows. Half-asleep from fatigue, she still wishes to relive her first encounter with romance. But sleep soon overtakes her. Her hand falls from her face, and the red rose slips from her fingers to the floor.

There is almost no sound for a moment, and then suddenly, buoyantly, the orchestra plays at full volume a quick, intoxicating waltz. As this rush of sound fills the room, through the open window the spirit of the rose leaps in a high, smooth trajectory to stand poised behind the girl's chair. He dances alone as the girl sleeps, moving about the room effortlessly, seeming to touch the floor almost against his will, dancing with the lightness of the rose petals that adorn his body.

He touches the girl, and now—awake in her dream—she dances with him. When the two dance together to the soaring waltz, the young girl moves with the grace of the spirit she has invoked; as they glide and leap about the room, their dance is absolutely continuous, never-ending, unbroken in its flow of movement into movement; the only thing that can stop it is the music. The girl is inspired by her partner as naturally as she held the rose to her cheek and—with his strong, but tender, aid—she becomes not simply a beautiful young girl in love with love, but a part of the romantic night.

The dream cannot last. The waltz melody fades. The girl goes to her chair and sits as before, her arm limp at her side, pointing to the rose on the floor. The spirit of the rose hovers gently over her head in farewell and in a continuous movement rushes toward the window. He disappears into the oncoming dawn at the high point of a leap that seems never-ending.

The light of the sun disturbs the girl. She moves in her sleep, then wakens lazily, rubbing her eyes, not yet aware of where she is. She is still thinking of the spirit of the rose and looks for her mysterious partner. He is not there! She sees she is alone in her own room and that she must have been dreaming. Then she sees the rose on the floor at her feet. She picks it up gently and holds it against her breast, content that the dream is still with her.

THE STILL POINT

Music by Claude Debussy. Choreography by Todd Bolender. First presented by the Dance Drama Company, 1954, with Emily Frankel and Mark Ryder. First presented in New York, April 10, 1955, at the YMHA. Presented by the New York City Ballet, March 14, 1956, with Melissa Hayden and Jacques d'Amboise in leading roles. Presented by the City Center Joffrey Ballet, September 24, 1970, with Pamela Johnson and Dennis Wayne. Lighting by Jennifer Tipton. Assistant to Mr. Bolender: John Mandia.

The Still Point, which takes its title from T. S. Eliot's poem *Four Quartets,* is a dance drama arranged to music by Debussy—the first three movements of the String Quartet, *Opus 10,* transcribed for orchestra by Frank Black. The drama is about a young girl who, lonely at first and rejected, finds love. She endures jealousy, embarrassment, and torment as her girl friends rejoice in young love. Rejected by them, she rejects herself and suffers. She so wants a young man of her own that she dreams, too, and simply waits, fearing a little a real encounter. Finally, a boy comes, watches her as she dreams, then touches her shoulder. She reacts at first as if she had been stung and appears to resist him. Realizing that he has found an extraordinarily sensitive girl, the boy is gentle with her. She watches him dance, then they dance together, becoming closer, too, in thought, as they touch. They find in each other, at the end, the dreams they have had.

NOTES Writing in *Dance Magazine* of *The Still Point,* the critic Doris Hering said that "Mr. Bolender has uncanny insight into the feelings of young women. His girl in *Mother Goose Suite,* his debutante in *Souvenirs,* and the tortured protagonist of *The Still Point* are all sisters under the skin—poignant sisters seeking fulfillment in romantic love. Of them all, the girl in *The Still Point* is the most touching because she is delineated with the most depth and at the same time with the most simplicity. In fact, simplicity is the prime virtue of this little ballet. Mr. Bolender has had the courage and the care to let the dancing speak out honestly without any mimetic overlay. And in Melissa Hayden and Jacques d'Amboise in the leading roles; and Irene Larsson, Roy Tobias, Jillana and John Mandia in secondary roles, he found responsive instruments. As the lonely girl, Melissa Hayden wove endless nuance and pathos into her portrayal, and yet the danced outlines were contained and beautifully clear. As her friend, Jacques d'Amboise communicated the steady masculinity that we have associated heretofore only with Igor Youskevitch."

SWAN LAKE

Dramatic ballet in four acts. Music by Peter Ilyich Tchaikovsky. Book by V. P. Begitchev and Vasily Geltzer. First presented, with choreography by Julius Reisinger, at the Bolshoi Theatre, Moscow, March 4, 1877, with Pauline Karpakova in the leading role. This incomplete and unsuccessful production was superseded by a new choreographic version by Lev Ivanov and Marius Petipa, which was presented for the first time in a complete, four-act production at the Maryinsky Theatre, St. Petersburg, February 8, 1895, with Pierina Legnani in the double role of Odette-Odile. *Act Two of this version was presented for the first time at the Maryinsky Theatre, St. Petersburg, February 29, 1894, with Legnani as* Odette. *Scenery by Botcharov and Levogt. First presented in western Europe in complete form in Prague, Czechoslovakia, June 27, 1907, with choreography by Achille Viscusi. First presented in the United States at the Metropolitan Opera House, New York, December 20, 1911, with Catherine Geltzer as* Odette-Odile, *Mikhail Mordkin as* Prince Siegfried, *and Alexandre Volinine as* Benno. *This production was staged by Mordkin after the Petipa-Ivanov choreography. Scenery by James Fox. First presented in England in complete form by the Sadler's Wells Ballet at the Sadler's Wells Theatre, London, November 29, 1934, with the Petipa-Ivanov choreography reproduced by Nicholas Sergeyev; Alicia Markova as* Odette-Odile, *Robert Helpmann as* Prince Siegfried. *Scenery and costumes by Hugh Stevenson. Presented complete by the San Francisco Ballet, in a version staged by William Christensen, 1940. The revised Sadler's Wells production, with scenery and costumes by Leslie Hurry, was first presented in the United States October 20, 1949, with Margot Fonteyn and Robert Helpmann. Presented complete with the original choreography of Lev Ivanov staged by David Blair, by the Atlanta Civic Ballet, August 24, 1965. Presented complete with Ivanov's choreography staged by David Blair by American Ballet Theatre at the Civic Opera House, Chicago, February 16, 1967. Scenery by Oliver Smith. Costumes by Freddy Wittop. Lighting by Jean Rosenthal. Presented in varied versions by many companies.*

Musically, and as a dance drama, *Swan Lake* is undoubtedly the most popular of all classical ballets. It is possible to see at least a major portion of the complete *Swan Lake*—the famous second act—danced by almost every ballet company in the world. And the ballet is a favorite of ballerinas as well as audiences. All leading dancers want to dance *Swan Lake* at least once in their careers, and all audiences want to see them dance it. To succeed in *Swan Lake* is to become overnight a ballerina. Petipa and Ivanov are to the dancer what Shakespeare is to the actor: if you can succeed in their choreography parts, there is a suggestion that you can succeed at anything.

Why is it that *Swan Lake* has been so consistently popular with both audiences and dancers for so long a time? What about its chief rivals in the classical repertory—*Giselle, The Sleeping Beauty*, and *Coppélia*—why are they not as popular? If we set aside practical considerations (unlike *Swan Lake*, these other ballets cannot successfully be shortened into one-act versions; the part does not provide the spirit of the whole), we find the answer in *Swan Lake*'s romantic and tragic story and the music that accompanies its unfolding.

The heroines of these other classics all have some relation to the real world—they are peasant girl or princesses. Strange things may happen to them, but they live within determined conventions. The heroine of *Swan Lake* has another story. She is a princess of the night; she is all magic, a creature of the imagination.

On one level, her story is a girl-meets-boy story: girl meets boy, girl loses boy, girl gets boy, and then both are lost. What prevents this from being silly is the character of the girl. She is Queen of the Swans, a beautiful bird, except for the brief time—between midnight and dawn—when the mysterious sorcerer, Von Rotbart, allows her to become a beautiful woman. In the world of sky and water she is at home, but in the real world, where romance is possible, she seems to be irretrievably lost. The great love she comes to have for a worldly prince is doomed at its start; she has no control over her destiny.

The Swan Queen is the opposite of the Firebird, the bird triumphant; she is immediately pathetic, a creature whose initial fear and consuming love interest us immediately. The dignity and courage and authority she possesses as Queen of the Swans become, in the ballet, the dignity of the woman in love. Humanly speaking, even in this magical world she inhabits, she is never unreal or absurd to us, because we see that love does not shatter her dignity; rather, it ennobles her beauty and explains her universal appeal.

ACT ONE—THE GARDEN OF PRINCE SIEGFRIED'S CASTLE Before the curtain rises, an overture warns us of the impending tragedy of the story. After the woodwinds have introduced the principal romantic theme, and the strings have taken it up, there is a faltering: a soft, gradually building questioning by the strings. And the answer comes in boldly asserted warnings by the crashing of cymbals and resounding trumpet calls. But soon, over these crescendos, the romantic theme returns at full, conquering volume. It quietens, and the curtain rises.

This is Prince Siegfried's twenty-first birthday, and the young prince is celebrating the occasion in the garden of his ancestral palace. Young people from the surrounding estates have come to pay tribute to him. Benno, friend to the prince, is talking to a group of twelve young men. Wolfgang, the prince's old tutor, comes in merrily and is almost immediately attracted to the bottles of wine that stand on a table at the right. The atmosphere is one of anticipation, and as the trumpets blare the climax of a spirited march, the host enters. The handsome prince is not haughty; neither is he familiar. He is delighted to see his friends, thanks them as they congratulate him, claps his old tutor on the back affectionately, and prepares to enjoy the festivities that have been arranged in his honor.

First there is a *pas de trois*, danced by two girls and a boy. (Since the Diaghilev company's second-act version of 1911, this *pas de trois* has often been performed as a *divertissement* in Act Two. Sometimes it is danced by Benno and two cygnets, sometimes by a first huntsman and two swan princesses, as in the production by the Sadler's Wells Theatre Ballet. Where the *pas de trois* is not interpolated in Act Two, the music for the variation of the *danseur* is almost invariably used for a variation by Benno.) For the dance of the two girls and a boy, the music is lightly melodic and flowing. Now each dances alone: the first girl performs to blithe, tripping music that increases in speed; the boy, to strongly accented rhythms that mark the precision of his *entrechats* and turns in the air; and the second girl, to a light, almost joking theme. Climactic music accompanies the final display of virtuosity that all three perform.

While most of the assembled guests have been watching the dance, the old tutor has been privately celebrating the prince's coming of age by drinking as much wine as possible. Just as everyone begins to enjoy the party, the conviviality is disturbed by the entrance of the princess mother and her four ladies in waiting. Siegfried goes to his mother and escorts her into the garden. She observes his friends with considerable disdain; there is an effort to hide the wine bottles, and poor old Wolfgang finds himself in obvious disfavor. The princess mother indicates to her son that his coming of age is hardly the occasion for levity. He responds to this opinion dutifully, but with apparent resistance. Siegfried is further disturbed when his mother points out to him that he must soon choose a wife. Her suggestion is in the nature of a command, and Siegfried turns stubbornly away. Tomorrow night, his mother reminds him, his birthday will be celebrated formally at a court ball, and there, from among the loveliest ladies of the land, he must select his future wife. Siegfried sees that argument is impossible; as he kisses his mother's hand and leads her out of the garden, he seems to bend to her will.

Wolfgang gestures his pleasure at the departure of the dominating princess mother. He attempts to restore the spirit of the happy occasion by claiming that, old as he is, he can dance better than any of the younger men. Everyone laughs at him, but Wolfgang is not to be outdone. He approaches one of the village maidens, who giggles as he takes her by the hand and begins to dance. The melody to which he partners her is subdued and charmingly sentimental, sweetly echoing the joys of youth. Soon Wolfgang is having such a good time that he tries to surpass himself by whirling his partner around and around. In the process he becomes dizzy and falls to the ground, taking his partner with him.

Now Prince Siegfried is convinced that the only thing to do is to enjoy himself to the utmost: tomorrow, after all, is another day. The prince signals that the celebration should continue. Wine is poured for all the guests, and village couples dance a vigorous polka that completely restores to the gathering its natural spirit of gaiety. Still Siegfried broods; the celebration has failed to dispel his apprehension in regard to the morrow.

Night begins to fall. Benno knows that Siegfried must be distracted for the remainder of the evening. He hears the sound of fluttering wings overhead, looks up, and sees in the sky beautiful wild swans in full flight. Against the sound of harp and strings, the oboe sounds softly the theme of these enchanted birds. Benno suggests that the prince form a hunting party and go in search of the swans. Siegfried consents; crossbows are brought, and flaming torches are provided to light the way through the woods. The village girls circle the stage and exit. Wolfgang alone is unwilling to accompany the hunting party. As the full orchestra takes up the mysterious and doomful theme that heralded the swans, Wolfgang tells Siegfried that he is too old, that he will remain in the garden. The young men bid him good-by and rush off into the night. The curtain falls as the old tutor stands alone in the center of the empty garden, his bottle his only friend.

ACT TWO—A LAKESIDE While the curtain is lowered, the music continues to develop the theme of strange foreboding. Then all is quiet for a moment. As the music resumes, the curtain rises on a forest scene; a great lake, its shining surface undisturbed by the wind, shimmers in the moonlight. The music begins again. The hunting party enters, led by Benno. All carry crossbows. The men look above them through the trees, searching for the swans; they are astonished to see that the swans have settled on the lake and, within a few feet of them, are placidly gliding by. Leading the group of swans is a beautiful white bird, apparently their queen. The diamonds in her crown reflect spangles of light over the dark water.

A flourish from the orchestra heralds the arrival of the prince. The hunting party bows to him. Benno hastens to point out to Siegfried that the swans can be seen close by.

The prince directs the men to hasten along the lakeside ahead of the swans; he is about to follow them off, when he sees something in the distance that gives him pause. He stops, close by the lakeside, then retreats hurriedly across the glade to conceal himself. He has seen something so strange and extraordinary that he must observe it closely in secret.

No sooner has Siegfried hidden himself than the most beautiful woman he has ever seen enters the quiet glade. He cannot believe his eyes, for the girl appears to be both swan and woman. Her lovely face is enclosed by swan feathers, which cling closely against her hair. Her pure white dress is embellished with soft, downy swan feathers, and on her head rests the crown of the Queen of the Swans. The young woman thinks she is alone. She poses in arabesque, then remains almost motionless, softly bending her cheek down against her shoulder in a gesture reminiscent of a swan smoothing its feathers. The music informs us of the pathos of this gesture, and Siegfried is so enchanted by the magical creature that he enters the glade. He moves quietly, lest he disturb her.

The girl is terrified, her whole body trembles, her arms press against her breast in an attitude of almost helpless self-protection; she backs away from the prince, moving frantically on points that drive desperately against the ground. Her arms seek the air for freedom, for escape. The prince, already in love, begs her not to fly away. The girl looks at him and gestures that she is afraid. Siegfried wonders why. She points to his crossbow and draws her arm back as if to let fly an arrow, then holds her arm over her face, cowering with fear. The prince indicates that he will never shoot her; he will protect her. The girl bows to him in gratitude.

The prince now asks her who she is, why she is here? The girl's hands enclose the crown on her head: she is Odette, Queen of the Swans. The prince salutes her and says that he will honor her, but how is it that she is the Swan Queen? The Swan Queen asks for his patience and points to the lake. The lake, she indicates, was made by her mother's tears. Her mother wept because an evil sorcerer, Von Rotbart, made her daughter into the Swan Queen. And swan she must always be, except between midnight and dawn, unless a man should love her, marry her, and never love another. Then she will be saved and be a swan no longer.

Siegfried holds his hands to his heart and says that he loves her, that he will marry her and never love another. He swears his faithfulness. Now angry at the fate of his love, he demands to know where this Von Rotbart hides himself. Just at this point, the magician appears at the lakeside. His owl-like face is a hideous mask; he reaches out his claws, beckoning Odette to return to him. [In one-act versions of *Swan Lake*, this lengthy mime passage is often shortened and the music is used to accompany a dance in which the prince, his bow set aside, follows the dancing Swan Queen, lifts her as they circle the stage, embraces her, and supports her gently in poses until she breaks away from him at the entrance of Von Rotbart.] Von Rotbart points menacingly at Siegfried. Odette moves between them, begging Von Rotbart for mercy. Trumpets sound in blaring, warning crescendo. The prince seizes his bow, kneels, and aims it at the magician. Odette beseeches him to stop and runs diagonally across the stage toward Siegfried. She touches his stretched bow and stands over it and her lover in extended arabesque. Von Rotbart disappears. Siegfried rises and embraces Odette. The music quietens. The prince puts his arm about the girl, and they go toward the forest.

The prince tells the girl that she must come the next evening to the court ball. He has just come of age and must marry and at the ball he will choose her as his bride. Odette replies that she cannot come to the ball until she is married—until Von Rotbart no longer has power over her—otherwise the magician will expose her and their romance will perish. She knows, she tells Siegfried, that Von Rotbart will stop at nothing to keep her in his power, that he will contrive artfully to make Siegfried break his promise to her, and that should he do so, should he be faithless, Von Rotbart will cause her own death. Siegfried again swears his faithfulness.

When the lovers have left the glade, Odette's charges, all the swans who, like herself, assume human form only between the hours of midnight and dawn, dance in from the lakeside.

They form a single serpentine line that moves toward the front, then face the audience in a triangular grouping.

Soon Benno, the prince's friend, comes upon the dancing swans. They encircle him, rushing past him with their fluttering arms. Benno, unaware of the mystery of these creatures, thinks only of the hunt. The swans cower in fear and rush together in a close group by the lakeside. Benno hails the rest of the hunting party. The huntsmen marvel at his discovery and aim their crossbows at the swans. Suddenly the music crashes warningly; Siegfried runs in and behind him comes Odette. The Swan Queen stands before the group of trembling swans and stretches out her arms to protect them; the huntsmen must kill her first. As Odette begs the men for mercy, Siegfried orders them to lower their bows and to respect the magical birds. When the huntsmen have learned that, like Odette, the swans are really unfortunate girls in the hands of an evil magician, they remove their caps and bow in apology to the maidens.

Siegfried and Odette again vanish into the forest, the huntsmen leave the scene, and the swan maidens come forward in three columns to dance. They dance to a charming waltz; their ensemble is dominated by two swan maidens who emerge from the group to dance in unison between lines formed by their friends. When the dance is over, the swans gather together in picturesque groupings to form a final tableau.

Now the swan maidens gather at either side of the stage. Siegfried enters with Benno. The harp sounds a series of arpeggios. The prince searches for Odette among the swans. He does not find her. The huntsmen return and stand among the swan maidens. Siegfried stands with his friend in the center of the glade. At the back, behind them, Odette enters softly. She touches Benno's shoulder, poses for a brief second in arabesque, then comes forward. It is as if she had not seen the prince. The harp is plucked gently. Odette rises on point, then sinks slowly to the ground. She rests on her left knee, her right leg stretched before her. She bends down low, her arms reach forward like enclosing wings, and to the quiet rhythm of the music her body stirs expectantly. Siegfried comes forward, reaches down to her hands, and raises her. The solo violin begins quietly the wistfully romantic theme of the adagio. Odette pirouettes with slow, romantic adroitness in his arms. Now her love supports her as she bends low in a deep arabesque. Each of the huntsmen, observing the beauty of this love duet, now stands between two swan maidens, his arms about their waists.

Odette moves to Benno, and the prince admires her loveliness as his friend holds her in arabesque. The beautiful Swan Queen returns to her lover, moves in supported attitude, then rests for a moment against his breast. She moves now slightly away, rises on point, takes Siegfried's hand, and then—raising her right leg straight before her—removes her hand from his; for a fraction of a second, as she lifts both arms up, the idyllic nature of this dance is luminously clear: the relation of Odette and Siegfried is one of complete sweetness and absolute trust. Odette falls back, and Benno catches her gently in his arms as her right leg closes against her left. Benno lifts her up, she returns to the prince, nestles against his shoulder as he embraces her softly, and the movement is repeated a second time. Siegfried puts his arms about Odette at its conclusion and leads her toward the lakeside. The swan maidens turn in arabesque, to the gently hopping rhythm of the woodwinds, and cross the stage before the lovers. As the solo violin resumes, Odette and the prince run forward quietly between the swan maidens. Siegfried lifts Odette high in his arms to the violin's music; he lifts her again, and then she pirouettes in his arms. He continues to lift her effortlessly to the demand of the theme; she turns to his encircling arms, then moves away on point with a gesture of obeisance and love.

Now a number of the swan maidens are arranged in a diagonal line across the stage. The huntsmen, standing in back, lift some of the girls to their shoulders. The prince moves back. Odette goes to him, and Siegfried opens his arms to her. She turns away then and, hopping softly, moves in arabesque down the line formed by her charges. Siegfried follows her adoringly and, taking her about the waist, lifts her at arm's length high above his head. He lifts her again, releases her, and, as she reaches the end of the diagonal, lifts her to carry her to the right side of the stage. The violin repeats the theme of the first lifts of the adagio, and this time, to the melody, Odette executes supported arabesques followed swiftly by pirouettes that she terminates with an open pointing of her leg to the left. These movements are repeated with the music.

The swan maidens are now grouped on the left. After the final pirouette, Siegfried stands close behind Odette. She leans back softly against him and balances. The prince opens his arms as Odette opens hers and gently he moves her arms close to her body, as if he were quieting her frightened wings. Siegfried moves slightly from side to side, gently rocking his love. Odette rushes away, seemingly compelled to resist the embrace, and balances in arabesque, both arms encircling her head. From behind, the prince takes her arms, moves them back close to her body, and Odette leans back against him, now confessing the power of her love for him.

The adagio nears its end. Siegfried turns the Swan Queen slowly as she stands on point, her right foot trembling in *petits battements*. She turns a final series of slow pirouettes in his arms and then is held by the prince; both arms over her head, her left leg extended to the side. Siegfried holds her thus, then releases her; she balances for an instant and then, holding her pose, falls to the side; at the last breathless moment she is caught in the arms of her lover's friend. The adagio is over. The two lovers and Benno leave the stage.

Four cygnets appear and dance with bright, youthful precision a *pas de quatre* that is accompanied by lightly bouncing music of great charm. This is followed by a dance for two swan princesses. Here the music is openly joyous, uninhibited in its bounding, youthful expression of happiness in newfound love.

Just as this dance ends, we notice that dawn is approaching. Odette returns and dances a variation that is at first modestly lyrical; her arms stretch back and her neck arches backward as she balances in arabesques, and we feel that to this beautiful woman such a pose is the most beautiful and natural thing in the world. The music increases in momentum, and the variation finishes with a dazzling diagonal of rapid pirouettes across the stage.

The swan maidens are alerted by the coming light and prepare to return to the lake. Odette, in their midst, comes forward and—from the front of the stage toward the back—executes to the driving rhythm of the rapid music a series of quick, desperate movements that reflect her fear at her departure from her lover. Siegfried beseeches her to stay, but she cannot. Benno kneels before her. Now impelled to become again the Swan Queen, she rushes toward Benno and stands in full flight on his extended knee. Siegfried reaches out for her, lifts her down gently. The swan maidens have responded already to the return of the mysterious music that presaged the first appearance of the magical creatures: Odette and Siegfried are alone. Von Rotbart appears by the lakeside, beckoning Odette to come to him. She is helpless and must obey. She holds out her arms yearningly toward Siegfried, but her feet carry her back toward the lake. Her body trembles with helplessness, and she glides farther and farther away from him, to disappear in the new dawn. Siegfried reaches out toward her, unable to console himself by her promise to return.

The huntsmen enter the glade. Benno comforts the prince, and then, at the sound of wings overhead, all look up to see the swans in full flight, led by their queen. The curtain falls.

ACT THREE—THE GREAT HALL OF PRINCE SIEGFRIED'S CASTLE

The time is the following evening. The ball that the princess mother has arranged in honor of her son is about to take place. After a long and regal musical introduction, the curtain rises on the hall of the palace. There is a roll of drums, and a march begins. Here in the great hall, the royal thrones are placed on a dais to the right; on the left, with a short flight of steps leading down to the ballroom, is the formal entrance. Across the back, stretching into the distance, is a long, curved colonnade.

A flourish of music marks the entrance of two royal pages. The prince and his mother enter the room. The assembled guests bow to them as they proceed to the dais. The princess mother turns to speak to her son. Siegfried looks out over the ballroom with a blank stare; he is thinking of his meeting with Odette and his vow to be faithful to her. His mother, jealous of his preoccupation, addresses him somewhat in the manner of Gertrude upbraiding Hamlet: "Are you ill? You must pay attention to our guests; they are beginning to remark your strange behavior." The prince throws off his thoughts and assures his mother that he will not fail in his obligations.

Ambassadors from foreign lands, attired in colorful native costume, have come to pay tribute to the prince on his coming of age. A trumpet sounds a flourish, and a herald announces the arrival of six beautiful girls invited by the princess mother as prospective brides for her son. The girls are attired identically in stunning evening dresses and each carries a large feathered fan. The princess mother nods to them, and they begin to dance before the prince to the strains of a courtly waltz.

Siegfried pretends to watch them, but actually he thinks only of the lakeside glade and his meeting with Odette. His mother taps him on the arm and warns him that he must dance with his guests. The prince descends from the dais and dances briefly with each of the would-be brides. He dances automatically, with no interest, holding the girls casually about the waist and scarcely looking at his partners. The girls are dismayed at his indifference, but cannot display their displeasure too markedly lest their hostess be disappointed in them. Siegfried returns to the dais and again sinks into melancholy.

The princess mother rises and approaches the prospective brides. She thanks them for the lovely waltz and congratulates them on their beauty. Now she turns to the prince, asking him to confirm her opinion. Siegfried gestures that the girls are very pretty, indeed, but he does not wish to marry any of them. He loves another. He bows coldly to the girls. As his mother upbraids him, the music is interrupted suddenly.

Again the trumpet sounds a flourish. All the guests turn to watch the door. A herald hastens to inform the princess mother that a strange couple has arrived. He does not know who they are, but avows that the woman is a creature of rare beauty. Siegfried looks expectantly toward the door. His mother orders that the guests be admitted. There is a crash of cymbals, the room darkens mysteriously, and the music hurries warningly into a repetition of the theme that marked the fate of the Swan Queen.

The light returns, and a tall bearded knight enters with his daughter. As the knight introduces himself and his daughter, Odile, to the princess mother, Siegfried—excited almost beyond control—stares at the beautiful girl. Although dressed in somber black, she is the image of his beloved Odette. [Although not originally designed for the same dancer, Odile for many years has been danced by the same ballerina who performs the role of Odette; Odette-Odile has become the most famous dual role in ballet.] Odile returns his stare with a steady glance of cold, but passionate, interest. In the distance, framed by an arch of the colonnade, Odette is seen holding out her hands to Siegfried. The prince is so enchanted by the girl he supposes to be the Swan Queen that he does not notice Odette's warning. The vision of the Swan Queen fades. Siegfried takes Odile by the hand. Now he foresees that the ball will be a happy occasion after all! He escorts Odile into the palace garden. Odile's father watches their departure with interest. Unknown to the prince, he is in reality not a knight at all, but Von Rotbart, the evil magician, who has transformed himself and his conniving daughter in order that Siegfried will be deceived and break his promise to Odette never to love another. Convinced that his trickery will doom Odette and Siegfried, Von Rotbart turns to the princess mother with a gracious smile. She is charmed by his flattery and—hopeful that her son will marry a lady of rank, as Odile appears to be—invites Von Rotbart to sit beside her on the dais.

Now the guests from foreign lands, who have come to honor the prince on his birthday, come forward to dance. First, two Spanish couples dance a quick and supple *divertissement* to the sound of music reminiscent of the melodies and rhythm of Spain. Next five Hungarian couples line up and, to the slow, anticipating measures of the music, commence a *czardas* that gathers in speed to end in a whirling finish. A vigorous Polish mazurka danced by eight couples concludes this series of *divertissements.* Von Rotbart indicates his appreciation of this entertainment to the princess mother and then suggests that his daughter, Odile, is the most beautiful dancer at the ball. Just as the princess mother is about to wonder where her son has taken Odile, Prince Siegfried appears with the stunning girl. Von Rotbart leaves the dais and tells Odile that the time has come for her to dance before the princess mother and Prince Siegfried. The orchestra sounds a rhythmic flourish, and the *pas de deux* between Odile and the prince begins. [When it is performed as a separate *divertissement,* this dance is known as the "Black Swan," or "Magic Swan," *pas de deux.* As a *divertissement,* the *pas de deux* necessarily lacks the dramatic impact it possesses as a part of the complete *Swan Lake.*]

This dance dramatically displays the cunning of Odile and the infatuation of the prince. In opposition to the adagio of Act Two, it has another kind of grace: it is full of pride and arrogance, rather than tenderness; it has the cold, dazzling light of a bright diamond. As Odile goes to Siegfried, Von Rotbart stands on the right, watching with guile and satisfaction. The prince welcomes his new love with joy: now his mother and the whole court will see how wonderful she is. Odile pirouettes across the ballroom floor, then turns rapidly in Siegfried's arms. Von Rotbart calls to her, and she goes obediently to her father, standing in arabesque with her hand on his shoulder. Von Rotbart whispers in her ear. Odile looks back at the prince and nods. She has grown confident with the success of her disguise and, when she returns to the prince, is determined to display her power over him with even more breath-taking skill. Siegfried supports her adoringly as she bends low in arabesque, but then Odile lets go his hand to stand alone, poised, balanced, splendidly self-sufficient. She goes back to Von Rotbart, and this time the impetuous prince follows her. After receiving more instructions from her father, she rejoins her lover, who supports her with glowing pride in bold and confident movements. For a moment the two are separated. They promenade across the ballroom floor, Odile walking with masterful authority and steely confidence, and meet in the center of the stage to resume the dance. Suddenly Odette again appears in the distant colonnade. Von Rotbart immediately notes her presence and signals to Odile, who steps between Siegfried and the vision. Odette extends her clasped hands to Siegfried, despairing of her fate if he abandons her. The enchanted Siegfried has no idea that she is there; the cunning Odile smiles at him—a cold, even smile in which he can discern nothing but warmth for his passion. The vision of Odette persists, and Odile becomes angry at this interference. She runs to Siegfried and places her hands over his eyes. Siegfried is so infatuated that he regards this gesture as flirtatious and fails to see that Odette, all hopes gone, has vanished, weeping, in the distance.

The *pas de deux* continues. Odile, now the winning seductress, carries her conceit still farther, and the innocent prince is utterly in her hands. The dance ends as the prince kneels before Odile and the proud, evil girl stands over him in high, conquering arabesque. With the final note of the music, she gives a curt, triumphant toss of her head.

The prince now dances a variation expressive of his great joy in rediscovering the girl he supposes to be Odette. Odile follows with a quick final dance designed to whip Siegfried's passion still further, and she succeeds in this brilliantly. Her variation contains a dazzling circling of the stage with small, swift turns, a series of quick, close movements performed in a straight line from the front of the stage to the back, and finally a series of thirty-two *fouettés*. These relentless, whipping turns sum up her power over the prince and, with disdainful joy, seem to lash at his passion. Helplessly bewitched, he rejoins his enchantress for a brief final dance.

Siegfried then approaches Von Rotbart and asks for Odile's hand in marriage. Von Rotbart immediately consents. Siegfried announces his decision to his mother, and Odile bows before the princess mother. Von Rotbart, still unsatisfied, addresses the prince further: he asks Siegfried to swear an oath of fidelity of Odile, asks him to promise that he will never love another. Siegfried's love for Odile is so great that he is offended by this request, and then, too, he knows that he has heard those words before. Why should they be asked again, he wonders. He looks at Odile, and his fate hangs in the balance. The music hesitates. He takes the oath. At that moment there is a crash of thunder. The ballroom darkens. The theme of the abandoned Odette screams above the orchestra. Quick flashes of light show the frightened courtiers fleeing the ballroom, the distraught princess mother, and Von Rotbart and Odile standing before the prince in a final triumph of self-revelation. Their hideous, cruel laughter Siegfried cannot bear, and he turns to see in the distance the pathetic figure of Odette, reaching out to him helplessly, her body racked with sobs. He falls to the floor in an agony of guilt.

ACT FOUR—THE LAKESIDE The swan maidens have gathered by the side of the lake. They are sad and wistful at the fate of their queen. Their grief is reflected in the still tableaux they form with a group of small black swans who have joined them and in the dance the little swans do with their elders to soft, tender music. They yearn for the return of Odette. When she appears, weeping, they try to comfort her, but she tells them they do wrong to give her false hope. "I have been betrayed and I must die: the magician has won."

The music cries out with her grief, and she runs toward the lake. Two swan princesses intercept her and urge her to wait. They remind her that Siegfried is only human, that he could not have known the power of sorcery and thus could have had no suspicion of Von Rotbart's design. "You must wait," they advise her, "and hear the prince." "No," she gestures, "I have lost him and could not bear it."

Some of the swans hear Siegfried in the distance, calling for Odette, and tell her that he approaches. The Swan Queen orders a group of little swans to stand before her so that the prince will not discover her. Siegfried rushes into the clearing and frantically searches for Odette among the swans. Desperate, he asks the swans if they have seen her; he is about to abandon hope when the swans that surround Odette bend down and he sees her standing among them. He runs to her and takes her in his arms, asking for her forgiveness, swearing his infinite love. They go into the forest, and the swan maidens continue their dancing. When the lovers return, Odette has forgiven her lover, but she tells him—with tears streaming down her smiling face—it is no use, for what is her forgiveness alongside her death, which now must surely follow. "Von Rotbart is relentless. My life was forfeit if I should be betrayed. Only in death am I released from his power."

Now Odette dances to music that is tenderly beautiful. She moves softly in a long diagonal enclosed by the swans and, at the moment of her imminent death, expresses her undying love for the prince. Von Rotbart, enraged at Odette's delay, hovers over the scene disguised as a monstrous owl. He vows vengeance on her and all the swans. The swan maidens tremble as Siegfried defies Von Rotbart, who is momentarily overpowered by the strength of the prince's love for Odette.

The lovers embrace as Von Rotbart disappears. Odette then reminds the prince that only in death will she be released from Von Rotbart, only in death will she be free to love him forever. Her gestures are dramatic and sure as she tells him this, and suddenly she rushes across the stage in a swift diagonal to the shore's edge and throws herself into the lake as the music reaches a surging climax. Siegfried is motionless for a moment and stands helpless among the grieving swan maidens. Then, knowing that life without Odette will be nothing, he declares that he will follow her. He runs down the same diagonal that Odette took to the lakeside and drowns himself.

Siegfried's sacrifice of his love that Odette might not be destroyed by the evil magician has caused Von Rotbart's downfall. Again the malevolent owl-like creature appears, but only briefly. He lingers among the distraught swan maidens only long enough to see that love has triumphed in the end. He dies.

The stage darkens. The music softens. The swan maidens form two diagonal lines at the right, and as the light of day gradually rises in a soft glow, we see their figures bent low to the ground in grief at the loss of their queen and in gratitude for their own liberation from the evil sorcerer. Then, on the waters of the lake, a gleaming jeweled bark glides into view, its ornaments brilliant in the morning sun. Odette and Siegfried, clasped in each other's arms, move in the magical bark to a new and perpetually happy life. The swan maidens raise their heads, and their arms move softly, like ripples on the water, in quiet farewell to their queen.

NOTES March 4, 1952, was the seventy-fifth anniversary of the first performance of *Swan Lake*. In observance of this occasion, Anatole Chujoy wrote the following authoritative article in the April 1952 issue of his informative and popular publication, *Dance News:* "Troubled less than it is in our days, a civilized world would have rested from its labors on March 4 to celebrate an important occasion in the history of ballet and music, the diamond jubilee of *Swan Lake,* the greatest romantic-classic ballet of all times.

"*Swan Lake,* as it were, stands at the highest point of the curve which represents the history of the source of all ballet as we know it today—the romantic-classic era which began with *Giselle* in 1841 and ended with *Les Sylphides* in 1909—the greatest period the classic dance has ever known. *Swan Lake* is often accepted as a strictly classic ballet; actually it is much more a romantic ballet. In conception, content, structure and emotion it is much closer to *Giselle,* for example, than to *The Sleeping Beauty*. In fact, it owes some of its choreographic invention to *Giselle*.

"*Swan Lake,* which has been variously called the greatest ballet of all times and an old war horse, was first presented on March 4, 1877, at the Moscow Imperial Bolshoi Theatre.

"Two years earlier, in the spring of 1875, the Director of the Bolshoi Theatre, V. P. Begitchev, commissioned Tchaikovsky to compose a score for a ballet then called *The Lake of the Swan,* based on a libretto written by the director himself, who was also a playwright of sorts, in collaboration with Vasily Geltzer (the future father of Catherine Geltzer, subsequently the famous prima ballerina of the Moscow Theatre [and the first to dance the complete *Swan Lake* in the United States]).

"Tchaikovsky hoped to create in *Swan Lake* a score that the Bolshoi Theatre would accept with the same regard as orchestras accepted his symphonic works. This hope was not realized. The choreographer assigned to the ballet was Julius Reisinger, a hack ballet master who possessed neither the talent nor the taste to choreograph a work to the music of a major composer.

"The ballerina, Pauline Karpakova, was a run-of-the-mill dancer past her bloom, who insisted upon interpolating sure-fire 'numbers' from other ballets in her repertoire to replace some of Tchaikovsky's music which she could not appreciate, understand or even count. The première of the ballet was to be a testimonial gala in her honor and she was not going to take any chances.

"When the première of *Swan Lake* took place it was a disappointment to everybody, especially to its composer. Herman Laroche, a well-known music critic, composer and friend of Tchaikovsky, wrote about the première as follows:

" 'If during the creation of the ballet he [Tchaikovsky] had pictured fairy-tale splendor and brilliance he must have felt a bitter disappointment when he saw the work of the ballet master on the stage. I must say that I had never seen a poorer presentation on the stage of the Bolshoi Theatre.

" 'The costumes, decor, and machines did not hide in the least the emptiness of the dances. Not a single balletomane got out of it even five minutes of pleasure. The greater, however, was the joy of the melomane. From the very first measures of the introduction one felt the hand of a true master; a few pages later we knew already that the master was in excellent humor, that he was fully at the height of his genius.'

"It cannot be said that *Swan Lake* was a total failure. It had a moderate success with the spectators and it remained on the stage until 1883 during which time it was given thirty-three performances.

"According to another contemporary of Tchaiskovsky, N. Kashkin:

" 'It [*Swan Lake*] was kept in the repertoire until the scenery was worn to shreds. The music also suffered a great deal. The substitution of the original numbers with others was practiced to an even greater extent, and toward the end almost a third of the music of *Swan Lake* had been substituted with that from other ballets, usually from the most mediocre ones.'

"When the scenery finally gave out the directorate of the Bolshoi Theatre took *Swan Lake* off the repertoire, and the ballet was not revived until January 1901, when Alexander Gorsky, a talented choreographer not sufficiently appreciated by his contemporaries and almost entirely neglected by historians, staged a new version of it.

"The version of *Swan Lake* which came down to our generation dates back to the St. Petersburg production choreographed by Lev Ivanov and Marius Petipa and first presented at the Maryinsky Theatre on January 17, 1895, more than a year after the death of Tchaikovsky.

"The production of *Swan Lake* at the Maryinsky came about in a rather unorthodox manner. The initiative for it stemmed from Ivanov, not from Petipa, as is generally supposed.

"After Tchaikovsky died of cholera on November 6, 1893, there was a general upsurge of interest in his work. His operas were being revived by Imperial and private opera houses, his orchestral compositions, even those which earlier had not been successful, were being played by symphonic organizations all over Russia.

"On March 1, 1894, an evening honoring the memory of Tchaikovsky was given at the Maryinsky Theatre. The program included several excerpts from the composer's operas and what is now called Act II of *Swan Lake,* independently staged for the occasion by Lev Ivanov, Marius Petipa's assistant who carried the unpretentious title of second ballet master and *regisseur,* the same Ivanov who had staged in 1892 Tchaikovsky's *The Nutcracker.*

"The role of Odette, the Swan Queen, was taken by Pierina Legnani, the great Italian ballerina, who had made her debut at the Maryinsky the year before in the ballet *Cinderella,* in which she introduced to St. Petersburg balletomanes her famous thirty-two *fouettés.* The short ballet caught the imagination of the audience.

"Petipa saw the performance and decided to profit by its success. He ordered a repetition of the performance at a gala evening and on that occasion placed his name alongside Ivanov's (and ahead of it) as choreographer. The second performance had an even greater success and Petipa decided to revive the whole ballet.

"Richard Drigo, the composer of the ballets *Talisman, The Magic Flute* and others, who was then conductor of the Maryinsky, was commissioned by Petipa to clean up the Moscow score. Drigo, on the whole, did a conscientious job, but found it necessary for some reason to eliminate several numbers from the ballet and substitute for them a few of Tchaikovsky's short 'salon pieces,' among them *Op. 72 Nos. 11, 12,* and 15, as well as one number in Act III by an anonymous composer (Drigo himself, perhaps).

"Outside Russia there has often been speculation about what choreographer staged which part of the ballet. Indeed on several occasions the entire ballet, through sheer negligence, has been credited to Petipa, which is not only historically incorrect but also a great injustice to Ivanov. It has been established beyond any doubt that Petipa staged Act I (called Act I, Scene 1 in the original St. Petersburg version) and most of Act III (called Act II in the original version). Ivanov staged Act II, which constitutes the familiar one-act version (called Act I, Scene 2 in the original version), and Act IV (called Act III in the original version).

"Unlike the Moscow opening, eighteen years before, the St. Petersburg première on January 17, 1895, was a huge success. The occasion was also a testimonial gala for Pierina Legnani, who danced the double role of *Odette-Odile* and could not restrain herself from injecting her thirty-two *fouettés* from *Cinderella,* this time as the coda of her *pas de deux* in the ballroom scene (Act III).

"The two acts of *Swan Lake* which Lev Ivanov was permitted to stage were a great achievement for the choreographer and the culmination of his long but frustrated career at the Maryinsky, too little of which is known to the outside world.

"In staging the two acts Ivanov went contrary to the basic artistic direction in ballet during the second half of the nineteenth century, which aimed to demonstrate the technical proficiency of the dancer and the spectacular solution of complicated technological choreographic problems. Ivanov built Acts II and IV on musical principles, thus breaking a strong and generally accepted tradition. An excellent example of this is the adagio in Act II.

"In Petipa's ballets the adagio usually unfolds against the background of a picturesque backdrop or an immobile group of dancers who do not take part in the action. Ivanov's composition of the adagio in Act II is a duet with an active ensemble which accentuates and participates in the dance of the two principals. It is motivated entirely by the construction of the music, which was inspired, according to memoirs of Tchaikovsky's friends, by the vocal duet in his opera *Ondine*, the score for which he had destroyed before the opera was ever produced.

"This may sound less than revolutionary now, but in 1894 it was quite a step forward, so much so, in fact, that no choreographer dared to take a similar step until Michel Fokine, at the very height of his avant-garde Fronde'ism, utilized Ivanov's idea in *Les Sylphides* in 1909. Fokine also made use of some of Ivanov's choreography in *The Dying Swan* which he staged for Anna Pavlova in 1905.

"But Ivanov did more than just violate the canonical principles of the construction of the adagio by subordinating it to the problems of the musical themes. His two acts of *Swan Lake* very effectively dethroned the ballerina as the alpha and omega and, one might say, the *raison d'être* of the ballet. For some forty years Petipa constructed his ballets *ad majoram ballerinae gloriam.* The ballerina was all that mattered and everyone and everything else was on the third plane. Not so in *Swan Lake.* Here Ivanov treated the ballerina only as one of the protagonists. Here she either participates in the dances together with other dancers or alternates with them, or, if she performs a solo passage, the other dancers echo or accompany her. But no one leaves the stage for her variation, no one freezes into the painted backdrop.

"The adagio in Act II is a remarkable example of Ivanov's choreography, a testimonial to his choreographic and musical genius, but it is not the only example. One has but to think of the witty and compositionally perfect *pas de quatre* of the cygnets, the man's variation, and especially the entire last act to realize the great talent of Ivanov that was never allowed to achieve full bloom because of Petipa's dictatorial position in the Imperial Theatre.

"An appreciation of Lev Ivanov in English and an analysis of his work on *Swan Lake* and *The Nutcracker* is still to be done, and this writer hopes to do it before very long. It can be said here, however, that Ivanov's two acts of *Swan Lake* have been an inspiration to many contemporary choreographers whose origin was in prerevolutionary Russia. If one man can be considered the precursor of modern ballet, especially in the musical approach to choreography, that man was Lev Ivanov.

"Since its St. Petersburg première *Swan Lake* has never left the stage. The greatest ballerinas of prerevolutionary Russia, among them Mathilde Khessinska, Olga Preobrajenska, Anna Pavlova, Tamara Karsavina, and Olga Spessivtzeva, have vied for the privilege of dancing it.

"The current production of *Swan Lake* in Russia is based on the Ivanov-Petipa version, revived by Agrippina Vaganova in 1935. It is being given both in Moscow and Leningrad and is unquestionably the most popular ballet of the repertoire of both state theatres. It is also the ballet always presented on gala occasions and it is safe to say that every American and Western European diplomat and dignitary visiting Moscow has seen it.

"In Western Europe the full-length *Swan Lake* is only being given by the two British companies, the Sadler's Wells Ballet and the International Ballet. Both productions are based on the St. Petersburg version and both were staged by Nicholas Sergeyev, a former *regissseur* of the Maryinsky Theatre.

"The familiar one-act version of *Swan Lake* dates back to the Diaghilev Ballets Russes, which presented the ballet first in two acts [November 30, 1911, at the Royal Opera House, Covent Garden, London, with Mathilde Kchessinska, *prima ballerina assoluta* of the Imperial Theatre and Vaslav Nijinsky. Mischa Elman played the solo violin passages for these performances] and later in one act (ca. 1925). With the exception of the small French groups, nearly all professional contemporary ballet companies in America and Western Europe have a one-act version in their repertoire, based more or less on the Ivanov choreography."

Swan Lake is always changing. That is as it should be. Tradition in performance is, unlike teaching, discontinuous, as my friend Lincoln Kirstein has said. It is always interrupted, depends on shifts of directorships, changes of parts, whims of choreographers, dancers, designers, musicians, and the public. Only recently has a way been found to make permanent a record of a performance and I imagine that in the future it will be posssible to know about a number of "definitive" *Swan Lakes*. But I also suspect that artists will want always to change it, to remake it for themselves. That is what many of us have done, and I hope will keep on doing.

My own version of Act Two, for example, first presented by the New York City Ballet November 20, 1951, retained then only the central *adagio* and the *pas de quatre*. But I have made many changes in the ballet since and we have new scenery and costumes, too, by Rouben Ter-Arutunian.

In England, the Royal Ballet, which has revised its production a number of times, has arrived at a useful compromise by retaining its older, Sergeyev version of the original in the repertory of its national touring company and presenting newer versions at Covent Garden and on international tours. This keeps the old well intact and at the same time makes possible innovation. The latest of the major revisions in the Royal Ballet's production was December 12, 1963, when Robert Helpmann staged a production with scenery and costumes by Carl Toms that had new dances by Frederick Ashton and restagings of other dances by Rudolf Nureyev and Maria Fay. Margot Fonteyn and David Blair danced the principal roles.

The Bolshoi Ballet and the Kirov Ballet productions of the complete *Swan Lake* have become familiar. Other productions of interest include a version by Vladimir Bourmeister for the Moscow Stanislavsky Ballet (1953), Rudolf Nureyev's staging for the Vienna State Opera (1964), with Margot Fonteyn and himself, and Erik Bruhn's production for the National Ballet of Canada (1967).

Bruhn's production was fortunately filmed for television in Canada. Produced and directed by Norman Campbell, with scenery and costumes by Desmond Healey, this National Ballet of Canada presentation featured Lois Smith, Erik Bruhn, and Celia Franca. In an hour and a quarter, Bruhn compressed for the television audience the entire ballet, employing new choreography and new arrangements, too, of the score. This version was presented in the United States by the Public Broadcasting Service, July 17, 1972, over Channel 13, New York.

On June 27, 1972, Natalia Makarova of American Ballet Theatre danced *Swan Lake* with the Royal Ballet in London. Clement Crisp wrote in London's *Financial Times:* "Odette and Odile are both magical beings, the one enchanted, the other an enchantress; the particular distinction of Natalia Makarova's interpretation was marvelously to convey this quality of magic.

"Her entrance as Odette is quite extraordinary; the Swan Queen is terrified, a fraught creature at Siegfried's appearance, trembling in his arms. Like Melisande when Golaud finds her, she is lost, a prey to unfathomable terrors, and throughout this first encounter we are made aware how heavily von Rotbart's spell lies upon her. Infinitely pathetic, she seems not of this world and the menace of the enchanter's presence never seems to desert her during the whole of the act. The result is a profoundly moving characterization, expressed through dancing of exquisite perfection.

"With the Kirov, Makarova's Odette was a marvel; now it seems even more amazing. The great sound-act duet pours out in an unbroken cantilena, long-breathed, phrased with the inevitability of genius. The pure, classic schooling, the lightness that imbues her every movement, make the dancing float on the music—albeit Makarova demands slow tempi and is not, I would hazard, the most musical of dancers. But an *assoluta* is to be allowed her own way with the score, and the means amply justify the end when it results in an interpretation at once classically controlled, in the Kirov manner, and totally communicative of the Swan Queen's tragedy.

"In her Kirov performances, Makarova's Odile was something below the standard of her Odette; this is now no longer true. She plays the third act with prodigious brilliance;

the choreographic variants she offers are acceptable since the enchantress in the ballroom shines with a hectic glitter that is totally compelling. No prince could resist this malign beauty, and Donald MacLeary's fine Siegfried is no exception. He is obsessed with her, and very properly so; Makarova's shining presence is hypnotically attractive—witness the fact that after prolonged stage calls following her variation, the truth of her impersonation seemed to carry right through them: we were not cheering a ballerina but Von Rotbart's creation.

"If the fourth act seemed slightly flat, I would blame the production rather than the interpreter; it is unfamiliar to Makarova, and not particularly effective anyway. What shone through the relative dullnesss of the staging here was the beauty of her style, with its delicacy and impeccable placing, the expressive force of her poses, and such small but thrilling things as a *pas de bourrée* which seems to meet the ground with a feathery lightness. I imagine that some viewers will consider Makarova 'cold' as Odette; her performance is still absolutely true to the canons of the Kirov style in which the very statement of the choreography must contain the essence of the role without any external 'acting'—and I find it entirely satisfying. My only hope is that her interpretation be preserved on film—it is essential for future generations to be able to study it, and to marvel at its magnificence."

There have been a number of films made of *Swan Lake*, or parts thereof (the Royal Ballet's Act Two, with Margot Fonteyn, for example). David Vaughan in *Ballet Review*, Vol. 4, No. 1, wrote at length of the Kirov Ballet's film.

When the first edition of this book of ballet stories first appeared, in 1954, there was only one complete four-act version of *Swan Lake* before the public in the West—the Royal Ballet's, described above. Since then, many other four-act productions have materialized, and in the United States it has been possible to see different versions by the National Ballet, American Ballet Theatre, in a notable staging by David Blair, the Bolshoi Ballet, the Kirov Ballet, the National Ballet of Canada, and the Stuttgart Ballet, among others. The one by John Cranko for the Stuttgart Ballet prompted these remarks by the choreographer: "I am always surprised by productions of *Swan Lake* that claim to have used all the music. Such a production would last about as long as *Die Meistersinger.* While opera lovers can take this length, balletomanes tend to enjoy shorter fare. Something must go and I have, therefore, cut the well-known waltzes and *pas de trois* from Act One and put in their place the equally beautiful but seldom performed *pas de six.* This gives Siegfried the opportunity to dance and also to develop the character. The Black Swan *Pas de Deux* remains in the place Tchaikovsky intended, and in the fourth act the Drigo *pas de deux,* which always seemed too slight for the situation, has been replaced by the beautiful *Elegy for Strings.* I have tried to base my own work on the classic/romantic style of Petipa, working freely and in my own manner, but not losing sight of the great man's direction. Consequently most of the second act has been retained in its usual form. For the opening of the fourth act and the famous elegaic entry of the swans I have 'borrowed' from various Soviet productions. However, all the musical repetitions have been cut and the drama has been strengthened accordingly so that the prince emerges as a living person who experiences a tragic ordeal, rather than being a human crane who simply lifts the ballerina. The national dances have been woven into an overall dramatic arrangement instead of being pointless *divertissements.* What of the ending? There have been many 'happy endings,' where the lovers are reunited after death in 'fairyland,' but I believe that Tchaikovsky intended to write a tragic ballet. Consider the situation: Siegfried proves unworthy, he breaks his vow and unconsciously confuses outward appearances with inner reality, . . . he is a tragic hero and must be vanquished. The tone of the music, especially in the fourth act, is tragic. In the imperial theatre the Tsar (surrounded by so many tragedies) made it an unwritten rule that everything must close happily. But Odette and Siegfried are not the sort of lovers who can 'live happily ever after.' "

LA SYLPHIDE

Ballet in two acts. Music by Jean Schneitzhoeffer. Choreography by Philippe Taglioni. Book by Adolphe Nourrit. Scenery by Pierre Ciceri. Costumes by Eugène Lami. First presented at the Théâtre de l'Académie Royale de Musique, Paris, March 12, 1832, with Marie Taglioni as La Sylphide *and Mazilier as* James. *Marie Taglioni danced the title role when the ballet was introduced to London (1832), St. Petersburg (1837), and Milan (1841). A version of* La Sylphide *was presented in the United States for the first time on April 15, 1835, with Mademoiselle Céleste in the leading role. It was subsequently danced in the United States by the same ballerina; by Augusta Maywood (1838); Amélie Galster (1839), sister-in-law of Marie Taglioni; and by Fanny Elssler (1840). In 1836* Sylphiden *was presented by the Royal Danish Ballet in a version by Auguste Bournonville with music by Herman Løvenskjold. Lucile Grahn danced the* Sylphide *in the first performance of this version, which has been in the active repertory of the Royal Danish Ballet ever since. Taglioni's* La Sylphide *was revived in 1946 by the Ballets des Champs-Élysées, Paris, with choreography by Victor Gsovsky, scenery by Serebriakov, and costumes by Christian Bérard. Nina Vyroubova and Roland Petit danced the principal roles. The Royal Danish Ballet danced the ballet in the United States for the first time at the Metropolitan Opera House, New York, September 16, 1956. Harald Lander staged* La Sylphide *for American Ballet Theatre in San Antonio, Texas, November 11, 1964, with Toni Lander and Royes Fernandez. Music arranged and composed by Edgar Cosma after Løvenskjold. On May 20, 1967, Carla Fracci and Erik Bruhn danced in this production at the New York State Theater. Erik Bruhn staged it for the National Ballet of Canada in Toronto, December 31, 1964, with Lois Smith and himself in the leading roles. These were later taken by Lynn Seymour and Rudolf Nureyev.*

Once a curiosity but now popular in repertories in the United States, Canada, England, and the continent, *La Sylphide* deserves continuing attention. Ballet history was changed completely by the work. Marie Taglioni who danced it and the men who created the role for her made a revolution in the art of dancing that we still witness whenever we go to the ballet and see a world of story—of sylphs, ondine, swan queens, and firebirds—that is both real and fantasy, settings that are both ethereal and natural, costumes of flowing white, satin toe shoes, and dancers who rise on *pointe* and are lifted magically into the air by their partners. The era of the romantic ballet begun by this ballet is still much with us.

ACT ONE The story of *La Sylphide* is a romance of old Scotland. The scene is the living room of a Scottish farmhouse. The time is 1830. The room is large and high. On the left a fire blazes in a great fireplace; a huge stone mantel rises from it to the rafters. The mantel is hung with trophies of the hunt—colorful stuffed birds, powder horns, and flintlocks. A staircase runs up the back of the room to the upper story, and a bright plaid decorates the banister. Near the first landing of the stairs is a high, peaked window through whose diamond-shaped translucent glass we can discern the break of day.

This is the wedding day of James Reuben, the young Scots peasant who lives in this house with his mother. The bridegroom sleeps restlessly in a high wing chair drawn close to the fire. He is dressed for his wedding: kilts, cap with high feather. His dark head stirs against the back of the chair; he is dreaming. His dream is with us in the room, and we understand his restlessness. For kneeling on the floor at his feet, her long white dress against the bridegroom's bright tartan, is the diaphanous, winged sylphide, who glances with quiet happiness about the room and seems with her penetrating gaze to look into the eyes of her dreaming lover.

Gurn, another young peasant, rests in a corner against the fireplace. In his deep sleep, Gurn is not disturbed by the realization of his friend's dream; he himself dreams of Effie, James's bride-to-be, and the love he will lose this day.

The sylphide rises effortlessly and circles about the chair. She looks down upon the sleeping James with wistful longing, moving around the room with a lightness and grace that make her wings more than a part of her costume. James turns his head as she dances about him; he is still asleep, but in his dream he watches every gesture she makes. Creature that she is from another world, the sylphide now seems a part of this room. Her smile is the considered smile of possession; she is both beautiful and serious, and her face tells us that her love is great enough to endure beyond James's dream. Should James respond to her love, we feel that this dream might become permanent.

James stirs in his sleep. He wakens suddenly and beholds the sylphide before him. He reaches out for her desperately. Frightened now by reality, the sylphide eludes his grasp. She rushes toward the fireplace. She disappears like the smoke from the dying embers. James moves his hand to his forehead in disbelief at the apparition: was she really there, after all? He becomes frantic and unable to understand the mystery and decides to question Gurn. He shakes his friend awake rudely. Did he see the beautiful vision? How long have we slept? Gurn is a little embarrassed at his own dream and is about to tell James yes, he saw the beautiful girl, but he sees that his friend is not talking about Effie, the bride, but about someone quite different. He wonders at his friend.

James is angry at Gurn for allowing himself to sleep so soundly. He is still trying to piece together the fragments of his dream when he hears his mother approach. She comes in from another room with Effie. Reminded by his bride's presence that he has scarcely thought of her, James is embarrassed. Gurn greets the bride first. The beautiful young lass smiles at him. Gurn can hardly control himself, he is so moved by her loveliness; meekly he presents her with a rare bird he killed yesterday while hunting. Effie accepts the gift, but turns to her fiancé. Why, she wonders, is he preoccupied? Has he no greeting for her? James shakes off his dream and kisses her fondly. They embrace. Effie cannot see James's face as he stares over her shoulder into the fireplace. His mother and Gurn watch him curiously.

Again James kisses his bride. Amused by his own formality, he kisses her hand and tells her that this is the day he has long awaited. Effie sees that he is sincere and his old self again. She is therefore a little annoyed when Gurn steps in, takes her hand and tries to kiss it too. She shakes her finger at him, and James, seeing that he has a rival in his friend, jokes with him about it. Gurn, however, is in no mood for jokes and walks away to nurture his private dream.

James's mother embraces her son and Effie. The lovers kneel before her; she blesses them and hopes for their eternal happiness. Effie and James look into each other's eyes; in her sight, he has forgotten his dream.

Now the music brightens and becomes festive with the arrival of Effie's bridesmaids. The young peasant girls, dressed in brilliant plaids, surround the lovers and wish them well. Gurn approaches. The girls giggle at his discomfiture: after all, he might choose one of them instead of Effie, who is already spoken for. The unhappy Gurn pleads with them to intercede for him; can't anything be done, he wonders, before it is too late? The girls put him off and bring out the wedding gifts they have for Effie: bunches of freshly picked flowers, decorative cloths, and simple jewelry. The bride is delighted with the presents, tries on the jewelry, and drapes the new material over her shoulder.

She and her friends do not notice James as he walks away from them and stares into the fire. Gurn watches him suspiciously. What can be wrong with his friend? James turns his head to look at the precise spot where he last saw the sylphide. He catches his breath and jumps back, startled. Someone is there! He reaches out his arms hopefully, and out of the dark corner steps not his sylphide, but a frightening figure: Old Madge, the village sorceress. The girls are pleased and run over to her. Old Madge stumbles forward, bent low over her crude walking stick. Her ragged clothes are filthy; her stringy gray hair hangs loose about her white, ghostly face. She cackles hideously and walks straight over to James and looks up into his face. His fear turns to anger. He orders her away. Madge cowers pathetically, and the girls are shocked at James's behavior.

The bridegroom stalks away. The girls persuade Madge to tell their fortunes. Effie is the first to hold out her hand. She asks the sorceress if her marriage will be a happy one? Effie does not really have any doubts; it is, after all, the conventional question. Old Madge nods her head and grins, "Yes, you will be happy in marriage." Emboldened by this answer,

Effie asks another question: does James love her? James looks over at the group. The witch says, "No," smiling the same toothless smile as she shakes her head. James will tolerate this no longer. Old Madge cackles ominously. He picks up a broom and drives the hag from the room.

Effie, reassured by James's indignation, tells him that she never doubted his love and that Old Madge is a proverbial liar. James believes her and is comforted. As long as Effie is with him and he can look into her eyes, he, too, has no doubt.

His mother comes to take Effie away. It is time for her to dress for the wedding. Mother Reuben laughs at her son when he doesn't want to let Effie go. She takes the girl by the hand and leads her and her bridesmaids up the stairs. Effie glances back at James, who smiles at her reassuringly.

But now, alone in the room, James has his doubts. He cannot get his dream out of his mind, though rationally he knows it is nonsense. Effie is his real love and so she will remain. But will the dream recur? What would he do if it did? Could such a vision really exist? As he asks himself these tormenting questions, he feels a draft. He turns around, and there—standing in the window—is the sylphide! She is leaning against the window frame; her hands are clasped before her; her expression is one of sweet sadness; and her eyes look down, refusing to meet James's glance. James goes to the window and asks her why she is so sad. Before she vanished so mysteriously, the sylphide was blithe and happy; what can be troubling so beautiful a girl? The sylphide replies that she loves someone who does not love her. James turns as if to move away, but the sylphide continues. He must know, she says, that she loves him. She is the one who brought him the beautiful dream; she is the one who will always watch over him and keep him from harm. Gurn, who has been sulking in a dark corner near the fireplace, emerges from the shadows to watch closely.

James reminds the sylphide that he is to be married this very day. The sylphide knows. Tears fall upon her cheeks. She murmurs that there can be no more beauty in her life: she must die. She starts to leave. James can suppress his secret no longer. He kneels before her and tells her that since she disappeared from his sight he has not been able to forget her for a single moment; he has tried, for he owed it to his love for his fiancée, but he could not: he has loved her as she loves him.

The sylphide dances about the room. James is enraptured to see his dream become real and to find the creature even more graceful in life. She moves toward the window, beckoning James to follow her. He does not move. She whispers softly into his ear. The unhappy bridegroom looks toward the stairs and hangs back. The sylphide watches him and sees the source of his anxiety. Lightly, without seeming to have the least idea of what it is, she takes up the plaid Effie has left behind on the chair, puts it around her shoulders, and poses demurely with downcast eyes as the bride. James can resist her no longer. When the sylphide kneels at his feet, he draws her to him and kisses her.

Gurn is now convinced of his friend's faithlessness and dashes up the stairs to Effie. James and the sylphide are frightened. Excited voices approach. Quickly the sylphide cuddles up in a corner of the huge chair. James throws the plaid over her just as Gurn and Effie, in her bridal gown, rush down the stairs. Her friends follow. Gurn accuses James of having kissed another woman in this room. But where is she? James asks him; he laughs and swears he has been quite alone. Effie and Gurn see no one, but Gurn notes the plaid that covers the chair. James trembles. Gurn pulls the plaid away, and underneath is . . . nothing! The sylphide was vanished! James is as surprised as his friend, but immediately reassures Effie, who now berates Gurn for allowing his jealousy to govern his sense of truth. The girls ridicule Gurn mercilessly, and he slinks out of the room.

James's mother enters with the wedding guests—her friends as well as the friends of the happy couple. Refreshments are served, toasts are made, the bagpipes tune up, and soon everyone is either dancing or talking volubly. Everyone, that is, except James. As all the other young men of the village surround the bride, James stands apart, reminded anew of the sylphide. Effie breaks away from her admirers and reminds the bridegroom that he has not asked her to dance. James is shocked at his forgetfulness, and the two begin to dance. The other guests stand back and watch them. The couple dance together happily until the formal pattern of the peasant dance forces them to separate for a moment. At this point the sylphide returns. She is seen only by James, and the other guests are astonished—when James rejoins Effie—to see him turn his head away from his bride. The *pas de deux* becomes a *pas de trois:* every movement of Effie's is imitated and elevated by the sprightly sylphide. The guests join Effie and James in a general dance, while the sylphide runs hither and yon, now visible, now concealed by the turning couples.

James tries not to lose sight of her and whirls Effie around and around as he frantically pursues the sylphide. Effie is so happy she doesn't notice his anxiety. The sylphide continually eludes him, and James can no longer see her. The dance stops, and some of the guests surround James and inquire about his strange behavior.

They are put off, however, by the beginning of the wedding ceremony. The guests stand in formal groups about the fireplace, where James and Effie stand with his mother. The ritual begins. The couple start to exchange wedding rings. James takes off his own ring and holds it at Effie's finger tip. He moves to slip it on her finger, when the sylphide darts out from nowhere and takes the ring from his hand. The guests gasp at the sudden disappearance of the ring. James turns away from his bride. The sylphide whispers to him that she will die if he marries anyone else. James is so appalled at this possibility that he now sees his course: he must prevent such a tragedy. The sylphide beckons to him and stands there in the room by the window before his wedding guests; the bridegroom vanishes.

Effie dissolves in tears. No one can understand how or why James has abandoned her thus. Gurn rushes in and announces that he has just seen the bridegroom running across the moor with another woman. Effie will not believe it. Gurn tries to comfort her, assuring her that she can be certain of his love. Mother Reuben and all the guests gather about the troubled bride. Effie sits down in the chair by the fire. The plaid is placed around her shoulders, her wedding veil is removed. Gurn kneels beside her.

ACT TWO Eerie music suggestive of an unnatural world marks the beginning of this second scene, which will unravel the mystery of the magical sylphide and confront the romantic James with his destiny. When the curtain rises, it is still night. On the left, a small fire throws grotesque shadows against the walls of a small, dark cave. The surrounding forest is impenetrably black. The witch, Old Madge, emerges from the cave and stands over the fire. Hovering over the flames, she invokes her demons, beseeching them to obey her commands. With her crooked walking stick, she draws a magic circle about the fire, then hurries into the shadows of the cavern. She returns with her sisters in witchcraft: hunchbacked, cackling hags who gather about the circle. The hideous women hang a huge black caldron over the fire and dance around and around it. Suddenly Old Madge orders silence and, walking up to stand over the caldron, she points her finger downward in unquestioning command. The other witches are silenced by this gesture and wait expectantly for some result. Old Madge orders them to dance again; as they circle the fire, smoke and steam and blue flame arise from the caldron, illuminating the forest for a few flashing moments. The conflagration in the caldron simmers down, and the old women crowd around to see what remains inside. With an imperious sweep of her arm, Old Madge tells them to stand back. The sun is about to rise, and they must hasten their work. Madge takes her stick and pokes it into the caldron; when she pulls it out, we see on the end of the stick, like a banner, a lovely shimmering scarf. The old women grab at it, but Madge holds it to her breast; only she is aware of the power of this beautiful scarf. She orders her sisters away, and all the witches disappear into the cave.

In the distance, the sun rises brightly over the fields of heather and we see a clearing in a thickly wooded glade. The green treees hang down over the scene, almost obscuring the witches' cave. Dew covers the ground as the morning mist settles on the earth.

On the right, James enters the forest. No longer dressed

like a typical Scots peasant, James wears a costume befitting the bridegroom of his sylphide: white tights and a plaid vest. He carries a bird nest in his hand. Carefully he examines the colorful eggs and replaces them. He looks about the forest for his love, but she is not to be found. As he begins to approach the cave, he discovers the sylphide standing by his side. He is astonished at the suddenness of her appearance and asks her where she has been hiding. The lovely girl smiles back at him so beautifully that James leaves off his questioning. As if to show him how she appeared so swiftly and silently, she dances about the forest like a magical sprite; the tips of her toes seem to require only the air to support them in flight. James is bewitched anew by her charm and becomes apprehensive when the sylph darts in and out behind the trees. He holds out the bird's nest and tells her he has brought her a gift. The sylph shrinks back; and we see suddenly that she is not frightened because James has probably harmed the eggs in the nest, but because the living birds who fly about the forest are moved by a power quite different from the mysterious force that makes her a sylphide as well as a woman. The sylphide is afraid of the nest. Scrupulously she takes it between her hands and runs to place it high on an overhanging branch. James smiles warmly at what he believes to be her tenderness; lightly the sylphide moves her finger tips over her diaphanous white gown.

James draws her to his side. The sylphide places her head on his shoulder for a moment, and James moves to take her face in his hands. Before he can do so, the sylphide has danced away toward the back. James observes her as she calls forth a band of sylphs, who pay homage to her and to him. The sylphs surround the happy lovers, and James would dance with his bride; but every time he turns to take her in his arms, she is mysteriously gone and before him stands another sylphide. This happens repeatedly, and James becomes frantic in his search. Then, just as if nothing had happened, the sylphide is at his side again, looking up into his eyes. James is satisfied, but again the vision disappears: all the sylphs seem to fly away in the blazing light of the sun.

Alone, James considers that he has made a mistake. Yesterday, in his mother's house, the sylphide was always appearing and vanishing mysteriously, but that he could understand—for there he alone shared her secret; but here in the forest with her, with no one to see, why should she wish to escape *him*? She had sworn that she loved him and would love him eternally, and yet she would be loved only from afar. Was his love an illusion, he wondered?

On the left, close to where he last saw his beloved, the branches rustle. James is startled to see Old Madge come out of her cave. In his present state of mind, he greets her like an old friend. He remembers his rudeness of yesterday and hastens to apologize. Old Madge tells him not to mind, she understands the momentary follies of youth—but why is he here in the forest? What has happened?

James tells her briefly that he has run away with his true love, the most beautiful girl in the world. Why then does he look so dejected, Madge inquires? "Because," James tells her, "the sylphide is never with me: I search for her, and she is not to be found; I reach out to touch her beside me, and she eludes my embrace."

Madge offers to help him with her occult powers. James, willing to try any device to still the sylphide's flight, beseeches the witch to ease his state of mind and secure his permanent happiness. Old Madge holds out the bright magic scarf and offers it to James. She instructs him to place this scarf about the sylphide's shoulders, and then the sylphide will never fly again: her light, transparent wings will fall to the ground and flutter no more; she will be his, on earth.

James is delighted with this magic and kneels before the witch in gratitude. Old Madge's eyes gleam with triumph as she looks down upon him. Then she hurries away into the dark cavern as she sees the sylphide approaching. James runs to his bride and embraces her. She responds warmly to his affection and seems to be charmed by the gift he offers her. James places the scarf about her shoulders. As the cloth touches her flesh, the sylphide clutches at her heart in a spasm of agonizing pain. Her wings fall to the ground. She stumbles forward. James, struck dumb by this outcome, tries to hold her in his arms and comfort her. The dying sylphide looks at him in horror and pushes him away. Slowly her body relaxes, and she lies dead before him, like a leaf fallen from a tree.

As James kneels beside her, weeping, the mirthful cackle of Old Madge ricochets against the dark walls of her hidden cavern. The sylphide's winged sisters emerge from the trees above. They do not comfort the despairing hero, but take the sylphide tenderly in their arms. As they lift her from the ground, they themselves are lifted up; the branches of the trees overhead move back, and high into the clear sky the winged creatures carry their dead queen.

James is inconsolable in his grief. The softness of the music that has carried his ideal love away forever is interrupted by the shrill, open sound of joyous bagpipes, reminding him of his home and the happiness he might have found there. Across the forest, in the distance, we see a wedding procession moving over the moor. Gurn and Effie, arm in arm, lead the happy party, and the curtain falls as the faraway church bells sound their welcome.

NOTES The National Ballet of Washington presented *La Sylphide* in the version by Elsa Marianne von Rosen in 1969. When Margot Fonteyn, dancing this ballet for the first time, appeared in this production October 3, 1969, the critic Clive Barnes wrote: "After seeing Dame Margot it seemed only remarkable that she had never danced the role before. It suited her perfectly, for she brings to these Romantic ballets a most exquisite sense of period style.

"The ballet is a kind of Victorian nosegay—sweet, sentimental and yet completely acceptable upon its own period terms. . . . Dame Margot fitted into its ardors with effortless grace. . . . she conveys the mystic character of the sylph with a seductive mixture of femininity and charm. It recalls her beguiling performance in Ashton's *Ondine*, all thoughtless wiles and innocent raptures."

When American Ballet Theatre staged a new production of *La Sylphide* in New York, July 8, 1971, the staging was by the Danish dancer, choreographer, and producer Erik Bruhn. Clive Barnes commented in the New York *Times* the next day: "By far the best aspect of the production is Mr. Bruhn's staging. This is far more authentic than the first production of *La Sylphide* he created for the National Ballet of Canada some years ago. Indeed, it follows the original fairly carefully and with considerable sensibility.

"The only major addition is a brief new solo for Effie, which is reasonable enough. As is common nowadays, the hero, James, dances the second male solo in this act, and his rival, Gurn, dances the first. Mr. Bruhn takes further than any other production the current trend to romanticize Gurn and to remove him from the original comic tradition, and I can see no harm in this, even though it eliminates some of the traditional pantomime.

"There were other details of the production I was less happy about. I would like to have seen more stage machinery used—this is part of that particular period. I regret the omission of some of the smaller touches that are usually introduced—such as the Sylphide, on persuading James to run away from home, bringing him his cap. There were even details of choreography missing—including James's quite celebrated turn-and-a-half, where he ends a sequence with his back to the audience facing his ballerina.

"These are quibbles, but perhaps the kind of details that give authenticity to the authentic. But at last Ballet Theatre has found a good and valid version of this very important classic, and it will fit well into the company's repertory.

"At this first performance, the Sylphide was danced by Carla Fracci, with Ted Kivitt as her swain, James. Miss Fracci, with her fugitive smile wreathing the corners of her mouth, her tarlatan skirt frothing, and her shy yet captivating manner, is the epitome of the Romantic ideal, when, poetically, women often meant to be more myth than reality. And her dancing had the right febrile grace.

"The Sylphide herself is all spirit—an image rather than a character, an unattainable sex symbol for an age that in polite literary terms had no explicit sex but merely its lost promise. James, the Highland lad, who, rather foolishly, throws away everything to follow her into the heather, has more of the dimensions of reality, and Mr. Kivitt acted with a simple forcefulness.

"Probably the most rewarding character in *La Sylphide* is that of Madge the Witch, who ruins James and insures all ends unhappily. This is now played by Dennis Nahat, who is wearing one of the two or three most interestingly twisted noses I have ever encountered, and glowers with genuine power. It is a good idea to have this role played by a man—it often is in Denmark—and Mr. Nahat, with his unfailing sense of style, is already good and will soon be even better."

Erik Bruhn performed the role of Madge in New York, in August 1974, in the production of *La Sylphide* he had staged for the National Ballet of Canada. Writing in *Dance Perspectives* about his famous roles in the essay "Beyond Technique," Erik Bruhn recalled the first time he appeared as James in *La Sylphide:* "It was a pretty difficult assignment—to do James at the age of 23. I would consider any age between 18 and 24 as the right age for James on the stage. Of course we are all that age at one time or another. But to play him that way is possible only if you can achieve and sustain an idea about how you see him. To play yourself or to play your own age is not enough; to play young when you are young is very hard. When you are mature you can look on youth from a certain distance and this makes you objective. But when you are terribly involved with what is happening to you at this age it is difficult to re-create this. Some people would say that when you look back it isn't the truth you are seeing anymore, it is what you think the truth is. Yes, the role is also what you think it is. It is what you bring to it—your thoughts, your mind. You give life to the role by bringing to it what is true for you at that moment.

"For me, James is the youngest in the gallery of Romantic ballet heroes. He is an idealist, a poet. In the end when he tries to grasp his ideal and tries to make her a real woman, he dies. Without this dream, this illusion, he can no longer exist. All he wants to catch is a dream which exists only in his head and which nobody else can see. He is a true escapist. Nobody can actually get hold of James. His mother, his fiancée—none of the real people understand him. But when he is alone with his dream he is quite himself; he is a total being. When the dream is gone, he must die with it. He believes only in this dream and it is sad that he could never grasp reality. James dies without knowing that he is licked, which becomes a very beautiful thing.

"Unlike James, Albrecht in *Giselle* is on the point of entering maturity. He realizes that he has done something terrible and that he must suffer. If he can survive his night of remorse he will come out the better for it. He pays the price as James never did. Therefore he can live."

LES SYLPHIDES

Classic ballet in one act. Music by Frédéric Chopin. Choreography by Michel Fokine. Scenery and costumes by Alexandre Benois. First presented by Diaghilev's Ballets Russes at the Théâtre de Châtelet, Paris, June 2, 1909, with Anna Pavlova, Tamara Karsavina, Maria Baldina, and Vaslav Nijinsky as the principal dancers. Fokine's first arrangement of this ballet was presented on March 21, 1908, in St. Petersburg, under the title Chopiniana. *The dancers were members of the Imperial Ballet; Pavlova and Oboukoff danced a classical* pas de deux *to the "Waltz," which was the only part of the original production without a realistic setting or suggestion of plot. The second production, given by Fokine's students, April 6, 1908, was wholly classical; like the first "Waltz," it had no plot, and the musical structure was altered. Preobrajenska, Pavlova, Karsavina, Nijinsky, and Bekeffy were the principal dancers. This second version was costumed in the long white ballet dress made popular by Marie Taglioni in* La Sylphide. *The title of this famous ballet of Taglioni's was Diaghilev's inspiration for the new name he applied to* Chopiniana *when it was first presented in Western Europe in substantially the same form as its second production. First presented in the United States in its authorized version by Diaghilev's Ballets Russes at the Century Theatre, New York, January 20, 1916, with a cast that included Lydia Lopokova, Lubov Tchernicheva, Xenia Maclezova, and Adolph Bolm. An unauthorized version, not credited to the choreographer and not supervised by him, was presented in the United States by Gertrude Hoffman's Saison des Ballets Russes on June 14, 1911, at the Winter Garden, New York, with Maria Baldina, Lydia Lopokova, and Alexandre Volinine as the principal dancers.*

No one knows exactly when the first *ballet blanc,* or white ballet, was first performed. It is probable that this kind of ballet, which involved a new conception of dance based on ethereal atmosphere, soft music, and diaphanous white costumes, was first performed before *La Sylphide;* but it was *La Sylphide,* and the dancing of its ballerina, Marie Taglioni, that made the *ballet blanc* famous. *Les Sylphides,* its twentieth-century namesake, has carried this fame into our time more than any other ballet.

For the *ballet blanc* did not remain popular. Théophile Gautier, who first used the phrase, was complaining in 1844 that since *La Sylphide* the Paris stage was so dominated by white gauze, by tulle and tarlatan, that the "shades became mists of snow in transparent skirts" and "white almost the only color in use."

And so the misty white ballets gradually passed out of fashion. The ballets that replaced them for half a century were more concerned with dancing than with mood—more devoted to elaborate, regal stage spectacle, and the development within this frame of the classic dance, than to simple stories of fantasy and ethereal romance.

Les Sylphides restored the *ballet blanc,* now embellished with the developed classic dance; but it did so without a story. Here, instead of characters with definite personalities and a narrative, we have simply dancers in long white dresses and a *danseur* in white-and-black velvet, whose movements to music invoke the romantic imagination to a story of its own. It is the music, and the care with which the classic dance embodies it, that tells us the story of these magical creatures who dance in the light of the moon.

The overture, *Prelude, Opus 28, No. 7,* to the ballet is quiet and contemplative. The curtain rises on a secluded wood near an ancient ruin, where lovely girls in white are grouped about the scene in a still, charming tableau. The light is bluish white, soft, and misty. As the *Nocturne, Opus 32, No. 2,* commences, some of the girls begin to dance to the light, airy melody. They are joined by the principal dancers, who stand in a cluster at the rear.

Now a girl dances a variation to a gentle but joyous waltz, music suggestive of beautiful and controlled happiness.

The next dance, like the *Mazurka, Opus 33, No. 3,* that accompanies it, is not as soft; it is bolder, more open and free, but still restrained in its exuberance as the ballerina bounds diagonally across the stage in *grand jetés,* over and over again.

A variation to another mazurka, *Opus 67, No. 3,* is danced by the *danseur* after the girls have formed a decorative tableau about the stage.

When the overture is repeated, the sylphs form picturesque groups, the girls kneeling about central figures. The *danseuse* who now enters comes softly, pauses, and seems to listen to a distant call. She moves among the groups adroitly and sweetly, but completely removed from them in her rapt attention to what she might hear.

The *Waltz, Opus 64, No. 2,* commences, and the *danseur* lifts the ballerina across the stage from the wings. She appears to be so light that it must require no effort to hold her. She is released, and the *pas de deux* begins. Throughout this dance, as the music increases in momentum, the girl responds with unhesitating swiftness and flight to the inspiration of the music and the night: she abandons herself to the air.

The stage is empty for a moment, there is no music; then, to the final buoyant *Waltz, Opus 18, No. 1,* the dancers return, move diagonally across the stage, mingle, brush past each other, and fill the stage with movement like the swift fluttering of butterfly wings. The principal dancers join them for short solos; and at the final chords, there is a swift, silent rush and all are standing still, in the same tableau in which we first saw them.

NOTES *Les Sylphides* is associated with many famous dancers. Fokine staged his work for the Royal Danish Ballet on October 21, 1925 (in a revised version), for René Blum's Ballet Russe de Monte Carlo in 1936, and for Ballet Theatre in 1940.

In the first Diaghilev production in Paris, the first solo, Waltz, was danced by Karsavina; the second, Mazurka, by Anna Pavlova; the third, Mazurka, by Nijinsky; the Prelude, by Maria Baldina; the *pas de deux,* Waltz, by Pavlova and Nijinsky; and the final Waltz, by all the soloists and the *corps de ballet.* Vaslav Nijinsky danced *Les Sylphides* in the United States on April 14, 1916, at the Metropolitan Opera House.

The music for Fokine's first arrangement of the ballet that was later to become *Les Sylphides* was orchestrated by Glazunov. Music for the second version was orchestrated by Keller and Glazunov. Music for the Diaghilev production was orchestrated by Stravinsky (his first Diaghilev commission),

Tcherepnine, Glazunov, and Liadov. Later orchestrations include those of Vittorio Rieti and Lucien Caillet.

On January 13, 1972, *Chopiniana*, the work on which *Les Sylphides* was based, was presented for the first time outside Russia:

Music by Frédéric Chopin. Staged by Alexandra Danilova after Michel Fokine. Pianist: Gordon Boelzner. First presented by the New York City Ballet at the New York State Theater, Lincoln Center, with Kay Mazzo, Peter Martins, Karin von Aroldingen, and Susan Hendl in the principal roles.

The title *Chopiniana* derives from a suite of four piano pieces by Chopin, orchestrated by Alexander Glazunov (*Opus 46*, 1894). Fokine, planning these for a charity performance ballet, asked the composer to add the *C Sharp Minor Waltz* (for Anna Pavlova and Mikhail Oboukoff, Nijinsky's teacher). This first *Chopiniana* was danced March 21, 1908, comprising five scenes: a Polonaise in Polish court dress; an evocation of Chopin and his Muse who repels nightmares of dead monks in his Mayorquin monastery; a Mazurka for a peasant wedding; the Waltz; and, as finale, a Tarantella based on Fokine's memory of a Capri festival.

A second (this current) *Chopiniana* introduced April 16, 1908, used different piano pieces orchestrated by Maurice Keller, retaining Glazunov's Waltz but eliminating all character dancing and mime for a visualized abstraction. Set in three days, Fokine described: "Some of the *corps de ballet* groups accompanying the dancing of the soloists were staged by me, just before curtain time." Diaghilev produced it in his initial Paris ballet season, June 2, 1909, under his own title as *Les Sylphides*, with Pavlova, Karsavina, and Nijinsky, in a long blond wig which the designer Alexandre Benois said "seemed a trifle comic when I saw it on stage . . . his slightly caricatured appearance made the artist look like a figure from some old beaded reticule or painted lampshade." Some critics frowned on piano music in arrangements made then (and later) by Keller, Liadov, Rieti, Malcom Sargent,

Sokolov, Stravinsky, Taneef, Tcherepnine, etc. Scenery was by Benois; later by A. Socrate, Leon Zak, etc. In 1932, for René Blum's Ballets du Théâtre de Monte Carlo under Balanchine's artistic direction, a Corot landscape was used. Fokine restaged his work for the Royal Danes in 1925 as *Chopiniana,* by which it was familiar in Russia before and since. In 1936, for Les Ballet Russes de Monte Carlo, he altered music and steps for the male solo. Other changes have crept in over sixty years, some due to individual dancers of which Fokine complained; others to the memories of rehearsalists after his death in 1942.

Costumes and scenery suggested the "romantic" (classic) lyricism of the 1830s. However much long skirts evoked Taglioni, Fokine's choreography surpassed any *tableaux vivants* inspired by static popular lithographs of the period. This was the first ballet as a whole (with precedents from Ivanov and Gorsky) in which movement itself projected from important music was a prime factor rather than a propulsive accompaniment. Fokine's fluent pattern held no pretext for virtuosity or pageantry. Layers of sentiment or sentimentality have tended to dull the force, logic, and ingenuity of this academic masterpiece. The original was planned for large opera house stages; later, scenic frames shrunk spatial possibilities due to the need for touring smaller theaters, while musical tempi increasingly decelerated. The present recension is not offered as a pious museum restoration but as a testimony of approximate efficiency in a context of its contemporary choreographic vitality.

Reviewing *Chopiniana* in *Dance News,* the critic Nancy Goldner wrote: "The decision to strip *Les Sylphides* of its scenery, costumes, orchestration, and by implication its sense of period, even genre—as the City Ballet has done with *Chopiniana*—will strike some as cantankerous and perverse; to others, like myself, a stroke of genius. While watching American Ballet Theatre's production during the last few seasons, I have been continually discovering that there is sturdy, tightly constructed, and subtle but unmistakable climax-building choreography underneath all the aspects that bring historicity to the ballet but have little to do with choreographic fact. One went to see *Les Sylphides* for great performances.

"Now we can more clearly see *Chopiniana* for great choreography as well. On the most obvious level, we can see what choreography is in the legs, since the girls wear short white tunics. It is easier to see that Fokine has been brilliantly economical. Alexandra Danilova's staging has also brought out the choreography's precision and deliberateness. The ensemble looks more vivid, more important. The placement of dancers now looks more linear, lending to the pretty formations a welcome touch of austerity. With this production, one also becomes more aware of lovely repetitions and the fact that *Chopiniana* is, in one aspect, a study on entrances and exits. The ballet is as beautiful as ever, but it is not of a genre. The City Ballet production, in other words, does not preclude style, just stylization. In its de-interpretation, it restores and preserves. This is useful."

NOTES *Ballet Review* (Vol. 4, No. 5) published in 1973 an interview with the ballerina and teacher Alexandra Danilova that is of special interest in view of her part in the staging of the New York City Ballet revival of *Chopiniana:*

"BALLET REVIEW How did you think the New York City Ballet's *Chopiniana* turned out?

"ALEXANDRA DANILOVA Well, I think the first performance was beautiful, and I think the angle that we took is very interesting, and it was very clever of Mr. B. to suggest all these things, because *Chopiniana* is usually done with long skirts, blue flowers—

"BR But this was really radical.

"AD But it is not, if you think that from the beginning it was done with the piano. Chopin never orchestrated. And in Paris people said it was illogical to orchestrate Chopin when he wrote strictly for piano.

"BR Was it the Glazunov orchestration?

"AD Yes, it was Glazunov, then it was Stravinsky, then it was Dorati. So Mr. Balanchine wanted to go right back as like it was done, and now we have the ballet done with the piano, so this time they say why is it not with orchestra?

"BR The principal criticism has been that the ballet was done for a particular reason with the costumes that it had, that when Fokine made the ballet the whole mood and the whole aura of the piece had a lot to do with the production and that these elements were very important to it.

"AD I think a little bit different. I don't know what they wore originally because it was done for annual school performance, and they probably, like we have, just had that white wardrobe tutu past the knee. But then when Diaghilev bought *Sylphides* from Fokine he asked I think Benois to do the costumes, and Benois did the costumes which we wear for forty or fifty years, let's say. And then the time come when the costumes are not necessary, like the scenery is not necessary. So it is a good angle to put just in tunic to see all the beauty of the movement.

"BR I, personally, thought it was very beautiful.

"AD But it is always—you can't please everybody. Don't forget that all our geniuses go twenty-five years ahead of the audience. The beginning, people spit when Stravinsky *Petrouchka* and *Firebird* was played. And now it's the classic. It took twenty-five years for public to catch up, and they love *Petrouchka*. They have such a habit of having *Sylphides* done the way Diaghilev did, but why not to show another angle? I know some people wrote me a letter that they just can't go and see old *Sylphides;* they think it's too heavy.

"BR I thought it was both interesting and beautiful, but many people thought a part of what the ballet meant to them was gone.

"AD Well it's too bad if they take so personally, but a lot of times you come to the rehearsal and admire the ballet before it's done with the costumes, and sometimes costumes ruin the ballet. But this was absolutely pure like crystal. There was pure art of Chopin and pure choreography of Fokine."

SYMPHONIC VARIATIONS

Classic ballet in one act. Music by César Franck. Choreography by Frederick Ashton. Scenery and costumes by Sophie Fedorovitch. First presented by the Sadler's Wells Ballet at the Royal Opera House, Covent Garden, London, April 24, 1946, with Margot Fonteyn and Michael Somes, Pamela May and Brian Shaw, and Moira Shearer and Henry Danton. First presented in the United States by the Sadler's Wells Ballet at the Metropolitan Opera House, New York, October 12, 1949, with the same cast but with John Hart replacing Henry Danton.

This classic dance ballet is arranged to Franck's *Symphonic Variations* for piano and orchestra. There is no story, only a mood created by the setting and costumes, the music, and the dancers' response to it.

When the curtain rises, six dancers are on stage. Three girls stand forward in a line parallel to the front of the stage. In the back, turned away from us, are three boys. The backdrop is of abstract design: curved and slanting black lines on a light green cloth.

The orchestra begins. The dancers do not move: they stand quietly in youthful meditation on the music. Directly the piano begins, the girls commence to dance. As if activated only by the instrument, they pause as the orchestra takes up the theme. A variation on the theme is stated, and one of the boys comes forward. He takes turns dancing with the three girls, then remains still as they dance about him. Now he holds the girls, one by one, as they whirl in his arms.

The girls rest as the two other boys join the leading male soloist in a line similar to that which was formed at the beginning by the three girls. The three dance—the two boys on the outside miming in motion the part of the orchestra, while the soloist, in the center, takes the part of the piano. The boys dance now to the girls, who respond to their statement of a theme. Two of the girls dance alone, then with one of the boys. They retire; another boy takes the center of the stage and dances a variation.

The principal ballerina now comes forward and, while the boys in the background dance quietly, she moves with sweet splendor to the music of the piano. The male soloist joins her, and they dance a *pas de deux*.

After this romantic sequence, all six dancers move together. Now they are not so much separate individuals responding to the music, as one group animated by the same theme. The boys and girls divide, come together in couples, and make swift, open patterns about the stage while the music rushes toward its conclusion. Their swift ebullience is broken at the end, as the dancers resume the meditative poses with which the ballet began.

NOTES Ashton has said of his ballet and the time it was composed, just after World War II, in *Frederick Ashton, A Choreographer and His Ballets:* "My mother died in 1939, just before the war. So I was independent at last, although it didn't do me any good. Almost as soon as the war started I had to go into the R.A.F. Everyone was being called up—all the dancers and everyone I knew in the theatre—and I wanted, I suppose, to share their agony. I must say, I thought it was the end of everything. It was a period of enormous frustration to me because I felt I hadn't said nearly enough to be ready to die on it.

"The importance of the war was that it gave me a period to think and read a good deal and also, because I was rather unhappy, I went in for mysticism. I read St. Theresa of Avila and St. John of the Cross and lots of books about mystics and mysticism. After all, one was told that it was the end of the world.

"During the war, the tendency in all the ballets seemed to become much too literary and dramatic. During the last part of the war, I was stationed at the Air Ministry as an Intelligence officer and I saw everything that was going on, although at this stage I couldn't do any work myself. It was very frustrating, and originally I think that *Symphonic Variations* was very much over-choreographed. I remember doing a tremendous amount of eliminating, especially in the finale;

I pared and pared and pared until I got the kind of purity I wanted. You see, when I started I was going to do something very complicated, with lots of people and a sort of seasonal theme. But then I thought one day that six dancers would be enough. When one begins to do things one is apt to overcharge everything, and if things get too intense, one blurs the vision of the audience. By simplifying, you make it easier for an audience to take in your intentions.

"With *Symphonic Variations* I had to do a lot of experimenting to find the sort of movement that I wanted. That was what took the time, but once I had achieved it the rest went fairly well. I was able to ride on the music quite a bit because I knew it very well and I'd listened to it during the war. I'd always hoped I would get round to using it one day."

Margot Fonteyn has also written of the time of the creation of this ballet: "When *Symphonic Variations* was almost finished, Michael Somes had to have an operation on the cartilage in his knee. The first night of *Symphonic* was postponed for something like two months while Michael had his operation and got back into training.

"When we started to rehearse it all again Fred took out a lot of things and simplified and purified the choreography. Instead of having his usual deadline for the dress rehearsal and the first performance, he had time to reassess the choreography. I think that's one reason why it turned out to be one of his masterpieces. I remember a lot of discussion and all sorts of different ideas and versions and several different endings, and Sophie Fedorovitch at the rehearsals and coming in each day to say what she thought. A lot went into revising *Symphonic*. It's probably the only ballet he's ever had the opportunity to revise before the first night."

The critic and dancer David Vaughan, writing in *Ballet Review*, has said of this ballet: "The postponed première of Ashton's *Symphonic Variations* was for him a kind of manifesto similar to *Apollo*—a clearing away of literary and scenic paraphernalia, just six dancers on an open stage, given an illusion of even greater spaciousness by Fedorovitch's airy decor. If Ashton had shown at various times in his earlier career the influence of Nijinski and Massine, to say nothing of Pavlova and Duncan, there were moments in *Symphonic Variations* that inevitably, maybe coincidentally, suggested Balanchine's masterpiece, especially in the passages of supported adagio involving three women and one man. But more important was the final distillation of Ashton's own classicism: it marked the beginning of his exploration of various motifs that became trademarks of his *pas de deux* at that time—the skimming lifts with *batterie* or *pas de bourrée* just off the floor, the scissor-like movements, the *arabesques élançées.* Notable also was the courage to be simple, to leave out anything extraneous to the piece's lyric utterance: there is never any sense of strain after the ingeniously original lift or step, indeed, some of the most eloquent passages are the transitions when the dancers join hands in a simple run.

"*Symphonic Variations* was, then, a kind of summation, and a consummation, of Ashton's career up to that point, made possible, no doubt, by the kind of fallow period he had been obliged to go through during his war service, however frustrating that must have been at the time. From there he could move on to the inevitable next step in the development of British ballet—or at any rate of the Wells, as it acquired official recognition as the national ballet in the form of the royal charter—the creation of full-length ballets that could stand alongside the classics of the repertory, *Giselle, Swan Lake, Sleeping Beauty,* and the rest."

SYMPHONY IN C

Classic ballet in four movements. Music by Georges Bizet. Choreography by George Balanchine. First presented under the title Le Palais de Cristal *by the Paris Opéra Ballet at the Opéra, July 28, 1947, with Lycette Darsonval, Tamara Toumanova, Micheline Bardin, Madeleine Lafon, Alexandre Kaliujny, Roger Ritz, Michel Renault, and Max Bozzoni as principals. Scenery and costumes by Léonor Fini. First presented in the United States by Ballet Society at the City Center, New York, March 22, 1948, with Maria Tallchief, Tanaquil LeClercq, Beatrice Tompkins, Elise Reiman, Nicholas Magallanes, Francisco Moncion, Herbert Bliss, and Lew Christensen in the principal roles.*

Symphony in C is not based on a story, but on the music to which it is danced. Bizet's symphony is in four movements; each of these movements develops different themes, different melodies. Correspondingly, in the ballet, there is a different dance scheme and development for each of these four movements. Each movement has its own characteristic ballerina, *premier danseur,* and *corps de ballet.* Toward the end of the ballet, when the different groups have danced their special parts of the symphony, all the groups combine with their ballerinas for a kind of dance summing up of all that has gone before. There is no scenery, only a blue background; the dancers are dressed in classical ballet costumes.

FIRST MOVEMENT—ALLEGRO VIVO The curtain rises before the music begins. Two small groups of girls begin to dance with the opening chord. As the orchestra plays the first theme and repeats it, the two groups dance in opposition, first dancing all together, then alternately following the movements of two leaders.

The ballerina appears as the second theme is announced by the oboe and strings. She dances forward in crisp, open movements to the rhythm of the melody, turning gracefully as she poses and balancing for a moment as she waits for the theme to begin anew. Her dance now becomes brisk and flourishing. She pirouettes swiftly as the two soloists join her, balances again briefly, and leaves the stage.

After the orchestra has given an intimation of the first theme and horns have played a short transition, two boys enter to support the soloists. The ballerina returns with her partner. She dances around the stage, retires to the rear, and, as the first theme of the movement returns, leads the ensemble. On the last clipped chord she stands supported in a quick, graceful pose.

SECOND MOVEMENT—ADAGIO The *corps de ballet* moves slowly to the introductory passage. A second ballerina enters with her partner as the soft central theme of the movement is sounded by the oboe. She is lifted low off the floor and moves as if in slow motion, then is lifted high, her legs describing sweeping arcs in the air. Her partner supports her in long, slow lifts and held poses while the *corps de ballet* gathers about her. As the movement ends, the ballerina falls back in her partner's arms.

THIRD MOVEMENT—ALLEGRO VIVACE Here the music is spirited and lively. Six girls, in a third *corps de ballet*, dance forward; two couples join them to leap across the stage; and, finally, a third ballerina and her partner enter to circle the stage in broad leaps. They dance together briefly, turning rapidly in the air together, and rush off into the wings. Soon they return, repeat their dance, and lead the *corps de ballet* to the bright, ebullient music. At one point the boy lifts the ballerina off the floor and drops her, pushing her forward, so that she seems to bounce to the music. The entire group joins in the final measures, the *corps de ballet* kneeling as the ballerina is held in a graceful pose at the last chord.

FOURTH MOVEMENT—ALLEGRO VIVACE In the final movement, the principals of the first three movements join with a fourth ballerina and her partner in an exhilarating display of virtuosity that becomes at times a contest. The fourth ballerina and her accompanying group dance first. They are followed by the ballerina of the first movement and her *corps de ballet*. The ballerina of the Adagio movement appears next, then the ballerina of the third movement.

The thirty-two girls who have made up the four *corps*

de ballet now line the stage at the sides and across the back. All four ballerinas dance in their midst, each executing the same brilliant steps. Their partners enter for their turn, while secondary soloists dance behind them. At the close, all forty-eight dancers—soloists and *corps de ballet*—join the principals in a brilliant finale. As the last chord of the music sounds, the ballerinas turn quickly and fall back over their partners' arms as the secondary soloists are lifted high behind them in a climactic tableau.

NOTES *Symphony in C* was originally mounted for the Paris Opéra during my visit there as guest choreographer in 1947. For the Opéra, I staged revivals of three ballets: *Apollo, Le Baiser de la Fée,* and *Serenade,* and although the two latter ballets had never been seen in Paris before, at the end of my engagement I wished to stage a new work especially for the principal dancers of the Opéra.

It seemed fitting to select for this new work music by a French composer. I accordingly chose the little-known *Symphony in C Major* written by the French master Bizet when he was only seventeen years old. Composition of the ballet was completed in about two weeks.

The ballet was staged for Ballet Society in New York the following spring. When this company became the New York City Ballet seven months later, *Symphony in C* was the concluding ballet on the first program. The ballet has been a part of the permanent repertory of the New York City Ballet ever since.

SYMPHONY IN THREE MOVEMENTS

Music by Igor Stravinsky. Choreography by George Balanchine. First presented by the New York City Ballet at the Stravinsky Festival, 1972, at the New York State Theater, Lincoln Center, June 18, 1972, with Helgi Tomasson, Sara Leland, and Edward Villella in principal roles. Lighting by Ronald Bates. Conducted by Robert Craft.

I remember Stravinsky's talking to me about this music during World War II, when I visited him in Hollywood. It is a magnificent, major work, and I had wanted for many years to make a ballet to the music. The appropriate opportunity came in 1972, when we were preparing the Stravinsky Festival at the New York City Ballet.

The score is a short one for a symphony—about twenty-one minutes—and is in three movements. Stravinsky has written that "the formal substance of the symphony exploits contrasts of several kinds, one of them being the contrast between the principal instrumental protagonists, harp and piano. Each instrument has a large obbligato role in a movement to itself, and only at the turning-point fugue . . . do the two play together and unaccompanied."

"Composers combine notes," Stravinsky said. Choreographers combine movements and the ones I arranged for this music follow no story line or narrative. They try to catch the music and do not, I hope, lean on it, using it instead for support and time frame. If I were to try to relate that a boy and sixteen girls begin the ballet, that would not be very interesting, or that a girl in purple dances with eight others to music for clarinet, piano, and strings soon follows. What is really interesting is the complexity and variety of the music, from the propulsive drive and thrust of the vigorous opening (which also closes the ballet) to the developed use, almost like a concerto, of the piano in the first movement, the harp in the second and the two together in the finale.

The central movement, Andante, is a *pas de deux*. One writer has called this a "strangely quiet, sensuous, meditative interlude with a pronounced Eastern tinge." I had not thought of that but paraphrasing Stravinsky, how and in what form the things of this world are impressed upon my dance is not for me to say.

After the ballet was in our repertory, I heard that the first movement of the symphony was actually composed as a possible accompaniment for a film about China and that the second movement was also composed (but not used) for a film project—the apparition-of-the-Virgin scene for the film of Werfel's *Song of Bernadette.*

TALES OF HOFFMAN

Ballet in prologue, three acts, and an epilogue. Music by Jacques Offenbach, arranged and orchestrated by John Lanchbery. Choreography by Peter Darrell. Design by Alistair Livingstone. Lighting by John B. Read. Scenario by Peter Darrell from stories by E. T. A. Hoffmann. First presented by Scottish Theatre Ballet at the Kings Theatre, Edinburgh, Scotland, April 6, 1972, with Peter Cazalet as Hoffman. First presented in the United States by American Ballet Theatre at the New York State Theater, Lincoln Center, New York, July 12, 1973, with sets and costumes by Peter Docherty and with Cynthia Gregory and Jonas Kage in the principal roles.

Those who are familiar with Offenbach's opera of this title, or with the popular film, will know all about E. T. A. Hoffmann, the German teller of tales whose stories have already made ballet history in *Coppelia* and *The Nutcracker*.

PROLOGUE—A TAVERN OUTSIDE AN OPERA HOUSE Hoffman is drinking with friends while awaiting the arrival of La Stella, his latest love, who is appearing at the opera. He is asked to explain the meaning of three souvenirs on his table but at first refuses. La Stella arrives and gives her maid a note for Hoffman which, unseen by him, is intercepted by Counsellor Lindorf. Hoffman, now a little drunk, agrees to tell the stories behind the three souvenirs and the tales proper begin:

ACT ONE (THE FIRST TALE)—THE CONSERVATOR IN SPALANZANI'S HOUSE Spalanzani, an inventor, has invited some friends to see his latest invention, the lifelike mechanical doll, Olympia. Hoffman as a very young man observes Olympia from afar and tries to meet her. Spalanzani announces that Olympia will dance for his guests, but first insists that Hoffman put on a pair of magic spectacles. Hoffman immediately falls in love with Olympia and asks her to marry him. Spalanzani, delighted with the success of his deception, agrees at once. Hoffman, whirling Olympia about in a dance, loses the magic pair of glasses. The doll thereupon falls apart and poor Hoffman realizes he has been tricked.

ACT TWO (THE SECOND TALE)—THE MUSIC ROOM OF ANTONIA'S HOME Ten years have passed. Hoffman, in love with Antonia, is taking music lessons from her father. Behind her father's back, Antonia flirts with Hoffman while dancing to his playing. When they are discovered, the father warns Antonia that too much exertion will be fatal to her. Doctor Miracle suddenly appears. He promises to cure Antonia and hypnotizes her into believing that she is a great ballerina. Hoffman returns and Antonia, enthralled by her vision, implores him to play so that she may dance again. Urged on by Doctor Miracle, Hoffman reluctantly does so until, overcome, Antonia dies in his arms.

ACT THREE (THE THIRD TALE)—DAPERTUTTO'S SALON Now an older and more serious man, Hoffman has turned to religion for comfort from his earlier disappointments. He finds himself in the salon of Dapertutto, who tries to lure him again to the enjoyment of sensual pleasures but without success until the arrival of Giuletta, a lovely courtesan. Encouraged by Dapertutto, Giuletta so seduces Hoffman that he even renounces his faith. Then he realizes, when his reflection disappears in a mirror, that he has lost his immortal soul. In his anguish he prays that he may be forgiven and, as his reflection reappears, Giuletta and Dapertutto are drawn into the mirror and vanish.

EPILOGUE—THE TAVERN Hoffman, his stories told, is offered more drink by the sinister Counsellor Lindorf. La Stella emerges from the opera house looking for Hoffman and finds him in a drunken sleep, her note crushed on the ground. Sad and disappointed, she is led away by Lindorf. Hoffman, roused from his stupor, realizes that yet again he has been duped by the evil presence that has pursued him throughout his life.

THE TAMING OF THE SHREW

Ballet in two acts after Shakespeare. Music by Kurt-Heinz Stolze after Domenico Scarlatti. Choreography and production by John Cranko. Scenery and costumes by Elizabeth Dalton. Lighting by Gilbert V. Hemsley, Jr. First presented by the Stuttgart Ballet at the Wurttembergische Staatstheater, Stuttgart, Germany, March 16, 1969, with Marcia Haydée and Richard Cragun in the principal roles. First presented in the United States by the same ensemble at the Metropolitan Opera House, New York, June 12, 1969.

The Taming of the Shrew turns out to be just as amusing to see in dance form as it is in the spoken theater. The action of the ballet follows closely that of the play:

ACT ONE, SCENE ONE—OUTSIDE THE HOUSE OF BAPTISTA, A WEALTHY NOBLEMAN Hortensio, a fop, Lucentio, a student, and Gremio, an elderly roué, serenade the beautiful Bianca, one of the nobleman's daughters. Their love songs are rudely interrupted by her sister, Katherine, who thinks herself just as beautiful. In addition, Baptista explains to the suitors that Kate, as the elder of the two, must be married first. Neighbors, awakened by the serenade and the rumpus, chase the thwarted lovers away.

ACT ONE, SCENE TWO—A TAVERN Here Petruchio, a gentleman of more generosity than means, is robbed of his last penny by two ladies of the streets. The suitors suggest that he, therefore, might be interested in the charms and fortune of Katherine. He readily agrees.

ACT ONE, SCENE THREE—INSIDE BAPTISTA'S HOUSE Bianca muses over her preferences among her three suitors. She is interrupted by a jealous outburst from Kate, a rowdy tomboy of a girl, who calls her a scheming flirt. This dispute is further interrupted by the arrival of Petruchio, who is accompanied by Bianca's suitors in disguise. Petruchio is none too favorably received by Kate. Alone with Bianca, the suitors throw off their disguises and continue their wooing in the form of singing, dancing, and music lessons. Bianca soon recognizes Lucentio as the most desirable.

Kate reacts violently against Petruchio's protestations of passion, thinking that they are a false mockery, but something in his manner convinces her, nevertheless, to accept his offer and they agree to get married.

ACT ONE, SCENE FOUR—A STREET Here neighbors on their way to Kate's wedding treat the whole matter as a huge joke. The three suitors, now in high hopes that Bianca will soon be released to marry one of them, join them.

ACT ONE, SCENE FIVE—INSIDE BAPTISTA'S HOUSE The guests have arrived. Kate in her bridal array is all expectant and waiting, but the bridegroom appears to have forgotten the day. When he does appear, in fantastic garb, Petruchio behaves very badly, ill-treating the priest and carrying off Kate before the wedding festivities have started.

ACT TWO, SCENE ONE—PETRUCHIO'S HOUSE Kate is a fiery-tempered girl and Act Two shows what Petruchio aims to do about it. In the first scene he finds fault with the food and the girl has to go without her supper.

ACT TWO, SCENE TWO—A CARNIVAL Meanwhile, in a scene at the carnival, two of Bianca's suitors, Gremio and Hortensio, encounter a masked and cloaked stranger. Both of them believing her to be Bianca are only too eager to take their marriage vows. Too late they discover that they have been duped and married to ladies of the street, who have been suitably briefed, bribed, and disguised by Lucentio.

ACT TWO, SCENE THREE—PETRUCHIO'S HOUSE When Petruchio finds fault with the new clothes that he has ordered for Kate, her weary resistance finally crumbles and she capitulates, only to find that her master is a kinder, wittier husband than she thought possible.

ACT TWO, SCENE FOUR—ENROUTE TO BIANCA'S WEDDING Petruchio indulges in more whims, fancies, and tricks, but Kate has learned her lesson and joins in the fun.

ACT TWO, SCENE FIVE—BAPTISTA'S HOUSE At Bianca's wedding the action is all tied up. Gremio and Hortensio have found out that the joys of marriage are a mixed blessing, and even Lucentio has reason to fear that Bianca is not the angel that she appeared to be. Kate, on the other hand, and to everyone's astonishment, turns out to be the truest, most obedient, most loving of wives. Which goes to show that women are not always what they appear to be or, in other words, never judge a book by its cover.

TCHAIKOVSKY SUITE NO. 2

Music by Peter Ilyich Tchaikovsky. Choreography by Jacques d'Amboise. Production designed by John Braden. Lighting by Ronald Bates. First presented by the New York City Ballet at the New York State Theater, Lincoln Center, January 9, 1969, with Marnee Morris, John Prinz, Allegra Kent, Francisco Moncion, Linda Merrill, and John Clifford as principals. Conducted by Robert Irving.

The first of a series of Tchaikovsky suites in the New York City Ballet, this dance ballet is performed to music from the composer's *Suite No. 2* for orchestra. In keeping with Tchaikovsky's music, which is fascinating in its Russian references, the ballet makes gestures to Russian, Georgian, and Ukrainian folklore or costumes, but the dances may be said to take place in any time and place. If you do not know this music of Tchaikovsky's, and it is no doubt the least famous of the four suites for orchestra, I with pleasure recommend that you become acquainted with it.

Reviewing the ballet for the New York *Times,* the critic Clive Barnes wrote: "Mr. d'Amboise, a strong dancer himself, of course, creates gratefully for dancers. Here in the first movement he has precisely caught in the delightfully skittish quality of Marnee Morris, the special lilt of laughter in her dancing, and contrasted this with the pouncing, very virile quality of John Prinz. Both dancers responded happily.

"The deep-set mystery of Allegra Kent and the somber power of Francisco Moncion have inspired the softer-toned second movement. Miss Kent showed just the right misty poetry, while Mr. Moncion, filled with a kind of animal nobility, made her an ideal partner.

"For the third movement the ballet reverts to the lighter-hearted tone of the beginning, and here Linda Merrill (in her first major created assignment) and John Clifford fly around blithely and impressively."

THE THREE-CORNERED HAT

Dramatic ballet in one act. Music by Manuel de Falla. Choreography by Leonide Massine. Book by Gregorio Martínez Sierra. Scenery and costumes by Pablo Picasso. First presented by Diaghilev's Ballets Russes at the Alhambra Theatre, London, July 22, 1919, with Leonide Massine as the Miller, *Tamara Karsavina as the* Miller's Wife, *Leon Woizikowski as the* Corregidor, *and Stanislas Idzikowski as the* Dandy. *First presented in the United States by the Ballet Russe de Monte Carlo at the St. James Theatre, New York, March 9, 1934, with Leon Woizikowski as the* Miller *and Tamara Toumanova as the* Miller's Wife.

The Three-Cornered Hat tells a love story of Spain with humor and warmth. The scene is a small Spanish village. The Spanish tone of the ballet is established immediately by the music, by cries of *"Olé! Olé! Olé! Olé!"* from behind the curtain, and by the sound of rhythmic castanets, dancing feet, and hand clapping.

The curtain rises on the village scene. The village miller stands before his house, whistling to a black bird who sits in a cage. The bird will not sing as he wishes it to. The miller's wife comes out of the house and teases her husband. He chases her and they embrace.

The couple go to the well to draw water. While the miller is busy at the well, a dandy passes by and blows kisses to his wife, who responds flirtatiously. The miller looks up and sees this exchange and chases the dandy off. He is not angry with his wife. He is delighted that other men find her as beautiful as he does. They are very much in love.

Now the governor of the province, the corregidor, enters with an escort. A doddering old fool, he looks absurd in his finery among the simple folk of the village. He wears a three-cornered hat, symbol of his class and position.

Almost immediately the corregidor eyes the miller's wife and decides that she must be his. The miller's wife is polite to him, but no more. He passes on. Noting that his wife is getting all the attention, the miller decides he'd better give another girl some favor. He playfully flirts with one of the lovely girls of the village. Now that both husband and wife have cause to be jealous, they are amused at each other and embrace.

The miller goes into the house. His wife, remaining outside, dances a brilliant *fandango.* The corregidor has come back and secretly watches her. Soon he approaches her and tries to make advances. The woman eludes him cleverly and flees. The old man, however, pursues her.

The miller has watched this scene from inside the house and runs out to help his wife. The corregidor can run no more and falls to the ground, exhausted. The miller and his wife pick him up, dust him off, and try to act as if it were all an accident, but the corregidor, furious with them, suggests that this is only the beginning of what they may expect of him. The husband and wife dance together.

Evening falls. The village folk come to the miller's house to join in a festival with the happy couple. The miller gives them wine and then dances alone a *farruca,* which everyone applauds. The villagers hear the approach of marching soldiers. The escorts of the corregidor enter. The men arrest the miller and take him off. Abandoned by her friends, the miller's wife is alone.

But not for long. The corregidor is back again, seeking her favor now with real determination. The miller's wife throws him to the ground as he clumsily holds her. He rises with difficulty and pursues her to the village bridge, which crosses a running stream. On the bridge, the corregidor again attempts to embrace the girl. In the process of pushing him away, the miller's wife pushes him off the bridge into the stream. She laughs at him, but helps the corregidor out of the water. But the old fool takes up the chase again. The miller's wife takes a gun from the house and, threatening the corregidor with buckshot, flees over the bridge away from the village.

The corregidor stands in front of the miller's house, alone, his clothes still dripping from the dunking he got in the stream. He takes off his outer garments and his three-cornered hat, lays them out to dry, and goes into the house to sleep.

Dawn comes. The miller has escaped the corregidor's henchmen and returns home. In front of his house he sees the corregidor's clothes and the three-cornered hat! Then he observes the corregidor himself, walking around in one of his own nightshirts! The miller decides there's only one thing to do. He will pursue the corregidor's wife, who is also young and beautiful! On the walls of his house he draws a caricature of the corregidor and leaves.

Now the poor corregidor is attacked by his own soldiers, who don't recognize him in the miller's nightshirt. He curses them, and the village folk come to see what the trouble is. The miller and his wife, who have found each other outside the town, come in. Their friends are told what the corregidor has tried to do, and in anger all the people rise up against the governor and his cohorts. The intruders are routed, and all dance triumphantly, led by the miller and his wife. A dummy representing the defeated corregidor is thrown higher and higher into the air by the crowd.

NOTES Although Leon Woizikowski first danced the miller at the American première of *The Three-Cornered Hat*, Leonide Massine later danced the role in the United States. The ballet was revived by Massine for Ballet Theatre in 1943 and for the Sadler's Wells Ballet in 1947.

Tania Massine, the choreographer's daughter, assisted by Yurek Lazowski, staged a revival of *The Three-Cornered Hat* for the City Center Joffrey Ballet in New York, September 25, 1969. Luis Fuente was the *Miller*, Barbara Remington the *Miller's wife*, Basil Thompson the *Corregidor*, Rebecca Wright the *Corregidor's wife*, and Frank Bays the *Dandy*. The original Picasso designs were reconstructed by William Pitkin.

THREE VIRGINS AND A DEVIL

Music by Ottorino Respighi. Scenario by Ramon Reed. Choreography by Agnes de Mille. Scenery and costumes by Motley. Setting designed by Arne Lundborg. First presented by Ballet Theatre at the Majestic Theatre, New York, February 11, 1941, with Agnes de Mille as the Priggish One, *Lucia Chase as the* Greedy One, *Annabelle Lyon as the* Lustful One, *Eugene Loring as a* Devil, *and Jerome Robbins as a* Youth.

The critic Robert J. Pierce has called this ballet a burlesque in the form of a medieval morality play. Arranged to Respighi's *Ancient Dances and Airs for the Lute*, this *danse caractère* personifies three typical but differing young women and shows what happens to them under devilish circumstances.

After a short overture the curtain rises on a medieval landscape, a monastery gate at the right, with door shut; a grotto at the left, leading to a cave. Three girls come in. Their leader, a priggish lass, is trying to drag her friends to church. She displays maximum piety in this undertaking, trying to persuade the Greedy One, who is decked out in finery, to put her belongings in the alms box. Not to be overlooked, the Lustful One, a child of nature with a garland of flowers, sees the directions things are taking and decides to renounce her wreath. When a prancing Youth enters to find all the virgins swaying in prayer, he is clearly astonished at such unanimous piety. He cannot persuade any of the girls to join him.

Now a hermit enters, asking the Greedy One for money. The beggar is a peculiar sort of fellow, almost spastic in his movements as he seems to try to hide one of his feet under his cloak. The foot keeps trembling and bothering him. When he can bear it no longer, he throws off the cloak and reveals himself as a Devil, tail, horns, cloven foot, and all.

The virgins, in their uniform piety, are appalled, but when he brings out a sort of cello and starts to play, they all dance lustily to his tune. They get so carried away by their revels that when the Youth returns, again beckoning to the Lustful

One, she jumps obligingly onto his back, whereupon he carries her swiftly into the grotto—a gate, of course, to hell.

The Devil tempts next the Greedy One, who responds to his offer of a bright jewel and follows her sister to the other world. The Priggish One, of course, is harder to tempt and the Devil has his own time of it getting from her the proper response. She mothers him and strikes terror into him by trying to get him into the monastery. Unable to bear such tactics any longer, he begins to chase her like a man possessed. In terror she flees, running from him in a wider and wider circle, but pursuing him, too, determined to have yet another convert. The widening circle of the chase leads to the grotto entrance, where the Devil stands aside and permits the lady to dash down to hell with her own momentum.

NOTES Agnes de Mille first produced a ballet to this theme in London, in 1934, at the Palace Theatre, in the musical comedy *Why Not Tonight?* Greta Nissen, Elizabeth Schooling, and M. Braithwaite were the Girls and Stanislas Idzikowski the Devil. The music was by Walford Hyden.

American Ballet Theatre revived *Three Virgins and a Devil* at the New York State Theater, Lincoln Center, New York, July 25, 1973, with Sallie Wilson (now called the Fanatical One), Ruth Mayer, and Christine Sarry as the Virgins, Dennis Nahat as a Devil, and Daniel Levins as a Youth. The conductor was Akira Endo and the lighting was by Nananne Porcher.

TRIAD

Music by Serge Prokofiev. Choreography by Kenneth MacMillan. Setting and costumes by Peter Unsworth. First presented by the Royal Ballet at the Royal Opera House, Covent Garden, London, January 19, 1972, with Antoinette Sibley, Anthony Dowell, and Wayne Eagling. First presented in the United States by the Royal Ballet at the Metropolitan Opera House, New York, in 1972.

The three principal dancers in *Triad* are a girl, a boy, and his brother. The two boys are devoted but from the start there is a problem. One of them is upset and cries. A girl comes to them and dances. One brother tries to shield the other from the effects of this dance of the girl's but the girl will not permit it. Now one of the boys dances for the girl, then she again for *him*. After a dance for all three, the girl tries to persuade one to come away with her. She goes but he stays. The two boys dance, one continuing to try to shield the other. But not for long. When three male "companions" enter, the stronger brother throws the weaker to them, only to rescue him at the last minute. After a passionate *pas de deux* between the stronger boy and the girl, the younger brother despairs. He leaves but returns, tries to separate them, fails, again despairs.

NOTES Writing in *Saturday Review* about *Triad*, the critic Walter Terry said that while the ballet "may seem to some to have homosexual overtones, I felt it to be rooted in something like the deep mystique of twins who are both dual and one. MacMillan captures this feeling tastefully but, what is more, imaginatively. The contours of his movements are generally balletic, but the dynamism is that of modern dance; that is, indeed, a striking integration of the elegance and dignity of classicism with the passionate, almost visceral, expressivity of free dance.

"In the cast I saw, Dowell and Wayne Eagling were most appealing as the brothers whose bond goes deeper than physicality, and Miss Sibley, as the girl, touched the heart with a portrayal involving need, desire, rejection. A most rewarding, adult ballet, rich in striking designs as well as in dramatic intensity."

TRINITY

Music by Alan Raph and Lee Holdridge. Choreography by Gerald Arpino. Lighting by Jennifer Tipton. Conductor: Walter Hagen. Rock Group: Virgin Wool. Organ: Hub Miller. Boys Choir: St. Luke's Chapel. First presented by the City Center Joffrey Ballet, October 9, 1969, with Christian Holder, Gary Chryst, Rebecca Wright, Dermot Burke, Donna Cowen, Starr Danias, and James Dunne in principal roles.

Named for its three parts, *Sunday, Summerland,* and *Saturday, Trinity* is a homage to youth, joyful and aspiring. It uses for music themes reminiscent of Gregorian chant and Baroque styles translated into rock, employing sections of the regular orchestra, a boy's choir, and a rock group, "Virgin Wool." There are two conductors, one for the orchestra and chorus, one who leads the rock group from the organ.

Thirteen dancers participate in *Sunday,* which is heralded by a brass chorale before the curtain rises. The dancers enter gradually until finally all are present to respond to the throb of the rock organ. This is a group dance, exuberant, demanding in its rhythm and pulse, persistent, rejoicing in companionship and celebratory of youth. There are a number of solos and small ensembles as the mixture of rock and baroque mounts in intensity. At the end, all lie in a circle on the floor as lead boy leaves.

In the part called *Summerland,* the pulse of the score slows down. The dancers rise from the circle and in varied ensembles suggest the sweetness of young love. Couple after couple now take the stage, one of them dancing a protracted adagio of affection. The accent here is on high spirits, too, shown in the many remarkable lifts in which the boys reach the girls up to the skies. All six couples rejoin as chimes sound twice and the boys carry the girls off.

Saturday, standing for the ancient Sabbath, begins as two boys enter the darkened scene carrying candles. The entire group follows, each bearing a lighted candle. They leave then and a boy comes forward to perform a dance to the hymn/rock beat, a version of the *Ite, missa est* that concludes the Latin Mass. He is joined by other male soloists and we have an impression that there is nothing on earth like lifting your arms and responding to the swell of the mighty organ that dominates the music here. The score intensifies in cracking crescendos of sound. All of the dancers then re-enter, each putting a candle on stage. The music gradually diminishes and the lights diminish, too, so that all we see on stage is the presentation of the candles.

NOTES Speaking of his ballet to Anna Kisselgoff of the New York *Times*, the choreographer of *Trinity*, Gerald Arpino, said, "I think I'm in tune with my time. . . . This is my Aquarius ballet. I wanted the classic idiom with its escape from gravity—for the highest reach man can assume. I don't want to sound corny, but this is a ballet about man seeking his inner self. When the kids leave the candles on the floor, it's not meant to suggest just the literal peace marches. In the end, each individual must express himself. All he can leave is the light of himself."

The critic Andrew Porter reviewed *Trinity* at the time of the City Center Joffrey Ballet's London debut in May, 1971: "Gerald Arpino's *Trinity* made a whizzing start. For here the company seemed to be the 20th century's answer to the Bolshoi Ballet: which is to say nothing prissy, and nothing pretentious, but tremendous vigour and soaring virtuosity; flashing, exhilarating achievement rather than refined niceties; punch rather than polish. But—unlike the Bolshoi—an imagery both on stage and from the players that belongs to the present day: thoroughly demotic images supercharged into a buoyant art.

"The score, for the company's own group The Virgin Wool, choirboys, electric organ and orchestra, strikes into plain chant and Palestrina, and turns them into rock—not self-consciously but exuberantly. The dancing strikes into classicism at times, and breaks it into modern movement. The whole is heady and joyful, a celebration of a youth that can effortlessly encompass and transform the past."

John T. Elson in *Time* magazine wrote that *Trinity* "represents a throbbing fusion of classic dance with the sound of now. It perfectly epitomizes the jaunty style and passionate, youthful temperament of the New York City Center's Joffrey Ballet."

Patricia Barnes, in *Dance and Dancers,* wrote: "*Trinity* is a hard ballet to describe for its vitality, sincerity and passion, its dynamic coloring, both choreographic and musical, must be seen. Nor can words alone convey the personality and power of dancers such as Gary Chryst, Christian Holder and Dermot Burke; these three did a great deal to make *Trinity* the success it was. However, the whole cast had a splendid exuberance that made the ballet a pleasure to watch."

In the *Village Voice,* writing of the work of choreographer Gerald Arpino, Deborah Jowitt said: "His new ballet, *Trinity,* never lets go of you, never stops pounding and hurling fast, smart-alecky movement at you. He ignores—or perhaps uses —several basic dichotomies with magnificent ease. The Joffrey dancers are young and phenomenal. The best of them may grow in artistry or sensitivity, but they will probably never be more indomitable. Although they are young, they already have a discipline that very few people their age possess. I think it is the combination of discipline and vigor that excites Arpino. The three-part *Trinity* is set to some very good rock music (written by Alan Raph and Lee Holdridge and played by Virgin Wool), and the whole dance seems a taut by-play between the freedom inherent in rock and the control necessary for ballet. The dancers progress from the flung *développés* of Broadway to perfectly centered pirouettes rendered dangerous and exciting by fast, off-balance head circles or contrary arm gestures. This gives the movement an odd duality; ballet with a loose, whizzing quality in one part of the body only.

"Rock is heavy, ballet light. In *Trinity,* the dancers skid and wiggle on top of the beat; they punch it, but rarely drop onto it. Another interesting paradox. The movement is, for the most part, fast and very intricate—except for a slow ritual with votive candles in the last section and a softer second movement that features those stunning one-arm lifts that drove the crowd wild."

UNDERTOW

Ballet in one act with prologue and epilogue. Choreography by Antony Tudor. Music by William Schuman. Libretto by Antony Tudor, after a suggestion by John van Druten. Scenery and costumes by Raymond Breinin. First presented by Ballet Theatre at the Metropolitan Opera House, New York, April 10, 1945, with a cast headed by Hugh Laing as the Transgressor, *Alicia Alonso as* Ate, *Diana Adams as* Cybele, *Nana Gollner as* Medusa, *Shirley Eckl as* Volupia, *Patricia Barker as* Aganippe, *and Lucia Chase as* Polyhymnia.

Modern ballets are continually enlarging the subject matter of the dance. It might seem strange to us now, but not until 1936—when Antony Tudor produced *Lilac Garden*—did we ever see on the ballet stage people, who looked and acted somewhat like ourselves, in a dramatic ballet. The women in *Lilac Garden* wore long party dresses, not romantic *tutus;* the men were anxious lovers, not mechanical cavaliers. And the characters in the ballet were caught up in a dramatic situation that was dominated by their inner feelings.

Undertow represents another effort to extend the dramatic dance. It attempts to show us why a young man, called the transgressor, commits murder. It shows us where he was born, the people he grew up with, and the people who influenced his life. All the characters in the ballet, except the hero, have names derived from mythology. They are thus not particular personalities, but universal characters recognizable in the life of every man. The time is the present.

PROLOGUE—BIRTH AND INFANCY The light is dim. We make out Cybele, great mother of gods, in labor. She gives birth to a son, who creeps out from between her limbs and cries. The mother is revolted by the sight of her son and the agony she has suffered. She abandons him and seeks a lover —Pollux, the immortal youth who is born anew each day. Her son instinctively despises his mother and nurtures his grief.

Even as a child, the transgressor discovers in the world no love.

THE CITY—ADOLESCENCE AND MANHOOOD The scene is a street in the slums of a huge city. We sense immediately the irony of the splendid statues that dominate the nearby square: great winged horses fly away from a place the inhabitants can never leave. Their life is so miserable that they cannot entertain the notion of accustoming themselves to anything else. A woman, made up hideously, stands pouting, waiting for someone to notice her. She is Volupia, here a bedraggled personification of sensual pleasure.

The transgressor, now a youth, enters with a pretty young girl. Her name is Aganippe and she is innocent inspiration. They appear to be having a good time together until the boy notices the streetwalker. He is fascinated by her and observes her with open curiosity. His girl abandons him. Volupia looks at the boy contemptuously and smartens up for a man who now struts onto the scene. He goes directly to her and follows, as she knowingly leads the way.

A rowdy bunch of boys race into the street. What seems to be playfulness on their part is genuinely mean and cruel. They are aware of nothing else in the world but the nuisance they may cause. The hero observes them. On the surface he has no reaction; underneath we suspect that he despises his life and is compelled to watch these people only because he seeks an explanation of their grossness.

Volupia, her first mission over, comes back looking for another man. An old man makes furtive advances toward her. He is so timid that the woman turns on him and ridicules him. He leaves the scene.

The youth's companion, Aganippe, comes back into the street. She is accompanied by another girl, Nemesis, with whom she is playing a private game. The man who has just recently finished his rendezvous with Volupia is attracted by Aganippe's beauty and innocence. He tries to strike up a conversation with her. The transgressor turns on him in a rage, orders him to leave the girl alone, and chases him off.

Polyhymnia, the muse of sacred music, enters as an overcheerful, pious busybody who is deluded into thinking she can change the lives of the people in this slum with the right word. She is recruiting an audience for a prayer meeting and invites all the passers-by to come. Several people join her: among them, Pollux, still the handsome youth, who is now courting the modest Pudicitia, and Ate, the hideous creature who would lead all men into evil. Ate's body is demure and innocent, her face and gestures grotesquely obscene. She accompanies the religious woman only out of malice and soon leaves.

Ate approaches the transgressor, but he is immune to her invitations and she seeks the company of Aganippe's discouraged admirer. In vivid contrast to this sordid couple, a bride and groom, Hymen and Hera, enter and—in a gay and tender dance—suggest to the young hero the true power of love. The transgressor watches them enviously, then disbelieves in their happiness to conceal his own misery.

Three lewd drunken women cavort about the scene noisily, braying and bawling Polyhymnia's call to prayer. Ate comes back to seek more mischief with the gang of dead-end kids. The transgressor and Aganippe watch her. She runs off with the gang, and the two innocents look at the ground in disgust. When Ate re-enters, this time alone, the youth goes directly to her and accosts her. He puts his hands around her neck and threatens to choke her to death. Aganippe flees. The transgressor proceeds to kill Ate, but stops, frightened, when the girl Nemesis comes in, guiding home one of the besotted women. Ate takes advantage of the youth's hesitation to elude him.

Still another kind of woman comes on the scene to disturb the hero. Medusa, true to her name, seems to be attractive, but her beauty is empowered to turn men to stone. She is so different, and yet so like the streetwalker and Ate, that the transgressor watches her with interest. She tries to take up with Pollux, but this youth has sense enough to repulse her. Medusa looks toward the transgressor: she must have someone. He is about to join her, when Polyhymnia begins to lead a revival meeting in the middle of the street. The youth participates in the meeting, hoping to escape. Medusa perceives this ruse and sends Polyhymnia and her crowd packing.

Now the transgressor is alone with a woman for the first time in his life. He is tense, expectant. The woman appears to control the youth as he responds to her advances. But gradually his true feelings become plain and we see that in reality he has control of the woman. Finally he can no longer conceal the hatred he has felt for women all his life. He becomes violent, and Medusa is afraid. The transgressor laughs. It is too late. He throws her to the ground, embraces her as she at first desired, and in the act, seizes her throat and chokes her viciously to death. The full orchestra is unleashed in a thundering, violent crescendo. The scene blacks out.

EPILOGUE—GUILT The hero is alone on the scene. In the back, the misty panorama of the city and the winged horses of the square gradually rise into the sky, as if the very scene of the crime would flee from the criminal. The transgressor moves as if recovering from a hideous nightmare, the dream that has been his life. Yet in remembering the end of the dream, he sees that he has destroyed his life. He wonders what else he could have done, what other ending such a dream could have had. He finds no answer. But perhaps no one knows what he has done! Perhaps he can escape!

Curious people come into the street to watch him. He ignores them. Surely, in every way, he is better than they. Then Aganippe comes in, playing with a balloon. She stops and stares at him. The transgressor recalls their early friendship, smiles at her, and walks toward her. But the girl knows. She points at him, and everyone watches as her forgotten balloon rises in the sky. His guilt reaffirmed by the one person in the world he respects, the hero walks away to meet his end.

UNFINISHED SYMPHONY

Music by Franz Schubert. Choreography by Peter Van Dyk. Costumes by Kalinowski. Lighting by Nananne Porcher. First presented in Paris, 1958. First presented in the United States by American Ballet Theatre at the New York State Theater, July 1971, with Cynthia Gregory and Michel Denard.

A dance ballet to Schubert's great *Unfinished Symphony*, the choreographer has created here a dance for two persons. They are lovers but there is a sense of experience and apparent detached civilization in their approach to each other. There is no radical discontent but there is a continuing sense of potential drama about their relationship.

Writing in *Cue* magazine, the critic Greer Johnson wrote of the ballet: ". . . This is a full-bodied if serenely understated hymn to two mature lovers so responsive to one another that touch and gesture are transformed into literally metaphysical poetry. The work is quiet; it enfolds you; it flows and caresses to make its unhurried, knowingly sensual point."

Deborah Jowitt, writing of *Unfinished Symphony* in the *Village Voice,* found the ballet "a curiously hypnotic duet performed by Cynthia Gregory and Michel Denard. They're both in blue-gray, and the lighting creates a blue ambience, and they move quite slowly with a smooth, barely inflected dynamic. Everything they do looks thoughtful and deliberate; even the more abandoned poses are carefully charted. They might even be sleepwalkers. Once they look sharply at each other and then at one corner of the stage, and the contrast is startling. . . . The calm heroism of some of the poses at times suggests a dream battle in which they are both engaged—sometimes as colleagues, sometimes as antagonists. Both Gregory and Denard sustain the gliding, weightless choreography beautifully, and the Schubert music provides the plangent tension that keeps the somnambulism from being soporific."

VIOLIN CONCERTO

Music by Igor Stravinsky. Choreography by George Balanchine. First presented by the New York City Ballet at the Stravinsky Festival, at the New York State Theater, Lincoln Center, June 18, 1972, with Karin von Aroldingen, Kay Mazzo, Peter Martins, and Jean-Pierre Bonnefous in the leading roles. Lighting by Ronald Bates. Conducted by Robert Irving. Violin soloist: Joseph Silverstein.

Stravinsky has written (see NOTES below) that he did not like the standard violin concertos. I myself have always preferred Stravinsky's. Some years ago, when the Original Ballet Russe happily gave me the opportunity, I made a ballet to this violin concerto of his. It was called *Balustrade,* largely after splendid scenery by the great artist Pavel Tchelitchew, who painted a décor that was dominated by a white balustrade in perspective in the background. *Balustrade* was first danced at the Fifty-first Street Theatre, New York, January 22, 1941, with Tamara Toumanova, Roman Jasinski, and Paul Petroff in the leading roles. I do not remember this ballet; but not, alas! What I did then was for *then,* and what I wanted to do to this same music for our Stravinsky Festival at the New York City Ballet represented more than thirty years' difference. The dancers were different and I liked the music even more.

The score is in four movements, the middle part being a center or core of two "Arias" enclosed by introductory Toccata and a final Capriccio.

And so is the ballet in four movements, the center being arranged as two *pas de deux* for different couples to accompany the Arias. The introductory Toccata introduces the principal dancers with a small *corps de ballet.* All four of the soloists participate in the Capriccio finale. The best guide to the character of these dances is a number of hearings of the music.

NOTES In the book *Dialogues and a Diary,* Stravinsky recalled that "The *Violin Concerto* was not inspired by or modeled on any example. I do not like the standard violin concertos—not Mozart's, Beethoven's, Mendelssohn's or Brahms's. To my mind, the only masterpiece in the field is Schoenberg's, and that was written several years after mine. The titles of my movements, Toccata, Aria, Capriccio, suggest Bach, however, and so to some extent, does the musical substance. My favorite Bach solo concerto is the one for two violins, as the duet with a violin from the orchestra in the last movement of my concerto must show. But the *Violin Concerto* contains other duet combinations, too, and the texture of the music is more often chamber music in style than orchestral. I did not write a cadenza for the reason that I was not interested in violin virtuosity. Virtuosity for its own sake plays little part in my concerto, and the technical difficulties of the piece are, I think, relatively tame.

"The ballet *Balustrade* (1940) by George Balanchine and Pavel Tchelitchew, and with the music of my *Violin Concerto,* was one of the most satisfactory visualizations of any of my theatre works. Balanchine worked out the choreography as we played my recording together and I could actually watch him imagine gesture, movement, combination, composition. The result was a dance dialogue in perfect coordination with the dialogues of the music. The dancers were few in number, and the whole second Aria was performed—and beautifully performed—as a solo piece, by Toumanova. *Balustrade* was produced by Sol Hurok, that master judge of the box *populi* (I imagine *Balustrade* must have been one of his few misjudgments in that sense). The set was a very simple white balustrade across the back of the dark stage."

Reviewing *Violin Concerto* in *The Nation,* Nancy Goldner wrote of the dance to the second Aria: "The duet for Kay Mazzo and Peter Martins is amazingly complex and dense, as is most of the ballet. It churns and seems to be a continuous process of knotting and unknotting. In their first phase, she faces him for a second, grabs his waist and slides to the floor, resting on her front haunch while her back leg is tensely stretched. He looks to the right. She looks to the left, her arm partly covering her face. There is discord here, which builds and builds as their sculptured and quickly changing poses become more multi-dimensional. Too, their relationship with the music becomes increasingly independent, until they finally seem to be in total counterpoint, though never in disharmony. Perhaps that is one reason why Mazzo's simple big movement to the one resounding chord in the score is such a shock. Another reason is that nothing is simple between this couple. But as soon as she has made that simple declaration the duet turns convoluted again. She collapses her knees inward and rotates away from Martins, who is grasping her ankles. The choreography is so innovative, intense and rich that detailed analysis of it, and clues as to why it seems to be a profound embodiment of inner turbulence, must await further performances. But first let me describe one luscious detail in it. Martins rolls Mazzo from one foot to another. In this little air voyage, she starts out with one foot pointed and the other flexed. With great deliberation and yet speed, she simultaneously points the flexed foot and flexes the pointed one. We can almost see each dot along the arced paths her feet trace. As the trip ends, she lands on one foot and whips her flexed foot along the floor into a point. This is an exclamation point to a juicy five-second game. Many choreographers have played with flexed feet in classical ballet, but Balanchine's version is now the definitive one."

WATERMILL

Music by Teiji Ito. Choreography by Jerome Robbins. Costumes by Patricia Zipprodt. Lighting by Ronald Bates. Décor by Jerome Robbins in association with David Reppa. First presented by the New York City Ballet at the New York State Theater, Lincoln Center, February 3, 1972, with Edward Villella, Penny Dudleston, Hermes Conde, Jean-Pierre Frohlich, Bart Cook, Tracy Bennett, Victor Castelli, Deni Lamont, Colleen Neary, and Robert Maiorano in the principal roles. Musicians: Dan Erkkila, Genji Ito, Teiji Ito, Kansuke Kawase, Mara Purl, and Terry White.

The score of *Watermill*, by the contemporary composer Teiji Ito, is radically different from the music we customarily hear in the ballet theater: it is quiet, full of pauses (what the composer calls "silent sounds") and stems mainly from the religious ceremonial and theatrical music of the Orient. It employs numerous percussion and wind instruments, including the Shakuhachi, a bamboo flute used in Japan in the thirteenth century. This flute was played mainly by Zen Buddhist priests whose compositions for the instrument still survive. These musical-religious works are usually contemplative evocations of nature and the seasons. So also is this ballet—a contemplation on a man's life as seen through the passage of the four seasons. However influenced by the music and theater of the East, the ballet—its world, people and events—are not to be taken as Oriental.

Writing of *Watermill*, Jacqueline Maskey in *High Fidelity/Musical America* aptly described the theme: a ritual of remembering.

"The man recalls: himself as a youth, light and graceful, boneless as a leaping fish; the ritual games that test and harden him; the perfections of love in which his partner seems woman, earth, moon-goddess; then the devils, irrational phantoms that tear and torment. Peasant figures—sowing, reaping, winnowing, gleaning—thread through his recollections. He recognizes, in a ceremony with grain stalks, nature and his oneness with it and, in a bent figure, the inevitability of old age. As he gazes, boys release curious and buoyant paper shapes which rise into nothingness as must his own dust, and the curtain falls.

"*Watermill* is a particular view of human existence, expressed in terms of the inexorable cycle of the seasons. Man matures and declines; the moon waxes and wanes; the earth is fruitful, then fallow; snow follows sun."

The six musicians, all in Japanese costume, enter and sit on the right of the stage. A framed scrim faces us. As the music begins with a plaintive sound, we discern behind it gradually three high mysterious shapes that we can't quite make out—they are not trees, for wasp-waisted, they spread out at the base, too; they are not giants or windmills. They stand in a field filled with mist under a crescent moon. As the mist lifts a bit, we see that they are high sheaves of grain, the stalks gathered in tightly at the middle. There is a fence in the distance, and before we know it, we see there is a man there, too, standing in the field in a long black cloak, his face hidden, a part of the natural landscape, too. What we have gradually seen here and made out patiently in the mist is characteristic of the voyage of recollection and discovery that now begins for this man and for us.

Slowly, slowly, looking up for a moment at the sky, the man comes toward us. He kneels, rises, leaving his cloak on the ground. He takes off his shoes then, and his shirt and trousers. Standing now almost naked, he stretches out his arms as figures bearing multicolored lanterns approach him. They come up to him closely, their lanterns poised at the end of long wands, as if to illumine his body fully, then go away. To a chanted song that rises from the music, the man begins to dance. But not for long. He sits down and youths enter with kites, an umbrella, etc.

A boy runs as men in the background till the fields. The man notices the boy, reaches out his hand to him, but the boy sees another man in the distance and goes to him. Five boys trot across the field, five more, too, these carrying sticks. The man walks among them. They do warlike gymnastics, as if preparing for battle. But the man runs off. He returns as the youths stop and remain motionless.

A woman enters in a long green dress and turban. In the background, a group of young persons arrange a picnic on the grass behind one of the sheaves of grain. The woman puts down a rug on the grass. There is a longer period of waiting. She lets fall her outer garment and her long hair, which she combs slowly. The man watches her some distance away. We have the impression that he is both with her and is remembering her, their contact is so close. She lies down to sleep; so does he. Darkness falls. A boy—the man in his youth?—enters and goes to the woman. He pulls her body to his and she stretches around him; to the light of the moon they embrace closely. They roll and undulate together on the blanket and stop. The picnickers in the back rise and go; the moon keeps on descending.

The man awakens and lifts his arm. The boy on the blanket raises his arm simultaneously. The girl, too, hails the descending moon. The man and the boy rise together; the man goes to the girl as the boy backs out. The man takes the girl's hand, then lies with his head in her lap as, on the right, the boy of the first scene sleeps. The girl gets up, takes her rug, and leaves as the man and boy sleep.

There is a menacing atmosphere. A bearded creature enters; two black figures follow. The man wakes up the boy, and to howls it seems of dogs and the beat of percussion, there is an attack of some sort. The man watches; the boy runs off. The man stretches out now as if dead. Figures enter with baskets to gather pebbles. Leaves flutter down in the autumn air. The man glances up, then sits bowed over, head on knees. Rose petals fall. Peasants enter, take shafts of wheat and let them balance and fall within their fingers. The moon rises and is seen in eclipse. The man kneels and watches the peasants as ever so slowly they wave the stalks of wheat in the still air, then return them to the shaft. One girl remains and gives the man two wheat stalks. He holds them aloft, balancing them carefully; they seem to be balanced extensions of his arms. Snow falls gently. The man dances as it were with the stalks of wheat; they quiver in the evening air. The man kneels within a cross they have made of the stalks. A girl and boy come in with more wheat stalks as the snow thickens. The man moves, holding the stalks; they seem extensions of his arms and tremble at his every movement. Snow falls. He dances as it were with the stalks of quivering wheat, crossing them and kneeling as they cross. A girl and a boy enter with wheat tassles. They soon leave and the man rises as the boy returns; the girl does, too. The man lays down the cross of wheat and the boy who died. The snow has stopped. The man is alone. He takes up his cloak and leaves as an aged figure with a stick comes in. So, also, do men who carry on their shoulders heavy burdens. They cross the stage, slowly, at the back. Suddenly their burdens begin to lift off their shoulders and rise into the air. The curtain falls.

NOTES Nancy Goldner reviewed *Watermill* for *Dance News:* "Jerome Robbins's *Watermill* is one of the most perfect productions I have seen. It is beautiful, by all means—but it is more than that. It is exquisite. The details are the thing, although the work deals with large themes. The ballet is a meditation on nature. There is a meditator. His world is populated by seeders, tillers, harvesters, and phenomena of nature—the moon, wind, snow, stalks of wheat. Even the music, written by Teiji Ito and played by him and friends on the side of the stage, is as natural sounding as it is sounds of music. But it is always the details. Some boys wave small kites; each bobs at a different altitude. They also carry lanterns at different heights. This sensitivity to slight variation is exciting and moving. Four of the lanterns are large, in primary colors. Two of them are tiny and white. They look so fragile next to the larger ones. In addition to going through its phases, the moon ascends and descends. It seems to move when you're not looking. Its changing aspects are always something of a surprise. The wind which causes the wheat bundles to rustle is slight; it becomes a presence, like the moon. When fall comes, the leaves float onto the stage one by one. Even the snow seems to have been sprinkled over the land by a Haiku poet-god, so gentle is the fall and isolated the flakes. The list could go on. . . .

"The Orientalisms are not only in the music, props, and use of props. The entire spirit of *Watermill* is Orientally meditative. It unfolds slowly. With the exception of the dance of the spring/youth figure and the running sequence, which in itself is a rare-faction of the action—the boys and protagonist do a trot-like stylization of a run—the dancers move slowly, very slowly. Time becomes thick, sliceable. Edward Villella, the meditator-dreamer, has a quality here that suggests great power beneath the stillness. It is this suggestion of action that makes him so compelling, and maddening. Like the wind and moon, he becomes a presence. Unlike the moon, he does not mark the passing of time but seems to be a second of time stretched into forever. You either settle into his state of consciousness, or go insane. Maybe you can settle on a compromise by coughing and fidgeting. But you can't go to sleep. Robbins gets at some part of you.

"There are some obscure sections. Some actions are not definable by line and verse, but they do make emotional sense. Some things make such sense that they become permanent images in the mind. One such moment was the sound of wind before the nightmare. It struck to the core. It was one of the great moments in the theater. Oddly enough, though, the nightmare itself hit sideways. For me, the totality of the piece was not equal to some of the parts. Not because the parts were unconnected to each other and to the larger theme; on the contrary, never have I seen a dance so perfectly interrelated. But because the ballet is not so much about nature, time, life cycles, and whatnot as it is 'about' a particular state of consciousness. And now I must confess that I was one of those who were going insane. The moments when I was thoroughly engrossed were the moments when I was most detached from the proceedings, when my attention was drawn away from the slow-moving dancers and from time. Only my aesthetic sense was engaged and heightened. Robbins wanted the whole being to be there. Those who find dwelling on a stalk of wheat exhilarating will find *Watermill* a masterpiece to end all masterpieces. I can only admire Robbins' essay."

Writing in *Dance and Dancers* magazine, Patricia Barnes said: "Every so often—but not that often—a ballet turns up which instantly convinces one of its place in dance history. It becomes a landmark. Such a one is Jerome Robbins's *Watermill*, a creation of such imagination, depth and profundity that no one seeing it can remain untouched in some way by it. The first night audience greeted it with a mixture of cheers and boos; some were clearly baffled by its newness and just sat looking stunned and perplexed. But it is not just that it is new and different: innovation alone does not make great art. *Watermill* is, in addition, a work of extraordinary beauty: a poetic and deeply felt work that seems to have been torn from the very soul of its creator. It has even been suggested that the ballet is part autobiographical, and certainly the title is the same as the island where Robbins has his country home.

"In 1964 Robbins studied the Noh technique, and clearly what he learned has been stirring in his mind ever since. *Watermill* incorporates much that can be traced to Noh—the deliberation, refinement and simplicity of movement, the stripping away of excessive gesture—but despite the influence of the music and theater of the East, this ballet's world, people and events, according to a program note, are universal and not to be construed as Oriental.

"Another influence on this particular world appears to be Robert Wilson, the fascinating and provocative young director who has forged a whole new theater style, and who recently performed in Paris with enormous success. But the creative genius of *Watermill* is Robbins alone. How incredible this choreographer is, never sitting back on the laurels of past successes, never choosing the easy way, but constantly challenged by new vistas and new ideas, a choreographer who can equally touch the heart and stimulate the intellect."

WHO CARES?

Music by George Gershwin, orchestrated by Hershy Kay. Choreography by George Balanchine. Costumes by Karinska. Lighting by Ronald Bates. Pianist: Gordon Boelzner. First presented by the New York City Ballet at the New York State Theater, Lincoln Center, February 5, 1970, with Karin von Aroldingen, Patricia McBride, Marnee Morris, and Jacques d'Amboise as the principal dancers.

This ballet is a set of dances to some songs by George Gershwin that I have always liked very much. "Who Cares?" goes back to 1931 and *Of Thee I Sing*. In Europe in the late 1920s and 1930s, we all knew Gershwin's music and loved it; it is beautiful, very American, too. Before I came to America I saw the Gershwin musical *Funny Face* in London and admired it. I did some work in musical comedies in London after that and continued to make dances for them after I came to New York. I don't think I would have done that if it had not been for George Gershwin's music. There are popular songs and popular songs; Gershwin's are special.

I was lucky enough to know Gershwin, who asked me to Hollywood to do dances for the movie *Goldwyn Follies*. Gershwin gave me a book of his songs, arranged in the way he used to do them in concerts. One day at the piano I played one through and thought to myself, Beautiful, I'll make a *pas de deux*. Then I played another, it was just as beautiful and I thought, A variation! And then another and another and there was no end to how beautiful they were.

And so we had a new ballet. No story, just the songs. Here they are, with the dancers who first danced them: "Strike Up the Band" (1927), Ladies and Gentlemen; "Sweet and Low Down" (1925), Ensemble; "Somebody Loves Me" (1924), Deborah Flomine, Susan Hendl, Linda Merrill, Susan Pilarre, Bettijane Sills; "Bidin' My Time" (1930), Deni Lamont, Robert Maiorano, Frank Ohman, Richard Rapp, Earle Sieveling; "'S Wonderful" (1927), Susan Pilarre and Richard Rapp; "That Certain Feeling" (1925), Deborah

Flomine and Deni Lamont, Bettijane Sills and Earl Sieveling; "Do Do Do" (1926), Susan Hendl and Frank Ohman; "Lady Be Good" (1924), Linda Merrill and Robert Maiorano; "The Man I Love" (1924), Patricia McBride and Jacques d'Amboise; "I'll Build a Stairway to Paradise" (1922), Karin von Aroldingen; "Embraceable You" (1930), Marnee Morris and Jacques d'Amboise; "Fascinatin' Rhythm" (1924), Patricia McBride; "Who Cares?" (1931), Karin von Aroldingen and Jacques d'Amboise; "My One and Only" (1927), Marnee Morris; "Liza" (1929), Jacques d'Amboise; "Clap Yo' Hands" (1926), Karin von Aroldingen, Patricia McBride, Marnee Morris, Jacques d'Amboise; "I Got Rhythm" (1930), Entire Cast.

NOTES The first performance of *Who Cares?* had only an orchestral beginning ("Strike Up the Band") because the composer Hershy Kay, who was arranging the songs for us, was busy with a musical. Gordon Boelzner, the pianist, played all the other songs except for "Clap Yo' Hands," where we played a recording of Gershwin doing the piece himself. We still do.

We did not have much scenery for the ballet at the beginning. This was provided later by Jo Mielziner, November 21, 1970, who gave us a scrim with two layers of silhouetted skylines of New York in a kind of fan shape for the backdrop and, for the sides of the stage, skyscraper cliffs.

When *Who Cares?* was first done, Lincoln Kirstein wrote an extensive note for our program: "*Who Cares?* is both the name of a new ballet in the classical idiom by George Balanchine and an old song George and Ira Gershwin wrote in 1931 for *Of Thee I Sing*. The dictionary says *classic* means standard, leading, belonging to the highest rank of authority. Once it applied mainly to masterpieces from Greco-Roman antiquity; now we have boxing and horse racing classics, classic cocktail dresses and classic cocktails. Among classic American composers we number Stephen Foster, John Philip Sousa and George Gershwin (1898–1937). First heard fifty years ago, the best of the Gershwin songs maintain their classic freshness, as of an eternal martini—dry, frank, refreshing, tailor-made with an invisible kick from its slightest hint of citron. Nostalgia has not syruped their sentiment nor robbed them of immediate piquancy. We associate them with time past, but when well sung or played, or preferably both at once, they not only revive but transcend their epoch. Lovely in themselves they are by way of becoming art songs, which that beautiful singer Eva Gauthier long ago realized when she first sang them in concert well after they had become familiar hits. The Gershwins wrote hit songs which were art songs. Most art songs pretend to be love songs; the Gershwin genre seem to be about playmates more than lovers. It was not by accident the best dance team of the time, Fred and Adele Astaire, were brother and sister.

"To the musician George Gershwin, perhaps their most important element was their potential as piano pieces. He played energetically, long and magically at private parties and in public. His semi-improvisational style was taken seriously even by 'serious' critics. Gilbert Seldes, our first popularizer of what we now call pop art (in painting as well as theater), indeed complained that *The Rhapsody in Blue* was a masterpiece marred by Liszt-like extended cadenzas; certainly Gershwin was a hypnotic virtuoso as well as a knowing and generous analyst of the jazz style of which he was a master. This he traced to the individual ragtimers at the turn of the century whose collective ingenuities in piano playing built up a tradition which he inherited, and which he used with a new articulate sophistication, flexibility and brilliance.

"But there is another serious aspect of the Gershwin songs which marks their sturdy structure—words supporting the tunes, mainly by his brother Ira. The wit, tact, invention, metaphor and metric of Ira's rhymes meant that you not only left the theater whistling melodies, but singing words. His phrasing was simple enough, his phrases sharp enough to impose themselves at one hearing; once heard, they were almost infectiously memorable. Love & dove, June & moon, true & you long comprised the pidgin English of Tin Pan Alley. Ira Gershwin not only transubstantiated such base metal; with condescension or parody he created a new prosody, a new means for lyric writing which incorporated the season's slang, references to local events, echoes of the vernacular rhythms of ordinary speech in a frame of casual thrown-away elegance which was never false, insistent or self-conscious. He seemed to have stumbled on what was right, fitting, appropriate, surprising and charming, as if such had been coins tossed in his path. But such coinage is art, not accident, and Ira incidentally was a poet and a master of mnemonics. He was also a satirist; there had always been comic ballads, but it is odd to find in 'Strike Up the Band' (1927), an ostensibly patriotic hit tune, its almost Brechtian tang. . . . Ira Gershwin's lyric style involved his skill in manipulating repetition, shift of breath, perfect punctuation, instinct for vulgarism in a mosaic of unusual context, plus a laconic polish. His vocabulary was small; both Noel Coward and Cole Porter were more literary; Lorenz Hart's smashing pastiches depended on a wide reading. These three derived from Gilbert and Sullivan, a more operatic or light-operatic tradition. Ira was in the line of minstrelsy—the minstrel show and the ancient descent from troubador soloists. All the songs sang 'I love you,' but Ira's hummed it with a unique American, or rather Manhattan (cocktail), simplicity and savor. Lyrics are to be sung, not enunciated like patter songs, or launched—like arias. In love songs, intense emotion is usually in inverse proportion to the heartbreak clarity of words. George Gershwin's tunes were not impassioned but playful. Their pretext was not profound feelings, but sportive sex, flirtatious games, gallantry in a tennis tournament: love, set, match. George Gershwin took forms and archetypes as he received them and composed something unheard before out of formulae. He did not so much write parodies of Negro spirituals, barroom ballads or cowboy songs; he appropriated familiar atmospheres and by his mastery whipped them into the strict form of the hit song, as someone might break a green colt into a pacer. He alternated tenderness with ironic narcissism, or contrasted a smashing climax with the most delicate expression of loss or confusion. And Ira's lyrics were indeed—lyric: personal, enthusiastic, eminently singable. The Gershwins were showmen; they gloried in hits, show stoppers, grand finales with everybody shouting in the aisles, but their brashest choirs never obscured the fragility of certain solos when George almost seemed to be singing to himself. Idiosyncratic serenades, at once self-deprecatory and wistful, they were as elegant, athletic and lonely as he was in life, which no one knew better than his brother.

"This faintly confessional residue of George Gershwin is a touching legacy. In 1930, for *Girl Crazy*, he and Ira wrote a deliberately paced number for a chorus of dubious cowboys, dude ranch gigolos leaning on the fence of a Reno divorce ranch. The wrangler of 1930 had already become a drugstore cowboy on his way to becoming a midnight cowboy; but forty years ago he was more the dandy than the hustler. And in Ira's deft quotation of the titles of four popular songs in his introduction, we have his compliments to colleagues in the song writing industry, a delicious in-joke of the era, as well as a not unjustified boast of the Gershwin superiority, as aristocrats of American lyricism, masters of music to the American electorate. The Gershwins' beautiful manners and high style, their instant melange of insouciance and shrewd innocence, their just estimation of the imaginative elasticity of an elite audience which they had developed, have left a body of words and music which lives, unblurred by vulgar rhetoric or machine-made sentiment. To combine an intensely personal attitude with a flagrantly popular language is a feat which few popular artists manage, and it is appropriate that Balanchine has used the songs not as facile recapitulation of a lost epoch, but simply as songs, or melodies for classic, undeformed, traditional academic dances, which in their equivalence of phrasing, dynamics and emotion, find their brotherly parallel."

Soon after the first performances, Arlene Croce, editor of *Ballet Review*, wrote about the ballet in the *Dancing Times*: "The title of Balanchine's Gershwin ballet, *Who Cares?*, has a double significance. It means, Who Cares what we call it ('as long as I care for you and you care for me'), and it suggests that the piece is an elegant throwaway. That's how it looks, too—like nothing much. The curtain goes up while the orchestra is playing 'Strike Up the Band' and we see a double exposure of Manhattan skylines projected in a pinkish haze on the backcloth. An excellent idea, but it stops there. The rest of the stage looks bleak. The girls wear their very well-cut Karinska tutus, this time in turquoise and lemon-yellow. The skirts have pleats and look 1920s and mini-mod at the same time. So do the boys' black bellbottom slacks. Like the title and the skyline, everything has a double impact, with one effect or style superimposed on another—Now on Then, ballet dancing on show tunes. The two planes of meaning are so shuffled that we're never completely in one world or the other, we're in both at once. Or rather, we're in four worlds since *Who Cares?* scrambles two elements, classical dancing and show dancing, and two eras, the Twenties and the Seventies, with equal paronomasiac facility. And since the Twenties was itself a period of classical revival, the play of references can grow almost infinitely complex. When Balanchine has five boys do double air turns (one boy at a time) in 'Bidin' My Time,' we're pleased with ourselves for thinking of the boys' variation in *Raymonda,* Act Three (the metrical swing of the music is pretty much the same), and even more pleased when we remember the masculine ensemble that made the song famous in *Girl Crazy.* That's simple enough. But when toward the end of the ballet his four stars fly across the stage to 'Clap Yo' Hands' in what is unmistakably a series of quotations from *Apollo,* we catch an unframeable glimpse of the multiple precedents *Who Cares?* is made of. It's then that we see, for just the flash of the moment that he gives us to see it, how comradely the links are between the Gershwin of *Lady Be Good!*, *Tip Toes, Oh, Kay!* and *Funny Face,* and the syncopated Stravinsky of *Apollon Musagete.* We notice that the dancers in the ballet wear necktie-belts in homage not only to Astaire but to the Chanel who in 1928 knotted men's striped cravats around the waists of Apollo's muses. But the allusion to 1928 isn't endstopped; it reverberates with *Apollo*'s own recapitulations of the Nineties and Marius Petipa—high noon at the Maryinsky—and so we are borne back ceaselessly into the past. To the question 'What is classicism?' Balanchine responds with a blithe shrug and a popular song. Classicism is the Hall of Fame viewed as a hall of mirrors. The Fun House. . . .

"The ballet suddenly . . . finds its own life—when the boys and girls start dancing out in pairs to ''S Wonderful,' 'That Certain Feeling,' 'Do Do Do,' and 'Lady Be Good'; the dance invention tumbles forth, so does the applause, and we realize that what we're going to see is not a clever foreigner's half-infatuated, half-skeptical view of a popular American art form, we're going to see the art form itself, re-energized. But this spectacle we see isn't like a musical comedy, it's more like a lieder recital with a few social mannerisms mostly in the pleasant, sappy, ingenue of Old Broadway. Just when you think that maybe the dancers do represent a musical comedy chorus full of stock types (with Linda Merrill as the company's inevitable redhead), they vanish and another ballet, or musical, or recital begins.

"The second half of *Who Cares?* has an *Apollo*-type cast—one boy (Jacques d'Amboise) and three girls (Patricia McBride, Marnee Morris, and Karin von Aroldingen). Each girl dances once with the boy and once by herself and then the boy dances alone. They are all four together in the Apollonian coda. The music is the same parade of Gershwin hits that has been going on since the beginning, only now, with the lights blue and the stars out, we listen more intently. If this is a musical comedy world, it's the most beautiful one ever imagined. In 'Fascinatin' Rhythm,' Patricia McBride holds a high extension in second and then in two or three lightning shifts of weight refocuses the whole silhouette while keeping on top of the original pose. It's so charming to see in relation to that unexpected stutter in the music which unexpectedly recurs, that it hits the audience like a joke, but that's fascinating rhythm, and that's *Who Cares?* Classical syntax, jazz punctuation. I couldn't begin to say what d'Amboise's solo to 'Liza' is composed of, though—it suggests soft-shoe virtuoso tap and classical lift and amplitude all at once, and d'Amboise, whose style in classical ballet has characteristically a casual, crooning softness played against sudden monkey-like accelerandos and sharp bursts of detail, dances it in total splendor. Everywhere the tight choreography sustains an almost unbelievable musical interest.

"As if it weren't enough for Balanchine to give us dances of extreme tension and wit and elegance, he also gives us back the songs unadorned by their usual stagey associations. 'Stairway to Paradise' isn't a big production number; it's one girl (von Aroldingen) covering ground in powerful colt-like jumps and turns. And in the duets, the emotion is more serious (the sense of receding hopes, for example, in 'The Man I Love') for not being acted out. It isn't emotion that dominates the stage so much as a musical faith that the choreography keeps, and that's what convinces us that the songs are good for more than getting drunk at the St. Regis by—that they have theatrical momentousness and contemporary savor. Gershwin in 1970, in the age of Burt Bacharach, has no trouble sounding classical, and that is how Balanchine hears him.

"I am also persuaded that Balanchine hears Gershwin the way Gershwin composed, i.e. pianistically, and this brings up the subject of orchestration and Hershy Kay. Kay had been set the task of orchestrating sixteen of the seventeen songs that Balanchine uses in *Who Cares?* (one number, 'Clap Yo' Hands,' is a recording made by Gershwin himself at the piano), but because of commitments to the Broadway show *Coco,* Kay has so far orchestrated only the opening ('Strike Up the Band') and closing ('I Got Rhythm') songs. The remaining fourteen songs were played for the three performances of *Who Cares?* that were given this season, with his customary sensitivity and attack, by Gordon Boelzner, from Gershwin's own concert arrangements. These piano arrangements were unvaryingly simple: verse followed by chorus followed (sometimes twice) by chorus repeat. But they are also beautiful examples of Gershwin's highly developed keyboard technique. Gershwin's pianism was comparable in its own time to Gottschalk's, and I hope Kay's further orchestrations of Gershwin are as good as the ones he did for the Gottschalk ballet *Cakewalk,* by far his best orchestration for the ballet theater. To my disappointed ear, his 'Strike Up the Band' and 'I Got Rhythm' were in the vulgarized idiom of his 'Stars and Stripes'-hotcha added to heat; and while the musical format of *Who Cares?* precludes his 'symphonizing' in the style of *Western Symphony,* orchestral thickening could destroy the bone-dry delicacy, the tonal transparency of this music and should be avoided like temptation. The more so as Balanchine has taken such evident delight in choreographing the countermelodies, cross-rhythms and abrupt syncopations out of which Gershwin built his compositions—it isn't all razz-ma-tazz—and not since the heyday of Fred Astaire have such felicities been observed.

"Fred and Ginger, Fred and Adele, George and Ira, George and Igor . . . it's easy to be seduced by the nostalgia of it all, but the remarkable thing about *Who Cares?* is how frequently it appeals to that nostalgia. It certainly makes no appeal on the basis of period glamor or period Camp. The multiple images, the visual punning, the sense of a classical perspective—all of that sweeps by with a strength of evocation more powerful than any individual moment of recognition. It's mysterious, the mythological intensity built up by a ballet that doesn't seem to have a thought in its airy head. No single cultural myth seems to be at the core of it. Manhattan in the Golden Twenties, penthouse parties, where composers of brilliance entertained at the baby grand until dawn, are lovely to think about but aren't the subject of *Who Cares?* any more than a rainbow on a wet afternoon is. To put it as simply as I can, this wonderful ballet enriches our fantasy life immeasurably, as works of art are meant to do. It's tonic, medicinal, too. Its fresh unclouded feeling seems to strike with special directness at the city's depressed spirits. Just before the première (on February 5), Balanchine received New York City's biggest award for cultural achievement, the Handel medallion, on the stage of the State Theater. He made a number of jokes in the disreputable manner of his hero on such occasions, Bob Hope, had what they call in show business a 'good roll,' and then rang up the curtain on a Gershwin march. The Higher Seriousness didn't have a chance, but who cares?—the ballet was a beaut."

INDEX

Aasen, Muriel, 132
Adam, Adolphe, 193
Adams, Diana, 2, 239, 245, 505
Adyrkhaeva, Svetlana, 426
AFTER EDEN, 1
AGON, 2–5
Ailey, Alvin, 345, 346
Albrecht, Angele, 266
Alcantara, Burt, 233
Aldous, Lucette, 119
Alonso, Alicia, 206, 245, 505
Alsop, Lamar, 126
American Ballet Caravan, 391
American Ballet Theatre, xiii, 11, 26, 28, 30, 41, 70, 73, 86, 146, 192, 220, 221, 229, 257, 258, 259, 274, 304, 316, 345, 351, 364, 367, 391, 432, 456, 457, 459, 469, 477, 489, 499, 509
ANASTASIA, 6–10
Anderson, Reid, 373
Anderson-Ivantzova, Elizaveta, 272
Andreyanova, Elena, 193
APOLLO, 11–16, 486, 524
Arpino, Gerald, 66, 234, 235, 379, 502, 503, 504
Arshansky, Michael, 277, 322
Arthur, Charthel, 130
Asakawa, Hitomi, 266
Ashley, Merrill, 90, 210, 339, 340
Ashton, Frederick, 47, 52, 64, 110, 129, 143, 152, 166, 170, 359, 368, 372, 384, 393, 410, 416, 455, 469, 480, 481–82, 483
Astaire, Fred and Adele, 521, 524, 527
ASTARTE, 17–20
AS TIME GOES BY, 21–25, 115
Atlanta Civic Ballet, 432
AT MIDNIGHT, 26–28
Australian Ballet, 118, 119

Bach, Johann Sebastian, 70, 210, 211, 259, 260
Bajetti, N., 193
Balanchine, George, ix, x, xiii, xiv, 2, 11, 46, 70, 89, 90, 91, 92, 99, 119, 126, 127, 128, 171, 222, 223, 224, 231, 239, 253, 277, 284, 322, 333, 342, 388, 410, 413, 484, 487, 510, 511, 512, 519, 520, 523, 525, 526, 527
Baldina, Maria, 473
Ballet Caravan, Chicago Opera, 34
Ballet of the Deutsche Oper, 6
Ballet of the Twentieth Century, 33, 178, 266, 269, 385

Ballet Rambert, 112
Ballet Russe, 11, 170, 237, 270, 272, 352
Ballet Russe de Monte Carlo, 87, 89, 90, 183, 273, 277, 347, 391, 475, 477, 495
Ballets des Champs-Élysées, 459
Ballet Society, 284, 484, 486
Ballets Russes of Diaghilev, 11, 170, 237, 270, 272, 291, 305, 315, 322, 330, 381, 393, 427, 454, 473, 495
Ballet Theatre, 112, 154, 160, 241, 246, 259, 317, 359, 366, 475, 497, 498, 505
Ballets U.S.A. (Robbins), 69
Bari, Tania, 385
Barnett, Robert, 68
Baronova, Svetlana, 273
Bauch, Alan, 129
BAYADÈRE, LA, 29–32
Bays, Frank, 66, 497
Beach Boys, 114
Beck, Hans, 237
Beethoven, Ludwig van, 47, 388
Begak, Dmitri, 424
Béjart, Maurice, xiii, 33, 178, 179, 266, 267, 269, 270, 385, 386
Bennett, Tracy, 132, 513
Bentley, Muriel, 154
Berg, Harry (Henry), 21, 23
Bergsma, Deanne, 143, 417
Beriosova, Svetlana, 6, 143, 145, 170
Bernard, Scott, 234
Bernstein, Leonard, xiii, 132, 133, 135, 136, 154, 343
Bessmertnova, Natalia, 425
BHAKTI, 33
BILLY THE KID, 34–40
Birkmeyer, Michael, 118
Bizet, Georges, 484, 486
Blair, David, 166, 432, 455, 457
Blankshine, Robert, 66
Bliss, Herbert, 284, 322, 484
Blum, Anthony, 93, 99, 107, 210, 218, 225, 226, 341, 342
Blum, René, 475, 477
Boelzner, Gordon, 126
Boerman, Jan, 256
Bolender, Todd, 2, 34, 430, 431
Bolm, Adolph, 305, 473
Bolshoi Ballet, 10, 49, 100, 116, 193, 354, 387, 421, 424, 426, 432, 449, 450, 455, 457, 503
Bonnefous, Jean-Pierre, 46, 47, 48, 151, 510
Bortoluzzi, Paolo, 46, 178, 266
Bourkhanov, Muzafar, 46, 47
Bourmeister, Vladimir, 455
Bournonville, Auguste, 236, 237, 263, 304, 459

Bozacchi, Giuseppina, 75, 92
Bozzoni, Max, 484
Brady, Eileen, 23, 130, 291, 295
Brae, June, 393
Brahms, Johannes, 41, 88, 228, 229, 239, 240
Brahms Quintet, 41
Braithwaite, M., 499
Brenaa, Hans, 237, 238
Brianza, Carlotta, 393
Brock, Karena, 32
Bruhn, Erik, 86, 207, 236, 346, 455, 456, 459, 469–70, 471
Burke, Dermot, 234, 502, 504
Burr, Marilyn, 65
Bustilio, Zelma, 316
Butler, John, 1
Butsova, Hilda, 138
Byron, John, 112

CAGE THE, 42–45, 342, 343
Caras, Stephen, 69, 132, 210
Carman, Adix, 23
Carozzi, Felicita, 75
Carter, Bill, 239, 253, 352, 353
Castelli, Victor, 132, 210, 513
Cazalet, Peter, 489
Cecchetti, Enrico, 170, 305, 314, 330, 393, 416
CELEBRATION, 46–48
Céleste, Mlle., 459
Cerrito, Fanny, 296–303 *passim*
Chabelska, Maria, 291, 295
Chambers, Russell, 379
Chase, Lucia, 112, 221, 317, 498, 505
Chausson, Ernest, 241
Chopin, Frédéric, 68, 69, 93–97 *passim*, 102, 103, 108, 146, 225, 226, 473, 476, 478, 479
Christensen, Lew, 11, 34, 484
Christensen, William, 277
Chryst, Gary, 291, 294, 502, 504
CINDERELLA, 49–65, 451, 452
City Center Joffrey Ballet, xiii, 1, 17, 21, 22, 66, 114, 130, 234, 236, 237, 291, 293–94, 315, 336, 379, 430, 497, 502–4
Clauss, Heinz, 147, 150, 228
Clayden, Pauline, 52
Clegg, Peter, 315
Clifford, John, 93, 99, 151, 210, 217, 218, 341, 342, 494
Clogstoun, Patricia, 112
CLOWNS, THE, 66–67
Coleman, Michael, 110, 417
Coleman, Richard, 130
Coll, David, 229, 230
Collier, Lesley, 417
CONCERT, THE, 68–69, 107
CONCERTO BAROCCO, 70–72
Conde, Hermes, 132, 210, 513
Connor, Laura, 110, 417

Conrad, Karen, 187, 241
CONSORT, THE, 73–74
Cook, Bart, 69, 132, 151, 513
Copland, Aaron, 34, 347, 352
COPPÉLIA, 47, 70, 75–92, 433
Coralli, Jean, 193
Corkle, Francesca, 336, 338
Cortesi, A., 193
Cosma, Edgar, 459
Cowen, Donna, 130, 291, 294, 502
Cragun, Richard, 228, 369, 371, 373, 491
Cranko, John, 10, 147, 148, 150, 228, 359, 366, 369, 371, 372, 373, 387, 491
Cuoco, Joyce, 373

D'Amboise, Jacques, 178, 231, 430, 431, 494, 519, 520, 525
DANCES AT A GATHERING, xii, xiii, 88, 93–111, 217, 226
Dance Theatre of Harlem, xiii, 159
Danias, Starr, 1, 379, 502
Danilova, Alexandra, 11, 86, 87, 89, 183, 476, 478
Danton, Henry, 480
D'Antuono, Eleanor, 41, 86, 304, 316, 345, 346
DARK ELEGIES, 112–13
Darrell, Peter, 489
Darsonval, Lycette, 484
Dauberval, Jean, 160
Debussy, Claude, 46, 97, 430
Delarova, Eugenia, 183
Delibes, Léo, 47, 75, 87, 90, 92
Delius, Frederick, 359, 360, 365
Dell-Era, Antoinette, 277
De Mille, Agnes, 100, 112, 347, 384, 498, 499
Denard, Michel, 509
Derman, Vergie, 129
DEUCE COUPE, 114–15
De Valois, Ninette, 393
D'Honau, Marilyn, 73
Diaghilev, Serge, 25, 170, 266–70 *passim*, 291, 313, 314, 315, 322, 330, 333, 384, 385, 427, 434, 473, 475, 479
Diaghilev's Ballets Russes, 11, 170, 237, 270, 272, 291, 305, 315, 322, 330, 381, 393, 427, 454, 473, 495
Dilena, Rennie, 129
Dobrievich, Pierre, 266
Dobson, Deborah, 32
Dolin, Anton, 46, 304, 322
Dollar, William, 70
Donizetti, Gaetano, 88
Donn, Jorge, 270
DON QUIXOTE, 116–25
Dowell, Anthony, 6, 46, 47, 48, 110, 129, 143, 145, 207, 247, 417, 419, 500
Dowland, John, 73

Doyle, Desmond, 143, 145
DREAM, THE, 129–31
Drew, David, 129
Drigo, Riccardo, 222, 223, 452, 458
Dryden, Richard, 210
Dubrovska, Felia, 11, 272, 322, 393
Dudinskaya, Natalia, 49, 415
Dudleston, Penny, 513
Duell, Daniel, 132
Duncan, Isadora, 260, 483
Dunleavy, Rosemary, 210
Dunne, James, 502
DUO CONCERTANT, 126–28
DYBBUK VARIATIONS, 132–36
DYING SWAN, THE, 47, 137–39, 453

Eagling, Wayne, 500
EARLY SONGS, 140–42
Ebbelaar, Hans, 345
Eckl, Shirley, 154, 505
Eglevsky, André, 91, 222, 277
Elgar, Edward, 143, 144, 145
Eliot Feld Ballet, ix
Ellington, Duke, 345
Elssler, Fanny, 195, 235, 297, 298, 303, 459
ENIGMA VARIATIONS, 143–45
Estopinal, Renée, 210
ETERNAL IDOL, THE, 146
EUGENE ONEGIN, 147–50
EVENING'S WALTZES, AN, 151

FAÇADE, 152–53
Falla, Manuel de, 495
FANCY FREE, 154–58
Farrell, Suzanne, 119, 231, 266, 270
Fauré, Gabriel, 231
Fedicheva, Kaleria, 29
Feld, Eliot, xiii, 26, 27, 28, 100, 140, 142, 220, 221, 229, 230
Fernandez, Royes, 258, 259, 459
FÊTE NOIRE, 159
Figueroa, Alfonso, 229, 230
FILLE MAL GARDÉE, LA, 160–69
FIREBIRD, 170–80, 313, 479
Flomine, Deborah, 519, 520
Fokine, Michel, 70, 112, 137, 138, 170, 305, 314, 315, 316, 427, 453, 473, 475, 476, 478, 479
Fonteyn, Margot, 9, 52, 170, 315, 373, 393, 410, 432, 455, 457, 469, 480, 482
FOUR TEMPERAMENTS, THE, 181–82
Fracci, Carla, 46, 86, 304, 366, 459, 470
Franck, César, 480
Franklin, Frederic, 183, 347, 391

Gade, Niels, 263
GAÎTÉ PARISIENNE, 183–86
GALA PERFORMANCE, 187–91
GARTENFEST, 192

Geltzer, Catherine, 432, 449
Gershwin, George, 519–27 *passim*
GISELLE, 48, 98, 193–209, 263, 296, 298, 427, 433, 449, 483
Glazounov, Alexander, 387
GOLDBERG VARIATIONS, 210–19
Gollner, Nana, 187, 505
Goodman, Erika, 66, 114, 115, 316
Gorsky, Aleksandr, 116, 451
Govrin, Gloria, 178, 253
Graham, Martha, 19, 381
Grahn, Lucile, 296, 299, 300–4 *passim*, 459
Grant, Alexander, 52, 129, 143, 145, 166, 315, 419
Gregory, Cynthia, 26, 28, 32, 41, 86, 88, 146, 192, 220, 345, 346, 489, 509
Grenier, Larry, 21, 24, 73, 130
Grey, Beryl, 52, 393
Grigorovich, Yuri, 421, 424, 426
Grisi, Carlotta, 193, 195, 296–301, *passim*, 303

HARBINGER, 220–21
Harkness Ballet, xiii, 1, 256
HARLEQUINADE, 88, 222–24
Haydée, Marcia, 147, 150, 228, 369, 371, 373, 491
Hayden, Melissa, 2, 239, 253, 430, 431
Haydn, Franz Josef, 21–24 *passim*
Helpmann, Robert, 52, 118, 119, 393, 432, 455
Hendl, Susan, 90, 210, 218, 339, 340, 476, 519, 520
Henri, Pierre, 266, 270
Hérold, Ferdinand, 160, 167
Hertel, William, 160, 167
Het National Ballet, 256
Hicks, Gloriann, 69, 210
Hoffman, Gertrude, 473
Holden, Stanley, 143, 166
Holder, Christian, 316, 502, 504
Holdridge, Lee, 502, 504
Horvath, 41, 346
Hoving, Lucas, 258, 259
Huffman, Gregory, 291, 295
Humphrey, Doris, 28, 150, 159

Idzikowski, Stanislas, 330, 393, 495, 499
INITIALS R.B.M.E., 228
INTERMEZZO, 229–30
International (British) Ballet, 454
IN THE NIGHT, 225–27
Ito, Teiji, 513, 516
Ivanov, Lev, 277, 432, 433, 451–55 *passim*

Jackson, Denise, 130
Janke, Elizabeth, 73
Janke, Olga, 74, 229, 230
JEWELS, 231–32

Jillana, 239, 253, 431
Joffrey Ballet, 1, 17, 21, 22, 66, 114, 130, 234, 258, 291, 293, 294, 315, 332, 379, 380, 497, 502–4 *passim*
Joffrey, Robert, 17, 19, 20, 237, 336, 338, 430
Johnson, Pamela, 236, 430
JOURNAL, 234

Karpakova, Pauline, 432, 450
Karsavina, Tamara, 118, 166, 170, 193, 305, 314, 330, 427, 454, 473, 475, 476, 495
Kay, Hershy, 66, 520, 526
Kaye, Nora, 42, 187, 245, 317
Kchessinska, Mathilde, 8, 9, 454
Kent, Allegra, 93, 104, 108, 494
KETTENTANZ, 234–35
Khachaturian, Aram, 421
Kidd, Michael, 315
Kirkland, 48, 151, 178, 210, 217, 218, 224, 341, 342
Kirkland, Johnna, 210, 341, 342
Kirov Ballet, 29, 30, 100, 354, 410, 413, 455, 456, 457
Kirov State Theatre of Opera and Ballet, 49, 206, 424
Kivitt, Ted, 86, 192, 316, 346, 470, 471
Kohner, Pauline, 258
Kokitch, Casimir, 347
KONSERVATORIET, 236–38

Laing, Hugh, 112, 187, 241, 246, 317, 359, 505
Lamont, Deni, 119, 513, 519, 520
Lander, Toni, 258, 259, 459
La Scala Ballet, 369, 386, 410, 411
Lavrovsky, Leonid, 10, 354, 359, 372, 373
Lavrovsky, Mikhail, 424, 425
Lazowski, Yurek, 316, 497
LeClercq, Tanaquil, 68, 245, 246, 284, 484
Lee, Elizabeth, 73, 229, 230
Lee, Keith, 345, 346
Legnani, Pierina, 432, 451, 452
Leland, Sara, 69, 93, 101, 108, 151, 210, 217, 218, 487
Levins, Daniel, 73, 74, 499
LIEBESLIEDER WALZER, 239–40
Liepa, Maris, 421, 425
Lifar, Serge, 11, 322, 371
LILAC GARDEN, 241–46, 505
Limon, Jose, 258, 259, 260
Littlefield, Catherine, 393–94
Lloyd, Maude, 112, 187, 241

London Ballet, 187
Lopokova, Lydia, 152, 291, 305, 393, 427, 473
Loring, Eugene, 34, 498
Lorrayne, Vyvyan, 143, 145
Ludlow, Conrad, 231, 239, 253, 341
Lyon, Annabelle, 317, 498

McBride, Patricia, 46, 87, 88, 89, 92, 93, 95–99 *passim,* 108, 132, 135, 151, 210, 218, 222, 225, 227, 231, 253, 304, 519, 520, 525
MacMillan, Kenneth, xiii, 6, 10, 247, 252, 359, 366, 372, 373, 374, 381, 410, 414, 417, 418, 500
Madsen, Egon, 228, 369, 371, 373
Magallanes, Nicholas, 42, 239, 253, 277, 284, 484
Mahler, Gustav, 26, 27, 112
Maiorano, Robert, 93, 99, 210, 217, 218, 339, 513, 519, 520
Makarova, Natalia, 30, 32, 86, 88, 91, 206, 207, 346, 386, 456–57
MANON, 247–52
Marie-Jeanne, 34, 70, 391
Markova, Alicia, 152, 193, 206, 208–9, 245, 277, 359, 432
Marks, Bruce, 26, 27, 258, 259, 316, 367
Martins, Kay, 126, 127, 476
Martins, Peter, 210, 218–19, 225, 226, 510, 511, 512
Maryinsky Theatre, 8, 29, 120, 137, 277, 278, 393, 432, 451, 452, 454
Mason, Monica, 110
Massenet, Jules, 46, 47, 247, 251
Massie, Robert, 6
Massine, Leonide, 183, 291, 292, 293, 294, 305, 315, 316, 330, 332, 381, 483, 495
Massine, Tania, 316, 497
Mathis, Bonnie, 367
Maule, Michael, 42
Maximova, Yekaterina, 421
May, Pamela, 52, 393, 480
Mayer, Ruth, 499
Maywood, Augusta, 459
Mazzo, Kay, 93, 108, 126, 127, 225, 226, 476, 510, 511, 512
Mead, Robert, 143, 145, 273
Mendelssohn, Felix, 129, 130, 253
Merrill, Linda, 494, 519, 520
MIDSUMMER NIGHT'S DREAM, A, 129, 253–55
Millberg, Barbara, 2
Minkus, Ludwig, 29, 31, 46, 116, 120
Mitchell, Arthur, xiii, 2, 159, 253
Moiseyev, Igor, 424

Moncion, Francisco, 69, 171, 225, 227, 231, 253, 284, 484, 494
MONUMENT FOR A DEAD BOY, 256–57
MOOR'S PAVANE, THE, 258–60
Mordkin, Mikhail, 48, 432
Morley, Thomas, 73
Morris, Marnee, 90, 494, 519, 520, 525
Moscow Stanislavsky Ballet, 455
Mounsey, Yvonne, 42, 246
Mozart, Wolfgang Amadeus, 21, 70, 192, 388
Mullowney, Kathryn, 388
Munro, Richard, 73
MUTATIONS, 261–62

Nabokov, Nicolas, 119, 120, 125
Nagy, Joan, 32, 41, 65, 86, 146, 192, 257, 345, 346, 366
Nahat, Dennis, 41, 345, 346, 471, 499
NAPOLI, 263–65
National Ballet, 60, 457
National Ballet of Canada, 112, 369, 410, 411, 414, 417, 455, 456, 457, 459, 470, 471
National Ballet of Washington, 410, 469
Naumann, Peter, 132
Nearhoof, Pamela, 23, 24
Neary, Colleen, 210, 513
Neary, Patricia, 231
Needham, Carole, 129
Nelson, Ted, 130
Nemtchinova, Vera, 330, 393
Nerina, Nadia, 52, 166, 315
Netherlands Dance Theatre, 233, 261
Neusidler, Hans, 73, 74
New York City Ballet, xiii, 2, 42, 47, 48, 68, 69, 93, 119, 125, 126, 132, 151, 171, 177, 210, 216, 219, 222, 225, 231, 239, 245, 246, 253, 277, 322, 333, 339, 341, 391, 430, 455, 476, 477, 478, 487, 494, 510, 513, 519
Nickel, Paul, 192, 277
Nijinska, Bronislava, 22, 23, 160, 272, 273, 274, 385, 393
NIJINSKY—CLOWN OF GOD, 266–71
Nijinsky, Vaslav, 266, 267, 268, 269, 270, 305, 314, 315, 381, 384, 385, 427, 454, 473, 475, 476, 483
Nikitina, Alice, 11
Nikitina, Varvara, 393
Nissen, Greta, 499
NOCES, LES, 95, 96, 108, 272–76, 385
Novikoff, Laurent, 330
Nureyev, Rudolf, xiii, 29, 30, 32, 110, 118, 119, 257, 281, 282, 315, 373, 386, 410, 411, 414–17 *passim*, 455, 459

NUTCRACKER, THE, 91, 223, 277–83, 451, 454

Oboukof, Mikhail, 473, 476
O'Brien, Shaun, 69, 91, 92
O'Connor, Patrick, 28
Offenbach, Jacques, 183, 489
Ohman, Frank, 519, 520
Orio, Diane, 130
Orloff, Nicolas, 359
Orlov, Alexandre, 305, 314
ORPHEUS, 2, 284–90
Orr, Terry, 26, 27, 41, 352, 353
Østergaard, Solveig, 92
Oxenham, Andrew, 373

PARADE, 291–95
Paredes, Marcos, 220, 345, 352
Paris Opéra Ballet, 178, 371, 391, 484, 486
Park, Merle, 206
Parkinson, Georgina, 143
Parlić, Dmitri, 359
PAS DE QUATRE, 296–304
Paul, Mimi, 41, 231, 346
Paulli, H. S., 236, 263
Pavlova, Anna, 32, 47, 48, 87, 118, 137, 138, 139, 193, 298, 453, 454, 473, 475, 476, 483
Penny, Jennifer, 417
Pergolesi, Giambattista, 330
Perrot, Jules, 193, 195, 296, 298, 299
Peters, Delia, 69, 210
Petipa, Lucien, 193
Petipa, Marie, 393
Petipa, Marius, 29, 30, 31, 46, 48, 70, 86, 89, 116, 118, 119, 120, 223, 303, 387, 393, 396, 410–17 *passim*, 419, 432, 433, 451–54 *passim*, 458, 524
Petit, Roland, 459
Petroff, Paul, 510
PETROUCHKA, 70, 305–16, 479
Philadelphia Ballet, 393
Pilarre, Susan, 210, 519
PILLAR OF FIRE, 317–21
Piltz, Marie, 381, 384, 385
Pitts, Bryan, 210, 218
Plisetskaya, Maya, 116, 424
Preobrajenska, Olga, 454, 473
Prinz, John, 93, 100, 104, 345, 494
PRODIGAL SON, 322–29
Prokofiev, Serge, 49, 52, 60, 151, 187, 220, 322, 354, 358, 367, 368, 369, 371–74 *passim*, 500
Pugni, Cesare, 296, 303
PULCINELLA, 330–35
Purcell, Henry, 258

Radius, Alexandra, 86, 345
Ralov, Børge, 315
Rambert, Dame Marie, xiii, 246, 384
Rambert Ballet Club, 241
Raph, Alan, 379, 502, 504
Rapp, Richard, 519
Rassine, Alexis, 393

Redpath, Christine, 69, 90, 151, 210
Reed, Janet, 154
Reiman, Elise, xiii, 11, 484
Reisinger, Julius, 432
REMEMBRANCES, 336–38
Remington, Barbara, 236, 497
Renault, Michel, 484
Rencher, Derek, 6, 129, 143, 145, 247
REQUIEM CANTICLES, 339–40
Respighi, Ottorino, 498
REVERIES, 341–44
Rhodes, Lawrence, 1, 256
Richardson, David, 210, 218
Ritz, Roger, 484
RIVER, THE, 345–46
Robbins, Jerome, xii, xiii, 42, 46, 47, 48, 68, 69, 93, 96, 97–112 *passim*, 132, 133, 135, 136, 151, 154, 177, 178, 210, 216, 217, 219, 221, 225, 226, 274, 276, 315, 322, 333, 334, 339, 342, 359, 498, 513, 516, 517, 518
Roberge, Giselle, 210
RODEO, 347–53
Rodriguez, Beatriz, 21, 23
Role, Donna, 336
Romanoff, Dimitri, 112, 160
ROMEO AND JULIET, 354–78
Rosati, Carolina, 303
Rosson, Keith, 315
Royal Ballet (London), xiii, 6, 29, 30, 32, 109, 129, 130, 143, 166, 170, 205, 247, 281, 315, 371, 373, 374, 381, 410, 411, 417, 418, 455, 456, 457, 500
Royal Danish Ballet, 92, 236, 263, 304, 315, 368, 372, 459, 475
Royal Swedish Ballet, 108, 281
Russell, Francia, 2
Russian Imperial Ballet, 86
Ryder, Mark, 430

Sabirova, Malika, 46, 47
Sackett, Francis, 210
SACRED GROVE ON MOUNT TAMALPAIS, 379–80
SACRE DU PRINTEMPS, LE, 313, 381–86
Sadler's Wells Ballet, 52, 80, 152, 277, 393, 410, 417, 432, 434, 454, 480, 497
Sahl, Vinod, 130
Saint-Léon, Arthur, 70, 75, 86, 92
Saint-Saëns, Camille, 137
Saland, Stephanie, 132
Samokhvalov, Nikolai, 116
San Francisco Ballet, 277, 432
Saratoga Performing Arts Center, 86, 216
Sarry, Christine, 26, 27, 28, 220, 229, 230, 352, 353, 499
Satie, Erik, 291, 292, 295
Sayers, Dido, 2
Scarlatti, Domenico, 491

Schaufuss, Frank, 92
Schermerhorn, Kenneth, 26
Schneitzhoeffer, Jean, 459
Schoenberg, Arnold, 88, 317
Schooling, Elizabeth, 499
School of American Ballet, xiii, 87, 342, 388, 390–92 *passim*
Schubert, Franz, 509
Schuman, William, 505
Scottish Theatre Ballet, 489
SEASONS, THE, 387
Seravalli, Rosanna, 367
SERENADE, 388–92, 486
Sergeyev, Konstantin, 49, 354
Sergeyev, Nicholas, 411, 454, 455
Seymour, Lynn, 6, 110, 459
Shabelevsky, Yurek, 273
Shaw, Brian, 143, 480
Shea, Mary Jane, 70
Shearer, Moira, 52, 152, 393, 480
Shelton, Polly, 210
Shollar, Ludmilla, 393
Shostakovich, Dimitri, 159
Sibley, Antoinette, 6, 46, 47, 48, 88, 110, 129, 143, 145, 206, 247, 417, 419, 500, 501
Sieveling, Earle, 519, 520
Sills, Bettijane, 69, 210, 519, 520
Singleton, Trinette, 17
Sizova, Alla, 410
Sleep, Wayne, 143
SLEEPING BEAUTY, THE, 46, 48, 70, 393–420, 433, 449, 483
Smith, George Washington, 193
Smith, Lois, 456, 459
Smuin, Michael, 146, 192
Sobotka, Ruth, 2
Sokolova, Lydia, 381, 393
Soloviev, Yuri, 49, 410
Somes, Michael, 52, 170, 480, 482
Sorkin, Naomi, 41
Sowinski, John, 73, 74, 229, 230
SPARTACUS, 421–26
SPECTRE DE LA ROSE, LE, 427–29
Spessivtzeva, Olga, 193, 393, 454
Spohn, Marjorie, 210
Stanislavsky Ballet, 455
Steele, Michael, 210
Stetson, Lynne, 210
Stevenson, Ben, 60, 64, 65
STILL POINT, THE, 430–31
Stirling, Christina, 73, 229
Stockhausen, Karlheinz, 261
Stolze, Kurt-Heinz, 491
Strauss, Johann, 234
Strauss, Richard, 140
Stravinsky, Igor, 2, 3, 4, 5, 11, 42, 70, 87, 95, 126, 170, 171, 178, 231, 232, 272, 274, 284, 305, 313, 314, 316, 330, 333, 334, 339, 343, 381, 384, 385, 393, 479, 487, 488, 510, 524, 527

Stripling, Jan, 369, 373
Stroganova, Nina, 112
Stuart, Virginia, 210
Stuttgart Ballet, 10, 147, 228, 369, 371, 387, 457, 491
Sultzbach, Russell, 130, 379
Sutherland, Paul, 236
SWAN LAKE, 31, 46, 222, 412, 432–58, 483
SYLPHIDE, LA, 194, 207, 208, 296, 297, 304, 459–72, 473, 474
SYLPHIDES, LES, 99, 107, 449, 453, 473–79
SYMPHONIC VARIATIONS, 480–83
SYMPHONY IN C, 484–86
SYMPHONY IN THREE MOVEMENTS, 487–88
Syrcus, Crome, 17

Taglioni, Marie, 194, 195, 296–303 *passim*, 459, 473
Taglioni, Philippe, 459
TALES OF HOFFMAN, 489–90
Tallchief, Maria, 106, 171, 222, 245, 277, 284, 322, 484
Talmage, Robert, 130, 291
TAMING OF THE SHREW, THE, 491–93
Tarakanova, Nina, 183
Taras, John, 386
Taylor, Burton, 130, 131
Tchaikovsky, Peter Ilyich, 6, 8, 46, 48, 70, 87, 147, 231, 232, 270, 277, 281, 341, 371, 388, 390, 391, 393, 396, 410–13 *passim*, 416, 417, 419, 432, 449, 450, 451, 453, 458, 494
TCHAIKOVSKY SUITE NO. 2, 494
Tchelitchew, Pavel, 511
Tchernicheva, Lubov, 11, 330, 473
Tennant, Veronica, 410, 416
Tharp, Twyla, 21–25 *passim*, 114, 115
Thomas, Robert, 130
Thompson, Basil, 497
Thorogood, Alfreda, 417
THREE-CORNERED HAT, THE, 495–97
THREE VIRGINS AND A DEVIL, 498–99
Tikhonov, Vladimir, 116
Timofeyeva, Nina, 421
Tobias, Roy, 2, 431
Tomasson, Helgi, 46, 91, 132, 135, 151, 210, 218, 257, 487
Tompkins, Beatrice, 284, 484
Toumanova, Tamara, 484, 495, 510
Tracy, Paula, 220
TRIAD, 500–1
TRINITY, 502–4
T'Sani, Nolan, 132, 210
Tudor, Antony, 112, 187, 241, 245, 246, 317, 359, 364, 365, 366, 367, 368, 384, 505
Turner, Harold, 277, 393

Ulanova, Galina, 206, 354, 359
UNDERTOW, 505–8
UNFINISHED SYMPHONY, 509

Vainonen, Vassily, 281
Van Dantzig, Rudi, 256
Van Dyk, Peter, 509
Vane, Daphne, 11
Vangsaae, Mona, 368
Van Hoecke, Micha, 266
Van Praagh, Peggy, 187, 241
Vasquez, Roland, 253
Vassiliev, Vladimir, 421
Vaughan, David, 482
Verdy, Antoinette, 46, 47
Verdy, Violette, 93, 99, 225, 226, 231, 239, 253, 304, 333
Verneuil, Cathérine, 266
Verso, Edward, 220, 316
Vestris, Auguste, 236, 237
Vienna State Opera, 455
Vikulov, Sergei, 29
Villella, Edward, 93, 95, 97, 98, 101, 102, 103, 108, 222, 224, 231, 253, 333, 487, 513, 517
VIOLIN CONCERTO, 510–12
Viscusi, Achille, 432
Vladimiroff, Pierre, 393
Volinine, Alexandre, 432, 473
Von Aroldingen, Karin, 210, 476, 510, 519, 520, 525
Von Rosen, Elsa Marianne, 469
Vossler, Heidi, 388
Vsevolozhsky, Alexandrovich, 411, 412, 417, 418, 419
Vyroubova, Nina, 459

Wagner, Richard, 336, 337
Walczak, Barbara, 2
Wall, David, 110, 247
Walton, William, 152
WATERMILL, 513–18
Watts, Jonathan, 2, 239, 336, 338
Wayne, Dennis, 1, 430
Weber, Carl Maria von, 427
Webern, Anton, 4
Weiss, Robert, 69, 99, 210, 217, 218
Wells, Bruce, 210, 217, 218, 339, 340
White, Glenn, 234
Whitener, William, 23
WHO CARES?, 88, 519–27
Wilson, Sallie, 192, 258, 345, 346, 499
Woizikowski, Leon, 272, 291, 315, 322, 495, 497
Wright, Rebecca, 130, 234 235, 497, 502
Wuehrer, Ully, 118

Yacobson, Leonid, 424
Young, Anita, 417
Young, Gayle, 41, 86, 346
Youskevitch, Igor, 183, 391, 431

Zajetz, Konstantin, 118
Zakharov, Rostislav, 116
Zhdanow, Yuri, 354
Zomosa, Maximiliano, 17, 66
Zverev, Nicholas, 291, 330